Prevention and Intervention in Childhood and Adolescence 17

Special Research Unit 227 – Prevention and Intervention in Childhood and Adolescence

An interdisciplinary project of the University of Bielefeld

conducted by *Prof. Dr. Günter Albrecht, Prof. Dr. Otto Backes, Prof. Dr. Michael Brambring, Prof. Dr. Detlev Frehsee, Prof. Dr. Wilhelm Heitmeyer, Prof. Dr. Klaus Hurrelmann (Coordinator), Prof. Dr. Franz-Xaver Kaufmann, Prof. Dr. Hans-Uwe Otto, Prof. Dr. Helmut Skowronek*

Diversion and Informal Social Control

Edited by
Günter Albrecht
Wolfgang Ludwig-Mayerhofer

Walter de Gruyter · Berlin · New York 1995

Prof. Dr. *Günter Albrecht*, Department of Sociology and Research Center 227, University of Bielefeld, Germany

Dr. *Wolfgang Ludwig-Mayerhofer*, Research Center 227, University of Bielefeld, and Department of Sociology, University of Munich, Germany

With 16 figures and 25 tables

∞ Printed on acid-free paper which falls within the guidelines of the ANSI to ensure permanence and durability.

Library of Congress Cataloging-in-Publication Data

Diversion and informal social control / edited by Günter Albrecht and Wolfgang Ludwig-Mayerhofer.
p. cm. – (Prevention and intervention in childhood and adolescence ; 17)
Originates from a conference held at the University of Bielefeld in 1991.
Includes bibliographical references and index.
ISBN 3-11-014948-6
1. Juvenile delinquency – Prevention – Congresses. 2. Pre-trial intervention – Congresses. 3. Social work with children – Congresses. 4. Social work with youth – Congresses. 5. Social control – Congresses. I. Albrecht, Günter, 1943– II. Ludwig-Mayerhofer, Wolfgang. III. Series.
HV9058.D58 1995
364.3′6′0973–dc20 95-30679
CIP

Die Deutsche Bibliothek – Cataloging-in-Publication Data

Diversion and informal social control / ed. by Günter Albrecht and Wolfgang Ludwig-Mayerhofer. – Berlin ; New York : de Gruyter, 1995
(Prevention and intervention in childhood and adolescence ; 17)
ISBN 3-11-014948-6
NE: Albrecht, Günter [Hrsg.]; GT

Printing: WB-Druck GmbH, Rieden am Forggensee. – Binding: Dieter Mikolai, Berlin. – Cover Design: Hansbernd Lindemann, Berlin. – Photo: Ullstein-Bilderdienst, Berlin.
Printed in Germany.

Preface

This volume originated from a conference organized by the Special Research Unit on Prevention and Intervention in Childhood and Adolescence at the University of Bielefeld. In November 1991, researchers from several countries met at Bielefeld to discuss problems of diversion and informal social control. As will readily be recognized, the aim of the conference was not to state a coherent theoretical position or to give a definite overview of established empirical results. Rather, we attempted to attract researchers who, together, might be able to highlight the very *different* viewpoints that presently co-exist within criminology. It is not our opinion that attempts at formulating a comprehensive theory are meaningless. But we are convinced that it is useful to point out from time to time the diversity of perspectives that eventually may have to be integrated if such attempts are to be successful.

The book is organized into five parts. Part I contains theoretical perspectives on diversion and informal social control, presenting a very broad spectrum of current positions in the field. Part II reports on the present state of diversion from the criminal justice system in three selected countries, the U.S.A., England and Wales, and Germany. The contributors in Part III discuss the effects of diversion on offenders. Part IV gives an overview of the broad range of mediation, reconciliation, and compensation procedures that are available as alternatives to formal processing within the criminal justice system. Finally, in Part V, the legal problems are discussed that emerge with the rise of informal justice, as well as alternative legal solutions that might be able to circumvent the pitfalls associated with the weakening of legal safeguards that often is entailed by diversion.

We would not have been able to successfully organize the conference and to edit the present volume without the generous help provided by many institutions and people. We are grateful to the German Research Foundation (Deutsche Forschungsgemeinschaft) for funding the conference and the Center for Interdisciplinary Research (Zentrum für interdisziplinäre Forschung) at the University of Bielefeld for its hospitality and organizational support. Petra Thünte assisted in the preparation of the conference and was a most charming receptionist during it. As the time of the conference grew nearer and the amount of work still left to be done seemed to grow larger every day instead of melting away, the help of Dorothea Rzepka proved invaluable.

The preparation of the volume profited enormously from the help of Jonathan Harrow, who translated several of the contributions and checked many others. In view of the heterogeneous disciplinary backgrounds of the authors, this was a difficult and prolonged task that he addressed with great patience and conscientiousness. In addition, we are thankful to Elfriede Kroppenstedt, Marina Walters, Marina Becker, Gisela Schneider, Frank Pütz, and Oliver Albrecht for all kinds of editorial and technical assistance. We also wish to thank Brigitte Friede for her help in setting up the final manuscript.

Finally, we want to thank all of the authors for their cooperation. We are most thankful to those who, having delivered their manuscripts very promptly, did not lose patience while we tried to gather the rest. But we also are indebted to those who eventually yielded to our persecution and provided papers when we had begun to lose our faith that the volume might ever be completed.

Bielefeld and Munich, December 1994

Günter Albrecht
Wolfgang Ludwig-Mayerhofer

Contents

Contributors

Albrecht, Günter, Fakultät für Soziologie and Research Center 227 (Prevention and Intervention in Childhood and Adolescence), Universität Bielefeld, P.O. Box 10 01 31, 33501 Bielefeld, Germany

Backes, Otto, Fakultät für Rechtswissenschaft, Universität Bielefeld, P.O. Box 10 01 31, 33501 Bielefeld, Germany

Barton, Stephan, Fakultät für Rechtswissenschaft, Universität Bielefeld, P.O. Box 10 01 31, 33501 Bielefeld, Germany

Bettmer, Franz, Research Center 227 (Prevention and Intervention in Childhood and Adolescence), Universität Bielefeld, P.O. Box 10 01 31, 33501 Bielefeld, Germany

Braithwaite, John, Department of Law, Research School of Social Science, Australian National University, GPO Box 4, Canberra, ACT 2601, Australia

Cornish, Derek, Department of Social Science and Administration, London School of Economics, Houghton St., London WC2A2AE, U.K.

Ezell, Mark, School of Social Work, JH-30, University of Washington, Seattle, WA 98195, U.S.A.

Frehsee, Detlev, Fakultät für Rechtswissenschaft, Universität Bielefeld, P.O. Box 10 01 31, 33501 Bielefeld, Germany

Heinz, Wolfgang, Fakultät für Rechtswissenschaft, Universität Konstanz, P.O. Box 55 60, 78434 Konstanz, Germany

Horwitz, Allan V., Dept. of Sociology and Institute for Health, Health Care Policy, and Aging Research, Rutgers University, New Brunswick, N. J. 08903-5070, U.S.A.

Korfes, Gunhild, Erich-Boltze-Str.17, 10407 Berlin, Germany

Lissenberg, Elisabeth, Criminologisch Instituut, Kloveniersburgwal 72, 1012 CZ Amsterdam, NL

Ludwig-Mayerhofer, Wolfgang, Institut für Soziologie der Universität München, Konradstr. 6, 80801 München, Germany

Matthews, Roger, Middlesex University, Faculty of Social Science and Education, Queensway, Enfield, Middlesex EN3 4SF, U.K.

Messmer, Heinz, Research Center 227 (Prevention and Intervention in Childhood and Adolescence), Universität Bielefeld, P.O. Box 10 01 31, 33501 Bielefeld, Germany

Micheel, Heinz-Günter, Research Center 227 (Prevention and Intervention in Childhood and Adolescence), Universität Bielefeld, P.O. Box 10 01 31, 33501 Bielefeld, Germany

Otto, Hans-Uwe, Fakultät für Pädagogik and Research Center 227 (Prevention and Intervention in Childhood and Adolescence), Universität Bielefeld, P.O. Box 10 01 31, 33501 Bielefeld, Germany

Plewig, Hans-Joachim, Institut für Sozialpädagogik, Universität Lüneburg, Wilschenbrucher Weg 69, 21335 Hamburg, Germany

Ransiek, Andreas, Fakultät für Rechtswissenschaft, Universität Bielefeld, P.O. Box 10 01 31, 33501 Bielefeld, Germany

Reiss, Albert J., Jr., Department of Sociology, Yale University, P.O. Box 1965, New Haven, CT06520, U.S.A.

Rössner, Dieter, Fakultät für Rechtswissenschaft, Martin-Luther-Universität Halle-Wittenberg, 06099 Halle/Saale, Germany

Schwartz, Ira M., Center for the Study of Youth Policy, University of Michigan, Ann Arbor, MI48104, U.S.A.

Steinert, Heinz, Fachbereich Gesellschaftswissenschaft, Johann Wolfgang Goethe-Universität, Robert-Mayer-Str. 5, 60325 Frankfurt/Main, Germany

Voss, Michael, Fachbereich 1, Institut für Kriminalwissenschaften, Johann Wolfgang Goethe-Universität, Senckenberganlage 31, 60325 Frankfurt/Main, Germany

Walgrave, Lode, Faculteit Rechtsgeleerdheid, Katholieke Universiteit Leuven, Hooverplein 10, 3000 Leuven, Belgium

Weitekamp, Elmar, Institut für Kriminologie, Universität Tübingen, Corrensstr. 34, 72076 Tübingen, Germany

Part I

Theoretical Perspectives

Introduction to Part I: Theoretical Perspectives

The papers in the first part of this volume discuss diversion with respect to general concerns of penal policy and prevention.

First, Heinz Steinert warns against the tendencies toward abstraction and reification inherent in the idea of prevention. These tendencies to view persons solely as targets of domination are, in Steinert's view, a result of the "dialectics of enlightenment", of the instrumental rationality that has been at the core of Western modernity and thus also of most state interventions and their underlying politics of exclusion throughout the 19th and 20th centuries. Therefore, he argues for modes of prevention and diversion that respect two principles. First, the focus of prevention should be not on changing people but rather on changing situations. Second, since changing situations still may involve intervention into the lives of people, the ultimate goal against which prevention is to be measured is the enhancement of individual autonomy.

Allan V. Horwitz applies the general theory of social control developed by Donald Black and others in order to explain the emergence of diversion as a means of social control, as well as the type of offenders that typically enter diversion programs. He maintains that diversion is a response of the formal control system to the weakening of informal control in families, schools, and neighborhoods. But why did the criminal justice system respond to this with a new style of control, namely, diversion? On the one hand, there are the stronger demands facing due process that evolved during the 1960s. These, together with an increased input into the criminal justice system, have led to the expansion of a less formally binding way of dealing with juveniles. On the other hand, the problems of the juveniles involved usually are defined as emotional problems, thereby eliciting a more therapeutic response. Precisely which youth enter diversion programs - in contrast to remaining within informal community control or entering the traditional correctional system - may be explained by such factors as the specific amount of parental control exercised on the offenders, the relationship between offenders and victims, or the offenders' class, gender, and age. Finally, the theory can be used to derive propositions regarding which factors may influence the effectiveness of diversion programs in changing delinquent youth. Most prominent among these are involvement of family and community members, empowerment of juveniles to deal more effectively with the conflicts they have with others, communities whose values coincide with those of the agents of change, minimization of distance between treatment agents and clients, and, finally, voluntary involvement of offenders in diversion programs.

Albert J. Reiss, Jr., deals with the role of theory in the creation and evaluation of diversion. He points out that the roots of diversion date back to the end of the 19th century when juvenile courts were created to divert delinquent youth from the adult courts under the label of "reform" instead of punishment. But this movement was not founded on any precise idea about how to change offenders. Instead, the idea was to create alternatives to criminal justice without a clear picture of what such alternatives should look like. As a result, the goals of interventions were never defined clearly, and little effort was made to assess which kind of treatment might be appropriate for which type of offender. In addition, we must face the possibility that interventions, at least under certain circumstances, might actually *increase* the risk of future delinquency. Reiss offers a few suggestions, arising from recent research, on how to achieve a better match between offenders and interventions, but ends with a warning that implementation of programs might lead to creation of new bureaucracies that will undermine the possibilities of further change.

Derek Cornish's starting point is similar to that of Reiss in that he emphasizes the weak foundation of current efforts at changing offenders. With this in mind, he compares two answers to the problems involved: diversion, as an attempt to direct offenders away from a seemingly ineffective system of criminal justice; and a situational crime prevention approach that focuses less on offenders and more on the crime-generating properties of situations. While there are some clear-cut differences, Cornish argues that both approaches have several features in common, for example, avoiding stigmatization of offenders and concentrating on first and casual offenders. Therefore, with respect to the aim of crime prevention, diversion might profit from incorporating some elements of situational crime prevention and the underlying rational choice perspective. Yet, more evaluation is needed, Cornish maintains, before we can ascertain whether diversion's attempts to reduce the stigmatization of offenders and interrupt involvement in delinquent behavior actually are successful.

The Idea of Prevention and the Critique of Instrumental Reason

Heinz Steinert

In recent years "diversion" - organizing ways out of the criminal justice system other than refusal to pursue, acquittal, or a formal sentence - has been offered and tried as the panacea for our problems with criminal justice: mostly that punishment does not work and is even suspected to make the situation worse. With some awareness of the history of punishment reforms, we are cautious and suspicious: Is this not punishment again? Even punishment that cuts deeper into everyday life than the old formal sanctions did? Or intervention into cases now that would not have been pursued at all in the absence of measures of diversion?

And what do we mean by "punishment does not work"? The answer is that we demand instrumental effects from this as from other types of state intervention into the lives of citizens. Liberals particularly demand it where the intervention is directed *against* citizens; where it inflicts pain and disadvantage upon them. But would this pain, which is inflicted deliberately by organized state intervention, be justified if it "worked"? Does an - always uncertain - preventive effect in the future justify the pain caused by state punishment now? And is "diversion" a way out of the dilemma?

I see the whole idea of prevention as part of one of the grave mistakes of this century. Or, to be more exact, one of the mistakes inherited from the 19th but having revealed its catastrophic implications only in this century: the prevalence of instrumental reason. But then, does not "prevention" sound so utterly rational? Who could possibly say anything against the idea that, instead of finding solutions to problems, we will ensure that these problems do not arise in the first place? We also have some excellent success stories to tell about this strategy: general protective vaccination against epidemic diseases; sewerage, clean water, and other hygienic measures against much of the urban misery of the 19th century; iodization of table salt against thyroid disorders and goiter, fluoridation of drinking water against caries; general and compulsory insurances of different kinds, bundled into what we now call the "welfare state", against the hunger, illness, homelessness, and disruption of social relations - not to forget the political radicalism - of the impoverished and demoralized laboring classes of the last and the beginning of this century. Could there possibly be anything wrong with all that?

In our narrower field, criminal law and punishment, many hope that "prevention" could at least alleviate some of the problems institutions in this field have: like the failure of the police whose model of intervention no longer fits today's reality of harmful social actions, or the uneasiness many people, including judges and prosecutors, have with the right of the state to punish, that is, to inflict pain upon and to exclude certain of its citizens. Would not the police be much more successful in creating the security we all expect from their activities if they did not have to wait for crimes to be committed but could instead concentrate on preventing them? And there is a hope to get rid of the offensive empowerment of the state to punish if we can - by preventing them - get rid of the actions that, and the people who, now have to be punished. What can be prevented by the state need not be prosecuted and punished by the state. The logic seems impeccable.

We have examples of another kind as well. Sociologists have sketched ironical scenarios of what life in the "punitive city", dominated by rehabilitative and preventive community services, would be reduced to (Cohen, 1979). They have identified and warned of "net-widening effects" to an extent that this word (which has no similarly elegant German equivalent) can today be heard from high-ranking public officials and in ministries of justice. We also have plenty of observations and documentations of how the police, coming along in the shining coat of "prevention", have acquired powers of covert observation, phone tapping, agent provocateur work, and similar highly problematic measures, and at the same time powers of open intimidation, searching, "encirculation"[1] on the one hand, banning from certain places on the other hand, up to preventive detention of "known trouble-makers" in some of the German-speaking countries.

There seems to be something wrong with the idea of prevention after all. What is it? Can we pin it down? Can history help us understand?

I shall - starting from such questions - introduce the topic in a somewhat general way by offering some reflections on the ambivalent character and the historical contradictions of the idea of "prevention" in order to be able to place "diversion" in this field and to be able to distinguish different forms of prevention and diversion. To do so I shall use - and thus have to discuss - the figures of thinking about history developed in Critical Theory and particularly by Adorno and Horkheimer (1947): "instrumental reason" and "dialectic of enlightenment".

I shall proceed in the following steps: First I shall place "prevention" in its historical context of the 19th and 20th centuries. Then I shall briefly discuss Horkheimer and Adorno's concept of "instrumental reason" and the "dialectic of enlightenment" as their figure of interpreting recent history. From this, I shall, in a third section, develop a differentiation of types of prevention that will also allow to place and again distinguish different forms of "diversion". In all, I hope to be able to draw our attention to some of the wider context in which we discuss prevention and diversion.

1 Glimpses From the History of Prevention

I shall draw on two items of historical evidence. The first one is well known among students of criminal law: "general prevention" as introduced into the legitimations of the state's power to punish by Feuerbach in Germany. Although not totally new, the strong reliance on this principle in Feuerbach's thinking about punishment originally had liberal and limiting functions. There should be no punishment in excess of what is necessary to reach the aim of preventing other people from doing what the punished person had done. This principle can be seen as a determined attempt to get the state's power to punish under the control of a rational calculus. No more metaphysics of an "offended order", no more "majesty of the law", all of which smacks of the religious justifications absolute monarchy mustered to arbitrarily maltreat and intimidate its unenlightened subjects. And above all: no recourse to the person and his or her properties, all of which are to be left alone by the state.

In the course of history, though, this has been turned around to mean: The state can or even has to use every measure, in this case every punishment, that is suited to reach the aim of general prevention. If it does not work, obviously more and sterner punishment is needed. Besides, there is no reason why the two, the recourse to the person in the form of special prevention and the abstract aim of general prevention, should not be combined and considered cumulatively. Such cumulation of principles and thus legitimations and alleged aims of punishment is what we have today. This can even be supplemented by "moral teaching" as one more principle, if the more "empirical" legitimations should not yet suffice. Compared to early liberal thinking, the license of the state to inflict pain on its citizens has acquired surprisingly wide and varied legitimacy. What started as a formula to limit the power of the state ended as a general and endlessly expandable legitimation of state intervention.

This example fits amazingly well into the model of historical progress that Max Horkheimer and Theodor W. Adorno have analyzed as "dialectic of enlightenment": critical rationality turned into oppressive rationality, the promise of liberation turned into technocratic domination.

My second example gives an even sharper edge to what I have tried to show so far. Research on Adorno and his experience of Schönberg's music (Steinert, 1989) has recently led me to take a very close look at fin-de-siècle Vienna and its culture again. What impressed me a lot is the racism and anti-Semitism prevalent at the same time in which the intellectual foundations of this century were laid in revolutionary breakthroughs in psychoanalysis, philosophy, literature, architecture, painting, and music in Vienna. This sinister background of the cultural achievements of the fin de siècle is largely played down in today's interpretations of that culture - also in Adorno's, by the way. So I started reading those disgusting newspapers, pamphlets, books, and journals. The well-known fact that we cannot understand the history of social formations and particularly of capitalism and its culture without studying the history of social exclusion and the forms it takes became very vivid to me. The glorious critical and ironic culture of fin-de-siècle Vienna had this dark side of racist, particularly anti-Semitic, and nationalist social exclusion, all of which was openly propagated politically and helped the populist christian-socialist party under Lueger to even rule in Vienna.

The interesting aspect is not so much the character of racism as irrational and a type of persecution mania but rather the self-reification and self-instrumentalization that it implies. Racism is the abdication of the individual. In racist terms, I am nothing but the bearer of my genes, and even these are only relevant as statistical particles of a "gene pool". Political measures oriented by this ideology go *through* the individuals who do not count. They are directed at (and against) great numbers of people in their abstract capacity as members of a "race". This type of political intervention is the prototype of instrumental rationality.[2]

Into this climate of social exclusion fits, as another aspect of the same thing, the institutionalization of empirical criminology at the end of the century - Hans Gross founded his journal, the *Archiv für Kriminal-Anthropologie und Kriminalistik*, in 1899 and his institute of criminology at Graz University in 1912. This founding father of modern criminology published articles on transportation and castration as rational measures of prevention and he only argued against the death penalty for "anarchists" because he thought they were mostly suicides anyway, so that denying them execution would actually prevent their attacks on crowned heads. This last example of unprejudiced thinking highlights the unprincipled and purely technocratic rationality for which the effect is all that counts. One of the constant sorrows of Hans Gross was "degenerates" who are apt to become a burden on the state. The danger he set out to prevent was not even any outright damage or threat but just people becoming "a burden", and not to society, but to "the state". The crumbling "ancien régime" mobilized enough fear and rage and authoritarian helplessness for quite extreme fantasies of social exclusion - and unfortunately they were openly voiced and organized politically.[3]

Criminology is but one - and not the most extreme - example of this "science of social exclusion" that sprang up with the political outcry for its practical realization. The journals with an explicitly racist program, like the *Politisch-anthropologische Revue* or the *Archiv für Rassen- und Gesellschaftsbiologie*, both founded shortly after 1900, exhibit the same cold rationality. These were not publications on the "lunatic fringe" like, for example, *Ostara* from which Hitler at the same time picked the fragments of his ideology. They were at least moderately respectable.[4]

From these "respectable" scientific documents, much more than from the openly agitating nationalist and racist pamphlets, we can get a strong impression of how the idea and the drive to prevent impending evil, to create perfection by eliminating all who might contaminate or diminish it, is the dangerous illusion - which, executed in a ruthless way, later led the way to Auschwitz. It is, therefore, no surprise that, as has recently been shown again by Aly and Heim (1991), economic plans and hopes developed by technocratic intellectuals joined into the complex web that had the destruction of Jews and the enslavement of Slavs and thus the system of labor and extermination camps as its center.[5]

From the early bourgeois control fantasies in the form of authoritarian utopias to the biologistic fantasies of improving the race by the new scientific endeavor of "eugenics",[6] we find the same technocratic preoccupation with eliminating - preventing - all deviance, all weakness, all that is not "healthy".

Once more, we can see here a "dialectic of enlightenment", an attempt to think rationally about society and its development that leads not to liberation but to a perfection of domination, a development of the forces of production that implies a development of the means of domination and social exclusion at the same time.

2 The Progress of Social Exclusion

I have repeatedly mentioned the "dialectic of enlightenment" as an interpretative pattern that could be applied to these developments of "prevention". Let me, therefore, briefly comment on this figure of thinking about history. Horkheimer and Adorno have sketched it in different approaches in their collection of "philosophical fragments" (1947) as an important modification of the Hegelian and Marxian dialectic of historical (mainly capitalist) progress. Instead of a more or less progressive development of reason coming to self-consciousness in history (Hegel), instead of a development of the forces of production opening up the chance for liberation by an increasing contradiction to the relations of production, that is, to domination by capital (Marx), they see a *parallel* and interlocking development of forces of production and means of domination. With the objective possibility of liberation also grows the willingness and capacity for repression - to the extremes of Nazism and Stalinism. Enlightenment, the attempt to liberate humanity by rational thinking, has been turned into an instrument of domination itself.

Let me briefly illustrate this by mentioning some of the crucial points and contradictions in the social history of industrializing Europe. Capitalist industrialization produced increased wealth in the 19th century - *and*, at the same time, an impoverished proletariat, bourgeois entrepreneurship *and* pauperized urban masses, the abstract freedom of a class of owners *and* its contradiction: a laboring class of people who have nothing to lose but their chains. Horkheimer and Adorno, in a somewhat abstract way, point to the opposite side of this contradiction: The threat of masses of hopelessly poor people open to socialist ideas and organized in a militant labor movement was answered by important modifications in the form of capitalist domination. The most important of these modifications can be named as: (a) a differentiation of the labor force into unskilled labor, the "labor aristocracy" of skilled workers, and the extra-privileged employees as administrators and other control agents, up to managers (who together let the owner disappear from sight); (b) obligatory, state-organized, and state-guaranteed insurance against the most typical risks of the proletarian way of life and work, like accident, illness, unemployment, and so forth, adding up to what we today know as the "welfare state". The most radical reorganization of the capitalist mode of production, though, was (c) the invention of mass production and concomitantly mass consumption, the development of a "consumer society" that has more aptly been studied and described under the name of "Fordism". This new formation of capitalism no longer has any need to actively and openly reduce the standard of living for workers in order to raise profits. Instead, it makes workers part of the broadened and accelerated circulation of commodities, it uses the labor force as a force of consumption as well, and controls them through the soft means of a culture and consciousness industry.

Horkheimer and Adorno developed this model that has the historical background indicated long before the Nazi seizure of power in Germany.[7] But, of course, the Nazi regime and its atrocities gave credibility to and reinforced their gloomy view of human progress. The willingness and ability of that regime to move millions of people from certain places and concentrate them in others, to selectively breed one "race" and enslave and exterminate others in order to conquer "living space" ("Lebensraum") for this "master race" ("Herrenrasse"), can be seen as the efficient application of "instrumental rationality".

"Instrumental reason" - that is thinking as domination, thinking as the result and with the intention of subduing "nature", including human nature. Domination over outside nature has the corollary and presupposition of treating human beings - including one's own self - in abstract terms of usefulness and exchange, in their abstract "function as" - and there are many such functions: work force, consumers, breeders of future workers and consumers, soldiers, "casualties", expendable or needed, a burden to the community, a threat - to the purity of the race or to the labor market position of others, a foreigner with no right to be here, down to parasites, vermin, and cancer of the social organism. Labeling theory, by the way, has described the same process of "reification" in its own (limited) way. And the existentialist philosophy of Jean-Paul Sartre can be read as an attempt to come to grips with this stark fact of reification and the contradiction between the individual self as experienced by itself versus the categorized and typed person as seen by others (plus the self-defining activities of the Ego).[8]

"Western Marxism", of which Horkheimer and Adorno's "Dialectic of Enlightenment" is an important and consequential formulation, has, in contrast to the technocratically over-optimistic and power-crazy Soviet version, always been aware of this dark side of progress. Against this, the "individual" has been kept in focus and as the perspective of history, even if the hope for a realization of that bourgeois promise was seen to decrease and vanish. Enlightenment had set out with the promise of the equal worth and dignity of every single individual and ended with treating these individuals as statistical units only (and thus individually expendable and negligible).

There is no need to share the diagnosis of quietism and self-discouragement that many readers give to the "Dialectic of Enlightenment".[9] Adorno at least has always claimed the classical way of liberation: by *work*, that is, interaction with nature, patient, concentrated, well-informed, and wide-awake handling and exploring and changing a material, which includes criticizing the form already stamped on it by social norms and which also includes developing my own capacities and sensibilities in the process. He deviated from the classical assumption that the subject of liberation is the proletariat, because he did not see them receiving any chance of experience and growth in work. Thus he did not see that the conditions of the possibility of a subject-object relation that could emphatically be termed "work" were often given in our type of "Fordist" social formation. He did see them as attainable, though, in two rare instances: in artistic and in theoretical work, for the artist and the social theorist. His "subject of liberation", therefore, was the individual, and the condition for liberating work was autonomy - both bourgeois achievements which are, at the same time, denied by bourgeois domination. But we can still look out for the instances and developments that may make them possible, as contradictory exceptions at least (and perhaps even on a larger scale).

3 The Idea of Prevention and Instrumental Rationality

From this perspective, "prevention" looks quite hopeless. In "prevention" we get exactly the same abstraction and reification that characterizes instrumental reason. Interventions oriented toward prevention do not look at the present situation and its demands and not at the person at whom (or against whom) the intervention is directed now. Instead, the orientation is toward some future state of affairs, toward other people than those present, even toward future generations. Prevention also is an effort to dominate the future by planning it - with the consequence that an uncertain future and the hopes and fears we have for it dominate the present. What is done to an individual in the name of "prevention" *now* reduces this person to a mere function and instrument for some future state - be it of that person him- or herself or even outside the person. Punishment for the sake of general prevention, to mention a strong example, is the instrumental use of a person and more: It is the deliberate and purely instrumental infliction of pain to a person for purposes outside this person and certainly against his or her will.

It may be useful to distinguish two types of prevention: Let us call them "prevention of people" and "prevention of situations". If I should, for example, want less shoplifting, there is quite a difference between a tactic by which I appeal to customers' moral restraint and threaten them with what I shall do if I can catch them and another tactic by which I simply have more personnel, a less tempting display of goods, and electronic alarm tags on them. If I should want to prevent speeding on the road, I could simply have slow cars only or, in the other tactic, I can let people buy vehicles that can be driven at 200 km/h and threaten to take away the driving license of anyone who actually drives that fast. Confronted with poor people who want to share our way of living, we can try to help reduce the poverty from which they flee or we can build barriers, fortresses, and ghettos to keep those "masses" from moving here and give us the opportunity to pick out those we want because of their "useful" personal properties. We can think of lots of similar examples.

The last example mentioned shows that this one criterion is not sufficient. We can add a second one: Does the intervention create and increase resources for *autonomy* or does it reduce them, take them away? Locking people out could, for instance, be seen as an intervention into the situation only. I would doubt such a definition, but if we accept it for the sake of the argument, it is still certainly not a liberatory intervention because it reduces possibilities and resources for all concerned (for those behind the wall too). I can reduce muggings and other "street crime" by making people stay at home - but at what cost in terms of a reduction of social life!

"Autonomy", therefore, is not just retreat into private life. It rather means augmented resources for managing our own affairs. Retreat into my own private cell and to my own private television set is not autonomy. "Autonomy" also is not privatization in the sense that state activities are taken over or imitated by private action. Thus, there is no progress in private search warrants, private bodyguards, or private prisons. There is no progress in state-organized or state-supporting vigilantism. In contrast, there is probably nothing wrong with neighborhood watch schemes in which people look after each others' homes during an absence.

4 "Diversion" at Last

Where does "diversion" fit into this? Reducing state punishment obviously does diminish the amount of instrumental treatment of people. But certainly there can be instrumentality outside the function of punishment proper as well. Most measures of diversion are still attempts to change, educate, resocialize, and morally fortify the person. But we can identify what makes the difference again: There could be diversion that concentrates on the situation instead of the person. This applies particularly to the "conflict resolution" or "victim-offender reconciliation" schemes that have become widespread recently (and could be a chance to radically change criminal law). They are just another instrumental intervention if they aim at reforming the person (or even the persons - plural) concerned - as they often do if the conflict is, for instance, taken as the opportunity for a social-work intervention. They can, on the other hand, have a liberating function if they concentrate on the problem at hand, if they limit themselves to creating an opportunity for the people concerned to rearrange the situation that has developed, to compensate damage done and reaffirm offended honor, and to disentangle the social knot in order to go on living (together or consensually separated) without an unresolved traumatic past. In short, if they concentrate on the *situation* and its management instead of on the person. Here, as in other cases, everything depends on the details, and the line between technocratic perfection of control and creating the conditions of autonomy is very thin.

Sociologists, of course, have long been aware of the absurdities of prevention and the hazards of diversion.[10] The more cautious among us have drawn the conclusion that it is not for us to invent programs to solve the state's problems. We have to stay strictly negative, they say: Our task is criticism and the struggle *against* projects of control or with control implications. This is the attitude of what I call "political abolitionism" which primarily wants to get rid of the death penalty, then of life imprisonment, then of the prison, then of the state's power to punish at all. We will probably find that no substitute for these institutions is necessary.[11]

But for what we could call "empirical abolitionism", no such rigorous self-denial is necessary. There is no need (and little theoretical justification) for a hypercriticality that suspects devilish plots in all reforms. It is much more useful to have criteria to distinguish more from less harmful from even useful reforms. To supply them is the task of "theoretical abolitionism", the empirical and historical critique of punishment and social exclusion. I have, in this little exercise in social theory, tried to find and supply some such criteria: noninstrumentality, individuality, autonomy and its resources, the situation versus the person as object of intervention. But we will have to live with the discrepancy between political tactics and theoretical radicality. As political realists, we have to demand the impossible. As political pragmatists, we will not look down on reforms that take place, as long as the general direction is not totally wrong, in which case we would have to fight them. We just will not permit pragmatism to corrupt the radicality of our theoretical thinking.

Notes

1 The word "Hamburger Kessel" has recently become the generally known name for a police tactic against demonstrations in Germany. In it a greater number of demonstrators are surrounded by police and let out only individually and after lengthy searching and identification. This means that the procedure can take many hours during which the demonstrators are out in the cold, are not allowed to sit down, can get no food, and have no access to toilet facilities. In the Hamburg example of 1986, the police officers commanding this action have now (1991) been found guilty of "deprivation of liberty", but the Senator responsible promoted them and told the press that they had his full trust. In this way, the purely military term "encirculation" ("Einkesselung") has become an everyday civil word in Germany.

2 We can get the same effect when the "nation" or the "revolutionary party" is made the subject of history. In all these cases, social exclusion becomes an easy political instrument because the individual who could suffer from it has already been eradicated in theory.

3 Hans Gross also acted on his willingness to have all burdensome persons excluded by having his son, the psychoanalyst, libertarian, sexual radical, drug taker, and "anarchist" Otto Gross, forcibly taken into psychiatric custody in 1914. Otto Gross' expressionist friends (Johannes R. Becher, René Schickele, Else Lasker-Schüler, Richard Huelsenbeck, Franz Jung, Erich Mühsam) started a literary campaign to have him released.

4 Alfred Ploetz, founder and editor of the "Archiv", was also a founding member of the "Deutsche Gesellschaft für Soziologie" otherwise associated with such venerable names as Weber, Sombart, or Simmel. Wilhelm Schallmeyer, one of the spokesmen of "scientific racism", argued vehemently against the hypocrites of "racial superiority" and for a cool, as it were "value-free" treatment of questions of degeneration or up-grading of races.

5 Aly and Heim's (1991) attempt to isolate the element of economic interest and planning in the complicated process that led to Auschwitz has been countered repeatedly by warnings not to "rationalize" Nazi politics (see the debate in Schneider, 1991). In answer to conservative attempts to reduce the Nazi horror to just another of those dictatorial and warmongering regimes that history has seen again and again, other historians have tried to establish the totally irreducible and unique character of Auschwitz and Nazi Germany. Dan Diner (1987) is the most energetic exponent of such a position. He holds that the only legitimate perspective on Auschwitz is that of the victims. And, from this perspective, Auschwitz was "destruction for its own sake" without any meaning or aims (p. 71). In consequence, there is no way of "understanding" it. I do not see what, on the other hand, can be gained by totally "irrationalizing" Auschwitz.

6 Founded by Sir Francis Galton and already flourishing in Great Britain as in Germany toward the end of the 19th century.

7 As I have shown in some detail in my recent book on Adorno, his model was in fact the development of musical composition (as he saw it) and particularly Schönberg's liberation of music and the later deterioration of that achievement into a "system" of "composition with 12 tones" (Steinert, 1989).

8 The labeling-theory motive is most explicit in Sartre's "Saint Genet" (1952). It is amazing and symptomatic of the state of German sociology at that time that we needed the reimport of labeling theory from the United States when we could have had the same theoretical model in a more elaborated version from European sources like existentialism and Western Marxism.

9 Including Habermas (1985: 144), who calls it "performative self-contradiction" - the radical critique of reason would, he argues, affect that critique itself and undermine its validity and credibility. This criticism is only possible when "work" as the central human and therefore also potentially liberating activity has been abandoned in favor of, for instance, "communication". Such a theoretical shift may or may not have its merits, but it certainly is a farewell to the Frankfurt school tradition and particularly to Adorno.

10 Not least, it has been sociologists who have produced the bulk of data demonstrating that a lot of preventive efforts, and certainly the punitive ones, simply do not work. Even within the context of instrumental rationality, punishment cannot be justified. This is more or less public knowledge. Nevertheless, juridical texts and particularly those consequential ones in which the reasons for convicting a person for 3 instead of 2 years in prison are argued, those in which the possibility of release for a person who has been kept in custody

for 16 years is denied, those numerous bureaucratic elaborations that future centuries - if there should be any - will study as documents of an incomprehensible intellectual hardness and inhumanity - all these routine theoretical texts that have very real human victims are full of appeals to and incantations of those metaphysical "preventions", individual or general, that cannot be proved. If there is enough power behind a concept, it is very real in its consequences.

11 I would hold that the only position that can be taken with some theoretical consistency here is to deny the democratic legitimacy of *all* punishment. Anything less than that is just pragmatism.

References

Aly, G., and Heim, S. (1991). *Vordenker der Vernichtung. Auschwitz und die deutschen Pläne für eine neue europäische Ordnung.* Hamburg: Hoffmann und Campe.

Cohen, S. (1979). The punitive city: Notes on the dispersal of social control. *Contemporary Crises, 3,* 339-363.

Diner, D. (1987). Zwischen Aporie und Apologie. Über Grenzen der Historisierbarkeit des Nationalsozialismus. In D. Diner (Ed.), *Ist der Nationalsozialismus Geschichte? Zu Historisierung und Historikerstreit* (pp. 62-73). Frankfurt: Fischer.

Habermas, J. (1985). *Der philosophische Diskurs der Moderne.* Frankfurt/M: Suhrkamp.

Horkheimer, M., and Adorno, Th.W. (1947). *Dialektik der Aufklärung. Philosophische Fragmente.* Amsterdam: Querido.

Sartre, J.P. (1952). *Saint Genêt, comédien et martyr.* Paris: Gallimard.

Schneider, W. (Ed.) (1991). *Vernichtungspolitik.* Hamburg: Junius.

Steinert, H. (1989). *Adorno in Wien. Über die (Un-)Möglichkeit von Kunst, Kultur und Befreiung.* Wien: Verlag für Gesellschaftskritik.

Diversion in the Juvenile Justice System and a Sociological Theory of Social Control

Allan V. Horwitz[*]

1 Introduction

In recent years Donald Black and his colleagues have developed the basis for a general sociological theory of social control (Black, 1976, 1984, 1989a; Horwitz, 1990). This theory addresses such questions as the conditions under which various types of control systems develop, the kinds of people who use them, and the case outcomes that emerge. At a macrosociological level, structural and cultural aspects of society predict the style, form, and quantity of social control. At a microsociological level, the social structure of cases, including the social characteristics of victims and offenders, their supporters, and third party adjudicators, explains outcomes.

The style of social control is the type of response normative violations elicit. Different styles of social control vary in the ends they seek, the way they allocate responsibility for actions, the identities they provide deviants, and the focus of sanctions. The major styles include the penal style that inflicts punishment on offenders; the compensatory style that extracts payment from an offender to a victim for some harm; the conciliatory style in which both parties to a dispute jointly reach a harmonious solution; and the therapeutic style that changes the personalities of deviants (Black, 1976; Horwitz, 1990).

The form of social control refers to the mechanisms through which people respond to grievances. Some forms involve the direct response of grievants to offenders, with or without the aid of supporters. These forms include tolerance, avoidance, or exit from conflict situations, self-help responses, and negotiations between victims and offenders (Baumgartner, 1988; Black, 1989b). Other forms involve third party agents who impose solutions upon disputants. Another dimension is whether the sanctioning agent is a legal authority whose specific task is to apply sanctions or a community member with no legally binding sanctioning authority (Weber, 1925). Finally, forms of social control differ on the degree to which they respond to disputes through formalized rules or specific case by case responses.

A sociological theory of social control uses patterns of relationships between the parties involved in a case to predict the styles and forms of social control. For example, relational distance refers to the degree of intimacy between parties to a dispute: whether they are family members, friends, acquaintances, or strangers. The relational distance between offenders and their victims predicts when social control systems develop, the kinds of cases that enter these systems, and the outcomes of disputes (Black, 1976, chap. 3). Disputes that arise between intimates, for example, typically are handled informally through negotiation or therapy while those between strangers are more likely to enter adjudicative forums and elicit penal styles. In general, as relational distance increases, therapeutic, conciliatory, compensatory, and penal responses become increasingly likely (Horwitz, 1990, chaps. 2-5). The relative status of victims and offenders, as well as their status compared to third party adjudicators, also predicts the style and form of social control. In general, downward social control when a lower status offender offends a higher status victim tends to be penal; upward control, compensatory (Black, 1989a). Or, authorities often ignore grievances among lower status persons but reconcile those among higher status ones. Note that it is not the status of the offender alone that predicts the control response but the status *relationship* between offenders and victims.

Traditional demographic variables such as age, gender, or race reflect underlying social statuses such as integration, power, and conventionality. Age, the primary variable of interest in this paper, reflects a variety of social statuses such as social integration, status, and conventionality, as well as cultural assumptions regarding age itself (Baumgartner, 1992). Youths are typically less integrated, powerful, and conventional than members of other age groups. Their status is also dependent on whether they are subject to no, some, or much parental control. Like other low-status categories, youths are typically treated informally and without due-process rights, and so they face more harassment, degradation, and surveillance than adults. In addition, authorities generally view their conflicts as unimportant and dismiss cases of physical violence, property damage, or theft between juveniles and pay even less attention to complaints teenagers press against adults (Black, 1980: 23-29, 152-55). In contrast, they take complaints adults make against juveniles much more seriously. Hence, formal social control that involves the young virtually always takes the form of adult complainants and juvenile offenders.

In this paper, I develop some ideas about how a sociological theory of social control explains juvenile diversion. I examine three questions about diversion. First, how do social factors explain the emergence, style, and form of diversion programs? Second, what factors predict the sorts of cases that enter these programs? Finally, what social conditions are associated with the effectiveness of diversion?

I emphasize how the answer to each question involves the relationship of informal social control systems, especially within families, to diversion programs. A central proposition of a general theory of social control is that law and formal control arise when informal control is weak or unavailable (Black, 1976, chap. 6; Horwitz, 1990: 142). Legal control by the state develops when social control of families, schools, and communities is inadequate. In addition, particular cases are treated more or less legalistically depending on the amount of family control over juveniles. Finally, diversion programs will be effective to the extent they mobilize family involvement in change efforts. In each respect, diversion is responsive to the degree of informal control over juveniles.

The perspective I take here diverges from most discussions of diversion. Many of these emphasize how several ideologies, including labeling theory, civil libertarian thought, and the delegitimation of most traditional institutions of social control, converged in the late 1960s and early 1970s to produce sustained and profound ideological assaults on juvenile justice and other control institutions (Polk, 1987; Schur, 1973). The result was both to avoid sending youths to the juvenile correctional system at all and to establish due process protection for those youths who did enter this system. Other accounts emphasize how diversion programs arose out of the ideologies and self-interest of professional groups, as well as the need of the state to extend hegemonic control over a widening net of juvenile misconduct (e.g. Abel, 1982; Austin and Krisberg, 1981; Cohen, 1985; Scull, 1977). In these accounts, diversion represents a more cunning way of extending state control over wayward juveniles.

Both of these explanations emphasize "supply side" factors that assume the independent power and authority of control agents and professional groups. The state is viewed as a largely autonomous body responsible for maintaining social control over juveniles. Although changing ideological currents and the interests of professional groups and control agents undoubtedly had some influence in the emergence of the diversion movement, these explanations neglect how formal systems of social control, including diversion programs, are responsive to "demand side" processes of informal social control.

Before proceeding to discuss diversion, I must make several disclaimers. First, I proceed deductively and predict what ought to be the case if the sociological theory of social control is true. To the extent that the actual data regarding diversion do not fit the expectations of the theory, the theory must be modified. Second, I rely only upon the social variables of the theory used here to explain diversion and neglect ideological, economic, and interest group factors that undoubtedly are also important. Third, although the goal of theory is to develop universal propositions, the limits of my knowledge about other societies restrict my speculations to juvenile diversion programs in the United States. The extent to which the hypotheses advanced here apply to settings other than the United States is an open question. In addition, even within the United States, there is great variation both in types of diversion programs and across different states (e.g., Schwartz, 1989). I ignore this variation and treat diversion as a unitary phenomenon. Finally, despite the voluminous literature about diversion programs in the United States, we have little information about the kinds of youth who enter diversion programs, the sorts of parties who refer offenders into them, the relationships between victims and offenders, or how these programs actually work. Until such data become available, what follows is speculative.

2 Diversion as a Type of Social Control

Diversion, in the sense of handling offenders informally or doing nothing rather than treating them in the formal system, has traditionally been the *most prevalent* way of dealing with delinquents. Every study of juvenile justice indicates that the police refer for further processing only a relatively small number of cases that come to their attention. For example, most studies of police-juvenile encounters indicate that only about 15% of incidents result in arrest (Black and Reiss, 1970; Lundman, Sykes, and Clark, 1978). Even those relatively small number of cases that do lead to arrests rarely result in formal sanctioning but are dropped before proceeding to the juvenile court.

The most prevalent response to juvenile misconduct has traditionally been to restore order to a situation without further action or to rely on parental control (Black, 1980: 11-13). For example, if a shopkeeper summons the police to deal with a group of unruly juveniles, the police may disperse the group and consider the situation resolved. Or, in the case of a juvenile caught breaking into a neighbor's home, the police may notify his parents and leave the matter in their hands.

Most discussions of diversion, however, use it in a second sense of avoiding formal correctional processes through the use of community treatment programs. In these accounts, diversion arose in the United States in the late 1960s out of the recommendations of the Juvenile Task Force of the President's Crime Commission of 1967 (Lemert, 1967). According to its original conception, diversion was a "process whereby problems otherwise dealt with in a context of delinquency and official action will be defined and handled by other means" (Lemert, 1981: 36). By 1974, diversion was embodied as a national policy implemented with federal monies from the Law Enforcement Assistance Administration. This policy discouraged the detention and incarceration of youthful offenders and instead encouraged the use of community-based options (Curran, 1988). Although some diversion programs are marked by arbitration (Ezell, 1989) or restitution (Staples, 1986), most are based on therapeutic principles of rehabilitation, counseling, or treatment. Hence, in its second sense, "diversion" refers to the treatment of offenders within community treatment programs who otherwise would have been referred to the more formalized juvenile justice system.

The new aspect of diversion is that it now occurs *within* the juvenile justice system as an explicit way of organizing programs. Diversion provides control agents additional options of either releasing offenders or referring them for formal processing. Although there have been some reductions in the long-term correctional handling of youths in public institutions, the great increase in the number of juveniles held in private correctional facilities has resulted in a stable overall rate of correctional placements between 1970 and 1983 (Curran, 1988: 367). However, there has been a great expansion in the number of youths placed in residential treatment settings in the child welfare system and in psychiatric units of private and general hospitals (Cohen, 1985; Lerman, 1980; Schwartz, 1989, chap. 7). For example, the number of children per 100,000 population in residential treatment centers for the emotionally disturbed grew from 4 in 1969 to 8 in 1981 to 10 in 1986 (Witkin et al., 1990). Overall, the number of juveniles handled within formal settings over the period between 1970 and 1985 when diversion programs were implemented has increased (Curran, 1988; Lerman, 1980; Sarri, 1981; Schwartz, 1989).[1] The stabilization of commitments to correctional programs, the growth of admissions to therapeutic programs, and the overall increase in the formal handling of juveniles, probably indicates that diversion programs deal primarily with youth who otherwise would have avoided formal processing, not so much those who otherwise would have entered correctional facilities (Ezell, 1989).

Within the juvenile justice system, diversion programs are therapeutic or restitutive rather than penal. Although these programs are ultimately coercive because they are backed by the authority of the state and somewhat restrict the liberty and privileges of offenders, punishment-oriented processes rarely predominate in these programs. Instead, most feature service or treatment orientations that provide counseling, education, job training, or recreational services (Ezell, 1989; Lundman, 1984, chap. 4).

As forms of social control, diversion programs represent less legality, distance, and exclusion than traditional correctional programs. Diversion programs typically operate with less formalized rules regarding substance and procedure than proceedings in the juvenile court. Peer and/or lay bodies rather than formal adjudicators impose sanctions so there is typically less distance between offenders and sanctioning agents. Offenders are not institutionalized but remain in the community. In each respect, diversion programs represent less formalized and exclusionary forms of social control than traditional alternatives. The critical question is what factors account for why more therapeutic and less formal modes of responding to juvenile misconduct developed in recent years?

3 The Development of Diversion Programs

3.1 Diversion and Informal Social Control

A theory of social control should explain why diversion has developed as a dominant way of handling juvenile offenders. The sociological theory of social control predicts that shifts in informal systems of control produce fundamental changes in formal systems of social control. The expansion of state-centered social control occurs as the control exercised by families, schools, and communities weakens.

I focus on informal social control because official agents of social control do not initiate most cases that enter the formal system. Rather, citizen complainants observe about three out of every four cases of juvenile misconduct that come to police attention (Black and Reiss, 1970; Reiss, 1971). Families are responsible for many referrals, especially for status offenses such as incorrigibility or running away. As well, when nonfamily members initiate referrals into the formal system, control agents will release offenders to their families if they are seen as capable and willing to exercise informal sanctions. Regardless of who refers a case to official attention, the response of control agents depends on the availability and willingness of families to exercise informal control.

The social control of delinquency in the United States has always been responsive to changes in informal control systems. Historically, the unit of responsibility for juvenile justice has not been the individual child but the child in the context of the family group (Staples, 1986). Before the development of specific correctional facilities for juveniles in the last half of the 19th century, parents, masters, or communities were responsible for sanctioning wayward juveniles (Mennel, 1972). Over the course of the 19th century, social life became marked by growing heterogeneity, mobility, and urbanization. Families could not as readily absorb vagrant youths as apprentices or servants, so were decreasingly able to serve as a locus for social control. Specialized police forces and, eventually, juvenile reformatories developed to control a "bachelor subculture" of transient young men who faced little or no informal social control (Lane, 1980). The largest class of entrants into the newly developed institutions were lower-class adolescent males, and occasionally females, who had either no family ties or conflicts with their families (Brenzel, 1980; Mennel, 1983). Often their fathers were dead or had deserted the family, leaving it bereft of informal control mechanisms. In other cases immigrant families felt that only formal sanctions could correct the strange and incorrigible behaviors of their children. Through the first half of the 20th century, the juvenile court and reformatory were especially likely to apply formal sanctions when kin groups were unable or unwilling to accept responsibility for offenders.

The emergence of diversion programs in the 1960s and 1970s likewise corresponds to drastic changes that occurred in American families. These changes weakened informal control systems and expanded social control institutions that could supply services previously provided within the community. Especially important has been the soaring rate of divorce. During the mid-19th century, the divorce rate was about 1 per 1,000 families. This steadily increased to about 10 per 1,000 families in the mid-1960s. At this time, divorces sharply rose, so 23 divorces for every 1,000 marriages occurred by 1979 (Sweet and Bumpass, 1987: 178). By 1988 the number of divorces each year was twice as high as in 1966 and three times higher than in 1950 (Mintz and Kellogg, 1988: 203). Because of rising divorce rates, female householder families without a spouse grew by 175% between 1950 and 1984 while married couple families only grew by 47%. Since 1960, the number of children involved in divorce has tripled, and nearly 20% of children under 18 live with only their mothers (Mintz and Kellogg, 1988: 225; Sweet and Bumpass, 1987: 264). Although over 80% of white children born in the early 1950s lived with two biological parents through age 17, over half of those born in the early 1980s will spend at least some time in a single parent family. The number of black children living with both biological parents until age 17 has dropped from 52% in the early 1950s to only about one of every six children today (Ellwood, 1988; Sweet and Bumpass, 1987).

We know that living with one parent is associated with a variety of negative experiences including delinquency, school dropout, and mental health problems (e.g. Furstenberg and Cherlin, 1991; Peterson and Zill, 1986; Uhlenberg and Eggebeen, 1986; Wallerstein, 1984). Of central interest here is that divorce and single parenthood, as well as the dramatic growth of married women's labor force participation, are also associated with a weakening of informal social control. The most direct effect is that single-parent families have less adult authority present to exercise social control. One monitor cannot control behavior as well as two. In addition, growing numbers of children are raised by fathers who are not their natural parents. One of every seven households with children involves a remarried parent and a child from a previous marriage (Mintz and Kellogg, 1988: 227). Because stepparents cannot exercise authority with as much legitimacy as natural parents, a further weakening of family social control arises. Finally, mothers who enter the labor force have less time to provide surveillance over their childrens' behavior.

Higher divorce rates and changes in women's labor force participation affect not only families but also neighborhoods. Many areas become free of informal controls during the day as adults abandon them for the workplace (Felson, 1986). Higher rates of divorce and geographic mobility also result in more frequent movement of families in and out of areas. The result is a declining capacity of communities to exercise strong informal social control.

The control exercised by the school is another traditional source of social control over youth. As with family and community control, discipline in schools has weakened. In addition, increased legal scrutiny over social control has led schools to abandon measures such as corporal punishment, suspensions, or expulsions without formal proceedings (Lieberman, 1981: 128-135).

All of these changes lead to the diminuition of informal control over juvenile misbehavior. Divorced parents have weaker ties to children who do not live with them and single parents have less ability to exercise informal control. Stepparents lack the legitimacy to exercise as much discipline as natural parents. Households with two working parents have less ability and time to control their children than those who have one parent at home. Neighborhoods that are abandoned by adults during the daytime have little capacity to control the activities of teenagers. Compared to prior generations, teenagers, especially girls, now face far less supervision of activities, are more likely to be away from home at night, and spend more time with peers and less with parents (Felson and Gottfredson, 1984). American families, communities, and schools cannot exert strong informal social control over teenaged children, who can easily evade adult surveillance.

Our theory predicts an increase in the amount of formal social control with the decline of informal means of social control over juveniles. Family ties weaken in single parent, reconstituted, and dual-worker households. This leads not only to less internal social control but also to greater social distance between family members. With greater distance comes a growing willingness to use formal systems of social control.[2] In addition, although the police and the juvenile court are reluctant to exercise authority over offenders in the presence of strong family control, they are unwilling to abandon authority over youth where no family is responsible. From this perspective, it is not so much ideological, economic, or professional interests that account for the net-widening effects of the diversion movement. Rather, formal means of social control expand when informal means of social control become weak or unavailable.

3.2 The Style and Form of Diversion

The growth of formal social control with the decline of informal control can account for the increasing number of juveniles entering the juvenile justice system. It also explains why diversion programs deal with offenders who previously would have been handled informally. It does not, however, explain why *diversion* rather than formal institutional programs has arisen to deal with offenders. What accounts for the style and form of diversion programs?

Several factors seem associated with the emergence of diversion programs. The heightened emphasis on due process in the juvenile court that began in the late 1960s had its greatest impact on the processing of status offenders (Schwartz,

1989). Parents could no longer use the court to sanction their incorrigible, truant, or sexually precocious children. We would expect that alternative programs emerge to satisfy parents who cannot control unruly children. In fact, there were large increases in the number of children and adolescents treated in psychiatric facilities (Lerman, 1981) and of status offenders in diversion programs in the private sector (Curran, 1988) after 1970. We infer from these increases that diversion programs are largely handling youths in conflict with their families (Lundman, 1984, chap. 4; Schwartz, 1989, chap. 7). The general principle that therapeutic social control is typically used to deal with conflicts among family members would account for the predominance of the therapeutic style in diversion programs (Horwitz, 1982, 1990, chap. 5).

A second reason for the therapeutic orientation of diversion programs is that the response to juvenile misconduct has always been congruent with therapeutic rather than penal styles. The cultural construction of juveniles attributes misconduct to emotional problems rather than to freely chosen evil actions. The therapeutic notion that problems stem from emotional difficulties or "acting out" behaviors is compatible with traditional images of children. The juvenile court has always relied on a relatively informal, person-centered philosophy that relies on the expertise of mental health professionals (Schlossman, 1977). Especially because diversion programs predominantly deal with first offenders or nonserious offenders, therapeutic orientations prevail.

Third, when neighbors, shopowners, and strangers demand that something be done with juvenile offenders, the growing legalization of the juvenile court burdens control agents who might otherwise prosecute offenders. Control agents can exercise formal control with less difficulty and fewer limits through diversion programs. In this way, they can satisfy complainants' demands that wayward juveniles be sanctioned while avoiding the time, trouble, and possible failure of formal prosecution.

Finally, the ideologies and self-interest of professional groups also play a role in the style and form of diversion programs. The emergence of these programs corresponded with the expansion of therapeutic social control in the United States (Conrad and Schneider, 1980; Horwitz, 1982). Between 1955 and 1983, treatment episodes in organized mental health facilities increased from 1.7 to 7 million (Mechanic, 1989: 10). At the same time, the number of mental health professionals, especially psychologists and psychiatric social workers, grew tremendously (Dial et al., 1990). Experts committed to the ideology and practice of individual treatment designed diversion programs that provide rehabilitative, treatment, and counseling services (Polk, 1987). They not only provide employment for many therapeutic professionals but do so in ways compatible with their occupational socialization.

Hence, diversion usually involves therapeutic social control over youths that families previously sanctioned. In cases that do not involve family complainants, they provide a less legalized alternative than the newly formalized juvenile court. In both ways diversion is compatible with one of the master trends of social control in the 20th century: the expansion of the therapeutic state.

4 Who Enters Diversion Programs?

A theory of social control uses the social characteristics of offenders and victims, as well as the relationship of offenders and victims to social control agents, to predict case outcomes.[3] A theory of diversion examines who offends whom in what circumstances to explain why some cases enter diversion programs, some avoid formal processing, and others enter the traditional correctional system.

The role of the family is influential in understanding the outcome of particular cases that enter diversion programs. Whether family members are complainants or supporters, whether they are willing to sanction offenders informally or desire formal help, and the kind of help they want should critically affect how cases proceed. In addition, family responses shape how control agents react to particular cases. These agents are usually sensitive to parental wishes. When families desire diversion alternatives they should be more likely to get them, while informal control should occur when parents are willing to apply strong sanctions. In contrast, processing through correctional institutions should be more common in the absence of parental control.

A powerful predictor should be the extent of adult authority to which juveniles are subject. In general, formal social control operates when juveniles are subject to little social control in the home, school, and community (Black, 1980). When strong families are present, police and prosecutors tend to avoid formal processing and rely on parental control. Compared to offenders who avoid official processing, diverted youths should more likely come from broken, single-parent, and disorganized families. These families, however, should not have abandoned all responsibility for the juvenile. Incarceration arises in a vacuum of parental social control (Dannefer, 1984; Staples, 1987).

The relational distance between offenders and victims is a second characteristic of cases associated with diversion. The use of authoritative social control is related directly to the relational distance between disputants (Black, 1976, chap. 3). Therefore, offenses that enter diversion programs should be less likely to involve strangers as complainants than those that are processed through the formal juvenile system. Conversely, therapeutic control is inverse to the relational distance between persons (Horwitz, 1990: 81). Because therapy emerges when family members have grievances against each other, we predict that youths who enter diversion programs are more likely to have offended family members than strangers. Therapeutic definitions of problems allow parents to see children as deserving of help rather than evil and at the same time protect the relational status quo within the family. Cases that enter diversion programs are likely to involve family members as complainants or families with weak, but not absent, informal control systems (e.g. Schwartz, 1989, chap. 7).

In addition to the presence of informal control and relational distance, social class should predict the entry into diversion programs. Therapy of all sorts is more compatible with the values, preferences, and cultural conceptions of self held by middle- than by working- or lower-class families (Horwitz, 1982, 1990). Middle-class people define therapists as interested in emotional health or social adjustment, rather than in overt social control (Baumgartner, 1988: 35). When middle-class parents find it necessary to use formal social control for their children, therapists are less objectionable than police and correctional agents. Likewise, when middle-class adults are *victims* of juvenile offenders, they too may find the therapeutic process more compatible than involvement in the juvenile court. Therapists are more likely to be of comparable class status and share a common culture with middle-class families and victims than police or correctional agents, so provide more acceptable outlets of conflict management.

Gender should also be associated with diversion. In general, girls are subject to more informal social control than boys so should typically avoid processing in the juvenile justice system (e.g., Kruttschnitt, 1981). However, girls who are not subject to informal control may receive less tolerance for their behavior than boys. In the past, girls free of informal control have had disproportionately high incarceration rates for status offenses such as vagrancy, running away, and incorrigibility (Chesney-Lind, 1977; Sarri, 1983). Because the therapeutic style is associated with females (Horwitz, 1990, chap. 5), when parental control is lacking, therapeutic diversion programs should be a particularly attractive alternative to incarceration for females. The notion that offenders need help, suffer from emotional problems, and should not be punished are congruent with cultural constructions of femininity.

Finally, age should be associated with entry into diversion programs. We would expect that the delicts of particularly young offenders, who culturally lack the free will and responsibility necessary for penal dispositions, are more likely to be treated therapeutically. As they enter late adolescence, however, their misbehavior should increasingly elicit penal responses (Graham and Rutter, 1977).

Hence, our theory of social control predicts that juveniles who enter traditional correctional facilities will be lower-class males who are subject to relatively little familial control. Compared with this group, youths who enter diversion programs will more likely be higher social status, female, younger, and have offended family members. Compared to offenders who avoid any contact with the formal juvenile system, diverted juveniles should have weaker family ties and have conflicts with their families.

The limited data on characteristics of diverted youth is consistent with our predictions: Compared to those who enter correctional facilities, they are disproportionately middle-class, young, female, minor offenders, and have no prior records (Ezell, 1989: 366; Lemert, 1981: 40). However, because the literature does not discuss the degree of informal control over offenders, the relationship of offenders to complainants, or how diverted juveniles compare to those who entirely avoid formal processing, we are not in a position to evaluate adequately the strength of the theory.

5 The Effectiveness of Diversion Programs

The final topic I address regards the social conditions that lead to effective diversion programs. A social theory of effectiveness predicts and explains the varying effectiveness of control efforts in social space. To what extent does the way people are embedded in different family, peer, and community groups as well as the relationship between clients and treatment agents affect whether diversion efforts are successful, counterproductive, or without effect? I assume that an effective diversion program leads to less repeated offending compared to the informal or correctional sanctions that offenders would otherwise receive.

Although a number of literature reviews compare the effectiveness of diversion programs with traditional programs, the results are uncertain and ambiguous. Some reviewers find that diversion programs are more effective than probation and parole or institutional-residential programs (Andrews et al., 1990; Lab and Whitehead, 1988), others claim treatment in institutional or community residential settings works as well as noninstitutional programs (Garrett, 1985), and some assert that no programs are effective (Lipton, Martinson, and Wilks, 1975). However, these studies neither compare juveniles in diversion programs to those who avoid treatment entirely nor examine the sorts of social characteristics of offenders, their families, peer groups, and treatment agents that might predict the effectiveness of the diversion process.

Several social conditions should lead to effective diversion programs. First, programs must mobilize or at least be congruent with the efforts of families, peer groups, and communities (Horwitz, 1990, chaps. 10, 11). Programs that link treatment with intensive efforts to strengthen family and community ties should produce the most successful results (Coates, 1981). The best programs work with families and peers, as well as the identified delinquent, to promote familial affection, parental monitoring and supervision, anticriminal role models, and positive peer associations (Andrews et al., 1990). Programs are also most effective when family and community members participate in shaming yet also reintegrate errant members into the group with little stigma or sense of difference (Braithwaite, 1989). In contrast, programs that focus on changing the individual through examining vague personal and emotional problems or bolstering self-esteem should be of limited usefulness. We expect that change efforts that ignore family, peer, and community networks will be unsuccessful (Coates, 1981).

Diversion programs should also recognize that much behavior such as running away, truancy, vandalism, or fighting involves grievances of youths against families, peers, and school authorities (Black, 1983). These programs should be sensitive not only to charges adults make against juveniles but also to the conflicts youths have with others. Empowering juveniles in their family and community environments might be one effective way of controlling behavior that is labeled as delinquent.

Second, the nature of the surrounding community will work to either reinforce or contradict the efforts of change agents. When delinquents are members of tightly knit communities whose values coincide with control agents, the efforts of informal community members are likely to strengthen treatment efforts (Braithwaite, 1989; Horwitz, 1990). Conversely, juveniles who live in communities whose values diverge from those of change agents and who are members of tightly knit oppositional groups, such as juvenile gangs, are least likely to benefit from these programs. Strong community ties can thus work to either facilitate or impede rehabilitation efforts, depending on the congruence of the values of communities and change agents.

A third aspect of effective diversion involves the relationship between service deliverers and clients. In general, programs that minimize the distance between treaters and clients ought to realize better results than those that feature much social and cultural distance (Horwitz, 1990: 217-218). Programs with treatment agents who relate to clients in interpersonally warm, flexible, and enthusiastic ways should be more effective than those with agents who act in more traditionally bureaucratic ways (Andrews et al., 1990; Lofland, 1969). Relatively unbureaucratic programs with counselors who share many characteristics with clients may produce the most positive change. In this regard, it is worth pursuing experiments that take diversion out of the juvenile justice system completely and use parents, teachers, and, especially, peers, as mediators and change agents.

Finally, because effective therapeutic programs require the voluntary participation of clients, coercive diversion programs should not work. Yet, the proper balance between penal and therapeutic efforts in diversion programs will always be difficult to achieve. On the one hand, these programs must communicate at least some blame and disapproval of the offender's action (Braithwaite, 1989). On the other hand, they must harness the commitment of the offender to participate in the treatment effort. Needless to say, it is very difficult to develop programs in which shaming and voluntary participation coincide.

6 Conclusion

The critics of diversion programs rightly conclude that youths who now enter diversion programs would not have entered the juvenile correctional system at all in prior decades. In this sense, diversion has indeed "widened the net" of formal social control. This has led most commentators to criticize the diversion movement as an unhealthy expansion of state-centered social control (e.g. Austin and Krisberg, 1981; Cohen, 1985; Curran, 1988; Lemert, 1981; Polk, 1987; see, however, Binder and Geis, 1984). In their view, diversion programs not only restrict the liberty of and increase control over juveniles but also have fewer restraints over the behavior of control agents.

These critical accounts neglect the social forces that lead to diversion programs. While it seems true that diverted offenders would, in the past, have been released to their families, it is also probably true that their families are now unable or unwilling to sanction their behavior. Most juveniles who enter diversion programs do not do so because of the interests of professional control agents but because some community member, often their parents, feels that some benefit would arise. We must examine families and family control systems to understand why diversion programs have developed, what cases enter them, and when they are effective.[4]

In the past, diverting youth to the care of their parents was probably an effective response to juvenile misbehavior. At present, when parents, teachers, and other adults do not effectively sanction youth, responses that avoid the formal system entirely may only exacerbate delinquent conduct. In societies that lack strong familial control, the only alternative to effective diversion programs may be more correctional responses. Therefore, it is critical to search for ways to enhance the effectiveness of these programs. The development of community forums that negotiate and mediate not only grievances against juveniles but also ones juveniles have with their families, peers, and other adults might provide the best alternative to enhanced systems of state imposed control. Ultimately, to deal with juvenile misconduct we must look for ways to strengthen institutions that provide informal social control and to empower juveniles themselves rather than rely on a growing therapeutic state of uncertain effectiveness.

Notes

* M.P. Baumgartner and Donald Black provided many helpful comments on a previous draft of this manuscript.

1 Another change brought about by the diversion movement in the United States has been a change from public to private forms of social control. Between 1950 and 1974, the percentage of youths resident in private facilities went from 21% to 48% and stabilized at that figure up to 1983 (Curran, 1988: 367). By 1983, the private sector accounted for

about 80% of community-based treatment while public facilities held nearly 90% of juveniles in institutional settings (Curran, 1988: 369).

2 Another consequence of growing familial distance might be a growing rate of conflict between youths and adults. Mothers who are the sole disciplinarian or who spend their days at work will probably meet more resistance and defiance from their children. In addition, greater family distance should lead to more participation in juvenile subcultures with values oppositional to adult authority. If so, changing family structures lead both to a greater amount of conflict between children and parents and to a greater willingness of parents to use formal control over their children.

3 In the present case, the characteristics of offenders will be relatively homogeneous since all are youths who are relatively powerless compared to adult complainants.

4 We now have the paradoxical situation in which the mental health system almost entirely lacks effective therapeutic programs for juveniles and adolescents. Too often, the only opportunities for therapeutic treatment now arise when juveniles break the law. Troubled, but lawful, juveniles who could perhaps derive more benefit from therapeutic programs cannot enter them while delinquents who resist therapeutic intervention are forced to participate.

References

Abel, R. (Ed.) (1982). *The politics of informal justice* (2 volumes). New York: Academic Press.

Andrews, D.A., Zinger, I., Hoge, R.D., Bonta, J., Gendrea, P., and Cullen, F.T. (1990). Does correctional treatment work? A clinically relevant and psychologically informed meta-analysis. *Criminology, 28,* 369-397.

Austin, J., and Krisberg, B. (1981). Wider, stronger and different nets: The dialectics of criminal justice reform. *Journal of Research in Crime and Delinquency, 18,* 165-196.

Baumgartner, M.P (1988). *The moral order of a suburb.* New York: Oxford University Press.

Baumgartner, M.P. (1992). War and peace in early childhood. *Virginia Review of Sociology, 1,* 1-38.

Binder, A., and Geis, G. (1984). Ad populum argumentation in criminology: Juvenile diversion as rhetoric. *Crime and Delinquency, 30,* 309-333.

Black, D. (1976). *The behavior of law.* New York: Academic Press.

Black, D. (1980). *The manners and customs of the police.* New York: Academic Press.

Black, D. (1983). Crime as social control. *American Sociological Review, 48,* 34-45.

Black, D. (Ed.) (1984). *Toward a general theory of social control,* Volumes 1 and 2. New York: Academic Press.

Black, D. (1989a). *Sociological justice.* New York: Oxford University Press.

Black, D. (1989b). The elementary forms of conflict management. In *New Directions in the study of justice, law, and social control.* Prepared by the School of Justice Studies, Arizona State University. New York: Plenum.

Black, D., and Reiss, A.J. (1970). Police control of juveniles. *American Sociological Review, 35,* 63-77.

Braithwaite, J. (1989). Crime, shame, and reintegration. Cambridge: Cambridge University Press.

Brenzel, B. (1980). Domestication as reform: A study of the socialization of wayward girls, 1856-1905. *Harvard Educational Review, 50,* 196-213.

Chesney-Lind, M. (1977). Judicial paternalism and the female status offender. *Crime and Delinquency, 23,* 121-135.

Coates, R. (1981). Community-based services for juvenile delinquents: Concept and implications for practice. *Journal of Social Issues, 37,* 87-101.

Cohen, S. (1985). *Visions of social control.* New York: Basil Blackwell.

Conrad P., and Schneider, J.W. (1980). *Deviance and medicalization: From badness to sickness.* St. Louis, MO: Mosby.

Curran, D.J. (1988). Destructuring, privatization, and the promise of juvenile diversion: Compromising community-based corrections. *Crime and Delinquency, 34,* 363-378.

Dannefer, D. (1984). "Who signs the complaint?": Relational distance and the juvenile justice process. *Law and Society Review, 18,* 249-271.

Dial, T.H., Tebbutt, R., Pion, G.M., Kohourt, J., VanderBos, G., Johnson, M., Schervish, P.H., Whitney, L., Fox, J.C., and Meuvin, E.I. (1990). Human resources in Mental Health. In R.W. Manderscheid and M.A. Sonnenschein (Eds.), *Mental health in the United States, 1990* (pp. 196-215). Washington, DC: U.S. Government Printing Office.

Ellwood, D.T. (1988). *Poor support: Poverty in the American family.* New York: Basic Books.

Ezell, M. (1989). Juvenile arbitration: Net widening and other unintended consequences. *Journal of Research in Crime and Delinquency, 26,* 358-377.

Felson, M. (1986). *The synchronized society.* Unpublished manuscript.

Felson, M., and Gottfredson, M. (1984). Some indicators of adolescent activities near peers and parents. *Journal of Marriage and the Family, 46,* 709-714.

Furstenberg, F.F., and Cherlin, A. (1991). *Divided families: What happens to children when parents part.* Cambridge, MA: Harvard University Press.

Garrett, C.J. (1985). Effects of residential treatment on adjudicated delinquents: A meta-analysis. *Journal of Research in Crime and Delinquency, 22,* 287-308.

Graham, P., and Rutter, M. (1977). Adolescent disorders. In M. Rutter and L. Hersov (Eds.), *Child psychiatry.* Oxford: Blackwell Scientific.

Horwitz, A.V. (1982). *The social control of mental illness.* New York: Academic Press.

Horwitz, A.V. (1990). *The logic of social control.* New York: Plenum.

Kruttschnitt, C. (1981). Social status and sentences of female offenders. *Law and Society Review, 15,* 247-265.

Lab, S.P., and Whitehead, J.T. (1988). An analysis of juvenile correctional treatment. *Crime and Delinquency, 34,* 60-83.

Lane, R. (1980). Urban police and crime in nineteenth-century America. In N. Morris and M. Tonry (Eds.), *Crime and justice: An annual review of research, Volume 2* (pp. 1-43). Chicago, IL: University of Chicago Press.

Lemert, E.M. (1967). The juvenile court: Quest and realities. In The President's Commission on Law Enforcement and Administration of Justice, *Task Force Report: Juvenile Delinquency and Youth Crime* (pp. 91-106). Washington, DC: U.S. Government Printing Office.

Lemert, E.M. (1981). Diversion in juvenile justice: What hath been wrought. *Journal of Research in Crime and Delinquency, 22,* 34-46.

Lerman, P. (1980). Trends and issues in the deinstitutionalization of youths in trouble. *Crime and Delinquency, 26,* 281-298.

Lieberman, J. K. (1981). *The litigious society.* New York: Basic Books.

Lipton, D., Martinson, R., and Wilks, J. (1975). *The effectiveness of correctional treatment: A survey of evaluation studies.* New York: Praeger.

Lofland, J. (1969). *Deviance and identity.* Englewood Cliffs, NJ: Prentice-Hall.

Lundman, R.J. (1984). *Prevention and control of juvenile delinquency.* New York: Oxford University Press.

Lundman, R.J., Sykes, R.E., and Clark, J.P. (1978). Police control of juveniles: A replication. *Journal of Research in Crime and Delinquency, 15,* 74-91.

Mechanic, D. (1989). *Mental health and social policy* (3rd ed.). Englewood Cliffs, NJ: Prentice-Hall.

Mennel, R.M. (1972). Origins of the juvenile court: Changing perspectives on the legal rights of juvenile delinquents. *Crime and Delinquency, 18,* 68-78.

Mennel, R.M. (1983). Attitudes and policies toward juvenile delinquency in the United States: A historiographical review. In N. Morris and M. Tonry (Eds.), *Crime and Justice: An Annual Review of Research, Volume 4* (pp. 191-224). Chicago, IL: University of Chicago Press.

Mintz, S., and Kellogg, S. (1988). *Domestic revolutions: A social history of American family life.* New York: Free Press.

Peterson, J.L., and Zill, N. (1986). Marital disruption, parent-child relationships, and behavior problems in children. *Journal of Marriage and the Family, 48,* 295-307.

Polk, K. (1987). When less means more: An analysis of destructuring in criminal justice. *Crime and Delinquency, 33,* 358-378.

Reiss, A.J. (1971). *The police and the public.* New Haven, CT: Yale University Press.

Sarri, R. (1981). The effectiveness paradox: Institutional vs community placement of offenders. *Journal of Social Issues, 37,* 34-50.

Sarri, R. (1983). Gender issues in juvenile justice. *Crime and Delinquency, 29,* 381-397.

Schlossman, S.L. (1977). *Love and the American delinquent: The theory and practice of 'Progressive' juvenile justice 1825-1920.* Chicago, IL: University of Chicago Press.

Schur, E. (1973). *Radical nonintervention.* Englewood Cliffs: Prentice-Hall.

Schwartz, I.M. (1989). *(In)justice for juveniles: Rethinking the best interests of the child.* Lexington, MA: Lexington Books.

Scull, A. (1977). *Decarceration: Community treatment and the deviant.* Englewood Cliffs: Prentice-Hall.

Staples, W. (1986). Restitution as a sanction in juvenile court. *Crime and Delinquency, 32,* 177-185.

Staples, W. (1987). Law and social control in juvenile justice dispositions. *Journal of Research in Crime and Delinquency, 24,* 7-23.

Sweet, J.A., and Bumpass, L.L. (1987). *American families and households.* New York: Russell Sage Foundation.

Uhlenberg, P., and Eggebeen D. (1986). The declining well-being of American adolescents. *The Public Interest, 82,* 25-38.

Wallerstein, J.S. (1984). Children of divorce: Preliminary report of a ten year follow-up of young children. *American Journal of Orthopsychiatry, 54,* 444-458.

Weber, M. (1925). *Max Weber on law in economy and society* (M. Rheinstein Ed.). Cambridge, MA: Harvard University Press.

Witkin, M.J., Atay, J.E., Fell, A.S., and Manderscheid, R.W. (1990). Specialty mental health system characteristics. In R.W. Manderscheid and M.A. Sonnenschein (Eds.), *Mental health, United States 1990* (pp. 1-138). Washington, DC: U.S. Government Printing Office.

Diversion and Social Control: Alternative Measures of Crime Control

Albert J. Reiss, Jr.

1 Introduction

The major goal of this paper is to explore ways that social control theory contributes to the prevention of juvenile offending and to the development of alternatives to juvenile and criminal justice systems for detecting, processing, and controlling law-breakers and law breaking. We begin by critically examining the ideas of *diversion* from criminal justice and *alternatives* to it. We then turn to consider how a few theories of social control can be linked to the idea of *alternatives* to criminal justice.

2 Diversion From and Alternatives To Juvenile and Criminal Justice

The roots of diversion and alternatives to criminal justice are found in retributive and deterrence theories of punishment and their embodiment in the criminal law and its enforcement, the processing of persons violating those laws, and their sentencing by justices to punishment and correction. This model prevailed for all criminal law violators until near the close of the 19th century when, in 1899, the Illinois legislature in the United States passed the Juvenile Court Act. The Cook County Juvenile Court created by this act became the model for all state juvenile courts in the United States and in many other countries.

The legislation separated the processing and disposition of juvenile from adult offenders under the legal doctrine of *parens patriae*. Under this doctrine, the State had the right and duty to act on behalf of the child whenever the child's welfare was not being protected by the parents. The Act not only diverted juveniles to a separate judicial branch, but the juvenile court was conceived as an alternative to punishment and incarceration, an alternative to insure that juveniles would be reformed. Accordingly, the court sought to determine what were the specific needs of the minor and to develop an individualized treatment program. The goal of the intervention was to determine the causes of the juvenile's misconduct and to find ways to induce conformity. Juvenile court proceedings lacked the formality of adult criminal court proceedings, because the State was presumed to act in the best interests of the child. There were few safeguards of the child's legal or moral rights.

Often overlooked in assessing the effect of this reform movement is the fact that the legislation substantially widened what constituted an offense. Not only were juveniles held accountable for all violations under the criminal law but for a host of new offenses that were created to insure they would not grow up to be adult criminals. They could become wards of the court, for example, for failing to attend school (truancy), for staying out too late at night (curfew violations), failure to obey parents (incorrigibility and running away from home), idling in the streets, and entering places prohibited to minors.

Diversion of juveniles from adult criminal courts posed the issue of what were the goals of processing juvenile offenders separately and what was to be the shape of the alternative. The goals of punishment and corrections were rejected for the alternatives of *reform* of offenders through education and their *individual treatment*. Yet, quite soon, the ideal was faced with the practical questions of *how* to reform and treat offenders, particularly since there was no alternative model for how the court was to process offenders to change them. Rejecting the model of adult corrections, over a period of years a number of major alternative institutions emerged. Born were alternative parenting institutions such as probation supervision, foster placement of dependent, neglected, and delinquent children, Big Brother and Big Sister programs, and the parental school for incorrigible and habitually truant youths. Born were institutions to change delinquent persons such as diagnostic and treatment clinics for those with defective personalities. And soon, confronted with the problem of recidivism and treatment failures, incarceration returned under the guise of training and reform schools, the juvenile version of adult penal corrections. Because the goal of juvenile justice was to reform offenders rather than to dispense justice, the length of time a juvenile was to spend in an institution, treated, or on probation was not fixed in advance but left to treatment agents and the court to decide upon recommendation and review of the offender's progress.

These then were the alternatives born of a diversion from adult criminal justice. By the 1960s, many of these alternatives were being challenged by research that questioned the effectiveness of the individualized treatment model and its inattention to prevention of delinquency. Acknowledging the failure of those alternatives to juvenile justice, the State nonetheless continues to proliferate their number as the search goes on for alternatives to present programs. With an attention to criminal careers, the focus shifts to alternatives that will reduce the prevalence of persistent delinquents who pass over into adult criminal careers. Moreover, some new alternatives focus on neglected aspects of justice such as the rights and responsibilities of offenders, of victims, and of communities and the State. There is a concern for victims in mediation programs. There is concern for the collectivity in reparation programs and community service orders. There are attempts to overcome bureaucratic recalcitrance to change by privatization of interventions. And, there is good reason to anticipate new alternatives to join the procession of limited successes (or failures), and that the pragmatic search for alternatives will go on.

With this history of failure in juvenile diversion and alternatives, it may seem surprising that we invest in parallel efforts at diversion from the adult criminal justice system and continue the search for alternatives to our failures in adult justice. Perhaps one reason why the State, practitioners, and criminologists continue to do so is that the alternatives are cast in terms of diverting individuals *from* justice systems rather than in terms of diverting individuals to alternative ways of dealing with the problem of delinquency and criminality. There is no seriously competing model of how to solve problems of crime and delinquency. Moreover, alternatives to criminal justice are conceived largely in terms of theories about how to *change persons* processed as criminal law offenders rather than in terms of an understanding of how to achieve personal and social control over behavior.

In concluding this section of the paper, I wish to emphasize that the idea of diversion is a reaction *against* criminal justice with its emphasis on deterrence and justice theories so that it is diversion *from* criminal justice and not a diversion *to* some alternative system which is a clear alternative to criminal justice. It therefore does not posit a set of alternative ways of dealing with either juveniles or adults in terms of either clear end goals or in terms of methods for the social processing of persons who continue to enter a criminal justice system. For the most part, the alternatives rest on a foundation of criminal justice with the diversion to alternatives never clearly specified in terms of an alternative conception of either persons or society.

3 Personal and Social Control Models

Let us explore the matter of alternatives further. In the United States, at least, the goals of alternatives are couched in the vague language of treatment, rehabilitation, community service, and social adjustment - goals that are difficult to evaluate. Stated succinctly, the question is: What outcomes do we expect for those who are subject to such generally stated alternatives as *treatment*? More specifically, what are the goals of a drug treatment program? Is the objective of a drug treatment program to reduce an offender's dependence upon drugs? Or, is it to reduce offending that is presumed a consequence of drug use (but not necessarily that offending which is not)? Is it to reduce offending by a given amount, to reduce the time between drug-related offenses so as to reduce the number of victims attributable to the offender, to reduce the seriousness of an offender's offending, or is it some combination of these? The goals can be quite unrealistic, as for example, by assuming that a treatment will on the average reduce an offender's offending to zero, that is, no recidivism or no relapse.

Not only are the goals for any given alternative to criminal justice unclear and consequently difficult to evaluate, but the goals of criminal justice often lack clarity as well. Accordingly, any comparisons of alternative models with criminal justice are ambiguous. Often it is difficult to discern what treatment programs have in common or what a given alternative of treatments has in common. This is readily apparent in the United States when one examines programs called intensive supervision on probation - a program involving not only increased supervision of the offender but a variety of rehabilitation programs. Such programs include almost any kind of imaginable intervention with offenders. An ISP program may include, for example, community service, drug treatment, group therapy, and increased surveillance of the offender. Each and all of these may also be administered separately for those not in the alternative ISP program. Indeed, in a recent study of three ISP experimental programs in the US state of California, each ISP program was compared with a regular probation program that employed one or more of these treatments. Petersilia and Turner (1990: 89-90) concluded that the only intervention that seemed to make a difference was the amount of surveillance; moreover, there was no significant relationship between an offender's characteristics and ISP program outcome. The amount of surveillance included compulsory urine testing for those with a record of drug use at the time of arrest. Additionally, there was the threat of incarceration for any offender violating the conditions of intensive supervision on probation. The amount of surveillance and the threat of an incarcerative sanction, I might add, are hardly alternatives to criminal justice, whatever criminal justice may be, other than an oxymoron.

Parenthetically, I note that those who hold to the social construction of criminal behavior as fundamental to any understanding of interventions fail to explore the implications of their deconstructions or alternative constructions. Accordingly, proposals for decriminalization usually engender policy debates around the wrong questions. As Zimring and Hawkins (1992) point out concerning the debate to decriminalize drug sales and use, the debate focuses on decriminalization rather than upon what role the criminal law should have in the government's efforts to control drugs.

4 Choosing Among Alternatives

A question that is closely related to what is the expected outcome for any alternative is how shall one choose among alternatives and, correlatively, choose among their expected outcomes? Usually this question is treated as a decision rule problem - just give us the rules for making choices among alternatives. Examination of the way decisions are made in the juvenile or criminal justice systems makes readily apparent that the more alternatives that have been tried for an individual violator and failed to achieve some objective, the narrower the range of alternatives perceived by decision makers. Rarely, if ever, is the problem treated in terms of some theory about changing people, situations, or macrosocial conditions.

Just how complex these considerations can be is apparent from the conclusions from recent experiments in the United States on the control of domestic violence. Those experiments compared law enforcement arrest of the violent spouse with alternatives such as counseling the couple and separating them temporarily - alternatives to a criminal justice sanction of arrest that was favored by the women's movement in the United States. Even though these were randomized treatments, it should have been evident that the arrest treatment is a far different intervention for a male (or female) partner arrested for the first time than for one with prior arrests. Indeed, an interesting question arises as to whether one should expect a treatment to work with someone who has previously failed the treatment.

From the perspective of selecting persons for alternative treatments, how often should a person be considered eligible for a treatment that by some standard he or she has failed previously? Many persons selected for treatments that are considered alternative to criminal justice sanctions have failed it previously, no matter what criterion is selected to evaluate its effectiveness. One should not conclude from this fact that no one should be exposed to the same treatment more than once nor that we should not expect repeated failure, but rather that we should try and understand whether there is some optimal exposure to the alternative. Peter Greenwood (1987) has argued in evaluating alternatives for persons who have been repeated failures that we focus more on criteria such as whether the treatment reduced the seriousness of the offenses or the frequency of offending in a continuing record of offending rather than on some superficial notions of recidivism in which all offenses are given equal weight and the desired outcome is a rate of zero.

When evaluating any alternative to criminal justice, it should be kept in mind that most adult offenders have failed one or more prior treatments either as a juvenile or an adult, and that many juveniles are subject to more than one treatment. The question thus becomes: What disposition shall be made when there are prior treatment failures? Should one continue with the failed treatment? Should one select some other treatment and, if so, which? Shall persons who are said to fail treatments then be sanctioned in the criminal or juvenile justice system - an alternative to treatment, so to speak? To illustrate with an example, shall the person who has a positive urine test while in drug treatment be continued in the treatment? If there is repeated urine test failure, should some other treatment be selected, and, if so, on what grounds will it be regarded as an alternative to drug treatment? If it is an alternative, why was it not selected initially? If none of these work, should one then resort to criminal justice sanctions that one assumed do not work? Is the alternative, then, to incapacitate the offender, seeking the deterrent effects of punishment and an expected reduction in victimization? The point I wish to make is: How do we evaluate alternatives to criminal justice sanctions and how do we select the alternative treatments when faced with evidence of a treatment failure, however failure has been defined. Above all, it should be evident that in evaluating any new or alternative disposition one should control for at least the number and kind of prior treatments each subject has experienced.

There is no need to belabor these points further. Diversion from a criminal justice system and alternatives to it are at best loosely grounded in a theory of an alternative system of interventions. More importantly, they lack grounding in some theory of not only what causes behavior but of how to change it, once caused. Most alternatives are not grounded in some theory of how to change behavior but in commonsense reasoning. As an example, if supervision on probation does not work, it is concluded that it fails because case workers have to supervise too many probationers, and therefore one should reduce their case load and make the supervision more intensive. The idea is rarely entertained that one should examine probation supervision with a view to learning whether it can achieve some particular goal.

Perhaps, as important as the lack of empirically tested theory for devising alternatives is the difficulty decision makers confront in choosing among viable alternatives in an individual case. Below we consider whether theories of social control may guide us in making such choices.

5 Criminal Careers and Selecting Alternatives

Before doing so, I want to suggest that the conception of a criminal career may aid us in thinking about diversion and alternatives. The onset of a criminal career is usually assumed to begin with the commission of some delinquent or criminal behavior - most usually in the adolescent or teen years. An offender is said to continue in the career until desistance from offending.

The most frequently observed behavior in any longitudinal study of youths is desistance after committing one or only a few offenses or desistance after only a short period of offending. We lack firm evidence on what leads to this high rate of early desistance after onset or entry into a population of offenders. Some speculate that detection by community persons who mobilize parental intervention leads to the early desistance while others speculate that early contact with law enforcement agents (e.g., cautioning) reenforced by family and parental sanctions is the main factor in early desistance.

Quite clearly, however, a person may desist from offending without intervention by any criminal justice agency or alternative formal system of control. The problem with which we must contend in considering alternatives to criminal justice is to understand whether and how interventions account for both persistence and desistance following onset. In evaluating interventions following onset, two questions are of special interest. One is: "Why do some persons desist without any criminal justice or alternative formal system interventions?" The other is: "Do criminal justice and alternative individual change interventions actually increase the likelihood of persistence and reduce the probability of early desistance?"

The problem of selecting alternatives revolves largely around persisters and particularly those who have persisted in offending beyond the juvenile years. Because persisters generally persist despite a large number of different interventions that include those we speak of as alternatives to criminal justice, we are faced with understanding what alternatives might work, given a pattern of failed interventions. That is no simple matter either theoretically or empirically.

The argument is readily advanced by some, however, that to be successful, intervention must occur prior to the onset of delinquent behavior, that is, preventive interventions based on identification of predelinquents are more effective than interventions after onset. A compelling question nonetheless has been raised: "Might early intervention actually increase the likelihood of delinquency onset and persistence into a criminal career?"

McCord's follow-up evaluation of youths randomly assigned to treatment and control groups in the Cambridge-Somerville Youth Study (McCord, 1990: 4-5) raises serious questions about the long-run effectiveness of treatment programs designed to prevent delinquency. Boys were in that program for an average of five and one-half years. The first full-scale evaluation of the effect of the program by Power and Witmer (1951: 337) concluded that while the program did not avert delinquency, early treatment moderated its seriousness. The evaluation of the program by McCord and McCord (1959) in the 1950s concluded that there were no benefits of the treatment program. A third follow-up in 1975 led McCord (1990: 4-5) to conclude that treatment of youths identified as predelinquent actually led to greater harm than those who were untreated, and that the longer and more intensive the treatment, the greater the probability of harm (1990: 7). Moreover, she concluded that not only is there evidence that the preventive treatment program failed but that both those who provided the social service, medical, and psychological treatments and the youths who were treated were poor judges of its effects. Objective evidence offered on their delinquent and criminal careers indicated treatment was harmful (1990: 21) even though both concluded it was beneficial.

McCord's work raises questions about whether we can intervene to prevent delinquent and criminal behavior without increasing the risk of young persons embarking upon a delinquent or criminal career. And she suggests that one may need to focus more on intervention in family and parenting contexts than upon intervening in the lives of young persons. Interventions aimed at changing parents, for example, may be more effective than those aimed at changing their children. Nevertheless, she seems quite skeptical that longitudinal studies of child development or theories about how delinquency develops will provide a sufficient basis for designing intervention programs.

6 Testing Control Theory

Despite reservations about past preventive interventions and the theories on which they were based, developmental models based on personal and social control theory seem to provide a promising alternative model to the criminal justice model of intervention. The strength of these models is that they substantially extend the age range at which interventions can occur and they focus on preventive interventions.

There are a number of different models of personal and social control of behavior. Early control models focused on the development of conformity, treating delinquency as the failure to develop an internal structure of conformity and the failure of external controls both as reinforcements of internal controls and as externally controlling (Reiss, 1951). Psychological control models focus on the early development of cognitive and moral controls (Killen, 1991; Kochanska, 1991; Kohlberg, 1969) or on the failure to develop self-control (Gottfredson and Hirschi, 1990). Others emphasize the importance of extra-individual controls such as family and peer controls. Few emphasize how changes in macrolevel controls affect conforming and deviant behavior, such as controls that operate in communities, schools, workplaces, or larger social networks (Reiss, 1986: 21-25).

Control theories are not easily tested, especially those that posit effects of both internal and external controls, because of the difficulty of measuring development and change in both control systems. Generally, most tests focus on individual development, treating other control systems as contexts that are properties of individuals. Moreover, few have longitudinal designs for testing individual and environmental change.

Tests of control theory are largely based on the formulation of control theory elaborated by Hirschi (1969), a formulation that focuses on the individual. The theory, known commonly as bonding theory, holds that persons who are closely bonded to conventional values are constrained from violating society's rules and regulations. It focuses on four elements that bond individuals to others in conventional conformity or law-abidingness. They are *attachment* to conforming others, *commitment* to conformity, *involvement* in conventional activities, and *belief* in moral validity of conventional values. Apart from the tautological nature of these elements, what is particularly striking is the relative inattention to the development and functioning of external controls and how they affect an individual's behavior. They are implicit rather than explicit in this formulation, a matter that Thornberry et al. (1991) have tried to correct in their formulation of interaction theory and that Elliott, Ageton, and Kanter (1979) have tried to take into account by including peer influences. Still, there is relatively little attention to how the organization of schooling and work and of social networks in society affects individual behavior nor of how family structure and functioning affects behavior.

Currently a number of longitudinal tests of control theory are underway in the United States, Canada, New Zealand, and the continuing study of the London cohort. These studies lead to a number of conclusions that are relevant for selecting alternatives to criminal justice interventions and may need to be taken into account in modeling the selection of alternatives. Summarizing, we can state the following:

First, there are different pathways to delinquency (Elliott, Ageton, and Kanter, 1979; Farrington, 1988; Loeber et al., 1990; Moffitt, 1990) that have implications for interventions. Although the number of types remains uncertain, it appears that there are at least two basic pathways to delinquency.

The first is characterized by the very early onset of delinquency and is preceded by a history of problem behaviors and conduct disorders (Moffitt and Silva, 1989). Indeed, there is some evidence from Moffitt's analysis of the Dunedin, New Zealand longitudinal study that it is possible to select them at a fairly early age - within the first years of life (Moffitt, 1990, 1991). These very early onset delinquents, while perhaps no more than 4% or 5% of all delinquents, appear to be a substantial proportion of the persisters in delinquency and later criminal careers. They are most likely to commit delinquencies alone even at an early age. They have been subject to a large number of alternative treatments for conduct disorders as well as delinquency and have survived many and diverse interventions. These persisters contribute disproportionally to our assessment of any treatment. Although the matter is speculative, it appears there may be temperamental as well as social and psychological factors that account for their conduct disorders and the link to the early onset of delinquency (Moffitt, 1990).

If the pattern isolated in these studies is confirmed in others, it suggests that interventions for these long-term persisters must begin early - in the first 4 or 5 years of life - and prior to the onset of delinquency rather than seeking alternatives following onset. The interventions then must focus on individual level attributes. There will be serious problems of false positives and negatives in early identification, however. For that reason, preventive programs should apply to all children rather than to a preselected group.

The second subgroup exhibits few if any behavior problems prior to adolescence and is the subgroup we typically associate with co-offending in delinquency. Although their numbers are large, they are characterized by short careers and early desistance following onset. Moffitt suggests that their prevalence may be explained in part by the structure of opportunities in the society, particularly those associated with educational and occupational achievement. The implications for intervention are not entirely clear, since their desistance appears to be a function of their acquiring investments in conventional society. In any case, there is reason to conclude that individual-level interventions with these offenders are largely ineffective and that macrosocial interventions are indicated, especially those that facilitate transition to adult status and independence.

These speculations about searching for subtypes who have different careers and pose different possibilities for intervention are not new. What is new is a growing body of evidence that suggests we must pay greater attention to the internal differentiation within a population of offenders when designing and choosing interventions.

A second conclusion that emerges from these theoretically based longitudinal studies is that preventive interventions will be enhanced when they affect factors that are associated with both initiation and escalation (Loeber, 1991) and that relate to changes in personal environments, which lead to increases in and sustained involvement in delinquent behavior and to transitions in the life career (Huizinga, Esbensen, and Weiher, 1991).

A third conclusion is that delinquent behavior contributes to its own causation and escalation. Thornberry et al. (1991: 31) attribute this to its reciprocal relationship to bonding variables. Although youths who are bonded to parents and significant others are at less risk of serious delinquency, delinquency, once initiated, causes a deterioration in the emotional bond of parent and child. This reciprocal causation reduces commitment to conventional values, thereby enhancing the risk of continuation of delinquency. From a treatment perspective, this suggests that interventions should be designed to mitigate the negative consequences of the delinquent behavior on attachment to family and commitment to school. These interventions must be comprehensive and holistic (Thornberry et al., 1991: 32) and begin soon after the onset of delinquency if one is to mitigate negative consequences.

7 Epilogue

One conclusion seems inescapable when we examine the treatment and sanctioning histories of offenders: Almost all adult persistent offenders have experienced a substantial number of different criminal justice dispositions and alternative treatments. Persisters in an important sense, then, are persons who have failed many of the alternatives we set up for diversion from the juvenile and the adult system of criminal justice. Similarly we can conclude that among persistent offenders, any intervention has a low probability of success. In selecting interventions for persistent offenders, consequently, it would seem important to understand just why previous interventions have failed. But that is precisely the knowledge that is lacking for the individual offender in choosing what might be the next intervention.

At a minimum, any consideration of alternatives must be viewed within the context of prior interventions. This suggests that we compound our misunderstanding of delinquent and criminal careers by simply looking at the offender's history of offending. What we need is to understand delinquent and criminal histories as sequential offending and intervention.

A few brief words about the implementation of any program of social control likewise are offered by way of conclusion. Implementation involves bureaucratic organization. By its structure, bureaucratic organization is recalcitrant and resists change. Any new interventions or alternatives consequently will be resisted through subversion of the process of the intervention. Process becomes standardized and routinized in bureaucratic intervention. Subversion occurs through informal means.

These risks of subversion are put succinctly in a recent paper by Gatti (1991: 307) in concluding: "An unhappy fate seems to await attempts at intervention within the juvenile justice system. Every intervention seems to be accompanied by heavy 'collateral damage' which often outweighs the positive results achieved." To recapitulate what was said at the outset: The individual treatment approach of the juvenile court soon gave way to institutionalization of juveniles and inattention to the rights of individuals. Recognition of the rights of individuals led to greater formalism in juvenile processing and increased sanctioning of an underclass in societies - especially of minorities and immigrants. Alternatives to prison have led to net-widening. Gatti suggests that the emphasis on mediation, private placements, and diversification of community and social-work-agency-based treatments results in the creation of new public and private administrative bureaucracies. These new bureaucracies may be as inattentive to the risks of collateral damage they introduce as was the old judicially centered bureaucracy (Gatti, 1991: 309).

References

Elliott, D., Ageton, S., and Canter, R.J. (1979). An integrated theoretical perspective on delinquent behavior. *Journal of Research in Crime and Delinquency, 16,* 3-27.

Farrington, D. (1988). Studying changes within individuals: The causes of offending. In M. Rutter (Ed.), *Studies of pychosocial risk* (pp. 158-183). Cambridge: Cambridge University Press.

Gatti, U. (1991). The future of juvenile justice. In *Crime and crime control: Past, present and future* (pp. 285-312). Korean Institute of Criminology.

Gottfredson, M., and Hirschi, T. (1990). *A general theory of crime.* Stanford, CA: Stanford University Press.

Greenwood, P., and Turner, S. (1987). *The Vision-Quest program: An evaluation.* Santa Monica, CA: The Rand Corporation.

Hirschi, T. (1969). *Causes of delinquency.* Berkeley, CA: University of California Press.

Huizinga, D., Esbensen, F.-A., and Weiher, A.W. (1991). Are there multiple paths to delinquency? *Journal of Criminal Law and Criminology, 82,* 83-124.

Killen, M. (1991). Social and moral development in early childhood. In W.M. Kurtines and J.L. Gewirtz (Eds.), *Handbook of moral behavior and development* (pp. 115-138). Hillsdale, NJ: Erlbaum.

Kochanska, G. (1991). Socialization and temperament in the development of guilt and conscience. *Child Development, 62,* 1379-1392.

Kohlberg, L. (1969). Stage and sequence: The cognitive-developmental approach to socialization. In D. Goslin (Ed.), *Handbook of socialization theory and research* (pp. 347-480). Chicago, IL: Rand McNally.

Loeber, R., Loeber, M.S., Kammen, W. van, and Farrington, D.P. (1991). Initiation, escalation, and desistance in juvenile offending and their correlates. *Journal of Criminal Law and Criminology, 82,* 36-82.

McCord, J. (1990). Crime in moral and social contexts. *Criminology, 28,* 1-26.

McCord, W., and McCord, J. (1959). *Origins of crime.* New York: Columbia University Press.

Moffitt, T.E. (1990). The neuropsychology of delinquency: A critical review of theory and research. In N. Morris and M. Tonry (Eds.), *Crime and justice: An annual review of research, Vol. 12* (pp. 69-99). Chicago, IL: University of Chicago Press.

Moffitt, T.E. (1992). *Adolescent limited and life-course-persistent antisocial behavior: A developmental perspective.* Unpublished manuscript, Program on Human Development and Criminal Behavior, Harvard University, Cambridge, MA.

Moffitt, T.E., and Silva, P. (1989). Self-reported early delinquency: Results from an instrument for New Zealand. *Australian and New Zealand Journal of Criminology, 22.*

Petersilia, J., and Turner, S. (1990). *Intensive supervision for high-risk probationers: Findings from three California experiments.* Santa Monica, CA: The Rand Corporation.

Powers, E., and Witmer, H. (1951). *An experiment in prevention of delinquency: The Cambridge-Somerville Youth Study.* New York: Columbia University Press.

Reiss, A.J., Jr. (1951). Delinquency as the failure of personal and social controls. *American Sociological Review, 16,* 197-207.

Reiss, A.J., Jr. (1986). Why are communities important in understanding crime? In A.J. Reiss, Jr. and M. Tonry (Eds.), *Communities and crime* (pp. 1-33). Chicago, IL: University of Chicago Press.

Thornberry, T.P., Lizotte, A.J., Krohn, M.D., Farnworth, F., and Jang, S.J. (1991). Testing interactional theory: An examination of reciprocal causal relationships among family, school, and delinquency. *Journal of Criminal Law and Criminology, 82,* 3-35.

Zimring, F., and Hawkins, G. (1992). *The search for rational drug control.* Cambridge: Cambridge University Press.

Diversionary Tactics: A Rational Choice Approach

Derek Cornish

1 Introduction

The rational choice perspective (Clarke and Cornish, 1985; Cornish and Clarke, 1986) was originally designed to assist in the further development of situational crime prevention policies. This chapter examines whether diversion might also benefit from taking a closer interest in the theoretical assumptions and practical applications of this approach. It begins by providing a brief historical context and outlining the rational choice approach to situational crime prevention. It goes on to explore several areas in which the interests of diversion programmes and situational measures may overlap, and concludes by suggesting practical ways in which collaboration to mutual advantage might be achieved. Cautioning is taken as the model for diversion, since police-regulated pre-trial diversion for offenders is the form most commonly found in the United Kingdom.

2 Situational Crime Prevention and Diversion: Common Origins

Like diversion, situational crime prevention arose in part as a response to the widely perceived failure of rehabilitation as the State's preferred crime-control policy (Clarke and Cornish, 1983). For rather different reasons, both were driven by the view that the criminal justice system's role in the reduction of crime was a limited one. For proponents of diversion, the message was clear: with the failure of rehabilitative (Lipton, Martinson, and Wilks, 1975; Romig, 1978) and of preventive programmes (Lundman, McFarlane, and Scarpitti, 1976; McCord, 1978; Spergel, 1973; Wright and Dixon, 1977) went much of the justification for unregulated, intrusive and costly interventions in the lives of potential and actual offenders. No longer could the benefits of changing offenders be set against the labeling and stigmatizing effects of criminal justice procedures and outcomes. As Adams (1974: 18) commented at the time: "For the present, it appears wise to focus more on changing the system than on changing the offender, accepting that at a later time the reverse emphasis might become more appropriate." For those advocating situational methods, the criticism was even more wide-ranging: that rehabilitative efforts were prejudiced by an insufficiently situational model of human behaviour and learning (Cornish and Clarke, 1975); and that, more importantly, traditional theories of criminal behaviour distracted attention from, and neglected the potential of, crime-control strategies based upon altering the situational contingencies that favour the occurrence of particular crime events (Clarke, 1980).

While, for both approaches, traditional methods appeared irrelevant and damaging, crucial differences were expressed in their contrasting objectives of, on the one hand, diverting offenders and, on the other, of preventing crimes. For diversion, the harm done to offenders by criminal justice procedures and outcomes was paramount, and damage limitation the goal. Crime control was to be enhanced by doing less to offenders, or doing it outside the criminal justice system. For situational crime prevention, the objective was to protect the targets and victims of crime from existing and potential offenders: Offender-centred policies were irrelevant and damaging to the extent that they directed money and resources away from this objective. In this respect, those involved in situational prevention shared the views of other commentators (Ehrlich, 1981; Van den Haag, 1982) that reducing crime rates is about considerably more than how - or how effectively - the criminal justice system deals with those offenders it catches.

3 Situational Crime Prevention and Rational Choice

3.1 Situational Crime Prevention

Situational crime-prevention is a collection of techniques (cf., e.g., Jeffery, 1971; Mayhew et al., 1976; Newman, 1972; Poyner, 1983) as much pragmatically as theoretically derived, that have in common a concern with the identification, analysis and modification of situational opportunities. (A full classification of the range of such techniques, and examples of their successful use can be found in Clarke, 1992.) While research was, and continues to be, directed at the solution of practical crime-prevention problems, the need to meet criticisms of the strategy soon led its exponents to take more interest in the theoretical aspects of the measures' operation. A satisfactory account of the utility and scope of situational crime prevention would, it was felt, have to achieve two things:

1. It must be able to counter arguments that situational measures merely displace criminal activity.
2. It must locate situational measures theoretically within the crime-control system, and provide convincing arguments for their greater use.

3.2 The Rational Choice Perspective

The outcome of these pressures was the development of what came to be termed the rational choice perspective. This was intended as a micro-level theory of action to guide thinking about the determinants of criminal events and criminal involvement. The perspective was explicitly designed to give due attention to the role of current situational factors in crime, and hence to offer alternative ways of conceptualising displacement, and examining its likelihood and limiting conditions. It was also intended (cf. Felson, 1986) to encourage a view of offenders as but one element in a multi-element "crime-event system" comprised, in addition, of victims, targets, facilitators and other relevant features of opportunity settings. This notion of a crime-generation system was seen as a way of widening the debate about crime-control policy. As well as stimulating thinking at the micro-sociological level, the routine activities/life-styles research (Cohen and Felson, 1979) which was developing at that time also promised to offer ways of relating opportunities as well as offenders to macro-sociological variables.

Briefly, the rational choice approach assumes the following:

1. the bounded rationality of human (including criminal) action;
2. its interactional, transactional, and adaptive nature;
3. the need to study offenders' perceptions and decision-making as indicators of these interactional processes and products;
4. a crime-specific approach, stressing the distinctive nature of different person-situation criminal interactions; and
5. the need for separate accounts of event and involvement processes, in order to reflect differences in the variables, decision sequences, and time-scales involved.

Most work has been put into developing the situational crime prevention aspects of the rational choice approach, that is, in examining the ways in which opportunities for particular crimes occur. This has been achieved by developing a decision-making approach to the understanding of target-selection and crime-commission methods. The approach has drawn on offenders' accounts and crime-site analyses in order to identify and control the salient situational variables for a variety of crimes. By viewing criminals simply as elements in a complex crime-event generation system, methods of crime control can be developed that, while taking account of the nature of offender motivation, are not dependent for their success upon attempting directly to modify the latter. Instead, situational measures aim to increase the effort and risks, and reduce the payoffs, of committing particular crimes in particular situations.

4 Situational Prevention and Diversion: Some Shared Concerns

4.1 Preliminary Remarks

What has the rational choice approach, one apparently so careless of the motives and, indeed, welfare of the offender to offer diversion - except the rather unhelpful view that traditional policies aimed at controlling the generation of offenders provide a very partial and inadequate response to the problem of crime control? A preliminary answer can, perhaps, be derived from the importance the rational choice approach ascribes to situational factors, and its advocacy of offender decision-making studies as one means of their discovery. The correct identification of the opportunity factors that influence the occurrence of criminal events may provide the most immediate payoffs for crime-prevention measures. But, in addition to analysing decisions taken while committing crimes, the rational choice perspective also calls attention to the usefulness of viewing other aspects of offenders' lives in the decison-making language of options, costs, benefits and choices. In so doing, it draws attention to the significance of immediate situational influences in relation to decisions about initial involvement and continuation in, and desistance from, particular forms of crime.

Traditional theories of involvement tend to be primarily concerned with the hypothetical influence of broadly drawn "past experiences" upon criminal propensities. The rational choice approach, however, is intended to offer the tools by means of which the present motives and actions that bring about criminal events can be related, not just (or even primarily) to past events, but to factors at work in the current settings and immediate preoccupations of offenders' daily lives. In a word, the rational choice approach facilitates the interactive linking, in the present, of criminal events to offender "life-styles". Situational measures will no doubt benefit from the more careful specification of motives which such analyses might bring. But the light that is shed on life-styles may also be of benefit to offender-centred measures like diversion. These shared concerns will be discussed in more detail below.

4.2 Choosing an Action Theory of Criminal Behaviour

It might appear that the rational choice perspective provides the most suitable framework, or "theory of action", for talking about aspects of criminal involvement or the occurrence of criminal events. But there are other candidates for this elucidatory role. Behavioural treatment programmes have encouraged the more explicit identification and use in criminology of psychological action theories of behaviour. Those provided by modern learning theory, for example, have many of the interactional features necessary to encourage a more situational approach to offending behaviour, and some diversion programmes have used a behavioural approach (Davidson et al., 1990). Recognition of the need to focus on criminal behaviour and its situational contingencies has been one of the few positive outcomes of preventive and rehabilitative research of the last three decades (Andrews et al., 1990; Hollin, 1990; Nietzel, 1979), although the definition of contingencies has often been narrow, and the desirability of studying the life-styles of delinquents in their natural environments as a prelude to designing behavioural treatments has not been so clearly understood.

But, apart from their use in treatment programmes, the criminological tradition within which radical behaviourist and social learning theory formulations have been applied has been one largely preoccupied with longer-term processual accounts. These action theories have therefore been used as a means of generating "explanation-sketches" of involvement processes (Akers, 1985), perhaps with the formation of early prevention policies in mind, rather than used as a means of framing situational accounts of crime commission, life-styles, or involvement. It may, of course, be that the clinical origins of such theories have also limited their suitability for this purpose. As will be discussed later, the more cognitive among these approaches and, in general, those assuming a "deficit explanation" of offending can very easily undermine the very strengths of the behavioural approach which originally made it so situationally aware, and so challenging to pathological explanations of crime.

Despite their potential, then, learning theories have failed, with some exceptions (Taylor and Nee, 1988), to exploit their ability to provide fully situational analyses either of crime or of criminality. The rational choice perspective, on the other hand, has a number of advantages which psychological action theories lack. As an alternative action theory, it provides a means for exploring person-situation interactions free from the distracting conceptual baggage and clinical preoccupations which inevitably accompany borrowings from psychology. It also has the practical advantage of being couched in everyday language, free from ties to particular hypothesized psychological mechanisms or processes of learning, and available for direct use when discussing conduct with offenders. More importantly, it has the heuristic value of making the explicit assumption that offenders behave as rationally as their non-offending peers - the "presumption of rationality", which provides some protection against the premature "pathologization" of behaviour. And lastly, it recognizes the importance at all times of situational sources of temporary motivations and inducements on behaviour.

Despite their differences of focus and purpose, however, both situational and behavioural analyses assume the need to study the interplay of the personal and situational variables in the individual case, whether the focus is upon understanding criminal behaviour or crime events. Because of these shared features, either rational choice or behavioural methods of analysis could, in principle, be employed as action theories both to give diversion a more situational outlook, and to relate its objectives more closely to those of situational prevention.

As far as diversion itself is concerned, it might well be the case that the offence-focused nature of situationally oriented approaches should make them less likely, at whatever level of diversionary practice, to attract unwelcome criticism for intrusiveness, and most able to engage offenders:

1. because they are understandable and consequential: they acknowledge and concentrate upon offending behaviour - the explicit justification for official action;
2. because they do not patronize or stigmatize the offender as psychologically defective; and
3. because their practical and active approach is more likely to secure the co-operation of offenders.

4.3 Emphasis Upon First and Occasional Offenders

Both diversion programmes and situational measures have their own good reasons for focusing their attentions upon first and occasional offenders. Advocates of situational measures have, for strategic purposes, always emphasized the opportunistic and temporary nature of most offending (Gabor, 1990), although the efficacy of the situational approach is not dependent on the relative proportions of casual as against hard-core offenders in the criminal population. Stressing opportunism, however, draws attention to the importance of situational contingencies in *all* offending, and provides an effective counter to those who argue the inevitability of displacement. It is also consistent with other persuasive accounts of occasional crime. Hepburn (1984: 79), discussing occasional property offenders, describes them as "... those whose criminal acts occur when there is an opportunity or situational inducement to such illegal behavior." He goes on to make a distinction between occasional offenders and vocational ones in terms of expertise, information networks, level of peer-group support, orientation of life around criminal activities, and self-definition.

Accounts of novice and youthful offending (Briar and Piliavin, 1965; Greenberg, 1977; Matza, 1964; Parker, 1974) are likewise particularly amenable to explanations in terms of opportunism, since they are concerned with exploring the "invitational edge" of casual offending, where situational inducements interact with temporary moods and motives to bring about particular types of crimes. Moreover, since children and young people are economically marginal at the best of times, it may well be that, unlike adults, their responsiveness to the presence (and growth) of illegal opportunities in their environment is less affected by changes in prevailing economic conditions (Field, 1990).

Such considerations point to the need to distinguish between initial involvement - which may be opportunistic, and driven by very temporary states of mind and temptations - and continuing involvement, in which the nature of the decisions, level of expertise, and ability to seek out and create criminal opportunities may be very different. The implications for situational prevention are clear. As Wilkins (1973: 22) has commented:

"Making crime more difficult may not prevent the professional; however, he who becomes a criminal begins his career as a non-professional. If the first crime, committed by any kind of criminal can be delayed - the first crime which a criminal commits taking place at a later age - we shall have reduced the volume of crime and also the probability of a criminal career as the probability of a serious and lengthy criminal career is most highly correlated with the age at first offense. To delay the first criminal act - not prevent it - may be an expected result of making crime more difficult."

Wilkins (1984: 156) returned to the subject later when he commented: "If it is *learned* that crimes can be carried out without the application of any special skill, subsequent punishment is not likely to change that learning experience." He uses this as a reason for suggesting that those kinds of crimes that attract the youngest offenders should be especially targeted in order to make them more difficult to commit. As Morris and Giller (1987) point out, reducing opportunities is another form of diversion from crime.

Pre-trial diversion strategies such as cautioning also tend to concentrate their efforts on young, less experienced and casual offenders (Evans and Wilkinson, 1990). In 1989, for example, no less than 73% of known offenders under the age of 17, a large proportion of whom will have been first offenders, were formally cautioned for indictable offences in England and Wales (Barclay, 1991). Since most forms of diversion deal with individuals after they have committed a crime, some degree of successful learning will already have taken place, and the objective of intervention will be either to avoid exacerbating or, more positively, to interrupt the learning process so that sporadic and opportunistic offending does not change into a more settled pattern of criminal activity.

The fact that targeting first or casual offenders may be a cost-effective way of reducing recruitment to recidivism does not mean that all methods of prevention are equally cost-effective. For example, talking of the mundane juvenile offender as drifter, Matza (1964: 30) comments: "Though his tenure is short, his replacements are legion." If this is so, then diversion is unlikely, on its own, to do much to stem recruitment. But the situational approach also has its drawbacks: Preventing many commonplace crimes - those, that is, particularly likely to be committed on an opportunistic basis - poses problems simply because such offences often require little in the way of expertise and offer an abundance of unprotected targets. These considerations suggest that there may be some scope for collaboration between strategies which are targeting this broad collection of offenders and offences.

4.4 Targeting Specific Crimes (and Offenders)

Diversion is particularly concerned with the reduction of commonplace crimes, such as shoplifting, theft, vandalism, autocrime and minor public order offences, committed by opportunist and inexperienced young offenders (Heal and Laycock, 1987). Barclay (1990: 21), for example, notes that the rise in the peak age for offending from 1986 to 1988 "... resulted entirely from a reduction in the annual number of offenders cautioned or convicted for theft from shops". This drop was most marked amongst those aged between 10 and 13 (in which shop thefts accounted for a half of known offending in 1986, compared with one third in 1989); and among those aged between 14 to 16 (where the drop was from one third to one quarter).

Situational prevention, too, has devoted much attention to such offences (see, e.g., Clarke, 1978; Ekblom, 1986; Hope, 1985). It has also been suggested (Cornish and Clarke, 1987) that the choice-structuring properties of particular crimes - those aspects perceived by offenders as being especially salient to their goals, motives, experience, abilities, expertise, and preferences - make them differentially attractive to offenders. If this is so, then crime-specific analyses may also suggest measures to target particular offender subgroups for the offence in question. It is true that evidence that juvenile offenders are generalists rather than specialists (but see Cornish and Clarke, 1989, on this issue) might suggest that targeting offenders for one type of offence would be unlikely to affect the commission of others. But for many juveniles - and especially, perhaps, young, inexperienced and opportunist offenders - their offending may well be quite limited in scope, and constrained by choice-structuring properties related to opportunity, expertise and effort particular to their subgroup. And such offenders may also be among those most often subject to diversion.

If the above analysis holds, then both diversionary and situational measures may sometimes, for pragmatic reasons, tend to become focused on a similar group of offenders. There is some tentative evidence from Barclay (1990) that this may be so for shoplifting. He offers three possible reasons for the fall in shoplifting among juvenile offenders: situational prevention measures; social crime prevention; and juvenile diversionary schemes, involving an increase in informal warnings. Since his evidence was rather anecdotal, it is impossible to disentangle the relative effects of each measure. What is does suggest, however, is that it may be worth exploring further the potential of using situational and diversionary measures as a planned strategy for dealing with specific forms of criminal activity.

5 Some Implications for Diversion Policy and Practice

Shared interests between situational and diversionary measures in terms of crimes, offenders and (sometimes) intervention procedures have been identified. But parallel interests do not necessarily provide a common cause. The next section develops some of the foregoing points in more detail in order to indicate how these interests might be turned to mutual benefit.

5.1 Making Diversion Practice More Situationally Oriented

Diversion strategies operate a policy of triage. Depending upon the offender and offence, the options range from pure diversion, through a graduated series of responses, some purely minatory, others providing "diversion-plus" - a variety of programmes intended to address factors assumed to have played a role in bringing about the current offence. In England and Wales, the police cautioning system is perhaps the most developed diversionary policy. While, in 1981, Lemert regarded the English police caution as coming closest to his notion of pure diversion (i.e., "planned non-intervention"), Evans and Wilkinson (1990: 164-165) have recently noted the increasing bureaucratization of procedures:

"The available range of pre-court decisions has become increasingly complex involving three main tiers with a number of options in each. The first tier consists of pre-caution decisions and involves no further action and informal warnings. The second consists of decisions to caution and includes instant cautions, deferred cautions with or without consultation and caution plus. By caution plus we mean cautions with a decision attached to them such as reparation or victim mediation. The third tier consists of decisions to prosecute with or without consultation."

Even this classification may understate the complexity of police decision-making in this area, because of the many reasons for "no further action", and variations in the location and formality of "informal cautions".

There is nothing intrinsically wrong with maintaining a variety of diversion options of differing degrees of intrusiveness - so long, that is, as they are applied consistently. Diversion by its very nature should be able to provide a range of carefully graduated, tentative course corrections to an offender's life. What these corrective processes should entail, however, is a more difficult question. Concentrating upon the offence and its circumstances, and drawing the offender's attention to the situational influences upon his or her behaviour (Tutt, 1984) would provide a circumscribed approach to intervention in keeping with the necessarily limited objectives of diversion. As has been indicated already, because of their emphasis upon the environmental determinants of behaviour, behavioural programmes might appear particularly suited to this objective.

Indeed, the behavioural treatment of offenders might, in principle, be used to complement a locally based situational approach to particular crimes and locations (see section 4.4), although at present there is little evidence that any such strategic alliances are being made. Thus, diversion programmes might, for example, use the situational information they generate to help the offender and his or her family to explore the role of opportunity, situational inducements and temporary, life-style-mediated motives and moods in bringing about involvement in particular offences. Knowledge so gained could also be used to develop ways of regulating the offender's access to particular local environments and activities within them. Where such offending behaviour was widespread locally, this information could also be used as a basis for crime-site analyses and situational measures.

Nor is there any reason why such approaches should necessarily confine themselves only to increasing situational constraints. As Davidson and Seidman (1974) pointed out at the end of their review of behavioural interventions, the identification of settings, such as schools and neighbourhoods, which appear to encourage offending, may also on occasion suggest environmental modifications which directly enhance offenders' lives.

5.2 Socio-Cognitive Accounts of Offending and Their Problems

There are, of course, many reasons for emphasizing the offence itself and the circumstances surrounding it when working with delinquents. Some rationales are less concerned with re-arranging situational contingencies for the future, and more concerned with changing the offender's evaluation of his or her behaviour. Events such as those involved in the arrest and cautioning process take the offence as their primary focus, and derive whatever impact they have from the sense of guilt or shame induced by public identification and confession. There is some evidence (Cameron, 1964: 164-167), for example, that an offence-centred emphasis may be beneficial where criminal behavior has not yet become a well-established part of an offender's life , and "... when the person finds that to continue the behavior he must define himself as a criminal with the consequent status changes."

There is also growing interest amongst juvenile liaison bureaux (Davis, Boucherat, and Watson, 1989), intermediate treatment schemes (Curtis, 1989; Tutt, 1984), and other programmes (Hollin, 1990) in encouraging the offender to reconstruct past criminal choices as a means of enabling joint exploration of the thinking patterns, cognitive strategies and problem-solving skills used by the offender. In so far as such techniques encourage the exploration of non-criminal options and alternative ways of coping with stress, need, unhappiness, anger, boredom, frustration (or whatever other condition is taken as fuelling offending), they too are essentially exploring the situational context of criminal behaviour. But the more these interventions base themselves upon theories stressing the cognitive mediation of criminal behaviour, the greater the risk they run of assuming offending to be a function of socio-cognitive incompetencies and deficits - such as inappropriate time-discounting strategies, inability to delay gratification, or lack of self-control. *A priori* assumptions of this nature, however sophisticated their expression (e.g., Gottfredson and Hirschi, 1990; Ross and Fabiano, 1985; Wilson and Herrnstein, 1985), can all too easily pre-empt proper discussion of social structural and situational influences on behaviour.

To take a more "present-oriented" view does not, of course, deny the importance of previous learning and experience. But it stresses the need to trace the intervening person-situation transactions which form such experiences - and which, by their consequences, both direct and sometimes continue to shape individual trajectories. Instead of assuming that previous experience at some distant point in the past gets turned into defective cognitive strategies - low self-control, low self-esteem, impulsiveness - which then carry the burden of explaining delinquent behaviour into the present, the rational choice approach is intended to encourage the investigation of the chain of situated transactions which lie between.

A simple example may make this clearer. When Brown and Harris (Brown, 1987) developed their model of the social origins of depression, they attributed this state to the interplay between adverse life-events and pre-existing vulnerabilities, whose continuing effect was mediated by the hypothetical socio-cognitive construct, low self-esteem. But examination of one particular source of vulnerability, early loss of the mother, suggested another explanation. Such losses, as Brown himself comments, often radically redirect the trajectory of an individual's life, bringing real, severe and continuing social, economic and familial deprivation as well as the cognitive changes. It may indeed be the practical and continuing effects of the former which carry most of the explanatory weight.

Since the recent history of criminology has been one of struggle to escape the premature "pathologising" of criminal behaviour (Cressey, 1954), treatments based upon assumptions about cognitive causes should, perhaps, be treated with some caution until rigorous and impartial evaluation has provided proof of their effectiveness. Until that time, those of a rational choice persuasion will tend towards the view that the acknowledged difficulty of changing offending behaviour is more a reflection of the adaptiveness of this response. Failure to locate offending in its situational context, and to recognize the distinctive pleasures that it provides (Katz, 1988) - failure, in other words, to consider "the healthfulness of bad actors" (Nettler, 1961: 280) as an alternative to the cognitive pathologization of offending - once again distracts attention from the matrix of situational variables which influences this and other behaviours.

5.3 Using Diversion-Generated Information

It may be thought from the above discussion that the rational choice perspective on offenders' behaviour offers little comfort to diversion. This, of course, is not so. Even if criminal behaviour is presumed to be more generally adaptive than some intervention theories might want to believe, situational analyses are still essential for uncovering the settings, motives and rewards which actually govern offending in the individual case. It is true that such initiatives may provide sobering evidence of the difficulty with which any planned intervention is faced when it competes with the opportunities and rewards for crime available within the offender's natural environment. But with the aid of such detailed information, it may be possible to devise ways of altering the balance of opportunities, risks and rewards for the individual offender and consequently of changing the choices he or she makes.

Additionally, the information gained may be useful in devising small-scale alterations to the local environment - schools, shops, leisure facilities - which will increase the risks and efforts, or reduce the payoffs of crime to their like-minded peers. Some diversion programmes seem to be well aware of the need to harness diversion projects to this goal: The juvenile liaison bureau observed by Davis et al. (1989), for example, has now apparently:

> "... become involved in local crime prevention efforts through various analyses of trends and the preparation of teaching packs for schools dealing, for example, with shoplifting and criminal damage. This work will receive renewed emphasis over the coming year with the more extensive collation of statistics on time, and location of offending, which should assist in the targeting of resources to reduce the incidence of juvenile offending." (O'Dowd et al., 1991: 189).

Even with regard to the least intrusive forms of diversion, then, and as a recognized *quid pro quo* for its most informal exercise, a situational approach to diversion would advocate requiring the offender to give as much detailed information about the crime in question as possible. Where necessary, this will directly address the offender's motives for offending, discuss with the offender the decisions which led to his or her involvement, trace the sequence of events which led to the offence in question, and ask for detailed crime-specific descriptions of the processes of target selection, crime commission and aftermath. Provided the appropriate legal safeguards are observed, and the bases for official action are met, this "situational analysis" should be mandatory.

Although offence rates are generated by the activities of an uncertain mix of known and unknown offenders, the information provided by such offence-related questioning would offer a further source of data about local patterns of juvenile crime, opportunities and techniques. This information, together with the more detailed knowledge of offenders' own motives and methods - in short, of their criminal decision-making - could be used as one source to guide local crime prevention strategy quickly and effectively (cf., also, Ekblom, 1988). Such data, collected over time, would also provide a longer-term picture of local crime and of patterns of victimization. Although it might be expected that the police already collect much of this information routinely, this does not in fact seem to be true - at least for diversion cases (Sanders, 1988: 522). The resource is, in consequence, poorly exploited by the police (Tremblay and Rochon, 1991), and unavailable to researchers or those involved in situational prevention.

6 Monitoring and Evaluating Diversion

6.1 Monitoring Diversion

There are, of course, other reasons for gathering more detailed offence-related information. Diversion was almost strangled at birth by its critics (Lemert, 1981; Lundman, 1976). And, although the debate over the reach of social control has been characterized more by conjecture and vivid rhetoric than by sound empirical research (Binder and Geis, 1984; McMahon, 1990), the nightmare vision of an implacably widening network of social control conjured up by radical commentators (Austin and Krisberg, 1981; Cohen, 1979, 1985) has remained a difficult one to dispel. Concern about the bases upon which the increasingly wide range of pretrial discretionary decisions are made by the police has been expressed by most United Kingdom commentators in the cautioning field (cf. Davis et al., 1989; Evans and Wilkinson, 1990; and Sanders, 1988 for discussions and earlier, related work). Fuller and more systematically collected information, including the circumstances of arrest, would help to answer this and other questions about the effects of expanding cautioning - as well as giving a clearer picture of the nature of the 73% of offenders under 17 whose offences currently attract police cautions (Barclay, 1991).

6.2 Using Offenders' Perceptions

There is now a growing literature on the proximal causes of criminal events, not only in relation to the commission of crime (Cromwell, Olson, and Avary, 1990; Wright and Logie, 1988 - on residential burglary), but also to the motivational accounts given by offenders (Agnew, 1990). Much of this information was collected from offenders' accounts, and it is clear that their perceptions can provide information useful for situational prevention. With the exception of studies of juvenile court procedures (cf. Morris and Giller, 1987, for a review), however, very much less information exists about offenders' perceptions of the criminal justice process and of the purposes and quality of the interventions it provides. As Dobash et al. (1990: 307) comment:

"Abstract issues regarding procedural 'justice', the operation of courts, and the responsibilities of court personnel are relatively meaningless to young people because they are invisible or seen as irrelevant. The significant element in criminal justice for the young is the police. Police are the most visible representation of the power of the state, and the exercise of this power on the streets has a significant impact on young people's perceptions."

Given the recent increase in the use of police cautioning as a disposition in the United Kingdom, it is somewhat alarming how little is known about the nature of the interaction between suspect and officer or its impact upon the offender. Despite the endless debates over the importance of ensuring fairness and due process, and the need to obtain informed consent, little is heard from the offender about these matters. Nor do we know whether offenders find the complex distinctions made between stages and degrees of diversion meaningful, or whether they discriminate between the activities of different parts of the system (Cressey and McDermott, 1974).

It is not even clear in what light they view what is done to them - or left undone - in the name of diversion. Is informal cautioning seen as judicious non-intervention or a lucky escape? Are multiple cautions viewed by the offender as an understanding kindness or as evidence of the law's ineffectiveness? How do they view their own role in the process? As Davis et al. (1989: 233) point out, referring to the lack of consultation about the decision to recommend non-prosecution: "Why should these young people be dealt with by reference to a policy which has been neither explained to nor endorsed by their victims or their parents?"

Surprisingly, evidence is lacking on one of the most fundamental and often quoted reasons for diversion - the avoidance of stigma and labeling. In the absence of research on offenders' perceptions, it is impossible to conclude, though all too often claimed, that one form of diversion is more or less stigmatizing than another, or that any are less damaging than other criminal justice dispositions. Moreover, since the avoidance of labeling may undermine deterrent effects by reducing the perceived seriousness of offending, it is important to investigate whether this is occurring. This is especially the case since the less intrusive forms of diversion seek only to avoid "making matters worse". Perhaps in this respect the warning of Wheeler et al. (1967) has been taken too literally. For though it may be true, as they remarked, that doing something is not necessarily better than doing nothing, it is equally dangerous to assume that inactivity has no costs.

6.3 Evaluating Outcomes: The Vanishing Offender

Most lacking of all is information about the long-term effects of the various measures currently being employed. In the first place, the lack of data on offenders and their assessment of outcomes is conspicuous. The contribution of diverson to offender decision-making about continued involvement and desistance requires investigation through detailed ethnographic and quantitative research. As Cressey and McDermott (1974: 33-34) comment:

"There is a pressing need to study the careers of juveniles who are diversion fodder. Most current concern ... has been for changes in the juvenile justice bureaucracies. Evaluation of the correlated change, if any, in the juveniles who have been processed is mostly an uncharted area ..."

Secondly, despite the growing sophistication of evaluative research design and analysis, there are fewer good evaluative studies of the outcomes of criminal justice interventions being carried out now than at any time in the last 30 years. This is true of diversion: The Davidson et al. (1987, 1990) series of controlled trials, for example, were carried out between 10 and 15 years ago, as were the considerably less well-controlled California Youth Authority diversion projects (Palmer and Lewis, 1980). It may be that the lesson learned by researchers from the methodological critiques of the 1970s was not to do evaluation better but, rather, not to risk doing it at all. Moreover, the apparent failure of rehabilitation was undoubtedly responsible for some re-direction of research efforts and funds. There may, however, be more to the dearth of evaluation in the United Kingdom than lack of money, time, or expertise. Instead, it almost seems that, out of an unholy alliance of divergent interests, a common cause against evaluation may have been forged. What else can account for the lack of readily available reconviction statistics, or the apparent lack of acknowledgement of any need for them?

Cost factors are likely to have been the major impetus basis behind any such alliance. The attractiveness of reducing costs as a major reason for community-based treatment and diversion was recognized early on in the rehabilitation debate by Harlow (1970: 38) when she ominously remarked:

"... a vast proportion of offenders could be managed in the community at least as effectively, and with much less cost, or diverted from the criminal justice system entirely, thus returning to the community its responsibility for dealing with behavior it defines as antisocial or deviant."

But as containing costs (by government) or maintaining budgets (by police, and official and voluntary treatment agencies) become priorities for all those involved in the criminal justice system, so does the scope for collusion grow. Add to this a natural desire to avoid public scrutiny and accountability, and the basis for a cosy complicity is formed, where it becomes in the interest of none to monitor the effectiveness of diversion at controlling crime.

It is certainly the case that the performance indicators chosen for diversion have largely been confined to those measuring its success at keeping juveniles out of the criminal justice system. Concern over the potential for "net-widening" (Austin and Krisberg, 1981) by the criminal justice system has altered views about the value of diversion policy during the 1980s (Davidson et al., 1990), but this has not, as might be expected, renewed calls for an evaluation of its effectiveness in reducing further criminal activity. Instead, conclusions about the success or failure of diversion remain centred on its diversionary potential as a measure to reduce the criminalizing effects of administering criminal justice. Everything else about it is assumed: Benign effects necessarily flow from good intentions.

The view by policy-makers that evaluation is a needless and self-imposed irritant has probably only been reinforced by the published outcomes of diversion projects. For example, Davidson et al.'s (1987, 1990) findings provide some evidence that official reconvictions were reduced by diversion. However, this result is hardly a vote of confidence in the crime-control capabilities of the juvenile justice system. Moreover, the results offer little reassurance that diversion itself has any positive effect upon criminal propensities: Self-reported offending and attitudes remained apparently unchanged amongst those subjected either to diversion or to conventional processing. These latter findings also question the role played by "labeling" in explaining diversion's impact, since the criminalizing effects of societal reaction on delinquents' self-concepts and motivation might have been expected to increase the self-reported offending of those processed via the juvenile justice system. Since this was not the case, a more convincing explanation for both the differences in offical reconvictions *and* the similarities in self-reported rates of offending might be sought in the differential ability of the criminal justice system to "track" diverted as opposed to otherwise processed offenders. This factor may, in addition, interact with the differential willingness of diversion agencies as against official ones to report on such offending as occurs - both during or after intervention.

Under these circumstances, it is scarcely surprising that calls to measure the effects of the system-wide changes brought about by diversion policies - that is, to provide a comprehensive range of intervention-related follow-up data on offending - are seen as beside the point, anathematized as dealing with "the sterile area of evaluation" (Morris and Giller, 1987), or as "social control talk" (Pratt, 1987). Talk, indeed, has been one of the main features of the debate over diversion (cf. McMahon, 1990) - and it is the rhetoric of "destructuring" (cf. Cohen, 1985), perhaps, which has sapped both the desire and the will to obtain a clearer picture of what the system now achieves.

7 Postscript: The Place of Offender-Based Interventions

7.1 Diversion and Crime Control

Diversion policy, while funded by governmental concern to reduce costs, was born of humanitarian concern about the potentially damaging impact of the criminal justice system, particularly on younger, less experienced offenders. Enhanced crime control - even in the modest sense of preventing the unnecessary exacerbation of existing criminal propensities - although theoretically a goal of diversion, can scarcely be considered to have been its primary aim. The present chapter has tried to make a case for exploiting the crime-control potential of diversion more actively. It has argued that even though, as an offender-based intervention policy, its crime-control role is likely to be a modest one, its effectiveness should be more closely monitored and evaluated than hitherto.

7.2 Controlling Crime by Changing Offenders

Traditionally, policy-makers have remained preoccupied with offenders, and with what the criminal justice process does, can, should do - or not do - to them. As Wilkins (1976: 154) puts it: "... we have attempted to simplify the problem of crime to the problem of the criminal." This concern seems to stem from two sources: legal requirements to allocate responsibility and blame; and assumptions that the major contributions to crime control, for good or ill, are made by what is directly done to or for offenders. These preoccupations are matched by those of criminological research, where attention has focussed more upon the acquisition, exacerbation and reduction of criminal propensities than upon the proximal origins of crime events.

7.3 The Crime Generation System

Motivated offenders are, however, only one element in the crime-generation system, other elements of which are also necessary, though not sufficient on their own to bring out crime events (cf. Cohen and Felson, 1979). It is clear, therefore, that whatever other good reasons there may be for paying attention to offenders, they need not, and should not be, the sole focus of crime-control policies. There are, in fact, as many potential intervention points for the purpose of crime control as there are strategies to reduce the likelihood of accidents, diseases or other harms. Diversion programmes, whatever their primary objectives, offer opportunities systematically to gather local information relevant to other crime-control strategies and, in particular, to situational crime prevention efforts. This, indeed, represents one example of how police knowledge of crime and criminal behaviour in local areas could be better utilized for crime control (Tremblay and Rochon, 1991).

7.4 A Rational Choice Perspective on Crime Generation

As an interactional theory of human action, the rational choice approach provides a particularly useful perspective on the crime-generation system and its intervention-points. Because of its "present-oriented" perspective, and its encouragement of crime-specific analyses of offenders' decision-making in relation to criminal events, it is able to give due attention to the practical role and theoretical importance of proximal influences on crime commission.

But the rational choice approach has something to say about offender motivation, too. Its concern to locate offending within its current interactional context is, indeed, what distinguishes it from traditional criminological accounts of involvement. As an action theory it is, of course, consistent with - and could be utilized by - any of the sociological accounts of criminal propensity or involvement. Each of these, after all, requires and assumes an action theory of some kind in terms of which to organize its particular motivational account (for an example of the use of social learning theory in this way, cf. Akers, 1985). But, in practice, such accounts all too easily lose their sense of the *contingency* of action in their eagerness to explain it in terms of the effects of past experience alone.

The rational choice perspective is primarily interested in emphasizing and exploring this missing interface between the offender and the motivating and opportunity-providing aspects of the current situation. For it is current patterns of behaviour, or "life-styles", which provide the contemporary sources of motivation and rewards for offending, and which expose and deliver the potential offender to the rest of the situational contingencies - of place, time, target or victim - which, together, generate the actual crime. By the same token, it is this interactional field that offers, perhaps, the most immediate hope for better crime control. The rational choice approach provides a way of developing policies which address this crime-generation system, whether through situational crime prevention, or by making offender-centred programmes, such as diversion, more aware of, and responsive to, situational factors.

References

Adams, S. (1974). Evaluative research in corrections: Status and prospects. *Federal Probation, 38,* 14-21.

Agnew, R. (1990). The origins of delinquent events: An examination of offender accounts. *Journal of Research in Crime and Delinquency, 27,* 267-294.

Akers, R.L. (1985). *Deviant behavior: A social learning approach* (3rd ed.). Belmont, CA: Wadsworth.

Andrews, D.A., Zinger, I., Hoge, R.D., Bonta, J., Gendreau, P., and Cullen, F. (1990). Does correctional treatment work? A clinically relevant and psychologically informed meta-analysis. *Criminology, 28,* 369-404.

Austin, J., and Krisberg, B. (1981). Wider, stronger, and different nets: The dialectics of criminal justice reform. *Journal of Research in Crime and Delinquency, 18,* 165-196.

Barclay, G.C. (1990). The peak age of known offending by males. *Research Bulletin, 28,* 20-23. London: Home Office Research and Statistics Department.

Barclay, G.C. (Ed.) (1991). *A digest of information on the criminal justice system.* London: Home Office Research and Statistics Department.

Binder, A., and Geis, G. (1984). Ad populum argumentation in criminology: Juvenile diversion as rhetoric. *Crime and Delinquency, 30,* 624-647.

Briar S., and Piliavin, J. (1965). Delinquency, situational inducements, and commitments to conformity. *Social Problems, 13,* 35-45.

Brown, G.W. (1987). Social factors and the development and course of depressive disorders in women: A review of a research programme. *British Journal of Social Work, 17,* 615-634.

Cameron, M.O. (1964). *The booster and the snitch: Department store shoplifting.* New York: Macmillan/Free Press.

Clarke, R.V. (Ed.) (1978). *Tackling vandalism.* Home Office Research Study No. 47. London: H.M.S.O.

Clarke, R.V. (1980). Situational crime prevention: Theory and practice. *British Journal of Criminology, 20,* 136-147.

Clarke, R.V. (1992). *Situational crime prevention: Successful case studies.* Albany, NY: Harrow and Heston.

Clarke, R.V., and Cornish, D.B. (Eds.) (1983). *Crime control in Britain.* Albany, NY: State University of New York Press.

Clarke, R.V., and Cornish, D.B. (1985). Modeling offenders' decisions: A framework for research and policy. In M. Tonry and N. Morris (Eds.), *Crime and justice: An annual review of research, Volume 6* (pp. 147-185). Chicago: University of Chicago Press.

Cohen L.E., and Felson, M. (1979). Social change and crime rate trends: A routine activity approach. *American Sociological Review, 44,* 580-608.

Cohen, S. (1979). The punitive city: Notes on the dispersal of social control. *Contemporary Crises, 3,* 339-363.

Cohen S. (1985). *Visions of social control.* London: Polity Press.

Cornish, D.B., and Clarke, R.V. (1975). *Residential treatment and its effects on delinquency.* Home Office Research Study No. 32. London: H.M.S.O.

Cornish, D.B., and Clarke, R.V. (Eds.) (1986). *The reasoning criminal: Rational choice perspectives on offending.* New York: Springer-Verlag.

Cornish, D.B., and Clarke, R.V. (1987). Understanding crime displacement: An application of rational choice theory. *Criminology, 25,* 933-947.

Cornish, D.B., and Clarke, R.V. (1989). Crime specialisation, crime displacement and rational choice theory. In H. Wegener, F. Lösel, and J. Haisch (Eds.), *Criminal behavior and the justice system: Psychological perspectives* (pp. 103-117). New York: Springer-Verlag.

Cressey, D.R. (1954). The differential association theory and compulsive crimes. *Journal of Criminal Law, Criminology, and Police Science, 45,* 29-40.

Cressey, D.R., and McDermott, R.A. (1974). *Diversion from the juvenile justice system.* Washington, DC: National Institute of Law Enforcement and Criminal Justice.

Cromwell, P.F., Olson, J.N., and Avary, D. (1990). *Residential burglary: An ethnographic analysis.* Washington, D.C.: National Institute of Justice.

Curtis, S. (1989). *Juvenile offending: Prevention through intermediate treatment.* London: Batsford.

Davidson, W.S., II, and Seidman, E. (1974). Studies of behavior modification and juvenile delinquency: A review, methodological critique, and social perspective. *Psychological Bulletin, 81,* 998-1011.

Davidson, W.S., II, Redner, R., Blakely, C.H., Mitchell, C.M., and Emshoff, J.G. (1987). Diversion of juvenile offenders: An experimental comparison. *Journal of Consulting and Clinical Psychology, 55,* 68-75.

Davidson, W.S., II, Redner, R., Amdur, R.L., and Mitchell, C.M. (1990). *Alternative treatments for troubled youth: The case of diversion from the justice system.* New York: Plenum.

Davis, G., Boucherat, J., and Watson, D. (1989). Pre-court decision-making in juvenile justice. *British Journal of Criminology, 29,* 219-235.

Dobash, R.P., Dobash, R.E., Ballintyne, S., Schumann, K., Kaulitzki, R., and Guth, H.-W. (1990). Ignorance and suspicion: Young people and criminal justice in Scotland and Germany. *British Journal of Criminology, 30,* 306-320.

Ehrlich, I. (1981). On the usefulness of controlling individuals: An economic analysis for rehabilitation, incapacitation, and deterrence. *American Economic Review, 71,* 307-322.

Ekblom, P. (1986). *The prevention of shop theft: An approach through crime analysis.* Crime Prevention Unit Paper No. 5. London: Home Office.

Ekblom, P. (1988). *Getting the best out of crime analysis.* Crime Prevention Unit Paper No. 10. London: Home Office.

Evans, R., and Wilkinson, C. (1990). Variations in police cautioning policy and practice in England and Wales. *The Howard Journal of Penology and Crime Prevention, 29,* 155-176.

Felson, M. (1986). Linking criminal choices, routine activities, informal control, and criminal outcomes. In D.B. Cornish and R.V. Clarke (Eds.), *The reasoning criminal: Rational choice perspectives on offending* (pp. 119-128). New York: Springer-Verlag.

Field, S. (1990). *Trends in crime and their interpretation: A study of recorded crime in post-war England and Wales.* Home Office Research Study No. 119. London: H.M.S.O.

Gabor, T. (1990). Prevention into the twenty-first century: Some final remarks. *Canadian Journal of Criminology, 32,* 197-212.

Gottfredson, M.R., and Hirschi, T. (1990). *A general theory of crime.* Stanford, CA: Stanford University Press.

Greenberg, D.F. (1977). Delinquency and the age structure of society. *Contemporary Crises, 1,* 189-223.

Harlow, E. (1970). Intensive intervention: An alternative to institutionalization. *Crime and Delinquency Literature, 2,* 3-46.

Heal, K., and Laycock, G. (1987). *Preventing juvenile crime: The Staffordshire experience.* Crime Prevention Unit, Paper No. 8. London: Home Office.

Hepburn, J.R. (1984). Occasional property crime. In R.F. Meier (Ed.), *Major Forms of Crime* (pp. 73-94). Beverly Hills, CA: Sage.

Hollin, C.R. (1990). *Cognitive-behavioral interventions with young offenders.* Oxford: Pergamon.

Hope, T. (1985). *Implementing crime prevention measures.* Home Office Research Study No. 86. London: H.M.S.O.

Jeffery, C.R. (1971). *Crime prevention through environmental design.* Beverly Hills, CA: Sage.

Katz, J. (1988). *Seductions of crime: Moral and sensual attractions of doing evil.* New York: Basic Books.

Lemert, E.M. (1981). Diversion in juvenile justice: What hath been wrought? *Journal of Research in Crime and Delinquency, 18,* 34-46.

Lipton, D., Martinson, R., and Wilks, J. (1975). *The effectiveness of correctional treatment.* New York: Praeger.

Lundman, R.J. (1976). Will diversion reduce recidivism? *Crime and Delinquency, 22,* 428-437.

Lundman, R.J., McFarlane, P.T., and Scarpitti, F.R. (1976). Delinquency prevention: A description of projects reported in the professional literature. *Crime and Delinquency, 22,* 297-308.

McCord, J. (1978). A thirty-year follow-up of treatment effects. *American Psychologist, 33,* 284-289.

McMahon, M. (1990). 'Net-widening': Vagaries in the use of a concept. *British Journal of Criminology, 30,* 121-149.

Matza, D. (1964). *Delinquency and drift.* New York: Wiley.

Mayhew, P., Clarke, R.V.G., Sturman, A., and Hough, M. (1976). *Crime as opportunity.* Home Office Research Study No. 34. London: H.M.S.O.

Morris, A., and Giller, H. (1987). *Understanding juvenile justice.* London: Croom Helm.

Nettler, G. (1961). Good men, bad men, and the perception of reality. *Sociometry, 24,* 279-294.

Newman, O. (1972). *Defensible space.* New York: Macmillan.

Nietzel, M.T. (1979). *Crime and its modification: A social learning perspective.* New York: Pergamon.

O'Dowd, D., Atkinson, J.R., Woodward, D., and Blackham, P. (1991). Pre-court decision-making in juvenile justice: Some comments. *British Journal of Criminology, 31,* 189-191.

Palmer, T.B., and Lewis, R.V. (1980). A differentiated approach to juvenile diversion. *Journal of Research in Crime and Delinquency, 17,* 209-229.

Parker, H. (1974). *View from the boys: A sociology of downtown adolescence.* Newton Abbot, U.K.: David and Charles.

Poyner, B. (1983). *Design against crime.* London: Butterworths.

Pratt, J. (1987). A revisionist history of intermediate treatment. *British Journal of Social Work, 17,* 417-436

Romig, D.A. (1978). *Justice for our children: An examination of juvenile delinquent rehabilitation programs.* Lexington, MA: Lexington Books.

Ross, R.R., and Fabiano, E.A. (1985). *Time to think: A cognitive model of delinquency prevention and offender rehabilitation.* Johnson City, TN: Institute of Social Sciences and Arts.

Sanders, A. (1988). The limits to diversion from prosecution. *British Journal of Criminology, 28,* 513-532.

Spergel, I. (1973). Community-based delinquency-prevention programs: An overview. *The Social Service Review, 47,* 16-31.

Taylor, M., and Nee, C. (1988). The role of cues in simulated residential burglary: A preliminary investigation. *British Journal of Criminology, 28,* 396-401.

Tremblay, P., and Rochon, C. (1991). Police organizations and their use of knowledge: A grounded research agenda. *Policing and Society, 1,* 269-283.

Tutt, N. (1984). Contemporary approaches to the understanding, assessment and treatment of delinquency. In J. Nicholson and H. Beloff (Eds.), *Psychology Survey No. 5* (pp. 369-396). Leicester, U.K.: British Psychological Society.

Van den Haag, E. (1982). Could successful rehabilitation reduce the crime rate? *Journal of Criminal Law and Criminology, 73,* 1022-1035.

Wheeler, S., Cottrell, S.L. Jr., and Romasco, A. (1967). Juvenile delinquency - its prevention and control. In *Task Force Report: Juvenile Delinquency and Youth Crime. President's Commission on Law Enforcement and Administration of Justice. Report on Juvenile Justice and Consultants' Papers* (pp. 409-428). Washington, DC: U.S. Government Printing Office.

Wilkins, L.T. (1973). Crime and criminal justice at the turn of the century. *Annals of the American Academy of Political and Social Science, 408,* 13-26.

Wilkins, L.T. (1976). Equity and republican justice. *Annals of the American Academy of Political and Social Science, 423,* 152-161.

Wilkins, L.T. (1984). *Consumerist criminology.* London: Heinemann.

Wilson, J.Q., and Herrnstein, R.J. (1985). *Crime and human nature.* New York: Simon and Schuster.

Wright, R., and Logie, R.H. (1988). How young house burglars choose targets. *The Howard Journal of Penology and Crime Prevention, 27,* 92-104.

Wright, W.E., and Dixon, M.C. (1977). Community treatment of juvenile delinquency: A review of evaluation studies. *Journal of Research in Crime and Delinquency, 19,* 35-67.

Part II

Diversion and the Juvenile Justice System

Introduction to Part II: Diversion and the Juvenile Justice System

The four papers that follow discuss the changes in the juvenile justice system and the place diversionary policies occupy therein with respect to the USA, England and Wales, and Germany.

First, Ira Schwartz, in a sobering account of the development of diversion and incarceration rates in the USA, establishes once more that the policies of diversion have not led to a decrease of criminal justice intervention in the lives of juveniles. Rather, given the growth of private correctional institutions during the last decade, an overall increase in the rate of institutionalized youth has been observed. But, in contrast to the lamentations we have heard so often in the past, Schwartz does not see this as a result of some obscure demonic forces that inevitably contribute to the widening of the net of control all over the world, but gives a very clear account of the precise political constellation that has led to this trend. Since diversion was largely a federally initiated program, but one which did not force states to reduce their incarceration rates, it is no wonder that the flow of federal dollars led to increased community-based intervention while, at the same time, leaving the traditional penal institutions intact. Such an analysis also gives rise to some hope for the future, since, as Schwartz points out, the fiscal problems to which decarceration policies were attributed in the past, actually are only beginning to turn critical at the state level, and this may force policy makers to consider diversion as a real alternative to incarceration in the future.

Roger Matthews gives an in-depth analysis of criminal policy trends in England and Wales. Here, we find a most interesting reversal of trends compared to the USA. While the British government, as is well known, promoted a policy of getting tough on offenders, incarceration rates of juveniles showed a dramatic decrease during the years 1980-1990. This, as Matthews explains, is largely due to a "corporatist" system developed during that time, in which increased interagency cooperation led to a skeptical view of incarceration as well as disdain of an overly personalized "welfare model" among practitioners in the field. Yet, the success of such a system is not unequivocal, since, at the same time, it leads to an increase in administrative discretion, to less judicial supervision, and decreasing emphasis on offender rights, as well as system accountability. Finally, Matthews suggests that a policy of "minimalism", while avoiding the stigma of formal justice procedures and incarceration, also tends to neglect the needs of youth in times of economic crises and growing inequalities.

The contribution of Wolfgang Ludwig-Mayerhofer attempts to evaluate diversion in the Federal Republic of Germany. Its starting point is the assertion that to be considered successful, diversionary policies should not simply lead to a growth of diversion but rather to significant changes in the formal criminal justice system. With this in mind, Ludwig-Mayerhofer's account of the changes brought about by diversion is rather negative in two ways: Diversion has led to a very small decrease in juvenile incarceration rates (especially if compared to the massive changes brought about by legislative reform some 20 years ago); and his analysis of juvenile court proceedings demonstrates that the scope of diversion is largely to keep petty offenders out of the system, while youth who might be considered to be in need of educational services still are more likely to be convicted by the courts. But, on the other hand, there has also been no increase of community-based interventions in the life of juveniles. The reason is that most of the allegedly "educational" measures for juveniles are community service orders, which replace financial payments in the case of juveniles who have no or little money of their own. In conclusion, according to this analysis, the rhetorics associated with juvenile justice have changed much more than its actual practice.

The chapter by Gunhild Korfes discusses the problems of diversion in the context of the transformation of the former German Democratic Republic. All in all, the abolition of the former system of "socialist justice" and the introduction of the Juvenile Justice Act of the Federal Republic of Germany have led to greater leniency in the dealings with juvenile delinquency. But this overall trend should not lead one to overlook the fact that, in some respects, the new system actually may be perceived as an extension of control. For, as Korfes shows, petty crimes could formerly be dealt with in the youths' social life-world, for instance, in the school; whereas now, criminal proceedings are invoked, even though they may be halted by the prosecutor or the judge at a later stage. But criminal policies should also be evaluated against the background of the actual social situation of the youth concerned. Korfes discusses the feelings of social uncertainty that arise from parental unemployment and family problems, and the possibility that violent youth gangs are formed in order to seek compensation for such feelings. Thus, diversionary and educational measures should mainly aim at these juveniles, while non-violent petty crimes should continue to be dealt with informally in the life-world (or social space) of the youth concerned.

Taken together, the contributions that follow seem to exemplify an old sociological wisdom: The unintended consequences of actions may be different from and sometimes even exactly the opposite of those that were intended in the first place. Thus, we have to conclude that criminal policies may not simply be assessed by looking at the labels attached to them (a lesson we have learned very well with respect to "offenders"), and that even the same label may have very different meanings according to the circumstances under which a criminal policy arises. In addition, the papers cast doubts on "globalizing" views of social control such as the concepts of the "control society" or the "surveillance society". While such concepts have strong merits inasmuch they direct our attention to phenomena that are easily overlooked and provide a unified framework of interpretation, at the same time, they support our tendency to neglect close empirical examination and to give too much weight to theoretical coherence. Another implication is that, despite two decades of research on diversionary politics, our knowledge about the effects of criminal policies and strategies is far from being conclusive.

The Impact and Role of Juvenile Diversion in the United States

Ira M. Schwartz

1 Introduction

There was considerable interest in diverting juveniles from the juvenile justice system in the United States during the 1960s and early 1970s. The broad support for this concept was codified in the federal Juvenile Justice and Delinquency Prevention Act of 1974 (Indexed Legislative History of the Juvenile Justice and Delinquency Prevention Act of 1974). Unfortunately, despite the interest and support for diversion on the part of juvenile justice professionals, public interest groups, social reformers, and policymakers at the federal and state levels, the best available evidence suggests this goal was largely unrealized. Moreover, there is research suggesting attempts to implement diversion programs have widened the net of social control (Ezell, in press).

This paper explores the impact of juvenile diversion in the United States. In addition, it discusses the current and potential role of diversion in the juvenile justice system.

2 Diversion from the Juvenile Courts

The federal Juvenile Justice and Delinquency Prevention Act encourages officials to divert status offenders and minor delinquency offenders from the juvenile justice system. In particular, the Act encourages officials to divert juveniles from the juvenile courts (Indexed Legislative History, 1974).

The data in Table 1 below presents information on the numbers and rates of delinquency and status offense cases disposed of by the juvenile courts in the United States between 1975 and 1988. As can be seen, there has been no decline in the overall rates during this period. Also, the sharp decline in the rates of status offense cases disposed of beginning in 1985 were essentially offset by increases in the rates for delinquency cases.

Table 1: Juvenile Court Case Rates 1975 - 1988

	Delinquency offenses		Status offenses	
	Number of case	Case rate	Number of cases	Case rate
1975	1,054,500	33.8	351,500	11.4
1976	1,089,660	35.1	307,340	10.4
1977	1,071,240	35.8	284,760	9.3
1978	1,019,160	34.6	321,840	10.7
1979	1,045,600	36.2	261,400	8.9
1980	1,089,450	38.3	255,550	8.9
1981	1,105,360	39.1	242,640	8.8
1982	1,075,680	39.1	220,320	8.1
1983	1,035,010	38.3	211,990	8.1
1984	1,030,160	38.7	273,840	10.1
1985	1,114,000	42.2	78,000	3.0
1986	1,148,000	44.1	83,000	3.2
1987	1,150,000	44.4	81,000	3.1
1988	1,156,000	45.3	82,000	3.2

Note :
1. "Case" refers to the number of cases disposed of by the juvenile court.
2. "Case rate" indicates the number of cases per 1,000 youth age 10 through the maximum age of original Juvenile Court jurisdiction for all 50 states and the District of Columbia disposed of by the courts.
3. Delinquency caseloads include cases disposed of both formally and informally by the courts.
4. Status offense caseloads before 1985 include cases disposed of both formally and informally by the courts. Status offense caseload rates after 1984 refer only to those cases handled formally by the courts.
5. Before 1984, estimation procedures changed frequently. Some changes in caseload can be attributed to changes in estimation procedures.

Source: Juvenile Court Statistics 1984 (caseload information for 1975-1984), Table 2, p.7; 1986 (caseload information for 1985-86), Table 2, p. 11, Table 6, p. 35; 1988 (caseload information for 1987-88), Table 2, p. 11, Table 6, p. 35; and 1987 (caseload information for 1987), Table 2, p. 11, Table 6, p. 35.

3 Diversion from Institutions

The Juvenile Justice and Delinquency Prevention Act also encourages juvenile justice professionals to reduce their reliance on secure detention and incarceration (Indexed Legislative History 1974). The Act calls upon officials to divert juveniles from pre- and post-adjudication institutions by developing community-based alternatives. Although juveniles placed in community-based programs are not diverted out of the system, their penetration into the system is limited.

Table 2 includes data on the numbers and rates of admission to juvenile detention centers (pre-adjudication confinement facilities). The table also contains one-day counts, or the numbers and rates of juveniles confined on a particular day. The data indicates there has been virtually no diversion from detention centers. The numbers and rates of admissions declined between 1971 and 1982 and increased thereafter. The rate of admissions was higher in 1988 than at any other time in which the data has been recorded. The one-day counts and one-day count rates were relatively stable until 1982 when they started to increase.

The data also indicates that the one-day count rates for females declined between 1971 and 1977. The rates increased between 1979 and 1985 and have been stable since that time. In contrast, the one-day count rates for males in detention centers have been increasing steadily since 1977. Also, virtually all of the increase is accounted for by black males (Schwartz, Willis, and Battle, 1991).

Table 3 below presents data on the numbers and rates of admissions to training schools. These data indicate the rates of admission were essentially stable between 1971 and 1989. This means juveniles have not been diverted from these institutions. The data also indicate the rates of admissions for females declined during this period. However, the decline for females was essentially offset by a corresponding increase in the rate for males.

The juvenile justice system in the United States includes private youth correction facilities as well as public institutions. A recent study by the National Council on Crime and Delinquency documents a substantial increase in the rates of admission to private juvenile training schools, group homes, halfway houses, and residential treatment centers (Krisberg, Thornberry, and Austin, 1989). This suggests that there has been not only no diversion from public training schools but also a sizeable overall increase in the rate of juvenile incarceration in institutions of all types.

Table 2: U.S. Public Juvenile Detention Centers Admissions and One-Day Counts, 1971-1989

	Admissions		Males		Females		One-Day Count		Males		Females	
Year	Number	Rate/ 100,000	Number	Rate/ 100,000	Number	Rate/ 100,000	Number	Rate/ 100,000	Number	Rate/ 100,000	Number	Rate/ 100,000
1971	496,526	1,655	349,407	2,329	147,119	981	11,767	39	7,926	53	3,841	26
1974	529,075	1,791	371,225	2,514	157,850	1,069	11,010	37	7,698	52	3,312	22
1977	489,694	1,681	375,728	2,530	113,966	798	9,977	34	8,058	54	1,919	13
1979	451,810	1,574	356,167	2,431	95,643	680	10,683	37	8,901	61	1,782	13
1982-83	410,688	1,488	325,461	2,311	85,227	630	13,048	47	10,833	77	2,215	16
1984-85	404,175	1,520	320,952	2,363	83,223	640	13,772	52	11,340	83	2,432	19
1986-87	467,688	1,799	374,461	2,823	93,207	732	16,146	62	13,587	102	2,559	20
1988-89	499,621	1,958	407,288	3,119	92,333	741	18,014	70	15,490	118	2,524	20

Note:

1. Totals pertain to all youth including those committed to a facility (placed following adjudication); detained youth (placed pending adjudication or awaiting formal court disposition or placement); and voluntary admissions.
2. Rates are based on the numbers of youths aged 10 through the age of maximum original juvenile court jurisdiction for each state and the District of Columbia.

Sources:

1. NCCD and Hubert Humphrey Institute of Public Affairs; Rethinking Juvenile Justice: National Statistical Trends, p. 43 (for years 1971 and 1974).
2. Juvenile Detention and Correctional Facility Census, 1977, 1979, 1982-83, 1984-85, 1986-87, and 1988-89.
3. U.S. Bureau of the Census, Current Population Reports, Series P-25, published and unpublished data.

Table 3: U.S. Public Juvenile Training Schools / Admissions and One-Day Counts, 1971-1989

	Admissions		Males		Females		One-Day Count		Males		Females	
Year	Number	Rate/ 100,000	Number	Rate/ 100,000	Number	Rate/ 100,000	Number	Rate/ 100,000	Number	Rate/ 100,000	Number	Rate/ 100,000
1971	67,775	226	53,089	354	14,686	98	35,960	120	27,874	186	8,086	54
1974	67,406	228	53,737	364	13,669	93	25,397	86	19,745	134	5,652	38
1977	66,098	227	56,427	380	9,671	68	23,408	80	19,998	135	3,410	24
1979	63,901	223	55,457	378	8,444	60	23,200	81	20,237	138	2,963	21
1982-83	56,568	205	48,639	345	7,929	59	25,071	91	22,213	158	2,215	21
1984-85	58,875	221	51,263	377	7,612	59	25,074	94	22,282	164	2,432	21
1986-87	61,399	236	53,466	403	7,933	62	27,034	104	24,075	181	2,959	23
1988-89	62,824	247	55,793	427	7,031	56	27,823	108	25,087	191	2,736	22

Note:

1. Totals pertain to all youth inluding those committed to a facility (placed following adjudication); detained youth (placed pending adjudication or waiting formal court disposition or placement); and voluntary admissions.
2. Rates are based on the numbers of youths aged 10 through the age of maximum original juvenile court jurisdiction for each state and the District of Columbia.

Sources:

1. NCCD and Hubert Humphrey Institute of Public Affairs; Rethinking Juvenile Justice: National Statistical Trends, p. 43 (for years 1971 and 1974).
2. Juvenile Detention and Correctional Facility Census, 1977, 1979, 1982-83, 1984-85, 1986-87, and 1988-89.
3. U.S. Bureau of the Census, Current Population Reports, Series P-25, published and unpublished data.

4 Discussion

The data in this paper indicates young people were not diverted from the juvenile justice system in the United States when this concept was in vogue. This raises the question of why the federal Juvenile Justice and Delinquency Prevention Act failed to influence diversion policies and practices in the states. In order to answer this question, one must understand the relationship and dynamics between national domestic policy and state government.

In the United States, the federal government does not administer social welfare programs. The federal government does not, with a few notable exceptions such as the Federal Bureau of Prisons and health services to veterans, provide or directly deliver social welfare and health services. Social welfare programs, such as child welfare and juvenile justice services, are administered at the state level and are largely governed by state laws. The federal government, through national legislation, U.S. Supreme Court decisions, and, to a lesser extent, Presidential directives, can both encourage and even mandate that states implement various social policies and programs. Mandated policies are almost always accompanied with federal funding to the states. Policies that are merely encouraged may also be accompanied with federal funding, but participation in these programs is usually voluntary on the part of the states. In other words, states can choose to participate or not as they see fit.

State participation in the federal juvenile justice program is voluntary. Moreover, the only requirements for state participation to receive federal juvenile justice funds are for state policymakers to agree to remove status offenders from secure institutions and juveniles from adult jails (Indexed Legislative History, 1974). The legislation does not require states to divert juveniles from the juvenile justice system or to reduce their rates of detention and incarceration as a condition for receiving federal dollars. While the legislation strongly encourages such policies and practices, they are not mandated as a condition for receiving federal resources. As a result, the concept of diversion, while an interesting and progressive concept, was largely ignored at the state and local levels.

Another factor that probably worked against the successful implementation of diversion policies in the United States is the general resistance to change on the part of the juvenile courts. Feld, for example, documents the inability of juvenile courts to insure young people receive the due process and procedural guarantees mandated by the United States Supreme Court in the landmark Gault decision in 1967 (Feld, 1989). In the case of diversion, juvenile court judges were not generally interested in seeing large portions of their caseloads diverted out of the system. This was particularly the case with juvenile court judges who administered probation services whose budgets were based upon the numbers of cases under supervision.

5 Policy Considerations

While the national data on the impact of diversion is disappointing, the concept of diversion should not be abandoned. Diversion should not be discarded, because the data from a few state and local programs is hopeful. For example, Davidson and Johnson evaluated programs in multiple sites using a randomized design that tested the "... effectiveness of diversion compared to traditional juvenile justice processing" (Davidson and Johnson, 1987: 17). The researchers were particularly interested in learning "To what extent is there evidence that diversion with services is more effective than outright release or court processing?" (ibid.: 163). They concluded that diversion with services, particularly the Family Support and Education Model, is superior in terms of reducing delinquency than either warn and outright release or traditional juvenile court processing (ibid.: 164). In addition, there are a number of examples documenting reductions in the rates of detention and incarceration in states and counties without compromising public safety (Austin, Joe, Krisberg, and Steele, 1990; Austin, Elms, Krisberg, and Steele, 1991; Schwartz, Barton, and Orlando, 1991).

These examples suggest diversion programs can work. However, policymakers and juvenile justice professionals need to take care to insure these programs are implemented properly, key officials are involved in the process of developing the programs and supportive of the program's goals, staff are properly trained and supervisedm and the programs are adequately funded, monitored, and evaluated.

Currently, the idea of diverting young people from the juvenile justice system is not on the public agenda in the United States. It is a concept that does not enjoy much popularity and is not even discussed at professional practice, policy, and academic meetings. It is also not discussed in state legislatures.

It would not be surprising, however, to see interest in juvenile diversion reemerge in the United States. The massive fiscal problems at the federal and state levels are forcing policymakers and professionals to consider program ideas and concepts that would have been almost unthinkable even just a few years ago (Eckl, Hutchison, and Snell, 1991). For example, the Governor and the legislature in Michigan are keenly interested in alternatives to the imprisonment of adults. This is the result of a large increase in Michigan's prison population, one of the most aggressive prison construction programs in the country, and huge fiscal deficits. If states are beginning to explore alternatives to the incarceration of adults, it would not be unreasonable to expect officials to be amenable to the diversion of juveniles from the juvenile courts, detention centers, and training schools. Moreover, if there is reason to believe juvenile diversion programs might reduce costs or, at the very least, prevent costs from rising, the prospects for this concept may be promising in the years ahead.

References

Austin, J., Elms, W., Krisberg, B., and Steele, P.A. (1991). *Unlocking juvenile corrections: Evaluating the Massachusetts Department of Youth Services.* San Francisco, CA: National Council on Crime and Delinquency.

Austin, J., Joe, K., Krisberg, B., and Steele, P.A. (1990). *The impact of juvenile court sanctions: A court that works.* San Francisco, CA: National Council on Crime and Delinquency.

Davidson, W.S., and Johnson, C.D. (1987). *Diversion in Michigan.* Final Report to Michigan Department of Social Services, Office of Children and Youth Services.

Eckl, C.L., Hutchison, A.M., and Snell, R.K. (1991). *State Budget and Tax Actions 1991* (Legislative Finance Paper, preliminary data). Denver, Co: National Conference of State Legislatures.

Ezell, M. (In press). Juvenile diversion: The ongoing search for alternatives. In I.M. Schwartz (Ed.), *Juvenile justice and public policy: Toward a national agenda.*

Feld, B.C. (1989). *The right to counsel in juvenile court: Fulfilling Gault's promise.* Ann Arbor, MI: Center for the Study of Youth Policy.

Indexed Legislative History of the Juvenile Justice and Delinquency Prevention Act of 1974 (1974, October). U. S. Department of Justice, Law Enforcement Assistance Administration, Office of General Counsel.

Krisberg, B.A., Thornberry, T.P., and Austin, J. (1989). *Juveniles taken into custody: Developing national statistics.* San Francisco, CA: National Council on Crime and Delinquency,

Schwartz, I.M., Willis, D.A., and Battle, J. (1991). *Juvenile arrest, detention, and incarceration trends 1979-1989.* Ann Arbor, MI: Center for the Study of Youth Policy, The University of Michigan, School of Social Work.

The Diversion of Juveniles From Custody: The Experience of England and Wales 1980-90

Roger Matthews

During the 1980s the number of juveniles in custody fell dramatically. This event in itself would have been remarkable enough but its significance is further underlined by the fact that this reduction occurred in a decade in which there was a widespread expectation that the juvenile custodial population would continue to rise. It was a decade which began with the establishment of a "law and order" conservative government which advocated the "experimentation" with tough militaristic custodial regimes for juveniles under the banner of the "short, sharp, shock" (Shaw, 1985). Moreover, this decrease occurred during a decade which was beset by growing political and economic divisions. In 1981 and 1985 the country was set alight politically by scenes of riots and disturbances in a number of major urban centres (Cowell, Jones, and Young, 1982). It was a decade of growing social and economic inequalities. Such processes have been repeatedly identified within criminological research as having a major impact on both the level of crime and the development of the implementation of more punitive crime control policies (Box, 1987; Field, 1990).

Underpinning these developments, there was - in the first half of the decade at least - a wave of liberal pessimism which expressed deep scepticism about the possibility of progressive reform in general and of reducing the custodial population in particular (Bayer, 1981). Some critics even began questioning the desirability of decarceration itself (Hudson, 1984; Matthews, 1987; Scull, 1977). Influential articles around these themes focussed on the "litany of impediments" which stood in the way of achieving effective forms of diversion (Klein, 1979).

The recent history of juvenile justice in England and Wales has confounded expectations. The juvenile custodial population since the mid 1980s has fallen dramatically, new forms of diversion have been established, and the recorded level of juvenile crime has decreased.

During the previous two decades a range of apparently radical measures were introduced in order to reduce or to limit the juvenile custodial population without much success. A range of strategies tied to "welfare" and "justice" considerations which were implemented in the 1960s and 1970s had a common objective of reducing the number of juveniles in custody. However, it transpired that by the end of the 1970s there were more juveniles locked up in England and Wales than at any time since the introduction of a separate system of juvenile justice in 1908. Surprisingly, it was under the banner of what has been termed "corporatism" in which the agencies in the juvenile justice system were brought into new alliances, that the objective of significantly reducing the number of juveniles in custody was realised (Pratt, 1989).

This achievement was clearly not anticipated within either criminological or government circles. The government was expecting an overall increase in the custodial population in the 1980s and embarked upon the largest prison building programme since Victorian times. The continuing expansion of the juvenile custodial population was clearly part of the basis for this expansionist policy.

However, the "successes" which have occurred in the juvenile sector are currently being redirected towards the young adult population (18-21) who now form a disproportionately high percentage of the custodial population. The types of corporatist policies which seemed to have worked well for juveniles are being directed to this older age group. It is not entirely clear, however, what particular elements of the diverse range of interventions which were implemented during the 1980s in relation to juveniles were actually effective. There has not as yet been any systematic research into what worked in this period. As a result, a certain number of assumptions have been made about the achievements of the last decade without any real empirical support. Out of the cocktail of measures which were implemented there is, in fact, considerable uncertainty about which were the most effective elements. If we are going to learn real lessons from these achievements and be able to apply them elsewhere it is necessary to examine these developments in some detail.

A recent, and very useful, attempt has been made by Rob Allen (1990; 1991) to uncover the key elements of this process of decarceration. In this paper we will follow the contours of Allen's argument, although ultimately placing a different emphasis upon developments. Before we engage in this discussion, however, it is necessary to make some introductory remarks on the precise nature of changes which have taken place in relation to the juvenile custodial population in England and Wales during the 1980s.

1 Juveniles in Custody 1980-88

The number of males between 14 and 17 sentenced to custody for indictable offences as well as in custody on the 30th June each year has fallen consistently throughout the 1980s (see Table 1).

Although it is clear that both the numbers of young males given custodial sentences as well as the numbers in custody decreased throughout the 1980, such decreases were not universal. There are, in fact, four important caveats which are obscured by these figures. The first is that the percentage of juveniles drawn from ethnic minorities increased in this period with some institutions reporting that over 30 %

of inmates were Afro-Caribbean. The second is that the use of custody for young women also increased from 52 in 1981 to 103 in 1985, and then dropped back down to 60 in 1988. Thirdly, that sentences for those committing "grave crimes" became longer in these years. Fourthly, that there were significant geographical variations in the use of custody with the north of England contributing disproportionately to the custodial population by the end of the decade.

Table 1: Males 14-16 Sentenced to Custody 1980-1988 and in Custody on 30th June

Year	Number sentenced to custody	Number in custody on 30th June
1981	7,700	1,637
1982	7,100	1,500
1983	6,700	1,397
1984	6,500	1,274
1985	5,900	1,078
1986	4,300	767
1987	3,900	788
1988	3,200	547

Source: Criminal Statistics 1989

Despite these variations, however, there has been a substantial overall decrease in the juvenile custodial population which requires explanation. A number of developments have occurred within juvenile justice in the 1980s which have been credited with producing this reduction. These include:

1. Demographic changes.
2. Increased use of cautioning.
3. The development of pre-court diversion.
4. Changes in sentencing policy and practices.
5. The development of competing alternatives to custody.

Competing explanations of the decrease in juvenile custodial rates have tended to argue in favour of one or more of these components. Allen has argued that these various changes have worked to reinforce each other often producing an unexpected "interactive" effect through different types of intervention working in mutually reinforcing ways to reduce the overall level of custody for juveniles. He writes:

"It seems clear, however, that a number of important changes have contributed to the use in sentences nationally. A declining population of juveniles and a declining population of sentenced juveniles do much to amount for the fall in custody. Changes in law, policy and practice have also played an important role. In as much as the juvenile justice system is a collection of local systems the relative significance of different factors will have varied between police force area, psd, local authority and probation areas and even within them" (Allen, 1990: 50-51).

This conclusion is partly an inevitable consequence of trying to assess the impact of a diverse number of processes on a national basis. Using national figures it is difficult to say very much about the specificity of each of these factors; while on the other hand the substantial variations between localities suggest that even specific and focussed studies may be unrepresentative. Clearly, if we are to understand more about the relative weighting of each of these factors in producing a reduction in the levels of custody a methodology needs to be constructed which can move between the general and the particular, and the local and national elements of this process. Only in this way will it be possible to develop a real understanding of the most effective mechanisms for promoting decarceration.

Any examination of this process needs to ask how far each of the various changes go in explaining the known facts about juvenile justice in the 1980s. The viability of any particular explanation must be evaluated in terms of the accuracy and comprehensiveness of its explanations of the known empirical findings. Although research of this issue remains partial and embryonic there are a number of empirical findings already available which have to be accounted for, some of which have been referred to above.

1. That over this period the decrease in the level of custody was most pronounced in the South with over 70 per cent of those receiving custody being resident in the North of England.
2. That custody rates for ethnic minority and females did not decrease in this period.
3. That the composition of the juvenile custodial population changed during the decade in relation to the types of offences for which young people were incarcerated.
4. That the decrease in the custodial population has not been even over the decade. It is only really since the middle of the 1980s that the juvenile custodial population has decreased significantly.
5. That the remand population has remained relatively high.
6. That although the number of juveniles coming before the courts has decreased sentence lengths have, on average, become longer.

One of the explanations which was consistently presented when it first became evident that a decrease in the juvenile custodial population was taking place was that there was a major demographic shift occurring which served to reduce the number of 14-17 year olds in the population. This reduction of numbers, it was claimed, would reduce the level of juvenile crime to a point where the delinquent would become a "scarce resource".

2 Delinquency as a Scarce Resource

Due to demographic changes the number of juveniles available to engage in offending and by implication to keep the juvenile justice agencies busy has declined. The assumption that delinquency would continue to increase indefinitely was undermined by the realisation that the number of males aged 14-17 in the population fell from 1.2 million in 1978 to 0.9 million in 1990 (Pratt, 1985). Paradoxically, during this period in which the government had planned for an expansion of juvenile custodial institutions the demand for such institutions was already beginning to wane. By the end of the decade a number of newly built custodial institutions stood empty.

The demographic downturn for juveniles aged 14-17 began around 1981/82 with an accelerated decrease after 1986/87. For boys aged 14-17 there is roughly a 25% decrease in this cohort between 1982-1991. Significantly, the number of males aged 14-17 per 100,000 found guilty or cautioned for an indictable offence increased up to 1983 and thereafter steadily declined. Between 1983 and 1990 there is a strong correlation between the decreasing number of 14-17 year males and the level of juvenile crime.

However, this decrease is able to explain at best 30% of the decline in the use of custodial sentences for juveniles. Although there can be little doubt that these demographic shifts have had a depressing effect upon the level of juvenile crime and in turn the use of custody it would be too simplistic to attribute a primary role to this process, since there are a number of examples of areas where the juvenile population has gone *up* but the custodial population has gone down.

One example of this paradoxical movement is Milton Keynes in Buckinghamshire, which became a magnet for many thousands of predominantly young working class-families who during the 1980s changed run-down, inner-city dwellings for less congested new towns. For our purposes this population shift was important in terms of the class and age composition of those involved. The new town of Milton Keynes had a significantly disproportionate amount of young males aged between 14-17 in the 1980s, and an above average percentage of these were drawn from the working and manual classes. Despite this increase, however, the developments in Milton Keynes followed a similar trajectory as other parts of the country with fewer custodial sentences being given through the 1980s. Between 1985 and 1991 the number of juveniles given custodial sentences, in fact, in Milton Keynes fell from 15 to 5.

This example indicates that demographic change may account for more limited effects than is usually supposed. The overall, and possibly most significant, effect of the declining juvenile population was on one hand to encourage a climate of increased tolerance on the assumption that juvenile crime was less of a problem, while on the other hand it allowed hard pressed social services departments to de-prioritise juvenile offending and to put greater resources into new areas of concern like child abuse. The apparent inability of demographic changes to explain more than a percentage decrease in juvenile offending has led to a focus on other possible explanations including cautioning.

3 Police Cautioning

The growth in the use of police cautioning of juveniles in England and Wales during the 1980s has been considerable. The numbers involved increased from 28,900 in 1979 to 48,000 in 1985, thereafter dropping back down to 37,500 in 1989.

In the earlier periods in which cautioning was adopted it was often associated with "net widening" (Ditchfield, 1976), but during the late 1970s and early 1980s, it became increasingly viewed as an effective form of diversion. Its impact on the custody rate is uncertain. The changing use of cautioning in this period does not correlate very well with changes in the use of custody. In fact, it is in the second half of the decade when the level of cautioning was being reduced nationally that the level of custody fell most sharply.

However, the significance of cautioning is not necessarily tied to the overall level of its use. Rather it is a question of which types of offences it is being used for. There is some evidence, for example, that by the end of the decade cautioning was being used for more serious offences - particularly violence against the person - and the effect of diverting these offenders from court might be significant (see Table 2).

Just as with demographic shifts, however, cautioning which at first sight appears as a potentially powerful explanatory variable is only probably responsible for a relatively small percentage in the decrease in juvenile custody rates. There are a number of reasons why its impact may be limited.

Firstly, in the majority of cases where cautioning is seen as appropriate a custodial sentence is probably a remote possibility. Secondly, although the use of cautioning was uneven across the country there is no evidence which indicates that custody rates were significantly lower in localities where cautioning was more extensive.

Cautioning, therefore, may have had an impact upon certain groups of offenders who were at risk of receiving a custodial sentence but the numbers involved were probably relatively low. Its most important contribution to the decarceration process may have been in reducing pressure on the courts and by implication allowing them to give more time and consideration to offenders who did appear in court.

At the other end of the spectrum it became evident that some 85% of the juveniles who received a caution did not come back into contact with the police. This suggests that for many young offenders it provides a response which deters them, and which was simultaneously able to deflect them from the mainstream of the juvenile justice system.

Table 2: Offenders Cautioned by Type of Offence (England and Wales); Indictable offences, Number of offenders (thousands)

	1979	1980	1981	1982	1983	1984	1985	1986	1987	1988	1989
Violence against the person	4.7	5.1	5.6	6.5	7.0	7.8	9.0	9.5	11.3	12.7	4.7
Sexual offences	2.8	2.9	2.8	2.7	2.9	2.8	2.9	2.9	3.2	3.6	3.5
Burglary	9.7	11.0	11.2	10.9	11.6	13.1	13.9	12.3	13.0	12.2	12.0
Robbery	0.1	0.1	0.1	0.2	0.2	0.2	0.2	0.2	0.2	0.2	0.4
Theft and handling stolen goods	74.9	77.0	79.2	85.9	86.9	92.3	109.9	100.3	106.5	92.6	81.9
Fraud and Forgery	1.2	1.4	1.4	1.4	1.6	1.8	2.2	2.7	3.9	4.0	4.0
Criminal damage	2.0	2.0	2.1	1.9	2.4	2.6	3.1	3.0	3.5	4.3	3.7
Drug offences	0.2	0.2	0.3	0.4	1.0	2.0	3.6	4.4	6.3	9.1	13.1
Other (excluding motoring offences)	1.1	1.3	1.3	1.4	1.4	1.5	1.5	1.5	1.8	1.9	2.9
Total	96.8	100.9	103.9	111.3	114.9	124.1	145.4	136.9	149.8	140.7	136.0

Source: Criminal Statistics 1989

In order to deflect the more persistent offenders a number of authorities set up multi-agency, pre-court diversion panels during the 1980s. These panels which were made up of representatives of all the principal agencies - police, youth service, social services, and probation - were developed in order to divert offenders from the courts.

4 Pre-Court Diversion: Multi-Agency Panels

It became increasingly apparent to many practitioners and observers that the juvenile courts were full of petty persistent offenders, who had "used up" their cautions. After the second or third caution it was felt, by the police in particular, that a more severe response should be given; although the nature of the offence was not considered to be serious enough to warrant a court appearance. This resulted in a growing emphasis amongst interested parties in developing and extending pre-court diversion.

Multi-agency panels which became widely known as Juvenile Liaison Bureaus (JLBs) sprang up around the country. The aim of these Bureaus was to make recommendations which could range from no further action, to a caution, to other relatively informal options. Based upon a commitment to diversion, a general adherence to the tenets of labelling theory, and a desire to reduce juvenile involvement in the juvenile justice system these panels aimed at reducing the number of people appearing in court.

Much of the interest in pre-court diversion panels has focused on the pioneering work of the Northamptonshire Juvenile Liaison Bureau. In their annual reports in the mid 1980s they claimed that the Bureau had been effective in considerably reducing the numbers of juveniles who were given a custodial sentence in this area. The numbers involved decreased from 37 in 1980/81 to 20 in 1985 (Northamptonshire Juvenile Liaison Bureau 1985). The Bureau dealt mainly with cases of burglary and theft. In 1985, in 69.5% of cases a formal caution was recommended, 16.3% of cases were put forward for prosecution and in the remaining 14% of cases no further action was recommended.

Throughout the 1980s there have been a number of multi-agency panels established following similar lines. They have, it is claimed, served to slow down the flow of juveniles through the system and to divert a considerable number of petty persistent offenders from the courts.

The major role of the panels is to check the progress of certain relatively minor offenders through the system. Thus their effect upon custody is in practice relatively limited. The presumption is that the majority of these offenders would not be eligible for a custodial sentence. At the same time "serious" cases are not referred to the panels. The range of disposals open to these pre-court diversionary panels is limited and they tend to be police led, with the police having the ultimate right to prosecute in court.

Thus, the real effectiveness of these multi-agency panels probably lies in their influence upon informal relations. By bringing the relevant agencies together to discuss cases, and particularly by bringing members of the judiciary into closer contact with other agencies, they are able to influence the process and objectives of sentencing. Since there is normally a strong anti-custodial ethos amongst juvenile justice practitioners these values will tend to be relayed in such meetings. It is therefore through the elaboration of these informal processes that changes in sentencing may have been achieved.

5 Sentencing in the Juvenile Court

The changes which have taken place on the informal level have been matched by equally significant formal changes. The 1982 Criminal Justice Act was important in that it set limitations on judicial discretion to make custodial orders. Any custodial order had to meet three now well established criteria: that the offender is unable and unwilling to respond to non-custodial penalties; that a custodial sentence is recurring for the protection of the public; or that the offence is so serious that a non-custodial sentence cannot be justified. The fact that the judge (magistrate) was required in court to publicly justify the use of a custodial sentence changed the way in which the use of custody was viewed. The Act also made provision for legal representation which was taken up in a growing number of cases (Burney, 1985).

Within the sentencing process itself, more dramatic changes took place in relation to juveniles. As Table 3 indicates, the number of juveniles sentenced to immediate custody decreased considerable in the second half of the 1980s. The percentage of cases given immediate custody fell from 12% in 1979 to 9% in 1989. Given the substantial reduction in the number of cases coming before the court this apparently small reduction in the percentage of cases given immediate custody is still significant. Also of considerable significance is the use of custody for different types of offences (see Table 3).

It is important to note that the use of custody increases for males aged 14-16 between 1979 and 1982 but thereafter decreases, with the most dramatic shifts occuring in 1985/86 and 1988/89. Also of interest is the fact that the use of custody decreases most noticeably for burglary, theft and violence against the person.

During the 1980s the total number of offenders given immediate custody decreased from 5905 in 1985 to 1922 in 1989; while the total number of 14- to 16-year-old males sentenced decreased from 56,000 in 1979 to 20,000 in 1989. Thus the number appearing in court went down by almost two thirds, of which a diminishing percentage were given immediate custodial disposals.

To some extent these changes may be attributed to a growing rejection of the use of custody amongst sentencers, arising from the changed formal and informal relations described above. However, there are indications that although there is a

Table 3: Receptions into Prison Service Establishments Under an Immediate Custodial Sentence (England and Wales): Males only, 1979-89; Number of persons

	1979	1980	1981	1982	1983	1984	1985	1986	1987	1988	1989
Males (total)	23,571	25,184	27,782	27,792	27,616	28,007	28,881	24,021	23,283	21,004	17,184
Aged 14-16	7,020	7,339	7,535	6,961	6,544	6,360	5,681	4,206	3,825	3,120	2,131
Violence against the person	809	913	993	942	906	751	758	566	516	523	207
Sexual offences	72	70	56	66	70	48	63	39	32	35	33
Burglary	3,269	3,760	3,969	3,542	3,227	3,083	2,559	1,890	1,683	1,312	806
Robbery	220	192	246	197	151	230	278	239	257	197	165
Theft, handling, fraud and forgery	2,345	2,128	1,924	1,880	1,840	1,596	1,339	987	853	615	433
Drugs offences	4	4	1	4	4	6	15	11	14	20	8
Other offences	301	272	346	330	346	645	669	474	460	385	378
Offence not recorded	*	*	*	*	*	*	*	*	8	32	101
Courts martial prisoners		-	-	-	-	1	-	-	2	1	-

Source: Criminal Statistics 1989

Table 4: Males aged 14 and under 17 sentenced for indictable offences by type of sentence or order (England and Wales): Number of persons (thousands)

	Total number of persons sentenced	Absolute or conditional discharge	Supervision order	Fine	Communitiy service order	Attendance centre order	Care order	Young offender institution	Otherwise dealt with	Total immediate custody
1979	56.3	9.8	9.0	20.9	*	7.1	2.2	6.9	0.3	6.9
1980	63.2	11.3	10.4	22.4	*	9.0	2.3	7.4	0.4	7.4
1981	62.0	11.9	10.4	19.9	*	9.6	2.1	7.7	0.4	7.7
1982	59.2	11.9	9.6	18.5	*	9.8	1.9	7.1	0.4	7.1
1983	54.4	11.7	8.9	15.7	0.5	9.4	1.2	6.7	0.5	6.7
1984	52.8	11.5	8.9	14.1	1.7	8.6	1.0	6.6	0.4	6.5
1985	47.9	10.7	8.4	12.0	1.9	7.8	0.8	5.9	0.5	5.9
1986	37.7	9.1	6.8	9.2	1.5	5.8	0.6	4.3	0.4	4.3
1987	34.2	8.4	6.3	7.8	1.6	5.3	0.5	3.9	0.5	3.9
1988	29.6	7.4	5.4	6.6	1.4	4.7	0.3	3.2	0.5	3.2
1989	20.1	6.1	4.0	4.3	1.0	3.2	0.1	1.9	0.5	1.9

Source: Criminal Statistics 1989

willingness to try to avoid custody for some categories of offenders, the number of juveniles on remand among this period remained relatively stable. Simultaneously, the overall length of sentences actually increased over this period. These considerations suggest that it was not so much a rejection of custody per se which motivated the judiciary but a growing sense of the inappropriateness of custody for certain types of juvenile offenders.

During the 1980s there were also some significant shifts in the use of sentencing options in the juvenile court. Most recently the use of the fine has decreased considerably, while both supervision orders and attendance centre orders also decreased (see Table 4). The use of care orders was reduced to a minimum level in this period following a growing disquiet about the suitability of placing vulnerable young people in "care".

If we look at the figures presented in Table 4 in percentage terms we see that the use of absolute and conditional discharges increased from 17% in 1979 to 29% of all disposals in 1989, while the use of the fine almost halves from 37% of cases in 1979 to 20% in 1989.

The changes of sentencing practices reflected in these figures is far-reaching. Clearly, without a change in attitude and in the use of disposals, the reduction of custody could, even with the demographic changes, the increased use of cautioning and the introduction of multi-agency panels, have been relatively limited. The judiciary, it would seem, have become more willing to use the available non-custodial sentences in a growing number of cases.

The use of non-custodial alternatives to custody has been beset by a series of problems in the 1970s (Harris, 1983; Smith, 1984). It became increasingly apparent that many of the available alternatives were relevant mainly for minor offenders. Subsequently, there had been a growing pressure towards the end of the 1970s to develop more intensive and competing alternatives which could be specifically used for those who were at real risk of receiving a custodial sentence.

In line with those developments the Department of Health and Social Services (DHSS) put forward a £15 million initiative which became known as LAC 83 (3) which was designed to promote the development of intensive intermediate treatment. This development was aimed principally at "heavy end" offenders who were identified as being likely to receive custodial sentences.

6 Intensive Intermediate Treatment LAC 83(3)

This initiative was designed to create non-custodial alternatives for juveniles which would be seen as competing with custodial sentences. They were to involve sanctions which would have an "interchangeability" with custodial sentences (Morris and Tonry, 1990). Implemented between 1983 and 1987, it involved 110 projects which were set up around the country offering over 3,000 places.

The rationale for the initiative centred around three main objectives. First, the development of competing alternatives to custody; second, the encouragement of inter-agency cooperation; and thirdly to encourage greater involvement of the voluntary sector. The DHSS provided £15 million "seed corn" funding for 2 or 3 years to selected projects. These projects were set up all with a slightly greater number being set up in the North of England.

Funding for these projects was organised on a "first come first served" basis rather by developing alternatives where they were most needed. This suggests that it was probably in the better organised localities that funding became available. Also, because of the short-term nature of these projects and the central role played by voluntary organisations some areas were reticent about engaging in this initiative. For these reasons it is difficult to make comparisons between the areas where the DHSS initiative was implemented and other areas. Assessing the impact of these "heavy end" alternatives is also made more difficult by the fact that areas which did not apply for funds may have felt that they already had a fairly comprehensive range of alternatives available.

Thus the comparisons which have been made between areas in which the initiative was introduced and other areas are not very convincing (NACRO, 1991). These problems are compounded by the fact that the agency principally responsible for monitoring this initiative - NACRO (National Association for the Care and Resettlement of Offenders) - was also principally responsible for promoting it.

The evidence collected by NACRO indicates that custody rates in the areas the initiative was implemented were around 10% in 1987 compared with a national figure for that year of 11.4%. This evidence indicates that the available places were on the whole taken up by those convicted of burglary, theft and violence against the person. As we have seen above, however, these were precisely the offences which the pre-court multi-agency panels were absorbing in some areas, while in other areas these offences were being dealt with by a caution.

Since these were funded as short-term developments which it was hoped would be sustained by local authority funding in the longer term, the refunding of each of these projects has been taken as an indicator of success. The results from 93 projects indicated that 58 of them continued to be funded by the local authority or by the voluntary agencies, although many of them changed their roles in the process. In order to secure longer term funding many of these projects had changed their range of activities to include work with non-offenders, crime prevention activities, developing bail support schemes and the like.

In consequence, it is hard to say what real effects this initiative has had nationally. Possibly, as the authors of the NACRO report suggest its real impact may have been twofold. On one side it was undoubtedly effective in developing inter-agency cooperation; while on the other hand it emphasised the need to develop a wider range of alternatives in most areas and to provide realistic alternatives for "heavy end" offenders. As Mike Nellis (1989) has argued the initiative was more concerned with consolidation rather than innovation. There are, however, serious questions to be asked about the appropriateness of developing these "privatised" alternatives, and whether the development of alternatives should more properly be carried out by the statutory sector on a more systematic basis.

An interesting dimension of this initiative was that it attempted to change, in the short term at least, the basis of funding. By, in a sense, subsiding local authorities to "hold on" to delinquent youths for longer in the community it changed the basis of funding. That is, it has historically been the situation that local authorities save money when a juvenile receives custody since the costs of confinement shift to the national state. This raises the important issue of "who pays?". In the past it has actually been cheaper for local authorities to hand over their troublesome juveniles to segregative forms of control. This initiative attempted in some extent to address this anomaly.

Also of importance was that the intensification of intermediate treatment signalled a new phase in the organisation of this form of provision. During the 1970s it had moved from a predominently individual "case work" to a "group work" approach. During the 1980s it increasingly became less concerned with face to face work, but under the aegis of working predominently with "high risk" offenders it became more of a monitoring agency. In this sense it has become less personally involved with local juveniles and more directly associated with monitoring and supervision.

Correspondingly, the DHSS initiative was based essentially on a "systems approach" or what has been termed "delinquency management" (Pitts, 1988). This is centred around an anti-Welfarism and more overtly concerned with diversion and "just deserts". Embracing elements of labelling theory, it propounds a minimalism which believes in doing "less harm" rather than "more good". As a form of minimalism it is able in more extreme variations to embrace non-interventionism and abolitionism. It is therefore less concerned with causes of crime and instead focuses both upon the reduction of both care and custody on the premise that segregation is invariably more harmful than "community" based or more informal forms of regulation.

Thus the debate around the development of more intensive forms of community- based alternatives remains open. It is tempting to believe that the DHSS initiative was effective in reducing the custody rate but the evidence is inconclusive. The most significant development it would seem was the judiciary's willingness to explore a wider range of alternatives and to adopt a growing array of non-custodial options.

Although there can be little doubt about the overall effects of the changes which took place in the 1980s there remains a great deal of uncertainty about whether or not it was the decline in the number of people coming before the courts that was critical or whether it was a function of changing sentencing practices. Interestingly, some comparisons have been made between recent developments in West Germany and England and Wales in order to throw some light on this issue. Evidence gained from an examination of the declining custody rates of juveniles in West Germany has been influential in giving weight to the contention that it was the number of juveniles appearing before the court rather than sentencing practices which is critical. This debate has important strategic implications for the development of decarceration and requires more detailed investigation.

7 Decarceration in West Germany and in England and Wales

Making direct comparisons between any two countries invariably encounters a number of problems, but the simultaneous decline in the juvenile custodial population in both countries invites comparison.

On the surface, at least, there are some remarkable similarities between the developments in the arena of juvenile justice in both West Germany and in England and Wales. Besides the fact that both places experienced substantial reductions in juvenile custody rates, they have both experienced a reduction in the number of 14- to 16- year olds in the population. They have also both experienced a considerable reduction in the number of offences subject to formal prosecution during the 1980s. Less tangibly, but no less importantly, both countries have witnessed a changing attitude towards the use of custody for juveniles (Feest, 1988; Graham, 1990).

In a recent article on juvenile decarceration in West Germany, John Graham, a Home Office researcher, has argued that what was significant about the reduction of the juvenile custodial population was that it was achieved primarily by reducing the number of people appearing in court rather than by a reduction in the overall length of sentences. This contention questions the widely held view that the most effective way to achieve a significant level of decarceration is by reducing sentence lengths.

The experience of West Germany, Graham argues, questions the conclusions which have been largely associated with the Dutch experience that sentence length is the key issue (Downes, 1988; Fitzmaurice and Pease, 1982). Graham finds some support for his argument in the recent study by other Home Office researchers (Walker, Collier, and Tarling, 1990) who examined incarceration rates in England and Wales and Australia.

In relation to the situation of juveniles in England and Wales during the 1980s Graham's argument appears to be in some respects accurate. The number of juveniles sentenced to immediate custody decreased from 5,905 in 1985 to 1,922 in 1989; while the percentage of juveniles receiving shorter sentences also went down during the period, the average length of sentence increased significantly (see Table 5).

The figures in Table 5 indicate a considerable reduction of the percentage of offenders receiving sentences of 3 months or less and a simultaneous increase of those receiving sentences of over 4 months. This is a function of a rigourously pursued policy of bifurcation, which aims to "get tough" on "hard core" and persistent offenders while limiting the use of custody for minor offenders. It has been widely assumed that such a policy would undermine a decarceration policy by sustaining a consistently high average daily population and by encouraging the general development of punitive responses. Graham and his Home Office colleagues believe they have found a vindication of recent government policy and shown that this apparently divisive strategy can still be associated with a reduction in the custodial population.

There are, however, a number of problems in adopting such an approach. Firstly there is a danger of creating a two-tier system divided between the salvageable and the unsalvageable based upon a differential aetiology. Secondly, in legitimating a policy of bifurcation it detracts from the arguments concerning the need to limit judicial discretion and control sentencing policy. Thirdly, it confounds notions of justice and of proportionality in sentencing. It encourages an emphasis upon administrative responses rather than a principled evaluation of the deployment of sentencing options.

It is almost certainly no accident that young black offenders have not been on the whole beneficiaries of this process of bifurcation. At the same time such a policy tends to heighten a sense of injustice and inequality. Decisions appear increasingly arbitrary and often inappropriate. The question of the role of incarceration for those who remain is unclear. The use of custody tends to be deontological rather than consequentialist and the implicit concern is with retribution and incapacitation (Braithwaite and Pettit, 1990). In short, such an approach tends towards instrumentalism rather than the question of "why punish?".

In the end however, the relation between reducing the numbers in court or reducing the length of sentences is a matter of arithmetic. Fitzmaurice and Pease (1982) argue, in fact, that "any attempt at reducing the number of people held in prison must involve either reducing the number of offenders who are sent there, the length of time for which they are sent or both." Clearly, a comprehensive decarceration policy would aim at doing both, not only because to do so would be more effective, but because it is more equitable and principled. The issue is not just how many juveniles there may be in custody at any time but the appropriateness of the disposal in each case or group of cases.

Table 5: Males aged 14-16 sentenced to immediate custody for indictable offences by length of sentence (England and Wales)

Year	Total Number of Immediate custody (=100%)	Percentage less than 3 months	Percentage 3 months and less than 4 months	Percentage 4 months and less than 6 months	Percentage 6 months and less than 12 months	Percentage 12 months and less than 2 years	Percentage 2 years and less than 4 years	Percentage 4 years or more (excl. life)	Average sentence length (months)
1985	5,905	36	25	17	19	3	-	-	3,4
1986	4,315	35	24	19	19	3	-	-	3,5
1987	3,898	35	22	20	20	3	-	-	3,6
1988	3,223	31	24	19	22	4	-	-	3,9
1989	1,922	26	22	14	28	5	-	-	4,4

Source: Criminal Statistics 1989

8 Summary and Discussion

In this paper we have reviewed some of the factors which have been associated with the reduction of the juvenile custodial population. Although the available evidence is far from comprehensive, it would seem that demographic changes and cautioning played a smaller part in this process than may have been assumed. The central determinants of the process appear to be changes in sentencing policy and practices together with greater use of non-custodial alternatives. This "sea change" in policy was a function of both formal and informal changes, linked to the establishment of new alliances and relations between the agencies involved in the juvenile justice process.

Many of these changes appear to be practitioner led. There were a number of official directives which were issued during this period but they often seemed to reinforce rather than introduce changes. They were more concerned with consolidation rather than innovation.

The development of inter-agency co-operation was undoubtedly important in effecting changes. Bringing together the relevant agencies - particularly the police and the judiciary - established new normative controls on prosecution and sentencing and did much to stimulate an anti-custodial ethos.

Based upon a systems approach and a delinquency management perspective, these agencies adopted what was seen as the central tenet of labelling theory that any involvement with institutions was likely to do more harm than good by drawing offenders ineluctably into the mainstream of the criminal justice process. Many practitioners, as a result, adopted a strategy of minimalism and even abolitionism. The creation of "custody free zones" and an overriding belief in the damaging effects of incarceration generated a general emphasis of keeping offenders in the "community" as long as possible.

At the heart of this approach was a disdain for what was seen as the overly punitive nature of the "justice model" on the one side and the overly personalised nature of the "welfare model" on the other. In attempting to avoid the pitfalls of these two models a new framework emerged which became known as "corporatism". This response which was based upon closer alliances between agencies and an emphasis upon the more effective administration of the juvenile justice system has been summarised in the following terms:

> "This sociological concept refers to the tendencies to be found in advanced welfare societies whereby the capacity for conflict and disruption is reduced by means of a centralisation of policy, increased government intervention, and the co-operation of various professional and interest groups into a collective whole with homogeneous aims and objectives." (Pratt, 1989)

This corporatist strategy when applied to juvenile justice involves according to Pratt, four central components. Firstly, it involves a shift in discretion away from the judiciary and towards other "gatekeepers". It also involves a greater degree of administrative discretion. Secondly, it involves a blurring of the boundaries between public and private realms and between the courts and other decision-making bodies. Thirdly, as a consequence, it involves a decreasing emphasis upon rights and a greater emphasis upon ends and policy objectives. Fourthly, it embraces less commitment to the purposes of punishment and instead tends to emphasise behaviour containment, harm minimalisation and monitoring.

Thus the essential components of this approach fit well within the dominant trends in criminal justice in the 1980s. The growing administration, the disdain of "welfare", and the movement away from "face-to-face" work and towards delinquency management, fit well within the dominant tendencies of the period. Not surprisingly, therefore, the changes which have occurred in juvenile justice are being held up as an example of "success" and attempts have been made to apply the same approach elsewhere.

But the achievements which occurred in juvenile justice in England and Wales were not wholly positive. They were based upon a complex and at times contradictory set of imperatives which while realising certain objectives overlooked others.

Its theoretical premises were particularly weak. Developments in the juvenile justice system in the 1980s were deeply influenced by labelling theory. While this perspective was important in encouraging a more appreciative stance towards the plight of offenders and a greater recognition of the damaging effects of certain forms of intervention, it often veered towards non-interventionism and abolitionism. However, countries with low crime rates are not those where people mind their own business. Rather they are, as John Braithwaite has argued, ones which adopt more constructive sanctioning techniques. Thus:

> "The labeling perspective has failed to distinguish the crime-producing consequences of stigma that is open-ended, outcasting, and person- rather than offense-centered from the crime-reducing consequences of shaming that is reintegrative. This is why there is such limited empirical support for the key predictions of labeling theory." (Braithwaite, 1989: 4)

The disdain for the "welfare" approach, questions of aetiology and the reduction of "face to face" work all militate against an approach which could deal adequately with the causes of crime. The commitment to non-interventionism, or at least to minimalism, has often centered around the belief that it was better to do less harm rather than more good. The road to custody, it was widely believed, is paved with good intentions.

These forms of minimalism tended to convey the impression that the juveniles who were coming into contact with the various juvenile justice agencies did not really have personal, social or economic problems but were really only the victims of an overly active juvenile justice system. In this climate dealing with juveniles becomes largely an administrative and management problem. It incorporated and encouraged the myth that non-interventionism is a position of neutrality. In this process, however, what initially appears as an altruistic strategy of harm minimisation can readily turn into neglect and indifference.

The real danger of non-interventionism - particularly during a period of growing inequalities, unemployment and poverty - is that it leaves people to the vagaries of the market. This stance becomes particularly problematic if we look at the use of care for young people. For many the damning critiques of existing forms of care for juveniles during the 1980s encouraged the objective of restricting the use of care. A slippage occurred in which the criticisms of particular institutions and practices became a critique of care provision itself. Many practitioners as a result became very self-satisfied with reducing the use of care facilities without developing other more constructive responses. Instead, many young people facing serious problems have been left largely to their own devices (Travis and Cullen, 1984).

The emphasis upon delinquency management and minimalism also led to a decreasing emphasis on the need for follow-up services. Instead, it was pure diversion which was favoured. As a result even potentially constructive options such as reparation have been devalued because they do not involve diversion out of the system.

The paradoxical nature of the corporatist approach is reflected in the workings of the Juvenile Liason Bureaus', which operated as a largely administrative organisation aimed at reducing the flow of juveniles into the court. But as Davis et al. have suggested:

> "Some might regard it as paradoxical that a whole new agency (the JLB) has been created in order to divert young offenders from systems of justice and welfare created (very expensively) for their reception. It is certainly intriguing that the state, having organized a network of statutory services intended to cater for the needs of children, should support this new hybrid organization which defines its brief in terms of keeping young offenders out of the clutches of those same agencies." (Davis, Boucherat, and Watson, 1989: 232)

This form of administrativisation not only plays down the needs of offenders but also of victims and their families. It involves an informal decision-making process which operates outside of public scrutiny or accountability. It is an agency with considerable powers but little ability to enforce decisions. It is based upon a series of informal and often ad hoc arrangements and is prone to all the problems of coordination and coherence which can beset inter-agency arrangements of this type (Sampson, 1988; Whittington, 1983).

Juvenile Liason Bureaus reflect the changing organisation of decision-making which has occurred in juvenile justice over the last decade. These new sites of decision-making are often less visible and accountable than in previous times. This development has been accompanied by a blurring of the boundaries between voluntary and statutory agencies and as a consequence a significant degree of "privatisation" has taken place.

Thus, this reorganised juvenile justice system was effective in reducing the custodial population and the number of juveniles appearing in court. It did not, however, provide an adequate response to the problem of juvenile crime or to the worsening predicaments in which many young people found themselves in the 1980s. It did not confront the judiciary, nor did it increase the accountability or fairness of the system. It effected important changes in the sites and modes of decision-making and created new hybrid agencies which functioned to divert juveniles away from the services and agencies which had ostensibly been established for their benefit. The series of relatively informal decision-making bodies have in the name of "corporatism" created new alliances and new relations. These relations are in many cases fragile and often dependent upon the good will of the agencies and the individuals concerned.

Whether or not these corporatist structures survive until the end of the decade will depend upon a number of factors. Their future will be conditioned by the continued existence of a consensus on the need for further decarcerating juveniles. This concern, in turn, is likely to be influenced by the degree to which these corporatist policies relate to the level of juvenile crime. If they are seen to be ineffective in containing juvenile crime or, even worse, encouraging juvenile crime by "going soft" on offenders relations may well begin to become strained. Similarly, if uses of "justice", particulary in relation to issues of equal treatment and proportionality, come to the fore on one side, or alternatively if the "welfare" of young offenders becomes an issue, the existing arrangements could come under pressure. Finally, the longer term viability of this corporatist response is also dependent upon the "depolitisation" of crime and punishment and the continuing acceptance of low levels of visibility and accountability in the system. If these tendencies can be contained the existing forms of corporatism could stabilise, but there are certain rumblings occuring within and around the juvenile justice system which may well begin to shake the foundations of these corporatist structures.

References

Allen, R. (1990). Out of jail: The reduction in the use of penal custody for male juveniles 1981-88. *The Howard Journal, 30,* 30-52.

Allen, R. (1991). Custody for juveniles - from elimination to abolition. *Youth and Policy, 32,* 10-18.

Bayer, R. (1981). Crime and punishment, and the decline of liberal optimism. *Crime and Delinquency, 27,* 169-190.

Box, S. (1987). *Recession, crime and punishment.* Basingstoke: MacMillan

Burney, E. (1985). *Sentencing young people.* Gower: Aldershot.

Braithwaite, J. (1989). *Crime, shame and reintegration.* Cambridge: Cambridge University Press.

Braithwaite, J. and Pettit, P. (1990). *Not just deserts: A republican theory of criminal justice.* Oxford: Clarendon Press.

Cowell, D., Jones, T., and Young, J. (1982). *Policing the riots.* London: Junction Books.

Davis, G., Boucherat, J., and Watson, D. (1989). Pre-court decision-making in juvenile justice. *British Journal of Criminology, 29,* 219-235.

Ditchfield, S. (1976). *Police cautioning in England and Wales.* London: HMSO.

Downes, D. (1989). *Contrasts in tolerance. Post war penal policy in the Netherlands and England and Wales.* Oxford: Clarendon Press.

Feest, J. (1988). *Reducing the prison population: Lessons from the West German experience.* London: NACRO paper.

Field, S. (1990). *Trends in crime and their interpretation.* London: Home Office (Research and Planning Unit Report).

Fitzmaurice, C., and Pease, K. (1982) Prison sentences and population. *Justice of the Peace, 18,* 575-9.

Graham, J. (1990). Decarceration in the Federal Republic of Germany. *British Journal of Criminology, 30,* 150-170.

Harris, K. (1983). Strategies, values and the emerging generation of alternatives to incarceration. *Social Change, 12,* 141-170.

H.M.S.O. (1989). *Criminal Statistics.* London: HMSO.

Hudson, B. (1984). The rising use of imprisonment: The impact of decarceration policies. *Critical Social Policy, 11,* 46-59.

Klein, M. (1979). Deinstitutionalisation and diversion of offenders: A litany of impediments. In N. Morris and M. Tonry (Eds.), *Crime and justice*, Vol. 1 (pp. 145-201). Chicago, London: University of Chicago Press.

Matthews, R. (1987). Decarceration and social control: Fantasies and realities. In J. Lowman, R.J. Menzies and T.S. Palys (Eds.), *Transcarceration* (pp. 338-357). Gower: Aldershot.

Morris, N., and Tonry, M. (1990). *Between punishment and probation.* Oxford: Oxford University Press.

NACRO (1991). Seizing the initiative. London: NACRO.

Nellis, M. (1989). Juvenile justice and the voluntary sector. In R. Matthews (Ed.), *Privatizing criminal justice.* London: Sage Publications.

Northamptonshire Juvenile Liason Bureau (1985). *The limits of diversion.* Second Annual Report. Northamptonshire: JLB.

Pitts, J. (1988). *The politics of juvenile crime.* London: Sage Publications.

Pratt, J. (1985). Delinquency as a scarce resource. *The Howard Journal, 24,* 93-107.

Pratt, J. (1989). Corporatism: The third model of juvenile justice. *British Journal of Criminology, 29,* 236-254.

Sampson, A., Stubbs, P., Smith, D., Pearson, J., and Blagg, H. (1988). Crime, localities and the multi-agency approach. *British Journal of Criminology, 28,* 478-93.

Scull, A. (1977). *Decarceration: Community treatment and the deviant.* Englewood Cliffs: Prentice Hall.

Shaw, S. (1985). Reflections on "short, sharp shock". *Youth and Policy, 13,* 1-5.

Smith, M. (1984). Will the real alternatives stand up? *New York University Review of Law and Social Change, 12,* 171-97.

Travis, L., and Cullen, F. (1984). Radical nonintervention: The myth of doing no harm. *Federal Probation, 48,* 29-32.

Walker, J., Collier, P., and Tarling, R. (1990). Why are prison rates in England and Wales higher than in Australia? *British Journal of Criminology, 30,* 24-35.

Whittington, C. (1983). Social work in the welfare network: Negotiating daily practice. *British Journal of Social Work, 13,* 265-286.

Sentence Without Conviction
Notes on Diversion from the Juvenile Court in the Federal Republic of Germany

Wolfgang Ludwig-Mayerhofer

1 Diversion in the Federal Republic of Germany - Promise Without Danger?

The concept of diversion was introduced to the F.R.G. in the late 1970s. Within a few years, it had become one of the most widely used concepts in the discourse about juvenile criminal justice. To understand more fully the meaning of this development, it is necessary to look back a few years.

The early 1970s had witnessed a vivid attack on juvenile criminal law. Taking up criticisms raised against the juvenile courts as institutions of repression, and inspired by hopes of overcoming the defects of society by means of social policy, the (social democratic) federal government had planned to restrict punitive social control - the application of juvenile criminal law - to cases of very serious crime and to develop a comprehensive system of aid to juveniles. After harsh protest, a milder version of this reform was proposed, which, if brought into effect, would have left the juvenile courts intact, albeit limiting their power to young people of age 16 or over. But even this minor reform failed because the state (*Laender*) governments opposed it, largely on the grounds of too heavy fiscal burdens that would be placed upon their shoulders if the reform were to be implemented, but also for political reasons. Thus, the hopes of a better way of dealing with juvenile delinquency, which clearly had been inspired by the liberal spirit of the late 1960s, had almost completely been paralyzed by the mid 1970s.

Ten years later, by the mid 1980s, the picture drawn by many criminologists concerned with juvenile justice had changed again. Diversion is the concept that is said to have been the guiding star of a "reform from within", that is, a reform from within the institutions of juvenile justice. With the help of social workers and criminologists committed to the idea of gradually changing juvenile justice by constantly propagating and offering better means of dealing with juvenile delinquency, the institutions of juvenile justice have achieved by themselves - so the story goes - the aims of the government's unsuccessful attempts at bringing about reform. More and more youths are diverted from the system, and traditional exclusionary repression has largely been replaced by community-based alternative sanctions.

There are many success stories, some of which are even true. The story of diversion in the F.R.G., as told by its advocates, clearly seems to be a success story. In the following, I will try to cast doubts on the notion that is one of those that are true. However, I will not contend that it is a story of failure in the sense that diversion has lead to a increase rather than a decrease of control - a position that is taken by authors such as Andrew Scull (1982) with respect to the U.S.A. or by Hans-Joachim Plewig (this volume) with respect to the F.R.G. I hope that my own position will become clear by what I am going to point out in the following.

Before continuing, I must clarify the notion of "diversion" that I will be using. In fact, there are two different notions. One refers to diversion in the strict or literal sense, that is, the disposition of the case by the prosecutor or the judge before a conviction is reached. But there is a second notion which also includes cases which are referred to other agencies without actually being diverted in the former, literal sense. This second, wider notion of diversion is shared by many German criminologists (see, for instance, Hering and Sessar, 1990), and in referring to the "diversion movement"[1] and its impact on criminal justice and policy, I will follow this usage. Positively stated, the reason is, in the words of Malcolm W. Klein (1976: 426), that although "(t)his meaning is not 'true diversion', (...) it does nevertheless imply a departure from past practices. To that extent, it is new." But not only do diversion in the literal sense and diversion as referral share the promise of a "departure from past practices"; they are also intertwined in reality. Many diverted offenders receive the same sentence (although in their case it is called "order") as their not so happy counterparts that were convicted; and as to the diversion programs, they usually make no difference whether the youths that are referred to them have been diverted in the literal sense or not. The obvious reason is that they, too, claim that they are offering something that "is new". Note, however, that in the empirical analyses I will present below, the term "diversion" will be used in the literal sense.

Returning to my main argument, I will start with the statement that in one respect the story of diversion *is* a success story. As all available statistics indicate, the proportion of youths whose cases are diverted by the prosecutors and the courts has been continually rising in the last decade. At present, we can guess that about as many youths are diverted from (or by) the courts as are convicted. Also, the courts are certainly using more and more "alternative sanctions" (see Heinz, 1990 and this volume). Many diversion programs that started on a provisionary basis as so-called "model programs" are now firmly established. If we take all this - the proportionate rise of diversionary decisions, the increase in community-based sanctioning and of diversion programs - as a measure of success, the story ends here.

The arguments I will present in the following take as a starting point the assumption that the goal of diversion should not and cannot be taken simply as the establishment or even the increase of diversion. This latter position, which is that of many practitioners and advocates of diversion, erroneously takes the means for the end. That this is not sufficient is especially clear in our case, since diversion inevitably entails the question: "Diversion *from what*?" That is, diversion is a strategy that aims at *avoiding* something that is worse. This is very clear from statements such as the following by the "President's Commission on Law Enforcement and Administration of Justice" (1967: 82):

"... the limited effectiveness of the formal processes of the juvenile justice system, the labeling inherent in adjucating children delinquents, (...) the limited disposition options available to the juvenile judge, the limitation of personnel and diagnostic and treatment facilities, the lack of community support - all these factors give pre-judicial dispositions an especially important role with respect to juveniles".

That is, the aim of diversion is to reduce the amount of involvement of youths in the juvenile justice system and to put something better in its place. "Something better" in the case of juvenile justice of course may also mean "nothing at all"; this is precisely what advocates of "true diversion" would consider desirable (Cressey and McDermott, 1973; Bullington, Sprowls, Katkin, and Phillips, 1978). Hence, the central problem with respect to a positive evaluation of diversion should not be: "Has diversion grown?" but rather: "Has diversion succeeded in reducing the amount of formal intervention into the lives of juveniles and, more generally, in departing from past penal practices?" While this point might seem obvious and trifling to most criminologists, it is my impression that it is sometimes all too easily forgotten and hence needs to be re-emphasized from time to time.

It is well known that a common (although not uncontested, see Binder and Geis [1984] concerning the U.S. or McMahon [1990] concerning Canada) answer to the question of diversion's success in reducing judicial intervention is negative, since diversionary control is said to have been superimposed on a constant or even rising prison population, thus augmenting rather than diminishing control (Austin and Krisberg, 1981). Concerning the F.R.G., however, I agree with most observers that such a net-widening effect can be ruled out (see, for instance, Pfeiffer, 1986; Kerner, 1989; Heinz, this volume). But here another trap opens up. By concentrating on the aspect of net-widening, the discussion in the F.R.G. implicitly has rested on the assumption that diversionary politics are to be considered a success if such a net-widening effect did not occur. On this point I disagree. First, diversion should not only have had no negative impact; rather, to be considered successful, there should be a decisive positive impact on the processing of juveniles away from the criminal justice system. Second, if diversion has not been detrimental with respect to net-widening, this does not exclude the possibility that other undesirable effects may have shown up.

2 The Impact of Diversion on Juvenile Justice in the F.R.G. - An Empirical Assessment

The first part of my account of the impact of diversion is somewhat provisionary, since it relates only to the overall changes of (post-adjucatory) juvenile detention (*Jugendarrest*) and prison sentences (*Jugendstrafe* or *Freiheitsstrafe* for young adults).[2] It would certainly be desirable to study these changes in more detail, for instance, with respect to different types of offenses. But for the time being let it suffice to have a look at the proportion of juveniles and young adults[3] who are sentenced to juvenile detention and to prison terms (Figure 1). From this it can seen that while indeed a decrease of juvenile detention and prison sentences has occurred in the years since 1982, this decrease is not very impressive if put into

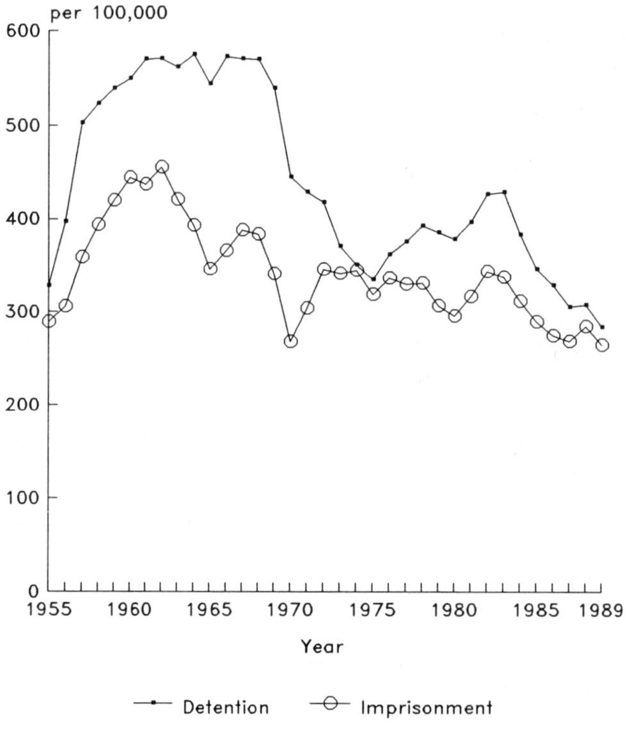

Fig. 1: Detention and prison sentences for juveniles and young adults in the F.R.G.
Source: Kerner (1989), supplemented by data from federal statistics.

a wider historical perspective. It has to be admitted that such a perspective can be misleading, since it may be argued that juvenile offenders in the 1980s differ from those in the 1970s or, for that matter, in the 1950s, with respect to relevant criteria. Yet, in my view the decrease of juvenile detention and prison sentences does not look very impressive given the fact that by the end of the 1980s we have just come up to the levels that had been reached in the year 1970 with respect to prison sentences or in the year 1975 with respect to juvenile detention. Furthermore, I would like to draw attention to the fact that much more drastic decreases have occurred before, notably the exceptional reduction of juvenile detention almost by half between the years 1968 and 1975, but also the reduction of prison sentences between 1968 and 1970. This decrease of prison sentences may be explained to a large extent by changes in the penal code for adults (transformation of prison sentences under 6 months into fines except for extraordinary circumstances), which clearly has affected the number of young adults sentenced to prison terms. However, in the light of this it seems even more impressive that the juvenile courts have made less use of juvenile detention instead of more (since the number of young adults sentenced to juvenile prison increased as a reaction to the legal change mentioned above, one might have expected the number of young adults sentenced to juvenile detention to rise even more). All in all, these figures make us aware of the fact that changes in penal practices may be determined by other forces than reform movements.

Still, I would not deny - though not take as established[4] - that probably at least part of the changes in the last years is due to the diversion movement's efforts. But does that really imply that the juvenile justice system is developing into a new, diversionary system built on the ideas of avoiding repression whenever possible and providing help where necessary?

In order to provide answers to this question, I will try to probe still deeper into the fabric of juvenile justice decision-making. To accomplish this, I will draw on research by the project "Changing Structures of Decision-Making in the Criminal Justice System: Implementation, Organization, Impacts" (directed by P.-A. Albrecht), at the Research Center "Prevention and Intervention in Childhood and Adolescence". During the past six years, procedures and impacts of decision-making with respect to juvenile offenders by the police in Bielefeld, prosecutors all over North Rhine-Westphalia and six juvenile courts in the districts of Bielefeld and Paderborn have been investigated.

The starting point for this research was a program developed by the Department of Justice of North Rhine-Westphalia, the Bielefeld youth prosecutors' office and the Bielefeld police to encourage prosecutorial diversion by having the police provide standardized information that might be pertinent to a decision in favor of diversion (see Herbort, Rzepka, and Voß, 1989; Rzepka, 1990; Voß, 1990).[5] The evaluation of this program was backed up by research on youth prosecutors in all of the 19 prosecutors' offices in North Rhine-Westphalia in the year 1987. Out of almost 18,000 files of cases against juvenile and young adult offenders, 11,500 were used for a detailed analysis of the prosecutors' decisions on whether or not to divert a case from the court (see Ludwig-Mayerhofer, 1990, 1992; Ludwig-Mayerhofer and Rzepka, 1993).

During 1990 and 1991, our research was directed at juvenile court procedures and outcomes in the districts of Bielefeld and Paderborn. One of the aims was to examine whether the high level of prosecutorial diversion in the district of Bielefeld would lead to a corresponding higher level of court diversion - that is, decisions by the courts to drop proceedings, usually on the condition that the offender successfully complete a court order (mostly community service orders, see below) -, or rather to the reverse, a harsher level of sanctioning by the Bielefeld courts. In the following, the more general problem of the factors underlying the courts' decisions on whether or not to divert a case will be addressed.

The research was carried out from August 1990 to November 1991. In each of the two disctricts, three courts were selected. All in all the cases of twelve different judges were involved in the research. Included in the sample were all cases of theft, assault against persons, and damage to property (also in combination), thus covering the most common juvenile offenses (with the exception of traffic offenses). At the same time, these offenses are also those where diversionary decisions are most likely to occur. 513 trials in juvenile courts were observed by means of a standardized observation scheme, including several ratings of offenders' and judges' behavior. In addition, data were collected from the courts' files, since although in principle court proceedings follow the rule of "orality" - that is, the judge is supposed to consider only those "facts" that were presented orally in the court's hearings -, it cannot be ruled out that the judges also take into account attributes of the offense or the offender that are mentioned only in the court's file.

The following analysis is restricted to those 492 cases in which the courts reached a decision on whether to divert (n = 193 or 39%) or to convict (n = 299 or 61%) an offender. Diversion means dismissal of the case according to Section 47 of the German Juvenile Justice Act (*Jugendgerichtsgesetz*; JGG) or to sections 153, 153a of the German Code of Criminal Procedure (*Strafprozeßordnung*; StPO). In the 21 cases not used here, the defendant was either acquitted (14 cases), the case was dismissed according to section 154 of the StPO, meaning that a decision was deemed unnecessary in view of another trial pending against the defendant (5 cases), and finally, 2 cases were dropped due to lack of responsibility on the part of the defendant.

In the following, I will try to make four points that in my opinion indicate that actually very little has changed with respect to decision-making in juvenile justice and that diversionary decisions by the prosecutors and the courts stand in opposition to core ideas of diversion. In addition to the results of our own research, reference will also be made to results of evaluation research on diversion programs in other districts.

1. According to the diversion movement, dispositions of juvenile offenders should be based on their needs for guidance and help. Clearly, this notion is not new to German juvenile criminal law, nor to that of other countries. Rather, it was inherent to the idea of the juvenile court from the outset (see Platt, 1969 for the U.S.A., Garland, 1985 for England and Voß, 1986 for Germany). However, one frequently repeated criticism against the juvenile courts during the 1960s and the 1970s was the assertion that they had not been able to live up to the expectations and to the hopes that had been placed in them. Contrary to the idea of the welfare

state, the juvenile courts were still adhering to the old notions of punishment and repression (Pfeiffer, 1983: 55-60). One clear expression of this was seen in the fact that decision-making in the juvenile courts was still largely based on attributes of the offense and on the offenders' prior record (see Hauser, 1980; Hermann and Wild, 1989). One of the hopes that were raised with the rise of diversion was that eventually prosecutors and courts would turn away from these old patterns of decision-making.

All available data indicate that this aim has rarely, if ever, been achieved. As to the *prosecutors*, there is ample evidence from the research report by Hering and Sessar concerning districts where prosecutors have adopted the politics of diversion to a relatively large extent that diversion is mostly restricted to cases with a very low value of stolen property or else little damage and almost exclusively to cases with no prior record (Hering and Sessar, 1990: 74-75). Very similar results have been obtained in our research on prosecutors in North Rhine-Westphalia (Ludwig-Mayerhofer, 1990; see also Heinz, this volume). With respect to the *juvenile courts*, there has been little systematic research up to now. However, our own results indicate that the courts, too, are still guided by similar notions. I will postpone a complete analysis of the courts' decision procedures to the next paragraph, but the data with respect to the number of offenses and to the prior records of the juvenile defendants are unequivocal (see Figure 2): First, the more offenses a juvenile defendant is charged with, the smaller his or her chance of being diverted is. Second, and even more obvious, if a defendant has been convicted before, his or her chances of getting a diversionary decision are almost zero. Generally, then, the decision to divert a case seems still to be based on notions such as severity of the offense or prior record. This will become even more clear in the following.

2. A second central idea of diversion programs, related to the previous one, is the notion of avoiding the stigmatizing label that is imposed on the juvenile offender when he or she is convicted and thereby formally defined as "delinquent" by the judge. However, it is obvious that not all youths will react in the same way to the courts' labeling procedures. Rather, we may hypothesize that some youths are more prone than others to assume a negative self-image when defined as a delinquent, to live up to their label and to develop into "career criminals". As one of the leading advocates of diversion in the F.R.G. puts it:

"Socially marginalized youths without a clear job perspective (e.g., unemployed youths) will take over the definition as a "delinquent" more frequently and more strongly into their self-concept than youths with the clear prospects of a middle-class or upper-class future.
Youths with socialization problems are more prone to take over the definition as "delinquent" into their self-concept than youths from families without structural or functional disturbances". (Pfeiffer, 1983: 33; my translation)

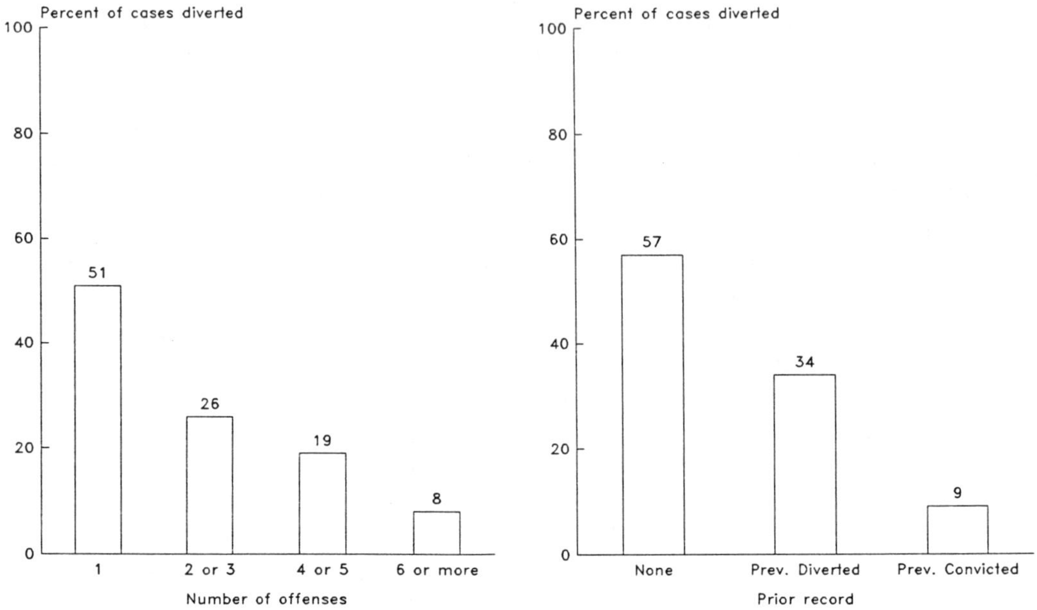

Fig. 2: Court decisions on diverting cases by number of offenses and prior record

Consequently, if diversionary strategies are to be judged as successful, we would like to see youths with job or family problems diverted more often than youths without such handicaps.

It can probably be guessed from the preceding paragraph that the practice of diversion should not be expected to match this idea very much; for it is well known that problem youths usually find themselves in the courts more often than others, as a consequence more often have prior convictions and therefore are no good candidates for being diverted. Also, according to another advocate of the diversion movement,

"we have reasonable cause to suspect that the 'new community-based measures' to a great extent are applied to groups for whom the customary less intrusive repertory of juvenile criminal justice - dismissal without measure, warning, reprimand, directives, orders - will suffice" (Heinz, 1989: 33-34; my translation).

The implication of this statement is that precisely those youths for whom "alternative" and "community-based" measures were developed - that is, problem youths - are largely excluded from them (see also Heinz, this volume).

Our own research supports the view that problem youths are not protected from the stigmatizing label "delinquent"; rather, they run higher risks of *not* being diverted. A juvenile offender's chance of getting a diversionary decision by the *prosecutor* is actually *diminished* if he or she is unemployed (Ludwig-Mayerhofer, 1990: 177-178). And again, our research on the *juvenile courts* yields similar results. Youths with family problems (trouble with parents) or with job problems (frequent job quits or unemployment, quarrels with their superiors) run higher risks of being convicted (Figure 3).

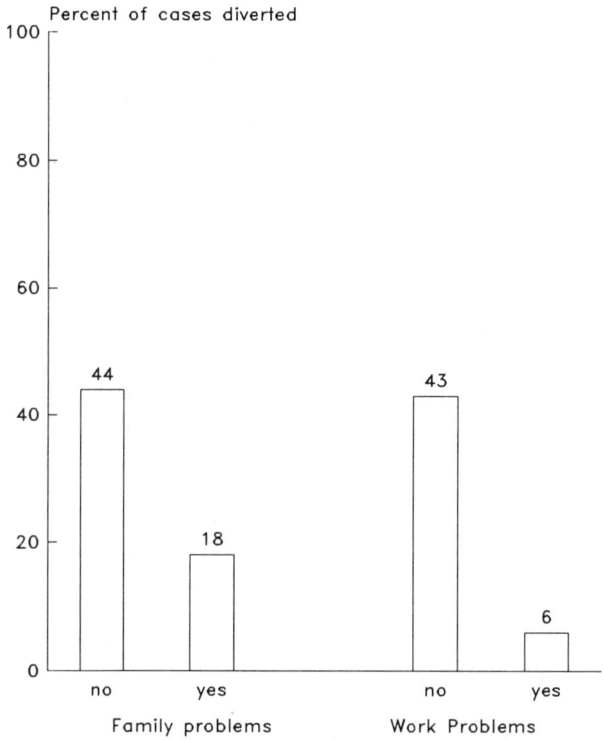

Fig. 3: Court decisions on diverting cases by family and work related problems

Here it might be objected, and with good reason, that bivariate analyses such as have been presented up to now are not sufficient to establish with validity a relationship between offenders' attributes and courts' decisions. Yet, the relationships I have mentioned stand the test of multivariate analyses. The possible influence of the following variables on the courts decisions to divert or not to divert a case has been tested: Number of offenses charged; type of offense(s); the type of the juvenile criminal proceedings which can be considered as another indicator of the seriousness of the offense(s); offender's sex, age and nationality; problems in family, school or on the job (which are usually discussed in the Juvenile Court Assistance social worker's report to the court); educational measures by offender's parents or other persons as a reaction to the offense(s);

restitution effected or announced prior to criminal proceedings; the defendant partially or completely denying his guilt (including denial of involvement in the case under consideration); and finally a measure from the observation of the court proceedings indicating how much the defendant and the judge agreed or disagreed with respect to the defendant's guilt (5-point Likert scale) (see overview in Appendix). A logistic regression analysis was performed, yielding eleven variables whose influence was significantly different from zero at $p < 0.05$ (see Table 1).[6] Its results show that (a) the most important determinants of the courts' decisions to divert a case or not are indeed the number of offenses, prior record, and the type of criminal proceedings, and that (b) controlling for these and other variables, family and job problems still appear as determinants of courts' decicions to convict an offender. In addition, it seems that courts also discriminate against youths with non-German nationality, especially from Turkey or Yugoslavia.

Table 1: Logistic regression model of juvenile courts' decisions to divert (districts of Bielefeld and Paderborn, n = 492)

Dependent variable: diversion (1) - conviction (0)

Variable	Coeff.	S.E.	Δ -2 LL[a]
Judge sitting alone[1]	-1.79	.346	31.70
Judge sitting with lay assessors[1]	-2.60	.535	26.66
Number of offenses	-.52	.112	25.93
Prior record: at least one conviction[2]	-1.65	.379	21.49
Prior record: diverted[2]	-1.11	.305	13.76
Disagreement defendant - judge on guilt	-.71	.195	15.14
Nationality: Turkish, Yugoslavian[3]	-1.12	.316	13.42
Complete denial of guilt[4]	1.88	.649	9.31
Partial denial of guilt[4]	.73	.358	4.17
Present family problems	-.99	.361	8.15
Job problems	-1.65	.682	7.78
Constant	3.10		
-2 Log likelihood of null model (incl. constant)	659.04		
-2 Log likelihood of actual model	426.24		
Pseudo-R^2	.35		

[a] Change of -2 Log likelihood (equalling LR-Chi-Square) if term is removed from model
[1] Reference category: "Simplified proceedings" according to Section 76 JGG
[2] Reference category: No prior record
[3] Reference category: All other
[4] Reference category: Admission of guilt by defendant

3. From the previous arguments, one might be tempted to infer that the net-widening effects so vividly described, for instance, by Stanley Cohen (1985), are also a characteristic of diversion in the F.R.G. After all, a well-known pattern seems to show up. Those youths who have always been the target group of the criminal justice system continue to receive harsh sanctions; the new diversion programs extend control to those who might otherwise have gone free. However, one difference to the scenario depicted by Cohen (or, with respect to Germany, Herriger, 1985) should be pointed out. Although diversion programs are staffed with social workers or even psychologists, and although it is often pointed out that one of the important characteristics of the last decade is the increase of so-called "educational measures", actually the only measure that has been introduced on a large-scale base is the community service order (*Arbeitsweisung* or *Arbeitsauflage*). While there exists a considerable number of programs offering "social competence training courses" (*Soziale Trainingskurse*) or other "alternative sanctions" (see Frehsee, this volume), the clientele they serve is quite small compared to the several hundreds or even thousands of juveniles and young adults that are channelled through an efficient community service order program (Ludwig, 1989: 57). It is true that community service orders are sometimes declared as therapeutic measures, opening up possibilities of social learning and helping youths to get a sense of achievement (Pfeiffer, 1983: 153). But such statements lack empirical support; rather, all of our knowledge hitherto accumulated indicates that most of the community service consists in dull and boring work such as clearing public parks, peeling potatoes in old people's homes or folding bedclothes in hospital laundries.

A clearer picture of the meaning of community service orders emerges from several sources. A first hint is provided by data from Heinz (1990). Figure 4 (relating to convictions only, since federal statistics do not indicate whether diversionary decisions have been accompanied by court orders or not) shows the growth of educational measures especially during the last decade. The federal statistics unfortunately do not indicate which kind of measures these are, but there cannot be any doubt that they consist mostly of community service orders. However, the rise of community service orders and other educational measures has not been leading to a significant decrease of the proportion of prison sentences or of juvenile detention during that time; the largest decrease is observed with respect to the so-called disciplinary measures (with the exception of juvenile detention). Again, the federal statistics do not clearly indicate the type of disciplinary measures, but it can be safely assumed that they consist largely of "fines".[7]

Thus, the truth about community service orders is that they replace fines in the case of those defendants who do not earn any money of their own. Consider the data in Figure 5 (from our research on the courts), which shows the distribution of fines and community service orders (both with and without diversion) to several categories of offenders. Clearly, most of the fines are reserved for youths and young adults who are part of the labor force (holding an apprenticeship or a job). Community service orders on the other hand are typically reserved for youths attending school or (rarely) university. The same conclusion can be derived from data provided by some diversion programs offering community service orders. Most of the participants in these programs are attending school or university or are unemployed, that is, have little or no earnings of their own (Ludwig, 1989: 67). This also helps to explain why the rise of the "educational measures" has not led to significant decreases in juvenile detention.[8] Community service orders rarely are conceived as alternatives to juvenile detention; rather, they offer the possibility of sentencing petty offenders for whom previously no measures were available with the exception of fines - which in the case of those juveniles with little money of their own are considered as rather inefficient by most of the judges.

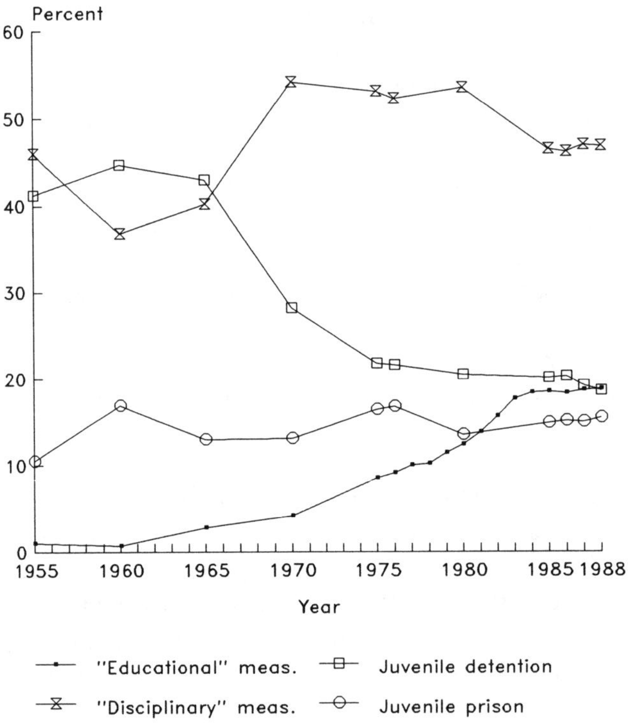

Fig. 4: Court sanctions in juvenile criminal law in the F.R.G.
Source: Heinz 1990, supplemented by data from federal statistics

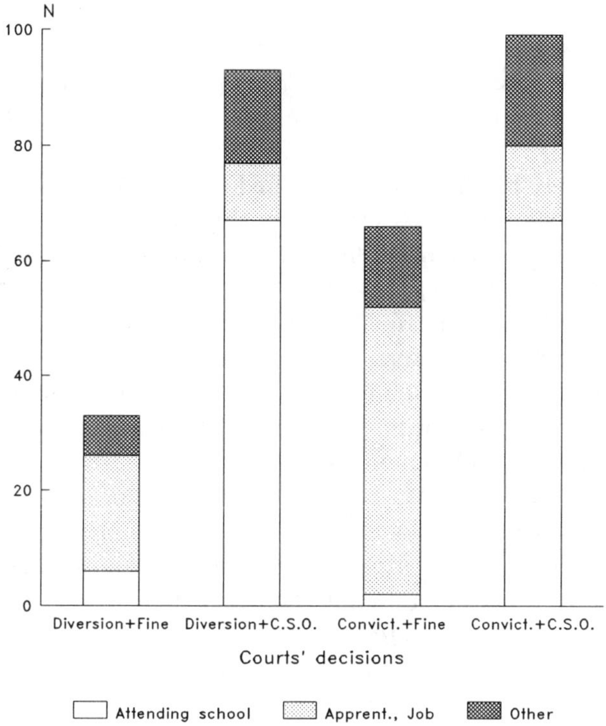

Fig. 5: Fines and community service orders by offenders' occupational status

4. Our observations of juvenile court procedures suggest one more cause for concern. In some cases, youths are "diverted" who actually should be acquitted according to legal standards because they deny their offense(s) and cannot be proven guilty on other grounds. This can also be seen from the results of the multivariate analysis in Table 1: Juveniles who deny their offense(s) more likely are diverted, all else being equal. In fact, this should not come as a surprise since the same observation has been made in studies of adult law (Hertwig, 1982; Weigend, 1984). That is not to say that judges avoid acquittals at all events; they make use of them if they are convinced of the defendant's innocence. The problematic cases seem to be those where the judge is undecided with respect to the defendant's guilt. Here, "diversion" seems to offer a way out of the conflict either to convict an innocent person or to let off someone who is actually guilty of a crime. I hasten to add that these cases are quite rare; they represent only a small percentage of our sample. But the main reason for this is that most juvenile defendants actually admit their offenses. Among those defendants who insist on their innocence, the risk of being "diverted" is about equal to the chance of getting an acquittal![9]

3 Conclusion

I will now try to summarize my observations and to develop a perspective by which we can do justice to the achievements of diversion, yet avoid the fallacy of taking its promises for reality.

First, although diversion possibly has had an effect of reducing incarcerations (juvenile detention and prison sentences), this effect probably has been rather small. It now can be seen why: On the one hand, the sentencing decisions of the courts (and of the prosecutors) have changed very little. The juvenile judges are still guided by the notion that each time an offender appears in court, his or her punishment has to be harsher than the time before. Problem youths, too, "deserve" harsher sanctions, and the fact that problem youths usually appear more often in the courts even aggravates this situation. On the other hand, the sanctions provided by the diversion programs - mostly community service orders, but also social education and the like - usually are restricted to the first-time or second-time offender, since although sometimes they imply 80 hours of community service or even more, they do not ususally exceed one, two or at most three weekends. The judges seem to feel that this is simply no adequate reaction to a repeat offender. Thus, it seems that *the main effect of diversion is to keep cases out of the system that are too trifling to require further action, not, however, to provide help for youths in trouble.*

Yet, the assertion that penal practices with respect to juveniles have undergone rather limited changes has the consequence that there also has not been much room for new forms of control, for more intense intrusion into the lives of juveniles and their families. Arguments that such changes have occurred are based on a reinterpretation of the promises of diversion: What is viewed by the advocates and the practitioners of diversion as benevolent distribution of the blessings of welfare, of guidance for the poor and help for the disadvantaged is conceived by the critics as coercion in disguise, as extension of discipline, as penetration of social control into the informal networks of society (for general statements of this kind, relating not only to diversion but to all sorts of informal justice, see, e.g., Hofrichter 1987: 70-71; Santos 1982: 262). However, this reinterpretation takes as established that the promises of diversion to replace repression by welfare, social education, and therapy have indeed been met. As I have tried to show, there is not much evidence to support this claim. What diversion programs have offered to the juvenile justice system is largely a means of more effective sanctions for petty crimes. There is little to indicate that community service orders contribute to an extension of discipline into the community. They are not used as a means of changing offenders' attitudes; they simply demonstrate the state's power to punish those who do not obey the rules. It is a much attenuated form of punishment, often reduced almost to a mere symbolic sanction, reflecting both the offenders' young age and the character of their offenses - mostly shoplifting, minor assault, damage to property. But nevertheless it is punishment and only rarely treatment or welfare.

My arguments concerning the character of social control in the 1980s and more specifically concerning the lack of dispersal of control are in line, at least it seems to me, with those advanced by Anthony Bottoms (1983) or, more recently, by John Pratt (1990). And in my opinion the reasons discussed by Bottoms why little "extension of discipline" from the criminal justice system into the community should be expected deserve further thought: Discipline is already promoted by society, by the family, the schools and the occupational system. Despite conservative claims of a decline of "moral order" - nurtured by rising crime rates -, most juveniles are well integrated into society's basic institutions and adhere to central values of our society - the striving for money and status. If such well-integrated youths commit a minor offense - as all of them do at some time - and become known to the police - as some of them do -, there is clearly neither a need for punishment nor a need for treatment, whereas the small minority of "real" problem youths still get the punishment they "deserve". The politics of diversion in the F.R.G. support such a strategy of "normalization" by providing the means of sanctioning petty offenders more efficiently - that is, smoothly and without much effort.

And, to conclude, this also helps to explain why diversion has been accepted to such a large extent by the criminal justice system and by policy-makers. Diversion has not been a strategy for a large-scale transformation of social control - neither for better nor for worse. Rather, it has helped the criminal justice system to keep in line with the modernization of society. It has provided the rhetorics of a liberal, up-to-date, benevolent juvenile justice system which are so attractive to many prosecutors and judges who want to get rid of the image of repressive, hard-core conservatives. But at the same time, the rhetorics - and even more the practice - of diversion have avoided any "radical" touch that would have been intolerable to those same people. But probably this is a characteristic of most reforms in our societies - giving the impression of change without actually changing much.

Notes

1 In using this term, I am referring to the view that social problems are not "given", but rather the result of claims of social groups that consider some social condition as problematic (Spector and Kitsuse, 1973). For a more extensive account, see Ludwig (1989).

2 (Post-adjucatory) juvenile detention is a custodial sentence ranging from one weekend up to four weeks that is served in special institutions. This form of short detention exists only in juvenile criminal law. Prison sentences according to juvenile criminal law range from six months up to five years (in the case of young adults up to ten years) and are served in special institutions set apart from those for persons convicted according to adult crimi-

nal law. Although they offer school and vocational training and the like, these institutions are prisons in legal terms and are also similar to prisons for adults in most other respects.

3 In the F.R.G., juvenile criminal law applies to juveniles proper (age 14 to 17), whereas young adults (age 18 to 20) may be handled either according to juvenile criminal law or to adult criminal law. Most of the young adults, however, are handled according to juvenile law. In the following, the terms "youth", "juveniles" or "juvenile defendants" should be understood as comprising those young adults that are treated according to juvenile law.

4 For instance, there has also been a decline, albeit small, in the number of young su spects known to the police (per 100,000).

5 It should be mentioned that in addition to the police-prosecutorial diversion program, Bielefeld has been the location of two further diversion programs in the past decade: In 1980, a program with emphasis on community service orders was initiated (Marks, 1981); and the local Youth Welfare Office has established a program to enhance informal control (see Otto, Bettmer, Messmer, and Micheel, 1989 and this volume).

6 The model building strategy was as follows. In a first step, all variables were entered simultaneously in the regression equation. Checks were accomplished concerning multicollinearity and inappropriate influence of single cases on results (using Cook's D and measures for changes in estimated coefficients [dfbeta], see Cook and Weisberg, 1982, chap. 5). Some *multicollinearity* occurred - quite naturally - (1) between type of court procedure and other variables (number of offenses, prior record) and (2) between defendant's denial of guilt and disagreement of judge and defendant with respect to the latter's guilt. As far as could be judged, this did not affect the results obtained. The cases with the most outstanding values with respect to *Cook's D* were those who were diverted despite an assessment of job problems. Deleting these cases lead to inestimability of the coefficient for job problems due to separability (Albert and Anderson, 1984), but left all other results virtually unchanged. In addition, these cases had high dfbetas only for the coefficient for job problems. Therefore, for the further steps these cases were not excluded from the analysis because high influence of "successes" with high predicted probability of failure (or vice versa) is common in logistic regression diagnostics (Jennings 1986). - In the second step, variables not significant at the .05 level were removed from the model in a stepwise manner. The final model was again checked with respect to influential cases; the results obtained were the same as above. Therefore, it was concluded that the statistical model might indeed yield an adequate picture of the decision process.

7 This can be seen from data provided by Dünkel (1990: 95). - I use the term "fine" for financial penalties both according to adult criminal law - fines proper - and according to juvenile criminal law, where they are called "orders to make financial payments" and are not paid to the state, but to a welfare organization - for instance, to a diversion program!

8 Pfeiffer's (1983: 222) view on this point is clearly different. His argument that, due to a newly implemented diversion project ("Brücke"), more than 500 cases of juvenile detention had been replaced by community service orders in the district of Munich in the year 1980 is based on the probably erroneous assumption that the absolute number of detention sentences otherwise would have increased. But above all he offers no explanation why more than 3,000 community service orders were necessary to achieve a reduction of only 500 cases of juvenile detention.

9 It should be added that this phenomenon was observed mainly in a single court. But given the small number of cases involved (altogether 15 to 20), any generalization is difficult.

Appendix: Variables tested in multivariate model on court decision
(R: reference category)

	n	%
Type of offense (R: shoplifting, bicycle theft)		
Other theft without aggravating circumstances	54	11
Theft with aggravating circumstances, automobile theft (also with other offenses)	139	28
Assault	43	9
Damage to property	20	4
Several (different) offenses, no theft involved	45	9
Type of proceedings (R: "Simplified Proceedings", Sect. 76 JGG)		
Judge sitting alone	287	58
Judge with lay assessors	119	24
Number of offenses		
One	302	61
Two	76	15
Three	30	6
Four	22	4
Five	10	2
Six or more	52	11
Prior record (R: None)		
Diverted only	88	18
Prior conviction	142	29
Sex female	83	17
Nationality Turkish or Yugoslavian	113	23
Family problems reported		
Present	88	18
In the past	107	22
Problems in school		
Present dissocial behavior	27	5
Past dissocial behavior	49	10
Present problems with achievement	48	10
Past problems with achievement	134	27
Job-related problems	50	10

Denial of guilt (R: Admission of guilt)		
Partial	105	21
Complete	62	13
Restitution effected or offender ready to provide restitution	98	20
Educational measures effected or announced		
By parents	60	12
By others	12	2
Disagreement judge - defendant on guilt		
None	368	75
.	50	10
.	23	5
.	22	4
Extreme	29	6
Age at (first of series of) offense(s)	Mean 16.9	S.D. 1.9
Number of trials scheduled for respective day	Mean 6.3	S.D. 3.3

References

Albert, A., and Anderson, J.A. (1984). On the existence of maximum likelihood estimates in logistic regression models. *Biometrika, 71,* 1-10.

Albrecht, P.-A. (1990) (Ed.). *Informalisierung des Rechts.* Berlin/New York: de Gruyter.

Austin, J., and Krisberg, B. (1981). Wider, stronger and different nets: The dialectics of criminal justice reform. *Journal of Research in Crime and Delinquency, 18,* 165-196.

Binder, A., and Geis, G. (1984). Ad populum argumentation in criminology: Juvenile diversion as rhetoric. *Crime and Delinquency, 30,* 624-647.

Bottoms, A.E. (1983). Neglected features of contemporary penal systems. In D. Garland and P. Young (Eds.), *The power to punish* (pp. 166-201). London: Heinemann.

Bullington, B., Sprowls, J., Katkin, D., and Phillips, M. (1978). A critique of diversionary juvenile justice. *Crime & Delinquency, 24,* 59-71.

Cohen, S. (1985). *Visions of social control.* Cambridge: Polity Press.

Cook, R.D., and Weisberg, S. (1982). *Residuals and influence in regression.* New York: Chapman and Hall.

Cressey, D.R., and McDermott, R.A. (1973). *Diversion from the juvenile justice system.* Ann Arbor, Mich.: University of Michigan.

Dünkel, F. (1990). *Freiheitsentzug für junge Rechtsbrecher. Situation und Reform von Jugendstrafe, Jugendstrafvollzug, Jugendarrest und Untersuchungshaft in der Bundesrepublik Deutschland und im internationalen Vergleich.* Bonn: Forum Verlag Godesberg.

Garland, D. (1985). *Punishment and welfare.* Aldershot: Gower.

Hauser, R. (1980). Der Jugendrichter - Idee und Wirklichkeit. *Monatsschrift für Kriminologie und Strafrechtsreform, 63,* 1-19.

Heinz, W. (1989). Jugendstrafrechtsreform durch die Praxis - eine Bestandsaufnahme. In Der Bundesminister der Justiz (Ed.), *Jugendstrafrechtsreform durch die Praxis* (pp. 13-44). Bonn: Bundesministerium der Justiz.

Heinz, W. (1990). Die Jugendstrafrechtspflege im Spiegel der Rechtspflegestatistiken. *Monatsschrift für Kriminologie und Strafrechtsreform, 73,* 210-226.

Herbort, U., Rzepka, D., and Voß, S. (1989). Police and prevention: A research report on cooperation in the criminal justice system. In P.-A. Albrecht and O. Backes (Eds.), *Crime prevention and intervention* (pp. 145-166). Berlin/New York: de Gruyter.

Hering, E., and Sessar, K. (1990). *Praktizierte Diversion: Das "Modell Lübeck" sowie die Diversionsprogramme in Köln, Braunschweig und Hamburg* (Hamburger Studien zur Kriminologie). Pfaffenweiler: Centaurus.

Hermann, D., and Wild, P. (1989). Die Bedeutung der Tat bei der jugendrichterlichen Rechtsfolgenbestimmung. *Monatsschrift für Kriminologie und Strafrechtsreform, 72,* 13-33.

Herriger, N. (1985). Familienintervention und soziale Kontrolle - Strategien der Kolonisierung von Lebenswelten. In M. Brusten, N. Herriger, and P. Malinowski (Eds.), *Entkriminalisierung* (pp. 53-73). Opladen: Westdeutscher Verlag.

Hertwig, V. (1982). *Die Einstellung des Strafverfahrens wegen Geringfügigkeit. Eine empirische Analyse der Handhabung der §§ 153, 153a StPO in der staatsanwaltschaftlichen und gerichtlichen Praxis.* Göttingen: Schwartz.

Hofrichter, R. (1987). *Neighborhood justice in capitalist society. The expansion of the informal state.* New York: Greenwood Press.

Kerner, H.-J. (1989). Unbeabsichtigte und unerwünschte Nebenfolgen der JGG-Reform durch die Praxis, insbesondere das Beispiel der Ausweitung des Netzes sozialer Kontrolle. In Der Bundesminister der Justiz (Ed.), *Jugendstrafrechtsreform durch die Praxis* (pp. 265-292). Bonn: Bundesministerium der Justiz.

Klein, M.W. (1976). Issues and realities in police diversion programs. *Crime & Delinquency, 22,* 421-427.

Jennings, D.E. (1986). Outliers and residual distributions in logistic regression. *Journal of the American Statistical Association, 81,* 987-990.

Ludwig, W. (1989). *Diversion: Strafe im neuen Gewand.* Berlin/New York: de Gruyter.

Ludwig-Mayerhofer, W. (1990). Die staatsanwaltliche Diversionspraxis im Jugendstrafrecht. In P.-A. Albrecht (Ed.), *Informalisierung des Rechts* (pp. 47-225). Berlin/New York: de Gruyter.

Ludwig-Mayerhofer, W. (1992). Jugendstrafrecht: Materiale Rationalität oder prozedurale Irrationalität? *Zeitschrift für Rechtssoziologie, 13,* 205-230.

Ludwig-Mayerhofer, W., and Rzepka, D. (1993). Zwischen Strafverfolgung und Sanktionierung. Empirische Analysen zur gewandelten Stellung der Staatsanwaltschaft im Prozeß strafrechtlicher Sozialkontrolle. *Zeitschrift für Rechtssoziologie, 14,* 115-140.

Marks, E. (1981). Das Modell Brücke - ein Versuch, mehr pädagogische Hilfen im Rahmen des Jugendgerichtsgesetzes zu realisieren. In Deutsche Vereinigung für Jugendgerichte und Jugendgerichtshilfen e.V. (Ed.), *Die jugendrichterlichen Entscheidungen - Anspruch und Wirklichkeit* (pp. 269-286). München: Selbstverlag der Deutschen Vereinigung für Jugendgerichte und Jugendgerichtshilfen e.V.

McMahon, M. (1990). 'Net-Widening': Vagaries in the use of a concept. *The British Journal of Criminology, 30,* 121-149.

Otto, H.-U., Bettmer, F., Messmer, H., and Micheel, H.-G. (1989). Alternative Sozialarbeit: Informalisierung sozialer Kontrolle im Bereich abweichenden Verhaltens. *Neue Praxis, 19,* 525-532.

Pfeiffer, C. (1983). *Kriminalprävention im Jugendgerichtsverfahren.* Köln: Heymanns.

Platt, A. (1969). *The child savers. The invention of delinquency.* Chicago: University of Chicago Press.

Pratt, J. (1990). Crime, time, youth and punishment. *Contemporary Crises, 14,* 219-242.

Rzepka, D. (1990). Polizei und Diversion - Das Bielefelder Modell der Informationsvermittlung. In P.-A. Albrecht (Ed.), *Informalisierung des Rechts* (pp. 341-458). Berlin/New York: de Gruyter.

Santos, B. d. S. (1982). Law and community: The changing nature of state power in late capitalism. In: R.L. Abel (Ed.) *The politics of informal justice, Vol. 1: The American experience* (pp. 249-266). New York: Academic Press.

Scull, A. (1982). Community corrections: Panacea, progress, or pretense? In R.L. Abel (Ed.), *The politics of informal justice, Vol. 1: The American experience* (pp. 99-118). New York: Academic Press.

Spector, M., and Kitsuse, J.I. (1973). Social problems: A re-formulation. *Social Problems, 21*, 145-159.

The President's Commission on Law Enforcement and Administration (1967). *The challenge of crime in a free society.* Washington, D. C.

Voβ, M. (1986). *Jugend ohne Rechte.* Frankfurt/New York: Campus.

Voβ, S. (1990). Staatsanwaltliche Entscheidung - Beeinflussung durch systematische Informationserweiterung? - Die Umsetzung des Bielefelder Modellversuchs durch die Staatsanwaltschaft. In P.-A. Albrecht (Ed.), *Informalisierung des Rechts* (pp. 461-566). Berlin/New York: de Gruyter.

Weigend, T. (1984). Strafzumessung durch den Staatsanwalt? *Kriminologisches Journal, 16,* 8-38.

Radical Social Change and Diversion: Problems With Diversion-Oriented Crime Policy in the Critical Transformation of Social Structures and Changes in the Living Conditions of Adolescents

Gunhild Korfes[*]

1 Introduction

This chapter discusses the problem of diversion-oriented crime policy in the new German states against the background of changes in penal social control. These changes are embedded in the construction of new institutional structures and social regulation mechanisms, a process that is occurring as a sudden transition from a system with an essentially centralistic organization and functioning to a constitutional state based on pluralistic structures.

One aspect of these changes was the introduction overnight of new penal norms, including those of the Juvenile Justice Act (*Jugendgerichtsgesetz*; JGG): These are also linked to changed strategies of social control and require corresponding structures if they are to be effective. Even just this aspect of the rapid transformation of penal social controls in the new German states represents an enormous problem. This is because new penal norms do not simply mean that previous characteristics of a criminal act are, for example, different; or, even more seriously, that certain behaviors are redefined as penally significant, but also that they are linked to new forms of control.

There can be no doubt that the introduction of the JGG has led to a liberalization of penal dealings with juvenile delinquency. This is shown not only in the much greater consideration given to youth-specific aspects but also in the differentiated possibilities of sanctioning juvenile delinquency. Finally, these differences are clearly seen in certain crimes that sometimes elicited a rigid reaction (in the sense of incarceration measures) in the German Democratic Republic (GDR). One example is how the GDR justice system dealt with vandalism (Section 215 of the GDR penal code). Nonetheless, despite the liberal intent of the JGG, a problem can be seen: Many petty crimes that now enter the scope of the JGG were punished as misdemeanors or regulatory offenses in the GDR.[1] Essentially, many petty crimes were punished by social courts or other forms of informal settlement without the initiation of criminal proceedings. Because of these differences in dealing with petty crime, I consider that there is a risk that the introduction of the JGG may lead to an expansion of penal social controls.

This latter aspect already draws attention to one of the issues that need to be discussed in the context of a diversion-oriented crime policy in the new German states. The goal of diversion is decriminalization and deinstitutionalization of the adjudication of juvenile delinquency. However, when it requires an extension of formal and state controls in the area of petty crime - compared to the GDR - will its clients, that is, juvenile delinquents, in any way perceive it as a decriminalization and accept it as a service for solving or dealing with conflicts?

Naturally, the issue of how far the JGG represents an extension of controls, at least in the area of petty crime, requires further comparative analysis, particularly of legal practise in the GDR and the new German states. The following discussion is only one possible contribution to such a complex issue.

This chapter addresses the following issues:

1. From the perspective of penal social control, how was juvenile delinquency dealt with in the GDR, or what differences can be ascertained between the GDR and the Federal Republic of Germany (FRG) in dealing with specific juvenile offenses? These considerations will be related to the impact of diversion; that is, also with reference to its reception as decriminalization and as an aid to coping with conflicts among adolescents in the new German states. In relation to this issue, I will present some preliminary findings from an analysis of attitudes toward sanctions and justice among the population of the new German states. In my opinion, general feedback on the new control system among the citizens who are currently living through a period of radical social change can also provide information on the impact of a diversion-oriented crime policy under the current social conditions in the new German states.

2. This will be supplemented by a brief sketch of the changes in the social situation of adolescents. The central issue is how far a penal control system developed in a completely different social context can adequately solve the conflicts that develop against the background of the collapse of GDR society and the restructuring of the entire network of social relationships and conditions. Restricted to adolescents, this means, which changes in their living conditions and their everyday life occur and produce conflict, or how far does the transformation process imply critical situations for adolescents?

2 Transformation of Penal Social Control and its Acceptance in the Population

One of the central topics in the history of the GDR is how criminal justice, police, and security services dealt with deviant behavior. This problem was intimately linked to the change in the GDR from the very beginning, when police assaults on the night of October 7th to 8th 1989 accelerated the protests in the population. This exposed a conflict that had long been latent between the people and the state, at least as far as the state's reaction to political deviance was concerned. In the following year, this problem area was continuously the focus of criticism of GDR society. This led to increasingly uncertain reactions from the justice system and, above all, the police, so that in the period up to reunification in October 1990, these authorities of control were repeatedly accused of not responding to the spread of anomic states - a criticism that still remained in 1991. Even though the restructuring of control authorities and personal problems played a role during the latter period, the duration of conflictual relationships between citizens and control authorities expresses a specific problem that remains characteristic for the crisis in the GDR and the current transformation process in the new German states.

That the effects of this long-term conflict have not simply been annihilated by the adoption of new control structures and norms is shown by some findings from a representative survey on crime trends in the new German states.[2] This survey, carried out in Spring 1991, also addressed attitudes toward sanctions and justice in the population.

The results show that skepticism toward the institutions of justice in the new German states is relatively high. For example, 49% of respondents said that they had little or no trust in criminal justice and the public prosecutor's office (27%) or that they did not know (22%). These response categories were chosen less frequently when the question referred to the police (35%), but were chosen much more frequently in ratings of prisons, the Office for the Protection of the Constitution, and the Federal Intelligence Service (65%, 72%). Similar to the ratings of justice and the public prosecutor's office were the responses regarding their actual tasks. For example, approximately one third of respondents were uncertain whether the legality of prosecution and the fairness of punishment were guaranteed, and approximately 20% considered that this was more unlikely or completely lacking. Responses to the question whether justice contributed to solving problems had a similar distribution.

A survey of offenders, which was included in the representative survey, addressed only 18- to 29-year-olds. Responses from young nonoffenders generally had exactly the same distribution as the rest of the population, while offenders had less or absolutely no trust in the system (nonviolent offenders: an average of 35%; but, above all, violent offenders: an average of 50%).

These responses can probably be explained in part through the current problems in setting up and reforming the justice system in the new German states. However, I consider that they also reveal a skepticism that can be viewed not only as a lack of trust in the work of the justice system that grew in the GDR but also as an indication of the difficulties in designing an alien control system so that it functions adequately and effectively under the conditions in the new German states.

As I consider that feedback from the population on penal social control demonstrates one of the conditions determining the effectiveness of a diversion-oriented crime policy, I shall return to the contradictory trends in dealing with juvenile delinquency in the GDR sketched above. They may be able to explain some of the causes for the much higher mistrust of the new justice system among the juvenile delinquents in the survey.

The rigid approach to violence and vandalism in GDR criminal justice has been mentioned briefly above. A study of selection processes for juvenile suspects in the GDR reveals that the proportion of incarceration measures for these offenses was higher than that for adult offenders, even in the years 1985 to 1989. As von der Heide (1992) reports:

"The proportion of incarcerated juvenile suspects dropped during the period of the study from 15.1% to 13.9%, while the proportion of adults dropped from 21.2% to 16.7%; that is, the relative difference fell from 6% to 3%. If we disregard the selection level of enforced incarcerations, it is generally justifiable to say that the criminal prosecution of violent juvenile offenders was even more repressive than that of adults in this crime category." (p. 15, translated)

Studies on the biographies of skinheads in the GDR also indicate that their violent behavior was frequently answered with incarceration. This resulted in "control and punishment processes leaving clear traces in the biographies of these adolescents and making a major contribution to the development of extreme right-wing attitudes." (Korfes, 1992: 56, translated)

These indications should suffice to show that a proportion of adolescents in the 1980s had experienced a massive application of restrictive penal sanctions by the state in its attempt to fight deviant and opposition behavior. Increased social control as the state's reaction to adolescent conflict was thus one of the basic social experiences of adolescents. This probably generalizes to viewing the reaction to more liberal sanctions as a continuation of negative experiences with state power.

Insofar as petty crime was prosecuted, much was dealt with by social courts (approximately 30% of all registered offenses). Transfer to social courts was used 15% to 20% more frequently for juvenile delinquents than for adult offenders. This trend nonetheless contrasted with the fact that the possibility of diverting adolescents from penal measures (according to Sections 75 and 76 of the GDR penal code) was hardly ever applied (von der Heide, 1992: 24).

This shows that persons who became entangled with the penal prosecution system in the GDR were punished by the courts much more frequently than persons in the FRG. However, in contrast, petty crimes often did not lead to criminal prosecution. This has been confirmed for adolescents in expert interviews with former judges, public prosecutors, police, and teachers (Korfes and Thiel, 1992).

Public prosecutors and judges reported that, in offenses with damages of less than 500 East German marks, the police could already check whether the case should be transferred to a social court, preliminary investigation should be commenced, or whether, following counseling with parents, school, or youth welfare, a penal response could be dropped completely (Section 75, GDR penal code) in favor of educational measures.

The section agent (similar to the contact police officer), who generally processed the complaint, played an important role in deciding whether charges should be preferred for petty crimes. This left discretionary powers regarding whether to press charges or simply enter the event in police records. Less severe offenses were frequently processed by the section agent without any further proceedings.

When an adolescent student committed a petty crime, it was common practice for the teacher and the section agent to evaluate the event in the student's classroom collective instead of pressing charges. The content of such an evaluation was the evaluation of the behavior of the student concerned, who was frequently instructed to work in order to make reparation for the damage.

This short sketch of the treatment of petty crime should suffice to show that, particularly in the field of misdemeanors and petty crime, there were discretionary powers for reacting to deviant behavior in all four control authorities of the GDR studied. This seems, at least in the opinion of the experts surveyed, to have been used in the sense of a liberal reaction. Nonetheless, there were also clear indications, particularly in the expert interviews with public prosecutors, that conformist behavior or a "positive family background" could have a favorable impact on the decision to press charges or use informal procedures.

Informal treatment of petty crime thus had a major status. It was important to strive toward the possibility of solving conflicts where they had occurred, that is, in the interaction between deviant juvenile and victim. However, there are some indications that, despite informal processing, control processes were nonetheless applied that had a selective and stigmatizing impact on the adolescents involved.

An example is the finding of a study in the GDR on juvenile delinquents of apprenticeship age. This revealed the following trend: 70% of the juvenile delinquents had already committed crimes while they had been at school. Regardless of whether they had been prosecuted by the courts or had been dealt with through the Regulatory Offenses Act, this had far-reaching consequences. Their vocational advance in the sense of choosing a profession corresponding to their interests was clearly impaired. The feature "delinquent at school" correlated highly significantly with having to choose a profession that did not correspond with one's own interests. Although only one third of the total population of apprentices were affected by this, it applied to 80% of delinquent apprentices. The relationship between delinquency and restricted vocational opportunities was clearly stronger than the relationship between school-leaving certificate and vocational choice, although this relationship was also very important (Korfes, 1987).

Despite these, as yet, insufficiently studied contradictory trends in the reaction to petty crime - contradictions between informal settlement and far-reaching forms of social control and selection - it can still be ascertained that the processing of petty crime certainly took decriminalizing forms. I consider that one consequence of this is that certain petty crimes are not linked to penal norms and criminal punishment in the minds of adolescents.

This raises the question of how today's adolescents react to the commencement of criminal proceedings for petty crimes. The assumption that they perceive this as a very strong reaction is confirmed by juvenile court assistants currently working in East Berlin. Even when criminal proceedings are later dropped, adolescents seem to retain this impression. This reaction may possibly also be explained by the fact that adolescents, regardless of whether a sanction follows or is dismissed, are now trapped in the net of formal penal social control for petty crimes as well.

The problems resulting from the contradictory experiences of adolescents with penal social control need to be taken into account in the goal of "education instead of punishment" stipulated in the JGG. In addition, current deficits make it more difficult to effectively implement the idea of diversion, and, thereby, the comparatively liberal goals of the JGG in the new German states. Striving to withdraw charges by introducing educational measures in the life space of the adolescent currently faces practical problems that seem to lead to two contradictory reactions: (a) mostly nonreaction or informal processing, and (b) when registered with the police, a trend toward formal and custodial processing due to a lack of alternatives (provisional information on the increase in incarceration rates suggests this assumption). The work overload of juvenile judges and the long periods between offense and trial play an important role in these problems. However, there is particularly a lack of private organizations that can implement noncustodial measures.

In view of these facts and the GDR experiences in processing petty crimes, it might be more meaningful to rely on or reactivate lifeworld forms of dealing with petty crime, and to apply diversion measures exclusively for intermediate and serious crimes by adolescents and young adults in the new German states.

This idea becomes increasingly relevant when the social situation of adolescents in the new German states is taken into account; a situation that is characterized by changes and conflictual experiences in all areas of the life of young adults.

3 Changes in the Everyday Life of Adolescents and Their Relevance for Diversion

Against the background of the transformation of social structures and relationships, the current problems in diversion-oriented crime policy are linked to a series of further issues.

Studies on crime trends in the new German states show that crime levels are lower than in the West German states (DFG-Projekt, 1992; Kury, 1991). In view of the extent of radical social change, it is questionable, against the background of this low crime growth, whether it is correct to implement the West German diversion model. Perhaps the given forms of conflict solution in this, to some extent, social experiment situation question the usefulness of an expanded net of diversion measures.

The current process of radical change is causing serious alterations in the life-worlds of adolescents. Particularly in this generation, an orientation crisis is being accompanied by the change or dissolution of social milieus. The confrontation with the completely new risks involved in an individual struggle for survival produces a critical situation in this context that possibly also encourages delinquency.

To illustrate the change in the everyday life process of adolescents, I shall present provisional findings from a survey of 16-year-old students in one of the large new residential developments in East Berlin.[3] The results reveal trends and problem areas that could be relevant to the questions posed above.

Some of the 16-year-olds seem to experience a probably serious change in the family. These changes seem to be linked closely to radical social changes and point to the formation of other, as yet nondominant, value structures. For example, one third of the 16-year-olds report that their relationship to their parents has deteriorated. In this context, frequent parental conflict and a tense atmosphere are particularly reported. Financial problems seem to play an important role here. How far such changes relate to parental unemployment or short time (19% of the students reported that this applied to their parents) cannot be stated until data have been subjected to further analysis.

However, that current problems in the parental home place the adolescents in critical situations seems to be confirmed by a study of the changes in the clients of a youth welfare emergency service in East Berlin (Ewald et al., 1992). While, at the beginning of 1990, the majority of adolescents who visited the emergency center came from residential care institutions, after monetary union and particularly after reunification in October 1990, increasingly more adolescents from family homes were attending the center.

"The increase in the proportion of those coming from family homes can be traced back to a real increase in conflicts within the family as a consequence of the breakdown of social structures and the attendant uncertainties regarding employment." (Ewald et al., 1992, translated).

In the school study, the current radical social changes were also accompanied by strong uncertainties regarding how to plan one's own life and future. Such tendencies were found in over 60% of the respondents. These included anxieties concerning their own or their parents' unemployment, and fears that the social situation could generally deteriorate. As yet, we cannot say how students cope with these anxieties. That they have an impact on the adolescents' willingness to engage in violence has proven to be a significant relationship.

A further important change in the social space of the young is seen in the perception of relationships between students. One third of the respondents reported a notable increase in the formation of cliques among the students, and that political discrimination played a relatively strong role in students' relationships. They considered that these discriminations were linked to confrontations that were becoming increasingly harsh and aggressive.

It is notable that these changes in the structure of relationships among students are perceived particularly strongly by those adolescents who report that they engage in violent behavior. Twelve percent of students reported that they had already participated in violent confrontations with foreigners, other groups of youths, or other citizens.

In general, this group of students who define themselves as violent seems to be particularly sensitive to the current process of radical social change. Inclusion in a violent youth culture seems to function as an aid in the sense of compensation.

In contrast to this group of adolescents, the symptoms of conflictual processing of the current upheaval seem to be less strongly marked in other groups of deviant youth. For example, the 19% of students who reported that they had already committed small shoplifting offenses revealed hardly any significant deviations from the total population that would indicate particular crises that essentially differ from those of other students.

It can be concluded from this study that violence should be evaluated particularly as a reaction to current conflict states. It can be assumed that violence is not only a defense against youth's social uncertainty but also an attempt to construct "action control over potentially threatening life conditions" (Heitmeyer, 1989: 13, translated).

If these findings are representative for 14- to 18-year-olds in the new German states, I consider that they permit the conclusion that it is not simply justified and meaningful to punish petty crimes within the scope of the JGG. Even if it can be assumed that petty crime will increase in the present period, informal adjudication in the social space of youth is probably generally sufficient, as this type of deviance does not seem to be an expression of any particularly conflictual reaction to the current situation of radical social change.

The situation is different among adolescents who commit violent and destructive offenses. Our study of students as well as other studies (DFG-Projekt, 1992) has revealed that these adolescents and young adults experience the critical process of radical social change with more intensity and conflict than the majority of respondents, although it can, nonetheless, be seen in them as well. This explains the reaction with violence, but simultaneously introduces a social learning process that seems to manifest an aggressive processing of conflict. With reference to this problem, it seems to be meaningful to confront violent delinquency with diversion-oriented measures.

The construction of a diversion-oriented crime policy focusing on deviance that is strongly related to the conflictual processing of radical social change would be meaningful for several reasons. First, focusing on specific offense categories would be easier to implement in light of the deficits in the structure of non-custodial treatment services. Second, adolescents who find themselves in a particularly critical situation would not simply become entangled in the net of institutionalized conflict processing and formal controls, but would experience an appropriate reaction to their problems. Finally, this orientation would counteract a trend that is currently extraordinarily dominant in the new German states: the tendency to counteract an increase in violent delinquency particularly by expanding the police and the justice system, which implies the threat that penal social control will become a major means of processing social conflict.

Notes

* Translated from German by Jonathan Harrow at the University of Bielefeld.

1 A misdemeanor was viewed as a minor violation of legally protected interests (Section 4 of the GDR penal code) and was dealt with separately with a special misdemeanor ordinance. Regulatory offenses were violations of law with a low extent of damages that were punished outside the penal code on the basis of the law against infringements of police and administrative regulations.

2 The representative survey is part of a project on radical social change and crime trends in the former GDR that is being conducted in Tübingen, Hamburg, and Berlin and is financed by the German Research Association (DFG).

3 The study was performed in June 1991 by students at the Institute for Sociology, Humboldt University, Berlin. A total of 175 students were surveyed in two urban districts of East Berlin.

References

DFG-Projekt (1992). *Sozialer Umbruch und Kriminalitätsentwicklung in der früheren DDR.* Berlin: Unpublished manuscript.

Ewald, U., Lautsch, E., D. Maron (1992). *Jugendberatung in Ost-Berlin während der Wende.* Materialien der kriminologischen Forschungsstelle Berlin. Unpublished manuscript.

Heide, F. von der (1992). *Selektionsprozesse jugendlicher Tatverdächtiger auf dem Gebiet der ehemaligen DDR in den Jahren 1985 - 1989.* Berlin: Unpublished manuscript.

Heitmeyer, W. (1989). Jugend, Staat und Gewalt in der politischen Risikogesellschaft. In W. Heitmeyer, K. Möller, and H. Sünker (Eds.), *Jugend - Staat - Gewalt* (pp. 11-47). Weinheim: Juventa.

Korfes, G. (1987). *Soziologische Untersuchung von Ursachen der Herausbildung sozialer Gefährdung - dargestellt an der Entwicklung von Jugendlichen im Lehrlingsalter.* Unpublished doctoral dissertation, Humboldt University, Berlin.

Korfes, G. (1992). Zur Entwicklung des Rechtsextremismus in der DDR. *Kriminologisches Journal, 24*, 50-64.

Korfes, G., and Thiel, K. (1992). *Wandel der strafrechtlichen Sozialkontrolle in den neuen Bundesländern.* Arbeitsbericht zum DFG-Projekt "Sozialer Umbruch und Kriminalitätsentwicklung in der früheren DDR". Berlin: Unpublished manuscript.

Kury, H. (1991). Crime and victimization in East and West: Results of the first comparative victimological study of the former GDR and FRG. In G. Kaiser, H. Kury, and H.-J. Albrecht (Eds.), *Legal protection, restitution, and support* (pp. 45-98). Freiburg: Eigenverlag Max-Planck-Institut für ausländisches und internationales Strafrecht.

Part III

Alternative Sanctions: Theoretical Ideas and Empirical Results

Introduction to Part III: Alternative Sanctions: Theoretical Ideas and Empirical Results

The contributions in the third part of this volume discuss diversion and its potential effects from very different points of view.

First, John Braithwaite undertakes the most important task of developing a consistent and philosophically well-founded theory that can function as a frame of reference for a rational criminal policy in modern societies. Braithwaite elaborates the central concepts and principles of this "republican theory" and their roots in social philosophy. This social theory, which is highly committed to the theoretical tradition of "communitarianism", is combined with Braithwaite's very interesting theory of "reintegrative shaming", which also owes a lot to communitarianism. In this way, this paper differs in a very important aspect from most other contributions to criminal policy, because it is not restricted to a mere discussion of criminological theories or to technical problems of law enforcement. Following Braithwaite's theory it is not only possible to understand why diversion may be a reasonable strategy to handle many cases of crime and delinquency. This theory can also explain why traditional forms of exclusionary social control on the one side and laissez-faire forms of diversion on the other side do not work with regard to special deterrence. Braithwaite is well aware that, since Durkheim, sociologists are searching for a societal strategy that might lead to the aims of communitarianism, but that most of them have ended in resignation. Braithwaite's several contributions try to show that most authors have been blinded by the example of the extreme individualistic society of the United States, though, even there, many examples also show the important role of communitarian ideas. Some readers may find Braithwaite's example presented here not absolutely convincing, because the issue is not to show that, in some contexts, reintegrative shaming is the "normal case" and an effective strategy. The main problem is how to change an extremely individualistic society into a (more) communitarian one. Nevertheless, Braithwaite's introduction to this theoretical tradition opens new horizons for the debates in criminal policy.

Second, Wolfgang Heinz's paper presents the empirical results of several very extensive and solidly conceptualized and conducted research projects on the development of diversion in Germany. Heinz is one of Germany's leading criminologists committed to the idea that diversion might be a very useful alternative to the traditional sanctioning practice that makes it possible to empower the principle of education as a guideline for juvenile criminal justice. For many years, Heinz and his research team have documented that diversion practices in Germany exhibit such broad local and regional differences that the principle of equality with respect to justice is offended. The fact that - after controlling for crime and delinquency structure - there is no relation between diversion rates and retrial or reconviction rates on this aggregate level can be interpreted as a first evidence that diversion by public prosecutors and judges of juvenile courts is a responsible form of social control. This practice is not only justifiable but preferable in light of the principle of minimal intrusion/interference. Using a very large-scale and complex cohort-study with data from the German central register as well as an exact analysis of case files on a special cohort, Heinz and his research team can show that diverted adolescents exhibit significantly lower reconviction and retrial rates compared to nondiverted youths matched on central parameters. Heinz comes to the firm conclusion that diversion has an important potential for solving some of the difficult problems related to juvenile delinquency. Some of the main advantages of Heinz's studies are the very broad empirical basis - avoiding the serious problems of selection and reliability typical for self-report studies. If some doubts have still remained about the impact of diversion on juvenile delinquents, these convincing results should help dispel them.

Albrecht reports on the aims and results of a longitudinal study on diversion. One of its central objectives was to evaluate short-term and long-term effects of diversion by the public prosecutor on juvenile delinquents by a panel-study with three measurement lags over three years using self-report data. In order to evaluate the effects of informal and formal social control reactions on the frequency of self-reported delinquency in a realistic manner, the study collected comparable data from a representative community sample of youths without official registration. The main objective of the study, which will be completed by a replication for another cohort, is not the mere impact evaluation, but the reconstruction of the complex processes by which diversion produces these results. For this purpose, the study combines ideas from control theory, rational choice theory, differential association theory, self-esteem theories, and especially labeling theory. These make available several rival and complementary hypotheses on the mechanisms by which different control reactions influence the behavior of delinquent youths. On the one side, the presented data document that many of the assumptions in the well-established theories mentioned above are not tenable or at least have to be modified. On the other side, the study comes to the provisional conclusion that the long-term effect of diversion just fails to reach the conventional significance level after controlling for other relevant factors. Nevertheless, it is of substantial importance. This is all the more so, because some results confirm Kaplan's theory of "deviant behavior in defense of self" as well as several assumptions in the labeling approach whose important theoretical potential has to be resurrected through an innovative integration of sociological and social psychological theories of the self with emphasis on the theory of emotions, especially shame.

There is no doubt about the fact that the following three papers are far from providing final conclusions on the potentials and constraints of diversion as a control strategy, but they should encourage further efforts to embed the discusions diversion into two broader encompassing discourses: one on central features of modern societies and their consequences for social control and the other on the processes of identity transformation with their contingencies on the one side and criminal careers on the other side.

Diversion, Reintegrative Shaming and Republican Criminology

John Braithwaite

It is appropriate to have someone from Australia contribute to an international conference on diversion since our country was the greatest diversion program in human history. Of course, from an English perspective, transportation to Australia was an exclusionary form of social control (to use Stan Cohen's, 1985, term); but from an Australian perspective it was inclusionary, a chance to join a country with a better cricket team. In some quite serious ways, I suspect transportation to Australia was not only the biggest, but also one of the more successful experiments in diversion (Braithwaite, 1991a). It had its horrors, for sure. But these were generally less than the alternative punishments of the time, because transportation was in practice reintegrative. The convicts were desperately needed to build the new Australia; so they were quickly pushed out into the community to work "on assignment" for free settlers and released convicts. There was an economic interest to make the assigned convicts feel "part of the team", and so economic imperatives resulted in transportation being the opposite of the exclusionary punishment its brutal architects had intended.

The boy convicts at Point Puer were pushed out into the Tasmanian workforce as soon as they had learnt skills that were needed in the new economy. Some of them became business leaders. And contrary to the predictions of everyone, the children of released convicts evidenced an extraordinarily low crime rate (Hughes, 1987: 357, 588). Twentieth century Tasmania enjoys lower crime rates than 20th century Britain. This when Tasmania was built on the most criminal of genetic stock: in the mid-19th century, almost half the population were still criminals under sentence, and almost half the free population were released convicts (Hughes, 1987: 551-552). Then one might count the children and grandchildren of convicts or former convicts. Citizen Toulongeon, a French advocate of the British experiment, described transportation as "the first time anyone has dared to fashion a society from all that is wicked in another" (*Moniteur*, 3 January, 1803). Toulongeon and I agree that the experiment was pretty much a success, because the stigmatization of the wicked was terminated by reintegration in a new community in which they were more accepted than in the old country and given economic opportunities. This will be a theme in this paper - that diversion works when it is reintegrative. But first, I will seek to embed this explanatory theme within a normative theory of when we should view diversion as a good thing or a bad thing. This theory is republican. I shall explain what republican theory is, what it has to say about diversion, and what its connections are to the explanatory theory of reintegrative shaming. Finally, I will argue that pockets of republican criminological praxis are to be found throughout the world, though the progressive reform does not march under the republican banner.

1 Paradoxes of Diversion

When white-collar criminals are diverted from the criminal justice system, progressive criminologists tend to view this as undesirable regulatory capture. Diversion is our standard way of dealing with white-collar crime. I am a part-time Commissioner with Australia's national antitrust and consumer protection agency, the Trade Practices Commission. More than 99% of the allegations of law-breaking that come to us are dealt with by diversion, and we are arguably the most enforcement-oriented business regulatory agency in Australia (Grabosky and Braithwaite, 1986). When juvenile offenders are diverted, progressive criminologists tend to view this as undesirable net-widening. When domestic violence offenders are diverted, feminists view this as a manifestation of patriarchal domination. One would be excused for thinking that progressive criminologists are rather arbitrary in the way they switch such judgments. What I suggest we should aspire to is a coherent theoretical position on when diversion and net-widening are good and bad things.

It may be that we should take the view that diverting 99% of white-collar criminals is a good thing, and that progressive criminologists ought to be advocates for dealing with our blue-collar criminals along the lines of the white-collar crime control model, rather than the reverse. My own position is actually pretty close to that. At the same time, I am an aggressive advocate of net-widening for white-collar criminals. As both regulatory theorist and practitioner, I have pushed the strategy of negotiating settlements with corporate criminals against the background of severe sanctions should negotiations break down (Ayres and Braithwaite, 1992). What we seek to accomplish in such negotiations is a package of private justice responses that takes net-widening to the highest form of the art: private discipline of responsible executives (including foreign executives who are beyond the reach of national criminal law), implementation of internal corporate compliance systems designed to prevent future violations, audited independent reporting on the performance of those internal compliance systems, industry-wide compliance education campaigns funded by the offending firm, compensation to victims of the offence, research and development to discover technological solutions to compliance problems (e.g., improved environmental control technology), and so on.

Brent Fisse and I are finalizing a fundamental rethinking of corporate criminal law that amounts to a net-widening strategy for controlling corporate crime (Fisse and Braithwaite, 1992). It seems to me that one can base such radical postures on a coherent theoretical position that is not contradictory to progressive positions one might want to adopt with regard to juvenile crime and domestic violence. Moreover, it is possible to render the net-widening one favours publicly accountable and fortified against abuse (see Fisse and Braithwaite, 1992, chap. 6). I will place on the table for consideration one possibility for such a theoretical position - republicanism. I would not suggest it is a theory that has all the answers. But of course I would not advance it if I did not think it had some answers that are not being supplied within the framework of the contemporary theoretical impoverishment of our field. So what is republicanism?

2 Republicanism Defined

Republican normative commitments direct us to take both political and economic inequality (Montesquieu, 1977, chaps. 3-4; Pettit, 1989) and community disapproval (Braithwaite and Pettit, 1990; Pocock, 1977) seriously. Sunstein (1988) advances four commitments as basic to republicanism: (a) deliberation in governance which shapes as well as balances interests (as opposed to simply doing deals between pre-political interests); (b) political equality; (c) universality, or debate to reconcile competing views, as a regulative ideal; and (d) citizenship, community participation in public life.

Consistent with these commitments, in *Not Just Deserts* Pettit and I (Braithwaite and Pettit, 1990) seek to define in a more foundational way the political objective republicans pursue. We develop a consequentialist theory that posits the maximization of dominion as the yardstick against which to measure the adequacy of policy. What is this dominion that we wish to maximize?

Dominion is a republican conception of liberty. Whereas the liberal conception of freedom is the freedom of an isolated atomistic individual, the republican conception of liberty is the freedom of a social world. Liberal freedom is objective and individualistic. Negative freedom for the liberal means the objective fact of individuals being left alone by others. For the republican, however, freedom is defined socially and relationally. You only enjoy republican freedom - dominion - when you live in a social world that provides you with an intersubjective set of assurances of liberty. You must subjectively believe that you enjoy these assurances, and so must others believe. Being a social, relational conception of liberty, by definition it also has a comparative dimension. To fully enjoy liberty, you must have equality of liberty prospects with other persons. If this is difficult to grasp, think of dominion as a conception of freedom that, by definition, incorporates the notions of liberté, égalité and fraternité. Then you have the basic idea.[1]

This conception of dominion as a target for the criminal justice system has two attractive political features for progressive criminologists. First, we show that it motivates a minimalism in state criminal justice interventions. This is the principle of parsimony. If in doubt, do less by way of criminal justice intervention.

Second, at the same time, dominion requires a highly interventionist state policy to secure equality of liberty prospects. This is the relational element built into the definition. When women or people of colour enjoy lesser liberty prospects, affirmative action, redistributive tax and economic policies are commended by the theory. So we have a theory that can require minimalism in criminal justice policy alongside interventionism in economic policy.

The principle of parsimony does important theoretical work. Pettit and I show that it motivates a theoretically driven incrementalism in criminal justice policy - actually a decrementalism. Republicans, we argue, are required to struggle politically alongside the budget cutting economic rationalists for progressive reductions in criminal justice interventions. The right level of punishment is not determined by the just deserts of offenders. The right level of punishment, according to the theory, is as low as we can take it without clear evidence emerging that crime has increased significantly as a result of cuts to the system.

Not Just Deserts argues that a consequence of implementation of this approach will be more equitable punishment practices than we have seen, or could ever see, by following competing philosophies. We argue that even though just deserts is based on a philosophy of equal punishment for equal wrongs (and republicanism is not), it is republicanism that in practice can deliver more egalitarian punishment practices. Because just deserts tend to be imposed successfully on the poor and unsuccessfully on the rich, a parsimonious policy will be more equitable than a policy of pursuing just deserts. Among other things, it will be mostly poor people who will be released from jail under a minimalist policy. Minimalist policies will tend to be more equitable than liberal desert policies because of the structural theory which we defend: Where desert is greatest, punishment will be least (Braithwaite and Pettit, 1990: 180-201).

3 Republicanism and Diversion

It follows from the principle of parsimony that we should have a presumption in favour of diversion, where diversion is a less intrusive intervention than formal punishment. Whether, in fact, diversion will be a less intrusive intervention than conviction and punishment is a matter for detailed empirical investigation in each context in which the question arises. A corollary is that we should have a presumption against net-widening where net-widening is taken to mean more intrusive interventions than formal processing policies would have delivered.

But the twin presumptions in favour of diversion and against net-widening are rebuttable presumptions. Rebuttal occurs by weighing the benefits to dominion from rejecting the presumptions. If net-widening will increase dominion more than the costs to dominion for those caught in the net - something that can be argued to be clearly true for many areas of business regulation - then the presumption against net-widening should be abandoned in that domain. One of the interesting features of dominion is that it is reduced when people are caught in nets of social control. So it requires us to balance the effects on dominion of those who are protected from crime against the effects on dominion for those who in some way have their freedom disciplined. It provides us with no simple algorithm for doing this. The theory merely supplies a framework for conducting debate that forbids voracious preoccupation with consequences on one side of the equation to the neglect of the other. Having set down this normative framework, let us now consider an explanatory framework I apply to problems of crime control.

4 An Explanatory Framework

Diversion risks counterproductive effects on criminal behaviour (and therefore on the dominion of crime victims) when diversion is transacted in a way I call stigmatic. This is why I think Günter Albrecht's paper in this volume is tapping into the crucial issue when it is looking at the effect of diversion on stigmatization. If, on the other hand, diversion is transacted in a way I call reintegrative, prospects for crime control are more likely to be positive. The emotion of shame is central to the understanding of social control processes relating to crime. The notion that shaming controls crime is an old one. But so is the seemingly contradictory notion that stigmatization makes crime problems worse. My book *Crime, Shame and Reintegration* (Braithwaite, 1989) attempted a theoretical resolution of this contradiction. Reintegrative shaming is posited as a shaming mechanism that prevents crime; stigmatization as a mechanism that increases the risks of crime by the shamed actor. Moreover, the partitioning of shaming mechanisms into two types, with these opposite effects, is advanced as a missing link in criminological theory. It enables us to integrate previously irreconcilable theories - control, subcultural, labelling, opportunity and learning theories.

Reintegrative shaming is disapproval extended while a relationship of respect is sustained with the offender. Stigmatization is disrespectful, humiliating shaming in which degradation ceremonies are never terminated by gestures of reacceptance of the offender. The offender is branded an evil person and cast out in a permanent, open-ended way. Reintegrative shaming, in contrast, might shame an evil deed, but the offender is cast as a respected person rather than an evil one. Even the shaming of the deed is finite in duration, terminated by ceremonies of forgiveness-apology-repentance.

Reintegrative shaming
1. Disapproval while sustaining a relationship of respect.
2. Ceremonies to certify deviance terminated by ceremonies to decertify deviance.
3. Disapproves evil of deed without labelling person as evil.
4. Deviance not allowed to become a master status trait.

Stigmatization
1. Disrespectful shaming, humiliation.
2. Ceremonies to certify deviance *not* terminated by ceremonies to decertify deviance.
3. Evil person, not just evil deed.
4. Deviance allowed to become a master status trait.

A crucial preventive effect of reintegratively shaming criminals occurs when the offender recognizes the wrongdoing and shames himself. Hence, a particular type of crime will be less common in a community when that type of crime is subjected to extensive and intensive reintegrative shaming. Extensive stigmatization, in contrast, will have equivocal effects on crime. On the one hand, it will reduce crime through the general deterrent effects of social disapproval. On the other hand, specific deterrence will be worse than a failure, because stigmatization will foster the rejection of one's rejectors and the formation of subcultures of resistance to the law.

Seeking to bring crime under control by community shaming seems more benign than relying on the punitive state. Shaming is not as oppressive as imprisonment. Nevertheless, shame can be a tool of extraordinarily powerful oppression. The most common and profound concerns that come to mind are not about shaming of crime, but concerns about the shaming of forms of deviance that are not criminal - unconventional political and religious views or unconventional sexuality. And the types of shaming of criminals which are most often raised as unconscionable are examples of stigmatization rather than reintegrative shaming. Reintegrative shaming, as a communicative, dialogic form of shaming that seeks to persuade offenders to disapprove of their own criminal conduct is not equivalent to ridiculing wrongdoers as persons by putting them in the stocks.

Even though reintegrative shaming has the virtue of being more respecting of persons than stigmatization, it can be oppressive. Just because it avoids the worst repressive excesses of the punitive state and the stigmatizing community, that is not to deny that reintegrative shaming is a dangerous game. Victims of violence, after all, are often ashamed of their victimization (Stanko, 1990: 55, 67). Republicans cannot support reintegrative shaming as the dominant crime control strategy unless they have a clear moral position on what should and should not be shamed. Pettit and I argue that conduct should never be criminalized unless we can be confident that its criminalization will increase dominion (the republican conception of liberty) in the community (Braithwaite and Pettit, 1990). Our contention is that republicans must reserve the reprobation of criminal conduct for conduct that passes this test. Republicans are therefore required to actively support the reintegrative shaming of conduct whose criminalization uncontroversially protects dominion (such as criminal acts of violence). They are also required to actively oppose the shaming of deviant conduct which poses no threat to dominion.

It follows that the republican will be required to support some forms of net-widening that amount to reintegrative shaming of offences that should be shamed. Let me give a case in point from Australian juvenile offending. In my home town of Canberra, domestic violence workers tell me we have a terrible, widespread, hidden problem of teenage sons assaulting their mothers. These days we talk a lot about domestic violence conceived as husbands bashing wives and children, but discussions at criminological conferences and in the popular press rarely focus on the shamefulness of sons who bash their mothers. Why is this? My hypothesis is that mothers tend to be the ones who are ashamed when it is their own sons who turn on them, and that we as a community are pretty supportive of this interpretation. The son's assault seems to the mother her own fault in a way that she may not perceive assault by the man she married as her fault. In a patriarchal culture, it is the job of the mother to rear her children right; so when they turn on her, that is as much a reflection on her as the son. There are three reasons, in my view, why a republican must support net-widening to mobilize community disapproval against sons who bash their mothers: (a) to tolerate this violence is to leave mothers unprotected against a very serious source of harm; (b) to tolerate this violence is to tolerate a patriarchy that strips mothers of dominion in the most fundamental way - there can be no equality of liberty prospects in a society in which mothers, but not other family members, must bear the responsibility and the consequences of violent children; (c) to ignore the violence of older sons is to leave unchallenged in the eyes of younger siblings the notion that violence is something about which we are allowed to be tolerant. These three reasons seem so profound in their implications for dominion that the adverse consequences of net-widening for the dominion of violent sons on the other side of the equation will be clearly less.

This does not mean that the republican has the green light for the most extreme vilification and punishment of violent sons. The principle of parsimony is still in play. The obligation of the republican is to find the least punitive, most-dominion-respecting way possible for protecting the mothers, while communicating the message that son-mother assault is a serious criminal matter (see Mugford and Mugford, 1991). If my explanatory theory is right, and of course it will not be in many particular contexts, that way will be reintegrative shaming rather than stigmatization or punishment. We as a community should seek to bring home to these sons that their behaviour is intolerable. This is not going to be accomplished if the police give the message that mother-son violence is something they tolerate by walking away from the problem, or by treating it as a matter for private dispute resolution rather than something which should mobilize public concern. But nor will mandatory arrest that risks stigmatization be a clever policy. Nor will putting him with a group of other violent sons to be lectured by a feminist on the evils of violence against women. To do this brings the criminogenic consequences of stigmatization together with the conditions for subcultural support from the other violent boys who are likely to reject their rejector (the feminist lecturer).

What reintegrative shaming recommends is mobilizing respectful disapproval from people whose positive regard the violent boy values. The job of the domestic violence caseworker, according to this strategy, is to find out who these significant others are, and to get them together in a problem-solving conference with the young offender. The objective of such a caseworker is to confront the unacceptability of violence, to discuss solutions to the situational problems that lead to the violence, to reason with the young person about exploitative attitudes towards his mother that underpin the violence, to give the young offender a dignified way of coming to accept that the violence is something about which he should feel genuinely remorseful and that he should want to change. The way to avoid a stigmatizing quality to the encounter is, in the words of Heinz Steinert's paper (this volume), to focus on the situation more than on reforming the person. When schoolmates are offering to take steps to avert the enraging situations at school that lead him to come home and take it out on his mother, when mates from the disco are offering to ensure that they cut down on their drinking to help with the problem, when the mother is promising to listen rather than provoke him when he comes home angry, when little sister is undertaking to interrupt him when his anger escalates and remind him of his promise to take time out to calm down, the risk that this will be seen as a degradation ceremony will be reduced. Even if some of the situational solutions are really not very fundamental to the causes of the violence, they help change the quality of the encounter away from a direct assault on the character of the offender. The message is communicated by the mobilizing of concern and help: "We still like lots about your character. We like you but we don't like this behaviour." So they work together on the situations that lead this essentially good person to do such a terrible thing. One respect, indeed, in which we do need to focus on the person (rather than the situation), contrary to Heinz Steinert's advice, is to assure the person that he is loved and/or respected. Moreover, we must be careful not to focus so exclusively on the situation that we communicate the message that we are morally neutral about the violence. Just as, according to Nils Christie's (1977) advice, we do not want our conflicts to be stolen by the police, nor do we want them to be stolen by a morally neutral situational crime prevention (see, also, Hackler and Garapon, 1987).

Really, I think Heinz Steinert was conceding all of this during the discussions at the conference when he referred to the importance of honour. The challenge is to analyse simultaneously the evil of the deed, the honour of the person and the ways of transforming the situation that leads to the evil deed. Competent human beings know how to manage this complex and subtle task. They do not need a degree in social work to be able to do it. The least competent of us have our moments of competence when we accomplish it. The most socially accomplished of us have our moments when we torpedo our own objectives by the contemptuous moralizing of the person-reformer. Let us next consider some places where reintegrative juvenile justice practices have made some headway.

5 Lessons from Wagga Wagga

In *Crime, Shame and Reintegration* I talked about reintegrative shaming and the successes of Japanese criminal justice. But successful pockets of reintegrative practice are to be found in all parts of the world. The communication of disapproval of violence within a continuum of love, respect and honour for young people is something that effective families accomplish probably in all Western countries. Reintegrative shaming, as I have said above, is not something that any of us is incapable of doing. While we have all done it successfully at some time, we are surrounded by a world of institutional practices that destroy reintegrative shaming with stigma, disrespect, humiliation and degradation ceremonies.

Some of the most interesting examples of institutionalizing reintegrative practices are to be found in the periphery of the world system. An Afghan criminologist at the University of Edinburgh, A. Ali Serisht, has told me of the institution of Nananate among the Pushtoon, the largest ethnic group in Afghanistan. The Nananate is a ceremony of reintegrative shaming where the criminal offender brings flour and other food and kills a sheep for a community feast. Often this will be held at the victim's house, where the victim will participate in cooking the food the offender brings. At the ceremonial part of the event, the offender will not be told that he is bad and in need of reform, but rather that "You have done an injustice to this person". However, the offender will be assured that "you are one of us and we accept you back among us". The police and courts have virtually no presence in communities that rely on the Nananate.

In my own region of the world, the Pacific, there are some strong instances of reintegrative shaming. Jim Hackler (1992) has written an interesting article on the reliance on reintegrative shaming in Fiji. New Zealand is the preeminent case of an industrialized society that has changed direction, jettisoning the institutions of stigmatic juvenile justice in 1989 to replace them with reintegrative institutions. The *Children, Young Persons and Their Families Act* of 1989 was landmark legislation that warrants the attention of all juvenile justice scholars (Office of the Commissioner for Children, 1991). It institutionalized diversion. During January-May 1989, 10,528 informations to take matters before the juvenile court were laid in New Zealand. For January to May 1990, this had dropped to 3,514 (unpublished police statistics quoted in Maxwell and Morris, 1990). There are fewer than a quarter of the institutional beds for young offenders that there were prior to the Act.

An important innovation under the Act is "family group conferences" as an alternative to the juvenile court. A total of 3,898 were held during the first 9 months of the Act. Even more interesting is that wherever the word "family" appears in the Act, Maori words for different types of kin groups also appear. The family group conference brings together the offender, the offender's family group, police, the victim and victim supporters where they are willing to participate. In the following discussion, I rely heavily on notes of conversations I have had with John McDonald, who was reporting on research conducted with Steve Ireland and Michael Hogan, and with Warren Young. I am told that wide interpretation of what constitutes a family group is allowed. Any type of friend or supporter of the offender might attend under this category, at the discretion of the Youth Justice Coordinator.

At these conferences, there is a lot of emphasis on ensuring that children who commit offences are held accountable. The word shame sometimes even comes up, I am told, quite an unusual phenomenon in the context of contemporary Western cultures where we are ashamed to be ashamed (Scheff and Retzinger, 1991). Shame is not the word used in official talk justifying the reform. "Encouraging young people to accept responsibility for their behaviour" is the preferred discourse. Obviously, it is a superior discourse to the discourse of shame for practical political purposes. It has been an important part of the surprising level of acceptance this reform has attracted from police in our part of the world, though not without considerable resistance as well. The Australian and New Zealand Police Federation carried a resolution at its 1991 conference supporting the New Zealand juvenile justice reforms. The philosophy of the conferences is to focus on the best outcome for the society, the victim and the offender - in Heinz Steinert's terms, to focus on the situation more than directly on reforming the person. Much of the talk about the situation, however, is about the offender "facing the consequences" of his or her actions, including the possibility of having to face the feelings of the victim. Stigmatization for past deeds is also avoided by a positive future orientation - reparation, community work, changes in patterns of leisure-time behaviour assisted by others at the conference are often agreed. Finally, ceremonies of apology and reconciliation with victims are regarded as important.

There are some innovative approaches to victim-offender reconciliation and community crime control. One case involved a Cambodian refugee who had experienced the horrors of Pol Pot. He felt he was being harassed and taunted by a young female who, with two others, broke into and damaged his restaurant, from which he was barely making a living. In addition to reparation to the Cambodian victim agreed at the family group conference, the young offender agreed to watch a video of "The Killing Fields", after which she agreed to "pass the word on the street" that there should be no more break-ins at the restaurant.

In my own country, reintegrative approaches to dealing with juvenile offending are not in the mainstream of criminal justice policy in the way they are in New Zealand. However, there have always been pockets of progressive practice - for example, juvenile court judges in central and western Australia dealing with young aboriginal offenders by diverting them to problem-solving with the elders of their community. A recent pocket of progressive practice has been in Wagga Wagga, the largest inland city in the vast expanses of Western New South Wales. Two case studies of reintegrative police cautioning in the Wagga Wagga police district written by Sergeant Terry O'Connell of the New South Wales Police appear in the appendix to this paper. These are both cases in which a family conference approach was used. Even more interesting, in that it breaks further from the limits of a "family" conference, is the approach the Wagga police adopted during a community furore over damage to property in high school senior breakup activity. The tradition of "muckup" activities for high school graduates got a little out of hand in 1991. A scavenger hunt was held in which a variety of types of property were stolen from local businesses.

The worst victim was a car-wash operator who suffered damage to advertising signs valued at $A3,000. The signs could not be repaired, had to be imported from the United States, and, as a result, a promotional campaign was cancelled, causing a person to miss out on a casual job for the duration of the campaign. When the local media picked up the story and the furious car-wash operator had his solicitor write to the police demanding action, some police felt they were under such community pressure that nothing short of laying charges would suffice. Instead, what the police tried first was to convene a meeting of all final year students at the school. At this meeting, the police explained the impact their actions had on the victim and was likely to have on a young worker who would miss out on employment. A representative of local businesses then addressed the students about how he and others felt about what had happened. The meeting led to the following procedure being written on a large blackboard:

1. Elect 5 representatives from the 240 students.
2. Report to a nominated location by 5 p.m. that day.
3. Return 3 outstanding signs.
4. Be prepared to meet with the victim, the company workers and police to work out an acceptable outcome.

The five elected students arrived at the car-wash, bringing three teachers and a parent with them. The dialogue occurred seated on the grass in front of the car-wash, in full view of an intrigued passing public. The police reported that

"The meeting dynamics could be described in the beginning as somewhat tense but by the end of the 1 hour session, the atmosphere was one of light hearted interactions and relief.

It appears after the Police left the school, the students have accepted collective responsibility, even though only about 10 students had actually removed the signs. They had also agreed to pay compensation with each student paying $15. They also agreed that it was necessary to issue an apology to the victim and the Wagga Wagga community."

At the meeting, it was agreed compensation of $A3,107.43 would be paid by the students (it was paid within two days), and that each student would work a minimum of 2 hours at one of the car-wash locations cleaning walls. The victim was fully satisfied with the outcome and delighted at the positive community support their business received for adopting such a conciliatory approach to the young people. The local newspaper ran a front-page story, "Students Apologise for Muck-Up Pranks", which fuelled a general community reaction of being impressed at the maturity of the students' response to the havoc they had caused. Apology and reparation transformed an angry community into a forgiving one, indeed one in whose opinion the stature of the students had grown. As the police report on the incident said: "The element of shaming effected all the students and the school. The positive affirmation within the community and the media to the students' response contributed significantly towards restoring the school and students' standing within the community."

Police standing in the community was also enhanced by the incident. The primary victim was so impressed that he made a donation to the Police-Citizens Youth Club in appreciation. The students and the school also expressed their thanks to the police and the media reaction was favourable. Of course, not all attempts at reintegrative shaming will have such win-win-win outcomes for offenders, victims and police. The purpose of the case study is merely to show that alternative models of reintegrative practice can be found and shown to be not only practical but capable of producing superior outcomes to traditional law enforcement. Demonstrating that they are capable of doing so in particular cases is no substitute for demonstrating empirically that they more consistently deliver protection of dominion than traditional enforcement.

6 Diversion in Perspective

I trust this paper will not create the impression that the most important policy implication of republican theory is diversion of the kind we have illustrated in Wagga Wagga. This is certainly a significant implication but far from the most significant one. The importance of shaming, according to the theory, is in preventing crime before offenders come to the attention of the criminal justice system. The importance of avoiding stigmatization is that stigmatization fosters criminal subculture formation. Elsewhere, I have argued that criminology places too much emphasis on state policies for dealing with offenders, once they have been so identified, as solutions to the crime problem (Braithwaite, 1991b). There I have argued that the types of crime that have become our deepest crime problems - domestic violence, white-collar crime and drink driving - have become the crimes that cause greatest harm because they are crimes that have been subjected to muted or ambivalent community disapproval. Fostering vibrant social movements against these forms of crime is the highest priority for reform. Ultimately, deeper cultural changes in respect for the autonomy of women that can be accomplished by the women's movement (and are beginning to be accomplished) are more important to responding to the problem of domestic violence than policing policies. The accomplishments of an environmental movement in constituting the shamefulness of environmental crimes is more important to protecting the environment than increasing the number of environmental inspectors, important as the latter is.

Progressive social movements are the important vehicles for crime control because they can tackle simultaneously the structures of inequality that cause exploitative conduct such as criminal violence and oligopolistic price-fixing (Braithwaite, 1991c; Dinnen, 1991) and the muted shame that allows offenders to excuse their crime. Moreover, there is a connection between the inequality effect and the shaming effect. The types of shame that have been most shielded from shame have been so shielded because of concentrations of power (Braithwaite, 1991b).

Even if long-term struggles for prevention via deeper cultural and structural change should be regarded as the main game, it is important that we have a theoretical position with some clear things to say about what to do with offenders after the event, when prevention has failed. I have argued in this paper that twin presumptions in favour of diversion and against net-widening are starting points for reaching such conclusions, so long as we are clear on the philosophy that should guide selective discarding of these presumptions. Then I have contended that diversion is likely to be an effective and desirable policy to the extent that the parameters of its implementation are reintegrative. Finally, I have given some practical illustrations of how diversion can be managed in a way that avoids stigmatization, while engaging offenders in a dialogue about the harm of their wrongdoing and how that harm can be remediated for the past and prevented for the future. Wagga Wagga, where England's dangerous classes and their descendants toiled during the 19th century to create one of the most efficient agricultural industries in the world, continues to be the centre of the criminological universe in the late 20th century! It is through spadework at sites like Wagga Wagga that one can begin to specify the conditions for successful reintegration ceremonies, a task to which Stephen Mugford and I are turning our attention.

Note

1 For the philosophers who are shocked by such a casual definitional gestalt, here is a formal definition:
"A person enjoys full dominion, we say, if and only if:
1. she enjoys no less a prospect of liberty than is available to other citizens;
2. it is common knowledge among citizens that this condition obtains, so that she and nearly everyone else knows that she enjoys the prospect mentioned, she and nearly everyone else knows that the others generally know this too, and so on;
3. she enjoys no less a prospect of liberty than the best that is compatible with the same prospect for all citizens."

Appendix

POLICE CAUTIONS IN WAGGA WAGGA
Prepared by Sergeant Terry O'Connell, 21 November, 1991.

1. WAGGA WAGGA INCIDENT

BACKGROUND:
15-year-old male offender was with a group of young people outside a Wagga High School, waiting to catch a bus. An incident in which the offender was hit on the foot with a stone by the 15-year-old female victim's brother resulted in an altercation between the offender and victim. The offender lost his temper and punched the victim in the face causing a black eye and swelling.

TYPE OF INCIDENT:
Assault Occasioning Actual Bodily Harm S.59.

POLICE INTERVENTION:
Statements were taken from the offender and victim. Offender admitted to the offence. The Detective in charge of the matter felt that in spite of the seriousness of the incident, there were a number of factors that supported the use of a formal caution. These were:
1. both families were well-known to each other, and in fact the offender's family had helped the victim's family over the years;
2. the offender had admitted the offence;
3. the offender had not been previously charged or cautioned;
4. the victim, the victim's family wanted the matter to be dealt with by way of conference;
5. it was felt more would be achieved for the offender, victim and their respective families than to proceed by way of formal sanction, i.e., charging.

CAUTION PROCESS:

The cautioning conference involved the following:

1. the offender, offender's mother, father and young brother;
2. the victim, the victim's mother, father and young brother;
3. the reporting Police Officer (Detective);
4. a Senior Constable as an observer;
5. Sergeant as the Cautioning Sergeant.

The offender was confronted about his actions, which he admitted publicly within the group. Everyone was provided with an opportunity of expressing what they felt about the incident and how in particular it impacted upon them. The offender's parents expressed embarrassment and shame about their son's actions. There was considerable emotion, blaming and excuses from both parties. Approximately 1 hour into the discussion, the victim's family started to express supportive sentiments about the offender, which basically said, "we still like him, we just didn't like what he did."

The mood of the discussions had turned from blaming and anger to one of support for both families.

OUTCOMES:

1. the young offender publicly apologized to the victim;
2. the victim was happy that she was able to tell the offender exactly how she felt;
3. both families believed that their relationships were greatly strengthened;
4. the young offender acknowledged that he needed to better manage his anger;
5. the young offender agreed to attend the Police Citizens' Youth Club for 20 hours to seek assistance with developing better skills and strategies for coping with his anger.

ISSUES:

1. it was likely that if the matter had been dealt with by way of charging it would have destroyed the family relationships;
2. the conference had the opposite effect in that it had strengthened these relationships;
3. there are considerable savings in not using the Courts;
4. the young offender is more likely to benefit from this type of intervention;
5. the victim and her family would have received far greater satisfaction than would have been possible at Court;
6. the Police involved have gained a valuable insight into how effective cautioning can be.

2. JUNEE INCIDENT

BACKGROUND:

The 12 year old male offender has a long history of problems that have involved school, family and Police. He is a product of a highly dysfunctional family and has experienced violence and trauma throughout his life. He is a fat boy and this becomes an issue at school because he is targeted by other children. On all the occasions he has come under notice, the young offender has been attempting to assault a teacher, other children or, as happened on the recent occasion, his mother. Many people within the Junee community were concerned about his behaviour and it has been suggested that the Police were not prepared to do anything.

The young offender had been seen by a number of welfare counsellors and other workers but generally this was ad hoc. The Police had a number of incidents which could have amounted to a caution, then charges, but because of the offender's young age, were reluctant to do so. The last incident which involved an assault on his mother, in which the offender threw a small iron bar, was yet another occasion when he was very angry and was not able to control this.

The Sergeant involved in this incident felt that the time had arrived when some formal process should be used.

TYPE OF INCIDENT:
Assault.

POLICE INTERVENTION:
Statements were taken from the offender, the offender's mother and the Family Support worker who had attended shortly after the incident. The Sergeant decided that the matter would proceed to a formal caution, even though the offender's mother was the victim. The caution was justified because:

1. there were a number of prior incidents which technically could have been dealt with by formal caution;
2. the young offender had not been previously cautioned;
3. the offender's mother wanted some formal Police intervention;
4. it provided a mechanism to involve other workers.

CAUTION PROCESS:
The cautioning conference involved the following:

1. the offender, the offender's mother and grandmother;
2. a school teacher, the school gardener;
3. two shopkeepers;
4. a Family Support Counsellor;
5. two workers from Department of Community Services;
6. an Army Major;
7. the Cautioning Sergeant;
8. a Co-ordinating Sergeant;
9. 4 other local Police who have dealings with the offender.

There was an attempt to assure the young offender that all of the "adults" involved shared a common interest, that is, they were concerned about his behaviour and the consequences that this behaviour was beginning to have on a number of different people within the community. All involved spoke about their experiences with the young offender, and, in the main, most of these experiences were very positive and supportive of the young offender. The issue for the young person was about handling his anger in a more appropriate way, and he acknowledged that he was not good at this. Whilst it does appear that, on the sheer weight of numbers, the experience would have been "daunting" for the young offender, it was a positive and useful experience because all those who attended were genuinely interested in the young person.

OUTCOMES:
1. the Army Major is to arrange a visit to Kapooka Army Camp (the offender has just joined the Army Cadets);
2. the Sergeant is to take the offender to the Riverina Youth Detention Centre to meet with other young offenders;
3. all the local people at the meeting offered to act as a reference point for the young offender;
4. the mother agreed to liaise on a regular basis with a newly developed network of people;
5. it has brought together all those involved with this young person but were acting alone.

ISSUES:
1. it provided the local community with an insight into the problems Police experience when dealing with difficult children;
2. it provided Police with an insight into how to effectively utilize resources within the community to assist with difficult young offenders;
3. it allowed the "gossiping" process to be turned about from a destructive to a constructive process, because a number of significant people were involved and this has ensured that only positive aspects would be promoted;
4. greatly enhanced the Police standing within the community;
5. has provided other Police with a range of new options in dealing with young offenders;
6. it demonstrated to all those involved that there is a high level of concern and commitment for young people within the community.

References

Ayres I., and Braithwaite, J. (1992). *Responsive regulation: Transcending the deregulation debate*. New York: Oxford University Press.

Braithwaite, J. (1989). *Crime, shame and reintegration*. Melbourne: Cambridge University Press.

Braithwaite, J. (1991a). The criminal class and the making and breaking of Australia. *Australian and New Zealand Journal of Criminology, 24*, 99-104.

Braithwaite, J. (1991b). *Inequality and republican criminology*. Paper presented at the American Society of Criminology Meeting, San Francisco. (Forthcoming in a Presidential volume from the conference edited by John Hagan, entitled "Crime and Inequality").

Braithwaite, J. (1991c). Power, poverty, white-collar crime and the paradoxes of criminological theory. *Australian and New Zealand Journal of Criminology, 24*, 40-58.

Braithwaite, J., and Pettit, Ph. (1990). *Not just deserts: A republican theory of criminal justice*. Oxford: Oxford University Press.

Christie, N. (1977). Conflict as property. *British Journal of Criminology, 17*, 1-26.

Cohen, S. (1985). *Visions of social control*. London: Polity Press.

Dinnen, S. (1991). *Big men, small men and invisible women - some comments on urban crime and inequality in Papua New Guinea*. Unpublished manuscript, Faculty of Law, Australian National University.

Fisse, B., and Braithwaite, J. (1992). *Passing the buck: Accountability and the control of corporate crime*. Unpublished Manuscript.

Grabosky, P., and Braithwaite, J. (1986). *Of manners gentle: Enforcement strategies of Australian business regulatory agencies*. Melbourne: Oxford University Press.

Hackler, J. (1991). Using reintegrative shaming effectively: Why Fiji has a juvenile justice system superior to the U.S., Canada and Australia. In J. Hackler (Ed.), *Official responses to problem juveniles: Some international reflections* (pp. 109-127). Euskadi, Spain: Onati International Institute for the Sociology of Law.

Hackler, J., and Garapon, A. (1987). Stealing conflicts in juvenile justice: Contrasting France and Canada. *Canadian Journal of Law and Society, 2*, 141-51.

Hughes, R. (1987). *The fatal shore: The epic of Australia's founding*. New York: Alfred A. Knopf.

Maxwell, G., and Morris, A. (1990). *A statistical overview of the juvenile offending before and since the Children, Young Persons and Their Families Act, 1989*. Institute of Criminology, Victoria University of Wellington.

Montesquieu, Baron de (1977). *The spirit of laws, abr. and ed. D.W. Carrithers*. Berkeley: University of California Press.

Mugford, J., and Mugford, S. (1991). *Shame and reintegration in the punishment and deterrence of spouse assault*. Paper presented at the American Society of Criminology Conference, San Francisco.

Office of the Commissioner for Children (1991). *An appraisal of the first year of the Children, Young Persons and Their Families Act 1989*. Wellington, New Zealand: Office of the Commissioner for Children.

Pettit, P. (1989). *Liberty in the republic*, John Curtin Memorial Lecture, Research School of Social Sciences, Australian National University.

Pocock, J.G.A. (Ed.) (1977). *The political works of Hames Harrington*. New York: Cambridge University Press.

Scheff, T., and Retzinger, S. (1991). *Shame, violence and social structure*. Lexington: Lexington Books.

Stanko, E. (1990). *Everyday violence*. London: Pandora.

Sunstein, C. (1988). Beyond the republican revival. *Yale Law Journal, 97*, 1539-1590.

Diversion in German Juvenile Justice: Its Practice, Impact, and Penal Policy Implications

Wolfgang Heinz[*]

1 Diversion in Juvenile Criminal Proceedings in the Federal Republic of Germany - Legislative Intentions and Their Implementation in Practice

Since the Juvenile Justice Act (*Jugendgerichtsgesetz;* JGG) of 1923, the possibility has existed in the German law of criminal procedure applicable to juveniles[1] to abandon criminal proceedings even where there is no reasonable doubt that a suspect is guilty of committing an offense. Instead of bringing a charge, the juvenile prosecutor can desist from prosecuting. Even after the charge has been brought, the *juvenile judge* may halt the proceedings instead of proceeding to a conviction (for German juvenile criminal proceedings, see H.-J. Albrecht, 1984; Heinz, 1990; Kerner, Galaway, and Janssen, 1986; Kerner and Weitekamp, 1984). These possibilities for procedural decriminalization are often referred to as (the German variant of) diversion in juvenile criminal law (see Blau and Franke, 1983; Herrmann, 1983).

The concept of diversion is rooted in ideas which developed in the United States of America. In its final report published in 1967, the "President's Commission on Law Enforcement and Administration of Justice" argued that in the case of juveniles the use of the formal sanctions should be reduced as much as possible. Instead less drastic forms of intervention should be used and new alternatives should be developed (President's Commission on Law Enforcement and the Administration of Justice, 1967). The second report of the "National Advisory Commission on Criminal Justice Standards" which appeared in 1973 defined diversion for the first time.

"...the term 'diversion' refers to formally acknowledged and organized efforts to utilize alternatives to initial or continued processing into the justice system. To qualify as diversion, such efforts must be undertaken prior to adjudication and after a legally proscribed action has occurred. In terms of process, diversion implies halting or suspending formal criminal or juvenile justice proceedings against a person who has violated a statute, in favour of processing through a noncriminal disposition of means (p. 73)."

This fundamental concept is also accepted in the Federal Republic of Germany where diversion is understood to embrace a number of very different penal strategies (see the sources cited in the bibliography of Heinz, 1989). Diversion in the wider sense is understood to include the totality of strategies of social control involving the criminal law, which aim to halt the proceedings as early as possible, and/or to impose the least onerous penal sanction (e.g. the replacement of custodial by non-custodial sanctions). In what follows diversion is understood as a strategy which is intended to ensure that a prosecution is not brought, even though the public prosecutor has established that there is at least a *prima facie* case against the accused.

In the German system of criminal justice the only diversionary strategies which are possible are those which use the procedural possibilities for the public prosecutor to halt the prosecution during the pretrial examination prosecutor or during the trial by the judge. Of particular relevance are the provisions relating to the halting of prosecution in sections 45 and 47 of the Juvenile Justice Act, which are applicable in proceedings against juveniles (that is, those aged from 14 up to 18 at the time of the commission of the offense) and young adults (that is, those aged from 18 to 21 at the time of the commission of the offense). German law excludes a number of means of diversion which, to a greater or lesser extent, are available in other countries. This applies in particular to "police diversion". The two provisions mentioned above apply to prosecutorial diversion (section 45 of the Juvenile Justice Act) and to judicial diversion (section 47 of the Juvenile Justice Act). One can therefore speak of a German variant of diversion. The following are characteristic of this type:

1. Both the material preconditions for a decision on diversion and the procedure for deciding whether to prosecute or not (prosecutorial diversion) or whether to halt the trial before proceeding to a conviction (diversion by the juvenile judge) are governed by statute; in several Federal States the statutory discretion of the prosecutors is more closely defined by guidelines,
2. a decision to divert may only take place after the suspect has been registered by the police,
3. a precondition for the decision to divert is that the prosecutor or the court confirm that at the respective stage of the proceedings there is no reasonable doubt of guilt,
4. the decision to divert may only be taken by the prosecutor or the judge,
5. referral to a diversion programme is not a precondition for halting proceedings,
6. the substance of the diversion decision is the halting of proceedings - with or without further measures; the primary objective is, therefore, the avoidance of a prosecution or a conviction and not the referral to a special diversion programme.

"Diversion" (or "informal halting of proceedings" or "informal sanctioning", which are used synonymously in what follows) serves various purposes (see Dirnaichner, 1990). In the case of juvenile and young adult accused persons, the objective is to diminish stigmatization and to provide increased opportunities for solving problems in order thereby to reduce the risk of recidivism - a risk which might be heightened by a conviction. From the point of view of the criminal justice system the objective is to lessen unnecessary social control and remove the burden of having to deal with petty offenses.

Although diversion means that in law there is no conviction, from the social scientific point of view a sanction is imposed, both because of the registration in the Federal Central Register (*Bundeszentralregister;* BZR) and because the juvenile has been assessed as having committed an offense with no reasonable doubt of guilt. Moreover, non-custodial sanctions can be proposed (e.g. restitution) or imposed (e.g. a warning, offender-victim mediation, community service, financial payments) as can be done after a conviction. From the point of view of the public prosecutor and the judge, diversion is an "informal decision", from the point of view of the affected party it is an "informal sanction".

It was suggested in the debates at the beginning of the 1960s in the USA that diversion represented a new departure in penal policy. In the German legal field this was certainly not the case. Diversion represents a return to old insights and legislative aims. Efforts to reduce to a minimum the damaging side-effects of formal criminal proceedings and convictions, particularly stigmatization and negative social consequences, did not come about for the first time as a result of the recent discussion about diversion. On the contrary, such efforts have been made in German legal circles since the end of the previous century.

These objectives were taken up by the German legislator and incorporated in the reforms to sections 45 and 47 of the Juvenile Justice Act by the First Juvenile Justice Amendment Act (*Erstes Gesetz zur Änderung des Jugendgerichtsgesetzes;* 1. JGGÄndG) of 1990, which strengthened them. In the justification of this Act the importance of diversion was emphasized:

"Investigations into the question of the extent to which it is important to renounce formal sanctions in favour of informal sanctions have led to the conclusion - at least with respect to petty and less serious juvenile delinquency - that informal decisions offer swifter, more cost effective, and more humane means of dealing with juvenile delinquency. This is also true from the point of view of penal policy considerations concerning prevention and avoidance of recidivism." (Government Bill for the 1. JGGÄndG [BT-Drucksache 11/5829]: 1).

Furthermore, the findings of more recent criminological research about juvenile crime and the effects of sanctions were grounds given for abandoning a "paternalistic" approach to juvenile criminal law:

"Recent criminological research has shown that juvenile criminality is mostly not a symptom of a lack of education, but is usually a deviation in the developmental process which disappears with approaching adulthood and is unlikely to recur. Juveniles should therefore be convicted in far fewer instances than the legislator required in 1953" (Government Bill for the 1. JGGÄndG [BT-Drucksache 11/5829]: 1).

The aims of the 1990 amendment to the Juvenile Justice Act correspond to the international tendency to expand and support diversion.

1. The 13th International Congress of Penal Law which was held in Cairo in 1990 (see Revue Internationale de Droit Pénale [1983, nr. 3/4] and [1985, nr. 3/4]) made diversion the subject of its proceedings and resolutions. In the resolutions of the Congress diversion is described as "a new and praiseworthy approach to current problems of the criminal justice systems".
2. The United Nations Standard Minimum Rules for the Administration of Juvenile Justice (the "Beijing Rules") provide that the possibility of using diversion should be considered where it is available.
3. The Committee of Ministers of the Council of Europe has declared its support for the further extension of diversion in juvenile justice in two recommendations (Recommendation nr. R [87] 20; Recommendation nr. R [88] 6).

The increased use to which the provisions relating to the abandoning of proceedings have been put has not been uncontroversial. In particular there has been criticism from three points of view:

1. Up to now there has been insufficient empirical support for the belief that diversion would ensure an equivalent or lower rate of recividism than would be the case with conviction.
2. It is feared that diversion is linked to a widening of the net of social control and a loss of the protection of the rule of law which is inherent in the "protective forms" of criminal proceedings. At least the danger is seen that diversion will lead to an increased burden being placed on the young people who are not diverted since it is feared that a "dual strategy" will lead to their being subjected to a harsher reaction than before.
3. More fundamental, but not empirically verifiable, is the criticism that the principles of the rule of law, in particular the presumption of innocence, are violated. The constitutional principle of the division of powers is also infringed if the provision of the Constitutional Law (*Grundgesetz*) that certain matters are reserved for the courts to decide, is undermined.

Whether and to what extent the empirical assumptions contained in the first two points of criticism are true can only be settled by appropriate research. Because of differences in overall conditions, findings based on foreign research cannot be summarily applied to German circumstances. Studies conducted in recent years by the author, which are described below (see also the studies by P.-A. Albrecht, 1990; Hering and Sessar, 1990; Kalpers-Schwaderlapp, 1989; Matheis, 1991; Pfeiffer, 1983), have demonstrated, however, that neither criticism has any empirical basis.

2 Research Projects on Diversion in Juvenile Criminal Proceedings in the Federal Republic of Germany: Research Subjects and Questions Posed

2.1 The Subject of the Research Projects

In order to establish empirically the answers to the questions mentioned earlier the Institute for Research into Legal Practice of the University of Constance has conducted several research projects:

1. *"Alternative Reactions in Juvenile Criminal Law":* The subject of this investigation, which was supported by the German Research Foundation, was a representative sample of all criminal proceedings in the State of Baden-Wuerttemberg which were dealt with in 1979 by the public prosecutors either under the terms of section 45 of the Juvenile Justice Act or by the bringing of charges under the juvenile criminal law. The study was based on data contained in the Federal Central Register in which not only all convictions, but also decisions not to proceed made under the terms of sections 45 and 47 of the Juvenile Justice Act must be recorded.
2. *"Educational Measures in German Juvenile Criminal Law"* (see Hügel, 1987): The subject of this investigation, which was supported by the Federal Ministry of Justice, was a national representative sample which was drawn from the databank of the Federal Central Register of those persons born in the years 1961 to 1966, who in 1980 had been sentenced to at least one non-custodial sentence recorded in the Register (directives, reprimands, disciplinary orders, i.e., restitution, apology, financial payments, or community service) or whose proceedings were dropped under the terms of sections 45 and 47 of the Juvenile Justice Act.
3. *"Reactions of the Juvenile Justice System and Recidivism"* (see Storz, 1992): This investigation, which was also supported by the Federal Ministry of Justice, was based on anonymous data from the Federal Central Register on all the juveniles registered there who were born in 1961.
4. *"A Cohort Study of Criminality and Penal Sanctioning"* (see Heinz, Spieß, and Storz, 1988): This pilot study for a cohort study, which is supported by the

German Research Foundation, is based on anonymous data from the Federal Central Register on all juveniles registered there who were born in 1967.

2.2 *Questions Posed in these Research Projects*

These research projects were concerned *inter alia* with the implementation of sections 45 and 47 of the Juvenile Justice Act, the factors determining sanctioning practice and the economic and practical advantages of informal as opposed to formal sanctions. They also compared rates of recidivism after the halting of proceedings under the terms of sections 45 and 47 of the Juvenile Justice Act (informal sanctioning) with those after conviction (formal sanctioning). Recidivism, defined as a further registration in the Federal Central Register[2] because of an offense (a felony or a misdemeanour) within a prescribed observation period after the original decision had come into effect, was examined closely. The criterion for evaluating recidivism was therefore renewed criminal conduct, which had been subject to informal or formal sanctions.

3 Results of Research on the Practical Implementation of the Possibilities for Diversion Offered by the Juvenile Criminal Law

The possibilities for halting a prosecution which are provided for under sections 45 and 47 of the Juvenile Justice Act have always been used in practice. It is noteworthy, however, that *a large increase* has been observable for some years (for an overview of the sanctioning practice in West German juvenile criminal law, see Dünkel and Zermatten, 1990; Heinz, 1986; Bundesministerium der Justiz, 1989a, b). Between 1980 and 1989 alone the proportion of persons subjected to informal sanctions expressed as a proportion of all those upon whom sanctions (both informal and formal) were imposed probably increased from 43% to 56% (see Table 1, Column 3). As may be expected, the proportion of "first offenders", defined as first registrations in the Federal Central Register subject to informal sanctions, is higher and has increased significantly in recent years. Of all the male juveniles born in 1961 and registered for the first time in the Federal Central Register during their youth, 53.5% were subjected to informal sanctions; for those born in 1967 the proportion was already 65% (see Table 2, Line 6). *The initial contact of first offenders - or, more precisely, of those about whom at least no reasonable doubt exists about their committing an offense - with the criminal justice system ends in the majority of cases with the halting of the prosecution rather than with a conviction.* In this way a subsequent conviction can also be avoided. As an analysis of the data of the "cohort study" showed, only one in seven of all "first offenders" in whose cases prosecutions were halted became recidivists while still juveniles in the sense that he oder she was convicted of a further offense (see Table 2, Line 9).

The halting of a prosecution under the terms of sections 45 and 47 of the Juvenile Justice Act does not mean, however, that a juvenile or young adult does not suffer any negative consequences. Apart from the fact that when it becomes known that a juvenile has committed an offense, there is a negative reaction from his oder her immediate social environment - parents, friends etc. - , the criminal justice system also usually imposes certain sanctions. The findings of the investigation into "Educational Measures in German Juvenile Criminal Law" show that the halting of the prosecution was linked in the majority (83%) of cases to a warning, a directive (*Weisung*) - particularly a work requirement - or an order (*Auflage*), in particular the order to make financial payments. It was also shown, however, that where the matter was disposed of informally, the sanctions imposed were less intrusive than after a conviction. The average number of hours of a work directive was less after a prosecution had been halted under the terms of section 45 of the Juvenile Justice Act than where the action had been taken under the terms of section 47 of the Juvenile Justice Act. This latter number in turn was smaller than after a conviction. The same finding was made about the amount of monetary penalties which were imposed (Hügel, 1987).

The *demands made on procedural resources* in cases which were disposed of informally as well as formally were also investigated. The *practicality* of formal and informal proceedings was compared in respect of the various directives and orders imposed from the point of view of non-fulfillment, the frequency of summonses to ensure fulfillment, and the number of admonitions. Hügel (1987) found that in terms of all three measures of practicality the informal procedure not only was not inferior, but was often superior, to the formal procedure. Difficulties were more common in proceedings which led to conviction than in informal proceedings. Disposal under the terms of section 45 of the Juvenile Justice Act resulted in significantly fewer cases requiring reconsideration. Admonitions relating to orders or directives had to be made least frequently where the prosecution had been halted under the terms of section 45 of the Juvenile Justice Act. So far as time for carrying out the orders and directives was concerned, Hügel found that for the same measures, the orders and directives were fulfilled more quickly in informal proceedings than after a conviction.

Until now diversion has generally been limited to first offenders and to petty offenses, as assessed by the nature of the offense and the extent of the damage. Hügel (1987) found that only a few factors had an influence on the decision to halt the prosecution. These factors related primarily to previous convictions, the number of alleged offenses and, in the case of property offenses, the extent of the damage. Additional, although less influential, factors were the age and occupation of the accused. Hering and Sessar (1990) found similar factors at work in the diversionary models applied in Brunswick, Hamburg and Cologne. The evaluation by Storz (1992) of the entries in the Federal Central Register of persons born in 1961 up to the end of the period of designation as juveniles, confirms these findings. The most important determinant of disposal (informal as opposed to formal sanctioning) was shown to be regional preferences for particular forms of reaction. The second most important determinant was the number of previous registrations and, after that, the nature of the offense.

It is noticeable that there were *significant regional and local differences* in the implementation of sections 45 and 47 of the Juvenile Justice Act. The comparison of the Federal States shows that there is significant variation. Thus, for example the diversion rate[3] in 1989 was 48% in Bavaria, and, in contrast, 87% in Hamburg (see Table 3).

These differences do not depend upon distinctive crime patterns or upon variations in the characteristics of the offenders in individual Federal States. As both Heinz, Spieß, and Storz (1988) and Storz (1992) have established in their evaluation of the entries in the Federal Central Register for all juveniles born in 1961 and 1967, the differences remain even when largely homogeneous groups of offenders and offenses are compared. Thus, for example, in the category of juvenile "first offenders" born in 1967, who were considered guilty of having "driven without a licence", 99.4% in Hamburg were disposed of with an informal sanction, whilst in Baden-Wuerttemberg in contrast only 36.9% were dealt with in this way (see Table 4, Column 4).

Regional differences in the implementation of sections 45 and 47 of the Juvenile Justice Act exist not only amongst the Federal States. They also exist within a State between the various state court districts. Heinz, Spieß, and Herrmann (1985) found that in 1979 within the 17 court districts of Baden-Wuerttemberg prosecutorial diversion rates for homogeneous groups[4] ranged from 9% up to 89%. These findings have recently been confirmed by a representative study of records of proceedings at 19 public prosecutors' offices in North Rhine-Westphalia, in which even more variables could be controlled. In a homogeneous sample of cases[5] diversion rates which lay between 39% and 99% were found (Ludwig-Mayerhofer, 1990: 213).

These discrepancies, which are revealed both in the comparison between states and between court districts within a state, are therefore not the product of characteristics of the offense or the offender, but appear to express different preferences concerning informal versus formal sanctioning.

The result of these different approaches to the halting of proceedings is that unusually high crime rates in a particular region are rendered less dramatic, i.e. the crime rate as a whole is evened out. In the research project "Alternative Reactions in Juvenile Criminal Law", it was found that, as a result of the regional differences in decision-making patterns, the local crime rates gradually, and in the final analysis completely, lost their significance as determinants of how often the formal sanctions of the juvenile criminal law would be used. No correlation could any longer be established between the crime rate[6] and the rate of conviction[7] (r=-0.01). The important question for penal policy which follows from this observation is whether the decision in favour of formal or informal disposal of cases has any measurable impact on the risk of further criminal offenses being committed by the juvenile or young adult.

4 Findings of Research on Recidivism Following the Application of Sections 45 and 47 of the Juvenile Justice Act

4.1 "Alternative Reactions in Juvenile Criminal Law"

As part of this research, which was carried out in Baden-Wuerttemberg, the recidivism rates of a representative and homogeneous group of first offenders who had committed less serious property offenses were studied. The extremely large range of decisions to halt proceedings - prosecutorial diversion rates ranged from 9% up to 89% - allowed a quasi-experimental design to be adopted. These natural differences, arising because of the variation in disposal strategies, were independent of the characteristics of offense and offender and so could be used to create groups with homogeneous characteristics.

The examination of recidivism on the basis of data extracted from the Federal Central Register for a period of three years after the first decision had come into force, revealed significant differences: When all subsequent registrations for felonies and misdemeanours - including traffic offenses - are included, the recidivism rate of first offenders who were only subject to "informal" sanctions is 7.9 percentage points below that of convicted offenders (see Table 5, Line 4). The differences become even larger when only further convictions excluding decisions under sections 45 and 47 of the Juvenile Justice Act are considered. The recidivism rate of the group of first offenders who were only subject to informal sanctions lay a full 11 percentage points below that of the convicted offenders (see Table 5, Line 6). The findings were also confirmed, at least in their overall tendency, when only those further convictions which resulted in sentences to juvenile or adult imprisonment were considered (see Table 5, Line 8). The statistical significance of the differences in this last case could not, however, be determined because of the small number of cases.

4.2 "Educational Measures in German Juvenile Criminal Law"

This investigation conducted by Hügel (1987) on the basis of a national representative sample, examined *inter alia* the extent to which recidivism followed after informal and after formal (but noncustodial) disposal of cases.

In order to conduct the study, the data which met the following criteria were drawn from the Federal Central Register:

1. Date of birth between January 1st, 1959 and December 31th, 1966;
2. at least one registration before the end of 1980.

For Hügel's analysis, a representative sample was drawn from the total data of proceedings relating to those juveniles born between 1961 and 1966, who in 1980 were involved in cases which were either disposed of under the terms of sections 45 and 47 of the Juvenile Justice Act or who were convicted and sentenced to a noncustodial sentence (a directive, a reprimand, or an order) under the Juvenile Justice Act. From a sample of 1,166 registrations, which was representative for Federal State, age and sex of the offender as well as outcomes of the proceedings, the court files and the records of the proceedings were consulted. Of these 1,134 were suitable for analysis. In order to determine recidivism and the previous criminal record of the juveniles concerned, the appropriate data were extracted from the Federal Central Register and evaluated. These data made it possible to gain an overview of an observation period of four years on average after the decision taken in 1980.

Groups of offenders were subsequently constructed, and the comparison of these groups showed that, where individual prevention was concerned, formal proceedings were not superior to informal disposal under the terms of sections 45 and 47 of the Juvenile Justice Act (see Table 6). This investigation was based on an *ex post facto* design in which for purposes of comparison, parallel groups are subsequently constructed in order to exclude possible selection effects. To this end the variables relevant to the selection of the form of procedure were first established (see above). The analysis of recidivism after controlling for these variables gave the following results:

"When both previous convictions and the nature of the offense are controlled for, it was shown ... that after informal disposal the number of new registrations for a recidivist offense in the Federal Central Register was less than after formal sanctioning ... With all groups of offenders constructed according to age, sex, occupation, previous criminal record and offense, and of non-custodial sanctions of all kinds (i.e. distinguished according to orders, directives, warnings and reprimands), a lower recidivism rate was found after diversion than after conviction" (Hügel and Heinz, 1987: 95).

4.3 "The Reactions of the Juvenile Justice System and Recidivism"

Hügel's findings, which had been based on documentary analysis, were tested and validated by Storz (1992) in this research project. Storz's study used all the entries into the Federal Central Register relating to persons born in 1961. The grand total (N = 90,599) included all of these juveniles who by the end of 1980 had at least one registration following decisions made under the terms of sections 45 and 47 of the Juvenile Justice Act, or following a conviction. The data which were extracted from the Federal Central Register in 1984 included all the informal and formal sanctions without exception which were reported to the Register for this birth cohort up until the end of their 22nd year.

Storz found that for persons against whom sanctions had been imposed for a first time the recidivism rate after informal disposal (under the terms of sections 45 and 47 of the Juvenile Justice Act) was 34.4% within four years, but after conviction, was 45.3%. The difference of 10.9 percentage points is statistically significant.

In order to control for possible selection effects further groups were created, which were comparable in respect of age group, previous criminal record and the category of offense.[8] These comparisons revealed two effects of diversion:

Firstly, it was shown that the rates of subsequent convictions were higher in all cases where the first sanction was formal (with the exception of criminal homicide[9]) than where it was informal. With the exception of two offense groups with poor representativity (sexual offenses and other offenses against the person) these differences are statistically significant for all classes of offenses.

When the groups studied were divided according to offense and the age and sex of the offender, the rate of subsequent registrations after sanctions had been imposed for the first time increased continuously in relation to the intensity of the first intervention. The intensity of the intervention was measured according to the rank order of halting the proceedings, conviction without custodial measures, conviction with juvenile detention (*Jugendarrest*) and conviction with juvenile imprisonment (*Jugendstrafe*). After the halting of the initial proceedings the number of subsequent registrations was below average. It was found, for example, that for juveniles where the offense was simple theft (*einfacher Diebstahl*) and the proceedings were halted, 27.4% were registered - including those in whose cases subsequent proceedings were again halted - as having offended again within three years. By contrast, in cases where there was a conviction as a result of a first offense of simple theft, 36.4% were registered again. This is 9 percentage points more than in the case of a decision to halt the proceeding (see Table 7, Line 6).

Secondly, it was shown that the type of sanction imposed on first offenders had an impact on subsequent decisions about sanctions. Where proceedings had been halted and the same person was subsequently charged with a new offense, this further case was also more likely to be settled by halting the proceedings than by a conviction. By contrast, where someone had already been convicted at a first appearance, he or she was not only more likely subsequently to have an offense registered against him or her, but was also more likely to be convicted again. This pattern holds for all sentences up to and including juvenile imprisonment. Where, under equivalent conditions - such as, for example, juveniles registered for the first time for simple theft - the first proceedings are dropped, only 2.9% are sentenced to juvenile imprisonment (with or without probation) on subsequent charges within the next three years. In contrast, where juveniles are already convicted at the first proceedings, they are twice as likely (7.2%) to be sentenced subsequently to juvenile imprisonment (see Table 7, Line 18).

The combination of these two effects of diversion means that juveniles who have proceedings against them dropped on the first occasion that they offend run a reduced risk of ever being subjected formally to sanctions. Of all the juveniles registered for simple theft in Hamburg - the Federal State with the highest diversion rate in Germany - only 20% had been convicted by the end of their adolescence. In contrast, in Rhineland Palatinate - the Federal State with the lowest diversion rate in Germany for young people born in 1961 - 65% were subsequently convicted (see Table 8, Column 4).

In a further analysis an attempt was made to examine the possible objection that the comparison groups were not adequately constructed on the basis of the variables controlled (i.e., age group, previous criminal record, type of offense).

The question was asked whether the discriminative power of a decision in regard to subsequent recidivism changes as a function of the degree of selection in the implementation of sections 45 and 47 of the Juvenile Justice Act. Selection might be dependent on an intuitive prognosis not accounted for by the statistical procedures and it could, therefore, be the case that the more selectively (i.e. the more cautiously) sections 45 and 47 of the Juvenile Justice Act were used, the greater the prognostic advantage for informal sanctions. The less selectively these reactions were used - in the most extreme case it was 91% - the less selective the decision regarding the recidivism rate would be. Against all odds the prognostic advantage in favour of the informally sanctioned is the highest where sections 45 and 47 of the Juvenile Justice Act were used the most (Table 9). Hence, we cannot explain the better recidivism rates after diversion on a notion that prosecutors or courts intuitively choose the "right" prognosis.

The same conclusion was reached in a further test which examined whether the differences in the rate of subsequent offenses could be explained by the different approach to selection adopted in the various States. If it is assumed that selections are made partly on the basis of "good" risks and partly on the basis of "bad" risks, then it may be expected in the States in which the number of halted proceedings is below average, i.e. those which select "good" risks, the rate of subsequent offending should be lower than in the States where selections are not made on the basis of "good" risks. This was not, however, the case.

The two tests therefore gave no support to the notion that the relation established between informal sanctioning and recidivism was an effect of the selection process. Nor could the lower recidivism rates which followed informal sanctions be explained by the assumption that in practice the "correct" prognosis was made intuitively, i.e. that only the "good" risks were selected. On the basis of the research findings there is *currently no empirical support for the assumption that - on the conditions of German Juvenile Criminal Law - formal disposal by a conviction is more effective as far as individual prevention is concerned than informal disposal. It follows that, from a legal point of view, informal sanctions should be preferred.* This is required not only by the principle of subsidiarity which governs German juvenile criminal law, but also by the fundamental doctrines of proportionality and humanity and the principles concerning social welfare responsibilities underlying the German constitution.

5 Results of the Research about the Widening of the Net of Social Control by Diversion

Finally, in the research project on "Alternative Reactions in Juvenile Criminal Law", a study was also made into whether the increased use made of sections 45 and 47 of the Juvenile Justice Act had led to an extension of the "net of social control". Building on discussions of this topic in the professional literature, the following three hypotheses were tested:

1. The "net-widening" hypothesis: Under this hypothesis, an extension of strategies designed to avoid the imposition of a formal conviction does not result in an accused person being "diverted" from the formal proceedings and dealt with informally, but instead results in an extension of the net of social control to persons who otherwise would not have been subject to sanctions at all.
2. The "sand heap" model: This model posits that as a result of the diversion from formal disposals (convictions) to informal disposals (halting of proceedings) there is a reduction of the severity of sanctions with respect to formal custodial punishments such as juvenile detention or juvenile imprisonment (see Pfeiffer, 1983: 224).
3. The "bucket" model: Under this model, the expansion of informal sanctions is merely the result of larger inputs from the police, i.e. the formal sanctions remain unchanged and only the increased number of suspects registered with the police is caught in the net of informal sanctions.

When the regional crime rates were examined, the conclusions in respect of these alleged effects of diversion were as follows:

1. With an increased use of diversionary measures the extent to which *formal* sanctions were imposed did show a tendency to decrease, but neither a reduction nor an increase could be found with respect to the total population subjected to formal *and* informal sanctions.

2. Where diversionary steps were taken at the level of prosecution, there was a tendency towards the imposition of fewer custodial sanctions. As far as the diversionary procedures adopted by juvenile judges were concerned, however, there was no evidence in the data of a reduction of the use of custodial sanctions. It appears more as if only non-custodial reactions have been shifted from the formal to the informal proceedings. Finally, no confirmation could be found for the proposition that the increased use of informal reactions had, in its turn, led to a tendency to impose more custodial sanctions.

Evidence that diversion led to a quantitative expansion of the "net of social control" therefore could not be found. From a *quantitative point of view* the findings are most compatible with the "bucket model", i.e. the effect of the increased application of sections 45 and 47 of the Juvenile Justice Act should be seen fundamentally as a diversion of the growing number of suspects registered by the police.

6 Summary and Conclusion

The possibilities for halting proceedings in German juvenile criminal law are intended to minimize the harmful side effects - particularly the stigmatizing and desocializing influences - of criminal proceedings and convictions. The legal position of the Federal Republic of Germany allows only diversion strategies which use the procedural possibilities for halting proceedings during the pretrial examination by the prosecutor or during the main trial by the judge. Section 45 of the Juvenile Justice Act, which governs diversion by the juvenile prosecutor, and section 47 of the Juvenile Justice Act, which governs diversion by the juvenile judge, are particularly important in this context. It is characteristic of these German variants of diversion that the preconditions and procedures for diversion are governed by statute, that a decision to divert can only be taken by the prosecutor or the judge, and that there is no requirement that the suspect be referred to a special programme.

The study made of the application of these procedural possibilities for the halting of proceedings revealed that in recent years they had been increasingly used in juvenile criminal law. In almost 56% of all those subjected to informal or formal sanctions the proceedings were informal, i.e. the cases were disposed of by the halting of proceedings. The percentage of first offenders whose first contact with the criminal justice system routinely ends without a conviction is even larger. However, in general, only first offenders and offenders involved in petty crime are reached by diversion procedures.

The extremely large regional differences in the application of sections 45 and 47 of the Juvenile Justice Act are noteworthy. These differences are not the product of differing characteristics of the offenses or the offenders, but appear to reflect preferences in respect of informal versus formal sanctioning.

Up to now there has been no reliable empirical confirmation as to whether the legislator and the practice itself of diversion are on the "right road" as far as individual prevention is concerned. It is often said to those who support diversion that juvenile offenders perceive the halting of proceedings as a form of acquittal and even a partial toleration of the offense. The research projects of the Institute for Research into Legal Practice of the University of Constance in recent years have been designed to settle this difference of opinion. Several research studies have been conducted using diverse data and various methods of controlling for the effects of selection. These studies have shown that there are at least two effects of diversion. First, for comparable groups of offenders and offenses, recidivism, measured in terms of renewed registration in the Federal Central Register, is regularly less frequent after proceedings have been halted than after a conviction. Second, it has been found that where a first offense was dealt with informally, a subsequent offense was also more likely to be settled by halting the proceedings than by a conviction. The combinaton of these two effects of diversion means that the risk of being subjected to repeated formal sanctions was reduced.

No empirical evidence could be found that the increased use of diversion had led to a widening of the net of social control in the Federal Republic of Germany. In the regions where diversion was used most often - and when the crime rates are controlled for - the incidence of persons subjected to sanctions - whether informal or formal - is not higher than in regions where diversion is used with restraint.

Practitioners, criminal justice administrators and the legislator, who appear to be increasingly receptive to notions of diversion, have therefore a sound empirical foundation upon which to increase and extend the use of, and the possibilities for, diversion.

Notes

* This article has been formerly published in "Studies on Crime and Crime Prevention", June 1992. Translation by Dirk van Zyl Smit.

1 For the period after 1949 attention is focused exclusively on the juvenile criminal law applicable in the Federal Republic of Germany as its territory was defined until 3 October 1990. In what follows no attention is paid to the juvenile criminal law of the former German Democratic Republic owing to the present lack of reliable data.

2 All convictions and all cases of proceedings dropped under the terms of sections 45 and 47 of the Juvenile Justice Act are registered in the Federal Central Register in Berlin.

3 The overall diversion rate in respect of decisions under the Juvenile Justice Act refers to the proportion of persons who have proceedings against them halted under the terms of sections 45 and 47 of the Juvenile Justice Act as a proportion of all persons who have

sanctions imposed against them under to the Juvenile Justice Act (i.e. both persons who are convicted and those who are diverted).

Similarly, the "diversion rate of the public prosecutor's office" refers to the proportion of persons who have proceedings against them halted under the terms of section 45 of the Juvenile Justice Act, as a proportion of all persons who have a pretrial examination into their case concluded either by a prosecution being brought under the Juvenile Justice Act or by the prosecution being halted under the terms of section 45 of the Juvenile Justice Act.

4 This group was composed of a sample representative for Baden-Wuerttemberg of 3,968 accused persons in 1979 who either had had prosecutions against them halted under the terms of sections 45 and 47 of the Juvenile Justice Act or who were convicted. This group met the following criteria:
1. Male juveniles recorded in the Federal Central Register for the first time who at the time of their offense were under the age of 18 years,
2. the first registered offense, without commission of a cumulative "secondary" offense, was a "petty" property offense.

5 This sample met the following criteria: a single instance of shoplifting, no previous convictions and also no registration in the central records of the prosecutors, a confession of guilt, and the value of the stolen goods not exceeding DM 50.

6 The number of suspects against whom the police had proceeded per 100,000 of the population of the same age.

7 Convicted offenders per 100,000 of the population of the same age.

8 A more extensive matching of the offender groups was not possible because of the shortcomings of the data. Except for the age and sex of the offender, the data in the Federal Central Register record no further characteristics. Only the actual criminal infringement and time of conviction are recorded as characteristics of the offense.

9 This finding, which in any event is not statistically significant due to the small number of cases (Chi^2 =.634, df = 3, p > .80), is not surprising. As a result of the large proportion of custodial sanctions the opportunities for committing further offenses during the postulated "recuperation period" of four years are limited, i.e. the rate of further offenses is necessarily below average as a result of the custodial sanctions during this period.

Table 1: Persons subject to informal sanctions in accordance with the Juvenile Justice Act (JGG)[1] in the Federal Republic of Germany[2] 1980-1989.

	All persons subjected to juvenile sanctions[3]	Ss 45 & 47 (JGG) total		S 45 II JGG (old)		S 45 I JGG (old)		S 47 JGG	
Year	N (1)	n (2)	in % of (1) (3)	n (4)	in % of (1) (5)	n (6)	in % of (1) (7)	n (8)	in % of (1) (9)
1980	239,000	102,000	43	30,000	12	27,000	11	47,259	20
1981	255,000	112,000	44	33,000	13	26,000	10	52,259	21
1982	270,000	118,000	44	40,000	15	23,000	9	55,886	21
1983[4]	276,000	125,000	45	45,000	16	22,000	8	58,675	21
1984[4]	261,000	126,000	48	52,000	20	19,000	7	53,721	21
1985[4]	244,000	123,000	50	58,000	24	16,000	7	49,636	20
1986	228,000	118,000	52	57,000	25	14,000	6	46,906	21
1987	209,000	107,000	51	54,000	26	11,000	5	42,074	20
1988	204,000	106,000	52	54,000	26	11,000	5	40,997	20
1989	195,000	109,000	56	60,000	31	12,000	6	37,367	19

1) In respect of sections 45 I and II of the JGG the statistics are estimates as the figures in the prosecution statistics had to be transformed from cases to individuals.
2) Figures for cases halted under the terms of section 45 of the JGG have only been available since 1989 for the whole of the Federal Republic of Germany (FRG), as it was before 3 October 1990. Statistics were not available for Berlin, Hessen and Schleswig-Holstein (1980-1984); Hessen and Schleswig-Holstein (1985-1987) and Schleswig-Holstein (1988). The figures for the States for which the statistics were incomplete were estimated on the basis of the population and inserted into the statistics for the entire FRG at the average for the other States.
3) Both persons convicted in accordance with the Juvenile Justice Act and persons whose cases were halted under the terms of sections 45 and 47 of the JGG.
4) Because of registration errors which led to fewer haltings under section 47 of the JGG being registered in 1983, 1984 and 1985 in Hamburg, the total number of persons subject to sanction and those dealt with under section 47 of the JGG may be to some extent an under-estimate.

Sources: Statistische Landesaemter of Baden-Wuerttemberg, Bavaria, Bremen, Hamburg, Lower Saxony, North Rhine-Westphalia, Rhineland Palatinate and Saarland: unpublished tables of the prosecution statistics 1980: Statistisches Bundesamt: Prosecution 1981-1989 (Working documents); Statistisches Bundesamt: Fachserie 10: Rechtspflege. Reihe 3: Strafverfolgung 1980-1989 (1986: corrected data).

Table 2: Rates of prevalence at the end of the juvenile years of male juveniles born in 1961 or 1967, as well as rates of transition in relation to the type of sanction.

Lines	Born 1961	Born 1967	Increase/Decrease Relative/Percentage
(1) Population*	511,700	523,300	+2.3%
(2) At least one registration	74,339	90,206	+ 21.3%
(3) Proportion of those sanctioned at least once formally or informally	14.5%	17.2%	+ 18.6% + 2.7%-points
(4) Proportion of those formally sanctioned	7.9%	7.7%	- 2.5% - 0.2%-points
(5) First informal sanction (N)	39,781	58,674	+ 18,893
(6) Proportion of those registered	53.5%	65.0%	+ 11.5%-points
Transition Rates			
(7) From first sanction to further registration	25%	27%	+ 2%-points
(8) From first informal sanction to further registration	23%	30%	+ 7%-points
(9) From first informal sanction to further formal registration	15%	15%	-
(10) From first formal sanction to further registration	28%	31%	+ 3%-points
(11) From first formal sanction to further formal registration	24%	26%	+ 2%-points

* Dec. 31, 1976 and Dec. 31, 1982, respectiveley. At these dates, there were 511,700 and 523,300 male juveniles aged from 15 up to 16 years in the two birth cohorts.

Source: Heinz, Spiess, and Storz, 1988: 647, Table 3; 655, Table 9.

Table 3: Diversion Rates[1)] in juvenile criminal proceedings in the Federal Republic of Germany 1981-1989

	1981	1982	1983	1984	1985	1986	1987	1988	1989
States	Percentages								
Baden-Wuerttemberg	36	36	38	43	44	44	43	45	49
Bavaria	42	40	43	46	45	46	45	47	48
Berlin	*	*	*	*	60	63	61	63	71
Bremen	75	72	74	75	75	76	77	77	82
Hamburg[2)]	76	74	75	71	81	84	85	85	87
Hessen	*	*	*	*	*	*	*	52	59
Lower Saxony	42	42	44	48	51	49	46	47	50
North Rhine-Westphalia	43	44	47	49	52	54	54	54	56
Rhineland Palatinate	37	35	33	35	40	44	45	50	51
Saarland	45	45	43	42	41	49	55	52	53
Schleswig-Holstein	*	*	*	*	*	*	*	*	64
All States:	44	43	45	48	51	52	52	53	56

* Missing data.

1) Diversion rates: Proportion of cases where proceedings were halted under sections 45 and 47 of the JGG (persons diverted) as a proportion to all persons subject to sanctions of the Juvenile Criminal Law (persons convicted and diverted).
The number of persons diverted was recalculated from the number of proceedings recorded in the prosecutorial statistics, in proportion to the number of persons involved. This was done on the basis of the relation between proceedings halted under sections 153a of thc Code of Criminal Procedure (StPO) and 45 (1) of the JGG and the number of persons for whom the conditional halting of proceedings was the most serious form of disposal.

2) In 1983, 1984 and 1985 there were technical difficulties with the recast of statistics in the city state of Hamburg. It was not possible to recast the statistics for 1983-1985. The statistics for the halting of prosecutions under section 47 of the JGG were affected inter alia by this error with the result that the figures for 1984 and 1985 were significantly below those of the previous years. The diversion rates for Hamburg appear therefore to be underestimates - at least for these two years.

Sources: Statistisches Bundesamt (Ed.), Staatsanwaltschaften 1981-1989 (Working documents); Statistisches Bundesamt (Ed.), Strafverfolgung 1981-1989 (1986: corrected data) by States (unpublished tables).

Table 4: Percentage of informal sanctions imposed in cases of driving without a licence and theft in respect of youths sanctioned for the first time. 1967 Birth cohort.

	Persons sanctioned		Driving without a licence[2]		Theft[1]	
	N	Informal (in % of 1)	n	Informal (in % of 3)	n	Informal (in % of 5)
States	(1)	(2)	(3)	(4)	(5)	(6)
Baden-Wuerttemberg	16,743	53.2	3,162	*36.9*	6,251	*40.5*
Bavaria	18,006	65.2	3,872	70.6	8,147	59.9
Berlin	3,888	86.1	184	96.2	2,570	85.8
Bremen	1,692	91.7	153	94.8	994	90.9
Hamburg[2]	3,442	*92.9*	485	*99.4*	1,895	*92.6*
Hessen	9,353	70.2	1,912	68.7	4,451	68.1
Lower Saxony	15,614	70.0	3,610	74.4	7,000	64.6
North Rhine-Westphalia	34,141	68.4	7,576	78.3	16,711	63.6
Rhineland Palatinate	5,774	*48.5*	1,435	48.6	2,607	44.4
Saarland	1,584	66.4	225	94.2	950	64.5
Schleswig-Holstein	5,575	82.1	840	90.0	3,091	80.2
Missing Data:	55					
Total:	115,867	67.4	23,454	69.5	54,667	63.5

1) Sections 242, 243, 244, 247, 248a StGB (Criminal Code).
2) Section 21 StVG (Road Traffic Act).

Source: Heinz, Spiess, and Storz, 1988: 653, Table 8.

Table 5: Recidivism within three years after decisions under sections 45 and 47 of the JGG and after conviction.
Results for juvenile males registered for the first time for minor property offenses[1]) in Baden-Wuerttenberg.

	Nature of the first decision		
	Ss 45 and 47 JGG	Concivtions	Total
(1) Persons sanctioned (N)	475	364	839
(2) *Percentage sanctioned*	*56.6*	*43.4*	*100*
(3) Persons subsequently subject to proceedings[2])	115	117	232
(4) *Percentage* (a) *of persons subsequently subject to proceedings*[2])	*24.2*	*32.1*	*27.7*
(5) Persons subsequently convicted[3]) (N)	89	108	197
(6) *Percentage* (b) *of persons subsequently convicted*[3])	*18.7*	*29.7*	*23.5*
(7) Persons subsequently sentenced to imprisonment[4]) (N)	17	20	37
(8) *Percentage of persons subsequently sentenced to imprisonment*[4])	*3.6*	*5.5*	*4.4*

(a) $Chi^2 = 6.091$; $p < .01$.
(b) $Chi^2 = 13.109$; $p < .01$.

1) Offenses against sections 242, 243(2), 246, 248a, 248b, 248c, 259, 263, 265a, 266, 267, 303, 304 and 309 StGB (Criminal Code).
2) Subsequent decisions under sections 45 and 47 of the JGG or convictions.
3) Only convictions without decisions under sections 45 and 47 of the JGG.
4) Sentences to juvenile or adult imprisonment.

Source: Heinz, W.; Spiess, G.; Herrmann, H.-J.: Reaktionsalternativen im Jugendstrafrecht. Determinanten und Auswirkungen unterschiedlicher Strategien der Strafverfolgung bei jugendlichen Erst- und Bagatelltätern. 2nd Interim Report. Unpublished manuscript, Constance 1985.

Table 6: Recidivism after decisions under sections 45 and 47 of the JGG and after conviction. Results of a documentary analysis of a representative sample of juveniles born in 1961-1966, who are registered in the Federal Central Register (N = 1134).

1. Subsequent decisions	Total n	S 45 JGG %	S 47 JGG %	Convict. %
1.1 Total[1)]	484	35.3	39.6	49.8
1.2 without previous record[2)]	326	31.8	33.7	41.6
1.3 with previous record[3)]	158	66.7	67.9	69.5
2. Recividism (formal conviction)				
Total[4)]	285	17.0	21.1	33.4
3. Recividists without previous record in cases of				
3.1 Driving without a licence[5)]	249	30.8	29.6	40.2
3.2 Theft[6)]	352	31.7	40.6	40.8
3.3 Traffic offenses[7)]	106	22.2	19.2	30.2
3.4 Other property offenses[8)]	106	52.0	37.2	55.3
4. Recividism in the case of property offenses				
	n	Ss 45, 47 JGG		Convict.
4.1 Pupils in further education[9)]	246	27.2		29.0
4.2 Pupils in secondary schools and in schools for educationally subnormal[10)]	209	50.0		50.0
4.3 Apprentices/skilled workers[11)]	365	46.3		41.7
4.4 Unemployed/unskilled workers[12)]	170	40.9		64.0

1) Chi^2 =	18.6; $p < .01$	2) Chi^2 =	7.6; $p < .05$
3) Chi^2 =	.1; $p > .05$	4) Chi^2 =	33.8; $p < .01$
5) Chi^2 =	3.8; $p > .05$	6) Chi^2 =	2.8; $p > .05$
7) Chi^2 =	1.3; $p > .05$	8) Chi^2 =	2.9; $p > .05$
9) Chi^2 =	.0; $p > .05$	10) Chi^2 =	.0; $p > .05$
11) Chi^2 =	.3; $p > .05$	12) Chi^2 =	2.1; $p > .05$

Source: Hügel, 1987: 62 et seq.

Table 7: Nature of the subsequent decision made within three years in relation to the initial sanction imposed on juveniles for simple theft[1)] (1961 Birth cohort)

	Nature of first decision				
Offense Group, Nature of subsequent decision (total)	Informal total	Formal total	Formal Non Custodial	total including Juvenile Detention	Juvenile Imprisonment
(1) Persons sanctioned (32,661)	18,293	14,368	11,802	2,448	118
(2) *Proportion of offense group (100%)*	*56.0*	*44.0*	*36.1*	*7.5*	*0.4*
(3) Persons **not** subsequently subject to proceedings (22,411)	13,280	9,131	7,860	1,239	32
(4) *Persons not subsequently subject to sanctions as percentage of line 1 (68.6)*	*72.6*	*63.6*	*66.6*	*50.6*	*27.1*
(5) Persons subject to at least one **subsequent sanction** (10,250)	5,013	5,237	3,942	1,209	86
(6) *Persons subject to at least one subsequent sanction as percentage of line 1 (31.4)*	*27.4*	*36.4*	*33.4*	*49.4*	*72.9*
(7) Persons subject to at least one **informal subsequent** sanction (3,630)	2,268	1,362	1,030	325	7
(8) *Persons subject to at least one informal subsequent sanction as percentage of line 5 (35.4)*	*45.2*	*26.0*	*26.1*	*26.9*	*8*
(9) Persons subject to at least one **formal subsequent** sanction (8,198)	3,570	4,628	3,448	1,095	85
(10) *Persons subject to at least one formal subsequent sanction as percentage of line 5 (80.0)*	*71.2*	*88.4*	*87.5*	*90.6*	*98.8*
(11) Under sections 45 and 47 of the JGG (2,052)	1,443	609	494	114	1
(12) *Under sections 45 and 47 of the JGG as percentage of line 1 (6.3)*	*7.9*	*4.2*	*4.2*	*4.7*	*0.8*

(contd. on next page)

(Table 7 contd.)

Nature of the most serious subsequent decision.

(13) Formal non-custodial (3,804)	1,813	1,991	1,649	332	10
(14) *Formal non-custodial as percentage of line 1 (11.6)*	*9.9*	*13.9*	*14.0*	*13.6*	*8.5*
(15) Juvenile detention (2,824)	1,226	1,598	1,173	417	8
(16) *Juvenile detention as percentage of line 1 (8.6)*	*6.7*	*11.1*	*9.9*	*17.0*	*6.8*
(17) Juvenile and adult imprisonment (1,570)	531	1,039	626	346	67
(18) *Juvenile and adult imprisonment as percentage of line 1 (4.1)*	*2.9*	*7.2*	*5.3*	*14.1*	*56.8*

1) Sections 242, 247, 248a StGB (Criminal Code).

Results of the test for significance for the comparison between the rate of *subsequent decisions* for informal and non-custodial formal sanctions. (The category "juvenile imprisonment" were not taken into account for the calculation of the level of significance on account of the small numbers in these categories at the time.):
$Chi^2 = 460.4$, $df = 2$, $p < .01$.

Results of the test for significance for the comparison between the nature of the *most serious subsequent decisions* for informal and non-custodial formal sanctions. (The category "juvenile imprisonment" were not taken into account for the calculation of the level of significance on account of the small numbers in these categories at the time.):
$Chi^2 = 686.7$, $df = 6$, $p < .01$.

Source: Storz, 1992, Table 14, Table 15.

Table 8: Diversionary effects of the type of sanctions imposed in specific states on persons born in 1961 and convicted of simple theft[1] as first offenders whilst juveniles, after a follow-up period of three years from the first decision. (Missing data for n = 1)

	Total number of juvenile sanctions	Diversion rates at first decision[2]	Juveniles sanctioned formally within three years	Persons subject to formal sanctions as juveniles as percentage of all persons sanctioned
	N	in %	n	in %
States	(1)	(2)	(3)	(4)
Baden-Wuerttemberg	4,020	43.4	2,637	65.6
Bavaria	4,610	56.0	2,578	55.9
Berlin	1,686	84.9	478	28.4
Bremen	584	88.9	139	23.8
Hamburg[2]	878	90.8	176	20.0
Hessen	2,533	63.6	1,197	47.3
Lower Saxony	4,149	46.3	2,658	64.1
North Rhine-Westphalia	10,061	50.8	6,056	60.2
Rhineland Palatinate	1,727	43.2	1,122	65.0
Saarland	688	66.4	310	45.1
Schleswig-Holstein	1,724	79.9	587	34.0

1) Sections 242, 247, 248a StGB (Criminal Code).
2) Proportion of decisions under sections 45 and 47 of the JGG, of all juveniles subjected to sanctions as first offenders for simple theft.

Source: Storz, 1992, Table 22.

Table 9: Subsequent decisions within three years imposed on juveniles in various States in relation to the first sanction for simple theft[1] (1961 Birth cohort: missing data for n = 1)

	First decision		At least one further decision after the first decision		Prognostic advantage
	N	Informal (in %)	Informal (in %)	Formal (in %)	(4)-(3)
States	(1)	(2)	(3)	(4)	(5)
Baden-Wuerttemberg[2]	4,020	43.4	26.9	34.2	7.3
Bavaria[3]	4,610	56.0	27.5	35.1	7.6
Berlin[4]	1,686	84.9	25.1	47.1	22.0
Bremen[5]	584	88.9	33.5	58.5	25.0
Hamburg[6]	878	90.8	29.5	60.5	31.0
Hessen[7]	2,533	63.6	25.1	36.4	11.3
Lower Saxony[8]	4,149	46.3	29.4	34.8	5.4
North Rhine-Westphalia[9]	10,061	50.8	29.0	38.2	9.2
Rhineland Palatinate[10]	1,727	43.2	24.3	31.3	7.0
Saarland[11]	688	66.4	18.6	32.0	13.4
Schleswig-Holstein[12]	1,724	79.9	25.6	45.2	19.6
Missing data	23	4.3			

1) Sections 242, 247, 248a StGB (Criminal Code).

Results of the significance test for the comparison between the rate of subsequent decisions for informal and formal sanctions.

2) Baden-Wuerttemberg $Chi^2 = 24.5$, df = 1, $p < .01$
3) Bavaria $Chi^2 = 36.3$, df = 1, $p < .01$
4) Berlin $Chi^2 = 51.4$, df = 1, $p < .01$
5) Bremen $Chi^2 = 15.5$, df = 1, $p < .01$
6) Hamburg $Chi^2 = 3.6$, df = 1, $p > .05$
7) Hessen $Chi^2 = 28.5$, df = 1, $p < .01$
8) Lower Saxony $Chi^2 = 13.9$, df = 1, $p < .01$
9) North Rhine-Westphalia $Chi^2 = 95.8$, df = 1, $p < .01$
10) Rhineland Palatinate $Chi^2 = 10.3$, df = 1, $p < .01$
11) Saarland $Chi^2 = 15.6$, df = 1, $p < .01$
12) Schleswig-Holstein $Chi^2 = 51.2$, df = 1, $p < .01$

Source: Storz, 1992, Table 19.

References

Albrecht, H.-J. (1984). Role and response of the juvenile justice system to delinquency in the Federal Republic of Germany. *Proceedings of the Third Asian-Pacific Conference on Juvenile Delinquency.* Seoul: San Jose, 63-87.

Albrecht, P.-A. (Ed.) (1990). *Informalisierung des Rechts. Empirische Untersuchungen zur Handhabung und zu den Grenzen der Opportunität im Jugendstrafrecht.* Berlin, New York: de Gruyter.

Blau, G., and Franke, E. (1983). Diversion and mediation. Federal Republic of Germany. *Revue Internationale de Droit Pénal, 54,* 929-940.

Bundesministerium der Justiz (Ed.) (1989). *"Diversion" im deutschen Jugendstrafrecht. Informelle Erledigungen und ambulante Maßnahmen.* Bonn: Bundesministerium der Justiz.

Bundesministerium der Justiz (Ed.) (1989). *Jugendstrafrechtsreform durch die Praxis. Informelle Reaktionen und neue ambulante Maßnahmen auf dem Prüfstand. Konstanzer Symposium.* Bonn: Bundesministerium der Justiz.

Dirnaichner, U. (1990). *Der nordamerikanische Diversionsansatz und rechtliche Grenzen seiner Rezeption im bundesdeutschen Jugendstrafrecht.* Frankfurt a.M., Bern, New York, Paris: Lang.

Dünkel, F., and Zermatten, J. (Eds.) (1990). *Nouvelles tendances dans le droit pénal des mineurs. Médiation, travail au profit de la communauté et traitement intermédiaire.* Freiburg: Max Planck-Institut für ausländisches und internationales Strafrecht.

Heinz, W. (1986). Jugendgerichtsbarkeit in der Bundesrepublik Deutschland. In: H.-J. Kerner, B. Galaway, and H. Janssen (Eds.), *Jugendgerichtsbarkeit in Europa und Nordamerika - Aspekte und Tendenzen* (pp. 527-641). Schriftenreihe der DVJJ, H. 16. München: Deutsche Vereinigung für Jugendgerichte und Jugendgerichtshilfen e.V.

Heinz, W. (1989). Auswahlbibliographie des deutschsprachigen Schrifttums seit 1980 zu Diversion und ambulanten Maßnahmen im deutschen Jugendstrafrecht. In: Bundesministerium der Justiz (Ed.), *"Diversion" im deutschen Jugendstrafrecht. Informelle Erledigungen und ambulante Maßnahmen. Thesen, Empfehlungen, Bibliographie* (pp. 65-135). Bonn: Bundesministerium der Justiz.

Heinz, W. (1990). Jugendgerichtsbarkeit und Jugendstrafvollzug. In: O. Speck and K.-R. Martin (Eds.), *Handbuch der Sonderpädagogik. Bd. 10. Sonderpädagogik und Sozialarbeit* (pp. 487-527). Berlin: Edition Marhold im Wissenschaftsverlag Spiess.

Heinz, W. (1990). Diversion im Jugendstrafverfahren. Aktuelle kriminalpolitische Bestrebungen im Spiegel empirischer Untersuchungen. *Zeitschrift für Rechtspolitik, 23,* 7-11.

Heinz, W., Spieß, G., and Herrmann, H.-J. (1985). *Reaktionsalternativen im Jugendstrafrecht. Determinanten und Auswirkungen unterschiedlicher Strategien der Strafverfolgung bei jugendlichen Erst- und Bagatelltätern.* 2nd (unpublished) preliminary report. Konstanz.

Heinz, W., Spieß, G., and Storz, R. (1988). Prävalenz und Inzidenz strafrechtlicher Sanktionierung im Jugendalter. Ergebnisse einer Untersuchung von zwei Sanktioniertenkohorten anhand von Daten des Bundeszentralregisters. In: G. Kaiser, H. Kury, and H.-J. Albrecht (Eds.), *Kriminologische Forschung in den 80er Jahren* (pp.

631-660). Freiburg: Max Planck-Institut für ausländisches und internationales Strafrecht.

Hering, E., and Sessar, K. (1990). *Praktizierte Diversion. Das "Modell Lübeck" sowie die Diversionsprogramme in Köln, Braunschweig und Hamburg.* Pfaffenweiler: Centaurus.

Herrmann, J. (1983). Diversion and mediation. Federal Republic of Germany. *Revue Internationale de Droit Pénal, 54,* 1043-1058.

Hügel, C. (1987). Ergebnisse der empirischen Untersuchung. In: W. Heinz and C. Hügel, *Erzieherische Maßnahmen im deutschen Jugendstrafrecht* (pp. 21-91). 3 ed. Bonn: Bundesministerium der Justiz.

Hügel, C., and Heinz, W. (1987). Ertrag und Folgerungen der Untersuchung über Bestandsaufnahme und Determinanten der Sanktionspraxis, Verfahrensökonomie und Praktikabilität, Legalbewährung und Wirkungsanalyse. In: W. Heinz, and C. Hügel, *Erzieherische Maßnahmen im deutschen Jugendstrafrecht* (pp. 93-96). 3 ed. Bonn: Bundesministerium der Justiz.

Kalpers-Schwaderlapp, M. (1989). *Diversion to nothing. Eine vergleichende Rückfalluntersuchung der gemäß § 45 Abs. 2 Nr. 2 JGG eingestellten bzw. im förmlichen Jugendverfahren abgeurteilten einfachen Diebstahlsverfahren von Jugendlichen in den Landgerichtsbezirken Koblenz und Mainz.* Diss. iur. Mainz.

Kerner, H.-J., Galaway, B., and Janssen, H. (Eds) (1986). *Jugendgerichtsbarkeit in Europa und Nordamerika - Aspekte und Tendenzen.* Schriftenreihe der DVJJ, H. 16. München: Deutsche Vereinigung für Jugendgerichte und Jugendgerichtshilfen e.V.

Kerner, H.-J., and Weitekamp, E. (1984). The Federal Republic of Germany. In: M. W. Klein (Ed.), *Western systems of juvenile justice* (pp. 147-169). Beverly Hills, London, New Delhi: Sage.

Ludwig-Mayerhofer, W. (1990). Die staatsanwaltliche Diversionspraxis im Jugendstrafrecht - Eine landesweite Aktenuntersuchung in 19 Staatsanwaltschaften Nordrhein-Westfalens. In: P.-A. Albrecht (Ed.), *Informalisierung des Rechts. Empirische Untersuchungen zur Handhabung und zu den Grenzen der Opportunität im Jugendstrafrecht* (pp. 47-225). Berlin, New York: de Gruyter.

Matheis, B. (1991). *Intervenierende Diversion. Eine empirische Untersuchung unterschiedlicher Verfahrens- und Reaktionsalternativen in Jugendstrafverfahren im Landgerichtsbezirk Kaiserslautern.* Diss. iur. Mainz.

National Advisory Commission on Criminal Justice Standards and Goals (1973). *Task Force on Corrections.* Washington, D.C.

Pfeiffer, C. (1983). *Jugendgerichtsverfahren und Kriminalprävention. Jugendrichterliches Handeln vor dem Hintergrund des Brücke-Projekts.* Köln: Heymanns.

President's Commission on Law Enforcement and Administration of Justice (Ed.) (1967). *Task Force Report: Juvenile Delinquency and Youth Crime.* Washington, D.C.

Storz, R. (1992). *Jugendstrafrechtliche Reaktionen und Legalbewährung. Abschlußbericht für das Bundesministerium der Justiz.* Bonn: Bundesministerium der Justiz.

Diversion in Juvenile Justice: Theoretical Expectations and Preliminary Results of a Treatment Outcome Evaluation of Juvenile Offenders

Günter Albrecht

1 Introduction

Supporters of diversion among the social sciences do not have an easy task in the Federal Republic of Germany: On the one hand, a whole series of different programs claim success - mostly on the basis of rather problematic self-evaluations by major proponents of diversion projects (see, e.g., Pfeiffer, 1983) - while, on the other hand, many parts of the country have a very hesitant justice system that continues to doubt the acceptability of any broad application of the long-established legal possibilities of diversion (see, e.g., as a short grasp of the development of diversion projects in Germany Albrecht, 1985: 607-612; Albrecht et al., 1988: 723-726 and with respect to the German literature on diversion Heinz, 1989a). Whether diversion as an alternative strategy to handle juvenile delinquency really expanded significantly during the 1980s is discussed controversially in Germany (see, e.g., Heinz, 1987: 142-143, 1989b, 1992; Pfeiffer, 1989, who argue affirmatively, and P.-A. Albrecht, 1990, who denies this development). Public prosecutors and judges have received unexpected, but very effective, support from critical German social scientists who have expressed a whole range of doubts about diversion (see Janssen, 1983; Ludwig, 1989; Voß, 1983, 1985). Such criticisms include: promotion of selective sanctioning of deviant adolescents (a tendency that is existent but not remarkable; see P.-A. Albrecht, 1990; Ludwig-Mayerhofer, 1990), widening the net of formal social control (Blomberg and Blomberg, 1985; Ludwig, 1989; Voß, 1985; on the one side, and for arguments and data that refute this apprehension, Kerner, 1989), the threat to constitutional guarantees of due process (P.-A. Albrecht, 1990; Backes, 1995, in this volume; Ludwig, 1989; Voß, 1985; but see, also, the arguments to the contrary by Dölling, 1989; Kerner, 1989) and the crippling of the demand for a comprehensive abolition or decriminalization of wide areas of juvenile delinquency (Backes, 1995, in this volume).

It would be foolish not to want to recognize that nearly all of these criticisms have a certain justification, and they make a critical and careful examination of diversion all the more important. Above all, arguments pointing to the unintended, but nonetheless possible, and undesired side effects would be fatal if the evaluation of legal diversion revealed that it was not at least as good as traditional sanctioning practice with regard to the development of adolescents.

2 Treatment Outcome Evaluation of Diversion

Because this issue is of such central importance to evaluating diversion policy, it is astonishing how little confirmed knowledge is available. First, the majority of studies come from English-speaking countries, hence, countries with completely different legal systems compared to Germany, so that there are considerable doubts about their generalizability (for the German situation, see Heinz, 1992; Walter, 1989; for a comparison between Germany and other countries, Kaiser, 1985; Kirchhoff, 1981; Kury, 1981). Second, the various Anglo-American programs differ to such an extent in design and treatment that, even within the USA, the external validity of the findings is exceptionally doubtful (see Klein, 1985; Lemert, 1985, for examples of short general introductions, and Davidson et al., 1990, for empirical data). This is the reason why it seems to be almost impossible to summarize the results of evaluation studies and why different authors come to very different conclusions: While Lab and Whitehead (1988) and Whitehead and Lab (1989) replicate the results of former studies that "nothing works" in correctional treatment for juvenile delinquency, Andrews et. al. (1990a) come to the very different conclusion that these programs work successfully when they are applied appropriately (but see the vivid discussion between both research teams: Lab and Whitehead (1990) and Andrews et al., 1990b)).

For these reasons, I do not even wish to attempt to present and analyze these research findings in detail. However, some brief comments are appropriate: From the very beginning, the relatively weak outcomes of diversion programs in the USA disappointed both the general public and scientists, probably because they were measured against unrealistic hopes. As the original philosophy underlying this movement (see, e.g., Lemert, 1971; Schur, 1973) in favor of abandoning official and professional intervention in most cases and waiting for processes of normalization soon got bogged down, and net-widening processes seemed to expand greatly, the movement lost its impetus. Therefore, only limited systematic evaluations are available. Hence, all the literature I have seen presents a diffuse discussion of inconsistent findings that are mostly hard to analyze methodologically. Even the latest and most comprehensive evaluation from Davidson et al. (1990) avoids any balanced evaluation of their own program.

In the Federal Republic of Germany, the state of research has improved greatly in recent years, as the previous paper by Heinz (see pp. 159-186 in this volume) has shown. In a series of admirable studies based on extremely comprehensive analyses of records and case files, Heinz and several colleagues (see Heinz, 1987; Heinz and Spieß, 1983; Hügel, 1987; Spieß and Storz, 1989; Storz, 1992) have confirmed that - when relevant parameters are controlled (prior offenses, severity of offense, etc.) - adolescents referred to diversion by public prosecutors or judges mostly showed improved, and nearly always equally good recidivism and retrial rates. Effects vary according to the type of offense, but they are generally notable, if not particularly dazzling.

3 Reasons for a Further Evaluation Study

In view of these findings, I need to justify why an additional study of the effects of diversion seemed meaningful and necessary.

Without wanting to belittle Heinz' and his colleagues' studies, I consider that some aspects indicate the need for a replication study with a different research design. Some of these aspects are:

First, concentrating on records and case files (as Heinz has done) strongly reduces the range of variables available for analysis. This applies, for example, to socio-demographic variables, data on the socialization background, informal social control, and so forth.

Second, the very small data base on prior problems and problem milieus in the subject makes it difficult to test whether diverted and nondiverted subjects really only differed in terms of treatment. If diverted adolescents are those for whom a better course can be assumed in any case because of favorable framing conditions, attributing low recidivism rates to the effects of diversion could lead to false conclusions.

Third, the use of case files to measure dependent variables (delinquency rates or recidivism) narrows research to officially registered delinquency and crime. Naturally, from the perspective of criminal law, this is the central outcome criterion, but from the perspectives of social science and social policy making, we are also interested in undetected delinquency, as this is also generally harmful to society. As other studies have suggested that the results of evaluation research can differ greatly depending on whether official or self-reported delinquency is analyzed (see Blakely, Kushler, and Davidson, 1980; Davidson et al., 1990; Dunford and Elliott, 1984; Farrington, 1989), it seems meaningful to also include self-reported delinquency in an evaluation.

Forth, although a purely quantitative confirmation of the effectiveness of diversion compared to the traditional form of sanctioning is of major value to science and crime policy, from a scientific perspective, and indirectly from a practical perspective, the detection of the mechanisms and processes by which diversion achieves this effect or, under certain conditions, does not achieve this effect, is even more important. To clarify this process, we must formulate and test specific theoretical hypotheses on how the diversion decision influences the clients or their social network in order to bring about reduced recidivism. We shall only be able to talk about a true gain in scientific knowledge when at least one of the various competing hypotheses is confirmed empirically by demonstrating that the decision for diversion takes effect across hypothesized links between variables.

Hence, we do not just want to know whether diversion demonstrates the intended effect, but we also want to study *how* it brings about this effect. Such a study represents a good opportunity to test general theories on deviant behavior and social control, as, to some extent, the theories generate very different hypotheses on the effects of diversion or explain the same effect through different processes (see, e.g., the very important analysis in Lamp, 1981). In fact, my colleagues and I view this possibility as the most stimulating aspect of the program, because it provides us with an opportunity to test central hypotheses from the labeling approach, self-esteem enhancement theory, control theory, and deterrence or rational choice theory, from which we borrowed the central ideas to build our model (see Albrecht, 1985; Albrecht et al., 1988a, 1988b; Albrecht et al., 1991a, 1991b; Albrecht et al., 1994a, 1994b; Albrecht and Karstedt-Henke, 1987).

4 Theoretical Foundations for an Analysis of the Effective Process in Diversion

As space is limited, I cannot deal with these theoretical approaches in detail. As most readers will be very familiar with them, I will sketch only the most important aspects.

Naturally, the labeling approach is of central importance (see Albrecht, 1973, 1982, 1992 for a general introduction). Although it is completely uninterested in etiological issues or considers them meaningless on the basis of fundamental principles in the theory of science (see Sack, 1978, as the most important German author committed to this radical version of the labeling approach), its concepts of secondary deviance (Lemert, 1967) and societal reaction have introduced the ideas that have mapped out the foundations of the diversion concept. The meaning of an act is defined initially by the quality of the societal reactions in three ways: (1) quite basically, insofar as "deviation" is only constituted as deviation through this reaction; (2) insofar as the generally negative, sanctioning reactions to the deviance of the "devaint" have a very important status, namely the attribution of the master status to the deviant that can lead to isolation from important roles (role engulfment, see Becker, 1963) and increase the probability of further deviance through the exclusion from conventional careers; and (3) in that interactionist identity theory predicts that the stigmatizing ceremonies of moral degradation (see, e.g., Garfinkel, 1956) in many formal processes of control generally lead to identity transformations that change a person who has arbitrarily performed a "deviant act" into a person with a deviant self-concept who correspondingly performs more deviant acts (see, e.g., Albrecht and Karstedt-Henke, 1987: 317-323, for an elaborated model of this relationship).

The theory of self-esteem or of "deviant behavior as defense of self" (Kaplan, 1980), which I cannot discuss suitably here in all its complexity, assumes that deviance (defined as a conscious violation of the norms of the reference group) is elicited by individuals' basic drive to obtain a positive self-image. A positive self-image can be obtained through positive evaluations from group members. If, for specific reasons, an individual is unable to obtain positive evaluation in the group or to cope effectively with the negative evaluations by others in order to build a positive self-concept, he or she can only defend his or her positive self-esteem by exhibiting behavior that does not meet the norms of the prior reference group, but offers opportunities of positive evaluation from members of another group.

Hence, in some circumstances, it is possible to increase self-esteem through deviance. Kaplan (1986, 1987) modified this simple model by arguing that there is no direct link between self-derogation and delinquency but an indirect connection via "delinquent tendencies". Kaplan, furthermore, postulates that only subjects with a very low level of self-esteem and without former delinquency will be successful in gaining a higher level of self-esteem by committing delinquent acts (for a partial confirmation see Czisch, 1994). If the threat to self-esteem evoked by the traditional sanctioning of punishment of juvenile delinquency places the juvenile in a situation in which self-esteem can be protected only through further deviance and through changing to a more delinquent reference group, then it could be anticipated that diversion would have a comparatively positive effect, because it does not generate the need for further delinquency in order to defend self-esteem.

Control theory (e.g., Hirschi, 1969) argues - in very broad terms - that deviant behavior always results when the various links to society or specific categories of persons or values are weakened or broken by social conditions or events (e.g., attachment to parents, commitment to norm compliant action guidelines, involvement in normative behavior patterns, belief in certain social values, etc.). The effects that societal reactions to the occurrence of deviance have on further development therefore depend on how societal reactions affect these links. If the judicial treatment of a juvenile delinquent elicits inappropriate reactions in parents that reduce attachment, further delinquency is more likely than when parents, alarmed by the authorities' interest in their child, try to show more understanding, intensify their interaction, and offer assistance. Or, if the judicial sanctioning of an adolescent leads to his or her exclusion from more norm-compliant peer networks, then this would reduce the involvement in conforming activity patterns and thus increase the probability of further delinquency, and so forth. As hardly any former research on diversion had addressed the highly significant processes of informal social control, at the beginning of our study, we could not state with sufficient certainty whether diversion - compared to penal sanctioning - either weakens or strengthens the mobilization of these informal control processes. However, we could assume that it would be necessary to explore the interdependencies between formal and informal social control and especially the ways in which different informal control reactions would be elicited by different forms of judicial handling (e.g., diversion vs. accusation) if we wanted to know how diversion brings about its effects. Such a research strategy has been underscored in the meantime by studies documenting that a longitudinal test of control theory in the version developed by Hirschi results in a lot of doubts with respect to its explanatory power (see Agnew, 1985, 1991).

Finally, one central theoretical perspective that conceivably influences diversion is the rational choice approach (see, e.g., Cornish and Clarke, 1986, as a general introduction, and Hirschi, 1986, for a discussion of the relationship between rational choice theories and social control theories; see, e.g., Tuck and Riley, 1986, for the relationship of the "theory of reasoned action", and Akers, 1990, for the relation of learning theory and rational choice theory). This approach is generally discussed in criminology in the shortened version of deterrence theory (see, e.g., Gibbs, 1975; Zimring and Hawkins, 1973) or the theory of general and special prevention. As our program is only dealing with the effects of diversion on individual delinquents, we shall initially leave aside general prevention. Deterrence theory should also be well known, so that it only needs a very short sketch (see, e.g., Gibbs, 1975, for a short introduction). The probability of delinquent behavior is viewed as a function of the expected probability of being sanctioned, the expected severity of sanctioning, and the celerity of sanctioning. While the latter generally proves to be relatively unimportant, attention focuses on the first two parameters.

The theoretical and empirical debates particularly range around five issues: (1) whether the subjective or objective probability of sanctioning or severity of sanctioning is relevant (Waldo and Chiricos, 1972); (2) whether the two independent variables have an additive or multiplicative effect on the dependent variable (Grasmick and Bryjak, 1980; Paternoster and Iovanni, 1986; Stafford et al., 1986); (3) whether the rational choice theory of delinquent behavior can be applied equally to all kinds of offense or whether it is necessary to differentiate between mala in se and mala prohibita (see, e.g., Liska, 1981: 109). This is closely related to the fourth issue: (4) whether hypotheses can be generalized to all types of offender, for example, to different age groups or to groups with different experiences with sanctioning by the criminal justice system (Smith and Gartin, 1989). Finally, (5) there is the important issue of the causal direction between expected sanctions and behavior: Do expectations determine behavior or are expectations the outcome of behavior and the experiences resulting from it (see, e.g., Bishop, 1984; Minor and Harry, 1982; Paternoster et al., 1983; Saltzman et al., 1982)?

In view of the many open questions and the major methodological problems involved in any valid test of deterrence theory, it is not surprising that the previous balance is not particularly positive. Nonetheless, major criticisms of deterrence theory can possibly be relativized if expected and experienced costs are not just related to formal reactions but also to informal control reactions; if not only objective reactions but also their subjective processing are observed; if appropriate longitudinal research designs are developed; and so forth.

When considering the effects of diversion, it has to be noted that the diversion decision does not change the probability of detection or sanction, as the diverted adolescent (just like the accused) has to pass through the preliminary phases of a formal proceeding and experiences the proceeding itself and the decision - even when this does not lead to punishment in a strict sense - as a sanction. As far as the severity of the sanction is concerned, the unpleasant experience of being detected, interrogation by the police, discussions with juvenile justice officials, parents, and eventually victims, as well as, in some circumstances, the imposition of reparations should make the subjective costs of deviance seem to be similarly high if not higher than for a delinquent who passes through the traditional formal proceedings and generally receives a relatively mild punishment.

So much for some selected elements of theories that we have drawn on to explain the content of the process of the effect of diversion - should it have any effect. It seems to be obvious that - on the one hand - in some cases, these different theories, which are in some respect complementary and in other respects contradictory, come to different conclusions regarding the expectable effects of diversion. On the other hand, in other cases, these theories come to the same result, though for different reasons.

Labeling theory, for instance, postulates that diversion will reduce the frequency of subsequent delinquency compared to accusation by protecting the self-esteem of diverted subjects - assuming that diversion really leads to a reduction of stigmatizing experiences.

Though stemming from the same theoretical tradition, the self-enhancement theory of crime and delinquency leads to a set of differing hypotheses for special subgroups of deviant youths: In some cases, accusation and not diversion should result in a decrease of subsequent delinquency - assuming that only accusation will be an event that symbolically documents a deviant status with respect to the original membership group (in former times, the source of feelings of self-derogation) and conformity with the standards of the new reference group (the source of positive social appraisals).

Arguments from control theory result in the hypothesis that diversion and not accusation will lead to a reduction of subsequent delinquency - if some assumptions are correct. The first assumption is that the experience of a formal accusation does not differ significantly in its potential for changing or intensifying the moral beliefs of juvenile delinquents compared with diversion by the public prosecutor. The second assumption is that - in most cases - diversion minimizes the risk of exclusion from conforming social groups, thus stabilizing the level of involvement instead of reducing it. The third assumption is that diversion does not undermine the commitment of the delinquent youth to conforming aims, because he or she will not come to the conclusion that he or she has lost all chances for the future. The fourth assumption is that the procedural involvement of parents connected with the diversion decision and its implementation leads to a reactivation of familial interaction and consolidates or increases attachment to parents, whereas an accusation does not afford so much family participation but bears the risk that family members will distance themselves from the delinquent.

Arguments from the rational choice theory of crime and delinquency will result in the hypothesis that diversion leads to a higher frequency of subsequent delinquency because it is connected with a lower level of subjectively experienced sanction severity, and will lead to a lower level of expected severity of sanctions for future delinquency that increases the probability of future deviant behavior - provided that some assumptions are given. The first is that an accusation is experienced as significantly more serious than diversion. The second is that an accusation triggers a higher number of informal sanctions and/or that these informal sanctions are connected with a higher level of social costs when they are caused by an accusation. The third assumption is that the experience of formal sanctioning, which is normally rather lenient, does not reduce the level of expected sanction severity - thereby undermining the basis of any deterrence.

Obviously, all these theories make a lot of assumptions that are difficult to appraise with respect to their tenability. In some cases, these assumptions seem to be rather plausible because they can be deduced from other theories; in other cases, they just contradict central hypotheses of a rival theory. In any case, they have to be tested empirically, because deductions from a theory that actually is correct will lead to false conclusions if the supposed marginal conditions are not given.

The modest objective of our analyses is to take a look at the tenability of these assumptions and at the causal chains postulated by the above-mentioned theories, or at least at parts of these chains.

5 The Design of the Present Study

Unfortunately, I cannot present final results of this test of rival theories, as our longitudinal design will only permit such statements in the near future. I shall report selected findings on the evaluation of the effect of diversion, although these should also be treated with caution. First, these findings are based on rather simple models and need to be checked carefully by controlling for several additional variables that might be theoretically relevant. Second, they concern the study of effects following the decision by the public prosecutor for only *one special cohort*. So we still cannot be certain whether these trends will be reproducible for another cohort, because there might develop something like "norm erosion" for later cohorts as a consequence of a very radical diversion practice (see, for example, Erickson, Stafford, and Galliher, 1984, who were the first to study the problem of "norm erosion" as a possible consequence of non-intervention).

Before presenting selected findings, I must provide some information on the design of the study, so that the limitations to the power of our data become apparent.

Legal restrictions to experimental design and its alternatives. First, it has to be emphasized that in the Federal Republic of Germany, unlike some other countries such as the USA, a true experimental design to evaluate sanctioning decisions is not only hard to implement but also legally impossible. Hence, subjects cannot be assigned randomly to a specific treatment, even though the enormous variety in judicial reactions to very similar cases, as Heinz (1987) has shown so impressively, creates the impression that referral to a particular treatment in the final analysis almost follows a random pattern.

In view of these framing conditions, we had hoped to tackle this problem by studying the effects of diversion through the development of delinquent adolescents in two court districts characterized by clear differences in the frequency of diversion decisions. The intention was to use a set of measures to increase the rate of diversion decisions in that court district that already showed a high level of diversion practice, whereas the court district using more traditional procedures would not be encouraged to implement such changes. If this had worked, we would have been able to assess a large number of cases that would have been generally very similar but had experienced a different treatment, so that an ex-post, quasi-experimental design would have been possible (see, for an introduction to the potential and constraints of evaluation studies, Albrecht, 1991). Though the real development deviated a little bit from our expectations and hopes, insofar as the "traditional" court district changed his practice into a more "progressive" direction and increased its diversion rate, the differences between both districts remained important though to pursue this research strategy (see, e.g., Crasmöller, 1995).

Characteristics of the study population and problems of access and representativity. It should also be pointed out in advance that we also succeeded in recruiting a high proportion of the adolescents who qualified as subjects for our study by being apprehended because of committing one of the acts typical for juvenile delinquents (larceny, theft, car theft, shoplifting, burglary, fraud, assault, bodily injury, damage to property, vandalism, etc.).

There is no room here to discuss the very serious problems of gaining access to personal data and addresses of delinquents from the criminal justice system because of individual and private data protection legislation in Germany since the 1980s, as well as the difficulties in overcoming the inhibitions and the reluctance of delinquent youths and their parents to participate in a study about delinquency (see Albrecht and Karstedt-Henke, 1989). These problems are of extraordinary importance, because we wanted to realize a longitudinal study with at least three measurement points (first measurement immediately after the decision by the public prosecutor, second measurement 9 months later, and third measurement about 2 years after the second measurement).

In order to be sure that our original sample did not differ from the population of apprehended delinquents in our court districts, we compared relevant data on the subjects of our study with those of the population, but did not find any hints of statistically significant differences.

Problems of population mortality. Second, we were increasingly confronted with the problem of "mortality" in our study population from one stage of the panel to the next. Though we had to fight against the additional problems raised by the fact that our research revolves around a very sensitive topic (Lee, 1993: 119-141) and that many of our subjects belong to an age group that implies a high probability of important changes that reduce accessibility (leaving the parental household, military conscription, changing the place of residence, etc.), we were rather successful in our efforts to reduce the attrition rate. Of our original sample of 617 adolescents, 437 were successfully interviewed a second, and 289, a third time. The (corrected) mortality rate was 35.3% or 28.8% respectively for the last interview (see Albrecht et al., 1994: 297; Crasmöller, 1994). In order to control for the threat of selectivity effects, we checked whether participants who took part in all phases differed significantly from those subjects who left the study. We could not find significant differences, though - of course - differences were observable (e.g., with respect to the academic or school status and prior registration by the police). Therefore, there is no reason to assume that the results of our analysis based only on those subjects who participated in every phase will be seriously biased in a certain direction by selection processes.

Adequate criteria for evaluation and the baseline problem. Before reporting on the design of each of the substudies analyzed in this paper, it should be mentioned that it would be very desirable to use a really realistic measure/criterion in later stages for a comprehensive and fair evaluation of diversion and traditional sanctioning practice. Unfortunately this is missing in nearly all previous studies. The absolute and not just the relative or comparative effectiveness of formal sanctions (be they diversion, or prosecution, etc.) - measured with the criterion of subsequent frequencies of delinquency - can only be determined by using participants with comparable undetected amounts of delinquency and framing conditions who are not officially registered and accused as a comparison group. Only such a comparison can provide an appropriate and fair evaluation of the effectiveness of diversion.

For these reasons, we have carried out a comprehensive representative community study of (officially!) nondelinquent adolescents in the same districts. This also has a longitudinal design and, to a large extent, uses the same instruments as those used with delinquents (N= 1480 subjects for the original sample [first interview] and N= 1053 for the second interview). Unfortunately, there is no chance to present first results from our efforts to perform such a comparison here. As far as I know, such an attempt has never been undertaken before, although the need is very obvious. We will present only some selected results of this (community) panel study here in order to answer some special questions.

Longitudinal design and its methodological and ethical problems. Wave 1 of our panel study on our experimental and control groups (adolescents who had been apprehended because they had committed at least one of the above-mentioned crimes) was carried out over an interval of 2 to 3 weeks after the public prosecutors had informed the adolescents that they would either be prosecuted or diverted. These dates, which could not be altered because of several procedural and methodological reasons, raised problems with the comparison between diverted and nondiverted adolescents: While proceedings were more or less finished for the diverted adolescents at the time of the first wave, the nondiverted adolescents only knew that a juvenile court process would follow, without actually yet having received a sanction.

The second wave was carried out 9 months after Wave 1 in order to study short-term effects, because, on the one side, there are many arguments that the impact of diversion - if there should be one - will appear as a short-term rather than a long-term effect. On the other side, there are arguments that postulate just the opposite: Formal sanctions will deter delinquents only for a short time and then lose their importance or even produce counterproductive effects.

The third wave of interviews took place about 24 to 27 months after the second, so that we have a follow-up study for a period of 3 years for these subjects. An interval of 3 years is a rather short one, but there were many reasons not to expand the duration of the study. First, it is not reasonable to assume that a small variation in a treatment (sanction by the criminal justice system) that, following an impressive research tradition, usually produces only "minimal effects" (see, e.g., Rossi, 1978: 574; Rossi and Wright, 1987: 48) will be investigable with respect to its consequences in a long-term perspective. This applies all the more because the period of adolescence is one that is characterized by turbulent development and a lot of changes in many life domains that will subdue the small consequences of being sanctioned by the juvenile justice system sooner or later. Second, we had to avoid the risk that a multiple repetition of a long and personally intrusive research interview revolving around the sensitive topic of delinquency and its consequences could result in stigmatization or self-stigmatization by the adolescents, because the delinquent act and its consequences attain an importance that would be impossible without the renewed interviews. Such a development would be intolerable on ethical grounds and because of methodological reasons. Third, we had to avoid the risk that a repetition of the interview after more than a few years could lead to the situation that additional persons, a new partner, for instance, may hear about the former delinquency of our subjects for the first time - a fact that might burden the intimate relationships.

All these considerations were serious objections against a longer research interval and a higher frequency of contacts. In order to be sure that our repeated interviews did not lead to the negative side effects just mentioned, we conducted a short special empirical study with the first 50 subjects to look for indications of such a problematic development. Though the empirical base is rather small, we got the firm impression that these negative side effects did not appear (see Albrecht and Karstedt-Henke, 1989).

Nonetheless, our design confronted us with major problems. If we regard the characteristic "diversion versus nondiversion" as a level of the sanction variables and relate this to subsequent delinquency frequencies in order to measure effectiveness, we overlook the possibility that, for example, in cases of nondiversion and sentencing, the punishment might only have been completed a few weeks before Wave 2, and its effects have only just begun to appear. Perhaps punishment has only just made the delinquent realize where delinquency leads (deterrence), or, due to inappropriate treatment by the juvenile court, perhaps the adolescent may feel stigmatized and provoked to secondary deviance in the sense of the labeling approach since a few weeks. This fundamentally raises the question whether we are justified in including, for example, delinquency during the period between Waves 1 and 2 or changes in self-concept during this period for both subsamples as a basis of evaluation.

For the results presented here, we have provisionally answered this question positively, as we assume that (1) nondiverted adolescents already experience the announcement of a juvenile court case as the beginning of a sanction, and (2) through the circumstance that most proceedings are completed approximately 3 to 4 months after the public prosecutor's communication, the difference in the temporal course between the samples is not as large as one might fear. At the end, we will come back to this critical point.

6 Selected Findings on the Relevance of Intervening Variables Between Sanction and Effect

To present our preliminary findings (see the remarks on p. 194-195), I have selected a few results that are spread across several aspects of our topic. Naturally, neither their content nor quality can provide the basis for a total evaluation of diversion.

Let us begin with some findings referring to identity theory, labeling theory, and Kaplan's interpretations of the relations between self-concept/identity and deviation and their implications for diversion.

One of the central arguments in the above-mentioned theories is that - roughly speaking - a bad or negative (deviant) self-image represents the primary (Kaplan) or the secondary cause (see Becker, Lemert) of delinquent behavior. Authors in the labeling tradition emphasize the idea that the kind of sanction plays a major role in the future development of the self-image. From this perspective, any form of social reaction that results in a definition of an act as deviant behavior is connected with the risk that a new identity is attributed to the actor that might be of severe consequences for the self-concept of the labeled actor. This is especially so when the social reaction is a public one or even a reaction by an agency of formal social control that can dispose of the means of power to organize a "successful degradation ceremony" (see Garfinkel, 1956).

Self-concept and subsequent delinquency. As far as the first part of this argument is concerned, our representative community study clearly reveals that such a relationship exists: Even in undetected adolescents, there was a negative correlation between the quality of self-image (measured by a German adaptation by Fend, 1984, of the Rosenberg Scale, 1979) and the frequency of delinquency. Although it was not particularly strong and differed across certain sociodemographic categories, it was nonetheless statistically significant. Interestingly, the various dimensions of the self-concept differed markedly in their relations to self-reported delinquency (the "self-concept of competence to cope with the future" being most important, see Albrecht, 1994: 66-72).

Societal reactions and self-concept changes. If we ask what relationship exists between self-image and societal reactions to delinquent acts, our findings provide an apparently unequivocal relationship: The less delinquency is followed by an official reaction, the better the self-image appears to remain. If we compare delinquent adolescents who have not been detected (our community sample) with (a) adolescents who were caught by the police, interrogated, and then diverted by the public prosecutor; and (b) those adolescents who were prosecuted, the groups differ significantly in self-image in the expected direction at Wave 1. Naturally, other variables such as the frequency of delinquency, prior convictions, parents' socioeconomic status, academic status, and so forth also contribute, but this relationship also remains as a trend among the controls, although on a modest level (see Albrecht and van Kampen, 1991: 23).

If we test some of the assumptions about the causes of this relationship, we obtain further confirmation for the hypothesis that stigmatizing experiences with the authorities of social control could be responsible for this finding. Our study of the perception of police interrogation among detected adolescents revealed that adolescents in general experienced police interrogation as being surprisingly fair. Nonetheless, a closer inspection was appropriate: Drawing on the literature, we specifically assessed how far the adolescents perceived the interrogation as severe, strict, and stigmatizing in the sense of an attribution of basically particularly negative characteristics (harmful tendencies) compared to other adolescents, and whether they possibly transform corresponding experiences into a self-stigmatization. While the experience of severe and strict interrogation did not correlate with self-stigmatization, it did correlate with stigmatization by the police. We thus have a preliminary confirmation that a "deviant self" can already be encouraged during the first phases of formal sanctioning, even though a causal interpretation would be subject to methodological objections (see Klinger, 1993, 1994).

Interestingly, there is a clear relationship between the sanctioning decision of the public prosecutor and the severity, strictness, and stigmatization by the police: Those who were subsequently diverted were treated with less severity, strictness, and stigmatization than those who were subsequently prosecuted. Hence, diverted and nondiverted adolescents not only experience differences in treatment by the public prosecutor, but this differentiation begins at an even earlier phase. Much of this difference is due to characteristics such as prior convictions, gender, family structure, socioeconomic status, and academic status, that all have a certain relevance for the public prosecutor's decision (see Klinger, 1993, 1994).

Our theoretical assumption that the quality and frequency of the interaction between representatives of informal and formal authorities of social control and delinquent adolescents play a role in their further development, and particularly in how they process their delinquency, is strongly confirmed by the following finding: In an extension of the interactionist theory of deviant behavior and social control, we have adopted the idea that societal interventions with an adolescent should be successful if they manage to persuade the adolescent to recognize that delinquency is a role with a high potential centrality, without the adolescent identifying with this role as a deviant. Let us look at the first of the two preconditions only, and study its determinants. One very important finding is revealed: High centrality of the role as delinquent correlates positively with perceived positive evaluation from others, for example, parents, teachers/supervisors, and police, and it is interesting that this correlation rises as a function of increasing social distance to the categories mentioned (see Albrecht and van Kampen, 1991:

22). Hence, if we want adolescents to process their delinquency in a constructive way, that is, a way that reduces the probability of future delinquent acts, this is linked to the adolescent believing that others rate him or her positively - despite the fact that he or she has committed a delinquent act that is not accepted by significant others. This precondition increases in importance as a function of how formal this relationship to the others is. It should be obvious what this implies for the idea of diversion. It is very interesting that this result is a fine confirmation of central elements of John Braithwaite's important theory of "reintegrative shaming" (see Braithwaite, 1989, and his paper in this volume).

However, we must warn against hasty conclusions, because our theoretical expectations regarding the relationship between societal reaction/sanction and self-concept preliminarily seem to be contradicted on a very important issue. We had expected that self-concepts, in particular, self-esteem, would develop differently between Waves 1 and 2 in diverted and nondiverted adolescents. In concrete terms, we had anticipated that the self-concept, especially self-esteem, in diverted adolescents would further improve or consolidate between Waves 1 and 2, whereas it would deteriorate in accused adolescents who had received their actual sanctions between Waves 1 and 2 as a function of the sanction and accompanying stigmatization. Self-concepts of diverted and nondiverted adolescents actually differed significantly at Wave 1, but this significant difference disappeared at Wave 2, due to the fact that the self-image of diverted adolescents hardly changed, whereas it improved significantly in accused adolescents! (see Albrecht and van Kampen, 1991: 22-24).

Before the opponents of diversion breathe a sigh of relief, I must emphasize that I consider that this result is essentially an artifact of our research design. Wave 1 was located just after diverted adolescents (about 2 to 3 weeks previously) had found out that they had been diverted, that is, there would be no subsequent court case and "no punishment". At the same time, nondiverted adolescents found out that their cases had not been dismissed but would be followed by accusation, a court case, and an indeterminate punishment. As we have no pretreatment data on either group, we cannot claim with any certainty, but consider it nonetheless very plausible, that the problematic effect of a formal sanctioning decision is exhibited in the clear and massive difference in self-esteem between diverted and nondiverted adolescents at Wave 1, even after controlling for relevant third variables. During the next 9 months, the accused adolescents recover to such an extent that the remaining difference between diverted and nondiverted adolescents is no longer significant. Hence, in no way can we state that prosecution leads to an improvement in self-esteem, but, in contrast, it clearly damages it, though, fortunately, this is not very permanent for the majority of participants. One reason for this could be that the experience of prosecution and of being involved in a court case does not seem to be perceived as being much worse than going through a police interrogation, so long as court proceedings are not accompanied or supplemented by other measures (e.g., from the youth welfare office).

One of our main tasks is to come to a new synthesis of general approaches to a theory of the self-concept (see, e.g., for a general discussion, Gecas, 1982; Markus and Wurf, 1987, and for a first step in this direction, Albrecht and van Kampen, 1991; Albrecht et al., 1994a, 1994b). Though there are some very fruitful attempts to develop a theory about the relation between the self-concept and crime and delinquency (Wells, 1978; Wells and Rankin, 1983), recent empirical studies (Matsueda, 1992; Rosenberg, Schooler, and Schoenbach, 1989) and summaries (Scheff, Retzinger, and Ryan, 1989) reveal that a lot of questions remain open.

Sanctions, expectations, and experiences. This brings us to the question on how formal sanction proceedings are perceived by the adolescents and how they influence the relevant variables of deterrence theory. I will briefly present a few findings that, once more, should not be taken as our final evaluation of the rational choice theory of deviant behavior. We can draw on the findings suggested above, but phrase it more pointedly: In order to test some central assumptions of the rational choice theory of crime, we developed several scales to measure the expected formal and informal sanctions and their subjective severity following a special act of criminal behavior on the one hand and the experienced informal and formal sanctions after apprehension by the police. As we have measured these expectations and experiences on one side and the frequencies of delinquent behavior on the other side at three points, we are able to differentiate between deterrence and experiential effects and avoid many of the serious weaknesses of former studies (see Saltzman et al., 1982; Minor and Harry, 1982, who demonstrated these shortcomings of former studies for the first time). Because of limited space, I shall present only some results for our first wave.

Diverted and nondiverted adolescents do not differ significantly in perceived severity of received sanctioning, as long as no further measures or impositions accompany the diversion or prosecution. It has to be considered that according to our participants' reports, approximately 80% of those who were diverted did not have to endure any further interventions, but experienced "diversion to nothing". The leap from "diversion to nothing" to "diversion with specific accompanying measures", such as social work, reparations, victim-offender mediation, and so forth, seems to be interpreted as a significant increase in the severity of the sanction. Further increases in the "objective severity" of sanctioning (measured as the amount and seriousness of formal sanctions) are no longer experienced as significantly more severe. Both these findings should be considered very carefully, because, first, pure accusation does not seem to be more stressful than "diversion to something" and should therefore be borne in mind by deterrence-oriented public prosecutors; and, second, educators and social workers should note that their preferred alternative to punishment (except "diversion to nothing") seems to be massively interpreted as punishment.

Our analyses also produced differences in the evaluation of the experiences of sanction between four groups of sanctioned adolescents differentiated according to the level of intervention intensity. Actually nondiverted but accused adolescents reduce their perceived and anticipated evaluations of sanctions on the basis of their experiences of delinquency and the following sanctions. Hence, it is not diversion - as assumed in deterrence theory - but the formal sanction that leads to a reduction in perceived severity. The application of punishment therefore undermines the preconditions on which the effectiveness of its threat is based (see Albrecht et al., 1991: 322; Wolterhoff, 1992: 18).

Because of limited space, we cannot analyze in detail the particularly important question on how far sanction expectations or sanction severity expectations specified by sanction experiences influence further delinquency. In global terms, there is an almost paradoxical finding: While it is precisely informal processing that seems to produce a deterrence effect on the perceived threat of sanction, formal processing also shows a preventive effect of the sanction event on the *change* but not the *pure frequency* of delinquent activities subsequent to the sanction. However, these findings are so complex, and in such great need of being tested when controlling for several theoretically important variables, that I would prefer to mention another nearly paradoxical finding instead of formulating a final conclusion.

If we take a look at the relations between the expectations of adolescents with respect to the informal sanctions in case of apprehension by the police because of a theft or delinquency in the next 2 years in our community sample, we can see just the opposite to deterrence: For those adolescents who expect some harsh reactions and complete rejection by their parents, the likelihood of becoming delinquent is significantly higher than for those youths without these expectations (Albrecht et al., 1994: 310). It is too early, to draw a firm conclusion, because, on the one hand, many authors believe that there is a close negative relation between perceived sanction severity and certainty on the one and delinquency on the other side (Grasmick and Appleton, 1977; Grasmick and Green, 1980; Jensen et al., 1978; Tittle, 1980), but, on the other hand, there is firm evidence that "formal risks of punishment have virtually no impact on criminal behavior" (Piliavin et al., 1986: 114). Our data show that the rational choice approach to the explanation of crime has to overcome a lot of contradictions, inconsistencies, and paradoxes that are still unresolved. Looking at our results and those of many authors, we feel sorely tempted to repeat the diagnosis by Tittle and Logan from 1973: "At this point we can savely say only, that sanctions apparently have some deterrent effects under some circumstances. It is now necessary to undertake careful research in an attempt to specify the conditions under which sanctions are likely to be important influences on behavior" (1973: 385).

One of the main problems with most studies testing this theory consists in the failure to adequately conceptualize and measure the objective and, especially, the subjective benefits of deviant acts. Most studies have concentrated almost exclusively on the costs of crime and delinquency. Explicitly asking for expected and experienced rewards received from different categories of people (e.g., peers, parents, teachers, supervisors, etc.) in connection with committing a crime or being sanctioned - as we have done - should be a step in the right direction. The same applies to our attempt to measure changes, especially gains, in self-esteem as a result of delinquent behavior. On the other hand, we face the problem of contradictory conclusions with respect to the consequences of gains in self-esteem as a result of crime and delinquency: Following the labeling tradition and the self-enhancement theory of crime, gains in self-esteem should reduce the probability of subsequent delinquency; following learning theory, we should expect the opposite.

So much for the first block of findings dealing with the intervening phase between sanction and effect. Now I shall move on to a preliminary estimation of the global effects of diversion, which should also be treated with sufficient caution.

7 Diversion and the Development of Delinquency: A Preliminary Global Analysis

7.1 Short-term changes in delinquency

A look on the changes in delinquent behavior in our sample of apprehended adolescents over the 9 months between Waves 1 and 2 reveals that the frequencies of delinquency for all subjects during the 9 months before Wave 1 and 9 months between Waves 1 and 2 clearly declined after sanctioning. In particular, almost one half of the participants reported that they had committed no further delinquencies during the previous 9 months. A test of whether diverted adolescents had transferred significantly more frequently to the delinquency-free category than accused adolescents was negative, though it only just failed to reach the conventional 5% level of significance ($p = .07$). If we do not use such strict criteria, but simply inspect the mean differences between the two groups, we see an initially surprising finding that the means of nondiverted adolescents drop much more than those of diverted adolescents (see Figure 1; for Figures 1 - 8b see Appendix).

Nonetheless, this finding should not be interpreted as a confirmation of the greater effectiveness of formal sanctions, because it is only due to the fact that the accused adolescents had a significantly higher base level. Basically it can be seen that - independent of the type of sanction - the probability of a decline in delinquency is a function of the original delinquency level (see Figure 2). For the same reason, we should not place too much importance on the relatively small but nonetheless significant relation between the public prosecutor's decision and subsequent delinquency (Kendall's Tau = .1504, p= .018), which makes it seem as if accused adolescents report more delinquent acts after the public prosecutor's decision than diverted adolescents. If relevant prior conditions such as prior delinquency over the years, delinquency in the 9 months prior to Wave 1, and so forth are controlled, this relationship disappears.

For these reasons, we shall now look at the development in delinquency after the sanction decision in diverted and nondiverted adolescents while controlling prior delinquency up to Wave 1. Figure 3 shows an interesting pattern: Accused adolescents with high prior delinquency show a particularly strong reduction in the number of offenses after the public prosecutor's decision. However, even if the decline in diverted adolescents with high prior delinquency, whose base levels are a little bit lower, is not so large, it is nonetheless significant. The diverted and nondiverted adolescents with less prior delinquency principally maintain their low offense frequencies from the 9 months prior to Wave 1. It should be noted here that significant declines in diverted adolescents with high prior delinquency only occur for theft, while the number of offenses in nondiverted adolescents with high prior delinquency declines significantly for all types of offense with the exception of physical injuries.

I do not have enough space to present corresponding findings on the control of age in any detail. I will merely state that there were no changes in the number of offenses following the sanction decision in either diverted or nondiverted 14- to 15-year-olds, while significant declines could be observed in older participants (see Figures 4 and 5).

Instead, let us turn to the effects of the prosecutor's decision as a function of gender (Figure 6). There is clearly a selective effect of diversion but not of prosecution. In male and female accused adolescents, who both had a particularly high base level, we can see clear and statistically significant declines in the number of offenses. In diverted adolescents, however, we can see a clear and significant decline only in female participants, although both genders started out from the same base level. Diversion seems to succeed more clearly in female participants than in males.

An important issue is whether the effects of diversion depend on socioeconomic status. We studied both subject's academic status and parent's occupation as moderator variables.

Figure 7 shows a somewhat irritating pattern regarding the participants' academic status: In accused adolescents with low academic status, we can observe a significant, 20% decline in offenses (approximately from 5.60 to 4.50). Interestingly accused adolescents with higher academic status show a clear decline in the mean number of offenses (approximately from 6.33 to 3.33). A closer inspection shows that this is due to the strong dispersal of scores in this category. This has to be interpreted as indicating that although there is a clear drop in the number of offenses in those accused adolescents with higher academic status in general, there seems to be a completely different development in a smaller proportion of the members of this group. Hence, we can see a polarization here, insofar as some participants with higher academic status react to prosecution with an increase in the number of offenses - in contrast to the general trend. Diverted adolescents show a completely different pattern: Those with higher academic status, despite their low base levels, show a significant decline in the number of offenses, whereas diverted adolescents with lower academic status, although they started from a higher base level, only show a minimal and nonsignificant decline.

If the parents' occupational status is used as a criterion of socioeceonomic status and also applied to the frequency of delinquency after the prosecutor's decision, a similar pattern emerges (see Figures 8a and 8b): Lower-class diverted adolescents do not change the frequency of their offenses, significantly, while those from the lower middle class change significantly. Upper middle/upper class adolescents show a decline that does not reach significance. Among accused adolescents, lower class youths show clear and significant declines, whereas accused adolescents from the lower-middle and upper middle/upper class do not reduce the frequency of their delinquencies significantly.

Naturally, it is tempting to neatly summarize these last two findings along with the findings on gender and state that each prosecutor's decision has addressees for whom it is particularly effective, namely, prosecution for male participants with low academic status and lower-class parents, and diversion particularly for female participants with a good academic status and higher-class parental homes. Nonetheless, we expressly wish to caution against such a conclusion. First, we must test precisely whether other variables are not at work here that may provide a better explanation of the findings. Second, it has to be seen that, even after diversion, the number of offenses - measured with means - does not increase but tends to decline systematically. However, and above all, detailed analyses must be further differentiated so that, for instance, type and long-term and short-term intensity of prior delinquency can be controlled.

7.2 Determinants of long-term changes in delinquency: Results of multiple regressions

Of course, the central criterion in evaluating diversion consists in the long-term future behavior of adolescents measured as a reconviction rate or future self-reported delinquency. Because of space limitations, I shall concentrate on self-reported future delinquency for our analysis of determinants of the subsequent development. I differentiate between short-term and long-term effects, that is, between frequency of delinquency in the first year after diversion or accusation and frequency of delinquency in the second and third year after the decision by the public prosecutor. I shall report results only, and cannot discuss the rather complex methodological problems in detail. All the arguments and information can be found in Crasmöller's (1993, 1995) very fine dissertation and paper (1994), from which I take the following table (Table 1).

We present three multiple regressions, one of them for *former* delinquency as dependent variable, the other two for the following frequencies of delinquency for different periods. For the second and the third analysis, we included "former registration by the police" as a control for potential selection effects, although it was obvious that this variable was not related systematically to the dependent variables. As we knew that the measurement of our variables was far from perfect, we decided to use the usual formulas to correct for attenuation and to run additional regressions with these corrected correlations.

Determinants of prior delinquency. The regression model with former delinquency as criterion (Model 0) that is included to control for some of the variables that might be of importance for the development of delinquent behavior - independent from any intervention by agencies of social control - documents the fact that the few sociodemographic and social status variables do not explain very much of the observed variance. Gender/sex and academic/school status are of some importance, whereas age nearly approaches significance, and social status (of parents) seems to be irrelevant.

Determinants of short-term developments of subsequent delinquency. When we turn to the regression model with the short-term (1 year after sanctioning decision) development of delinquency as dependent variable (Model 1), we find a moderate to impressive amount of explanation of the variance in the dependent variable (R-Square = .283 or .478 respectively for the model with correction for attenuation). Second, we observe a confirmation of the general law that the best predictor of delinquency is former delinquency (Beta = .488 or .669 respectively). Third, sex/gender - the most important predictor of former delinquency - is irrelevant for the short-term development of delinquency after diversion or accusation, respectively. Fourth, age has some importance when we look at the model with the corrected coefficients: The older the subjects the smaller the number of delinquent acts during the first year after the sanctioning decision, controlling for the other variables. Fifth, academic status/school status and social statuts of the parents prove to be relevant for short-term effects, though in different directions: While adolescents with high school status commit fewer delinquent acts in the first year, the opposite is true for social status of the parents. Sixth, former registration by the police is irrelevant for the short-term development of delinquency.

*Table 1: Frequency of self-reported delinquency before and after decision by the public prosecutor (diversion vs. accusation): Multiple regressions with observed coefficients and coefficients corrected for attenuation**

Criteria	(0.) Prior delinquency			(1.) Delinquency during the first year after decision			(2.) Delinquency during the second and third year after decision		
Predictors	B (S.E.)	beta <beta>	Sig <Sig>	B (S.E.)	beta <beta>	Sig <Sig>	B (S.E.)	beta <beta>	Sig <Sig>
Sex/Gender (1=m; 0=f)	.656 (.168)	.251 <.281>	.000 <.000>	.025 (.148)	.010 <-.027>	.862 <.595>	.324 (.161)	.119 <.120>	.045 <.016>
Age (0=14,15; 1=16,17)	.229 (.145)	.102 <.114>	.115 <.074>	-.198 (.124)	-.094 <-.126>	.110 <.012>	-.210 (.135)	-.090 <-.107>	.120 <.029>
Academic/School Status (0=low; 1=high)	-.279 (.148)	-.124 <-.138>	.060 <.033>	-.328 (.131)	-.155 <-.170>	.013 <.001>	.018 (.144)	.007 <.033>	.900 <.525>
Social Status (parents) (0=low; 1=high)	-.098 (.152)	-.042 <-.047>	.517 <.463>	.236 (.129)	.108 <.133>	.069 <.009>	-.040 (.141)	-.016 <-.029>	.775 <.555>
Former Registration by police (0=no; 1=yes)				.084 (.151)	.035 <.023>	.578 <.671>	.040 (.164)	.015 <.004>	.806 <.934>

(Table 1 contd.)

Formal Decision (0=diversion; 1=accusation)				-.104 (.131)	-.049 <-.079>	.425 <.132>	.196 (.142)	.084 <.095>	.169 <.063>
Prior delinquency				.460 (.057)	.488 <.669>	.000 <.000>	.320 (.071)	.308 <.369>	.000 <.000>
Delinquency in the first year after decision							.290 (.073)	.262 <.362>	.000 <.000>
Constant	1.418 (.177)		.000	-.084 (.174)		.628	-.205 (.189)		.278
N=227	R^2 = 0.102 d.f.= 4/222 <R^2 = 0.127>	F=6.33 Sig(F): p=.000		R^2 = 0.283 d.f.= 7/219 <R^2 = 0.478>	F=12.367 Sig(F): p=.000		R^2 = 0.312 d.f.= 8/218 <R^2 = 0.523>	F=12.386 Sig(F): p=.000	
Correlations of residuals	$r(e_0,e_1) = .000$;			$r(e_0,e_2) = .000$;			$r(e_1,e_2) = .000$;		

*Values in < ... > are corrected for attenuation

Source: Crasmöller 1994: 27

Seventh, the most important result, the type of decision by the public prosecutor (diversion vs. accusation) is statistically irrelevant with respect to following delinquency (first year only!). Interestingly, we see a small deterrence effect, but it is *far* from being statistically significant. Though this result is no confirmation of deterrence theory, it nevertheless may irritate proponents of diversion. However, if our former remarks on our research design are recalled, we may have the solution of this problem. Those subjects who did not receive a diversion decision had to live for several months (up to 7 or 8 months) with the pending process that could lead to a disastrous end if the subject was apprehended again. Therefore, the pressure for the accused subjects to continue to conform was exceptionally high and may have had two complementary effects: reducing the number of delinquent acts - at least for some time - in order to get a lenient sentence and/or not reporting absolutely correctly in the self-report of delinquency in order to reduce any risk if the subject was not really convinced of the absolute secrecy of the data. Part of the small and - we stress it once more - not significant deterrence effect may be caused by these methodological problems (for a discussion of the general problems of reliability and validity of self-report data on crime and delinquency see Huizinga and Elliott, 1986; for an analysis of these aspects with regard to our data see Howe, Karstedt-Henke, and Wolterhoff, 1991; for a discussion of the advantages and disadvantages of cross-sectional or panel data in the realm of self-report data, see Green, 1990; Weitekamp, 1989).

Determinants of long-term developments of subsequent delinquency. If we look at the third regression model (2) that, in principle, replicates the prior model but applies for long-term effects, we observe a confirmation of some parts of the former model as well as some interesting differences. First, we achieve an explanation of more than 50% of the variance in the dependent variable. Second, we acknowledge the special importance of prior delinquency again. In this case, the frequency of delinquency before diversion is as relevant as the frequency of delinquency in the first year after the diversion decision - an impressive proof of the eminent importance of the self-dynamic of early delinquency. Third, we discern that the gender of the juvenile offender becomes relevant for the long-term development: While in a short-term perspective, apprehended youth of both sexes do not differ in their reaction with respect to future delinquency, this is different in the long run. Males rather than females continue their delinquent behavior. Fourth, we once again see that older adolescents begin to desist from crime and delinquency, controlling for other variables. Fifth, an important difference to prior results is observable for academic/school status and social status of parents: In the long run, both variables lose any significance when the other variables are controlled.

Sixth, we can discern now that the type of decision by the public prosecutor is not irrelevant if we look at the long-term effects. Our data document that diverted adolescents will, in the long run, commit fewer delinquent acts than accused juveniles - controlling for other relevant variables. Admittedly this interpretation has to be handled with caution: We find only a rather small beta coefficient (.084 or .095 respectively) for this variable that fails to meet the conventional significance level of 95% by a narrow margin (p= .063). If we were to be very strict, we would have to ignore this result, but I think this would be a mistake. First, I would argue that although the diversion variable actually fails to reach statistical significance, it is nevertheless of *substantial* significance because the difference to the traditional level is very small, while, on the other hand, our result makes much sense from a theoretical point of view. If we consider the fact that our number of cases is rather small and that we excluded a number of cases because of technical problems when there was the slightest suspicion with respect to the assignment of our data to the court files, it would not make sense to bother about missing the significance level by one and a half percent. This is all the more so as our model includes several variables that do not contribute to the explanation (e.g., the status variables and prior registration by the police) but influence the significance level in a disadvantageous direction.

8 Conclusion

Our findings indicate that diversion in the long run brings about a slight reduction in self-reported delinquency compared to prosecution, although this effect just fails to reach the conventional significance level. If we are extremely cautious and do not accept this interpretation, we nevertheless come to a positive evaluation of diversion. At least we can say that diversion in no way threatens the positive development of delinquent youth if we look at it on an aggregate level. This result does not preclude the possibility that, in *individual* cases, diversion leads to disastrous consequences just as an accusation may have fatal results. One of our theoretically important future questions will be to investigate which juveniles gain optimal profit from which type of decision by the public prosecutor, although such a study might be very problematic from a political point of view. Its results could be used as a legitimation of "selective sanctioning", though we have every reason to assume that a prognosis for individual cases that could be the foundation for judicial sanctioning is impossible.

It should not be forgotten that an appropriate evaluation can only be obtained by a comparison with matched officially nonsanctioned adolescents. This will be completed in the following years (for a first analysis of the delinquency development in the comparable community sample, see Albrecht and Howe, 1994).

Up to now, we have only differentiated between diverted and nondiverted adolescents without considering what diversion and prosecution have actually involved. Both treatments should be viewed differentially, e.g., we should have a look at different forms of diversion and different forms of non-diversion. This could produce different results. This is also a task that we will be facing in the future. Because of space limitations and because of the rather provisional character of our analysis with respect to the theoretical traditions we mentioned and discussed in earlier parts of this paper I want to restrict myself to a few general remarks.

First, we come to the conclusion that theories that postulate a causal relation between self-concept and delinquency and vice versa are partly confirmed and partly disconfirmed by our data. Apparently, existing theories are too general and have to be modified in several respects.

Second, central ideas of the control theory of delinquency (especially with respect to the dimensions attachment and commitment) are confirmed more or less by our data (not shown here), whereas Hirschi's original assumptions about involvement have to be modified insofar as involvement in some types of networks increases the probability of delinquency.

Third, our data, on the one hand, document the enormous importance of informal control reactions, but, on the other hand, we still do not know how far the triggering of informal reactions depends on special forms of official reactions (see, for instance, much data indicating that such a dependency exists, in Becker, 1993: 78-100).

Fourth, most of our data are not compatible with central assumptions of the rational choice theory of crime and delinquency in its simple versions. On the other side, we see the necessity and possibility of an integration between labeling theory and rational choice theory that might solve several of the difficulties that both theoretical traditions have when confronted with empirical data.

Of special importance will be the analysis of "deviant cases", for example, of individual developments that do not fit into the "usual" development pattern: Though all predictors, for instance, lead to the expectation of desistance from crime and delinquency, a subject may not desist but even prolong and intensify his or her "criminal career". We have collected data on about 40 "deviant cases" 2 years after completion of the third wave of our main study with a semistructured interview in order to search for an explanation for these "deviant cases of deviance".

If I had to draw a firm conclusion, I would state that although our preliminary findings indicate that diversion is no wonder weapon, it is nonetheless defensible. It obviously does not threaten the development of adolescents by dropping formal prosecution proceedings. However, we need to examine more closely whether its effects will be even more favorable when it is applied in a way that minimizes intervention and stigmatization. This attempted "reintegrative shaming" should not surreptitiously - but informally - revive the negative side effects of prosecution. I am skeptical about the chances of reinstitutionalizing or revitalizing premodern forms of social control that could guarantee that "organized shaming" would be applied in a reintegrative manner. But, nevertheless, we should examine these ideas very seriously, both theoretically and empirically. Though we observe some progress in the sociology of emotions, especially of shame (see, e.g., Neckel, 1991; Scheff, 1988, 1990a), we have to acknowledge the problem that, till now, there has been a deep cleavage between the sociology of shame and the sociology of shaming (see Scheff, 1990b: 744)

Before we develop ideas on how to organize formal control structures that might implement John Braithwaite's ideas, we should take a critical look at the majority of delinquent acts that trigger the activities of the criminal justice system in Germany and that are solved by diversion. In my opinion, we are still too far removed from "radical nonintervention" to be able to evaluate it properly, because diversion is still focusing on those delinquents with minor offenses and with relatively few former contacts with the agents of formal social control.

Appendix

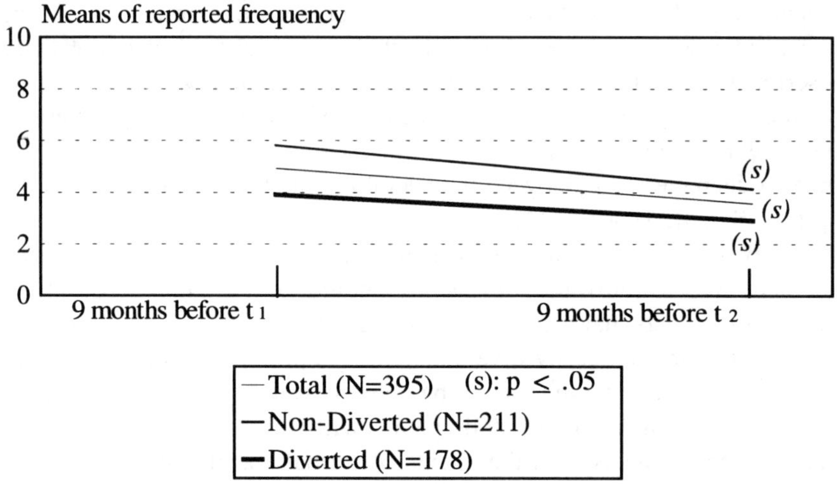

Fig. 1: Change in self-reported delinquency (comparison of means) t_1 - t_2: Total / Diverted / Non-Diverted

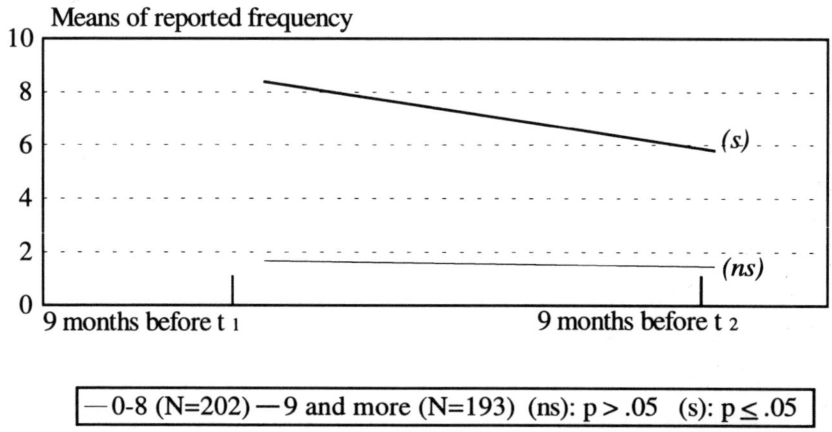

Fig. 2: Change in self-reported delinquency after decision by the prosecutor (comparison of means) t_1 - t_2, controlling for lifetime delinquency (0-8= 0-8 delinquent acts during lifetime before t_1; >8 = 9 and more delinquent acts during lifetime before t_1)

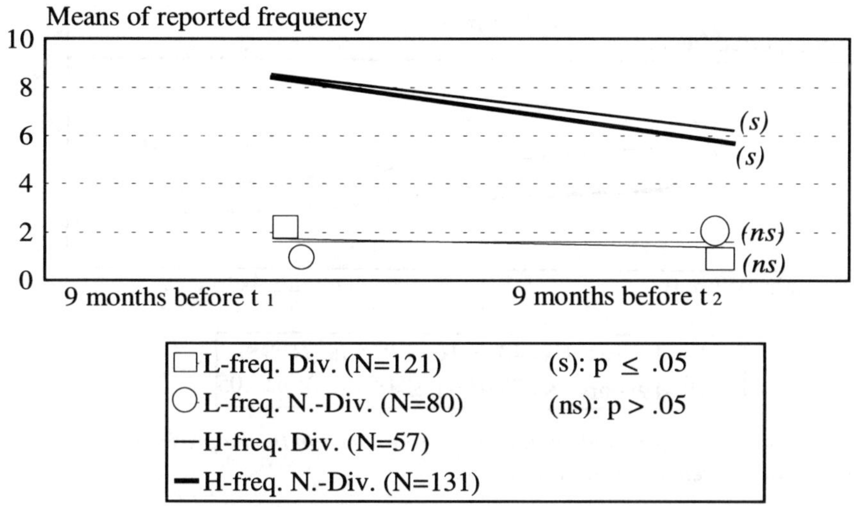

Fig.3: Change in self-reported delinquency after decision by the prosecutor (comparison of means) t_1 - t_2 for diverted and non-diverted adolescents, controlling for lifetime delinquency before t_1

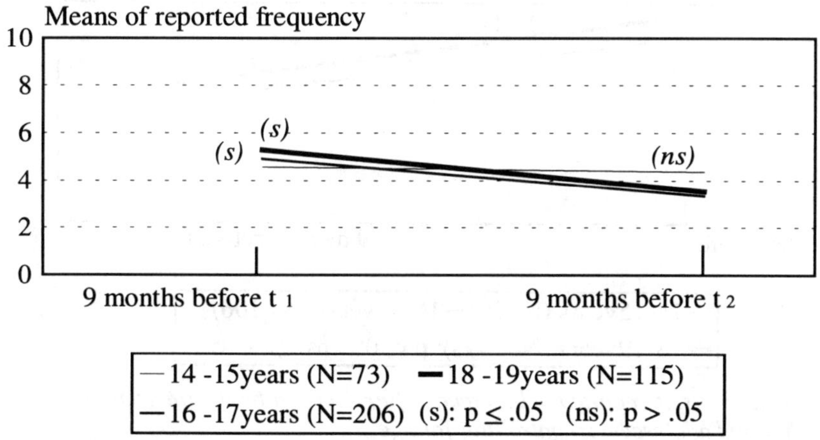

Fig.4: Change in self-reported delinquency after decision by the prosecutor (comparison of means) t_1 - t_2, controlling for age (at t_2)

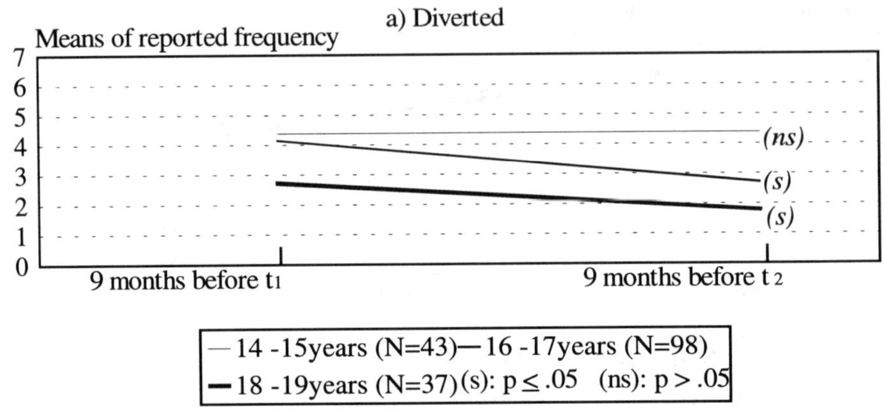

Fig.5a: Change in self-reported delinquency after decision by the prosecutor for diverted adolescents, controlling for age

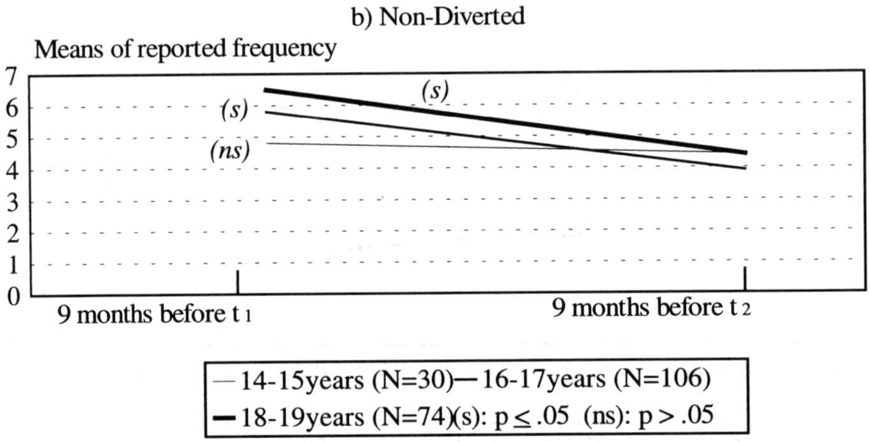

Fig.5b: Change in self-reported delinquency after decision by the prosecutor for non-diverted adolescents, controlling for age

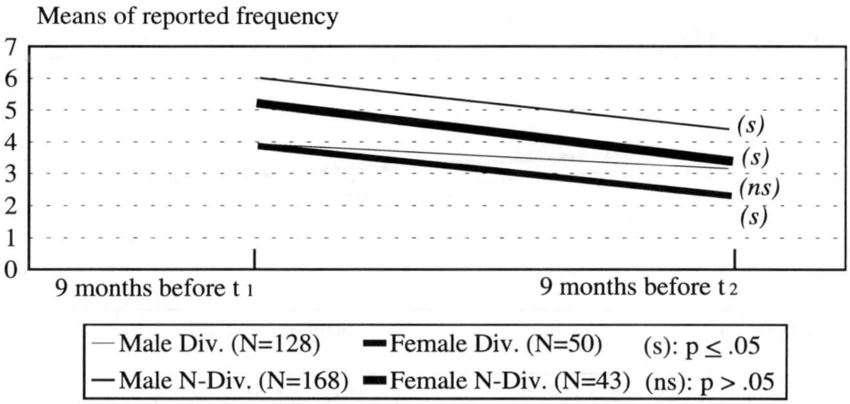

Fig.6: Change in self-reported delinquency after decision by the prosecutor (t_1 -t_2) for diverted and non-diverted adolescents, controlling for sex

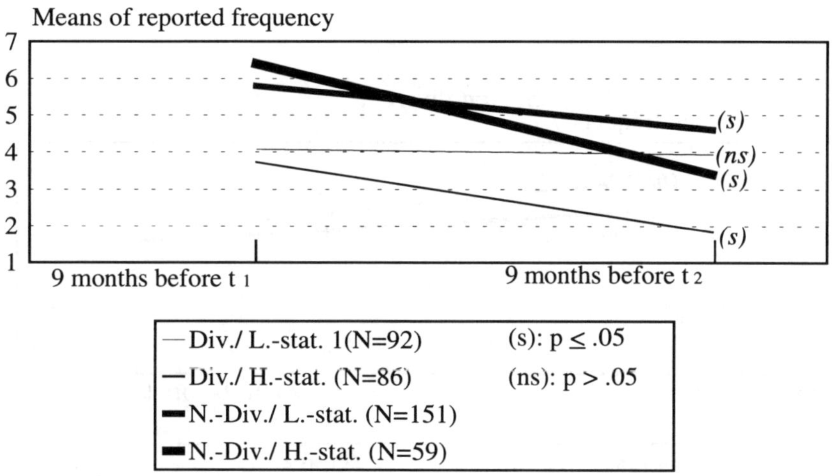

Fig.7: Change in self-reported delinquency after decision by the prosecutor (t_1 - t_2) for diverted and non-diverted adolescents, controlling for school status

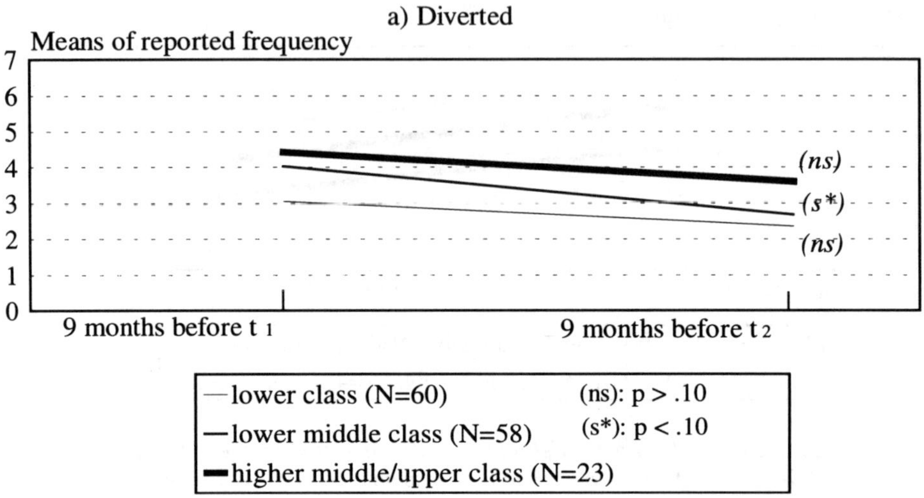

Fig.8a: Change in self-reported delinquency after decision by the prosecutor (t_1 - t_2) for diverted adolescents; controlling for social status of parents and type of decision by the prosecutor

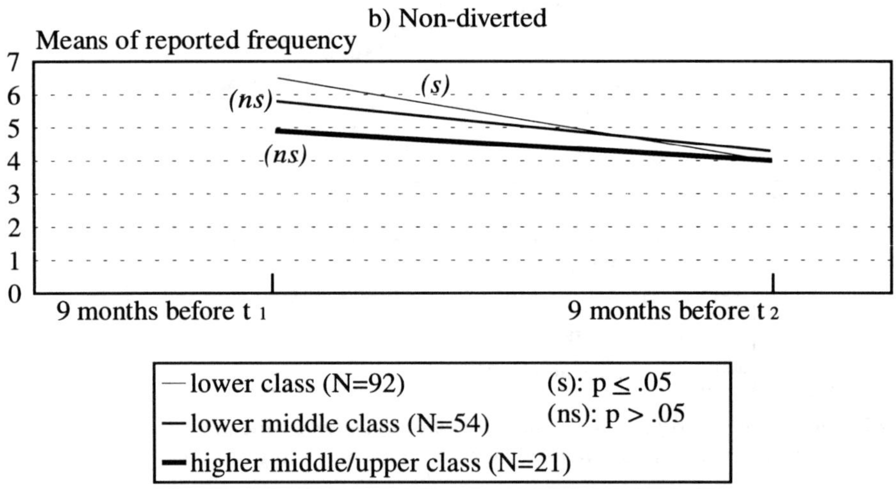

Fig. 8b: Change in self-reported delinquency after decision by the prosecutor (t_1 - t_2) for non-diverted adolescents, controlling for social status of parents

References

Agnew, R. (1985). Social control theory and delinquency. A longitudinal test. *Criminology, 23*, 46-61.

Agnew, R. (1991). A longitudinal test of social control theory and delinquency. *Journal of Research in Crime and Delinquency, 28*, 126-156.

Akers, R.L. (1990). Rational choice, deterrence, and social learning theory in criminology: The path not taken. *Journal of Criminal Law and Criminology, 81*, 653-676.

Albrecht, G. (1973). Die "Erklärung" von Devianz durch die Theorie des Symbolischen Interaktionismus. In G. Albrecht, H.-J. Daheim, and F. Sack (Eds.), *Soziologie. Festschrift für René König* (pp. 775-803). Köln-Opladen: Westdeutscher Verlag.

Albrecht, G. (1982). Muß angewandte Soziologie konforme Soziologie sein? In U. Beck (Ed.), *Soziologie und Praxis. Erfahrungen, Konflikte, Perspektiven. Soziale Welt, Special Issue* (pp. 161-204). Göttingen: Schwartz.

Albrecht, G. (1985). *Finanzierungsantrag des Projektes C3 "Alternative Konfliktlösungs- und Sanktionspraktiken: Auswirkungen auf strafrechtlich Auffällige" an die Deutsche Forschungsgemeinschaft*. Bielefeld: Sonderforschungsbereich "Prävention und Intervention im Kindes- und Jugendalter".

Albrecht, G. (1991). Methodological dilemmas in research on prevention and intervention. In G. Albrecht and H.-U. Otto (Eds.), *Social prevention and the social sciences. Theoretical controversies, research problems, and evaluation strategies* (pp. 397-428). Berlin, New York: Walter de Gruyter.

Albrecht, G. (1992). Jugend, Recht und Kriminalität. In H.-H. Krüger (Ed.), *Handbuch der Jugendforschung* (pp. 495-525). 2nd ed. Opladen: Leske + Budrich.

Albrecht, G. (1994). Anomie und Kriminalität. In W. Heitmeyer (Ed.), Anomietendenzen und ihre Folgen für interkulturelle und interethnische Konflikte. Frankfurt am Main: Suhrkamp (in preparation).

Albrecht, G., and Howe, C.W. (1994). *Delinquenzentwicklung im Längsschnitt: Ein Vergleich zweier Wellen einer repräsentativen Längsschnittstudie*. Preprint Nr. 86. SFB 227. Bielefeld

Albrecht, G., and Karstedt-Henke, S. (1987). Alternative methods of conflict-settling and sanctioning: Their impact on young offenders. In K. Hurrelmann, F.-X. Kaufmann, and F. Lösel (Eds.), *Social intervention: Potential and constraints* (pp. 315-332). Berlin, New York: Walter de Gruyter.

Albrecht, G., and Karstedt-Henke, S. (1989). Ethical problems of survey research on delinquency: An empirical analysis of accessing and interviewing young offenders. In P.-A. Albrecht and O. Backes (Eds.), *Crime prevention and intervention. Legal and ethical problems* (pp. 249-271). Berlin, New York : Walter de Gruyter.

Albrecht, G., and van Kampen, N. (1991). *Auswirkungen der Diversion auf die Entwicklung des Selbstbildes delinquenter Jugendlicher*. Preprint Nr. 45, SFB 227. Bielefeld.

Albrecht, G., et al. (1988a). *Arbeits- und Ergebnisbericht des Teilprojektes C3 (Phase 1) "Alternative Konfliktlösungs- und Sanktionspraktiken: Auswirkungen auf strafrechtlich Auffällige" an die Deutsche Forschungsgemeinschaft*. Bielefeld: Sonderforschungsbereich 227 "Prävention und Intervention im Kindes- und Jugendalter".

Albrecht, G., et al. (1988b). *Finanzierungsantrag des Teilprojektes C3 "Alternative Konfliktlösungs- und Sanktionspraktiken: Auswirkungen auf strafrechtlich Auffällige" für die zweite Förderungsphase (1989-1991) an die Deutsche Forschungsgemeinschaft.* Bielefeld: Sonderforschungsbereich 227 "Prävention und Intervention im Kindes- und Jugendalter".

Albrecht, G., et al. (1991a). *Arbeits- und Ergebnisbericht des Teilprojektes C3 "Alternative Konfliktlösungs- und Sanktionspraktiken: Auswirkungen auf strafrechtlich Auffällige" (Phase 2) an die Deutsche Forschungsgemeinschaft.* Bielefeld: Sonderforschungsbereich 227 "Prävention und Intervention im Kindes- und Jugendalter".

Albrecht, G., et al. (1991b). *Finanzierungsantrag des Teilprojektes C3 "Alternative Konfliktlösungs- und Sanktionspraktiken: Auswirkungen auf strafrechtlich Auffällige" (3. Phase: 1992-1994) an die Deutsche Forschungsgemeinschaft.* Bielefeld: Sonderforschungsbereich 227 "Prävention und Intervention im Kindes- und Jugendalter".

Albrecht, G., et al. (1994a). *Arbeits- und Ergebnisbericht des Teilprojektes C3 "Alternative Konfliktlösungs- und Sanktionspraktiken: Auswirkungen auf strafrechtlich Auffällige" (3. Phase: 1992-1994) an die Deutsche Forschungsgemeinschaft.* Bielefeld: Sonderforschungsbereich 227 "Prävention und Intervention im Kindes- und Jugendalter".

Albrecht, G., et al. (1994b). *Finanzierungsantrag des Teilprojektes C3 "Alternative Konfliktlösungs- und Sanktionspraktiken: Auswirkungen auf strafrechtlich Auffällige" für die vierte Phase (1995-1997) an die Deutsche Forschungsgemeinschaft.* Bielefeld: Sonderforschungsbereich 227 "Prävention und Intervention im Kindes- und Jugendalter".

Albrecht, P.-A. (1990a). Exekutivisches Recht - Eine Einführung in empirische Analysen zur staatsanwaltschaftlichen Diversion in Nordrhein-Westfalen. In P.-A. Albrecht (Ed.), *Informalisierung des Rechts* (pp. 1-44). Berlin, New York: Walter de Gruyter.

Albrecht, P.-A. (Ed.) (1990b). *Informalisierung des Rechts. Empirische Untersuchungen zur Handhabung und zu den Grenzen der Opportunität im Jugendstrafrecht.* Berlin, New York: Walter de Gruyter.

Andrews, D.A., Zinger, I., Hoge, R.D., Bonta, J., Gendreau, P., and Cullen, F.T. (1990a). Does correctional treatment work? A clinically relevant and psychologically informed meta-analysis. *Criminology, 28,* 369-404.

Andrews, D.A., Zinger, I., Hoge, R.D., Bonta, J., Gendreau, P., and Cullen, F.T. (1990b). A human science approach or more punishment and pessimism: A rejoinder to Lab and Whitehead. *Criminology, 28,* 419-429.

Becker, H.S. (1963). *Outsiders: studies in the sociology of deviance.* New York: Free Press.

Becker, M. (1993). *Informelle soziale Kontrolle - Eine empirische Untersuchung im Bereich der Jugendelinquenz.* Unpubl. Diplomarbeit, Bielefeld: Faculty of Sociology.

Blakely, C.H., Kushler, M.G., and Davidson, W.S. (1980). Self-reported delinquency as an evaluation measure. Comparative reliability and validity of alternative weighting schemes. *Criminal Justice and Behavior, 7,* 369-386.

Blomberg, Th., and Blomberg, J. (1985). Die Ausdehnung des Netzes sozialer Kontrolle durch Diversion. In M. Brusten, N. Herriger, and P. Malinowski (Eds.), *Entkriminalisierung* (pp. 111-123). Opladen: Westdeutscher Verlag.

Braithwaite, J. (1989). *Crime, shame and reintegration.* Cambridge: Cambridge University Press.

Bundesministerium der Justiz (Ed.) (1989a). *Jugendstrafrechtsreform durch die Praxis. Informelle Reaktionen und neue ambulante Maßnahmen auf dem Prüfstand. Konstanzer Symposium.* Bonn: Bundesministerium der Justiz.

Bundesministerium der Justiz (Ed.) (1989b). *"Diversion" im deutschen Jugendstrafrecht. Informelle Erledigungen und ambulante Maßnahmen.* Bonn: Bundesministerium der Justiz.

Cornish, D.B., and Clarke, R.V. (1986a). (Eds.). *The reasoning criminal. Rational choice perspectives on offending.* New York: Springer.

Cornish, D.B., and Clarke, R.V. (1986b). Introduction. In D.B. Cornish and R.V. Clarke (Eds.), *The reasoning criminal. Rational choice perspectives on offending* (pp. 1-16). New York: Springer.

Crasmöller, B. (1993). *Wirkungen strafrechtlicher Sozialkontrolle jugendlicher Kriminalität. Eine empirische Analyse der spezialpräventiven Effekte.* Bielefeld: unpubl. Diss., Faculty for Sociology.

Crasmöller, B. (1994). *Kurz- und längerfristige Effekte staatsanwaltlicher Diversion.* Preprint Nr. 83. Bielefeld: Sonderforschungsbereich 227 "Prävention und Intervention im Kindes- und Jugendalter".

Crasmöller, B. (1995). *Wirkungen strafrechtlicher Sozialkontrolle jugendlicher Kriminalität. Eine empirische Analyse der spezialpräventiven Effekte (rev. edition of Crasmöller 1993).* Freiburg: Centaurus (in preparation).

Czisch, J. (1994). *Veränderungen im Selbstwert nach delinquentem Verhalten.* Preprint Nr. 84. Bielefeld: Sonderforschungsbereich 227 "Prävention und Intervention im Kindes- und Jugendalter".

Davidson, W.S., Redner, R., Amdur, R.L., and Mitchell, Chr.Ch. (1990). *Alternative treatments for troubled youth.* New York, London: Plenum.

Dölling, D. (1989). Rechtsprobleme der Jugendstrafrechtsreform durch die Praxis. In Bundesministerium der Justiz (Ed.), *Jugendstrafrechtsreform durch die Praxis* (pp. 243-266). Bonn: Bundesministerium der Justiz.

Dunford, F.W., and Elliott, D.S. (1984). Identifying career offenders using self-reported data. *Journal of Research in Crime and Delinquency, 21,* 57-86.

Erickson, M.L., Stafford, M.C., Galliher, J.M. (1984). The normative erosion hypothesis: The latent consequences of juvenile justice practices. *The Sociological Quarterly, 25,* 1984, 373-384.

Farrington, D.P. (1989). Self-reported and official offending from adolescence to adulthood. In M.W. Klein (Ed.), *Cross-national research in self-reported crime and delinquency* (pp. 399-423). Dordrecht, Boston, London: Klüwer Academic Press.

Fend, H., et al. (1984). *Inventar zu Selbstkonzept und Selbstvertrauen.* Konstanz: Universität Konstanz.

Garfinkel, H. (1956). Conditions of successful degradation ceremonies. *American Journal of Sociology, 61,* 420-424.

Gecas, V. (1982). The Self-Concept. *Annual Review of Sociology, 8,* 1-33.

Gibbs, J.P. (1975). *Crime, punishment and deterrence.* New York: Elsevier.

Grasmick, H.G., and Appleton, L. (1977). Legal punishment and social stigma: A comparison on two deterrence models. *Social Science Quarterly, 58,* 15-28.

Grasmick, H.G., and Bryjak, G.J. (1980). The deterrent effect of perceived severity of punishment. *Social Forces, 59,* 471-491.

Grasmick, H.G., Green, D. (1980). Legal punishment, social disapproval and internalization as inhibitors of illegal behavior. *Journal of Criminal Law and Criminology, 71,* 325-335.

Green, D.E. (1990). Measuring self-reported deviance: Cross-sectional or panel data? *Social Science Research, 19,* 301-321.

Heinz, W. (1989a). Auswahlbibliographie des deutschsprachigen Schrifttums seit 1980 zu Diversion und ambulanten Maßnahmen im deutschen Jugendstrafrecht. In Bundesministerium der Justiz (Ed.), *"Diversion im deutschen Strafrecht. Thesen, Empfehlungen, Bibliographie"*. (pp. 65-135). Bonn: Bundesministerium der Justiz.

Heinz, W. (1989b). Jugendstrafrechtsreform durch die Praxis - eine Bestandsaufnahme. In Bundesministerium der Justiz (Ed.), *Jugendstrafrechtsreform durch die Praxis* (pp. 13-44). Bonn: Bundesministerium der Justiz.

Heinz, W. (1990). Diversion im Jugendstrafverfahren. Aktuelle kriminalpolitische Bestrebungen im Spiegel empirischer Untersuchungen. *Zeitschrift für Rechtspolitik, 23,* 7-11.

Heinz, W. (1992). Diversion im Jugendstrafverfahren der Bundesrepublik Deutschland. Gesetzgeberische Zielvorstellungen, kriminologische Grundlagen, Umsetzung in der Praxis, kriminalpolitische Folgerungen. In W. Heinz and R. Storz, *Diversion im Jugendstrafverfahren der Bundesrepublik Deutschland* (pp. 3-130). Bonn: Forum Verlag.

Heinz, W., and Spieß, G. (1983). Alternativen zu formellen Reaktionen im deutschen Jugendstrafrecht. Ein Forschungsvorhaben zu §§ 45, 47 JGG und erste Ergebnisse. In H.-J. Kerner, H. Kury, and K. Sessar (Eds.), *Deutsche Forschungen zur Kriminalitätsentstehung und Kriminalitätskontrolle* (pp. 896-955). Köln: Heymanns.

Hering, E., and Sessar, K. (1990). *Praktizierte Diversion. Das "Modell Lübeck" sowie die Diversionsprogramme in Köln, Braunschweig und Hamburg.* Pfaffenweiler: Centaurus.

Hirschi, T. (1969). *Causes of delinquency.* Berkeley, Los Angeles, CA: University of California Press.

Hirschi, T. (1986). On the compatibility of rational choice and social control theories of crime. In D.B. Cornish and R.V. Clarke (Eds.), *The reasoning criminal. Rational choice perspectives on offending* (pp. 105-118). New York: Springer.

Howe, C.-W., Karstedt-Henke, S., and Wolterhoff, J. (1991). *Wie dunkel ist das Dunkelfeld? Die Validität selbstberichteter Delinquenzangaben bei Jugendlichen.* Preprint SFB 227. Bielefeld.

Hügel, C. (1987). Ergebnisse der empirischen Untersuchung. In W. Heinz and C. Hügel, *Erzieherische Maßnahmen im deutschen Jugendstrafrecht* (pp. 21-91). 3rd ed. Bonn: Bundesministerium der Justiz.

Hügel, C., and Heinz, W. (1987). Ertrag und Folgerungen der Untersuchung über Bestandsaufnahme und Determinanten der Sanktionspraxis, Verfahrensökonomie und Praktikabilitität, Legalbewährung und Wirkungsanalyse. In W. Heinz and C. Hügel, *Erzieherische Maßnahmen im deutschen Jugendstrafrecht* (pp 93-96). 3rd ed. Bonn: Bundesministerium der Justiz.

Huizinga, D., and Elliott, D.S. (1986). Reassessing the reliability and validity of self-report delinquency measures. *Journal of Quantitative Criminology, 2,* 293-327.

Janssen, H. (1983). Diversion: Entstehungsbedingungen, Hintergründe und Konsequenzen einer veränderten Strategie sozialer Kontrolle. Oder: Es gibt viele zu packen, tun wir es ihnen an. In H.-J. Kerner (Ed.), *Diversion statt Strafe? Probleme und Gefahren einer neuen Strategie strafrechtlicher Sozialkontrolle* (pp. 15-54). Heidelberg: Kriminalistik Verlag.

Jensen, G.F., Erickson, M.L., and Gibbs, J.P. (1978). Perceived risk of punishment and self-reported delinquency. *Social Forces, 57,* 57-78.

Kaiser, G. (1985). Möglichkeiten der Entkriminalisierung nach dem Jugendgerichtsgesetz im Vergleich zum Ausland. In M. Brusten, N. Herriger, and P. Malinowski (Eds.), *Entkriminalisierung* (pp. 159-189). Opladen: Westdeutscher Verlag.

Kaplan, H.B. (1980). *Deviant behavior in defense of self.* New York: Academic Press.

Kaplan, H.B., Johnson, R.J., Bailey, C.A. (1987). Deviant peers and deviant behavior: Further elaboration of a model. *Social Psychology Quarterly, 50*, 277-284.

Kaplan, H.B., Martin, St.S., and Johnson, R.J. (1986). Self-rejection and the explanation of deviance: Specification of the structure among latent constructs. *American Journal of Sociology, 92*, 384-411.

Kerner, H.-J. (1981). Diversion - eine wirkliche Alternative? In H. Kury and H. Lerchenmüller (Eds.), *Diversion. Alternativen zu klassischen Sanktionsformen,* Vol. 2 (pp. 688-728). Bochum: Studienverlag Dr. N. Brockmeyer.

Kerner, H.-J. (1983). Statt Strafe: Diversion? Zur Einführung in die Thematik. In H.-J. Kerner (Ed.), *Diversion statt Strafe? Probleme und Gefahren einer neuen Strategie strafrechtlicher Sozialkontrolle* (pp. 1-13). Heidelberg: Kriminalistik Verlag.

Kerner, H.-J. (1989). Unbeabsichtigte und unerwünschte Nebenfolgen der JGG-Reform durch die Praxis, insbesondere das Beispiel der Ausweitung des Netzes sozialer Kontrolle. In Bundesministerium der Justiz (Ed.), *Jugendstrafrechtsreform durch die Praxis* (pp. 265-292). Bonn: Bundesministerium der Justiz.

Kirchhoff, G. (1981). Diversionsprogramme in den USA. Diversion zwischen Entdeckung und vor Verurteilung im Juvenile Justice System. In H. Kury and H. Lerchenmüller (Eds.), *Diversion. Alternativen zu klassischen Sanktionsformen,* Vol. 1 (pp. 246-284). Bochum: Studienverlag Dr. N. Brockmeyer.

Klein, M.W. (1985). Die Reform der Jugendgerichtsbarkeit in den Vereinigten Staaten und ihre Konsequenzen für die Delinquenzprophylaxe. In M. Brusten, N. Herriger, and P. Malinowski (Eds.), *Entkriminalisierung* (pp. 145-156). Opladen: Westdeutscher Verlag.

Klinger, Th. (1993). Die polizeiliche Vernehmung von Jugendlichen. Zusammenhänge von erlebten Kontrollreaktionen, Selbstzuschreibungen und Diversion. *Soziale Probleme, 4,* 101-138.

Klinger, Th. (1994). *Wahrgenommene Etikettierung, deviantes Selbstbild und Delinquenz.* Preprint Nr. 85. Bielefeld: Sonderforschungsbereich 227 "Prävention und Intervention im Kindes- und Jugendalter".

Kury, H. (1981). Diversion - Möglichkeiten und Grenzen am Beispiel amerikanischer Programme. In H. Kury and H. Lerchenmüller (Eds.), *Diversion. Alternativen zu klassischen Sanktionsformen,* Vol. 1 (pp. 165-245). Bochum: Studienverlag Dr. N. Brockmeyer.

Lab, S.P., and Whitehead, J.T. (1988). An analysis of juvenile delinquency correctional treatment. *Crime and Delinquency, 34,* S. 60-83.

Lab, S.P., and Whitehead, J.T. (1990). From "nothing works" to "the appropriate works": The latest step on the search for the secular grail. *Criminology, 28,* 405-419.

Lamp, R. (1981). Probleme der theoretischen Analyse von Diversionsprogrammen. In H. Kury and H. Lerchenmüller (Eds.), *Diversion. Alternativen zu klassischen Sanktionsformen,* Vol.2 (pp. 657-687). Bochum: Studienverlag Dr. N. Brockmeyer.

Lee, R.M. (1993). *Doing research on sensitive topics.* London, Newbury Park, New Delhi: Sage.

Lemert, Ed.M. (1967a). *Human deviance, social problems, and social control.* Englewood Cliffs, N.J.: Prentice-Hall.

Lemert, Ed.M (1967b). The concept of secondary deviation. In Ed.M. Lemert (Ed.), *Human deviance, social problems, and social control* (pp. 40-64). Englewood Cliffs, N.J.: Prentice-Hall.

Lemert, Ed.M. (1971). *Instead of court. Diversion in juvenile justice.* Washington, D.C., 1971.

Lemert, Ed.M. (1985). Diversion im Rahmen der Jugendgerichtsbarkeit: Was wurde eigentlich erreicht? In M. Brusten, N. Herriger, and P. Malinowski (Eds.), *Entkriminalisierung* (pp. 124-144). Opladen: Westdeutscher Verlag.

Lemert, Ed.M. (1985). Alternativen zur gerichtlichen Verarbeitung abweichenden Verhaltens - Diversion auf der Ebene polizeilichen Handelns. In M. Brusten, N. Herriger, and P. Malinowski (Eds.), *Entkriminalisierung* (pp. 37-52). Opladen: Westdeutscher Verlag.

Liska, A.E. (1981). *Perspectives on deviance*. Englewood Cliffs, New York: Prentice-Hall.

Ludwig, W. (1989). *Diversion: Strafe im neuen Gewand*. Berlin, New York: de Gruyter.

Ludwig-Mayerhofer, W. (1990). Die staatsanwaltliche Diversionspraxis im Jugendstrafrecht - Eine landesweite Aktenuntersuchung in 19 Staatsanwaltschaften Nordrhein-Westfalens. In P.-A. Albrecht (Ed.), *Informalisierung des Rechts. Empirische Untersuchungen zur Handhabung und zu den Grenzen der Opportunität im Jugendstrafrecht* (pp. 47-225). Berlin, New York: Walter de Gruyter.

Markus, H., Wurf, E. (1987). The dynamic self-concept: A social psychological perspective. *Annual Review of Psychology, 38*, 299-337.

Matsueda, R.L. (1992). Reflected appraisals, parental labeling, and delinquency: Specifying a symbolic interactionist theory. *American Journal of Sociology, 97,* 1577-1611.

Minor, W.W., and Harry, J. (1982). Deterrent and experiential effects in perceptual deterrence research: A replication and extension. *Journal of Research in Crime and Delinquency, 19,* 190-203.

Neckel, S. (1991). *Status und Scham: Zur symbolischen Reproduktion sozialer Ungleichheit*. Frankfurt, New York: Campus.

Paternoster, R., and Iovanni, L. (1986). The deterrent effects of perceived severity: A reexamination. *Social Forces, 64,* 751-777.

Paternoster, R., Saltzman, L.E., Waldo, G.P., and Chiricos, T.G. (1983). Estimating perceptual stability and deterrent effects: The role of perceived legal punishment in the inhibition of criminal involvement. *The Journal of Criminal Law and Criminology, 74,* 270-297.

Pfeiffer, Ch. (1983). *Jugendgerichtsverfahren und Kriminalprävention. Jugendrichterliches Handeln vor dem Hintergrund des Brücke-Projektes.* Köln: Heymanns.

Pfeiffer, Ch. (1989). Diversion - Alternativen zum Freiheitsentzug, Entwicklungstrends und regionale Unterschiede. In Bundesministerium der Justiz (Ed.), *Jugendstrafrechtsreform durch die Praxis* (pp. 74-100). Bonn: Bundesministerium der Justiz.

Piliavin, I., Gartner, R., Thornton, C., et al. (1986). Crime, deterrence and rational choice. *American Sociological Review, 51,* 101-119.

Rosenberg, M. (1979). *Conceiving the self.* New York: Basic Books.

Rosenberg, M. (1985). Self-concept and psychological well-being in adolescence. In R.L. Leahy (Ed.), *The development of the self* (pp. 205-246). Orlando: Academic Press.

Rosenberg, M., Schooler, C., and Schoenbach, C. (1989). Self-esteem and adolescent problems: Modeling reciprocal effects. *American Sociological Review, 54,* 1004-1018.

Rossi, P.H. (1978). Issues in the evaluation of human services delivery. *Evaluation Quarterly, 2*, 573-599.

Rossi, P.H., and Wright, J.D. (1987). Evaluation research: An assessment. In D.S. Cordray and M.W. Lipsey (Eds.), *Evaluation studies review annual* (pp. 48-69). Newbury Park: Sage.

Sack, F. (1978). Probleme der Kriminalsoziologie. In R. König (Ed.), Handbuch der empirischen Sozialforschung, Vol. 12 (pp. 192-492). 2nd ed. Stuttgart: Enke.

Saltzman, L., Paternoster, R., Waldo, G.P., and Chiricos, T.G. (1982). Deterrent and experiential effects. The problem of causal order in perceptual deterrence research. *Journal of Research in Crime and Delinquency, 19,* 172-189.

Scheff, Th. (1988). Shame and conformity: The deference-emotion system. *American Sociological Review, 53*, 395-406.

Scheff, Th. (1990a). *Microsociology: Discourse, emotion, and social structure.* Chicago: University of Chicago Press.

Scheff, Th. (1990b). Review Essay: A new Durkheim (Crime, shame and Reintegration. By John Braithwaite). *American Journal of Sociology, 96*, 741-746.

Scheff, Th., Retzinger, S., and Ryan, M.T. (1989). Crime, violence, and self-esteem: Review and proposals. In A.N. Mecca, N.J. Smelser, and J. Vasconcellos (Eds.), *The social importance of self-esteem* (pp. 165-199). Berkeley: University of California Press.

Schur, E.M. (1973). *Radical non-intervention. Rethinking the delinquency problem.* Englewood Cliffs, New York, 1984.

Smith, D., Gartin, P.R. (1989). Specifying specific deterrence: The influence of arrest on future criminal activity. *American Sociological Review, 54*, 1989, 94-106.

Spieß, G., and Storz, R. (1989). Informelle Reaktionsstrategien im deutschen Jugendstrafrecht: Legalbewährung und Wirkungsanalyse. In Bundesministerium der Justiz (Ed.), *Jugendstrafrechtsreform durch die Praxis* (pp. 127-153). Bonn: Bundesministerium der Justiz.

Stafford, M.C., Gray, L.N., Menke, B.A., and Ward, D.A. (1986). Modeling the deterrent effects of punishment. *Social Psychology Quarterly, 49,* 338-347.

Storz, R. (1992). Jugendstrafrechtliche Reaktionen und Legalbewährung. Ergebnisse einer Untersuchung zur erneuten justitiellen Registrierung nach formeller und informeller jugendstrafrechtlicher Sanktionierung von Jugendlichen des Geburtsjahrgangs 1961 anhand von Daten des Bundeszentralregisters. In W. Heinz and R. Storz, *Diversion im Jugendstrafverfahren der Bundesrepublik Deutschland* (pp. 133-221). Bonn: Forum Verlag.

Tittle, Ch.R. (1980). *Sanctions and deviance. The questions of deterrence.* New York: Praeger.

Tittle, Ch.R., and Logan, C.H. (1973). Sanctions and deviance: Evidence and remaining questions. *Law and Society Review, 7,* 371-392.

Tuck, M., and Riley, D. (1986). The theory of reasoned action: A decision theory of crime. In D.B. Cornish and R.V. Clarke (Eds.), *The reasoning criminal. Rational choice perspectives on offending* (pp. 156-169). New York: Springer.

Voß, M. (1983). Über das keineswegs zufällige Zusammentreffen von Gefängnisausbau und der Einrichtung ambulanter Alternativen. In H.-J. Kerner (Ed.), *Diversion statt Strafe? Probleme und Gefahren einer neuen Strategie strafrechtlicher Sozialkontrolle* (pp. 95-116). Heidelberg: Kriminalistik Verlag.

Voß, M. (1985). Widersprüche im Konzept und bedenkliche Erfahrungen. Lohnt die Einführung von Diversion? In M. Brusten, N. Herriger, and P. Malinowski (Eds.), *Entkriminalisierung* (pp. 190-230). Opladen: Westdeutscher Verlag.

Waldo, G.P., and Chiricos, Th.G. (1972). Perceived penal sanction and self-reported criminality: A neglected approach to deterrence research. *Social Problems, 19,* 522-540.

Walter, M. (1989). Jugendkriminalrechtliche Zielvorstellungen und die Reichweite der Reform des JGG durch die Praxis - Perspektiven für systemimmanente Entwicklungen und Verbesserungen. In Bundesministerium der Justiz (Ed.), *Jugendstrafrechtsreform durch die Praxis* (pp. 230-243). Bonn: Bundesministerium der Justiz.

Weitekamp, E. (1989). Some problems with the use of self-reports in longitudinal research. In M.W. Klein (Ed.), *Cross-national research in self-reported crime and delinquency* (pp. 329-346). Dordrecht, Boston, London: Klüwer Academic Press.

Wells, L.E. (1978). Theories of deviance and the self-concept. *Social Psychology Quarterly, 41,* 189-204.

Wells, L.E., and Rankin, J.H. (1983). Self-concept as a mediating factor in delinquency. *Social Psychology Quarterly, 46,* 11-22.

Whitehead, J.T., and Lab, S.P. (1989). A meta-analysis of juvenile correctional treatment. *Journal of Research in Crime and Delinquency, 26,* 276-296.

Wolterhoff, J. (1992). *Diversion statt Abschreckung? Spezialpräventive Effekte einer alternativen Sanktionsform auf die Delinquenzaktivität Jugendlicher.* Preprint Nr. 48. Bielefeld: Sonderforschungsbereich 227 "Prävention und Intervention im Kindes- und Jugendalter".

Zimring, F.E., and Hawkins, G. (1973). *Deterrence: The legal threat in crime control.* Chicago: University of Chicago Press.

Part IV

Diversion, Social Work, and Restitution

Introduction to Part IV: Diversion, Social Work, and Restitution

The increasing involvement of "prevention professions" - social workers, psychologists, and others - in the social control of deviant behavior has been an important cause and, at the same time, possibly one the most conspicuous consequences of diversion policy. This is also one of the most significant aspects of the accusation that diversion has led to increased control over the lives of juveniles. While this observation serves as a starting point for most of the contributions that follow, rather than further belaboring this well-known fact, they try to redirect the focus of diversion away from individual, offender-related treatment and toward victim-offender mediation and restitution.

Lode Walgrave, starting from the observation that the growth of diversion has occurred despite a lack of clarity regarding its content and aims, explores the restitutive approach toward juvenile justice as a paradigm that might overcome the limits of both traditional penal law and the welfare or educational approach inherent to most diversion programs. His very thorough investigation into the underpinnings and the applicability of restitution clearly elaborates not only the advantages but also possible limits and dangers of restitution. Yet, if we keep these dangers in mind, we have a strong guideline for the necessary restructuring of juvenile justice.

Elmar Weitekamp points to one of the greatest perils facing the restitutive approach: that its application will, just like diversion in general, be restricted predominantly to petty offenses and first time, nonminority, and middle-class offenders. With such foundations, restitution programs will not be able to play a major role as an alternative to incarceration. Data on the sentencing behavior of a Philadelphia judge show that the application of restitution does not have to be bound by such limits. Also, according to Weitekamp, the effectiveness of restitution can be equal, or even superior to, imprisonment in a group composed of predominantly minority, repeat offenders who have committed mostly violent crimes.

Mark Ezell gives an overview of the various methods for assessing the possible net-widening effects of diversion programs. His discussion covers the comparison of client characteristics, the analysis of pre- and postprogram transition probabilities, and time series analysis. In addition, he points out the ambiguities inherent in the notion of diversion. In his empirical example, he found that although diversion did occur, it was largely diversion away from the courts but not from the overall system of juvenile justice. In addition, those appearing in court were put on probation or sent to prison more often after the implementation of diversion than before.

The chapter by Hans-Uwe Otto serves as an introduction to the three contributions that follow. Their object is a pilot scheme of the youth welfare office at Bielefeld. While there are clear limits to this program - initial case selection as well as the final responsibility for the decision rest with the juvenile prosecutor - it was developed with the aim of overcoming some of the weaknesses of previous diversion programs. Most notably, there is neither a predefinition of the kind of offenses to which the program is limited nor to the type of interventions that should take place. Thus, the aim is to "tailor" the decision to the individual case and to take into account the perspectives of both the offender and the victim.

Heinz Messmer, starting from the observation that traditional procedures within law give offenders few possibilities of influencing the content and outcome of discursive negotiations, analyzes conversations that have taken place between social workers and defendants in the Bielefeld program, partly also including victims. According to these analyses, offenders have quite large shares in the communication with social workers in diversion-oriented procedures, and the conversations center much on the offenders' concerns. This picture changes when, in addition, victim-offender mediation becomes an aim of the conversation. Here, naturally, the interests of the victim are also at stake, and offenders often respond to this with justifications that are meant to play down their role in the offense and their responsibility for it. This opens up the possibility of conflict, which, however, often results in more extensive confrontations over right and wrong - clearly an aim of a more "proceduralized" justice.

Franz Bettmer explores the program staff's decision-making criteria in the disposal of cases. Although criteria that are related to the model of formal justice still play a certain role, Bettmer demonstrates that the program is quite successful in striving for restitution or mediation whenever meaningful. Also, responses to a juvenile's offense that occurred in his or her life-world, most notably restitution effected by the offender or his or her parents, are taken into account in quite a number of cases. Thus, at least to some extent, not only formal justice but also "organized informal justice" like mediation programs may be of secondary importance in comparison with the settlements that offenders and victims can reach of their own accord.

The third contribution relating to the Bielefeld project investigates the question of net-widening. Data from the preprogram period enable Heinz-Günter Micheel to estimate the probabilities for dismissal or further prosecution as a function of the characteristics of the case. These estimations are then applied to the cases from the postprogram period. Micheel establishes that while about 30% of the cases that ended with some kind of measure during the program period would have been dismissed by the prosecutors prior to the program, about twice as many would have been brought to court, but were actually dismissed with or without measure. Therefore, the overall effect of the program is indeed one of less, and not of more, intervention into the juveniles' life-world.

In the following chapter, Hans-Joachim Plewig shows that, all in all, diversion in the Federal Republic of Germany is much more similar to what Walgrave has termed "wild diversion" than to a theoretically grounded crime policy. In his opinion, diversion has not succeeded in freeing itself from the "logic" of juvenile criminal law and thus has led to an usurpation of social work as an instrument to serve the interests of the penal institutions. In addition, he points out that while the idea of diversion is based on insights from labeling theory on the possibly stigmatizing effects of formal control, most diversion programs get along very successfully without any indication whether the proposed effects actually did occur. This, again, shows that a more rationally grounded crime policy is urgently needed.

Finally, Elisabeth Lissenberg points to the importance of "fantasies" about crimes and criminals. Such fantasies are both a result of and an influence on crime policies. Most important, they are a means of social control, both of others as well as of the self. Her research shows that children's perceptions and moral judgments about "prisoners" and "bad persons" have, in some important respects, changed very little during the last decade, even though on the surface - for instance, with respect to the predominance of "drug offenders" - some changes have occurred that reflect changes in the official ways in which "criminality" is dealt with an reported. Such judgments about "good" and "bad", "respectable", and "deviant" serve as moral capital in everyday life, and attempts at transforming crime policy are well advised to take into account such deeply imbedded feelings and world-views.

Diversion? It Depends on What We Divert to: Some Comments on Diversion and the Restorative Alternatives

Lode Walgrave

In Belgium, about 75% of the juvenile delinquents registered at the level of the public prosecutor are not prosecuted before the court.[1] We estimate that 10% of these cases are requalified as "children at risk" and treated according to that qualification. Other cases are sent directly to welfare agencies. Finally, approximatively 10% of the juveniles, known by the public prosecutor as delinquents, are sent as such to the juvenile court. But still then, no punishment will be pronounced, because the Belgian Juvenile Protection Act of 1965 is purely welfare-oriented and it provides only measures "in the best interest of the child", till the age of 18 (with a few exceptions).

Is all this "diversion"? The use of that term is so inflated that it has lost its distinctive meaning. If we consider criminological diversion as "every procedure that diverts known delinquents from being convicted as a delinquent", we may conclude that about 90% of all juvenile delinquents in Belgium are diverted. This is no reason for any triumphalism. The system has been criticized severely, and a reform of the Belgian Juvenile Protection Act is considered to be very urgent. A comeback of more punitive sanctions, according to more strict legal procedures, is expected.

It shows that diversion is not a panacea that solves all problems within the societal reaction against juvenile delinquency. Diversion as such does not guarantee either the "embetterment" of the delinquent or the avoidance of stigmatization. It all depends on what we are diverting to.

Actually, diversion is a negative concept. It only refers to avoiding, not letting something happen that is considered as undesirable (the judicial intervention and judgment). It does not say anything about where the diversion is oriented toward, as if anything would be better than the judicial circuit. That is not evident at all. Research has indicated repeatedly that stigmatization is not the monopoly of the judicial intervention. A lot of treatment, welfare, and school institutions can have stigmatizing effects as well. A body of evaluative research results confirms that most of the treatment programs, regardless of whether or not they are working under judicial supervision, do not lead to satisfying results in improving delinquents. Very often, diversion procedures result in the loss of legal safeguards and in net-widening. Rather than pleading for "wild diversion", we have to search for alternatives to the traditional judicial circuit, guided by a concern for socially and individually constructive intervention schemes. In general, four criteria must be met:

1. The safeguard of correct legal procedures that guarantee controllable and proportionate societal reactions.
2. The reassessment of the victims' position in the procedures following an offense.
3. The meaningful significance and the social constructiveness of the societal reaction against an individual delinquent.
4. The effectiveness in promoting social order of the forms of reaction scheduled and applied.

It seems that the reactions tending toward real or symbolic restoration respond best to these criteria. Both mediation and community service are the prototypes of such a "restorative justice".[2]

1 The Restorative Model in the Societal Reaction to Juvenile Delinquency

In traditional *penal law*, retribution is the primary concern: By deliberately inflicting a harm, one attempts to restore the disturbed balance in the legal order. Recent legal doctrine also ascribes a resocializing effect to the operation of penal law, although empirical evidence for it is hardly found. One also assumes that punishment satisfies (to a certain extent) the victim, which may imply a certain form of compensation.

In the *welfare* or educational approach, the rehabilitation of the offender comes first: By means of an adapted individualized measure, one intends to influence the offender to such an extent that he or she refrains from further criminal offenses. The restriction of freedom, part of the imposed measure, can also imply an unpleasant harmful element. This is, however, not pursued, it is only an expected side effect. The rehabilitative reaction is understood by many victims as unfair: Offenders are not punished but helped, while they themselves have great difficulty in being recognized as victims.

In the *restorative paradigm* ("restitutive approach"), the restitution of the damage caused is the most important element. The damage can be material, as well as mental or social. The victim can be an individual citizen or the community.

Restorative interventions also contain harmful and educative elements. The obligation to restitution is a restriction of freedom which can be most unpleasant. In contrast to penal law, the infliction of grief is not strived for, but it can be a side effect (Wright, 1991). Moreover, the obligation to restitution demands a personal dedication that can also lead to insight (and repentance). However, this is not the first aim either, but a possible positive side effect. Important is, thus, that the restitutive approach is not simply a variant of penal intervention, nor of the educational paradigms. It may develop toward a new third way (Galaway and Hudson, 1990; Van de Kerchove, 1986; Walgrave, 1981, 1985a, b).

Depenalizing the offense and the restitutive approach to it *do not imply that the norm violation is trivialized*. It is partly redefined. The offense, with its connotations to the questions of guilt and penalty, is now considered in the first place as a (pos-sibly serious) "conflict" and a (serious) "problem" that requires the most advantageous social solution possible (Steinert, 1986). In mediation, the conflict is handed back, so to speak, to the parties concerned (the offender and the victim; Christie, 1977), but the state monitors that conflict regulation actually takes place and that no misuse of power is being exercised, either by the offender or by the victim (Council of Europe, 1990; see, also, the "two-track approach" proposed by Van Ness, 1990). If restitution is impossible because, for example, negotiations between offender and victim cannot take place, then an indirect reparation can be imposed via community service.

This last type of reaction *prevents* the official reponse to whatever offense *being limited to a kind of civil settlement of damages* between two (groups of) citizens. Next to the offender and the victim, a third party is involved in an offense, the community, represented by the state. The fact that the state can take legal action against offenses proactively, and that so-called "offenses without victim" exist, indicates that more general and fundamental norms are also at stake in an offense (Orlando, 1992). In this paper, I cannot go into the important question about the presupposed consensus underlying the norms applied at present and about the selectivity of social control. But in every regime, society is a party concerned in the case of an offense, and, therefore, it cannot let itself be side-tracked (Van Ness, 1990, distinguishes between "community" and "government").

The restitutive approach toward norm violation is *not new*. It is, on the contrary, an old principle that was being used before the public penal systems (Steinert, 1986; Weitekamp, 1992 and this volume). In less structured communities, the compensation of the victim was the most important or even the only purpose of the reaction of the community to the norm violation. The central power limited itself originally to interfering and/or producing piece-rate schemes whose main purpose was the compensation of the victim, not punishment. Gradually, this authority became more and more involved with structured legal proceedings and came to the fore as demanding party (Schafer, 1977). At present, victims are put into a tight corner. They are used only as witnesses, and their own restoration is only a second-order consideration.

The *ethical basis* for the punishment of an offense is the Kantian principle claiming that the punishment of evil is necessary in order to maintain the norm and to restore the social balance. Evil must be answered by evil, and equal suffering must be imposed on the one who makes others suffer. Great problems arise, however. "Balancing the harm done by the offender with further harm inflicted on the offender; that only adds to the total amount of harm in the world" (Wright, 1992: 525). The retributive function of penal law comes down to a canalizing of revenge within the systems of the legal state. As the basic ethical principle for the regulation of community, it does not seem right to me.

Evarts (1990), on the other hand, defends the Platonic ethical principle "never to cause harm". To restore harm, the obligation to do good is preferable: The one who causes harm should restore or compensate it (Del Vecchio, 1975; Wright, 1991, 1992). The motives of mediation, restitution, reconciliation, and forgiveness are communicative and human patterns that are socially more constructive than display of power, infliction of harm, refusal, or revenge (see, also, Harris, 1987, cited in Van Ness, 1990). They contribute more to a harmonic community and to collective emancipation (Mackay, 1992).

Forgiveness, one of the most important factors in restorative intervention, also yields *psychological profit* (Gehm, 1992). Forgiveness does not diminish the seriousness of the harm nor the blameworthiness of it to the offender. It does, however, imply that victims consciously renounce their "right to pay the offender back in his own coin". This makes them psychologically the strongest, while being the most noble-minded. Certain psychotherapeutic practices consciously apply the gesture of forgiveness in order to resolve bottled-up rage feelings about earlier experiences of injustice (Gehm, 1992).

Many ethical, judicial, psychological, and social reasons are available to plead for a judicial reaction to norm violation in which the restorative function is stressed more than the penal or even the therapeutic. The question is, however, if and to what extent these principles are applicable in practice.

2 The Applicability of the Restorative Approach

During the last 10 to 20 years, there have been elaborate experimentations with intervention models with a restorative perspective. Several recent surveys exist (see, e.g., Dünkel and Zermatten, 1990; Galaway and Hudson, 1990; Hudson and Galaway, 1980). Moreover, a very current and critical discussion of the present state of affairs, especially concerning mediation, took place at the *Advanced Research Workshop on Conflict, Crime and Reconciliation* (Lucca, April 1991) (see Messmer and Otto, 1992).

One of the special problems is the *legal status* of the restorative models and of those concerned.

In general, *victim-offender mediation* is seen as a kind of diversion (Feest, 1990). The possibility that the victim can be satisfied without the whole penal law procedure being completed diminishes the necessity for appeal to the penal system. The victim can be less inclined to complain; the public prosecutor can stipulate a successful mediation as a condition to dismiss the case; the judge can use compensation, for example, as a condition for probation.

Community service, on the contrary, is explicitly seen as a sanction and should thus be reserved as a judgment after the completion of the whole procedure. The immediate reparation is dropped so that the link between the offense and its consequence is less strict and more delicate to determine. Moreover, community service is not an agreed upon claim settlement as a result of a negotiation. Community service is explicitly an imposed restriction of freedom because of an offense. The culpability of the offense and the extent of the restriction of freedom should thus be determined. In our legal system, this is only possible in court.

With regard to mediation, the state should make sure that the rights of those concerned are guaranteed. The rights of the victim should be respected in case the victim does not want to take part in an initiative for mediation (Wright, 1991). Making the procedure less formal can lead to a lessening of the attention paid to the legal rights of the offender (Feest, 1990). It is possible that young offenders, through lack of knowledge or defence, are pressured to eventually accept a mediation result that implies more serious consequences for them than when they would have followed the normal legal procedure (Orlando, 1992).

The most important threat to the legal statute of the restitutive approach is, however, the confusion about the concept *"alternative sanctions"*. This concept can be understood in many ways. Because of the confusion, these so-called alternative sanctions are sometimes added as an odd collection to the already existing set of sanctions and measures (see Frehsee, this volume). Of course, their reformative appeal gets lost this way.

The confusion has led, for example, to an *incorporation* of mediation and community service in the *welfare approach*. "Alternative sanctions" have become "alternative treatments". The aim of mediation is then no longer reparation of the harm, but to have an educational influence on the offender (Dongier and Van Dosselaere, 1992; Scieur, 1990; Thys, 1987). The character and the extent of the sanction is no longer dependent on the offense but on the characteristics of the offender. The victim and the harm are no longer respected as elements as such, but only as "demonstrative elements" in the treatment of the offender. Of course, the educational importance of mediation or community service is real, but they should primarily remain sanctions connected with an offense. If not, the disadvantages of a purely rehabilitative approach to the offender remain: The legal guarantees for the offender are minimal, the position of the victim is subordinate, and the risks of net-widening are real (Austin and Krisberg, 1982; Houchon, 1984; Orlando, 1992; Van de Kerchove, 1986; Vass, 1981).

On the other hand, the obligation to restitution is often *misused in a punitive discourse*. Compensation of the victim or even community service are then additionally imposed on top of a penal sanction (Dünkel, 1990; Houchon, 1984; Wright, 1991), or they are imposed on young offenders who would not have received any sanction at all if these restitutive measures had not existed. In both cases, it is a matter of net-widening and more specifically of "additive sanctions" rather than "alternative sanctions".

In order to avoid both cases of recuperation of the restorative ideas into the traditional intervention models, the basic principles need to be outlined very clearly. The distinction on the basis of legal-theoretical and social-ethical principles should be made as explicit as possible and should be applied logically in practical circumstances. Especially in the beginning, their correctness should be monitored in a "puristic" manner.

Gradually, more is also known about the *experience of those concerned* in the restorative paradigm, that is, the victims, the offenders, and "the public".

With regard to the *victims*, experience with mediation is obviously essential. Not all victims are willing to participate in a mediation program. The participation rate stated in research is 50% to 70%. Next to a number of personal characteristics, more systematic factors also play an important role, such as the type and circumstances of the offense and the way in which mediation is presented. But also the victims of serious physical violence (even rape) are sometimes willing to participate in mediation (Marshall, 1992; Umbreit, 1989; Weitekamp, 1992).

Depending on the practice, the agreed upon restitution or compensation is actually executed in 64% to 100% of cases (Marshall, 1992; Umbreit, 1989).

An exhaustive investigation was done by Umbreit (1989, and, especially, 1992) in the USA about the victims' experience of the mediation process. His samples contained to a considerable extent victims of juvenile delinquency, mainly of house-breaking and, to a smaller extent, robbery. The general degree of satisfaction of the cooperating victims was very high and was mainly ascribed to the possibility of actively participating in the completion of "their" case, the correctness of the procedure, the experienced equity of the eventual agreements, and the emotional satisfaction.

Perchance, the often very emotional and punitive reaction of the victim immediately after the offense is to a large extent due to unfamiliarity with other possibilities. Repeatedly, it seems that later the victims are concerned mainly about the respectful recognition of their victimship, the restoration of the harm (both emotional and material), and the certainty that the offender will not recommence (vis-à-vis themselves or others) (Coates and Gehm, 1985; Dünkel, 1990; Haley, 1992; Steinert, 1986; Voss, 1990).

Literature provides a number of reasons why one could expect the *effects on the offenders* to be more favorable. The fact that offenders are confronted more directly with the consequences of their acts, that an active effort is demanded of them to restore or compensate the harm, may imply that they will realize more the significance of the norm, that they become aware of an appeal to responsible co-citizenship, and that they can partly escape the negative side effects of the criminal judgment. Also, in comparison with the protective model, the obviousness of the norm and the sensitization for responsibility, both included in the restorative approach, are essential points scored (Pelikan, 1992; Van der Laan, 1991; Walgrave, 1985).

Whether this is also true in practice is not yet indicated clearly by empirical evidence. Investigating the effects on offenders is extremely difficult (Cornejo, 1981; Mair, 1990; Umbreit, 1992; Walgrave, 1992; Weitekamp, 1992). Not only are the characteristics of the offenders, and consequently of the possible effects, very diverse, but it is also difficult to determine in measurable variables the aims of the intervention. Prevention of recidivism seems the easiest measure, but a reliable confirmation is very difficult and is often not sufficient to register the side effects (Cornejo, 1981; Landreville, 1982). Moreover, the methodological problems of evaluation research also concern the composition of control groups, controls over possible influences of intervening variables, and the resistance against the interest-biased registration and interpretation by criminal policymakers and by field workers (Mair, 1990).

Up to now, there has been no in-depth investigation into the effects of restorative sanctions on offenders. Yet, two data come to the fore and are parallel with regard to mediation and community service.

1. Offenders who experienced a mediation and who executed the agreements are, in general, left with a far greater feeling of reasonableness and equity than those who went through a traditional punishment (Umbreit, 1992). Similar data are mentioned with regard to community service (Junger-Tas, 1981).
2. Some authors state a distinct decline of recidivism among participators in mediation programs (Haley, 1992; Marshall, 1992; Rowley, 1990; Schneider, 1986); something which is relativized by others (Umbreit, 1992). Neither does community service lead right away to a decline of recidivism (Junger-Tas, 1981; Schneider, 1982; Van der Laan, 1991). Possibly, the processes of selection, of provision, and of coaching are very important. It is clear, however, that restorative sanctions do not result in more recidivism.

The replacement of the punitive judicial reaction by a nonpunitive restorative reply, which is often executed outside the judicial circuit (but always under supervision), raises questions about the *opinion of "the public"*. Indeed, very often "the public" is appealed to in order to justify the repressive approach of delinquency. Systematic inquiry in no way confirms this.

Whenever the possibility for restitution is proposed in a realistic manner, the population interviewed prefers, to a large extent, this approach to the repressive and even the rehabilitative schedules. The seriousness and the kind of offense play a less important role than one could presume (Doble, 1987; Dünkel, 1990; Galaway, 1984; Wright, 1989).

Yet, the question remains: *What are the boundaries of the restitutive approach?* Is it really a valuable alternative to penal law intervention, or should it be restricted to a specific category of (less serious) offenses and/or (younger) offenders? In practice, the restorative paradigm is mostly used for less serious (property) offenses and for young delinquents. Gradually, however, the target group is also being extended to adult offenders and more serious delinquents (Dünkel, 1990; Umbreit, 1989; Weitekamp, 1992).

It can be assumed that the societal reaction with regard to *serious offenses cannot be restricted to a simple victim-offender mediation.* The seriousness of an offense also implies the seriousness of violation of public order, so that the restoration should be more than a simple compensation of the victim.

Still, it is *difficult to* think of good reasons to *exclude offenders committing serious offenses from community service* (Walgrave, 1990).

1. The idea that serious offenders should experience a real punitive sanction originates in the purely retributive opinion of the societal answer to delinquency. We do not believe that revenge, unless canalized within a legal framework, can be a sound basis for a civilized social policy. Other arguments are necessary.
2. The idea that "the public" would not accept a community service for serious offenders is based on a stereotype. As demonstrated above, the punitive attitude does not seem to be as general as some comments seem to suggest.
3. The assumption that offenders who have committed serious offenses would be less persuaded by community service is based on a naive etiological opinion, as if a delict's judicial seriousness would coincide with the seriousness and impressionability of a psychosocial disturbance. Empirical research refutes this. Also offenders who have committed serious offenses are capable of bringing restitutive sanctions to a good end and of deducing the rehabilitating advantages, without this involving heightened recidivism (De Martelaere and Peeters, 1985; Dünkel, 1990; Umbreit, 1989; Weitekamp, 1992).

Finally, the boundaries of the restitutive approach are double.

The *willingness to co-operate* is, in principle, easy to determine. But the way in which the offer is made causes a very diverse extent of willingness (Marshall, 1992; Umbreit, 1989), and it often requires some time before the willingness indeed comes about. Nonetheless, a number of victims refuse to cooperate in a restoration procedure. This should be fully respected, yet, it should not be a reason to simply subject the offender to a traditional punishment. In such a case, the offender can still be obliged to do community service.

It becomes more difficult when the offenders themselves are not willing to cooperate in a direct mediation with the victim, and/or when they do not accept community service. A denial is relative here. Also the traditional penal package deals with imposed restrictions of freedom and conditions, and the preference of the accused is only considered to a minor degree. The obligation to community service and even to mediation can be introduced, for example, by analogy with the existing conditions for probation, as it is already the case in some countries (Galaway, 1992; Junger and Van Hecke, 1989). If an ambulant community service is impossible, then a service to the community or to a fund for victims can be imposed within a residential framework (whether or not together with confinement). This brings us close to the second possible boundary of the restitutive approach.

In principle, *security reasons* can be of the kind that a mediation or community service in (be it controlled) freedom bear too many risks for serious recidivism. But this boundary for restorative sanctions is difficult to determine. There are two considerations here:

1. The security of imprisonment is not absolute. The wide diversity in the modalities and regimes of imprisonment practices often result in periods of unguarded contact with free society. The fact that relatively few "accidents" occur proves that security reasons should not be exaggerated. A large number of actual detainees could, without risk, complete an ambulant restorative sanction.
2. Imprisonment does not necessarily imply the end of its restitutive aim. Several authors have suggested models in which, for example, the duration of imprisonment is made dependent on the extent to which one, through the proceeds of prison work, contributes to a fund for victims or even to the restoration of the victim (Weitekamp, 1992).

It is, however, obvious that the *boundaries of the restitutive approach are not yet known*. Experiences are still too limited. As these increase, its applicability could also increase.

Finally, the implementation of the restorative approach in justice has revealed many *practical problems*, such as the need for a specific methodology, the requirement of a well-trained and time-investing professional staff (Messmer, 1989; Pelikan, 1992; Umbreit, 1989). Too often, good ideas and opportunities get lost because of bad implementation skills.

Special attention has to be given to the role of private agencies. Their involvement in restorative sanctioning holds considerable risks. When private organizations are engaged with the execution of sanctions, new professionalization, including tendencies toward particularism and defence of interests might arise (Curran, 1988; Pratt, 1989; Vass and Menzies, 1989). They might limit themselves to the less difficult cases with which easy success can be obtained and the necessary allowances can be acquired more easily (something Orlando, 1992, called "creaming": creaming the easiest cases and leaving the difficult ones for governmental organizations). Thus, privatization undoubtedly includes net-widening risks that should be accurately followed.

3 Diverting the System Instead of the Offender?

Diversion in itself is an empty concept. It tells something about what seems to be avoided, but it in no way contains any option about what should be done instead. As a consequence, evaluating diversion programs appears to be rather artificial, if the evaluation does not address the program that is being replaced (or systematic nonintervention).

But if we want to avoid so desperately the traditional judicial system, why would we not simply tend to replace the system in itself? Rather than trying to divert some individual delinquents from the traditional penal or protective sanctions, we have to try to change the system as a whole. Otherwise, diversion seems to be an alibi for letting the "bad" system exist and for delivering up the nondivertible delinquents to it.

Recent trends in experiments into mediation and community service and thoughts about restorative justice seem to lead to a coherent view on the societal reponse to delinquency. It can serve as an alternative paradigm, beside the retributive or the welfare approach, and it opens up promising pathways toward a realistic new criminal policy.

Of course, a lot of questions and problems arise and a long period of experience and research will be needed. The traditional penal system had several centuries to develop, and it was sustained by the authorities with massive means. We cannot expect that the recent revival of restorative thinking will have all the answers and solutions at once. A long path will have to be taken involving interaction among theoretical thinking, practical experience, empirical evaluation, and support by the political and judicial authorities.

However, the fundamental option is needed now already. It must offer a theoretical (utopian?) framework, helping to avoid the definitive satisfaction with small technical modifications such as diversion or community service. If so, we would simply contribute to the unburdening of the traditional system, while at the same time widening the net of social control.

Diversion in itself is no solution for whatever problem. It can only serve as an opportunity for experimenting (with mediation) in view of a more global change of the judicial system in the long term. In my opinion, that change will have to take a restorative direction.

Notes

1 The mentioned figures have to be estimations. The quality of Belgian Criminal Statistics is extremely low and their publication is always very late. For the time being, only data for 1985 are available. Their reliability is doubtful and they are not complete.

2 Both terms, mediation and community service, are used here as collective nouns. Mediation means all intervention schedules that focus on the communication between the victim and the offender (the excuse, the restitution, the compensation, the reconciliation) accomplished before, during or after the judgment. Community service stands for all tasks performed by a delinquent to the benefit of a social institution, as a reparation for the committed transgression, sanctioned by a judicial institution.

References

Austin, J., and Krisberg, B. (1982). The unmet promise of alternatives to incarceration. *Crime and Delinquency, 28,* 374-409.

Christie, N. (1977). Conflicts as property. *British Journal of Criminology, 17,* 1-15.

Coates, R., and Gehm, J. (1985). *Victim meets offenders: An evaluation of victim-offender reconciliation programs.* Valparaiso: PACT.

Council of Europe (1990). *Nouvelles stratégies sociales et système de justice pénale.* Strasbourg, Conseil de l'Europe, 19ième Conférence de Recherches Criminologiques, novembre 1990 (publication in preparation).

Cornejo, J. (1981). *Le problème de l'efficacité et de l'évaluation des interventions de prévention de la délinquance.* Louvain-La-Neuve, UCL, Ecole de criminologie.

Curran, D. (1988). Destructuring, privatization and the promise of juvenile diversion: Compromising community-based corrections. *Crime and Delinquency, 34,* 363-378.

De Martelaere, G., and Peeters, J. (1985). Een experiment van alternatieve sancties aan de jeugdrechtbank te Mechelen. *Panopticon, 16,* 34-44.

Del Vecchio, G. (1975). The problem of penal justice. In J. Hudson and B. Galaway (Eds.), *Considering the victim* (pp. 85-101). Springfield, IL: Thomas.

Double, J. (1987). *Crime and punishment: The public's view.* New York: E. Mc Connelle Clark Found.

Dongier, S., and Van Doosselaere, D. (1992). Approaching mediation in juvenile court: Rationale and methodological aspects. In H. Messmer, and H.-U. Otto (Eds.), *Restorative justice on trial: Pitfalls and potentials of victim-offender mediation* (pp. 501-511). Dordrecht: Kluwer.

Dünkel, F. (1990). Médiation délinquant-victime et réparation des dommages. Nouvelle évolution du droit pénal et de la pratique judiciaire dans une comparaison internationale. In F. Dünkel and J. Zermatten (Eds.), *Nouvelles tendances dans le droit pénal des mineurs. Médiation, travail au profit de la communauté et traitement intermédiaire* (pp. 2-81). Freiburg: Max-Planck-Institut für ausländisches und internationales Strafrecht.

Dünkel, F., and Zermatten, J. (Eds.) (1990). *Nouvelles tendances dans le droit pénal des mineurs. Médiation, travail au profit de la communauté et traitement intermédiaire* (Kriminologische Forschungsberichte aus dem Max-Planck-Institut, Vol. 42). Freiburg: Max-Planck-Institut für ausländisches und internationales Strafrecht.

Evarts, W. (1990). Compensation through mediation: A conceptual framework. In B. Galaway and J. Hudson (Eds.), *Criminal justice, restitution and reconciliation.* Monsey, NY: Criminal Justice Press.

Feest, J. (1990). Courses of action designed to avoid entry in the criminal justice process or to interrupt the process. In Council of Europe, *Nouvelles stratégies sociales et système de justice pénale.* Strasbourg, Conseil de l'Europe, 19ième Conférence de Recherches Criminologiques, novembre 1990 (publication in preparation).

Galaway, B. (1984). A survey of public acceptance of restitution as an alternative to imprisonment for property offenders. *Australian and New Zealand Journal of Criminology, 17,* 108-117.

Galaway, B. (1992). The New Zealand experience implementing the reparation sentence. In H. Messmer and H.-U. Otto (Eds.), *Restorative justice on trial. Pitfalls and potentials of victim-offender mediation* (pp. 55-79). Dordrecht: Kluwer.

Galaway, B. and Hudson, J. (Eds.) (1990). *Criminal justice, restitution and reconciliation.* Monsey, NY: Criminal Justice Press.

Gehm, J.R. (1992). The function of forgiveness in the criminal justice system. In H. Messmer and H.-U. Otto (Eds.), *Restorative justice on trial. Pitfalls and potentials of victim-offender mediation* (pp. 541-550). Dordrecht: Kluwer.

Haley, J. (1992). Victim-offender mediation: Japanese and American comparisons. In H. Messmer and H.-U. Otto (Eds.), *Restorative justice on trial. Pitfalls and potentials of victim-offender mediation* (pp. 101-130). Dordrecht: Kluwer.

Harland, A. (1983). One hundred years of restitution: An international review and prospects for research. *Victimology, 8,* 190-203.

Harris, M.K. (1987). Moving into the new millenium: Toward a feminist vision of justice. *The Prison Journal, 67,* 27-38.

Houchon, G. (1984). A la recherche du temps perdu. *Panopticon, 15,* 199-206.

Hudson, J., and Galaway, B. (1980). *Victims, offenders and alternative sanctions.* Lexington, MA: Heath & Co.

Junger, M., and Van Hecke, T. (1989), Schadevergoeding als straf. *Panopticon, 20,* 350-368.

Junger-Tas, J. (1981). Community service en dienstverlening: Een kritische beschouwing. *Delikt en delinkwent, 11,* 5-23.

Landreville, P. (1982). La récidive dans l'évaluation des mesures pénales. *Déviance et Société, 6,* 375-388.

Mackay, R. (1992). Restitution and ethics: An aristotelian approach. In H. Messmer and H.-U. Otto (Eds.), *Restorative justice on trial. Pitfalls and potentials of victim-offender mediation* (pp. 569-583). Dordrecht: Kluwer.

Mair, G. (1990). Evaluating the effects of diversion strategies on the attitudes and practices of agents of the criminal justice system. In Council of Europe, *Nouvelles stratégies sociales et système de justice pénale.* Strasbourg, Conseil de l'Europe, 19ième Conférence de Recherches Criminologiques, novembre 1990 (publication in preparation).

Marshall, T. (1992). Restorative justice on trial in Britain. In H. Messmer and H.-U. Otto (Eds.), *Restorative justice on trial. Pitfalls and potentials of victim-offender mediation* (pp. 15-28). Dordrecht: Kluwer.

Messmer, H. (1989). Tackling the conflict. In B. Galaway and J. Hudson (Eds.), *The state as a parent* (pp. 187-192). Dordrecht: Kluwer.

Messmer, H., and Otto, H.-U. (Eds.) (1992). *Restorative justice on trial. Pitfalls and potentials of victim-offender mediation - International research perspectives.* Dordrecht: Kluwer.

Orlando, F. (1992). Mediation involving children in the United States. Legal and ethical conflicts. In H. Messmer and H.-U. Otto (Eds.), *Restorative justice on trial. Pitfalls and potentials of victim-offender mediation* (pp. 333-342). Dordrecht: Kluwer.

Pelikan, C. (1992). The Austrian Juvenile Justice Act 1988. A new practice and new problems. In H. Messmer and H.-U. Otto (Eds.), *Restorative justice on trial. Pitfalls and potentials of victim-offender mediation* (pp. 163-178). Dordrecht: Kluwer.

Pratt, J. (1989). Corporatism: The third model of juvenile justice. *British Journal of Criminology, 29,* 236-254.

Rowley, M. (1990). Comparison of recidivism rates for delinquents processed in a restitution diversion program to a matched sample processed in court. In B. Galaway and J. Hudson (Eds.), *Criminal justice, restitution and reconciliation.* Monsey, NY: Criminal Justice Press.

Schafer, S. (1977). *Victimology. The victim and his criminal.* Reston, VA: Prentice Hall.

Schneider, A. (1986). Restitution and recidivism rates of juvenile offenders: Results from experimental studies. *Criminology, 24,* 533-552.

Schneider, P. (1982). *Restitution as an alternative disposition for serious juvenile offenders.* Eugene, OR: Institute of Policy Analysis.

Scieur, Y. (1990). La prestation communautaire: Une logique pour le magistrat de la jeunesse. In F. Dünkel and J. Zermatten (Eds.), *Nouvelles tendances dans le droit pénal des mineurs. Médiation, travail au profit de la communauté et traitement intermédiaire* (pp. 143-155). Freiburg: Max-Planck-Institut für ausländisches und internationales Strafrecht.

Steinert, H. (1986). Beyond crime and punishment. *Contemporary Crises, 10,* 21-38.

Thys, P. (1987). Les prestations communautaires au tribunal de la jeunesse de l'arrondissement judicairé de Liège. In L. Walgrave (Ed.), *Changement de société et délinquance juvénile, Actes des Sixièmes Journées d'études Internationales de Criminologie Juvénile,* 2 Vols. (pp. 141-155). Leuven: Acco/OGJC.

Umbreit, M. (1989). Violent offenders and their victims. In M. Wright and B. Galaway (Eds.), *Mediation and criminal justice* (pp. 99-112). London: Sage.

Umbreit, M. (1992). Mediating victim offender conflict: From single-site to multi-site analysis in the USA. In H. Messmer and H.-U. Otto (Eds.), *Restorative justice on trial. Pitfalls and potentials of victim-offender mediation* (pp. 431-444). Dordrecht: Kluwer.

Van De Kerchove, M. (1986). Signification juridique de la sanction en matière de délinquance juvénile. In C. De Troy, F. Tulkens, and M. Van De Kerchove (Eds.), *Délinquance des jeunes. Politiques et interventions* (pp. 163-189). Bruxelles: Story.

Van Der Laan, P. (1991). *Experimenteren met alternatieve sancties voor jeugdigen.* Arnhem/Den Haag: Gouda Quint/WODC.

Van Ness, D. (1990). Restorative justice. In B. Galaway and J. Hudson (Eds.), *Criminal justice, restitution and reconciliation.* Monsey, NY: Criminal Justice Press.

Vass, A. (1981). Community service for juveniles? A critical comment. *Probation Journal, 28,* 44-49.

Vass, A., and Menzies, K. (1989). The community service order as a public and private enterprise. *British Journal of Criminology, 29,* 255-272.

Voss, M. (1990). Victim expectations, diversion and informal settlement: Results of a victim survey in Bielefeld. In B. Galaway and J. Hudson (Eds.), *Criminal justice, restitution and reconciliation.* Monsey, NY: Criminal Justice Press.

Walgrave L. (1981). Recht tegenover jeugddelinquentie: Beteugelen en herstellen, maar niet straffen? *Tijdschrift voor Familie- en Jeugdrecht, 4,* 106-118.

Walgrave, L. (1985a). La repénalisation de la délinquance juvénile: une fuite en avant. *Revue de Droit Pénal et de Criminologie, 65,* 603-623.

Walgrave, L. (1985b). De restituerende gemeenschapsdienst: Een uitweg uit de impasse? In OGJC (Ed.), *Alternatieve Sancties: een praktijk-kijk, Verslag van een studiedag* (pp. 3-19). KU Leuven: OGJC.

Walgrave, L. (1990). Synthèse et conclusions. In Council of Europe, *Nouvelles stratégies sociales et système de justice pénale.* Strasbourg, Conseil de l'Europe, 19ième Conférence de Recherches Criminologiques, novembre 1990 (publication in preparation).

Walgrave, L. (1992). Mediation and community service as models of a restorative approach: Why would it be better? Explicating the objectives as criteria for evalation. In H. Messmer and H.-U. Otto (Eds.), *Restorative justice on trial. Pitfalls and potentials of victim-offender mediation* (pp. 343-353). Dordrecht: Kluwer.

Weitekamp, E. (1992). Can restitution serve as a reasonable alternative to imprisonment? An assessment of the situation in the USA. In H. Messmer and H.-U. Otto (Eds.), *Restorative justice on trial. Pitfalls and potentials of victim-offender mediation* (pp. 81-103). Dordrecht: Kluwer.

Wright, M. (1989). What the public wants. In M. Wright and B. Galaway (Eds.), *Mediation in criminal justice: Victims, offenders and community.* London: Sage.

Wright, M. (1991). *Justice for victims and offenders: A restorative approach to crime.* Milton Keynes: Open University Press.

Wright, M. (1992). Victim-offender mediation as a step towards a restorative system of justice. In H. Messmer and H.-U. Otto (Eds.), *Restorative justice on trial. Pitfalls and potentials of victim-offender mediation* (pp. 525-539). Dordrecht: Kluwer.

Concentration on the Wrong Offender Groups: An Assessment of Current Mediation and Restitution Programs

Elmar Weitekamp

1 Introduction

Quite unlike laws found in today's societies, the laws of more primitive societies contained monetary evaluations for most offenses as compensation to the victims, not punishment of the criminal. Although it had nearly disappeared, restitution was rediscovered in the 1970s. However, evaluations of current restitution programs limit their clientele seriously by admitting primarily only property and/or first-time offenders, by applying the programs mostly to juveniles who belong to the middle class, and by excluding minority offenders. This study examined the cases of 605 adult offenders who were tried before a judge from the Philadelphia Common Pleas Court between 1974 and 1984 and who received sentences of incarceration, probation with restitution, or probation. Over 50% of the offenses committed were violent ones; and in 28.6% of all cases the judge imposed a restitution sentence. The majority of the offenders belonged to the lower SES group and to a minority group. Our analysis showed no differences between the incarceration group and the restitution group (both groups represent about two-thirds of the sample) with regard to violent offenses, weapon use, and the victim's injury. With the exception of prior arrest and pretrial detention, no differences could be found between the groups with regard to the criminal history of the offenders. At first glance, it appeared that the restitution group had the highest recidivism rate (measured by the probation revocation rate). However, if one considers the total probation time, we found that the restitution group had the lowest recidivism rate of the three subgroups and that 61.2% of this group were not reincarcerated. The policy implications of our findings are that it is possible to use restitution as an alternative to incarceration and that such programs can include a clientele which comes from a large metropolitan area, belongs to the lower SES group, to a minority group, and commits serious, violent offenses.

2 Restitution: Recent Rationale, Purpose, and Issues

The commonly accepted definition of restitution is payment to victims of crime by an offender to cover losses incurred from the crime. Payment can take the form of money and/or services to the victim or the state. According to Black's Law Dictionary (1968: 1477), restitution is an "Act of restoring; restoration of anything to its rightful owner; the act of making good or giving equivalent for any loss, damage or injury; and indemnification".

In their literature review on restitution Hudson, Galaway, and Novack (1980) found that 85% of the 336 articles, books, and reports they identified had been published since 1970. They further pointed out that the literature prior to 1970 focused mainly on the role of restitution in criminal law and theory, whereas, since 1970, the literature has dealt more often with program development, implementation of restitution programs, and research on these programs.

In their annotated literature review on restitution and community service, Nutter, Hudson, and Galaway (1989) found 940 items published on the topic of restitution, of which 394 were about program description, 479 theoretical and conceptual, 39 historical, 16 cross-cultural, 146 formative evaluations, 103 evaluated the outcome of programs, 58 dealt with public opinion on restitution, 141 considered legal aspects of restitution, and the rest were general summaries and studies of the use of restitution. Of the 930 dated documents, 607 were published prior to 1983 and 323 since then, indicating a substantial interest in restitution and community service.

There are several reasons for the rediscovery of restitution as a penal sanction. The first reason was the rediscovery of the victim in the criminal justice system. Viano (1978), amongst others, has pointed out that promoting restitution as a program to help crime victims is popular but questionable. No doubt the victim, in the case in which an offender is apprehended and convicted for the crime, can benefit from recompense for the losses suffered; but, as Edelhertz (1977) noted, in its historical connotation, restitution was designed to benefit the offender and his or her kin group to avoid more severe sanctions by the victim's kin group.

A second purpose of restitution is to provide less severe and more humane sanctions for the offender. As Tallack (1900: 7) claimed:

> "For injuries both to person and property, it (former societies or our ancestors) enacted restitution, or reparation, in some form, as the chief, and often the whole element of punishment. And this was wiser in principle, more reformatory in its influence, more deterrrent in its tendency, and more economic to the community, than the modern practice, of so often substituting an unremunerative or very costly imprisonment for the ancient mode of treatment."

Restitution in its current context is considered to be a viable alternative to incarceration. Not only does the offender in particular benefit from this approach, but society benefits in general. As Berrini (1921: 42) wrote: "The State spends enormous sums on intensive breeding of dangerousness and criminality of offenders: and thereafter restores to society offenders more fearful than before." Furthermore, the family of an offender, who may actually be innocent, does not suffer from the imprisonment; and the offender, in order to make his or her restitution payments, has to work, which means that taxes will be payed or community service will be delivered, which is beneficial to society but would not be the case if we imprison the offender. Especially today, as correctional administrators struggle with the dilemmas of overcrowded prisons and record incarceration rates, restitution seems to be a viable way to ease some of today's correctional system problems in the United States of America. Just to illustrate the dilemma of the correctional crisis in the United States: As Huang (1989) pointed out, the growth of the prison populations in the United States has remained stable with only minor fluctuations until about the mid-1970s. The incarceration rate increased from 94 per 100,000 in 1968 to 132 and 426 per 100,000 for the years 1978 and 1989 (Huang, 1989; The Sentencing Project, 1991). Between 1980 and 1988 alone, the prison population increased by 90.2%, meaning that this population almost doubled in 8 years. The United States of America, having now 1,057,875 persons behind bars, has the highest incarceration rate in the world: 426 per 100,000, followed by South Africa with 333, and the Soviet Union with 268 per 100,000 (The Sentencing Project, 1991). If one thinks that black Africans are treated badly in South Africa, a look at the incarceration rates reveals that the rate for black Africans in South Africa is 729 per 100,000 and 3,109 per 100,000 for Afro-Americans in the United States of America (The Sentencing Project, 1991).

Third, a conceptionally distinct purpose for restitution is the rehabilitation of the offender. As Cohen (1942), Del Vecchio (1975), Eglash (1958a, b, 1959), Galaway and Hudson (1975a, b), Mowrer (1978), Newton (1976a, b), Schafer (1970a, b, 1974, 1975a, b), Spencer (1975), and Tallack (1900) have pointed out, restitution might be more rehabilitative than other correctional measures because it is related rationally to the amount of damages done and might be perceived as more just by the offender. Furthermore, the offender is an active participant in the treatment program; that is, the program puts the burden almost totally on him or her and much less on society. In addition, it provides the offender with a concrete way to express guilt; and the stigma for the offender who makes restitution is far less than for the offender who is sent to prison.

Fourth, restitution also offers a fairly easy-to-administer sanction for the criminal justice system. Restitution programs can be administered at the pretrial stage in the prosecutor's office and community correctional facilities and as part of probation and parole sentences. Galaway (1977a, b) has suggested it as part of diversion; and Cohen (1942) thought the right place for restitution was the probation department. Regardless of which form one prefers, we know that there are many established organizations in the criminal justice system in which restitution programs could easily be added. Their main goal would be a reduction of either (a) offenders who would not have been processed through the complicated and expensive court system or (b) incarcerated offenders who are the most costly for society.

Finally, the last advantage of restitution programs is that society at large would benefit from a more humane approach that would lead to a reduced need for vengeance and retribution. If society sees that offenders take an active step to undo the harm they have done and that the victim is involved in the criminal justice process, people might develop different attitudes toward offenders.

These five possibilities are not mutually exclusive and may not be complete. They are, in practice, defined more definitely by specific restitution programs. Over the past 20 years, we have experienced a booming business in the creation and operation of these programs.

3 Restitution Programs in the 1970s and 1980s

While restitution and victim-offender reconciliation sounds very promising in theory, it is plagued by shortcomings in practice.

First, despite a tremendous amount of legislative decisions with regard to the implementation of restitution and victim-offender reconciliation programs, they are applied in a very unsystematic manner at the discretion and initiative of criminal justice administrators who support such programs at very different levels. According to Waller (1990), legislation in the USA and Canada over the past 15 years has created over 2,000 new laws and procedures to improve the situation of victims of crimes and to implement various forms of restitution and victim-offender reconciliation programs. Unfortunately, these laws and procedures were passed in a very unsystematic manner, thus leading to quite different applications depending on the jurisdiction one looks at. Furthermore, according to Hudson and Galaway (1989) and Shapiro (1990), these laws and procedures are mostly applicable at the discretion of the police, the prosecutor's office, and the courts and are not mandatory, thus leading to confusion or to the fact that the laws and provisions provided by legislation are not used by practitioners (Robinson, 1990).

Second, almost all restitution and victim-offender reconciliation programs use restitution or mediation only for property offenses and/or first-time offenders. There is no reason why these programs are restricted to this clientele; and one looks in vain to find a theoretical explanation. In the restitution/mediation literature, we were unable to find evidence suggesting such limitations, although in the more practise-oriented literature of the 1970s and 1980s, these limitations are taken for granted without a reasonable explanation.

Third, having found such a limitation, we are not surprised that restitution and mediation as an alternative to incarceration, although heavily advocated by proponents of restitution/mediation, is nearly nonexistent. Hudson and Chesney (1978) found that restitution is commonly added to probation and parole requirements and, as Austin and Krisberg (1982) found, expands rather than reduces control over the offender. Harland's (1981a, b) reviews of community service statutes revealed that community service is not intended as an alternative to incarceration, although it is claimed as such in the literature. The national surveys on victim-offender reconciliation programs (Coates, 1990; Daniels, 1988; Gehm, 1990; Umbreit, 1986, 1992) clearly show that these programs do not serve as an alternative to incarceration, because they serve an offender population charged with minor offenses who would not receive a prison sentence in the first place. Weitekamp (1989) found the same patterns to be true for restitution programs. At the Advanced NATO Workshop on Conflict, Crime, and Reconciliation in April of 1991 at Il Ciocco, the participants agreed that this shortcoming is life-threatening for the restitution/mediation movement. If restitution/mediation programs cannot turn the wheel around and provide a viable alternative to incarceration, the impact of such programs will be mediocre at the most and a complete failure at the worst (see Messmer and Otto, 1992).

Fourth, Hudson and Galaway (1980) reported that restitution programs in Pima County, Arizona; British Columbia; and Minnesota admit only a disproportionately small number of minorities, indicating that programs indeed select very carefully whom they admit. Simular results were obtained by Daniels (1988), Gehm (1990), Coates (1990), Umbreit (1986, 1992), and Marshall (1992) for mediation programs as well as by Weitekamp (1989, 1992) for restitution programs. The only exception seems to be the restitution program in Philadelphia in which 73.1% of the restitution group belonged to minority groups (Weitekamp, 1989).

Fifth, the majority of restitution/mediation programs are applied to juveniles more often than to adult offenders. In addition, the majority of the clientele have a white, middle-class background. Again, juveniles probably constitute a lower risk group for which criminal justice officials might be more willing to use this penal sanction.

Sixth, another important aspect would be whether restitution and mediation in their various forms have reduced the recidivism rate. Hudson and Chesney (1978), in a study in Minnesota, reported that 6% of the experimental group (released from prison to a restitution center) versus 24% of the control group (served their prison sentence and were released on parole) were returned to prison because they were convicted of a new crime. However, only 10% of the control group were returned because of technical violations, whereas 40% of the experimental group were returned. In general, 46% of the experimentals versus 34% of the controls were returned to prison, indicating that the experimentals were under much tighter control and that this control was responsible for their higher recidivism rate.

Finally, a major problem of restitution and mediation programs is their planning, implementation, and evaluation. According to Hudson and Galaway

(1989), Shapiro (1990), and the participants of the Advanced NATO Workshop on Conflict, Crime, and Reconciliation (Messmer and Otto, 1992), restitution and mediation programs are often planned and implemented in a very unsystematic manner. In addition, these programs are implemented with no concrete goals and are often combined with other criminal justice and welfare programs, thus making evaluations of the effects of restitution and mediation programs impossible. Furthermore, net-widening effects are almost never considered. In order to improve the quality of restitution and mediation programs, major changes in the planning and the evaluation of the effects of the programs seem to be unavoidable and necessary.

4 The Philadelphia Study

The purpose of this study was to examine the criminal cases of the Honorable Lois Forer of the Philadelphia Court of Common Pleas from 1974 to 1984. The dataset of this study is unique and valuable because studies on restitution usually examine specially invented restitution programs in which eligible offenders are seriously screened before they can participate, therefore, leading usually to the inclusion of first-time offenders, property offenders, and predominantly white, middle-class offenders. This study, on the other hand, has used data from a large metropolitan court of Common Pleas in which the cases were assigned randomly to the judge and she imposed restitution sentences on her own; and to enforce such sentences, she had to rely on existing criminal justice agencies. Thus, this study examined a different type of offender: Coming from a large metropolitan area, most of the offenders belonged to a minority group; and over 50% of their offenses were violent.

Of the 605 offenders in our study, 198 were incarcerated, 173 received a restitution sentence, 196 received probation, 26 were found not guilty, and 10 were found not guilty by reason of insanity; in two cases we were unable to determine the outcome. In the sample, 57.7% had a prior arrest record, and 28.6% had been incarcerated before. The offenders in this sample were charged with homicide (5.1%), rape (4.0%), robbery (23.1%), aggravated assault (20.2%), burglary (15.0%), larceny (9.4%), automobile theft (3.3%), arson (2.5%), kidnapping (0.8%), fraud (3.3%), and other offenses (13.3%). A weapon was used in 45.6% of the cases, and the victim was injured in 46.6%. Females constituted only 9.8% of the sample; and the mean age was 27.6. With regard to race, 74.2% of the offenders were Afro-Americans, 20.3% were white, 4.5% were Hispanic, 0.7% were Asian, and 0.2% were American Indian; race was unknown for 0.2%. The majority of offenders were single (55%) and were high-school dropouts, while 23.6% were illiterate or semiliterate and 39% were unemployed.

To determine which offender received a particular sentence, we constructed three different subsamples that constituted our dependent variable: an incarceration group, a probation/restitution group, and a probation group. We created a model containing variables that described the criminal history of offenders: prior offense(s), juvenile record, adult record, number of prior arrests, number of prior convictions, and previous incarceration(s). A second independent set of variables was created to describe the type of offense committed and the resulting damage: Homicide, rape, robbery, aggravated assault, burglary, larceny, automobile theft, arson, kidnapping, fraud, and other offenses constituted the offense variables, and plea, pretrial detention, gang membership, weapon use, whether there was a codefendant, victim's injuries, and victim's property loss comprised the independent variables for determining which offender received a particular sentence. In addition, we created a third set of variables describing the offenders' demographic background: age, gender, marital status, education, occupation, number of children, literacy, whether they lived with parents or relatives, and whether their earnings were sufficient.

We employed various forms of statistical measure to analyze the data. Besides univariate descriptive measures, we used discriminant and logistic regression analysis to predict group membership and to determine the best predictors.

The logistic regression analysis for the criminal history model showed that only a prior arrest had a significant effect on receiving an incarceration sentence over a restitution sentence. The odds of being incarcerated were three times as high if the offender had a prior arrest. By comparing incarceration with probation we found, again, that if an offender had a prior arrest, he or she was 2.5 times more likely to receive an incarceration sentence; no other variables were significant. We also found no significant effects when we compared the criminal history variables with whether an offender received restitution or probation.

For the offense-related model we found that pretrial detention, property of $101-$500 involved, and property over $1,000 involved had a significant effect on whether an offender received an incarceration sentence or a restitution sentence. An offender who was detained before trial was more than twice as likely to be imprisoned; an offender who committed a property offense valued at $101-$500 was twice as likely to receive a restitution sentence. An offender who committed a property offense valued at over $1,000, on the other hand, was three times as likely to be incarcerated. By comparing the effects of these variables on incarceration and probation, we found that, in the case of rape, robbery, and aggravated assault, an offender was more than twice as likely to receive an incarceration sentence; this was also the case for pretrial detention and gang membership. An offender who committed a property crime valued at $501-$1,000 was twice as likely to receive a probation sentence. By comparing the effects of these variables on restitution and probation, we found that an offender who committed a property crime valued at $1-$100 was 2.3 times as likely to receive a restitution sentence, while a property crime valued at $501-$1,000 doubled an offender's chance of receiving a probation sentence.

A comparison of the effects of the demographic background variables on incarceration, restitution, and probation revealed that the only significant effect was being illiterate/semiliterate.

Looking at the results of the 2-year follow-up period of the offenders who were placed on probation/parole, we found that the restitution group had the highest percentage of probation revocations (51.0%), followed by the probation (30.8%) and incarceration (27.8%) groups. However, we must be cautious about the results for the two latter groups, because a great deal of information was missing. Reasons for probation revocation for the restitution group included commission of a new crime (35.4%) and technical violations (45.6%). However, in 32.7% of these cases, a new probation term was imposed, and 61.7% of the offenders served their new term successfully.

5 Policy Implications and Conclusions

The present study clearly indicates that without outside interference, a judge can impose restitution sentences in combination with probation on a large scale and that the official establishment of restitution programs might have a negative effect on its use because of too rigid screening. We found in this study that restitution, contrary to its current use, can be applied successfully in a large metropolitan court in which the majority of the offenders belong to a minority group, have a previous criminal record, and in which most of their offenses are violent.

An evaluation of the results indicates that in terms of the criminal background of the offenders, only prior arrest made a difference in whether an offender was imprisoned or given a restitution sentence. If we look at the offense-related model, we find that only pretrial detention made a difference between incarceration and restitution. Weapon use, whether an offense was a violent one or a property offense, gang membership, and victim's injury made no difference. Because these variables are usually used to determine the seriousness of a crime and the penal sanction, it was surprising that they made no difference in this study. These results indicate that today we could return to the ancient concept of restitution for very serious crimes. That prior arrest and pretrial detention made a difference in determining who was incarcerated and who received a restitution sentence was expected. However, since the number of prior arrests, being convicted before, the number of prior convictions, being incarcerated before, as well as the number and length of prior incarcerations had no effect on the imposition of an incarceration sentence, we could argue that we should overlook the obstacle of a prior offense and pretrial detention since the latter variables indicate a much less serious behavior.

The analysis further revealed that the amount of money involved in property offenses affected imprisonment and restitution. While a value of $101-500 led to a restitution sentence, a value of over $1,000 led to imprisonment. These results are astonishing if we compare them to the victim's injuries. The extent of the injuries had no effect on the imposition of the sentence. It is no surprise that a more costly property offense is punished more severely; but if bodily injuries and even death make no difference, why should property values make such a difference?

To no one's surprise, the only demographic variables that had an effect on incarceration were being male and being illiterate/semiliterate. It is well known that males commit more crimes of a more serious nature and are more likely to have few marketable skills. Before the illiterate/semiliterate offenders could make restitution, they would have to learn how to read and receive job training. Restitution programs such as those in Minnesota and Georgia could serve such a population.

Besides these results, we obtained some more when we compared the incarceration group with the probation group and the restitution group with the probation group, but since they are not as important as the above-mentioned results and because of limited space, we are unable to present them in this context.

The results of this study clearly favor a wider use of restitution for more serious offenders than is now the case. Although the restitution group in the present study had the highest percentage of probation revocations (51.0%), 61.2% served their probation term successfully. The large number of revocations can be explained through the net-widening effect of restitution. Because restitution is an added - although just - burden on the offender, it is controlled by representatives of the criminal justice system; and failure to make restitution payments can lead to the revocation of probation. However, the net-widening effect - viewed negatively in the literature because it leads to more social control - can be viewed positively in the context of restitution. In the context of this study, offenders also profited from the imposition of a restitution sentence and the extended social control since they were not incarcerated, and despite their large number, most of the probation revocations led to the imposition of new probation terms, emphasizing to the offenders the need for them to make their restitution payments.

One concern is whether the increased use of restitution might lead to an unsafe society. The data do not support such a claim: 61.2% of the offenders completed their probation time successfully, and only 24.5% were incarcerated. If we compare this rate with the fact that among released prisoners in the United States, 41.4% are expected to be reincarcerated within 3 years (U.S. Department of Justice, 1989), it appears that society is much better off in applying restitution as an alternative to incarceration.

To summarize our results, the implications of this study are that restitution can and should be used in large metropolitan courts for more serious offenders and for violent offenses. Although the data comprising this study come from the files of a single judge in a Philadelphia court, which might limit their generalization, we believe the results are encouraging and should lead to a wider use of restitution as an alternative to incarceration. The winners of such an approach will be the victim, the offender, and society in general, which desperately needs new alternatives and approaches to deal with the current crisis in the criminal justice system.

References

Austin, J., and Krisberg, B. (1982). The unmet promise of alternatives to incarceration. *Crime and Delinquency, 28,* 374-409.

Berrini, B. (1921). *La giustizia. Problemi giudiziari italiani.* N.p.

Black, H.C. (1968). *Black's law dictionary.* St. Paul, MN: West Publishing Comp.

Coates, R.B. (1990). Victim-offender reconciliation programs in North America: An assessment. In B. Galaway and J. Hudson (Eds.), *Criminal justice, restitution, and reconciliation* (pp. 245-265). Monsey, NY: Criminal Justice Press.

Cohen, I.E. (1942). The integration of restitution in the probation services. *Journal of Criminal Law, Criminology, and Police Science, 33,* 315-321.

Daniels, R.A. (1988). *Making things right: An evaluation of a victim restitution program.* Paper presented at the Annual Meeting of the American Society of Criminology, Chicago.

Del Vecchio, G. (1975). The problem of penal justice. In J. Hudson amd B. Galaway (Eds.), *Considering the victim* (pp. 85-101). Springfield, IL: Charles C. Thomas.

Edelhertz, H. (1977). Legal and operational issues in the implementation of restitution within the criminal justice system. In J. Hudson and B. Galaway (Eds.), *Restitution in criminal justice* (pp. 63-76). Lexington, MA: D.C. Heath Comp.

Eglash, A. (1958a). Creative restitution: A broader meaning for an old term. *Journal of Criminal Law, Criminology, and Police Science, 48,* 619-622.

Eglash, A. (1958b). Creative restitution: Some suggestions for prison rehabilitation programs. *American Journal of Corrections, 20,* 226-232.

Eglash, A. (1959). Creative restitution: Its roots in psychology, religion, and law. *British Journal of Delinquency, 10,* 114-119.

Galaway, B. (1977a). Is restitution practical? *Federal Probation, 41,* 3-8.

Galaway, B. (1977b). Restitution as an integrative punishment. In R. Barnett and J. Hagel (Eds.), *Assessing the criminal* (pp. 331-348). Cambridge, MA: Ballinger.

Galaway, B., and Hudson, J. (1975a). Issues in the correctional implementation of restitution to victims of crime. In J. Hudson and B. Galaway (Eds.), *Considering the victim* (pp. 351-360). Springfield, IL: Charles C. Thomas.

Galaway, B., and Hudson, J. (1975b). Restitution and rehabilitation: Some central issues. In J. Hudson and B. Galaway (Eds.), *Considering the victim* (pp. 255-264). Springfield, IL: Charles C. Thomas.

Gehm, J. (1990). Mediated victim-offender restitution agreements: An exploratory analysis of factors related to victim participation. In B. Galaway and J. Hudson (Eds.), *Criminal justice, restitution, and reconciliation* (pp. 348-360). Monsey, NY: Criminal Justice Press.

Harland, A.T. (1981a). Court-ordered community service in criminal law: The continuing tyranny of benevolence. *Buffalo Law Review, 29,* 425-486.

Harland, A.T. (1981b). *Restitution to victims of personal and household crimes.* Washington, DC: U.S. Department of Justice.

Huang, V. (1989). *Prison crowding in Pennsylvania: An exploration of its causes and condition.* Philadelphia, PA: Pennsylvania Prison Society.

Hudson, J., and Chesney, S. (1978). Research on restitution: A review and assessment. In B. Galaway and J. Hudson (Eds.), *Offender restitution in theory and action* (pp. 131-148). Lexington, MA: Criminal Justice Press.

Hudson, J., and Galaway, B. (1980). A review of the restitution and community-sanctioning research. In J. Hudson and B. Galaway (Eds.), *Victims, offenders, and alternative sanctions* (pp. 173-194). Lexington, MA: D.C. Heath.

Hudson, J., Galaway, B., and Novack, S. (1978). Research on restitution: A review and assessment. In B. Galaway and J. Hudson (Eds.), *Offender restitution in theory and action* (pp. 131-148). Lexington, MA: D.C. Heath.

Hudson, J., and Galaway, B. (1989). Financial restitution: Toward an evaluable program model. *Canadian Journal of Criminology, 31,* 1-18.

Marshall, T. (1992). Restorative justice on trial in Britain. In H. Messmer and H.-U. Otto (Eds.), *Restorative justice on trial. Pitfalls and potentials of victim-offender mediation - international research perspectives* (pp. 15-28). Dordrecht: Kluwer.

Mowrer, O.H. (1978). Applications and limitations of restitution. In B. Galaway and J. Hudson (Eds.), *Offender restitution in theory and action* (pp. 67-72). Lexington, MA: D.C. Heath.

Newton, A. (1976a). Aid to the victim, Part I. Compensation and restitution. *Crime and Delinquency Literature, 8,* 368-390.

Newton, A. (1976b). Alternatives to imprisonment: Day fines, community service orders, and restitution. *Crime and Delinquency Literature, 8,* 109-125.

Nutter, R.W., Hudson, J., and Galaway, B. (1989). *Monetary restitution and victim/offender contact: An annotated and cross referenced bibliography.* Washington, DC: U.S. Department of Justice.

Robinson, J. (1990). *Bill C-89: An Act to amend the Criminal Code.* Paper presented at the VIIth International Course on Victims and the Criminal Justice System, Dubrovnik.

Schafer, S. (1970b). *Compensation and restitution to victims of crime.* Montclair, NJ: Patterson Smith.

Schafer, S. (1970b). Victim compensation and responsibility. *Southern California Law Review, 43,* 55-67.

Schafer, S. (1974). Compensation of victims of criminal offenses. *Criminal Law Bulletin,* 605-636.

Schafer, S. (1975a). The proper role of a victim-compensation system. *Crime and Delinquency, 21,* 45-49.

Schafer, S. (1975b). The restitutive concept of punishment. In J. Hudson and B. Galaway (Eds.), *Considering the victim* (pp. 102-115). Springfield, IL: Charles C. Thomas.

Shapiro, C. (1990). Is restitution legislation the chameleon of the victims' movement? In B. Galaway and J. Hudson (Eds.), *Criminal justice, restitution, and reconciliation.* Monsey, NY: Criminal Justice Press.

Spencer, H. (1975). Prison ethics. In J. Hudson and B. Galaway (Eds.), *Considering the victim* (pp. 71-84). Springfield, IL: Charles C. Thomas.

Tallack, W. (1900). *Reparation to the injured and the rights of victims of crime compensation.* London: Wertheimer, Lea and Co.

The Sentencing Project (1991). *Americans behind bars: A comparison of international rates of incarceration. Project Report.* Washington, DC.

Umbreit, M. (1986). Victim-offender mediation: A national survey. *Federal Probation, 50,* 53-56.

Umbreit, M. (1992). Mediating victim-offender conflict: From single-site to multi-site analysis in the U.S. In H. Messmer and H.-U. Otto (Eds.), *Restorative justice on trail. Pitfalls and potentials of victim-offender mediation - international research perspectives* (pp. 431-444). Dordrecht: Kluwer.

U.S. Department of Justice (1989). *Attorney General's Survey of release procedures: Probation.* Washington, DC.

Viano, E. (1978). Victims, offenders, and the criminal justice system: Is restitution an answer? In B. Galaway and J. Hudson (Eds.), *Offender restitution in theory and action* (pp. 91-100). Lexington, MA: D.C. Heath.

Waller, I. (1990). *Implementing the Victims Declaration of the United Nations.* Paper presented at the VIIth International Course on Victims and the Criminal Justice System, Dubrovnik.

Weitekamp, E.G.M. (1989). *Restitution: A new paradigm of criminal justice or a new way to widen the system of social control?* Ann Arbor, MI: University Microfilms.

Weitekamp, E.G.M. (1992). Can restitution serve as a reasonable alternative to imprisonment? An assessment of the situation in the USA. In H. Messmer and H.-U. Otto (Eds.), *Restorative justice on trail. Pitfalls and potentials of victim-offender mediation - international research perspectives* (pp. 81-103). Dordrecht: Kluwer.

Measurements of Net-Widening

Mark Ezell

Net-widening is considered the major unintended consequence of diversion. Although some might question whether net-widening is, in fact, unintended, few of those who have observed the implementation of diversion over the last 20 or 25 years will dispute the near maxim that "Where there is diversion, so shall there be net-widening". Controversy abounds, however, over the goodness or badness of net-widening.

The purpose of this paper is to describe and discuss several approaches to measuring net-widening, but in order to do this, the conceptual underpinnings of diversion and net-widening will be articulated first. Debates about the impact of net-widening are generally grounded in different conceptual views of diversion. After discussing the conceptualization of diversion and the definition of net-widening, three techniques for measuring net-widening will be described and discussed.

1 Juvenile Diversion

Diversion is a relatively recent juvenile justice reform which is intended to reduce the penetration of cases into the traditional juvenile court system by creating alternative procedures and programs for alleged delinquents. There are many different conceptual definitions of diversion and even more variations of how diversion is applied in practice. Although somewhat obvious, "net-widening" takes on different meanings with various definitions of diversion.

Frazier, Richards, and Potter (1983) describe two distinct views of diversion which differ as a result of one's assumptions about the cause of delinquency. The first view accepts the theory that labeling produces delinquency and that the goal of diversion is to reduce the number of youth and types of behaviors labeled delinquent by the juvenile court. From this point of view, when diversion programs deal with youth who otherwise would not have gone to court, they contribute to juvenile delinquency by treating more youth as delinquents. Net-widening, then, is undesirable because it compromises the goals of diversion.

The second view of diversion holds that delinquency is deviant behavior and can be best reduced by early intervention and treatment. When youth who would not normally go to court are involved in diversion programs, this provides an opportunity to intervene and reduce delinquency. From this point of view, net-widening - serving youth who would not have gone to court - is not a major concern.

More specifically, diversion involves a decision to turn youth away from the official system and handle them via alternative procedures and programs. The expectation is that diverted youth will be more successful than similar youth processed in a traditional manner. This much can be agreed to by both camps, but they would disagree over the reasons why diverted youth will recidivate less. The first view - the labeling viewpoint - predicts that secondary delinquency will be reduced because diversion procedures and programs avoid official labeling. The second view - the early interventionists - predicts less secondary delinquency because of the social services provided by diversion programs.

Diversion, therefore, involves two distinct elements: a) the decision by a justice official (e.g., law enforcement, prosecutor, court intake or probation worker, judge, etc.) to turn the youth away from usual juvenile justice system handling; and b) a program that provides a destination for the youth who has been turned away. The first element - the decision - is absolutely necessary, but there does not have to be a diversion program. In fact, the diversion decision has always been actively used in the juvenile justice system as a result of the broad discretion that court officials have. Diversion programs, the second element, have evolved and proliferated in the last 25 years largely from the influx of federal and state dollars. Separating the two elements of diversion is important for understanding net-widening, because diversion will not happen without the decision to turn a youth away, but, without the programs, there would be no net-widening, because the programs produce the magnetic draw for youth who would not have been sent to court.

Programs for diverted youth usually consist of services for the youth such as counseling, remedial education, job training and placement, drug and/or alcohol treatment, and recreation. Many diversion programs also attempt to involve the youth's parents in the programs, such as those that offer family counseling and parent education. In recent years, a new style of diversion programming has emerged and is gaining popularity because of the public's increased desire to hold youth accountable for their misbehaviors. These newer diversion programs are more sanction- than service-oriented. For example, diverted youth must appear before an individual, judge-like arbitrator or panel of community members (e.g., community accountability boards) who utilize a process of mediation or arbitration to decide on appropriate sanctions for the youth. Frequently ordered sanctions include restitution, fines, writing essays and making apologies, attending a class on victims or the consequences of crime, and hours of community service. The new style of diversion is interesting because it is unclear whether the avoidance of labeling is a goal, and there is little emphasis on the provision of services.

Most diversion programs - whether focused on services or sanctions - are funded from public resources, are staffed with professionals, and seek to involve community volunteers. Once a youth, and sometimes his or her parents, agree to be diverted, there are numerous rules and regulations with which the youth and the family must comply. The day-to-day practices of diversion programs and the enforcement of program rules are the mechanisms by which social control is extended over the youth.

There is some debate over the proper auspice of diversion programs. Is it really diversion if the agency hosting the diversion program is part of the justice system or should diversion services or sanctions be implemented by nonsystem agencies? For example, some diversion programs are run by the court, the prosecutor, or the probation department, while others are operated by nonprofits or agencies of local government. Again, the answer to this question is highly related to one's original view of diversion. Generally, proponents of labeling theory insist that the service agency to which the child is diverted be independent of the juvenile justice system so that stigmatization is less likely; Empey (1982) believes that allowing justice agencies to operate diversion programs subverts the goals of diversion. Others, however, are unconcerned about program sponsorship and feel that diversion's real value comes from minimizing a youth's penetration into the system. Research findings by Elliott, Dunford, and Knowles (1978) make this a meaningless debate. They found that diverted youth perceive high levels of labeling regardless of whether services are delivered in a traditional justice setting or a diversion agency.

More important than the auspice of a diversion agency, however, is the question of whether the court has closed a divertee's case or has retained jurisdiction by leaving the case open pending successful completion of the diversion program. Does the youth voluntarily receive services from the diversion program? If a youth's case is still considered open by the court, then the agency, notwithstanding its official auspices, can be considered an agent of the court. Agency personnel will be expected to report the youth's attendance and/or performance to the court. If the youth is cooperative and successfully completes the requirements of the particular diversion program, the case will usually be closed, but if the youth fails to attend, cooperate, or in some way violates the conditions of the diversion program, the court has the option to schedule an adjudicatory hearing and prosecute the original charges. In order for this scenario to occur, the youth and his or her parents probably would have agreed to waive their rights to a speedy trial. If diversion is voluntary, as many insist it should be, the youth's decision on whether to cooperate with the diversion program should have no legal ramifications.

This is a crucial consideration that impacts the potential for diversion programs to widen the net. The net cannot be widened if the court terminates its jurisdiction once the diversion decision is made. However, it is rare for this to happen, because most prosecutors, judges, and diversion program personnel feel that the threat of formal court processing must remain an option in order to have leverage on the youth and to get his or her "cooperation."

Some view diversion as any action, decision, or program that minimizes a youth's penetration into the juvenile justice system. In this view, probation is considered diversion when the youth might otherwise have been committed to a residential program; or placing a youth in a group home diverts him or her from an institution. This paper specifically focuses on pre-trial diversion, that is, those practices and programs which divert alleged delinquents from juvenile court prior to an adjudicatory hearing. The concept of diversion as used here specifies that a youth not headed toward the court cannot be turned away; "... diversion programs must handle only youngsters who otherwise would enter ... the justice system" (Klein, 1979: 153).

2 Definitions of Net-Widening

Empirical studies of diversion programs have documented these programs' propensity to widen the net of the justice system, an unintended increase rather than an alteration of the court's reach. Rather than providing a true alternative to court, diversion programs have merely supplemented the court function and increased both the number of youth brought to the attention of the juvenile justice system and the number under court jurisdiction. A substantial proportion of youth served by diversion programs would not have received services and/or been supervised by the court had these programs not existed.

Saul and Davidson (1983) describe net-widening as the major unintended consequence of juvenile diversion. Instead of reducing the number of youth under court supervision, as intended, diversion has increased it. Blomberg (1983) uses a similar definition by pointing out that net-widening extends the reach of the juvenile justice system by increasing the overall proportion of the population subject to court services or control.

Thus far, we have not reached agreement on a specific definition of net-widening (Esbensen, 1984). The following question helps to frame the concept: "Is diversion serving as a process for moving young persons who have 'penetrated' the justice network outward and away from that system, or has it become a device for incorporating a whole new class of clients inside an expanding justice system?" (Polk, 1984: 654). Therefore, if the class of clients served by a diversion program is examined and it is determined that they have not been moved out and away from the juvenile justice system, the reach of the system has been extended. Net-widening occurs if the probability of being subject to court jurisdiction and control increases and the increase can be shown to be a result of the implementation of diversion. If youth are engaged in activities no different than before diversion and they are more likely to be arrested, to be placed in a program under court control, or to be sent to court, diversion has widened the net (notwithstanding however benevolent the intentions of the policy makers and program staff).

3 Methods to Measure Net-Widening

3.1 Client Characteristics

Klein (1979) described a method for determining whether a diversion program is serving youth who would have be formally processed. He suggests comparing the demographic and legal characteristics of diverted youth to those who were released without diversion or court processing. The profile of diverted youth should be older, disproportionately male, with prior offenses, and be currently charged with a relatively more serious offense. If the comparison does not meet this expected profile, the diversion program is judged to have widened the net by serving youth who otherwise would have been released. Others have taken Klein's logic and extended it and compared diverted youth to youth who were formally handled by the court.

Frazier, Richards, and Potter (1983) point out several criticisms of this method. First, there is no consensus on how large the differences between the groups need to be before the research can conclude that net-widening has occurred. Second, what does it mean if some of the client characteristics are different and others are not?

Table 1: Comparison of Youth Handled Through Arbitration and Informally

		Arbitration	Informal
Age*			
	Under 16	64.2%	37.0%
	16 and over	35.8%	63.0%
Offense*			
	Felony	20.5%	41.1%
	Misdemeanor	79.5%	58.9%
Priors*			
	None	85.1%	53.4%
	One or more	14.9%	46.6%
Total *N*		215	73

* χ^2 statistically significant, $p < .01$.
Data from Ezell (1989)

Table 1 is an example of a comparison of client characteristics for youth who were diverted to a juvenile arbitration program to those who were handled informally by court intake (Ezell, 1989). The data from this example would support a conclusion of net-widening because diverted youth tend to be younger, charged with less serious offenses, and have fewer prior offenses than youth whose cases were closed after an initial contact with an intake worker.

3.2 *Pre- and Posttransitional Probabilities*

Another very popular methodology for measuring net-widening involves comparing transitional probabilities from the time period prior to the start of the diversion program to those from a post-program time period. Transitional probabilities are derived from aggregate data and represent the likelihood that any given youth will penetrate the juvenile justice system beyond given decision points (Blomberg, 1983). The transitional probability of greatest interest when studying diversion and net-widening is the probability that an arrested youth's case will be taken to court. Formal judicial handling is narrowly equated with being subject to the court's jurisdiction or under state control, the concepts of interest in the study of net-widening. The importance of this narrow operationalization will be important later.

The transitional probabilities can be used in two ways. First, if they increase after the program initiates services it is concluded that net-widening occurred. The juvenile justice system has expanded its reach. Second, the pre-program transitional probabilities can be used to project the number of youth who will be judicially handled in the future. The projections can be compared to the actual number to estimate the level of diversion or net-widening. If more youth actually go to court, for example, than estimated, then the system has extended its reach.

Table 2: Pre- and Postdiversion Transitional Probabilities[*]

	Prior to diversion	After diversion	Percent change
Average no. of arrests	1,759.2	1,748.8	- 0.6%
Average no. of judicially handled cases	556.3	645.8	16.1%
Average rate of judicial handling	31.8	36.9	16.1%
Increase in judicially handled cases due to net-widening[a]	n/a	89.7	n/a
Average no. of cases under court jurisdiction	556.3	1,278.8	129.9%
Increase in no. of cases under court jurisdiction due to net-widening[b]	n/a	722.7	n/a
Remainder of the state			
Average rate of judicial handling	31.8	50.0	57.2%
Average no. of cases under court jurisdiction	6,732	10,116	50.3%

[*] All data are quarterly.
[a] (645.8) - (.318)(1,748.8)
[b] (1,278.8) - (.318)(1,748.8)

Again, sample data are used to illustrate this technique (see Table 2). Before the diversion program started, the rate of judicial handling was 31.8 cases per 100 arrested youth (this is an average rate for 16 quarters); after the diversion program began handling cases, it rose to 36.9 cases per 100 arrested youth. (For ease of communication, transitional probabilities are represented as rates per 100 cases.) The probability of an arrested youth going to court increased in the years following the start of the diversion program, and net-widening - at least the narrow operationalization of it - has resulted in approximately 360 more cases per year being sent to court.

However, if we used a broader operationalization of net-widening we would include all arrested youth who are under the court's jurisdiction. This would include not only those whose cases have gone to court but also those who have been referred to the diversion program because the diverted youth signed agreements that gave the prosecutor the option to take their cases to court should they fail to cooperate or complete the diversion program. The diversion program "served" an average of 668.2 youth per quarter, meaning that an average of 1,278.8 youth per quarter were under state control after the start of the diversion program. Using this method to measure net-widening, we see that the implementation of this diversion program extended the reach of the court to almost 2,800 youth in a three-county area. Prior to the implementation of the diversion program, these youth's cases would have been handled informally and closed shortly after arrest.

This method has serious shortcomings however. We cannot conclude that increase in the number of cases going to court result from the start of the diversion program. Suppose that the Governor and Legislature of the state had decided to crack down on juvenile crime by implementing new, get-tough policies and practices throughout the state. This or other factors (e.g., increasingly serious delinquency) could be the cause of increased judicial handling rates, not the diversion program, and until we eliminate this rival explanation for the results, above, we are in a weak position to conclude that the diversion program caused net-widening.

One way to improve the method of comparing pre- and post-program transitional probabilities, and one that will help eliminate some of the rival explanations for the results, is to add a comparison or control group. This helps control for changes in policy, practice, and/or behavior beyond that included in the implementation of a diversion program. For this example, the remainder of the state was used as a comparison group, and, as can be seen from Table 2, the rate of judicial handling showed a much greater increase in the remainder of the state than in the three counties served by the diversion program. The diversion program of interest here seems to have had a suppression effect on the broad and rather steep increase in judicial handling. But, the implementation of diversion programs in the rest of the state accounted for a smaller increase in the number of juveniles under court supervision than was the case in the catchment area for this diversion program.

3.3 Time Series

Both of the techniques discussed so far take static snapshots of net-widening and are insensitive to change over time. Neither approach would discern the fact that rates of judicial handling and/or rates of being under state control might be changing and that the implementation of the diversion program could increase, decrease, or reverse the trend. For example, if the pre- and post-diversion transitional probabilities for judicial handling are equal, we might conclude that diversion is having no effect, or if the post-diversion transitional probability is larger, then we would conclude that net-widening occurred. But if the transitional probabilities are observed over time, it could be that the chance of going to court increased every year before diversion started, but the start and continued operation of diversion causes a shift in this pattern and the longer the program operates the lower the probability of going to court.

Figure 1 shows the quarterly rate of judicial handling for approximately 8 years. Before diversion started, the rate was increasing every quarter by an average of 2.3 cases per 100 arrests. This trend does shift downward once diversion starts, which means that the prosecutor changed his decision-making patterns after diversion began operating (slope = -1.0). The trend which is of greater interest to those concerned about net-widening, however, is the steep increase in the rate of court jurisdiction which shows that this three county juvenile justice system was not reducing its reach at all (slope = 2.3). Certainly, there are both expected and unexpected changes going on as a result of diversion, and it remains to be determined whether they may be viewed as positive.

Just like with the transitional probabilities, we cannot be sure that the observed shift in decision-making practices is caused by the diversion program alone; again, adding a comparison group will strengthen the research design. As can be seen in Figure 1, the trends in judicial handling rates were increasing in the remainder of the state (slope = 1.0) and the increase slowed but did not reverse direction after diversion as was the case in the three counties in which the diversion program operated (slope = .4). Also, the rate of court jurisdiction for the remainder of the state continued to increase slightly but not as much as in the diversion area.[1]

3.4 Other Unintended Consequences

Diversion is an intervention directed both at individual youth and at the operation of the juvenile court. Since a major goal of diversion is to alter the flow and mix of cases going to court, it is not too surprising, therefore, that other decision patterns will change. Either transitional probabilities or time series analysis can be used to monitor possible changes in decision-making relating to probation or institutionaliza-

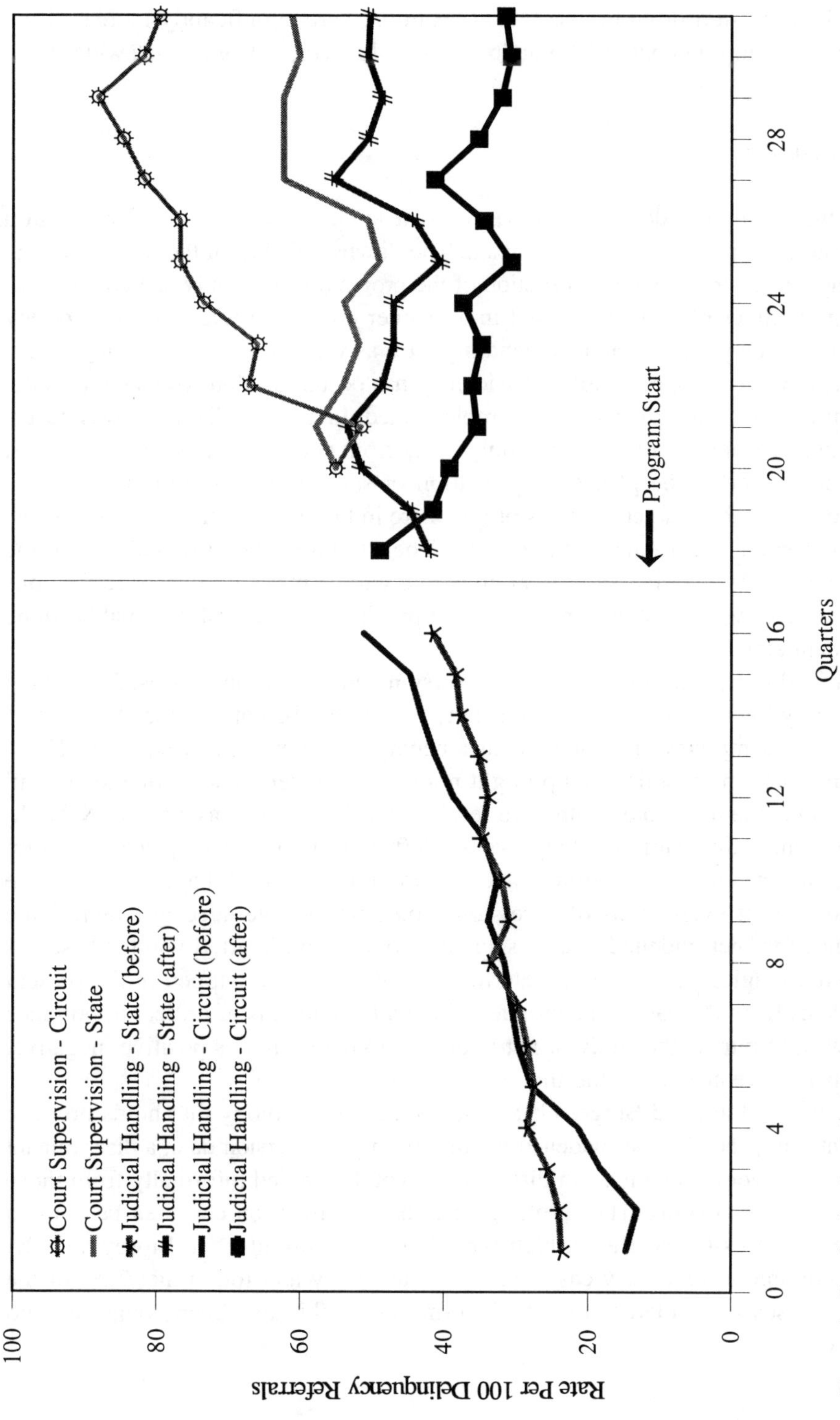

Figure 1: Graph of judicial handling and supervision rates for 3-county arbitration program and the remainder of state (starting with quarter beginning 4/74, ending 12/80).

tion. The diversion program used as an example here significantly increased the probation and institutionalization rate in its area while controlling for statewide shifts.

4 Discussion

Using the techniques described above, we can see that the impact of diversion on a local juvenile justice system was mixed. The downward shift of the rate of judicial handling demonstrates that the operation of the program significantly altered decision-making practices of court personnel in a manner consistent with diversion policy goals. Based on predicted judicial handling rates as well as an examination of client profiles, however, it appears that net-widening has occurred. More youth came under court jurisdiction after diversion was implemented. In a sense, diversion was occurring, but not away from the system, only away from court, and those going to court were more likely to be placed on probation or sent to an institution than before diversion. Therefore, larger numbers of youth are in the system longer and are subject to more system requirements and control. Their failure to comply with any of the conditions set by the diversion program is likely to be met with further restrictions of liberty. This would not have been so if the pre-diversion rates of informal handling been maintained.

As a final note, depending on which diversion conceptualization is used - labeling versus early intervention - these results may or may not be bothersome. Those from the labeling camp view net-widening as a negative unintended consequence. Those from the early intervention camp might not see net-widening as unintended at all and would argue that more youth have received needed services as a result. Notwithstanding one's diversion ideology, we are left with the major empirical question "What impact does net-widening have on individual youth?" To answer this, we need to look at evaluations of diversion programs, but we need to examine the outcomes for "net-widened youth" separate from "truly diverted youth." It seems we need a magical technique to determine what would *not* happen in the present if practices from the past had continued. Such a technique is of critical importance if we wish to pursue the study of net-widening to determine its positive, negative, and other consequences at the individual level.

Lipsey, Cordray, and Berger (1981) utilized a methodology that holds promise for identifying specific "net-widened youth." With pre-diversion data, a discriminant analysis is developed which can differentiate youth handled informally from those who were sent to court. The resulting discriminant function can then be applied to diverted cases to ascertain which type they most resemble. In Lipsey's study, they were able to reclassify cases with 88% accuracy and found that 76% of the diverted cases resembled those which formerly would have been counseled and released.

5 Conclusion

In conclusion, if either the client characteristics or the transitional probabilities approaches had been used alone, it is likely that some of the subtleties of the impact of diversion and the nature of net-widening would have been missed in the sample data presented here. Neither approach is adequately sensitive to shifting patterns in the decision-making practices of court personnel. A time series approach is the recommended method to determine diversion's impact on the entire juvenile justice system. It should be noted that the time series approach described here was more than a simple, one-variable model, however, because it tracked four variables over time - rate of judicial handling, rate of court supervision, rate of probation, and rate of commitment - and used a comparison group.

Even though a time series approach is more powerful and sensitive, the client characteristics approach remains a useful tool. By examining the characteristics of youth who went to court prior to the start of diversion, court and program staff can develop a profile of those youth who are most appropriate for diversion. After diversion starts, they can determine whether they are targeting the appropriate youth for diversion by comparing the characteristics of the diverted youth to the profile. Staff can get specific guidance to alter client selection practices by noting the differences between the profile and the characteristics of diverted youth.

Note

1 Simonton (1977) suggests the following regression model to test whether the pre- to post, and experimental to comparison group differences are significant:

$$Y_t = b_1 + b_2X_t + b_3Z + b_4t + b_5X_tZ + b_6X_tt + b_7Zt + b_8X_tZt$$

Y_t is the judicial handling rate measured at each quarter for both the diversion area and the remainder of the state. X_t is a dummy variable that equals zero for quarters 1 through 16 and equals 1 for quarters 17 through 31. Z equals one for the experimental area and 0 for the remainder of the state. t represents the particular quarter number transformed so that t = 0 for the quarter when the program started, - 1.0 for the prior quarter, and + 1.0 for the quarter after program startup, etc. b_8 is the coefficient of interest because if it is significant then the rate of judicial handling in the diversion area is significantly different from that of the remainder of the state while controlling for historical trends.

References

Blomberg, T.G. (1983). Diversion's disparate results and unresolved questions: An integrative evaluation perspective. *Journal of Research in Crime and Delinquency, 20,* 24-38.

Elliott, D.S., Dunford, F.W., and Knowles, B. (1978). *Diversion: A Study of Alternative Processing.* Boulder, CO: Behavioral Research Institute.

Empey, L.T. (1982). *American Delinquency: Its Meaning and Construction.* Homewood, IL: Dorsey.

Esbensen, F. (1984). Net widening? Yes and no: Diversion impact assessed through a systems processing rates analysis. In S.H. Decker (Ed.), *Juvenile Justice Policy: Analyzing Trends and Outcomes* (pp. 115-128), Beverly Hills: Sage Publications.

Ezell, M. (1989). Juvenile arbitration: Net-widening and other unintended consequences. *Journal of Research on Crime and Delinquency, 26,* 358-377.

Frazier, C.E., Richards, P., and Potter, R.H. (1983). Juvenile diversion and net widening: Toward a clarification of assessment strategies. *Human Organization, 42,* 115-122.

Klein, M.W. (1979). Deinstitutionalization and diversion of juvenile offenders: A litany of impediments. In N. Morris and M. Tonry (Eds.), *Crime and justice: An annual review of research,* Vol. 1 (pp. 145-201). Chicago: University of Chicago Press.

Lipsey, M.W., Cordray, D.S., and Berger, D.E. (1981). Evaluation of a juvenile diversion program: Using multiple lines of evidence. *Evaluation Review, 5,* 283-306.

Polk, K. (1984). Juvenile diversion: A look at the record. *Crime and Delinquency, 30,* 648-59.

Saul, J.A., and Davidson, W.S. (1983). Implementation of juvenile diversion programs: Cast your net on the other side of the boat. In J.R. Kluegel (Ed.), *Evaluating Juvenile Justice* (pp. 31-45), Beverly Hills: Sage Publications.

Simonton, D.K. (1977). Cross-sectional time-series experiments: Some suggested statistical analyses. *Psychological Bulletin, 84,* 489-502.

Alternative Social Work: Informalization of Social Control in the Field of Juvenile Delinquency - An Empirical Study

Hans-Uwe Otto

1 Introduction

Investigations into the labeling approach carried out in the 1970s viewed the social welfare service as a further instrument of criminalization and control that seemed to fit almost seamlessly into the definition and punishment processes of the criminal justice system. Nor has this impression changed with the import of diversion from the USA and the establishment of alternative interventions. Rather, a discussion has arisen as to whether social control is not extended by the social welfare service, because the interventions it offers create additional potential instead of providing alternatives to the repressive sanctions of detention. Moreover, it is argued, the pedagogical claims do not only merely represent the conventional penal practice in a different rhetorical guise but also result in subjecting the personal and social situation of the persons concerned to intensified controlling intervention.

Such fears are well-founded because the relationship between the social welfare service and the criminal justice system is marked by a specific distribution of competencies. From the legal standpoint, cases are reduced to the aspect of norm violation, and this continues to be crucial for the decision concerning the action to be taken or the sanctions to be imposed. According to the prevailing view, it is left to the social welfare service to fill out the factual findings of the individual case with the personality features of the accused person and to supplement the sanctions imposed with the necessary sociopedagogical interventions. It may be that sociopedagogics is subsequently doomed to failure because of the need to operate in a problem field determined by others and is therefore bereft of the special conditions which it needs to function properly by the decisions already taken by the criminal justice authorities.

In this situation, an integrated concept coordinated between the sociopedagogical and social welfare services for tackling officially registered juvenile delinquency seems subject to substantial restrictions. In any case, it is pointed out, social welfare work does not have its own "dogmatics", that is, a classification of delinquency situations that could be brought into a systematized context with interventions outside of the penalties legitimized by the state, which means that in the concepts it offers for diversion projects and field interventions, the social welfare service is to a correspondingly greater extent obliged to find the smallest common denominator between the problem definition of the criminal justice authorities and the approach to problem solving of sociopedagogics. It is claimed that instead of differentiating the problem situations of young people which may lead to delinqency, the generalizing attitude of the criminal justice system to the delinquency problem is adopted and sociopedagogical intervention becomes directed toward the postulate of combating crime.

Criminal justice takes the abstract view of crime as the violation of a norm, and this is said to find its sociopedagogical counterpart in the "deficit model", that is, in the interpretation of a crime as a symptom of a deeper seated personal deficit that can be remedied by pedagogical means. For the field of minor delinquency, in which this symptomatic character of crime is questionable, the figure of the "first crime" as the potential beginning of a criminal career has been mobilized to legitimize pedagogical intervention. By generalizing and applying the problem definition to this alleged symptomatic character, which also means foregoing any attempt at closer definition of the actual pedagogical problem, the orientation of the criminal justice system to the gravity of the offense may become permeated with pedagogical terminology: the stronger the symptom manifested in the norm violation, the more serious is the underlying deficit, and, consequently the more interventionist the action that needs to be taken. Social welfare work can, it is concluded, evidently not transcend the principle of individual guilt assignment because it does not have the necessary competence in the area of case definition. Furthermore, it is argued that social welfare work is at the same time fixed on the principle of personality modification in accordance with the deficit model in so far as the application of its resources is predetermined by judicial sanction decisions and made compatible with the needs of the criminal justice system by the goal of combating crime through individual prevention.

The "pedagogization" of criminal justice established in the conception of the German Juvenile Justice Act (JGG) has evolved as a central aspect of the developments in the system in the two decades up to the mid-1980s. However, reinforced by criminological research, juvenile crime has in the last few years come to be seen as a more or less ubiquitious and development-related natural phenomenon, and both this impression and the emphasis on the position of the victim have meant that the scope for pedagogical interventions in juvenile criminal proceedings has come under increasing pressure. Calls for the retreat of pedagogically fixed social welfare work from the field of criminal justice as a whole or at least from the areas of petty or moderately serious crime (see Haase-Schur, 1985; Walter, 1986) have been nourished above all by the fears of an extension of controls. Other positions, conversely, stress that the dilemma of social work as a pedagogically legitimized instrument for sanctions must be solved by freeing it from the "basement of criminal justice" (Müller and Otto, 1986). As the precondition for the development of an independent quality in the social welfare service's dealings with juvenile crime, changes to trial proceedings or a definition of the legal rights of juveniles in respect of assistance by the social welfare service have been called for (see Feltes, 1988).

In view of the present ministerial drafts for the Juvenile Justice Act and Juvenile Assistance Law, calls for legislative changes currently seem to hold no prospect of realization. Regional pilot schemes that do not exceed the framework of the Juvenile Justice Act are, on the other hand, even more restricted in their reforming impact; but they can be established relatively unproblematically and provide insight into what effect changes in the conditions of cooperation between criminal justice and social work would have. The subject of the present investigation is a pilot scheme at the Bielefeld youth welfare office that has been implemented in cooperation with the juvenile public prosecutor's office with the aim of rendering trial proceedings in court unnecessary. Possible sociopedagogical interventions have not been predefined. Instead, the social workers concerned have been given the opportunity to participate in the decisions of the public prosecutor. In each individual case referred to the scheme at the pretrial stage, they examine whether any alternative ways of dealing with the matter are available, and if so which. Where certain interventions appear appropriate, they are also responsible for their implementation - subject to the agreement of the public prosecutor's office and the other parties involved. In this way, social workers are able to establish the preconditions for the proceedings to be dismissed pursuant to Section 45, Subsection 2, No 1, Juvenile Justice Act.

By consciously not predefining the delinquency problem and the corresponding interventions to be adopted, the social welfare service is, in principle, in the position of being able to coordinate the problem definition and the action for dealing with it on the basis of informal proceedings and using independent criteria. This also enables the advantages of the traditional approach of dealing with individual cases, resulting from the mobility between the definitions of the relevant authorities and the positions of the persons involved, to come into play (see Matthes, 1973). The social workers may be guided in their proposals for handling the matter by considerations that transcend both the offender orientation of the deficit model and the reductionist view of crime as held by the judicial authorities. To the extent that the particular action proposed to the public prosecutor also requires the agreement of the parties involved, their participation in the informal proceedings would necessarily also be of increased importance. It is true that this cannot be apostrophized as "voluntary participation", but the particular proposal for dealing with the case should not be made without taking into account the subjective views of the persons involved. In this way, the pilot scheme could enable the conditions leading to the crime and its consequences for the accused and the victim or the normality of juvenile crime to be taken into account more substantially.

Utilization of this increased scope, in which independent decision-making criteria are to be developed with the participation of the parties involved, is, however, not free of influence from the institutions of criminal justice. As the cases to be handled by this pilot scheme are for the most part referred by the criminal justice authorities, there is an initial dependency on their selection criteria. Moreover, the action to be taken by the social workers is always dependent on acceptance of their proposals by the public prosecutors, as otherwise the willingness of the public prosecutors to cooperate might be endangered. In this way, the crime orientation of the criminal justice authorities could prevail just as could efficiency criteria in the field of legal conduct.

2 Research Questions

First, the possibilities of participation of the accused and the victims in the decision-making process: The form, content, and quality of social worker/client and offender/victim interactions will be analyzed.

Second, the structural conditions and forms of implementation of the informal proceedings will be looked at, and the question of what connections exist between the case structure and the proposed action will be investigated.

Third, the impact of the pilot scheme on the decision-making behavior of the criminal justice authorities within the overall volume of pending juvenile delinquency cases will be investigated. Here, particular attention will be paid to the question of whether and to what extent the action of the social workers in the context of criminal justice leads to an increase or decrease of social controls.

In the following papers each of these questions will be adressed in detail by researchers in the project "Alternative Social Work" (Special Research Center 227, Prevention and Intervention, University of Bielefeld).

3 Summary

On the basis of the results available at present, the prospects for influencing the juvenile offenders on the level of bargaining at the youth welfare office must be viewed as good. They are given adequate opportunity to articulate the assessment standpoint; in the bargaining process with the social workers, they have sufficient scope to present their subjective perceptions. The talks focus primarily on the reasons for and the significance of the offense and hence on subjective attitudes, social and situative problem aspects, and specific consequences for the offender and less on the actual events of the offense itself. For bargaining processes at the youth welfare office - and also for the victim/offender relationship - this basis also opens up the way to a special preventive orientation.

On the level of decision-making conditions within the proceedings, however, it is apparent that the social welfare service, even if furnished with extended decision-making powers in the individual case, is strongly and directly confronted with the dependencies that fundamentally determine the relationship between the social welfare service and criminal justice authorities. On the basis of initial trends, the influence of the orientation of the criminal justice system to offense severity or the deficit model can be perceived in some areas. The statement that a considerable number of cases could have been expected to be dismissed by the public prosecutor in normal proceedings suggests that the pilot scheme has, in some instances, been instrumentalized for the sanction purposes of criminal justice. On the other hand, however, criminal justice intervention has also been minimized to an equally large extent. The social welfare service has therefore proved able to justify nonintervention or to provide alternatives. The pilot scheme thus presents an opportunity for social welfare work to improve its position in relation to the criminal justice system by introducing other perspectives into the proceedings and thus advancing from being merely an informative executive instrument to playing a certain role within the decision-making process.

With the inclusion of a further survey carried out at another youth welfare office, it will be possible to see how far the trends visible so far are confirmed or are subject to change. A tendency was already emerging in the first phase of the pilot scheme for the referral practice of the public prosecutor's office to change in favor of more serious cases. Also, the interventions proposed by the social workers are likely to undergo development with the consolidation of the pilot scheme. As the data base is extended, particular attention will be paid to the question of whether and in what way the pilot scheme influences the decision behavior of the criminal justice system within the overall volume of juvenile criminal cases.

References

Feltes, T. (1988). Pädagogik und Justiz. Ein Plädoyer für mehr Gerechtigkeit und Ehrlichkeit und weniger Pädagogik im Jugendstrafverfahren. *Neue Praxis, 18*, 315-327.

Haase-Schur, I. (1985). Jugendhilfe und Diversion. Zum Verhältnis von Jugendhilfe und Jugendgerichtsbarkeit im Spannungsfeld einer neuen Legitimationskrise des Jugendstrafrechts. *Theorie und Praxis der sozialen Arbeit, 36,* 209-218.

Matthes, J. (1973). Sozialarbeit als soziale Kontrolle. In H.-U. Otto and S. Schneider (Eds.), *Gesellschaftliche Perspektiven der Sozialarbeit,* Vol. 1 (pp. 107-128). Neuwied: Luchterhand.

Müller, S., and Otto, H.-U. (1986). Sozialarbeit im Souterrain der Justiz. Plädoyer zur Aufkündigung einer verhängnisvollen Allianz. In S. Müller and H.-U. Otto (Eds.), *Damit Erziehung nicht zur Strafe wird* (pp. VII-XXII). Bielefeld: KT-Verlag Böllert.

Walter, M. (1986). Angebote der Jugendhilfe und Jugendkriminalrecht. *Zentralblatt für Jugendrecht und Jugendwohlfahrt, 73,* 429-436.

Informal Justice and Communication: The Case of Diversion and Victim-Offender Mediation

*Heinz Messmer**

1 Introduction

An increasing amount of research in criminal sociology today is showing how ineffectively traditional criminal law fulfills its goals of special and general prevention. Research on undetected crime is revealing that juvenile delinquency is more the rule than the exception, and that it mostly declines with increasing age, even without formal criminal sanctions. Cohort studies also suggest a negative relationship between criminal sanctions and legal compliance: Penal interventions often reinforce deviant behavior.[1] Juvenile criminal law has started to respond to this with decriminalization. Two such measures have gained particular attention: diversion and victim-offender mediation (see Messmer and Otto, 1992).

However, little is known about the actual practice of diversion and mediation. Reports by programs and practitioners generally provide only a rough sketch of the specific treatment practice, and this is illustrated only with single case reports. In most cases, the program's "inner life" is treated as a "black box".[2]

In the following, I shall consider this generally rather neglected field of research and report what can be found when the practice is subjected to systematic observation. The present study is based on analyses of interactions between social workers and clients within the diversion and mediation practice at the Bielefeld Youth Welfare Office. First, I shall use some ideas on negotiation theory to formulate a framework for the decision-making process in diversion and victim-offender mediation. This framework then provides the background to present the methods and data of the study. This is followed by quantitative and qualitative analyses of findings on the practice of diversion and victim-offender mediation. Finally, the importance of these findings for improving communication between professionals and their clients is discussed.

2 Law and Negotiation

A negotiation paradigm views the construction of meaning as an activity that the parties involved perform while carrying out their interaction (see Kallmeyer, 1981:

89). Negotiations always arise when there is a lack of agreement on reality (see Strauss, 1978: 15), and they unfold within "challenge-and-response" encounters (see Zartman, 1976). Negotiation moves react to prior situational definitions of others in such a way that future situational definitions will be influenced according to one's own criteria of suitability. With regard to social reality - or that which should become social reality - negotiations are both constitutive and universal; they are product and precondition for all that which attains meaning in social interaction. The question is then no longer what social reality objectively is, but under which conditions we consider something objective to be real.[3] Social reality depends on different meaning-giving devices that relate to the various types of organizing principles of social experience. Adjudication is no exception to this. Its aspects of relevance culminate in the production of binding decisions about right and wrong. A decision is achieved through normatively safeguarded assumptions about reality: In the legal system, such premises follow norm expectations and are taken as objectively right regardless of whether this is true or not. Correspondingly, deviations from this impinge norm expectations and are viewed as normatively wrong.[4]

As a result, law has established typical negotiation procedures, namely, those of jurisdiction. These form a particular kind of communication system in which factual information is made available according to its normative suitability. Oral communication before the court links together various tasks such as explaining the facts, making a decision, and the legitimacy of proceedings into an apparently rationally calculable sequence of procedures. However, communication according to the imperatives of the legal system also has side effects on the legitimacy and justice of its procedures. As long as the court has to provide clear, legally binding, and also rapid decisions between right and wrong, it also has to reduce the particularities of socially relevant facts to a limited number of typical ideal case characteristics until these can be assigned to a generally valid norm.[5] Law protects its rationality by carrying out a decision-making program that does not have to be identical to the psychological and situational experience of its clients. While court proceedings are predominantly concerned with the maintenance of this decision-making program, the client is more interested in the "net effect of change in being" (Schumann, 1979: 11, translated). This leads to the problem of incongruent perspectives in the perception of law.

Several empirical studies have focused especially on this issue. Despite national differences in court proceedings,[6] analyses nonetheless all agree in showing asymmetrically distributed spheres of influence between the status groups involved. In German procedural law, above all, judges have unequal powers of influence, particularly in their procedural rights and their habitually regulated interaction standards. Judges rule over the course and duration of a case, they steer the flow of discussion by granting the right to address the court, and they control the investigation with special interrogation techniques (see, e.g., Kallmeyer, 1983; Wassermann, 1985). Risky side effects exist particularly in the judges' self-immunization through preconceived situational definitions and - complementary to this - in their practice of preventing clients' from giving complex case descriptions. Research has confirmed that the ability and willingness to provide complex case descriptions depends on the possibilities to realize the preconceived communication plan. If the cohesive structure of such plans is interrupted, broken up by specific questioning techniques, or the flow of presentation is cut off inconveniently,[7] this will lead to decreasing eloquence - even in professionals with court experience (see, also, Knuf, 1982: 271). Empirical observations in Germany have shown that lay persons generally have a low negotiation relevance in both civil (e.g., Grüner, 1984) and criminal justice procedures (for more detail, see Muth, 1984; Soeffner, 1983). The restricted opportunities for lay persons to present their case can additionally suffer from the loss of the appearance of a competent mode of speech, which also has a strong impact on the credibility, attractiveness, and acceptance of a speaker's utterances.[8] As long as clients' opportunities to articulate themselves are restricted, they will feel themselves to be insufficiently understood before the court.[9]

Unequally distributed opportunities to exert an influence before the court frequently express themselves in communication patterns that are aimed more toward eliminating rather than bridging incongruent patterns of perception. When subjective and legal orientations are based on different premises regarding the attribution of meaning, which situational definitions can finally impose themselves becomes an issue of communicative structures. In the following, specific features of informal law are evaluated against this background. The thesis is that informal procedures in general - and victim-offender mediation in particular - will correspond better to the specifics of a problem situation as viewed by the parties themselves, and therefore lead to decisions that are more appropriate to the problem at hand.

3 Method

Since 1986, the Youth Welfare Office at Bielefeld has been engaged in a diversion program that also includes victim-offender mediation. It is being implemented by specially appointed social workers. From 1986 to 1989, the program was subject to a scientific evaluation on several levels (for more details, see Bettmer, Messmer, and Otto, 1989). On a systems level, we evaluated the relationship between criminal justice (public prosecutor's office) and program implementation (social work), and also used a control group in order to study possible net-widening effects (see Micheel, this volume; Otto et al., 1989). On a program level, the individual steps in the social workers' measures were studied in detail (see Bettmer, 1991, and this volume). Finally, on the interaction level, we were interested in the interactional properties of the decision-making procedures during diversion and victim-offender mediation. This last aspect will be addressed in more detail in the following. The investigation is based predominantly on observations of conversations between social workers and clients. To perform a detailed analysis, we tape-recorded almost 60 conversations with the permission of all participants. Forty-six of these conversations were analyzed for the present study. Twenty-eight of them contain a decision on diversion, while 18 are carried out with the intention of preparing or implementing a victim-offender mediation. Victims are present at 10 of these conversations.

The conversations between social workers and their clients were analyzed in two ways: First, all conversation sequences of a speaker were quantified in the form of conversational moves. Each conversational move consists of a certain type of move and a certain negotiation level. *Types of move* describe the particular form of a statement (e.g., questions, answers, or unrequested proposals) as well as different levels of appraisal (e.g., understanding vs. nonunderstanding, acceptance vs. rejection of a proposal). *Negotiation levels* indicate the topics on which information is given. They may refer to procedural issues, to the offense and the offender, to the consequences of an offense for the offender or the victim, as well as to the procedural decision that has to be made. The combination of types of move and negotiation levels results in a total of 70 different classifications of conversational moves to which each single conversation sequence could be classified.[10] In addition, several of the conversations recorded during victim-offender mediations were transcribed in full for further single case analyses. These analyses focused on the process of the procedure and the dynamics of the conversation. We were particularly interested in how victims and offenders coped with conflict and the various intervention techniques used by social workers in their role as a third party.[11] However, before dealing with these in more detail, I shall first report on the analysis of the conversational moves.

4 Negotiation Structures in Conversations Between Social Workers and Clients

4.1 *Conversational Profile According to Conversational Moves*

In the following, conversations between social workers, offenders, and, at times, also victims and relatives are conceived as negotiations and interpreted as bilateral action. The analysis reveals that an average of 700 conversational moves per conversation are used to explain and define the facts of the case. Slightly more than one half of all conversational moves (53%) are made by social workers; and 39%, by offenders.[12] Conversational moves are far less frequent in all other groups of speakers: victims (4%), relatives of offenders (3%), and relatives of victims (1%). The distribution of conversational moves across speakers indicates the central position of social workers and offenders. Both groups are present at all conversations, and their negotiation position is correspondingly balanced. The situation is different for victims: Even when it is taken into account that they are present at only 10 of the 46 conversations, their conversational moves are still clearly underrepresented in terms of quantity. The reasons for this will be discussed below.[13]

4.2 Conversational Profile According to Negotiation Levels

Negotiation levels reveal which topics are being discussed. In social workers and offenders, the distribution of conversational moves according to negotiation levels is almost identical. Both focus their messages on explaining the backgrounds and motives of deviant behavior. Almost 33% of all their conversational moves address causes and motives (why it happened) while only an average of 14% address the facts of the offense (what happened). A further 14% discuss the consequences of the offense for the offender in terms of the informal reactions that the offender had possibly already experienced before legal proceedings were initiated. Discussions on the type and extent of the procedural decision that had to be made during the conversation cover about 11% of all conversational moves. Questions regarding the formal course of the procedure take up an equal proportion. The consequences of the offense for the victim are discussed far less frequently (4%). The distribution of conversational moves according to negotiation levels generally shows that conversations focus, above all, on the underlying causes of deviant behavior involved in an offense. In combination, the clarification of motives and the clarification of facts form central points of orientation for determining attributions of responsibility, although discussions on causal constellations are more important. The consequences of the offense for the offender are discussed in detail, but not so for the victim. In general, the conversations revolve very predominantly round the concerns of the individual offender.

Particularly in victim-offender mediation, we were interested in the role of victims in the negotiation process. It was surprising that 24% of the conversational moves of victims address the facts of the offense. This is a much higher frequency compared to social workers and offenders. Apparently, there is a great need for corrective situational descriptions to complement or contradict those of offenders. Victims seem to fulfill a "state's evidence" function here. In contrast, victims are scarcely interested in the offender-related causes of delinquency or the consequences of the offense for the offender. However, as could be anticipated, the consequences of the offense for the victim are mentioned most frequently by the victims themselves (12%). Furthermore, far more than all other groups, victims have a disproportionately strong influence on the outcome of negotiations

(17%). As the direct sufferers, victims are particularly involved in the type, extent, and implementation of a reparation measure. The procedural alternatives available to the offender are very dependent on their acceptance by the victim.

4.3 Conversational Profile According to Types of Move

Types of move characterize the way in which information is exchanged between conversation partners. As could be anticipated, conversations between social workers and offenders reveal a complementary role structure: Social workers dominate the flow of information through demands for information in 20% of their conversational moves. Offenders respond to these demands and answer the social workers' questions with 26% of their conversational moves. The strict complementarity of roles between givers and receivers of information is weakened in that offenders also made unrequested proposals (28%), that is, they exhibit the dominant proportion of free speech. Nonetheless, the role structure remains specific: The social worker controls most of the situational definitions while the offender has more control over their contents.

Alongside the forms of conveying information, types of move also reflect the reciprocal evaluation of the information conveyed. Twenty-nine percent of all conversational moves in social workers are statements expressing understanding used to register information given by the offender. In contrast, the proportion of statements of understanding among offenders is only 13%; this lower figure could be anticipated because of their role as a giver of information. In contrast, nonunderstanding plays hardly any role in either social workers (1%) or offenders (2%). As a result, conversations between social workers and offenders are shaped predominantly by mutual understanding. Explicit statements of agreement amount to 2% in social workers and almost 7% in offenders. The situational definitions of the offenders seem to be understood by the social workers, but they do not necessarily have to be accepted as such. Vice versa, although the situational definitions of social workers are quantitatively fewer, they seem to be qualitatively more important for proposals requiring agreement or rejection. This conclusion was supported by explicit rejections, which make up 1% of the social workers' conversational moves compared to 3% in the offenders. A final type of move signalizes reservations about acceptance and doubts about the correctness of the other's situational definitions. These make up almost 3% of the social workers' conversational moves compared to less than 2% in the offenders.

In the present conversations, the social worker's role is predominantly to ask for information from offenders, check their information through statements of understanding, critically test their content, and, without being asked, guide the conversation toward more decision-relevant situational definitions in line with the circumstances of the negotiation. The offender's role complements this: Offenders are mostly givers of information who express themselves following a demand but, even more, make unrequested proposals. They communicate mostly descriptions of facts that are evaluated and collated by the social worker in terms of their relevance to a decision. The offenders then respond to these descriptions with agreement, rejection, or skepticism.

The types of moves of victims are very similar to those of offenders. Like offenders, 24% of the victims' conversational moves are responses to demands from others. Likewise, there is a dominant proportion of free speech in their negotiation strategies (31%). In contrast, their proportion of conversational moves in the area of understanding/nonunderstanding is lower than all other groups, while it is highest for statements of acceptance (agreement, rejection, casting doubt). When present, victims are thus the primary partners for decision-relevant situational definitions, and they are particularly the addressees of proposals that require agreement. Which procedural outcomes will be available for mediation depends on their agreement.

4.4 Diversion and Victim-Offender Mediation: A Comparison

Unlike the communication situation in courts, the present analyses have shown that the form and content of negotiations are not dominated by any single group of speakers alone. Instead, the specific role of the social workers is implemented on the basis of critical empathy linked to the effort to match attributions of responsibility for deviant behavior to kinds of prospective intervention that would be suitable for reaching a decision on how to react to the underlying problem. It could also be seen that clients possess sufficient negotiation scope to express their subjective experience. On the other hand, victims apparently reduce the offender orientation in mediation by complementing and correcting both the antecedents and the consequences of the offense from their own perspective. Although victims make a smaller quantitative number of interventions, their interventions seem to be qualitatively more powerful.

The data demonstrate that the conversational goals (diversion or victim-offender mediation) have a recognizable impact on the negotiation structure of the participants. A comparison of the conversational profiles of social workers and offenders in diversion and victim-offender mediation reveals clear differences on the negotiation levels: Victim-offender mediations show a general decline in discussions on both formal procedures and on the causes of delinquency; in contrast, discussions on the consequence of the offense for the victim almost double. Questions on the facts of the offense and its consequences for the offender remain roughly the same. There is also a sharp rise in conversational moves concerned with a procedural decision: Conversations on the outcome of the procedure almost quadruple. It is very clear that conversations aimed at "resolving conflicts" or "reparation" contain a disproportionately greater potential for a variation in solutions than diversion, and this is reflected in a greater need for conversational moves dealing with this goal.

With regard to the types of conversation (types of move), the comparison between diversion and victim-offender mediation reveals further important differences in social workers and offenders. In conversations dealing with mediation, both social workers and offenders show a notable increase in strategies to impose their own interests on the other. Both parties intervene more frequently in the course of the conversation with unrequested proposals; the social workers through more undemanded situational definitions and the offenders through more demands on others. A corresponding weakening of the role complementarity between demanding social workers and reacting offenders can be traced. In conversations on mediation, statements of understanding decrease by one third, while statements of nonunderstanding double. All this suggests that there is a higher level of activities in dealing with conflictual situations: Both parties are more interested in influencing the situational definitions in question rather than in trying to understand them. Expressions of doubt also more than double in mediation; while there are almost half as many more explicit rejection statements. Nonetheless, the proportion of explicit agreement statements remains nearly unchanged. Although this suggests that the desire for cooperation still exists, the style of confrontation has changed.

Much of our data suggests that the multiplicity and openness of the procedural ends of mediation places stronger demands on the individual interests of the parties involved. The attribution of responsibility and the outcome of the procedure are linked together more directly. Discussing issues of material reparation or coping with emotional conflict encourages the active assertion of particular and individual interests. The presence of victims strengthens the confrontation, because they introduce additional perspectives and expectations regarding the outcome. In contrast to diversion, the interests of the offender in rehabilitation are no longer the focus in victim-offender mediation, but have to be balanced against the victims' views of the case and their expectations regarding reparation. With reference to the outcome of the procedure, there is a notable increase in demands in conversations on victim-offender mediation: The conversation becomes more demanding and more contradictory as well.

5 Negotiations in Victim-Offender Mediation

5.1 Victim-Offender Mediation as a Procedure

Typically, the processing of criminal behavior in victim-offender mediation addresses the experience of conflict and the needs of the participants in a very transparent way: This begins with the voluntary decision to participate in the attempted mediation, covers the unimpeded exchange of opinions on the offense and its consequences, and ends with questions concerning acceptance or denial of a proposed reparation. The procedure focuses strongly on evaluations of the facts of the offense as well as on responsibility and guilt: Consensus over reparation of damages can be attained only after clarifying the responsibilities for the injustice at stake. Whether the discussion of injustice resolves conflict depends to a great extent on how far victim- and offender-specific interests and perceptions can be balanced out in the negotiation of an agreement on reparations. The conversational profiles of the parties involved show that the confrontation concentrates more strongly on the facts of the offense and the subsequent solutions than in diversion, while motives and problem backgrounds of the offense, in contrast, become less prominent during the ongoing procedure. It can also be seen that the assertion of interests intensifies in social workers and offenders, and the conversation becomes generally more contradictory. These findings are supplemented by the results of qualitative case analyses on victim-offender mediation. The following investigation will show in which way conversations in mediation help to clarify the causes of juvenile delinquency. A closer look will demonstrate that the confrontation between the parties involved reactualizes the content of the conflict in a verbal form, encourages confrontations on decision-relevant norms, and stimulates problem-appropriate paths toward a solution.

5.2 Injustice and Justification

In the 1950s, Sykes and Matza formulated a criminality paradox according to which generally binding norms are simultaneously recognized yet can nonetheless be violated. Although people generally know what is wrong and prohibited, they put legal constraints to one side. Sykes and Matza (1957) use various neutralization techniques[14] to explain how individual ethics can render general norm prescriptions powerless. According to this theory, neutralization techniques leave the general validity of the norm untouched, while locating the incriminating behavior beyond the norm. As a result, offenders retain their positive self-image, stifle feelings of guilt at their very origins, and neutralize injustice-related attributions of responsibility.

The results of our qualitative case analyses agree essentially with Sykes and Matza's postulate. In victim-offender mediation, offenders typically explain their incriminating behavior in terms of a continuously repeated pattern of justifications. Although the facts to which they are linked vary from case to case, their intention and implementation are always the same. In mediation, justifications prove to be a distinctive barrier on the path toward consensus between victim and offender, and they have to be overcome before any solutions become possible. In contrast to Sykes and Matza, the present conversation material reveals four rather than five typical patterns of justification. Two patterns are conflict-related and oriented toward the cause and consequence of delinquency. Two further patterns are more norm-related and oriented toward the attitudes and behavior of the victim and the offender.[15]

Competing versions of conflict. Deviant behavior implies cause and effect. Correspondingly, attributions of responsibility are always successful when damaging behavior is blamed causally on the offender and can be classified motivationally as an action. As a result, an accusation discriminates victim and offender according to their responsibility for the causes of a criminal act. One first basic possibility for justifications is linked to this: Offenders offer an alternative causal structure for the events that triggered the deviant behavior. According to our analysis, the events that have triggered offenses, especially those involving insult, aggression, or violence, cannot always be characterized unequivocally. A chain of actions and reactions is far more typical, and exactly this can be instrumentalized for justifications. While in the official accusation, the (aggressive) offense is classified causally as an action initiated by the offender, justifications invert the structure of causality: Offenders who use this pattern do not see their incriminating behavior as a cause, but as an effect, that is, as a reaction to prior actions by their opponents. From this perspective, the actual (provocative) actions proceed from the victim. This generates a competing version of the offense. The pattern of justification succeeds by inserting a prior disappointment or injury from which the offender supposedly suffered before reacting with the incriminating behavior.[16] The precondition for this is a continuity of action that makes it possible to shift and relocalize trigger events for the incriminating behavior at different times. With competing conflict versions, it is possible to externalize at least some of the causes to the victim. In this way, the victim shares responsibility for the triggering events. Apparently unequivocal role positions between victim and offender are now ambiguous and complex; the relationship between cause and effect becomes relative and reversible; responsibility is redistributed; and, finally, the role positions between victim and offender are changed.

Casting doubt on the consequences of the offense. A second pattern of justification addresses the effects of deviant behavior instead of the causes, that is, it deals with the consequences of the offense. Offenders are not just characterized by being the cause of an offense. Their actions are aimed toward advantages whose acquisition is not accepted normatively. Correspondingly, victims are defined as those who lose through deviant behavior: They are deceived, injured, or damaged in some other way. Hence, the accusation also discriminates victims and offenders according to who has suffered the consequences of normative misbehavior. This is where the second pattern of justification is applied. According to the conversations, offenders introduce the effects of their behavior into the discussion. Justifications that refer to the consequences of an offense try to play down these consequences until the victim status becomes questionable. Two principle approaches are available here: First, the offender may play down the seriousness of his or her own misbehavior. Points of access here are the motives for the act or its implementation. The unjust content of one's own behavior is made as harmless as possible so that the victim status of the injured party loses its legitimacy. The second option is to question the injured person's account of the actual consequences of the offense. The extent of injury is not always unequivocal and objectively quantifiable but is experienced and evaluated individually by each victim. The reference point here is the victim. Characteristic differences in individual experience can be exploited for this pattern of justification. The consequence of both kinds of justification is to make the victim's interest in reparation seem exaggerated. This weakens the role relationship between offenders and victims and may even invert it. Exaggerated demands for reparations (for merely trivial offenses) put victims themselves in the wrong and transform offenders into victims.

Competing norm concepts. A third pattern of justification is oriented toward individual attitudes about normality. The point of reference here is the offender's perspective on standards of correct behavior. In the conversations, we often find a tension between generally accepted legal norms and particular or situational ethics of the offender. As a result, this pattern of justification concerns offender-specific arguments that their own behavior is not as unjust as the official version of the offense implies. This introduces the offender's norm orientations into the discussion. Justifications of this kind contrast norms with other norms; they produce normative contradiction. The present transcriptions contain indications for habitual rights that offenders used to legitimize their behavior. Class- and culture-specific patterns of behavior become directly relevant here. There are also justifications that point to a lack of reciprocity: According to these, the incriminating behavior is a reaction to disappointments with the other. Here, justifications legitimize incriminating behavior by introducing a competing normative construction. Their standard is necessarily different from that of formal law, on whose legitimacy doubt is cast. The principle of inverting victim and offender is similar to that found in the competing versions of conflict: Here as well, the normative expectations of the offender have been violated. Justifications based on competing versions of the conflict deny the legitimacy of the other's action, while justifications based on competing norm concepts, in contrast, cast doubt on the legitimacy of the other's right not to act.

Negative characterization. A final pattern of justification also refers to norms. However, instead of trying to re-evaluate the individual standards of the offender's own expectations, those of the opposing party are degraded in normative terms. In this way, the offender undermines the official accusation that assigns norm deviation to the offender and norm compliance to the victim. The normative behavior of the opposing party is introduced into the discussion. The more characteristics of the opposing party are known, the easier it is to label him or her with behaviors that can be claimed to be normatively wrong. According to this justification, the behavior of the victim appears to comply with norms only from a distance. On closer inspection, it is no better than that of the offender. This argument is often linked to the damaged party's demands for reparation. Damages or other claims for reparation are often perceived to be exaggerated from the perspective of the individual offender, especially when the offense is not just attributable to the offender alone, when the consequences of the offense seem exaggerated, or when the incriminating behavior seems to be legitimate because of a particular situational ethic. Thus, negative characterizations also aim to invert the role relationships between victims and offenders: Because the behavioral goals of the victim are characterized as questionable, the legitimacy of their claims is denied.

5.3 Summary

Injustice is - at least in part - a product of social definitions and essentially depends on how persons perceive and judge a situation. Mediation, therefore, primarily serves to process criminal behavior on the basis of the individual experiences of the victims and offenders. The analyses of conversations have shown that the participants mostly judge the injustice at stake according to different criteria. Contradictions arise during the clarification of responsibility for an offense. The pattern of a justification depends on the points of reference: The first pattern of justification addresses the causes, and defines the incriminating behavior as a reaction to prior events. The second justification pattern addresses the consequences of the offense and plays down the injustice of the offender's behavior. The third justification pattern addresses individual norm orientations and emphasizes their legitimacy. The fourth justification pattern addresses the victim's behavior and characterizes it as morally and normatively deviant.

Justifications are directed toward increasing the tolerance for deviant behavior. The borders between conformity and deviance, between what should be and what is, are locally negotiated in favor of what is. The justifications in this study typically defend the accused from attributions of responsibility by externalizing attributions of guilt to the opposing party. In this way, justifications effect a change of roles between victim and offender, between conformity and deviance, between good and bad. The proportions of conflict between the parties are reweighed through justifications. This elicits contradictions and finally renews conflict.

6 Communications About Right and Wrong

The findings from the analyses of conversations on diversion and victim-offender mediation indicate a procedural rule that can be roughly summarized as follows: The more comprehensive the communication between those involved in processing the injustice, the more probable it is that the procedural outcome will correspond to the underlying causes of the problem that the procedure was initiated to solve. The increasingly equal distribution of possibilities of definition and negotiation on decision-relevant facts raises the potential for a free expression of opinions as a precondition of what is procedurally just. A procedural decision can be appropriate only when the character of the problem to which it reacts is recognized and considered.[17] The more communication is permitted, the more clearly the causes of deviant behavior can be recognized, named, and assessed in terms of possible reactions. Therefore, the importance of communicative permissiveness should not be underestimated. It can in no way be taken for granted that only one standard is available for the normative evaluation of social behavior. Morals have become unreliable as a judgment criterion, and historically handed down values can no longer be drawn upon unconditionally. It is worthwhile to follow Christie's (1977) statement that more attention has to be paid to decisions on the relevance of what is considered to be important in the discussion about right and wrong. We should note that law loses its legitimacy when its decisions disassociate themselves too far from the sense of justice of the clients involved. In this context, communication creates a useful corrective to a mere legal and only formal correctness in the application of law.

Above all, the effectiveness of communication proves to be clear in victim-offender mediation. The confrontation over right and wrong necessarily pays attention to the offense from various perspectives. The victim's interest in negotiating the outcome gains in importance. However, the variety of perspectives increases the complexity of the procedure and can also intensify conflict: The greater the number of judgment perspectives that are relevant for decisions, the more probable the communication of contradiction. In negotiations, communication will continue the conflict by other means: Party-specific statements aim to influence the perceptions and behavior of the other in a way that increases the chances of asserting one's own interests and goals. Explanations, justifications, and similar patterns of persuasive communication are used to work out but also legitimize one's own negotiation position. However, further analysis of the conversations also shows that the verbal means for constructing - under certain circumstances, conflict-raising - negotiation positions are simultaneously the same ones that can, in turn, be used to ease the conflict at stake.

To the extent that communication about justifications is a means of presenting the legitimacy of one's own interests and actions, it simultaneously contains those preconditions that can neutralize misconceptions. Every bit of information conveyed is a bit of additional knowledge for the other party; the credibility of each presentation has the potential of being checked; and every explanation can be judged regarding its correctness. Communication becomes an element of unintended self-disclosure, since everything that is said can be used as a basis for contradiction and comment.[18] Thus, communication permits discoveries about the other, but also about oneself. Further analysis of the conversations has confirmed that justification itself provides the opportunity to counter its intentions. During the presentation and counterpresentation of different versions of what happened, it mostly becomes clear how the offense actually occurred, which consequences have resulted from it, and which normative judgment perspectives are decisive for the special case. To the extent that it is possible to defuse the intention of justifications to neutralize injustice, the injustice can no longer be rationalized by the offender.

In a time when numerous traditional values are losing their power to convince, the difficulties in gaining insight into the motives of adolescents will also increase. Jurisprudence often is unable to pay much attention to this, because it is primarily interested in the phenomenal level of delinquency and less in the underlying causes. Instead, the legal system sets clear priorities: The application of law comes first, while the discussion of the norms that underlie justice is circumvented. However, more than ever, there is a need to come to an understanding on norms that can achieve consensus, because traditional assumptions no longer suffice to hand down a sense of justice in a rapidly changing society. Deviant behavior is not just a problem for society but also its product - and, as such, in turn, a problem for the adolescents involved. An appropriate response to deviant behavior requires a discussion on norm orientations that must not remain one-sided if it is to contain possibilities for learning. Nils Christie (1986: 113) has pointed out an interesting analogy that aptly describes the acquisition of both language and a sense of justice: Although a human being enters the world with a predisposition for learning to speak and acquiring a sense of justice, both can be achieved and developed only through a community life. Accordingly, interactions that ensure mutual understanding are a constitutive precondition for a problem-adequate application of law: Both controller and controlled have to learn to recognize what is cause and what is effect if they are to achieve an appropriate solution to problems. As a result, the correct response to deviant behavior is not the mere application of law, but also requires the practice of justice. A major condition for this is provided by procedures in which the voices of the people involved are heard and their individual norm orientations are taken into account.

Notes

* Translated from German by Jonathan Harrow at Bielefeld University.

1 Studies on undetected crime and cohort studies seriously question the premises underlying the legitimacy of criminal law: If, on the one hand, juvenile delinquency is ubiquitous (see, e.g., Heinz, 1989), while, on the other hand, the perception of the reality of prosecution is practically irrelevant to legal behavior (see, e.g., Schumann et al., 1987), and prosecution can additionally even be counterproductive in terms of its own goals (see West, 1982; West and Farrington, 1977) - then, the principle of appropriateness is violated by punishment, as sanctions are applied to offenses whose repetition is less probable than their nonrepetition.

2 Note, however, as an exception, the study of Gwynn Davis (1992a, b) and his colleagues, who offer sample protocols of mediation sessions in various English programs at the time when they were initially set up.

3 The assumption that social reality is "constructed" in accordance with personal interests and available experiences has a long theoretical tradition (see James, 1905), and leads over phenomenological (see Schütz, 1932), symbolic (see Blumer, 1969), or ethnomethodological concepts to the currently well-known constructivist theoretical approaches.

4 Some of the ideas formulated in this context have been inspired by systems theory (see Luhmann, 1982, 1985).

5 Social facts are transformed into legal ones. This reduces the complexity of the everyday world. For legal experts, this makes a case practicable; for clients, in contrast, unreal. Galtung (1965) and Brinckmann (1973) have discriminated between conflict and metaconflict to express this transformation.

6 This particularly refers to differences between "adversary" and "inquisitorial" procedures. In the former, the lawyer is responsible for ascertaining the facts, while the decision is the responsibility of the judge. In the latter, ascertaining and judging are both equally the responsibility of the judge. Adversary procedures are mainly found in Anglo-American countries, while inquisitorial procedures are closer to German or French adjudication. The differentiation between adversary and inquisitorial is based on research by Thibaut and Walker (1975).

7 Here, I am particularly thinking of forms of habitual degradation as described by, for example, Garfinkel (1956).

8 The results of several studies overlap at this point. See, for example, Leodolter (1975: 250-299), Erikson et al. (1978), Atkinson and Drew (1979: 198), Conley and O'Barr (1990).

9 According to surveys by Eilsberger (1969: 307) and Boy and Lautmann (1979: 61), about two thirds of clients feel that they have insufficiently understood the jurisdiction of formal proceedings.

10 This method is reported in more detail in Messmer (1988, 1991).

11 Various case analyses have already been used to present different aspects of proceedings in Messmer (1989, 1990).

12 For social workers and offenders, this corresponds roughly to a relation of 5 to 4. However, if paraverbal statements of understanding such as "hm" are neglected, which contain little information and are disproportionately frequent in the social workers, then

the conversational situation between social worker and offender shifts toward a balanced relationship (33.9% to 36.1%).

13 The negotiation profiles of relatives are not dealt with in this study.

14 The neutralization techniques of Sykes and Matza (1957) are: (a) denial of responsibility; (b) denial of the injury; (c) denial of the victim; (d) condemnation of the condemners; and (e) appeal to higher loyalties. At first glance, they seem to be very similar to the justification patterns classified in our conversations. However, closer inspection reveals some basic differences concerning their structure and points of reference. A more detailed consideration of this cannot be presented here.

15 The following presentation of the justification patterns is extremely concise and a summary of mostly small particles of argumentation dispersed throughout a conversation. They first had to be joined together through the analysis before, like pieces of a mosaic, a recognizable pattern appeared that permitted conclusions on their structure and function.

16 The inversion of chains of action and reaction is easily comprehended in bodily harm offenses in which provocation and subsequent behaviors may well be a question of perspective. The same applies to long-term relationships of conflict in which it may well be impossible to disentangle the chain of reciprocal accusations. For illustrations of this and the following justification patterns, see Messmer (1989, 1990).

17 Clear differences can be seen here between formal legal problem definitions and those of informal programs like diversion and victim-offender mediation. The direct contact between social worker and client under conditions of voluntary communication generally leads to major deviations from the evaluations of an offense recorded in the public prosecutor's files. This outcome has also been confirmed by other similar studies. Komter (1991: 6) concludes from a study of 48 observations of courts: "Only one of the defendants in my material agreed totally with the version of events as proffered by the public prosecutor."

18 This should be compared particularly with Gulliver's (1979) anthropological and theoretical conclusions. These show a high level of agreement with the results of more recent studies that were also carried out in other cultural contexts (see, e.g., Nothdurft, 1987).

References

Atkinson, J.M., and Drew, P. (1979). *Order in court. The organization of verbal interaction in judicial settings*. Atlantic Highlands, NJ: Humanities Press.

Bettmer, F. (1991). Auswege aus der Pädagogisierungsfalle. Ergeben sich für die Sozialarbeit neue Perspektiven aus der Informalisierung strafrechtlicher Sozialkontrolle? *Neue Praxis, 21*, 250-261.

Bettmer, F., Messmer, H., and Otto, H.-U. (1989). Informal justice and conflict solution - A research report. In P.-A. Albrecht and O. Backes (Eds.), *Crime prevention and intervention* (pp. 129-143). Berlin/New York: de Gruyter.

Blumer, H. (1969). *Symbolic interactionism. Perspective and method*. Englewood Cliffs, NJ: Prentice-Hall.

Boy, P., and Lautmann, R. (1979). Die forensische Kommunikationssituation - soziologische Probleme. In R. Wassermann (Ed.), *Menschen vor Gericht* (pp. 41-67). Neuwied: Luchterhand.

Brinckmann, J. (1973). Konflikt, Konfliktregulierung und Recht. Ein vorläufiger Problemkatalog. *Soziale Welt, 24*, 79-93.

Christie, N. (1977). Conflicts as property. *British Journal of Criminology, 17*, 1-15.

Christie, N. (1986). *Grenzen des Leids*. Bielefeld: AJZ.

Conley, J.M., and O'Barr, W.M. (1990). Rules versus relationships in small claims disputes. In A.D. Grimshaw (Ed.), *Conflict talk: Sociolinguistic investigations in conversations* (pp. 178-196). Cambridge: Cambridge University Press.

Davis, G. (1992a). *Making amends*. London: Routledge.

Davis, G. (1992b). Reparation in the UK: Dominant themes and neglected themes. In H. Messmer and H.-U. Otto (Eds.), *Restorative justice on trial. Pitfalls and potentials of victim-offender mediation*. International research perspectives (pp. 445-459). Dordrecht: Kluwer.

Eilsberger, R. (1969). Die Hauptverhandlung aus der Sicht jugendlicher und heranwachsender Angeklagter. *Monatsschrift für Kriminologie und Strafrechtsreform, 52*, 304-313.

Erikson, B., Lind, E.A., Johnson, B.C., and O'Barr, W.M. (1978). Speech style and impression formation in a court setting: The effects of "powerful" and "powerless" speech. *Journal of Experimental Social Psychology, 14*, 266-279.

Galtung, J. (1965). Institutionalized conflict resolution. *Journal of Peace Research, 2*, 348-397.

Garfinkel, H. (1956). Conditions of successful degradation ceremonies. *American Journal of Sociology, 61*, 420-424.

Grüner, H. (1984). Kommunikation in Arbeitsgerichtsverhandlungen - Versuch einer Analyse. In H. Rottleuthner (Ed.), *Rechtssoziologische Studien zur Arbeitsgerichtsbarkeit* (pp. 165-200). Baden-Baden: Nomos.

Gulliver, P.H. (1979). *Disputes and negotiations: A cross-cultural perspective*. New York: Academic Press.

Heinz, W. (1989). Jugendstrafrechtsreform durch die Praxis - eine Bestandsaufnahme. In Bundesministerium der Justiz (Ed.), *Jugendstrafrechtsreform durch die Praxis* (pp. 13-44). Bonn: Bundesministerium der Justiz.

James, W. (1905). *Principles of psychology*. (Vol. 2). New York: Holt.

Kallmeyer, W. (1981). Aushandlung und Bedeutungskonstitution. In P. Schröder and H. Steger (Eds.), *Dialogforschung* (pp. 89-127). Düsseldorf: Schwann.

Kallmeyer, W. (1983). Mündliche Kommunikation vor Gericht. In R. Wassermann and J. Petersen (Eds.), *Recht und Sprache. Beiträge zu einer bürgerfreundlichen Justiz* (pp. 139-151). Heidelberg: Müller.

Knuf, J. (1982). *Polizeibeamte als Zeugen vor Gericht. Eine kommunikationswissenschaftliche Untersuchung*. Wiesbaden: Sonderband der BKA-Forschungsreihe.

Komter, M. L. (1991, June). *Accountability in the courtroom*. Paper presented at the International Law and Society Conference, Amsterdam.

Leodolter, R. (1975). *Das Sprachverhalten von Angeklagten bei Gericht*. Kronberg: Skriptor.

Luhmann, N. (1982). *The differentiation of society*. New York: Columbia University Press.

Luhmann, N. (1985). *A sociological theory of law*. London: Routledge.

Messmer, H. (1988). Zur Quantifizierung qualitativer Daten. Probleme der methodischen Fixierung von Interaktionsprozessen im Rahmen der Aushandlung außergerichtlicher Verfahrenserledigungen. *Kriminologisches Journal, 20*, 101-120.

Messmer, H. (1989). Tackling the conflict: A framework analysis of dispute settlement. In J. Hudson and B. Galaway (Eds.), *The state as parent: International research perspectives on interventions with young persons* (pp. 187-192). Dordrecht: Kluwer.

Messmer, H. (1990). Reducing the conflict: An analysis of victim-offender mediation as an interactive process. In B. Galaway and J. Hudson (Eds.), *Criminal justice, restitution, and reconciliation* (pp. 59-71). Monsey, NY: Criminal Justice Press.

Messmer, H. (1991). Sozialarbeiter und Proband in Verfahren jugendamtlicher Diversion - eine gesprächsanalytische Zwischenbilanz. *Monatsschrift für Kriminologie und Strafrechtsreform, 74*, 90-105.

Messmer H., and Otto, H.-U. (Eds.) (1992). *Restorative justice on trial. Pitfalls and potentials of victim-offender mediation. International research perspectives*. Dordrecht: Kluwer.

Muth, J. (1984). Die Jugendgerichtsverhandlung aus der Perspektive des Angeklagten. In J. Reichertz (Ed.), *Sozialwissenschaftliche Analysen jugendgerichtlicher Interaktion* (pp. 58-110). Tübingen: Stauffenburg.

Nothdurft, W. (1987). Die Ordnung des Konflikts. Gesprächsanalyse der Konfliktbehandlung in einer Güteverhandlung vor dem Schiedsmann. In K.-F. Röhl (Ed.), *Die Güteverhandlung vor dem Schiedsmann* (pp. 565-609). Köln: Heymanns.

Otto, H.-U., Bettmer, F., Messmer, H., and Micheel G. (1989). Alternative Sozialarbeit: Informalisierung sozialer Kontrolle im Bereich abweichenden Verhaltens. *Neue Praxis, 19*, 525-532.

Schumann, K.-F. (1979). Aushandeln von Sachverhalten innerhalb des Strafprozesses. In H.-G. Soeffner (Ed.), *Interpretative Verfahren in den Text- und Sozialwissenschaften* (pp.10-23). Stuttgart: Metzler.

Schumann, K.-F., Berlitz, C., Guth, H.-W., and Kaulitzki, R. (1987). *Jugendkriminalität und die Grenzen der Generalprävention*. Neuwied: Luchterhand.

Schütz, A. (1932). *Der sinnhafte Aufbau der sozialen Welt*. Eine Einleitung in die verstehende Soziologie. Vienna: Springer.

Soeffner H.-G. (1983). Ursachen von Kommunikationsstörungen vor Gericht. In R. Wassermann and J. Petersen (Eds.), *Recht und Sprache. Beiträge zu einer bürgerfreundlichen Justiz* (pp. 73-97). Heidelberg: Müller.

Strauss, A. (1978). *Negotiations: Varieties, contexts, and social order*. San Francisco: Jossey-Bass.

Sykes, G.M., and Matza, D. (1957). Techniques of neutralization: A theory of delinquency. *American Sociological Review, 22*, 664-670.

Thibaut, J.W., and Walker, L. (1975). *Procedural justice*. Hillsdale, NJ: Erlbaum.

Wassermann, R. (1985). *Die richterliche Gewalt. Macht und Verantwortung des Richters in der modernen Gesellschaft*. Heidelberg: Müller.

West, D. (1982). *Delinquency: Its roots, careers, and prospects*. London: Heinemann.

West, D., and Farrington, D. P. (1977). *The delinquent way of life*. London: Heinemann.

Zartman, I.W. (Ed.) (1976). *The fifty percent solution*. New York: Doubleday.

Diversion and Extrajudicial Programs: Preventive Claims and the Decision-making Process

Franz Bettmer

The basic issue in the discussion about diversion and extrajudicial programs, as well as criminal justice in general, is to find a relation between offenses and sanctioning that can be objectified and justified. We can differentiate two substantial models, which are used to formulate criteria for the application of sanctions to offenses. The first one is a technological model: Criteria are defined by causal relations between social factors and the offense. Sentencing decisions are justified by predicted or supposed effects regarding recidivism. In the second model, criteria are defined in the context of a formal relation between offenses and sanctioning, according to severity. This model rests on the principle of retaliation, but it is also justified by the purpose of reducing criminality. The idea is that this formal relation is a precondition for the criminal norm to be accepted and thus followed.

Neither in criminal justice nor in extrajudicial programs shall we find a clear preference for one of these models, but always a mixture. Extrajudicial programs claim to offer better measures with respect to the first model and to render a more adequate relation regarding the second model. Both models, however, start from the common view that criminal norms reflect rules of social behavior, which are preconditions of social order. Objectified criteria for the application of sanctions tell us in which cases and with what kind of measures the criminal norm has to be validated in order to maintain rules of social behavior against deviance. This validation, however, is no easy business. The objectified and formalized criminal norm has to gain acceptance as a signification of preconditions of social order, and it must prove to be practicable as a guiding principle in the varied contingencies of everyday life. The attempts to translate a criminal norm into an accepted rule of social behavior may be successful to a certain extent. But the preconditions for such a success - as well as the reasons for failure - are not quite clear. As we know from Max Weber, the validity of a norm does not originate with obedience but depends on the norm being a point of reference for activity and behavior. Thus, the conception that social behavior might automatically follow rules is very doubtful. It is more plausible that "rules" of social behavior are more or less "invented" while acting takes place. Social behavior does not start from formal norms and rules but rather from a certain perception of how social reality is organized and how individual activity can be situated inside this organization. Thus the crucial point is the condition of the norm to give a correct or "true" description of the preconditions of social order - a description that people agree with.

While this problem is neglected by the technological model, the formal model at least indicates an important aspect that belongs to this context, namely the perception of the people who are expected to comply with the norm. This model concedes the possibility of a discrepancy between social life's perspective of reality and the description of social order given by criminal norms. Beyond this discrepancy, however, another problem has to be taken into account. According to Habermas, the legitimation of law is gained from being a compensation of the weakness of an autonomous morality. In this view, society is a predominantly self-regulated order which sometimes is afflicted by pathogenic tendencies that exceed self-regulating capacities. If criminal justice can manage to overcome the discrepancy mentioned, that is, if the criminal norm is in accord with what is accepted as a true description of the preconditions of social order, then criminal justice still has to consider its relation to those capacities from two perspectives. First, it has to ensure that the norm violation cannot be left to self-regulation, because this would increase the threat of pathogenic tendencies. Second, regulative modes of social life, if practicable, should not for minor grounds be displaced or destroyed by a judicial proceeding and its consequences.

In summary, prior to any preventive effort, criminal justice must to some extent meet the perspective (Habermas would even say: the demands) of social life in order to gain legitimation. This concerns the claim of the criminal norm to signify sociopathogenic behavior as well as the methods of norm validation which claim to compensate failures of social self-regulation. Criminal justice always has to face discrepancies with the perspective of social life, and the question is not only how to overcome these discrepancies but, first of all, how to handle them. According to these considerations we can identify three well-known demands to which the criminal justice system is exposed. These are:

1. The demand of decriminalization, in which the criminal norm's qualification to signify a certain behavior as sociopathogenic is doubted.
2. The demand of subsidiarity, in which criminal justice is accused of cutting off regulative capacities of persons or institutions which belong to or at least are closer to social life.
3. The demand for proceedings which consider victim's interests. This concerns the maintenance of regulative modes which are common or preferred in social life.

It is quite difficult for criminal justice to meet these demands. If criminal justice is not willing to give up its authority, it must continuously differentiate its decision criteria in order to maintain a correspondence with the perspective of social life. But this differentiation is subjected to limitations. The failure of preventive efforts is due partly to the fact that a transgression of the formal relation is possible only to a certain extent. Nowadays there is quite a wide range of minor delinquency in which criminal justice has difficulties in adjusting its decision criteria to the perspective of social life.

Such problems are solved typically by shifting decisionary competencies to executive institutions. This could be a substantial motive for criminal justice to accept the measures offered by extrajudicial programs. Thus, these programs serve predominantly as intermediate institutions between criminal justice and social life. Their task may not be solely or not even primarily to attain norm obedience but to bring the perspective of social life in line with objectifiable criteria for the application of sanctions. The programs provide an investigation of whether the case at hand is submitted correctly to the norm not only for legal grounds but also in accordance with the perspective of social life. The question here is whether the norm violation can also be signified as a violation of the preconditions of social order. Furthermore, the programs are a lot more flexible in varying the intervention - for example, its degree of intensity - with respect to responses which have been carried out or seem to be adequate in social life. And, last but not least, they can try to "reconcile" the punitive demands of criminal justice with regulative modes and demands of social life.

These performances, however, cannot be read off the diversionary decisions or measures alone. Especially with customary programs, which are limited to offering certain predefined measures, they only appear in a so-to-say "coagulated" form. That is, the adjustment has taken place in a process of structuring referrals to programs without completely revealing decision criteria. It is a matter of bargaining between criminal justice and the programs, which to a large extent is already finished when the program starts operating.

In the Bielefeld program, however, decisions have to be made within the program and for every single case. This program is based on a cooperation between the public prosecutor and a youth welfare department set up for this particular purpose. Referrals to this department are made by the public prosecutor if case characteristics do not obviously suggest either a dismissal or further prosecution with trial. The staff of the program then makes a proposal on how to settle the case. They may suggest dismissal of the case without a measure, continuation of judicial proceedings with a trial, or dismissal of the case after a measure. Realization of such a measure has to be ensured by means of the program. Offenders and their parents have to be asked for their agreement. The final decision on case settling has to be made by the public prosecutor who usually follows the proposal made by the program staff. Rejection by the public prosecutor is so rare that it can be neglected empirically.

It is the particularity of this program to be limited neither to certain measures nor to fixed and well-defined criteria for case selection. If the public prosecutors combine a referral with a suggestion concerning a certain measure, the staff of the program may, but is not obliged to, follow that suggestion. Thus the Bielefeld program differs considerably from extrajudicial programs which realize certain predefined measures according to a judge's order. Decisionary competences of the program staff are restricted under three aspects: Case selection is done by the public prosecutor; the final decision on case settling remains with the public prosecutor; if measures are to be realized, agreement of additional participants in the proceeding (offender, parents, victims) is a precondition.

In principle, however, the program staff is in a position to structure and control the decision-making process to a large extent. They have to decide whether a referred case should be settled in the course of the diversionary proceeding. Furthermore, they dispose of the intensity of the intervention regarding the provision of information about the case as well as the feasibility and extent of an eventual measure. Besides, they may develop new types of measure in accordance with singular case characteristics. The main point, however, is the fact that case criteria which are crucial for the decision may be defined and installed within the actual diversionary proceeding. Finding criteria, thus, is part of the performance of the program.

Due to this conception, we had a very good opportunity to collect data about case processing in the program. This will probably answer two questions: (a) Which characteristics of the case determine the program's proposals to settle the case? (b) How do different characteristics influence certain proposals? Table 1 shows some comprehensive results of logistic regression models.

The proposals are differentiated into six alternatives which constitute the dependent variable. Actually, these are six different regression models, in which every type of proposal is set against all others. The first proposal favors a definite non-intervention, a refusal of any activities. The second one is meant to dismiss the case after it has been discussed with the offender. The following three are proposals to dismiss the case after a negotiated measure has been realized. The type of a proposal for restitution or mediation is used only if no additional measures are under consideration. Punitive measures of a very moderate character, that is, either a community service up to 9 hours or, in a few cases, a fine of not more than DM 50 (about $30) are understood as a "symbolic" sanctioning, summarized in the fourth type. Only the fifth type represents measures which are assigned a seriously punitive intention. This type, above all, consists of community service of more than 9 hours, but it also includes fines of more than DM 50 and combinations of different measures, for example, a community service in addition to mediation or restitution. The proposal for trial is used if a proceeding within the program is considered to be inappropriate.

Table 1: Factors Influencing Decision-Making in Bielefeld Extrajudicial Program

Decision criteria	Proposals					
	With no measure		Dismissal after measure			Trial
	Without contact	After hearing	Resti-tution/ mediation	"Symbolic" sanctioning	Punitive sanctioning	
1. Degree of severity	(1) .045	(3) .084	(1) .013*	(1) .012	(1) .016*	(3) .115*
2. Social deficits, causal relations		(3) .074			(1) .043*	(2) .068*
3. Sensitiveness, normality	(1) .016*	(1) .019*			(1) .041*	(1) .030
4. Responses in social life		(2) .029*	(1) .057		(1) .023*	(1) .018
5. Offense suitable for mediation		(2) .047	(2) .386*	(3) .070	(3) .072	(1) .040
6. Proposal urged by other institutions					(1) .052*	
7. Demands of the public prosecutor	(1) .011		(1) .021			
8. Male offenders	(1) .027*					
9. Age > 15			(1) .040*	(1) .029		
10. Victims are juveniles			(1) .018*	(1) .018		
Sample (*N*)	323	290	290	290	290	290
Events (*n*)	33	83	62	43	79	23
Pseudo-R^2	.615	.436	.742	.534	.333	.876

Note: For each set of predictor variables, the first row indicates the number of predictor variables, the second row the difference between the explained variance of the regression model including all predictors, and the explained variance of the regression model in which the respective predictors are excluded. The asterisk indicates positive direction of the influence on the proposal, its absence negative direction. The level of significance throughout is $p < .05$. The null model for computing Pseudo-R^2 is a model without a constant.

Regarding the assignment of cases to the different proposals, we can find a predominance of predictor variables which, in accordance with the theoretical considerations, can be summarized to five "decision-criteria":

1. Variables regarding the severity of the offense, prior records, and so forth, which are used to construct a formal relation between offense and proposal;
2. variables regarding social deficits, and suggestions that these deficits might be causes of the offense.

This second criterion must not necessarily lead to preventive efforts according to the technological model. Obviously, the proposals do not contain measures which are conceived explicitly to influence social or individual factors of deviance. Thus, the criterion rather indicates that the application of the criminal norm and of any measures to validate the norm is suitable because self-regulation is estimated to be too weak. It is used in a way similar to the first criterion and refers also to the formal model.

The following three criteria represent the perspective of social life:

3. If the offender can be labeled normal or sensitive to the norm, an intervention is questionable.
4. If persons or institutions situated in the social life of the offender have already responded to the offense, further validation of the norm might not be justifiable.
5. If the case is suitable for measures like restitution or mediation, a penalty can easily be displaced.

These decision criteria each consist of several different predictor variables, while not all of these variables have a significant influence on every single proposal. In order to obtain a comprehensive presentation, the single variables are not specified in the table. Variables belonging to the same criterion in any case show an identical direction of influence regarding the actual proposal. The number of predictor variables representing a criterion and showing a significant influence on the actual proposal is indicated in parentheses. In the lower part of the table, some further variables are presented which do not fit in the criteria above but also have a significant influence. The exceptional sample *(N)* used in the regression model regarding the first proposal is due to the fact that all cases proposed to be settled in this way (n = 33) had to be excluded from the regression models concerning the other proposals. This exclusion was necessary, because the first proposal naturally is based on a restricted set of information, namely from official records.

The results show that, first of all, the "degree of severity" and an attribution of "social deficits" are critical for the decision between dismissal without measures on the one hand and having recourse to punitive measures or to a formal proceeding with trial on the other. So far, the decision structure within the program follows judicial principles in accordance with the formal model. The criteria representing the perspective of social life, however, take the opposite direction of influence: Here "suitability for mediation" is obviously the predominant criterion. This is no surprise, because mediation and restitution provide an ideal combination of punitive components and a way of case settling that is appreciated in social life. "Suitability for mediation" also indicates a certain need for regulation, which might explain the negative effect on a dismissal without measure. The negative effect of "responses in social life" on a restitution proposal indicates that the program adheres to the principle of "subsidiarity". The significant predictor variable here concerns restitutional activities of the offender or the parents. Beyond that, "responses in social life", which also include punitive or educational reactions, may suspend the demand for a norm validation by criminal justice. A similar effect can be observed if the offender is sensitive to the norm. Furthermore, this criterion may even induce a rejection of a norm application and thus lead to nonintervention. The impact of these criteria on a dismissal without measure, however, is rather small compared to the impact of a low "degree of severity" and an absence of "social deficits".

What might be irritating is the positive effect of "sensitiveness" and "responses in social life" on the fifth proposal, which can be considered as a predominantly punitive measure. These effects, however, relate to some further aspects of decision making. The "sensitiveness" variable concerns the fact that the offender is taking responsibility for his or her offense, and as a consequence agrees to a measure. This agreement actually can be viewed as a precondition for the realization of a measure being unlikely to fail, which otherwise would necessitate a resumption of the proceedings. Of course, there is an interest in a smooth and successful proceeding within the program. With regard to the decision between trial or case settling by means of the program, we can identify another influence on decision-making that is due to this interest: A very high damage (of more than DM 1,000; about $600) as well as financial difficulties are conducive to a proposal for trial. Under such circumstances, it would be difficult to realize a restitution within the program, while any other proposal would neglect the claims of the victims.

Another aspect of decision-making refers to the situation that the most appropriate case-settling cannot always be realized. Then a "second-best" alternative might be proposed in order to keep the case within the program and to prevent a trial. The unexpected promotion of the fifth proposal by "responses in social life" probably can be explained in this way. The particular predictor variable indicates restitutional efforts of offenders or parents. In these cases, it might be unnecessary to carry out further restitutional activities by means of the program. This same predictor variable also influences the decision about the second and the fifth proposal. In a regression model in which all alternatives are specified in a multinomial dependent variable, it is possible to see how predictor variables influence the decision between two or more specified alternatives. This regression model (which is too complex to be presented here in detail) shows that the negative impact on a restitution proposal exerted by restitutional efforts in social life corresponds both to a positive effect on the second and a positive effect on the fifth proposal. That is, if restitutional efforts in social life impede a restitutional measure within the program, the staff has recourse either to a dismissal without measure or to a community service of more than 9 hours. The decision for the latter alternative may depend on specific characteristics of the respective cases (in which restitutional efforts in social life occur and the fifth proposal is made). These cases in fact show one or another characteristic (such as prior records, demands of the public prosecutor, or further offenses during the proceeding) which is likely to evoke a more serious reaction but is of no significant influence within the regression model regarding the fifth proposal and with respect to the whole sample. Thus the fifth proposal does not result directly from restitutional efforts in social life but rather is a substitute in cases which, for some reasons, cannot be left to self-regulation, while restitution cannot be used as a particular measure of the program.

The proposal for more than 9 hours of community service may also result from an intervention by other institutions, as shown in the lower part of the table (Predictor variable 6). These are usually social work institutions in which the offender resides. Naturally they are already dealing with the offense, and the program staff follows the proposals made by these institutions, albeit their own standard of decision-making is not matched. "Demands of the public prosecutor" are of surprisingly low influence. They might induce the staff of the program not to end up with nonintervention or nothing else but restitution or mediation. This result, however, does not explain very much. As mentioned above, the proposals usually are accepted by the public prosecutors. Thus it is not possible to decide here whether the proposals comply with the expectations of the public prosecutors or whether the public prosecutors only agree to the proposals in order to provide a rapid proceeding. The positive effect of male sex on a proposal for nonintervention probably indicates the common prejudice that male delinquency is more normal, and intervention is less necessary than in cases of female delinquency. If the offenders are older adolescents (Predictor variable 9) or if "victims are juveniles", restitution and mediation might be considered to have a better chance for a smooth realization, while the more symbolic measure of up to 9 hours community service is not regarded as being very useful.

In summary, decision-making in the program is to a considerable degree guided by the formal model. In view of the proposals' contents, preventive aims according to the technological model are insignificant. The formal relation between "degree of severity" or "social deficits" and sanctioning, however, is modulated by some aspects representing the perspective of social life. Primarily, a restitution or mediation is striven for wherever possible. These efforts are fruitful, because naturally a more serious offense most often results in a higher need for regulation. Thus, an optimum combination of the formal model and the perspective of social life can be reached. Apart from the restitution proposal, attempts to exceed the formal model in order to give way to the perspective of social life are rather hesitant. But while the program, of course, has to meet the punitive demands of criminal justice, to a certain degree, it puts forward a common sense of what might be necessary and suitable to settle cases of juvenile delinquency and thus strengthens the link between criminal justice and social life.

A Discrete Outcome-Model to Measure Net-Widening Effects

Heinz-Günter Micheel

1 Introduction

In the following, I will present an empirical study on a diversion program involving cooperation between the public prosecutor's office and the Youth Welfare Office at Bielefeld. The study investigates whether this diversion program has led to increases in social control. This general criticism of diversion models has been adopted from the USA, where many studies, although they are not all particularly convincing (see, e.g., Ezell, this volume), have reported net-widening effects of diversion (e.g., Blomberg, 1980, 1983; Ezell, this volume; Klein, 1979). In this context, an expansion of social control can take three forms:

1. Intervention could extend to adolescents who have not come to the attention of the police but have been assigned to diversion programs for reasons of social proximity.
2. Adolescents could be assigned to diversion programs whose cases would otherwise have been dismissed without any measure or sanction being applied.
3. A criminal justice reaction might have been less intensive (and thus less stressful) than intervention within a diversion program.

However, American experiences cannot be transferred simply to the Federal Republic of Germany, as diversion programs differ in their institutional and legal frameworks. American experiences have yet to be either confirmed or rejected in the Federal Republic of Germany. Although changes in the control and sanction practices of the criminal justice system have often been observed to accompany the implementation of diversion programs, nationwide trends toward an increase in dismissals make it difficult to state whether this trend is increased or decreased in the population of a diversion program (e.g., Heinz, this volume). This faces evaluation studies in the Federal Republic of Germany with the problem that longitudinal analyses cannot assess this trend with sufficient accuracy to provide a satisfactory answer to the question on the expansion of social control.

The conception of the Bielefeld Diversion Program permits another evaluation design. There are no content-related case criteria for referral to diversion programs. The program should receive cases in which there is no clear option for dismissal or prosecution (e.g., Bettmer, this volume; Otto, this volume). Hence, it is theoretically available for all cases of minor to intermediate criminality. As the Bielefeld Program has only limited personnel resources, it has only a restricted capacity, and, consequently, only a subpopulation of the cases suitable for the diversion program are actually referred. Most suitable cases are dealt with in formal criminal proceedings. Hence, it is possible to form both a model group and a control group from a temporally and spatially identical population. This provides a quasiexperimental design (e.g., Cook and Campbell, 1976).

2 Method

A standardized questionnaire was used to collect data from the juvenile crime records of the Bielefeld County Court covering two periods, 1987 and 1989. The program populations were assessed completely. This resulted in data on 173 accused cases in the first wave and 144 in the second wave. For both periods, control group data were collected with random samples. For the first wave, this was data on 200 accused cases and for the second wave, 250.

Usually, empirical social research is predominantly directed toward explaining relationships. The present analysis is additionally concerned with predicting outcomes. The data were analyzed with a discrete outcome model. In mathematical terms, this model is formally identical to models in econometrics, where they are known particularly as discrete choice or qualitative-response models (see Greene, 1990, chap. 20; e.g., Amemiya, 1981; Maddala, 1983; McFadden, 1976, 1984).

The specific research question in the present study was: Which decision would have been anticipated in formal justice proceedings for the program population: dismissal or prosecution? Hence, this particularly concerns the prediction of a hypothetical outcome, naturally, on the basis of determining the predictors from which such an outcome results.

The general model equation of the discrete outcome model is:

$$(1)\ P(y_j=j) = F(x_i\beta),\ i = 1,\dots,n.$$

The probability p that the ith study unit will take the value i instead of an independent alternative y depends on the known predictors x_i and the unknown parameters β. F is a cumulative distribution function. Research practice particularly uses the following logistic distribution function for F:

$$(2)\ F(x) = \exp(x)/(1 + \exp(x)) = 1/(1 + \exp(-x))$$

If Equation 2 is entered into Equation 1, under the assumption of two possible alternatives ($p_{ij} = 1$, $p_{ij} = 2$), the following binominal logit equation is obtained:

$$(3)\ P(y_i{=}1) = P_{j1} = 1/(1 + \exp(x_{jk}\beta_k)$$
$$= 1/(1 + \exp(\beta_0 + x_{i1}\beta_1 + \ldots + x_{im}\beta_m),\ k = 1, \ldots, m.$$

Equation 3 represents a logistic regression equation. By transforming Equation 3 into the estimation equation of the logit model,

$$(4)\ p_{i1}/(1 - p_{i1}) = \exp(X_{ik}\beta_k),$$

and introducing the logarithmic form,

$$(5)\ \text{Ln}\ p_{i1}/(1 - p_{i1}) = (x_{ik}\beta_k),$$

the parameters β are estimated with the maximum-likelihood method. The estimated parameter values are individual probabilities. Their sum in Equation 3 provides the probability ratio between the two possible alternatives in the relation p_{i1} to p_{i2}. Hence, individual probabilities can be predicted.

3 Results

To determine which formal penal decisions would be expected for the model population, I first had to calculate the relevant criteria for the public prosecutor's decision in the random sample - the dichotomous goal variable: dismissal versus prosecution - using a logit model.

3.1 Model estimation

These analyses initially used all cases to form 38 offense clusters based on content criteria. The same analysis was also performed on the model cases. Then the analysis samples were adjusted. Cases that could not be assigned to the offense categories because of the nature of the offense or which had been dismissed for special legal reasons were dropped. In the first wave, this left 180 cases in the control group and 156 cases in the model group. The second wave was left with 224 cases in the control group and 132 cases in the model group. Initial bivariate analyses left 14 offense clusters. Different combinations of these remaining offense clusters were used for calculations in the logit models. The analysis of the first wave finally resulted in three offense clusters that differed significantly from each other regarding the public prosecutors' decision-making behavior, and the second wave in two offense clusters:

Offense clusters 1987:
Offense cluster 87A: Minor offenses (shoplifting up to DM 100) (ca. $60)
Offense cluster 87B: Intermediate offenses (e.g., other theft, fraud, material damage up to DM 100, driving without a license)
Offense cluster 87C: More serious offenses (e.g., theft, fraud, material damage above DM 100, assault, burglary).
Offense clusters 1989:
Offense cluster 89A: Minor and intermediate offenses (e.g., theft, fraud, material damage up to DM 250 [ca. $150], driving without a license, assault without injury)
Offense cluster 898B: More serious offenses (e.g., theft, fraud, material damage above DM 250, assault with injury, burglary).

In both waves of the random sample, further significant criteria for the public prosecutor's decision between dismissal and prosecution were:

Number of offenses: Metric variable with the levels 1, 2, 3 (and more) offenses
Prior offense: Dummy variable with the value 1
Several prior offenses or serious prior offense: Dummy variable with the value 1
Joint offense: Dummy variable with the value 1
Negative police record: Dummy variable with the value 1.

In addition, the following predictors (all consisting of dummy variables with value 1) were also significant in the first wave:

Limited responsibility
Criminal offense arising from a conflict situation
SES 2 (Intermediate socioeconomic status).

In the second wave, the following predictors (again consisting of dummy variables with value 1) were also significant:

Assault arising from a conflict situation
Joint assault
Turkish nationality or German immigrant from Eastern Europe
Positive police record
Public prosecutor No. 3.

The following tables present the results of the logit model for the control groups in the first wave (Table 1) and the second wave (Table 2).

Table 1: Logit Model for 1987 Control Group: Prosecution Versus Dismissal

Variable	β^1	SE[2]	E(x)[3]	sp[4]	p[5]
Constant	-4.683	2.165			
Offense cluster 87A	-4.908	1.693	135.37^{-1}	.0913	.004
Offense cluster 87C	3.261	1.395	26.08	.0299	.019
Number of offenses	4.716	2.067	111.72	.0502	.023
Prior offense	6.231	1.743	508.26	.1645	.000
Several or serious prior offense(s)	7.334	2.678	1531.50	.0996	.001
Joint offense	3.280	1.341	26.58	.0352	.014
Negative police record	4.263	1.867	71.02	.0321	.022
Limited responsibility	-4.606	1.715	100.08^{-1}	.0457	.007
Offense arising from conflict	-5.830	2.216	340.36^{-1}	.0525	.009
SES 2	1.788	0.836	5.98	.0199	.032

Likelihood-Chi^2: 192.51 with 10 d.f.; $p < 0.0001$[6]; Pseudo-R^2 (McFadden) = .797[7]

1 Estimated parameter values report the direction and magnitude of effect.

2 Standard errors (SE) are *T* values. For a 5% significance level, β/SE must be higher than 1.96 (Ben-Akiva and Lerman, 1985: 161).

3 The effect coefficient (which is derived directly from the estimated parameter value) corresponds to a factor for the change in the individual probability relationship p_{i2}/p_{i1} when a predictor is changed by a value of 1 while all other predictors are held constant (Long, 1987).

4 The semipartial (pseudo-)coefficient of determination reports (analogously to linear regression) the relative importance of the predictor within the total set of predictors (Cohen and Cohen, 1983: 88-102).

5 *p* reports the significance of the values of individual predictors (sp^2): It can be calculated from the difference between the likelihood Chi^2 of the total model and that of a model reduced by one predictor. The degree of freedom then corresponds to the number of alternatives reduced by one; in this case: df = 1.

6 The likelihood-ratio Chi^2 tests the significance of the total model. Degrees of freedom *(df)* are given by the number of parameters minus one (Ben-Akiva and Lerman, 1985: 164-167; McFadden, 1973: 121).

7 The coefficient of determination pseudo R^2 (McFadden) or (alternatively) likelihood-ratio index p^2 reports the proportion of explained variance. It is roughly equivalent to R^2 of a linear regression though generally somewhat lower (Amemiya, 1981: 1505; Ben-Akiva and Lerman, 1985: 167; McFadden, 1973: 121). The null model used here was a model without a constant.

Table 2: Logit Model for 1989 Control Group: Prosecution Versus Dismissal

Variable	β^1	SE^2	$E(x)^3$	sp^4	p^5
Constant	-6.439	1.465			
Offense cluster 89B	4.469	1.255	87.27	.0721	.000
Number of offenses	2.843	1.146	17.17	.0287	.013
Prior offense	3.046	.0896	21.03	.0442	.001
Several or serious prior offense(s)	3.871	1.096	47.99	.0457	.000
Joint offense	2.506	1.341	12.26	.0161	.036
Negative police record	3.057	1.196	21.26	.0210	.003
Assault arising from conflict	-4.949	2.252	142.03^{-1}	.0206	.028
Joint assault	6.698	2.932	810.78	.0268	.022
Nationality Turkish or Immigrant	1.542	0.732	4.67	.0130	.047
Positive police record	-3.525	1.071	33.95^{-1}	.0188	.001
Prosecutor # 3	2.474	0.715	11.87	.0432	.001

Likelihood-*Chi*^{2}: 213.71 with 11 d.f.; $p < 0.0001$[6]; Pseudo-R^2 (McFadden) = .73[7]

Notes: See Table 1.

Both models produced very good saturation. This is also confirmed by the number of correctly predicted alternatives, that is, the predicted individual probabilities that cases would be dismissed was compared with the actual decisions of the public prosecutors: For both the first and second waves, the level of agreement was 94%.

3.2 *Individual Probabilities*

Individual probabilities can be calculated with Equation 3. For example, the predictive equation of the logit model of the random sample in the first wave is generally expressed as follows:

Example 1:

p_{i1} = 1 / (1 + exp(-4.68 + offense cluster 87A · -4.91 + offense cluster 87C · 3.26 + number of offenses · 4.72 + prior offense · 6.23 + several/serious offense(s) · 7.33 + joint offense · 3.28 + negative police record · 4.26 + limited responsibility · -4.61 + offense out of conflict · -5.83 + SES 2 · -1.79)).

If the variables are replaced with appropriate values, probabilities like the following are produced:

Example 2:

p_{j1} = 1 / (1 + exp(-4.68 + 1 · -4.91 + 0 · 3.26 + 1 · 4.72 + 0 · 6.23 + 0 · 7.33 + 0 · 3.28 + 0 · 4.26 + 0 · -4.61 + 0 · -5.83 + 0 · -1.79)) = .99 = 99%.

The individual probability that the case will be dismissed (p_{i1}) is 99% if one minor offense has been committed, while no further significant predictors are observed.

Example 3:

p_{j1} = 1 / (1 + exp(-4.68 + 0 · -4.91 + 0 · 3.26 + 1 · 4.72 + 0 · 6.23 + 0 · 7.33 + 0 · 3.28 + 0 · 4.26 + 0 · -4.61 + 0 · -5.83 + 0 · -1.79)) = .49 = 49%.

The individual probability that the case will be dismissed (p_{i1}) is 49% if one offense with intermediate severity hase been committed (both offense cluster 87A and 87C have value 0; cluster 87B is a reference category which is not specified in the logit model), while no further significant predictors are observed.

Example 4:

p_{j1} = 1 / (1 + exp(-4.68 + 1 · -4.91 + 0 · 3.26 + 1 · 4.72 + 1 · 6.23 + 0 · 7.33 + 0 · 3.28 + 0 · 4.26 + 0 · -4.61 + 0 · -5.83 + 0 · -1.79)) = .21 = 21%.

The individual probability that the case will be dismissed (p_{i1}) is 21% if one minor offense has been committed and one prior offense is present, while no further significant predictors are observed.

Hence, values for the variables that serve as predictors of the public prosecutor's decision can be applied to each case in the model group. This produces a value that reports the probability that the public prosecutor would have dismissed the case. Using this principle, the logit prediction equation from the corresponding control group was used to calculate the hypothetical probability of dismissal for all cases from both model populations.

3.3 Population Probabilities

Table 3 compares the actual outcome of diversion with the probable outcome of a criminal justice proceeding. The outcome of diversion corresponds to dismissal in formal proceedings if the social worker proposes dismissal without considering any measure and without making contact with the accused, that is, when no intervention is performed on the accused. If the social worker recommends a court proceeding, this corresponds to prosecution in formal proceedings. In cases that were dismissed after intervention within the diversion program, it is assumed that the intensity of intervention lies above dismissal but below prosecution in formal proceedings.

Table 3: Comparison Between the Actual Outcome of the Program and the Predicted Outcome of a Formal Proceeding

Program outcome	Predicted outcome of a formal proceeding					
	1987			1989		
	Dismissal	Prosecution	Total	Dismissal	Prosecution	Total
	n (%)	n (%)	n (%)	n (%)	n (%)	n (%)
Unconditional dismissal	7 (4)	12 (8)	12 (12)	11 (8)	6 (5)	17 (13)
Dismissal						
- After conversation	19 (12)	33 (21)	52 (33)	14 (11)	21 (16)	35 (27)
- After measure	25 (16)	49 (31)	74 (47)	23 (17)	47 (36)	70 (53)
Prosecution	1 (1)	10 (5)	11 (7)	1 (1)	9 (7)	10 (8)
N (%)	52 (33)	104 (67)	156 (100)	49 (37)	83 (63)	132(100)

In cases in which prosecution was predicted and the social worker did not recommend a court proceeding, it can be seen that if formal proceedings had been implemented, the clients would have experienced a higher sanction and a longer duration of proceedings. The severity of sanctions was clearly lower than that assigned by the courts: In 1987, sanction was merely a discussion at the Youth Welfare Office in 33% of cases; in 1989, in 27% of cases. Community service assignments were also clearly lighter than the measures assigned by the courts in the comparative cases in the random sample. The duration of proceedings was on average 30 days less than in cases that went to court. In addition, all measures are completed at the time when dismissal is passed in the diversion program, while clearly higher sanctions still have to be implemented after court decisions in a formal proceeding.

The predictions for both program populations were very similar:

Sixty percent of the program cases in 1987 and 56% in 1989 actually were settled by dismissal with or without measure, while a continuation of formal proceeding of these cases would have led to prosecution. Since prosecution usually implies a punishment, which is more severe than a measure within the program, this part of the program population is concerned with a reduction of social control.

In 11% of the model cases from the first wave (1987) and 15% of the model cases from the second wave (1989), the prediction corresponds to actual outcome, namely, either unconditional dismissal or prosecution. Thus, the extent of social control in these cases is equivalent.

In both the first (1987) and second (1989) wave, 29% of the program cases actually were settled after an intervention (conversation, measure or prosecution), while a formal proceeding probably would have led to dismissal without any further intervention. This must be viewed as an expansion of social control resulting from applying the program.

4 Conclusion

In conclusion, results showed that the Bielefeld diversion program tended to decrease rather than increase social control. This is strengthened by very similar distributions in both waves.

References

Amemiya, T. (1981). Qualitative response models: A survey. *Journal of Economic Literature, 19,* 1483-1536.

Ben-Akiva, M., and Lerman, S.R. (1985). *Discrete choice analysis: Theory and application to travel demand.* Cambridge, MA: MIT Press.

Blomberg, T.G. (1980). Widening the net: An anomaly in the evaluation of diversion programs. In M. Klein and K.S. Teilmann (Eds.), *Handbook of criminal justice evaluation* (pp. 572-592). Beverly Hills, CA: Sage.

Blomberg, T.G. (1983). Diversion's disparate results and unresolved questions: An integrative evaluation perspective. *Journal of Research in Crime and Delinquency, 20,* 24-38.

Cohen, J., and Cohen, P. (1983). *Applied multiple regression/correlation analysis for the behavioral sciences* (2nd ed). Hillsdale, NJ: Erlbaum.

Cook, T.D., and Campbell, D.T. (1976). The design and conduct of quasi-experimental and true experiments in field settings. In M. Dunnette (Ed.), *Handbook of industrial and organizational psychology* (pp. 223-326). Chicago: Rand McNally.

Greene, W. (1990). *Econometric analysis.* New York: Macmillan.

Klein, M.W. (1979). Deinstitutionalization and diversion of juvenile offenders: A litany of impediments. In N. Morris and M. Tonry (Eds.), *Crime and justice: An annual review of research, Vol. 1* (pp. 145-201). Chicago: University of Chicago Press.

Long, J.S. (1987). A graphical method for interpretation of multinominal logit analysis. *Sociological Methods & Research, 15,* 420-446.

Maddala G. (1983). *Limited dependent and qualitative variables in econometrics.* Cambridge: Cambridge University Press.

McFadden, D. (1973). Conditional logit analysis of qualitative choice behavior. In P. Zarembka (Ed.), *Frontiers in econometrics* (pp. 105-124). New York: Academic Press.

McFadden, D. (1976). Quantal choice analysis: A survey. *Annals of Economic and Social Measurement, 5,* 363-390.

McFadden, D. (1984). Econometric analysis of qualitative response models. In Z. Griliches and M. Intriligator (Eds.), *Handbook of econometrics* (Vol. 2) (pp. 1395-1457). Amsterdam: North Holland.

Evaluation of Diversion Program Concepts

Hans-Joachim Plewig

Diversion has been established in Germany within a specific historical context. The background of the so-called inner reform (see Chapter 2) indicates the function of the new instrument in juvenile crime policies as well as the interests of its protagonists. In this paper, I shall stress the argument that the doubtful circumstances of its implementation correspond to the rather inadequate situation on the level of research.

1 Diversion in Germany: Implementation Context

The late 1960s and early 1970s in West Germany witnessed a serious argument on the role of democracy, the state, and the individual. Authority was questioned on various levels, including social and law policies. Institutions like the prison, psychiatry, residential public education, and detention centers came under heavy attack. Some wanted to abolish them, others at least wanted to open them up, while some relied on therapeutical approaches (which they thought to be less repressive). In addition, since both jurisdiction and social education practice are dependent on and influenced by law, the two major legal codes dealing with the broad group "youth at risk" were examined critically.

The new perception of "youth" at the end of the last century had led to a system of comprehensive social control. The historical context of its genesis tells about the motivations and "inner logic" of dealing with young people supposed to be at risk or deviant. The basic concept of dealing with young people at risk has not changed until today.

1.1 Youth Laws and Their Structure

In the early 1920s, the state completed the system of social control by establishing a Youth Welfare Act (JWG)[1] and differentiating penal law by adding the Juvenile Justice Act (JGG)[2]. The preceding debate covered the wide range of possible arguments and motivations from repression to criticism of the capitalistic system as the cause of deviance. In between there were "child savers" insisting on social education within the community (*Gemeinschaft*).

The result of the controversy was the following tripartite system (which - indirectly - gave an answer to the question "Whose side are we on with regard to young people?"):

1. Civil (family) law in charge of "normal" families and parent-child conflicts.
2. The Youth Welfare Act consisting of two focal parts: (a) welfare work in the context of ordinary youth work (*Jugendpflege*); (b) juvenile care for those minors who are defined as socially maladjusted, neglected, or in need of care or protection (*Jugendfürsorge*).
3. The Juvenile Justice Act (JGG), differentiating between educational measures (court order/directive, educational guidance, and educational supervision) and youth imprisonment. In 1943, juvenile detention was added as another repressive instrument.

Therefore, the whole complex of youth laws was based on a three-tier structure. All participants in that reform shared the firm belief that there were "the good and the bad ones" whom they were able to identify: the juveniles who can be (socially) educated and the ones who are either not able or not willing "to be reached". The latter group would not "deserve" the merits of "educational grace"; they should be selected and locked away from the *Gemeinschaft*.

This procedural logic expressing the basic approach of a preventive concept will be discussed later on in the context of constitutional law principles and criteria for the evaluation of diversion.

1.2 The "Lost Battle" and the Emergence of "Inner Reform"

Two trends were responsible for the attempt to create a comprehensive reform of the Youth Welfare and Juvenile Justice Act in the 1970s:

1. The rising trend of rehabilitative intervention, expressed by therapeutic approaches (prison, psychiatry, residential homes; the Netherlands and Scandinavia were reputed to be positive examples).
2. Partly overlapping and following this trend, the so-called labeling approach supported by a movement that criticized state policies in general, leading to a lasting anti-institutional attitude.

The slogan of the reform movement in the early 1970s was "Forward Youth Welfare" (*Offensive Jugendhilfe*). Its primary goal had been to abolish or reduce the discrimination predominant since the 1920's between the "Good One" (the juvenile who is supposed to be social educable, capable of being treated, etc.) and the "Bad One" (the juvenile who is no longer "open" to social educational measures, who shows, as the JGG states, criminal tendencies (*"schädliche Neigungen"*). Thus, a new Youth Welfare Law should give up the mere law-and-order perspective and change from intervention to a concept based on services and voluntariness.

Part of the reform should have been the *abolition* of repressive institutions (e.g., detention centers) and a preference for youth welfare activities over youth criminal justice sanctions, for example, by raising the age of responsibility to 16 years. The attempt failed completely. This was not only for fiscal reasons but also, or even mainly due to, the basic governmental conviction that traditional ways of controlling youth should not be given up. That position involves specific assumptions on the genesis of deviance, responsibility for deviance, and limits of "welfare intervention".

The therapeutic and social educational approach, which gained in interest and influence about 1970, led to the invention of the "social competence training course". The concept was inspired by "community treatment programs" like those developed in California. The reason for this proposal had been the - then still realistic - hope of replacing detention with this kind of "ambulant sanction". A little later, another model came up: the community service order as a tool for a meaningful sanction, based on strong guidance by the people in charge of this juvenile court directive.

Caring and training are therefore two categories that characterize the trend in the 1970s. Reformers pleaded for nonresidential sanctions and the reduction of institutional sanctions.

By the mid-1970s, the discussion in the field of youth welfare broke down completely. In youth penal law, a purely positivistic, pragmatic debate remained. Further reform attempts were labeled "inner reform". The developing practice described above was suddenly justified as diversion.

2 German Diversion: Some Introductory Remarks

The transfer of diversion from the United States had its formal limits: Not the police but only the prosecutor could handle the new instrument. Two major principles of German Constitutional Law have to be considered:

1. Discretionary power is only available to the prosecutor (*Legalitätsprinzip*).
2. The less intensive intervention has priority (*Subsidiaritätsprinzip*). This principle forms the basis of youth laws, their general principle, as well as several of their specific regulations.

Even before looking at the diversion practice that has grown up, it can be stated that:

1. Diversion on the level of discretionary police powers (as doubtful as it may be) is ruled out by law in Germany.
2. Diversion in Germany means *intervention* with the instruments of social work. Nonintervention is contradictory to the inner logic of the youth law system.
3. Diversion is propagated mainly with the argument that "juvenile delinquency" is supposed to be normal - due to adolescence. Practically no expert in this country is interested in tackling the logical hurdle combining this empirical argument with interventions based on a social educational approach.
4. From the beginning of the diversion debate onwards, critics raised the formal accusation of net-widening. The efforts to support this - no doubt plausible - argument have been very poor, however. One major critic hinted at the number of new juvenile prisons planned but never corrected his thesis when reality showed a different picture.[3]

Diversion led to a situation that was difficult to survey in the 11 (West) German states. German diversion - first of all - means widening the opportunities of intervention. "Inner reform" of the Juvenile Justice Act did not mean the abolition of any of the previously criticized sanctions but an extension of the variations of penal interventions: First, as the police have no discretionary power, the prosecutor became the "hidden judge". Second, he or she became responsible for a new dimension of dismissing cases either without any intervention or after some "social educational measure" has taken place. This meant that the prosecutor not only had the juvenile but also an understanding of his or her psychology (attitude, motives, guilt, etc.). Through more or less intensive information on personality and personal/social background, the prosecutor gets to know more than ever before about the offender. This "expert" knowledge is part of the decision procedure on whether or not to stop the intervention of justice. Naturally, we do not know whether the prosecutor actually possesses the necessary knowledge and insight into the problems of deviant youth. German diversion relies on "educational measures." Its main characteristic is the functionalizing of social work. Whereas during the first 60 years of the Juvenile Justice Act, social education fulfilled its role within penal institutions (especially youth prison), diversion now led to a pact between the justice system and part of the welfare system. In contrast to the major trends during the late 1960s and early 1970s - and apart from social work groups that insisted on a gap between police and justice on one side and the juveniles and their advocates on the other side[4] -social work began to establish projects initiated by the law system especially for offenders and in cooperation with justice. All these projects were founded more or less only to serve this disciplinary purpose. This fact has consequences for their status (negotiationary power; political and theoretical quality).

The logic of the youth laws, especially of the Juvenile Justice Act, calls for intervention. This logic has - among others - two consequences:

1. The juvenile offender must not get away without any distinct reaction.
2. If the juvenile offender is not capable of appreciating the so-called milder "educational" sanction, the next punishment must be more severe (laymen's learning theory).

This doubtful background and context has its specific influence on diversion practice and the state of research on it.

3 Diversion Approaches and Concepts in Germany

Statements concerning any kind of "evaluation" of diversion in Germany have to be of a very modest kind. Keeping in mind the genesis of this criminal policy, it is not surprising that very few efforts are undertaken to reflect the whole movement in a self-critical way. As far as I know, there are three different approaches to "evaluating" this subject:

The typical conventional way of analyzing sanctions is to look for data on "recidivism." There is a strong belief that the fact of an offender being sentenced again indicates some "causal" connection to the quality of the prior sanction. The argument raised by labeling theory, that the fact that an offender gets caught and sentenced anew tells more about the institutions of control than about the offender, is never considered seriously in this kind of research. Because no experimental research projects are available,[5] the main source of information is the analysis of statistics (files; Federal Educational Register), in other words: a specific construction of reality.

An alternative to this rather broad and abstract research is the evaluation of a specific project or program. Not one of the various diversion projects throughout Germany has undertaken or accepted a systematic evaluation of their theory (if ever existing), concept, and practice.[6] This fact allows the conjecture that neither the protagonists in the Ministries of Justice, nor the supporting criminologists, nor the social workers involved have a real interest in clarifying this issue. A number of German states (*Länder*) have introduced a statewide diversion program by passing diversion directions on the level of the general prosecutor.[7] In those cases, there is a *political will* to enforce a specific criminal reform policy. It is no surprise that under such circumstances there is a different kind of interest situation. Against this background, Hamburg has decided to evaluate its first years of diversion.[8]

One of the great dilemmas and, in fact, an unacceptable constellation for social-pedagogical approaches and objectives is the usurpation of social work (*Sozialpädagogik*) as an instrument to further the interests of penal sanctioning. But apart from that, any kind of realistic research makes it indispensible to look at the side of practice. If diversion projects are considered to be so effective that prosecutors or judges can rely on their effect and therefore dispense with (so-called) more severe sanctions, then a differentiated view of those interventions is needed.

Any kind of social educational approach that does not include the actor and objects of those efforts - that is, does not emphasize the life world and perspectives of the youth involved within its processes and context[9] - provides only insufficient information.

A subsidiary path of evaluation is to look at the concepts available and to try to analyze them on a secondary level. Under the title of "Diversion within the JGG", an attempt has been made to give an overview of the practice (Plewig, 1990). Some of the main initial results are presented in the following.

3.1 Evaluation of Diversion by Files and Statistics

Conventional criminology believes that a sophisticated juridical sanction is directly responsible for "positive" or "negative" effects on the offender, that is, it has a causal effect on "recidivism." It is regretted that differentiated experimental investigations cannot be undertaken for practical, legal, and ethical reasons. Therefore this criminological position argues from a different point of view: It claims that - formal or informal - "educational measures" are positive per se, and that ambulant (i.e., nonincarcerative/noncustodial) measures are "better" than custodial ones.

The next argument then seems to be easy: From the point of view of *prevention* (individual or general prevention), there is reason to prefer ambulant sanctions. As the main proof, it is argued that "recidivism" following ambulant sanctions is lower than after custodial intervention. This logic provokes the cautious question as to whether the constellation of locking up (in detention or youth prison) is not a different situation (life circumstances of the selected offenders, criminal career/secondary deviance) from that of other offenders. The line of argument comes to an end with the statement that there is no empirical evidence for "harder" sanctions.

To make it clear: All these arguments are filtered purely from the perspective of data analysts. What is considered to be "positive", "better", "milder", and so forth or the opposite is simply defined from a sociologist's point of view. It does not necessarily have much to do with "real life."

To explain the critics: The labeling approach puts forward plausible arguments for *possible* effects. Whether or not they happen has to be evaluated as well. The leading German criminologist following the statistical approach is Heinz (1989). The conclusion from his evaluation is that not only petty offenses but also delinquency on a medium level could be handled on an informal juridical level. This program is called "youth penal law reform by practice". In addition to arguments from the data and his interpretation, he points to the *Subsidiaritätsprinzip* (priority to the "milder" interventions).

Heinz has stressed an important aspect of diversion implementation. As prosecutors or judges need specific information on the offender, the Juvenile Justice Act established the Juvenile Court Assistance System (*Jugendgerichtshilfe*: JGH; something like court liaison office). The juvenile court assistant is asked to investigate the personal background of the offender and make proposals for the sanction from a social educational point of view. Another function of this institution is to support, care for, guide, and supervise young persons during and after the proceedings taken against them. It is obvious that the Jugendgerichtshilfe *can* influence sanction practice. It is therefore of importance if the proposals made by the Juvenile Court Assistance are diversion-minded in the way criminologists like Heinz argue (pleading for "milder" forms of intervention). Heinz and Hügel (1986: 48-53) provoked those social workers by their findings that they are not always in favor of this policy but sometimes make sanction proposals that are "more severe" than even judges expect.

The first insight into German diversion reveals that internal demands of criminological evaluation are of modest quality. The information that it may give is more indirect than "to the point". Yet this conclusion still does not tell much about what is really worth knowing.

3.2 Diversion: A Statewide Program (Hamburg)

In 1985 the Hamburg Senate decided to introduce "Diversion in juvenile criminal procedure". Its basis was a directive addressed mainly to prosecutors, as they are - in contrast to independent judges - subject to directions. This document included a list of offenses that are supposed to be divertable.

Diversion had to be accepted by different authorities: Department of the Interior (police), as the body that has to prepare the case; Department of Justice (prosecutor and judge), who have to decide whether the case is divertable. Last but not least, the Department of Youth Welfare is involved because it is supposed to take over the implementation of the educational measures in its administrative section of Juvenile Court Assistance.

The debate on the implementation was highly controversial. *All* signs indicated that the attempt failed. A new senator of justice surprised all critics, especially among prosecutors and judges, by supporting the reform. But decisions at the top do not necessarily have anything to do with practice "at the bottom". Therefore any debate on evaluating reform models has to include a specific analysis of the concrete conditions of (non)realization. History is not made by persons, but personalities can be decisive by using the options in a specific historical situation. At Hamburg, three alternatives of Diversion became part of the concept:

1. Before court trial and after police registration, the prosecutor stops the procedure conditionally.
2. Formal intervention is replaced by an informal one either (a) during a court trial, or (b) before that stage. "Informal sanction" represents a typical German diversion variation. The variety of "educational measures" will be explained in the next section.
3. Diversion can also be defined as reducing "formal intervention" (e.g., youth detention or probation instead of youth prison).

The research undertaken at Hamburg aims at two different levels. One approach concentrates on the situation in 1988. The passage of the report concerning just this specific phase is of very limited value. Its facts are imprecise and - above all - do not include any hint toward developments in later years. Rather excitedly, it assures a rise in the rate of youth detention and youth prison. This conclusion is and was wrong. Data from 1990 and 1991 were available before the report was published. It anyway fails to analyze the development of implementing diversion over a period of about 7 years.

A secondary evaluation has been undertaken in order to overcome this deficit (pp. 377-400). It comes to the conclusion that prosecutors and judges increasingly use the possibility of dismissing the case.

A preliminary summary of a first evaluation of Hamburg diversion practice could be:

1. The justice system does not hesitate to accept diversion, but it uses it as an additional instrument.
2. There is little doubt that mainly minor offenses lead to an "educational measure."
3. There is also no controversy that the situation at juvenile prison is determined primarily by drug offenses. An increase or reduction of figures does not necessarily have anything to do with diversion.

The evaluation of the Hamburg diversion program gives some hints about the reality produced by a political reform program. It tells something about fantasies in the justice system: the way and manner in which different kinds of "educational measures" are mixed, about the length of diversion intervention, and the - law-oriented - expectations behind it.

The levels of evaluation are complex. It is necessary to analyze the administrative level, the level of making decisions, the level of producing offenders by selection, and - last but not least - the level of interaction (social education and dealing with "the offender"). With regard to this high, complex expectation, the Hamburg research report is not a helpful resource.

4 Diversion: What Are They Doing?

From a critical point of view - considering theory of society, theory of youth and youth welfare, theory of science of education, especially including historical analysis - it is irritating to look at German diversion practice. It just happens. In Germany, diversion regularly means: Something has to happen. A "social educational" approach within the context of youth law intervention is based on the inner logic of intervening in the best interest of the juvenile. As youth in general is considered to be at risk and in need of preventive measures (Gillis, 1974), there is no reason to hesitate with "helpful offers". Therefore, the unofficial parole is: *care instead of locking up*. The variety of intervention includes "social educational courses"[10], work orders or supervision orders, intensive intervention at the early level (first offenses, minor offenses) by intervening at the family level and claiming "remorse" in the offender, or, finally intensive talks by the prosecutor with the offender (not to find out the reasons for juvenile delinquency but to test the motivation and remorse of the delinquent).

Diversion therefore can mean an intensive cooperation between prosecutor and court liaison aid and/or police and social work in order to identify the underlying problems. Basically this means a very intensive intervention into the individual life world. This approach is also defined as "colonization" (*Kolonisierung von Lebenswelt*; see Müller and Otto, 1986).

A new chapter is added to the history of political reforms and evaluation by looking at the way of arguing for the advantages of diversion in Germany. It is as funny as it is astonishing that almost all protagonists of this criminal policy reform refer to the so-called Uelzen project. Probably it is an unique phenomenon on a world level that practitioners, state governments, and even the Federal Department of Justice quote this place and practice.

But what is so exciting about diversion practice at Uelzen (a small town in Lower Saxony)? At one time, the only judge in this small town had decided to reduce the number of juvenile offenders who were being locked up. He was influenced by typical humane arguments about the "ineffectiveness" of prisons. He founded an organization to take over the care of young delinquents whom he sanctioned to accept its offers. Not surprisingly, local statistics changed. His production of judge-produced reality became *the* proof of "successful" diversion. Independent of what social work did "in cooperation" with their judge, it has to be stated: That kind of unquestioned practice represents "the making of diversion success in Germany".

The structure of the German Juvenile Justice Act allows almost any kind of reaction because any sanction can be assumed to have an educational value. Consequently, evaluation actually is superfluous. It only needs to convince "conservative" critics. They, on the other hand, do recognize sooner or later that their idea of repression is not needed presently. Social control continued to function. And it never gave up its basic structure. It just became a little more flexible.

The search for "valid" facts on diversion ends at this point. There are some indications; there are some kinds of scientific approach. But - as a hard fact - there is nothing but some theoretical, abstract arguments that doubt the sense and effect of the diversion movement: Disciplinary action has opened up a new, additional dimension and, as one effect among others, created the "nondivertible" (van den Boogaart, 1989).

Notes

1 The Youth Welfare Act was replaced by the *Kinder- und Jugendhilfegesetz* (KJHG) in 1990. Despite new options, whose quality has to be tested in future, the basic structure of help and social control has not changed.

2 Age of responsibility: 14 years; young adults: 18 to 20 years.

3 A number of juvenile prisons have never been built. Some juvenile prisons were or are not full. The average age of prisoners is about 20 to 21 years. Therefore, the problem is a different one.

4 An impressive example for this move for separation is the Netherlands.

5 See, for Great Britain, Berg, Brown, and Hullin (1988); for another review, see Plewig (1990).

6 Pfeiffer has analyzed the "Brücke-Projekt" at Munich. His research leaves many questions open, especially with regard to the evaluation of intervention and the new practice of "soft social control" by social workers cooperating with judges.

7 Hamburg prepared its political decision through a series of hearings with experts and on the basis of scientific material. The way arguments are used and stressed is well documented.

8 See Sack (1991). This research has been financed by the Federal Ministry for Youth.

9 The first German comprehensive qualitative study on "Genesis of Deviance" (in early youth) between 1911 - 1981 was undertaken by Plewig and Wegner (1984).

10 Once planned as an alternative to detention that is part-time at weekends or lasts between 1 and 4 weeks.

References

Berg, I., Brown, I., and Hullin, R. (1988). *Off school, in court: an experimental and psychiatric investigation of severe school attendance problems*. New York: Springer.

Boogaart, H. van den (1989). Mind the gap: The creation of the non-divertible. In J. Hudson and B. Galaway (Eds.), *The state as parent* (pp. 207-211). Dordrecht: Kluwer.

Gillis, J.R. (1974). *Youth and history. Tradition and change in European age relations 1770 - present*. New York: Academic Press.

Heinz, W. (1989). JGG-Reform durch die Praxis. Eine Bestandsaufnahme. In Bundesministerium der Justiz (Ed.), *Jugendstrafrechtsreform durch die Praxis. Konstanzer Symposium*. Bonn: Bundesministerium der Justiz.

Müller, S., and Otto, H.-U. (Eds.) (1984). *Verstehen oder Kolonialisieren?* Bielefeld: B. Kleine Verlag.

Müller, S., and Otto, H.-U. (Eds.) (1986). *Damit Erziehung nicht zur Strafe wird*. Bielefeld: KT-Böllert.

Pfeiffer, C. (1983). *Kriminalprävention im Jugendgerichtsverfahren*. Köln: Heymanns.

Plewig, H.-J. (1990). Diversion im Rahmen des Jugendgerichtsgesetzes. In D. Kreft and H. Lukas (Eds.), *Perspektivenwandel der Jugendhilfe*. Material zum 8. Jugendbericht. Band II: Expertisentexte "Neue Handlungsfelder in der Jugendhilfe" (pp. 247-272). Nürnberg: Institut für Soziale und Kulturelle Arbeit.

Plewig, H.-J., and Wegner, Th. (1984). *Zur Genese von Devianz im frühen Jugendalter*. Arbeitspapiere aus dem Institut für Kriminologie der Universität Heidelberg, Bd. 4. Heidelberg: Universität Heidelberg.

Sack, F. (1991). *Entkriminalisierung Jugendlicher durch innere Reform des Jugendgerichtssystems - Eine Begleitforschung zum Hamburger Diversionsmodell*. Unpublished Manuscript, University of Hamburg.

References

Fantasy and the Embodied Moral Capital: Children's Moral Judgments of Crime and Criminals

Elisabeth Lissenberg[*]

1 Introduction

During the enduring process of socialization, both children and adults have to come to grips with problems of control in interpersonal relations on which any code of penal law depends. During this process, we learn or have learned to make classifications, to distinguish between appropriate or inappropriate, and good or bad forms of behavior and between deviant and respectable people. These judgments partly reflect the ways by which the State more or less perceivably exerts external control by criminalizing behavior and by punishing (some of the) offenders (cf. Elias, 1969, Vol. 2: 325-326). As children and as adults, we are influenced by the State's definition of "crime" and its labeling of people as "criminals". On the other hand, we as citizens influence the legislator and the law-enforcement agencies by putting pressure on political parties to change the criminal code and by informing the police, thus structuring and restructuring the field of penal law whose field overlaps the moral field.

In the form of its representations or symbols, criminal law is omnipresent in everyday life: The police officer is the living symbol of the State's monopoly of violence; prisons have a particular architecture which can be noticed from the outside; traffic rules are visualized in traffic lights and signs. These phenomena facilitate children's apprehension of the penal law. Their moral judgments of crime and criminals have a base in reality.

However, I want to introduce fantasy as an additional means of social control to clarify the processes involved in legal socialization. I shall describe these particular processes as the incorporation of moral capital by discussing the manifested amalgam of knowledge and fantasy of crimes and criminals in the context of moral capital. The above-mentioned arguments will be illustrated empirically by moral judgments on crimes and criminals gathered from compositions written and questionnaires answered by children during the first half of the 1970s and the latter half of the 1980s.

2 Moral Capital

Pierre Bourdieu distinguishes three forms of capital or symbolic forms of power: economic, cultural, and social capital. As I have argued elsewhere, these are not enough.[1] A fourth category is necessary, that of moral capital. Moral capital, just like the other forms of capital, functions as a substantive source of power to structure and restructure social reality, however symbolic. It functions as yet another marker, as a measure of social distinction.

I see moral capital as the capacity to influence others, individuals or groups, in the sphere of moral behavior, moral judgments, and perceptions of good and evil, as well as the capacity to maintain, create, or change moral rules and other relevant social institutions. People try, overtly or not, to convince others in moral realms, and by doing so they can and do distinguish between themselves based on their respective evaluations of moral behavior. The capacity to discriminate between good and evil is a social product. Morality is not a gift; one is not born more or less moral, one is made that way. During the process of socialization, moral judgments and strategies to convince others are transmitted within the family, the church, and the peer group. People need time to acquire capital in whatever form, and they have to divide their time in their quest for whatever form of capital: Time spent on the acquisition of moral capital cannot be used to obtain economic capital.

Moral capital can be transmitted into the other forms of capital and vice versa. Take the example of children gradually developing their "feel for the game" to deal with moral dilemmas. One needs time to draw their attention "inconspicuously" to possible solutions to moral problems which arise in the playground, or to read them fairy tales in which judgments of good and evil are abundantly illustrated.

People differ in their capacity to influence or convince others of their moral ideas or to impose their moral standards. Moral capital is distributed unequally, just like the other forms of capital. It also has its own legitimations, its own vocabularies of motives, its own "morals" (cf. Elias, 1976).

Moral capital, as the other forms of capital distinguished by Bourdieu, functions at three different states, the *objectified* state, the *embodied* state, and the *institutionalized* state.[2] These various states are interconnected; inducing, producing, and reproducing one another. And different forms of capital, different sources of (symbolic) power, come into the picture depending on the fields and the problems under study as well as on the interests of the people involved. In this paper, I shall go more deeply into the incorporation that is the acquisition of embodied moral capital than into the other two states, and I shall also draw attention to the role fantasies play in connection with the incorporation of this form of symbolic power.

3 Fantasy as a Means of Social Control

Fantasy as a means of social control is discussed as the missing link between the biographical and the sociohistorical processes in relation to the development of moral judgments of crimes and criminals. This concept may also facilitate the connection between the two prevalent lines in psychological theories of socialization: the psychological cognitive developmental theories (Piaget, Kohlberg, Tapp, Gilligan) and the social-environment theories.[3] Fantasies have psychological as well as social aspects, or to put it in other words, psychological fantasies can both be transhistorical, yet inflated or curtailed by changing socio-historical circumstances (Brennan, 1991: 20-21). Psychoanalysts presuppose the human capacity to have fantasies as a primal disposition, while, as a sociologist, I want to stress that the contents are socially induced, produced, and reproduced.

In the course of their upbringing, children gradually learn to cope with problems that arise because they have to live with and are therefore dependent on other people (Goudsblom, 1977: 138). Fantasies are part of the means that helps them to solve and resolve these problems, while these solutions inform, produce, and reproduce their everyday theories (see, for example, Bettelheim, 1976; Lurie, 1990).

These fantasies function not only as a means to control other people's behavior but also as a form of self-control. And they stimulate and are stimulated by the fantasies and the constructed realities of oneself and others. This works at the institutional level, that is, through press releases of the Public Prosecutor's Office making mention of successful escape attempts by "dangerous" prisoners. In reacting to this kind of news, most people "rely" on their fantasies while projecting images of those escapees. At the interactional level, the human imagination operates through gossip and small talk about crimes and criminals or indirectly via crime serials on television or in comic books in which always at least one "bad" character figures to expose the "goodness" and "justice" of the "hero". The international character of many television programs and many comic books may inform the social construction of an internationally - or, to be more precise, an American - flavored image of offenders.[4]

Adults, at least partly, "cherish" the same images of criminals as children do. I made a comparison between the research of a Dutch colleague and my own data (see Rood-Pijpers, 1987, and Lissenberg, 1990b). This prompted me to define adults' images as infantile. Adults and children daydream about the "big catch" which would leave them rolling in money. However, laws and practical needs intervene between dreams and deeds. Imagination and fantasies keep us in control at least on two interconnected levels, namely, on the internalized or embodied level as a means of self-control and as a means to accept external constraint in the form of official punishment of crimes and their perpetrators; and this institutional reaction produces social control at the embodied level and reproduces indirect social constraint in a more or less fantasied form.

Fantasy and reality, in my opinion, are distinct, while both are connected to moral capital. Fantasy functions at a level more enduring than and relatively autonomous from reality. However diffuse and however repressed fantasies can be, everyone of us - children or adults - continuously copes with visions of the bad or the evil "other(s)". The contents of these visions change biographically over time, with reality, however constructed, overlaying fantasies. They vary with the acquisition of knowledge about those "others" and/or with the changing images of crimes and criminals presented by governmental as well as mass media rhetoric. This rhetoric is contingent on other social developments (see Cremer-Schäfer and Steinert, 1991).

This point of view is in discordance with the basic assumptions of labeling theory. According to labeling theorists in the 1960s, fantasy and reality were highly interconnected, with fantasy being more powerful than reality. Jock Young (1971), for example, describes the negotiations between the marihuana smoker and the police about reality and fantasy stereotypes of drug usage. The expected and predicted outcome of these negotiations was then depicted as "the translation of fantasy into reality" with the fantasy of the police overwhelming the reality of the drug users, consecutively creating a "new" reality for both the police and the drug users (Young, 1971). We are now also familiar with the reverse process in which the reality of drug users is an accepted or anyway an acceptable reality for a larger part of the audience including the police. The labeling process, in my view, is better described as a process of negotiating different social constructions of reality.

The process I want to describe, however, is a process in which one or more groups try to maintain or achieve moral dominance and growth of moral capital by successfully linking their conceptions or descriptions of reality with other people's fantasies about the evil "other" that more or less lie in wait for the imposed descriptions. The outcome of this process is dependent on the prevailing hierarchy of credibility of the groups or persons involved (Becker, 1966).

4 Research Methods

In the first half of the 1970s, 332 seven- to 12-year-old boys and girls in three elementary schools at Amsterdam wrote compositions in reply to the question we phrased as: "You know there are people in prison who have been caught by the police. What kind of people do you expect to be in prison?" During the same time span, 318 six- to 12-year-old boys and girls from three elementary schools at The Hague answered a questionnaire with open-ended and closed questions. In both cities, Amsterdam and The Hague, the three schools were selected in such a way that a division could be made into upper, middle, and lower social backgrounds.[5]

In the second half of the 1980s, the research format I designed in the 1970s has been replicated in part in the framework of two separate educational programs in two other cities in the Netherlands. In Rotterdam, 11- to 12-year-olds from lower- and middle-class backgrounds wrote compositions responding to the question: "Who is a bad person?"[6] This formulation is more suggestive than the one used earlier, but it is more in accordance with ordinary language. A classroom discussion on this very topic preceded the composition writing, which must account in part for various similarities in the descriptions given by the children from the same classroom. Fifty compositions written by pupils in the highest grades of four different elementary schools were analysed. The schools were located in neighborhoods with different socioeconomic compositions. At two schools, the majority of children were of non-Dutch origin.

In the fourth city, Nijmegen, my questionnaire research was repeated in part. Some of the closed questions/statements from the questionnaire used earlier in The Hague were answered by male and female secondary school students who were approximately 15 years old.[7]

5 Results

In presenting the results, I shall concentrate on the compositions written by the pupils of the highest grade in elementary schools in the first half of the 1970s and the second half of the 1980s. When writing the compositions they were approximately between 11 and 12 years old. I shall refer to some comparable results from the questionnaire research I did in The Hague at the beginning of the 1970s and the replication conducted by a colleague in Nijmegen at the end of the 1980s to clarify certain information from the compositions. The analysis will be predominantly qualitative with the aim of discerning possible changes in children's images, fantasies, and representations of offenders over 15 years.

There has not been much change in the forms of behavior children associate either with prisoners or "bad persons". In both surveys, crimes against life, like murder and manslaughter, and, indeed, crimes against property, like shoplifting, breaking and entering, and bankrobbery are emphasized. The stolen items continued to be money and jewelry, but radios changed into videos. A change over time can be discerned in connection to victimization of significant others. Breaking and entering in the night or during the holidays with nobody present in the house is described as an event to which significant others have fallen victim. This has become a topic for some of the children in the 1980s, whereas these events were hardly mentioned in the 1970s.

A marked change has come about in connection with the use of drugs. In the 1970s, the use of drugs was mentioned as a form of behavior that could lead to imprisonment. Children did not specify the kinds of drugs nor did they distinguish between soft and hard drugs. In the 1980s, the use of specific hard drugs like heroin and cocaine is mentioned in direct relation to crimes of property. This relationship is regularly posited as a spiral movement. Children expect addiction to hit hard right after the first time hard drugs have been used. They expect these forbidden goods to be quite expensive, creating a need for money which will develop into a greed caused by the steady increase in quantities of hard drugs necessary to meet the addiction.

People expected to trespass the penal code are classified as outsiders. According to at least half of the 1980s' group, this can be perceived by characteristic differences in dress like wearing black clothes, a black cap, and a black mask. This will make "bad persons" less visible after dark, which time of night is supposed to be the normal working time of criminals. In the 1970s' group, distinct physical looks were only mentioned by the youngest age group of 6- to 7-year-olds. Among the older children in that research group, discernable dress appearances could then be gathered from the drawings added to the compositions. Black and white striped prisoners' uniforms were abundantly present, as well as masked persons dressed in black carrying bags to contain the "loot". The visibly discernable exterior possibly stands for a symbol of the invisible interior of the "others".

Characteristics attributed to offenders also show them to be perceived as outsiders or "others". We shall see that this is a recurrent aspect of the relevant fantasies, although their social dressing changes. In both questionnaires - in the 1970s and the 1980s - positive and negative adjectives had to be underlined when they were thought to be applicable to a bankrobber and a drunken driver. No positive attributes in either of the two surveys were underlined. Also, no change in the attribution of adjectives to the two types of offender can be perceived. Bankrobbers are typified by words like dangerous, mean, greedy, and dishonest pertaining to the total image of the person. Drunken drivers as well are indicated as dangerous but also as dumb, stupid, and crazy. The two types of offender were introduced in order to discern possible variations in representations of offenders and possible variations in behavior which are labeled judicially as *mala in se* and *mala prohibita*. This division also clarifies the overlap of the moral field and the field of penal law. Crudely stated, *mala in se* refers to both legally and morally condemned behavior, whereas *mala prohibita* refers to legally forbidden behavior.

The dangerousness as well as the other characteristics of the drunken driver apparently refer to his or her temporary state and form of behavior. Drunken drivers are seen as "outside-insiders" who will return to their insider status after sobering up. Apparently this form of behavior hardly stimulates fantasy. In terms of pronouns, they could be typified as "you". Bankrobbers, prisoners, and "bad persons" are portrayed as "they", as socially distant from the children themselves. However, in some of the compositions written in the 1980s, a number of children take the role of the "bad person". This "persona" does exciting things but inevitably ends up in a police station or in prison.

Indeed, imprisonment is regularly referred to as a successful judicial activity. Occasionally children require harsher reactions from the judges whom they expect to punish leniently. Contrary to these demands are the fears that the wrong persons will be imprisoned. Then the children find themselves confronted with the insoluble problem of proving innocence in the case of innocence. They do not as yet know that in penal process, the burden of proof is on the other side, which induces them to produce fantasies about the struggles and strategies necessary to establish the truth.[8]

In comparing the compositions over time no change has come about in the self-constraint children practice with regard to their wish for capital punishment. Children in the Netherlands hardly make any mention of this kind of punishment, which has been abolished since 1870.

In the questionnaire research in the 1970s, the children were asked expressly to account for the origin of criminal behavior. It then turned out that girls and children from lower-class backgrounds tended to refer to *need*, to "objective" circumstances like poverty, bad friends, unemployment, and bad schooling, whereas boys with higher social background predominantly referred to *greed*, to subjectively motivated and goal-oriented behavior like the wish for enrichment or the quest for fun and excitement. Looking at the compositions, it appears to be specifically characteristic of children from middle- or higher-class backgrounds to assume and to suggest unquestioned explanations for why crimes are committed. Those appear to be similar to the ones mentioned in reply to the questionnaire.

However, there appears to be an interesting change in the accounts mentioned as far as responsibility, guilt, or intentionality of the perpetrators are concerned. In the 1970s, regular mention was made of psychological disorders and the necessity of treatment for the offenders. This sort of account is completely absent in the compositions written in the 1980s. Some children implicitly raise the problem of guilt by mentioning feelings of shame or spite which the offender experiences after being caught. These can be interpreted as an allusion to their assumption that the person involved could have acted otherwise and can be held accountable for his or her behavior.

6 Discussion

Eleven- to 12-year-olds do have the capacity to make moral judgments about a restricted kind of behavior which they label as criminal or expect from someone portrayed as a "bad person". They specifically make mention of crimes of property and crimes of violence and associate those forms of behavior with imprisonment. The latter association shows their awareness of the state's capacity to react in an organized way. These moral judgments of crimes and criminals are partly a cognitive product: They *know* that certain forms of behavior are punishable, and they *know* that the police can be involved in order to solve these kinds of problems. They are also able to make *judgments* about crimes and criminals, to classify in categories of good and bad, in deviant and respectable. As with the need for an "outsider", such divisions into two types (good and evil) are common to all fantasies regardless of all social circumstances. This tells us something important about the process of incorporation of moral capital. It relies both on fantasies with recurrent themes (the outsider, the division into good and evil) and on social perceptions which shape or dress the fantasies according to changing social circumstances.

However, the concept of moral capital not only pertains to moral judgments. It also pertains to the capacity to convince others of one's judgments. In other words, it refers to symbolic power. The above-mentioned research material was mainly aimed at gaining insight into the contents of moral judgments and shows how some fantasy "universals" operate together with changing social representations. Little can be said here about the differential distribution of moral capital within and between the various groups studied. The compositions in the 1980s' research were written after class discussion, and they indicate the production of a certain consensus in moral judgments within the same class. No follow-up research was conducted on the process through which this consensus was reached, so it is not possible to clarify the relative symbolic power of either the teacher or the students in the construction of this part of social reality. Shortly, I shall return to the transcultural aspects of fantasies in concluding this paper. But at this point, more needs to be said about their specific social aspects.

In the diachronic comparison of the results from the 1970s and the 1980s, some changes in the representations of crimes and criminals can be discerned. The most obvious changes are the reference to the use of drugs and drug-related crimes, and to the victimization of significant others. These changes in children's moral judgments and representations reflect changes on other levels, especially changes in prevalence of drug usage as well as changes in the drugs policy of the Dutch authorities. It was only at the beginning of the 1970s that hard drugs really entered the Dutch drugs market, and, during that very period, the Dutch government changed its law enforcement policy. In 1973, a guideline for the public prosecution was adopted to separate markets for marihuana (hashish) and hard drugs and to remove the sale and consumption of marihuana from the hard drugs scene. The intentional effects of this policy have been accompanied by unintended but welcome effects like a decrease in the number of young people using marihuana despite the de facto decriminalization which has made soft drugs available for any interested consumer (Rüter, 1986: 150).

The development of the hard drugs market went together with other social developments like rising unemployment especially among the newcomers from the Maghreb countries and from Surinam, a former Dutch colony, as well as rising rates in crimes of property. More people than before have been victimized in the sphere of property. One might say that, together with other democratization processes, the chance to become a victim has also become an equal opportunity in the Netherlands. These developments produced tantamount media coverage about drug-related property crimes. These changes on the macro level had effects on a change in the production of moral capital on the institutional level. Governmental rhetoric changed from moral to technical-legal discourse in connection with perpetrators, while the police and the public prosecution gradually started to pay more attention to the problems of victims (Lissenberg, 1990).[9]

The shift in children's accounts with reference to responsibility, guilt, and intentionality of the offenders clearly indicates that changes in social reality as produced at the institutionalized level are reproduced in their perceptions. During the 1980s, the notions of individual responsibility and accountability of offenders returned into the legal discourse and into the courtroom (see Komter, 1991). The children's accounts reflect these changes, at the same time as they are combined with the recurrent aspects of fantasies already discussed. In the above-mentioned respects, the changes in children's judgments are produced and structured by changes in reality construction on other social levels. This relationship also shows when considering the self-control children practice in connection with their wishes to impose capital punishment. This gives an intriguing illustration of the interconnectedness of moral capital at the objectified, the institutionalized, and the embodied level. As stated above, capital punishment was abolished in the Netherlands in 1870, and since then it no longer forms part of the objectified moral capital materialized in the penal code. Consequently, the officials structuring the penal apparatus do not have the institutionalized symbolic power to impose and execute capital punishment. In countries in which the death penalty is still part and parcel of the organized reactions of the State, I expect that children will mention the death penalty more frequently.

Their frequent reference to murder in the 1970s' and the 1980s' research gives the impression that these crimes of violence happen regularly. This is not matched by reality in the Netherlands. Although the number of deaths caused by deliberate infliction of bodily harm in our country is increasing, it only rose from 0.56 per 100,000 inhabitants in 1970 to 0.78 per 100,000 in 1985 and to 0.98 per 100,000 inhabitants in 1989.[10] Homicide is closely linked to fear and specifically to fantasied fear. The extensive media coverage of each separate case of homicide adds fresh fuel to this.

7 Conclusion

The way in which children construct and structure social reality pertaining to crimes and criminals is not only a reconstruction and restructuring of reality as presented by others, but is also "informed" by their fantasies, which have recurrent or transcultural aspects as well.

The images of prisoners constructed by children in the framework of my research in the 1970s were unequivocally negative. The same goes for the representations of "bad persons" given in the 1980s. While knowledge about crimes and about the possible reactions of the State has changed over time, the images of offenders have not. They seem to have transhistorical contents. The fantasied images hardly bear on reality nor can reality ever match them. However, socially constructed images can easily be linked to these fantasied images when the former matches the latter in some way, for instance, through the connection of the fantasy of the evil other(s) with an attribute like dangerousness. I formerly interpreted these constructions as a magical form of problem solving, deploring the imagined threat, and, at the same time, legitimating exclusionary reactions toward offenders. And I continued to explain the reactions as a distant form of external control toward offenders (Lissenberg, 1979: 100). However, fantasies about criminals and their behavior should also be interpreted as a means of self-control. In fantasy, children do indeed picture themselves as "bad persons", but, at the same time, they imagine the possible negative reactions they will then experience, which restrain them. And also by having fantasies about "dangerous others" who will be or have been punished, they more or less consciously come to grips with problems of social control.

The social constructions of criminals seem to be an amalgam of restricted knowledge and judgments and more or less frightening and exciting fantasies which children will project in fantasied images either of themselves or of socially distant others. They function as a means of social control, self-control as well as external control, and they are a vehicle for the incorporation of moral capital as I have defined it.

Notes

* I am deeply grateful to Teresa Brennan for her comments on an earlier version of this paper, wich has been presented at the XIth Biennial Meetings of the International Society for the Study of Behavioural Development, July 3-7, 1991, Minneapolis, Minnesota.

1 For a more extensive elaboration in English, see my *Moral capital and the penal code*, paper presented at the International Law and Society Conference, Amsterdam, June 25-29, 1991. This paper is part of the full-length study I am writing on moral capital; see also my publications in the list of references.

2 Bourdieu (1986: 245-247) uses cultural capital to discuss the three levels or states in which capital is manifested and functions. Cultural capital in the *embodied* state is, as the phrasing implies, linked to the body and presupposes embodiment. It is bound to individuals and it is not transferable unless symbolically: "It has the same biological limits as its bearer." Cultural capital in its *objectified* state has a number of properties which are defined only in relation to cultural capital in its embodied form. The cultural capital objectified in material objects and media, such as writings, paintings, monuments, instruments, and so forth, is transmissible in its materiality. In the objectified state, cultural capital can be seen as the *means of production*. Indicating what he means with cultural capital in its *institutionalized* state, Bourdieu switches to educational capital and points at academic qualifications, certificates of cultural competence which have a relative autonomy vis-à-vis their bearers and even vis-à-vis time and place.

3 See Cohn and White (1990, in particular Chapter 2 and Conclusion) for the current "state of the art" in this field.

4 In an international comparative analysis, the uncovering of the various forms of international dissemination may be facilitated by the use of the recapitulation theory as a heuristic device, provided that fantasy is added to that recapitulation theory, thereby avoiding the problems of assumptions that there are unchanging biological givens in behavior; if there were, the same processes would be repeated across civilizations, when evidently, and as I have noted, they are not. In other words, fantasy permits us to talk of recapitulation, without condemning us to cross-cultural or historical universalism.

5 An extensive quantitative and qualitative analysis of this research has been reported in my book *Kinderen spreken recht* (Lissenberg, 1979).

6 I am thankful to Robert Pohlkamp who used to be coordinator of the educational program "Delinquency and Society". He handed me the output of his "replication" study of my research in the 1970s, see note 5.

7 See Project poenale voorlichting. Over effect van repressievoorlichting op crimineel gedrag in het bijzonder van jongeren [Project penal education. About the effects of education on criminal behaviour in particular of youngsters], Nijmegen, 1990.

8 I expect the majority of adults in the Netherlands not to be aware of this most important characteristic of criminal law procedure.

9 Cremer-Schäfer and Steinert (1991) discuss a similar development in the FRG.

10 In absolute figures, this refers to 48 male and 26 female victims in 1971, 88 male and 38 female victims in 1985, and 106 male and 41 female victims in 1989. In the USA in 1989, the number of deaths caused by infliction of bodily harm per 100,000 inhabitants was 8.9. I would like to thank Herman Franke for handing me these data.

References

Becker, H. (1966). Whose side are we on. *Social Problems*, 239-247.

Bettelheim, B. (1976). *The uses of enchantment.* New York: Knopf.

Bourdieu, P. (1979). *La distinction. Critique sociale du jugement.* Paris: Editions de Minuit.

Bourdieu, P. (1986). Forms of capital. In J. G. Richardson (Ed.), *Handbook of theory and research for the sociology of education* (pp. 241-258). New York: Greenwood Press.

Brennan, T. (1991). The age of paranoia. *Paragraph, 14.*

Cohn, E.S., and White, S.O. (1990). *Legal socialization. A study of norms and rules.* New York: Springer.
Cremer-Schäfer, H., and Steinert, H. (1991). Herrschaftsverhältnisse, Politik mit der Moral und moralisch legitimierter Ausschluss. *Kriminologisches Journal, 23,* 173-188.
Elias, N. (1969). *Über den Prozess der Zivilisation,* 2 vols. Bern und München: Francke.
Elias, N. (1976). *Introduction* to the Dutch translation of N. Elias and J. L. Scotson, Established and outsiders. A sociological enquiry into community problems. London: Frank Cass & Co, 1965 (Gevestigden en buitenstaanders, een studie van de spanningen en machtsverhoudingen tussen twee arbeidersbuurten, Uitgeverij Het Spectrum, Utrecht/Antwerpen, pp. 7-46).
Gilligan, C. (1982). *In a different voice. Psychological theory and women's development.* Cambridge, MA: Harvard University Press.
Goudsblom, J. (1977). *Sociology in the balance.* Oxford: Basil Blackwell.
Komter, M.L. (1991). *Accountability in courtroom interaction,* Paper presented at the International Conference of Law and Society, Amsterdam, June 25-29.
Lissenberg, E. (1979). *Kinderen spreken recht* [Children's jurisprudence]. Alphen aan den Rijn: Samsom.
Lissenberg, E. (1989). *Verlagen en verheffen* [Degrade and elevate]. Alphen aan den Rijn: Samsom H.D. Tjeenk Willink.
Lissenberg, E. (1990a) *Het morele kapitaal* [The moral capital], in: Justitiële Verkenningen.
Lissenberg, E. (1990b), Book review of Elly Rood-Pijpers' People on crime and punishment, in: *Rechtshulp.*
Lissenberg, E. (1991). *Moral capital and the penal code,* Paper presented at the International Conference of Law and Society, Amsterdam, June 25-29.
Lurie, A. (1990). *Don't tell the GROWN-UPS.* London: Bloomsbury.
Piaget, J. (1968). *The moral judgment of the child.* London: Routledge and Kegan Paul.
Piaget, J. (1973). *The child's conception of the world.* London: Paladin.
Rood-Pijpers, E. (1988). *Mensen over misdaad en straf* [People about crime and punishment]. Arnhem: Gouda Quint.
Rüter, F. (1986). Drugs and the criminal law in the Netherlands. In J. van Dijk, C. Haffmans, F. Rüter, J. Schutte, and S. Stolwijk (Eds.), *Criminal law in action. An overview of current issues in Western Societies* (pp. 147-165). Arnhem: Gouda Quint.
Tapp, J., and Kohlberg, L. (1971). Developing senses of law and legal justice. *Journal of Social Issues, 27,* 65-92.
Tapp, J.L., and Levine, F.J. (1970). Persuasion to virtue. A preliminary statement. *Law & Society Review, 4,* 565-582.
Young, J. (1971). The role of the police as amplifiers of deviance, negotiators of reality and translators of fantasy. In S. Cohen (Ed.), *Images of deviance* (pp. 27-61). Harmondsworth: Penguin Books.

Part V

Legal Aspects of Diversion

Introduction to Part V: Legal Aspects of Diversion

The final part of this volume discusses issues related to diversion from the viewpoint of legal science.

First, Otto Backes raises the question of the constitutionality of diversion. This entails two criteria that any crime policy has to meet: First, the principle of "ultima ratio", which says that penal law is only a means of last resort that has to give way to other, less intrusive measures when such means are available; and second, the principle that only the lawgivers are entitled to determine which behaviors should be subject to criminal prosecution and punishment. Both principles are violated, Backes argues, when crime policy makes heavy use of diversion. The lawgivers' discussion about the appropriateness of the means of control is replaced by administrative rules that are not limited by law but tend to determine in which realms of crime policy law is applied and in which it is not.

Michael Voss points out that diversion is to a large extent guided by the principle of efficiency, which stands in stark opposition to the "rule of law". He goes on to identify and investigate three powerful interest groups that, he argues, are the driving forces behind the rise of diversion observed during the last decade in Germany: First, in the realm of politics, we find demands toward increased use of criminal law accompanied by the growing insight that regulation of societal problems is impossible by state intervention. The result is informal justice that emphasizes the symbolic power of the law, while, at the same time, leaving its application to arbitrary administrative rules. This is, second, also in the interest of the administration, primarily of the Ministries of Justice who have to meet the public's demands toward criminal law with scarce resources. Third, the "professions of prevention" prefer "soft law", governed by the principles of "good intent" and education, to "hard law", which emphasizes close observation of legal rules, due process, and the defendants' rights.

Detlev Frehsee, with bitter irony, shows how the principle of treatment or "Erziehung" (the problematic meaning of this German term, which is covered neither by the concepts of treatment, education, or welfare, is expounded in his introductory section) guiding the German discussion on diversion leads to insoluble contradictions with the repressive aims of juvenile criminal law and is also quite inconsistent in itself when applied to delinquent youth. Why should juveniles acquire, in a diversion program set up for delinquent youth, skills like dexterity, concentration, and perseverance, which are useful not only in legal activities but also in illegal behavior? Why, if such skills are deemed so valuable by society, are such programs not offered to all youth, and predominantly to the law-abiding among them? But he also points out the weakening of legal safeguards that arises when, as a reaction to a petty offense, youth have to take part in social education programs that extend over considerable periods of time and may, indeed, be much more intrusive than the reactions an adult would receive for the same type of offense.

Stephan Barton compares diversion to defense as an institution in criminal law whose aim is decriminalization, that is, the lessening of the amount of intrusion of criminal law into the lives of delinquent youth. While, on the surface at least, this aim is common to diversion and to defense, their methods and strategies differ widely. Diversion means informal justice, leading to the abandonment of legal guarantees while at the same time necessitating a harmonious stance toward the institutions of law enforcement. In contrast, defense uses all the formal provisions of law that may be in the interests of its clients, and hence very often has to attack, and not to bargain with, prosecutors and courts. Diversion takes the norms that define criminal behavior for granted and seeks the easiest way out; defense, instead, in its critical attitude toward the state's claim of the right to punish, may initiate learning processes about those norms and cast doubts on this claim.

Dieter Rössner's starting point is the assertion that diversion, in seeking decriminalization by way of criminal procedure, leaves the material norms of criminal law intact, those norms that define certain behavior as "crime" in the first place. These norms often stand in contrast to the life-world of adolescents that is characterized by its own norms that therefore sometimes may clash with those of the adult world. In addition, from a life-course point of view, norm violation may be considered a necessary stage of development that, however, in most instances, results in conformist behavior when commitment to and integration into the adult world develop. With this in mind, he discusses several proposals that try to harmonize criminal norms with the adolescent life world.

Finally, Andreas Ransiek provides a thorough discussion of the privilege of self-incrimination, which protects the interest of suspects prior to and during police interrogation. This principle is most important, given the fact that - in the Federal Republic of Germany - some, although not all, rules of juvenile criminal law regulating diversion assume that suspects have made a confession. Clearly, the prospects of working toward a diversionary decision (even if this is ultimately made by the prosecutor) may be used by the police as means of putting pressure on an otherwise recalcitrant suspect to confess. In the light of this, Ransiek's interpretation of police interrogation not as a fight between the police who want to "discover" the "truth" and the suspect who wants to "hide" it, but as an interaction between two parties who have to have equal chances in the process of construction of truth, can serve as an important guideline for the evaluation of diversion practices from the legal point of view.

The lessons to be learned from these contributions obviously should not just be important for legal scientists. They reveal the wide range of questions that might and should be considered in evaluating the outcomes of crime policy. The fact that some contributors, notably Dieter Rössner, have to point out the imperfection and provisional character of the ideas they discuss, is significant in itself. It shows how much energy has been absorbed by the discussion on diversion, with the result of neglecting other, possibly more comprehensive and radical roads toward decriminalization.

Diversion and Constitutional Crime Policy

Otto Backes[*]

1 Introduction

When I received the topic of this symposium, my opinion was that, although diversion - viewed from the perspective of constitutional crime policy - raised some problems, it could ultimately be brought into line with constitutional crime policy. Nowadays, I would summarize this topic differently and more precisely: Diversion *instead of* constitutional crime policy.

What does "constitutional" crime policy mean? The German constitution does not have much to say about this. But the little that it does say, as well as that which has additionally grown out of the principles of the constitution of the Federal Constitutional Court, should be considered. There are, above all, two basic principles:

1. In forming the social order, penal law must be the ultima ratio in the instruments of the lawgivers.
2. The lawgivers themselves - and none other - must have legally determined the implementation of this means.

Now why should diversion not meet these constitutional demands?

Diversion grew out of the recognition that the application of penal law was inappropriate for certain behaviors that its wording does not cover, could even be counterproductive, and must therefore be circumvented. From this viewpoint, diversion was nothing less than the classical case of a reinstatement of the basic principle of ultima ratio that had been insufficiently considered by the lawmakers; and whoever practiced diversion would in no way usurp penal competence but would far more reduce the competence exercised by the lawgiver to an acceptable level. How does this oppose the constitution?

2 The Principle of Ultima Ratio

The basic principle of ultima ratio states that only careful and hesitant use should be made of penal law. According to the ruling of the German Federal Constitutional Court, two prerequisites must be met before penal law should be applied as a means of control:

1. There must be a lack of suitable means that take a milder form, or their application must have proved to be ineffective.
2. The penal sanction must be appropriate and necessary in order to attain the desired goal at all or to facilitate its attainment.

Decisions on the presence of these prerequisites are made by the lawgivers; the constitutional court has only limited powers to examine them. Although practitioners and scientists can and should discuss these prerequisites, they cannot make binding decisions on them; they are allowed to engage in criminal policy but not in legal ruling. However, diversion is not just crime policy. It is (applied) crime policy through proceedings and thereby legal ruling. I shall consider this and the violation of the principle of democracy that it entails further below. Here, it is only of interest that the crime policy of diversion also impairs the basic principle of ultima ratio, and it does this in two ways.

2.1 The Lack of Milder Alternatives

The basic principle of ultima ratio first requires a search for suitable milder means. When certain types of case arc not considered appropriate for a criminal trial (e.g., because the stolen object was of low material value, the offender has confessed, and there is no prior criminal record), and these cases generally circumvent legal proceedings, then - in the context of diversion - the crime policy issue regarding effective means of a milder kind is either no longer or only insufficiently raised. I shall give two examples.

Example 1. The increase in the number of thefts of automobile radios and, recently, also automobile telephones was predictable. It is fairly certain that this trend could have been avoided by the introduction of quick-out mountings or instruments with easily removable but essential components. "Proactive circumvention", "before the offenders exploit the new technology" would also have been possible in other fields such as the use of credit cards and would have had at least an inhibiting impact on crime.

Example 2. In the 1950s and 1960s, the criminal courts were not insubstantially burdened by fraud processes against so-called commission salespersons who had palmed off some worthless product on buyers. Buyers could only free themselves by challenging their contract on the grounds of serious fraud and taking it to court. The number of such processes dropped abruptly after the legal option was introduced of withdrawing from contracts made with door-to-door salespersons within 8 days without having to give any reason. Similar shifts to civil or insurance law solutions could also be developed for other sectors such as nonpayment on public transportation or shoplifting.

Now, one can certainly raise the objection that the lawgiver is free to organize social order through proactive technical prevention or through sectorial civil or insurance law solutions, but that this cannot also be a task of diversion.

However, this criticism falls down, because the search for alternatives is precisely a necessary element of constitutional crime policy. If this search for alternatives is eliminated, as is the case in diversion, a constitutional prerequisite of crime policy is removed. In this way, opportunities for far-reaching decriminalization are lost. This field cannot be made good even approximately through diversion, because its limitations - material value, confession, and no prior record - are rapidly reached, and, beyond these limits, criminal law is engaged, although it would actually be possible to do without its applications in these fields.

2.2 *Appropriate and Necessary Sanction*

The second aspect of the basic principle of ultima ratio is that the criminal sanction must - given a lack of milder alternatives - be appropriate and necessary to attain the goal at all or facilitate its attainment. This aspect is also not taken into account sufficiently in the diversion approach.

Example 1. When fines were introduced in 1985 for failing to wear seat belts in automobiles, a district court judge in Swabia declared them to be unconstitutional. In the judge's opinion, not wearing a seat belt obviously did not violate any third person's rights. The encroachment into general freedom of action, which could be seen in punishment through fines, could therefore be justified only if it was in agreement with constitutional order, in particular, the basic constitutional principles of necessity and reasonableness. As the judge actually said (AG Albstadt, 1985, translated):

"Measured against these basic principles, punishment ... through fines cannot be upheld. The lawgiver has violated above all the basic principle of reasonableness. He is, so-to-speak, shooting down sparrows with cannons while, in other fields, in which things are very urgent, he shows a passivity that is almost grotesque .... While the lawgiver shows his full severity to those who drive without seat belts, who are, no doubt, potential victims of traffic accidents, he undertakes far too little against the sources of danger that actually lead to accidents in which the seat belt should prove its worth.

An example of this is the practically unrestricted use of motorbikes on the open roads. Here, one is almost tempted to speak of a perverted market economy in which the desire for profits is even allowed to walk over dead bodies .... Motorbikes with 1,200 cc, that develop 100 horsepower, that can accelerate from 0 to 100 kilometers per hour in 4 seconds, and achieve top speeds of 230 kilometers per hour are no rarity. An 18-year-old is allowed to buy such 'hot seats', also on credit, and he can drive them as long as he has gained the necessary driver's license, without any personal driving practice. The judge making this ruling is very familiar with the mentality of young persons as a juvenile court judge; and as a traffic judge with many years experience, he is not unfamiliar with the particular dangers of overpowerful motorbikes. So he can do no other than name the slowness of the lawgiver in this field a crime against our youth." (p. 928)

The local district judge continues - in this pathetic tone - to denounce the campaigns against speed limits by "an unholy alliance consisting, among others, of automobile manufacturers and a motorbike association that campaigns one-sidedly for the interests of a speed-obsessed minority." (p. 928)

Although this ruling was soon overturned by the court of appeal at Stuttgart, among other reasons, because the court could not prescribe to the lawgiver which measures it had to undertake within the range of its far-reaching formal freedom, the ruling clearly reveals that constitutional sanctions are directed more toward potential victims of traffic accidents than against those who consciously create or permit such sources of danger. In other words, those who only introduce criminogenic situations or opportunities, who merely tempt, can feel safe from the intervention of criminal law, because such behaviors located in the vanguard of legal property violations that can hardly be assigned to a specific individual are miles away from the criteria of the criminal law system that are oriented toward individual behavior. Therefore, they cannot be assessed.

The same picture is obtained from a look at shoplifting in self-service supermarkets. Almost as a matter of course, criminal law takes the side of the shopkeepers in representing their interests against the shoplifter, even in situations in which the violation of these interests is almost provoked and the wares are consciously presented in such a way that the buyer will want to grab them and take them, so that, as a conclusion, increases in shoplifting are seen as confirmation of successful marketing.

Diversion, which is applied here and protects the shoplifter from criminal sanctions, remains one-sided. It continues to be attached to the umbilical cord of criminal law. Even when it abstains from criminal sanctions and criminal procedures, it presumes - like criminal law - offense and offender, and only these. However, whoever prepares the form of the situation of the crime or introduces the opportunity; whose interests are possibly one-sidedly protected here; how, for this reason, this sector of society can be organized more effectively; these and similar structural issues are not and cannot be the topic of a crime policy that remains fixated on a starting point of criminal law that is centered on the individual.

Constitutional crime policy has to reach further. It must not be satisfied with the issue of how certain interests can be protected by applying criminal law to an individual, but has to address the issue of how these interests can be determined effectively outside of criminal law so that the implementation of criminal law becomes unnecessary.

Example 2. We all know that environmental law has hardly any impact on the large-scale polluters who place massive burdens on the environment with their production. For these polluters act within the bounds of law. Their activities are justified by administrative regulations, permits, and the like. If one wants to influence this environmental pollution and change it, then it is necessary to try to change permit procedures, to introduce public liability insurance, product liability, tax incentives, or the like. The only thing that is certain is that direct environmental protection through the means of criminal law would have no prospects of success. For the criminal justice system would generally fail in the face of the complex and complicated procedures of large companies. A concrete proof of guilt could hardly ever be obtained, and there would be a strong risk that, in the jungle of industrial in-service competences, only marginal figures would be caught and the sanctions imposed on them would then be absurd. Criminal law and criminal procedures, in conclusion, are not the place to tackle structural problems in society. Therefore, the goal of crime policy cannot be to suggest a penal pseudo-solution to this problem by demanding a criminal law against "the powerful of this world".

However, for diversion this is no topic. In contrast, it only strengthens the false impression that a criminal law from which petty crimes have been removed is intrinsically "in order".

3 The Lawgiver's Monopoly in the Implementation of Law

If crime policy manages to reach the conclusion that control over a certain area of life can only succeed through the means of criminal law, the application of this means must be defined legally by the lawgiver. The basic principle of certainty suffices for the lawgivers only when they specify limits for both the inclusion as well as the exclusion of types of case. It would therefore be unconstitutional for the lawgiver to formulate far-reaching operative facts and hand over their restriction to a socially acceptable measure of adjudication.

Now, it naturally seems reasonable to refer to Sections 153, 153a, 154 of the German Code of Criminal Procedure or Sections 45 and 47 of the Juvenile Justice Act that prescribe the dropping of charges and thus the abstention from material criminal law under certain conditions. Recourse to these regulations certainly represents a correction to far-reaching penal provisions. There can be no objections to this as long as charges are only dropped after the examination of the facts in the *individual case*. When, in contrast, guidelines or general criteria are set up that serve to drop charges in the case of a *general* presence of facts - that is, with disregard for the single case - and, as a result, criminal law is not applied, then this is an encroachment into the lawgiver's competences. Diversion represents such an encroachment.

Although this emphasis on the constitutional separation of powers may seem formal and insistent, the reasons are more far-reaching. I shall mention only two:

1. Separation of powers is separation of competences, that is, it may be assumed that the lawgivers possess more possibilities of appropriately solving conflicts than the criminologists and jurists who move within the field of criminal law. There are, as the Federal Constitutional Court ruled in the context of Section 218 of the Penal Code on abortion (BVerfGE, Vol. 39):

"various possible solutions ... depending on the judgment of actual conditions, the concrete goals and their priority, the suitability of conceivable means and paths. The decision, which frequently follows compromises and is carried out in procedures of trial and error, belongs ... within the jurisdiction of the ... lawgiver." (p. 71-72, translated)

Even the Federal Constitutional Court does not consider itself to be competent to take over this decision from the lawgiver. Then "otherwise, the court would be forced into a role for which it is neither competent nor equipped." (p. 72, translated)

2. When crime policy, and thus also diversion, is applied in procedures and thus raised to a means of control, then legality no longer has an independent value. Laws no longer limit crime policy; it is far more the case that crime policy determines the limits of the law. Such trends may currently seem acceptable, and even agreeable, because the crime policy is well received. However, as a result, other crime policies will have to be accepted when the application of criminal law is no longer legitimized by law but by need for punishment. We know where this leads. Werle (1989) has formulated this as follows for the judicial criminal law and the police fight against crime in National Socialist Germany:

"Judicial penal decisions are not legitimized by reference to norm texts but through agreement with the will to punish of the political leadership that uses the law, among others, to control the administration of justice .... Criminal law itself is only *one* means by which the state intervenes intensively in the fight against crime; the judiciary is only *one* organ for implementing penal authority." (pp. 733-734, translated)

4 Conclusion

My conclusion regarding diversion is that it tends to hinder rather than encourage more fundamental and comprehensive reforms of criminal law. Diversion redefines the relationship between crime policy and criminal law in a way that threatens the constitution.

Note

* Translated from German by Jonathan Harrow at the University of Bielefeld.

References

Werle, Gerhard, 1989. Justiz-Strafrecht und polizeiliche Verbrechensbekämpfung im Dritten Reich. Berlin/New York: de Gruyter.

Cases

AG Albstadt, in Neue Juristische Wochenschrift 38, 1985, 927-928; overturned by the court of appeal at Stuttgart, in Neue Juristische Wochenschrift 38, 1985, 3085-3087.

BVerfGE: Entscheidungen des Bundesverfassungsgerichts [Rulings of the Federal Constitutional Court], Vol. 39, No. 1: Urteil vom 25. Februar 1975 (Schwangerschaftsabbruch, "Fristenlösung"), 1-95.

Efficiency Interests and the "Rule of Law" in Informal Proceedings

Michael Voss

1 Introduction

The "efficiency" of criminal justice can be related, first, to the preventive effects of proceedings, educational measures, or penal sanctions. Even the avoidance of penal procedures or sanctions can be examined with regard to its preventive effects. Second, the administration of scarce criminal justice resources can be evaluated under aspects of efficiency, for instance, the management of personnel, courtrooms, or prison cells. Third, the criminal justice system can be assessed as a steering medium of the state and classified in this regard as efficient or nonefficient.

Such interests in efficiency are in fundamental contradiction to the formality of the criminal proceedings (see Hassemer, 1990a: 266): Educationally oriented juvenile court hearings should not be limited in their good intentions through mandatory sentencing guidelines or a time-consuming appeal system. Calculating costs and benefits of the proceedings should not unnecessarily become prolonged through far-reaching rights to produce evidence or participatory rights of the accused. Finally, political steering interests - in the net of conflicting and highly variable social interests - should not be denied the possibility of political maneuvering through steadfast definitional elements of an offense or legal obligations to prosecute ("principle of legality" - principle according to which prosecution of an offense is mandatory for the public prosecutor).

Formality binds. Criminal proceedings yielding the pressure of future oriented steering interests inevitably reduce legal links which tie penal interventions to conditions existing in the past. Limiting or strengthening power, guaranteeing the rule of law, or administrative efficiency: Each aim demands specific legal regulations. Steering efficiency - in the sense of the optimization interests outlined above - and the rule of law cannot be achieved by one and the same procedure (see Naucke, 1990: 254-255).

Which specific problems concerning legal safeguards are related to the widespread informalization of criminal proceedings? Comparing the basic principles of constitutionally based criminal proceedings with the modern strategies of informalization - known as "diversion" - an unaffected observer is forced to argue that unequivocal administration of law and informal strategies of case settlement are incompatible.

The principle of the separation of powers should avoid, for instance, that the power to punish is monopolized in one hand. The separate assignment of functions should guarantee reciprocal control. The independent judge is responsible only to the principles of law and not subject to political direction; instead, he or she has to check the legality of state action. Diversionary proceedings, on the contrary, are characteristically in the hand of a state executive agency; normally, they are decided by the public prosecutor autonomously.

The principle of the commitment of the adjudicative power to the law demands that the citizen has to be informed beforehand about the legally protected objects and the sanctions directed against infringements of law. Diversionary rules typically modify the normative prerequisites for prosecution in a way that erects additional conditions for criminal liability through criteria such as the amount of damage or the criminal record of the accused. And the diversity of legal consequences frankly counts as a quality mark of a diversion policy oriented toward particular case decisions.

Does the informal juvenile justice system therefore have to accept the verdict of Hassemer: "Social control with the sharp means of the criminal law without formalization of this control is barbarism" (1990b: 93)?

Not at all. At least dogmatically experienced criminal law teachers have no problems in certifying that the informal juvenile justice system is not in contradiction to the constitution. After a detailed test of the "legal problems of juvenile criminal law reform", Dölling (1989: 264) ascertains that the flexible system of the Juvenile Justice Act (JGG) and its practical implementation would "stand up to a constitutional examination". The independent suggestion of educational measures on behalf of the public prosecutor would not infringe the sentencing monopoly of the court, since the juvenile accepts voluntarily a "service" offered according to Section 45 II of the Juvenile Justice Act; also, the presumption of innocence (of the accused until he or she is found guilty) is not endangered, since a determination of guilt remains undone (1989: 251-252). On the contrary, he argues, the diversion-oriented juvenile justice reform renders outstanding service to the legal principle of proportionality (between offense and legal consequence) and the thought of subsidiarity of judicial reactions (see, also, Heinz, 1989: 39-40). And, finally, the avoidance of unnecessary burdens for the accused - which is a programmatic claim of diversion - has to be valued likewise as a constitutional gain (Dölling, 1989: 264).

In this chapter, no attempt is made to provide a contribution to this dispute. One author "proves" with precision that intervening diversionary measures on behalf of the public prosecutor necessarily represent a violation of the presumption of innocence (see Kuhlen, 1988: 32, 52). Other authors "prove" not less precisely the contrary (see Dölling, 1989: 252; Ostendorf, 1991: 426 et seq.). Obviously, dogmatic legitimations of the criminal justice system are quite arbitrary. This judgment corresponds to general observations made by the "Critical Legal Studies Movement" whose members maintain: "to each statement of dogmatics the exact contrary can be derived with its assistance too" (Teubner, 1989: 12, citing Unger, 1983). In the following sociological statement, conditions shall be addressed which support an informalization of the criminal justice system. The consequences of informalization policy in the course of the "diversion movement" will be analyzed as well.

2 Informalization of the Juvenile Justice System

In a long-term perspective, it should be indisputable that the criminal justice system in general and the juvenile justice practice in particular have developed toward "informalization".

Juvenile delinquents arrested by the police for offenses of lower severity hardly experience formal criminal proceedings. Under recourse to generally formulated opportunity norms, preliminary proceedings are dismissed by the public prosecutor or the court hearings are dismissed by the judge - with or without conditions. Informal regulations appear as a concession to counter threatening consequences (stigmatization). However, they may appear as a burden in terms of the rights of defense and participation stipulated in the Code of Criminal Procedure which are unable to come into force through the early closure of the proceedings (see Kühl, 1987: 145).

In reference to statistics from 1988, the public prosecutor's offices in the Federal Republic show a "diversion rate" of 27.1% (dismissals according to Section 45 of the Juvenile Justice Act in reference to all indictable cases); if dismissals by judges are included, the diversion rate reaches 52.5% (see Heinz, 1990a, and this volume). If one refers to all prosecutorial decisions combined (including dismissals according to insufficient evidence for a charge based on Section 170 II of the Code of Criminal Procedure), only 46.3% of indictable cases are brought to prosecution (see Ludwig-Mayerhofer, 1990: 83).

Sanctions defined by law and carried out by state agencies (e.g., fines) are being replaced increasingly in the informal juvenile court proceedings by educational measures which emerge freehand - and disappear again. They are offered mostly by private organizations. With recurrence to unspecific legal terms, public prosecutors, judges of the juvenile court, youth welfare services, or private project managers develop alternative sanctions at their pleasure. A wide range of community service, educational aids through social workers, or social competence training courses can be found. Creative forms of leisure-time or adventure pedagogics like camping tours, sailing courses, or mountain-climbing are part of the modern juvenile justice sanction system (see Frehsee, 1988, and this volume). In modern victim-offender-reconciliation programs, the decision on a suitable measure is achieved finally within the free discourse of the conflict partners under the instruction of social workers or gifted private citizens.

Strategies of informalization adopt legal rules which differ strongly from the conditional structure of formal law. The discretionary norms of the Juvenile Justice Act or the Code of Criminal Procedure open up the decision on dismissal or prosecution to extrajudicial criteria. Indefinite legal terms, for instance, "educational measure" (Section 45 of the Juvenile Justice Act) or "directives" (Section 10 of the Juvenile Justice Act) allow for a high variability in criminal justice practice.

3 Conditions for the Informalization of Juvenile Court Procedures

What are the driving forces behind the triumphal march of informalization within the criminal justice system? At least three spheres of interest in different social subsystems can be distinguished which each require strategies of informalization and flexibility in specific ways. These are the spheres of interest of politics, criminal justice administration, and prevention professions.

3.1 Politics

In the social subsystem of politics, legislation and law application - like political programs in general - are evaluated less on the grounds of their practical utility but calculated merely for their political "exchange value". The support of broad and heterogeneous voter groups has to be secured; powerful and frequently conflicting social interests need to be considered and balanced. Hence, political strategies follow in which "the greatest possible variety of available options becomes institutionalized" (Stangl, 1985: 26). In his inquiry into criminal law reform in Austria, Stangl concludes that the "tendency in the modern civil and penal law legislation to take recourse to discretionary norms and unprecisely defined legal terms" (p. 26) is an expression of such a political market logic.

On the one hand, within a "risk society" (Beck, 1986), the political system is confronted continuously with growing demands for the protection from threats. From the perspective of legal science, this is mourned as the "almost boundless free disposability of legally protected interests" (Lüderssen, 1989: 7). Lüderssen (1989) mentions a multitude of legal interests which have been newly created or recently proposed by the legislator: threats to nature (law on protection of the environment), protection of communication (information processing act), protection of economy (credit card fraud), state security (right to demonstrate), or protection of the human being (gene technology restrictions). In all these areas, an application deficit of crime control is preprogrammed. It is caused alternatively by the procedural suspending of the material norm (case dismissal) or through its self-suspension by a norm construction which filters the range of law application by administrative regulations (e.g., limiting values in pollution control laws). The particularized validity of law is necessarily joined with the instrumentalization of the (penal) law as a means of symbolic problem intervention. "The formulation of clear conditional programs in the swirl of the balancing of political interests" cannot be successful - just as the citizen is incapable of a "parallel understanding of the injustice of this type of criminal law" (Herzog, 1991: 64).

Comparing the normative claim for the rigorous protection of legal interests with the discretionary power of modern law enforcement procedures, this appears to be a retreat to a symbolic form of criminal justice. The legal claim for norm obedience is openly opposed to the perception of system-based violations of the law: On the one hand, the state is obliged to apply criminal law with its categorical principles to stop the destructive utilization of soil, air, and water for the protection of humanity. On the other hand, the state finds itself obliged to hold the utilization costs of soil, air, and water down in order to protect economic world market interests. Under the verdict of its claim for crime prevention, the criminal justice system has to stop juvenile delinquency. But the law enforcement agencies are forced simultaneously to accept a certain amount of socially grounded or educationally necessary juvenile delinquency for the further welfare of youth.

Juvenile delinquency, which can be attributed to all juveniles, settled within the criminal justice system in the majority of cases without formal hearings and without a need of prevention, irritates our traditional idea of criminal law and criminality. The criminal norms and the criminal justice system are evidently less in a position to stabilize the difference between conformity and deviance independently of space and time (see Bettmer, 1991: 41-42). In addition, the procedural particularization of prosecution is underlined by the creation of penal norms disclaiming universal validity by means of politically steered principles of application (see, e.g., the regulations in the environment protection statutes, Sections 324-330d of the Penal Code). The political manipulation of the legal obligation to prosecute leads, on the one hand, to renunciation (typical juvenile mass delinquency; overloaded urban court districts); on the other hand, to consistent application of the norm program (drug dealing; relieved rural court districts). The publicly discussed delinquency is freed in this way from a binding categorization as crime. Therefore, it is once more open to competing definitions of meaning (e.g., nuisance, resistance, civil disobedience). In this way, the majority of juvenile delinquency has become normal.

The weakening of the obligation to prosecute reflects the dissolution of social standards of normality and differences in the social perception of deviance. At the same time, it points to a changed functionalization of criminal law as a means of social control. Society is differentiated today into far-reachingly independent functional and cultural areas with their own specific normative demands. Original meaning becomes lost and is replaced by always new definitions of meaning. The range of available conduct models expands explosively; normatively bound images of normality decrease (see Kreissl, 1987: 104-105). In the fundamentally "disenchanted world" (M. Weber), everything can be argued, and deviance can also become recognized as an attribution and be rejected. The social sensitivity toward visible deviance has declined just as the susceptibility for deviating conduct styles has increased - if the deviation, measured against the traditional standards of normality, is still recognized at all. The criminal justice system logically now perceives society itself as crime-provoking and pursues new crime prevention strategies by using diffuse definitions of danger and suspicion (see Preuss, 1989: 489).

Of course, criminal law instrumentalized through discretionary norms by given political needs does not solve the conflict between system-produced norm violations and normative claims on the inviolability of the norm. It allows, however, on the one hand, the maintenance of the demand for the legal protection of interests by the means of individual prevention. Material law remains untouched: Shoplifting or joy-riding remain (normatively) criminal. On the other hand, the law enforcement administration accepts by its systematic dismissal of proceedings that societal problems cannot be steered by criminal law principles of guilt: The criminal sanctioning of shoplifting or joy-riding is suspended. This kind of decentrally modifiable criminal law functions almost as a buffer between the symbolically raised claim on universal norm validity and the actual disposability of the norm. The prosecution of crimes becomes procedurally flexible; it is left to the discretion of the administration. In this way, the symbolic validity of the norm can be linked with massive renunciation of intervention in one offense group and with intensified law enforcement in other offense groups (see Albrecht, 1990: 36).

Accordingly, Naucke (1986: 203) states as an essential character of "current law": "Bound to the rules and to know, however, that you have to apply them only if you look upon them as appropriate - you can escape the norm if you want". Remembering how rapidly conceptions of normality change, the legislators free themselves from the long-term bindings of the law. Laws are no longer enacted for all eternity, but for a period of time or on demand.

3.2 Administration of Justice

Politics disposes of needs for symbolic intervention and, in this way, steadily increases the amount of rules. The administration of justice is held to manage scarce system resources. Furthermore, the political expectations concerning symbol-carrying law enforcement campaigns are naturally extended to the responsibility of the administration. By the application of informalization strategies the administration of justice strives toward:

1. relief of time- and cost-intensive proceeding stages;
2. flexibility in the coordination of jurisdictional resources with the caseload; and
3. selectivity in steering the tight court hearing resources considering the changing definitions of offense severity.

Sentencing guidelines enacted by the justice administration authorities provide an opportunity to re-evaluate criminal offenses without any public attention. Criminal norms which seem unsuitable or secondary with regard to political or administrative interests can be suspended without really touching the norm and the interests of norm lobbyists. Cases can be filtered as they arrive by varying criteria of severity while neglecting the written definitions of criminal law. In this way, a generous liberal attitude toward ubiquitous minor offenses can be joined with get-tough strategies against system-endangering crimes.

Accordingly, the success of the diversion movement is explained mainly in economic terms.

In his inquiry into US diversion policy, Andrew Scull presents the assumption of the fiscal crisis of the state. The welfare state finds itself compelled to cut down expenses within the criminal justice system as well. Alternatives to expensive and inflexible formal proceedings and custodial institutions are needed. Under recourse to the economic analysis of O'Connor, Scull locates the origin of the fiscal crisis in the growing burden of the state budget through measures directed at the social and economic infrastructure, through production subsidies, or ecological follow-up costs (see Scull, 1980: 159-168). These continually growing budget shares are governed by strong organizations and social interests. Cheap and privately offered counseling services and noninstitutional sanction alternatives for the least powerful members of the society thus gain budgetary attraction. This is reinforced by the fact that the noninstitutional alternatives compete with institutions whose proverbial inefficiency ("school of crime") at the same time receives scientific confirmation ("nothing works", Martinson, 1974).

One criticism of such a fiscal argumentation is that actual diversion policy cost savings are not provable in pre-post comparisons. On the contrary, diversion policy has been stimulated especially in the USA, to which Scull refers, through state subsidy programs. Besides, the institutional sector - side by side with diversion policy - has been further expanded, which is also criticized by the "net-widening" assumption (see Ludwig, 1989: 15-16; Matthews, 1989: 4).

In fact, it can be shown easily that cost savings in the criminal justice budget cannot have been achieved. The mere fact that the prison system has expanded speaks against it. This has come about parallel to the growing utilization of noninstitutional measures (see U.S. Department of Justice, 1983). Also comparisons of open and institutional forms of crime control show that the costs for staff-intensive counseling services are very similar to the costs of institutional accommodation (see, for the State of Massachusetts: Schumann and Voss, 1981: 217). Evaluations like those undertaken by Pfeiffer (1983: 315-320) to verify cost reduction after the implementation of non-institutional forms of control rest ultimately on the requirement that the institutional system is diminished proportionate to the growing use of the open measures. Up to now, either in Germany or in the USA, nothing similar has happened.

Even if absolute cost reductions are not demonstrable, it would be presumptuous to dismiss the fiscal thesis. A decline in cost increases also has to count as budget saving. In this regard, diversion policy might work quite effectively. Influenced by the state-sponsored diversion policy, the cheapest form of procedural settlement shows a high ratio of increase at the public prosecutor's offices, namely unconditional dismissal ("diversion to nothing"). By this means, an increase in prosecutorial proceedings can be absorbed with least expense. But also the privatization component of diversion policy together with the per capita payment for services has made the justice budget more flexible and avoided subsequent costs in the shape of state officials or state institutions.

The assumption of a fiscal crisis explains diversion policy in the wake of a general redistribution within the public budget. The resource assumption, on the contrary, starts much more concretely from the consideration that the relationship between dismissals and charges is steered simply by the caseload. Accordingly, diversion policy is due not only to global budgetary decisions but also to economic and technical (rooms, specialists) pressures within the justice system; indeed, their boundaries are described correctly by the fiscal thesis. The origin of procedural rules of discretion in the German Code of Criminal Procedure ("Emminger reforms" in the 1920s) has been explained already with reference to capacity limitations within the criminal justice system. Accordingly, the increase of regulatory demands on the state has drastically expanded the extent of material law and forced procedural simplifications (see Kunz, 1980: 25-26). Because of the strong increase in prosecutorial proceedings in the Federal Republic in the 1970s, the public resources for "granting law" have been exhausted again (see Feltes et al., 1983: 846-847; Heinz, 1984: 24). Much empirical evidence supports the assumption of a capacity-influenced informalization policy. A regional study on "Alternative Reactions in Juvenile Criminal Law" confirmed that a connection exists between the crime rate and the application of dismissals (see Spieß and Storz, 1989: 149; Heinz and Spieß, 1984: 57; see also Heinz, this volume). A longitudinal study on the district attorney's office statistics likewise showed that periods of high caseload are accompanied by high rates of dismissal according to Sections 170 II and 153 I of the Code of Criminal Procedure (see Hergenröder, 1986: 162).

4 Professions of Prevention

Up to now, I have dealt with informalization lobbyists who naturally look after their interests persistently but, however, tend not to publicly articulate these interests in order to avoid threats to the legitimation of law. Those in the interest groups addressed below have delivered the political legitimation for diversionary reform. Criminological scientists, pedagogical professionals and social workers belong to the interest groups which deal with the optimization and implementation of crime prevention measures.

Criminology substantiates the informalization of criminal proceedings by referring to the labeling approach and the control paradigm. According to labeling theory, crime is nothing but a common expression for the only phenomenon which has to be explained: criminalization. Accordingly, it is not the technical inefficiency of the institution which hinders the solution of the crime problem. Instead, it is the institution that constitutes the crime problem. Thus, the institutions of social control achieve a new role with respect to criminality. As part of an offender-based explanation of crime, courts and prisons could also be discussed as places of criminal infection or therapeutic inefficiency. Precursors of today's familiar criticism of imprisonment can be found already in great numbers in the scientific literature of the last century (see, e.g, Scull, 1980: 131-143). In this kind of traditional criminological literature, the agencies of control appear as an amplification of crime which is basically caused by the criminal personality. The control paradigm, on the contrary, defines the criminal justice system as an imperative condition in the emergence of a social meaning of "crime". There is simply no crime without a corresponding authorized attribution of social meaning. Consequently, the conclusion has to be: Let's do less (Martinson, 1974: 48; Wilkins, 1964: 103) or nonintervention (Schur, 1973: 153-173).

The diversion strategies of the 1970s and 1980s inspired by the control paradigm thus represent a thoroughly new phenomenon compared to the dismissal of criminal proceedings in the 1920s (Heinz, 1990b: 8, on the contrary, points to this as a continuous development). Of course, the economic calculation of justice administration also had an effect on the rate of dismissals, which increased again in the 1970s. Nevertheless, the scientific and, with its offender- and offense- related restraints, also the arguments on behalf of the Ministry of Justice recognize that a new argument is now entering the debate. In the scientific reasons for diversion, the crime-generating function of criminal prosecution outlined by the control paradigm is stated frankly (see, e.g., Sessar, 1984: 39). The avoidance of prosecution becomes a preventive means sui generis: prevention of crime through the renunciation of prosecution, or more clearly: the avoidance of criminalization. In contrast, the diversion policy of the Ministries of Justice still justifies dismissals as a means of providing education: Through a rapid informal reaction to offenses, which is carried out within the social surrounding, the educational process is furthered in a youth-related way.

Both criminal policy positions differ clearly from the belief in the possibility of a technical and professional solution of the person-related crime problem still included in the Prison Act (*Strafvollzugsgesetz*) of 1977. At this time, the task of rehabilitation was still regarded completely as a task of specialized clinics and treatment experts who should fight criminogenic tendencies with the help of thorough personality diagnoses and elaborated treatment programs (see Heinz and Korn, 1973: 149-231). Only 10 years later, these hopes rest on the self-healing forces of socialization and - at best - on interventions within the community. "The usefulness of inaction" is a typical headline of the early scientific debate on diversion programs (Kerner, 1981: 690).

To provide necessary space for pedagogics or other purpose-oriented criminal policy, there is an imperative need for the departure from formalized law. Insofar, modern youth criminal law reform ("diversion") stands completely in the spirit of the early Juvenile Court Movement. Due process, granting subjective rights of the accused, has been perceived above all as a barrier to the realization of educational aims in the history of youth criminal law. The reduction of formal legal rules was seen as a basic requirement for the evolution of a flexible decision program oriented toward educational purposes. The judge bound up in classical criminal law thinking executed the conditional program, which tied pertinent legal consequences to exactly fixed requirements of application. The juvenile court judge of the modern school - today, this is mainly the public prosecutor - should be guided by the general clause of good intent, that is, the educational purpose of the law. In this model, the criminal offense has lost its limiting function against state intervention (see Voss, 1986).

The rejection of due process categories by the education-oriented reformers of the Juvenile Court Movement was consequent insofar as education is not compatible with conditionally programmed law. Both the old and the modern legal requirements called for by the educational reformers demand complete closeness instead of constitutionally demanded distance, continuous relations instead of momentary sanctioning, and normative vagueness of the legal consequences instcad of normatively given sanctions. As a consequence, juvenile law reform has been directed toward the abolition of legal dogmatics and the formality of law since the beginning of the century (see Voss, 1986).

5 Effects of Informalization Policy

Whether an informalized criminal justice system has to count as constitutional or not might arouse little interest in an accused who benefits from noninterventive strategies. The accused will comment positively on the informal proceedings, looking on the favorable result. The debate on whether informalization is congruent with the constitution or not might appear purely academic to him or her.

Indeed the question of constitutionality cannot depend on the accused's evaluation of the outcome of proceedings. Free discretion typically does not precede the result of the proceedings. Therefore, discretion cannot be accepted because presently it seems to be politically opportune to use discretion in favor of informal strategies. The policy of informalization can be interrupted at any time or used for other offenses by the very norms which now lead to informalization. To prolong the current informalization policy into the future, a legislative solution is needed, finally based on material law reform.

However, I shall first continue to discuss the practical consequences of the diversion movement for the accused. The essential aspect is not the interests of a single accused but the outcome of informalization policy. It has to be asked to what extent a decline in the rate of charges and in the rate of institutional sanctions in favor of dismissals and noninstitutional measures has been stimulated by the diversion movement during the 1980s.

First, I shall consider the level of case dismissals in the Juvenile Court. In 1980, the conviction rate (related to the number of adjudicated persons) was 57.4%. In 1989, the conviction rate was almost unchanged at 58.3%. An increase of dismissals by the juvenile court judge has not occurred as a result of the diversion movement - in complete contrast to developments in the 1970s. In 1970, the conviction rate was still 70.6% (see Pfeiffer, 1983: 52, and own calculations from the statistics of convicted persons - *Strafverfolgungsstatistik* - 1970-1989)!

The sanctioning tendencies of juvenile court judges also show only minor changes. In 1980, 20.4% of the convicted juveniles were sentenced to juvenile detention ("Jugendarrest"), and 5.1% received youth imprisonment without probation. In 1989, the rate of juvenile detention was 18.3%, which indicates a minor decline. At 5.5%, an almost constant number of juveniles were sentenced in 1989 to prison without probation. In this field as well, diversion policy has caused only insignificant changes.

These statistical findings may appear unimportant since the efforts of diversion policy were directed essentially at an expansion of prosecutorial dismissals. But, again, there is no clear effect. Using statistics presented by Pfeiffer (1989: 78) for the years 1981 to 1986/1987, it can be shown first that the prosecution rate (formal charges including propositions according to Section 76 of the Juvenile Justice Act leading to a simplified, informal proceeding by the judge of the juvenile court, in reference to all prosecutable proceedings) dropped from 82% to 73.2%. But the efforts of diversion policy were directed, however, particularly toward the avoidance of formal court hearings. If the formal charges in the comparison are decreased by the propositions leading to an informal court proceeding (Section 76 of the Juvenile Justice Act), 63.9% of the prosecutable proceedings led to formal court hearings in 1981. In 1986 this rate fell to 61.1%, which is a decline of 2.8%. In 1987, this "cleared" prosecution rate was 63.2%; in 1989, 62% (see prosecution statistics - *Staatsanwaltschaften* - 1987, 1989). These minor variations cannot be regarded as a success of diversion policy (see, on the contrary, Pfeiffer, 1989).

Within the different kinds of prosecutorial dismissals, an increase in decisions according to Section 45 II of the Juvenile Justice Act can be found (decision of the public prosecutor taken without participation of the judge). The increase stems from two sources: Dismissals according to Section 45 III of the Juvenile Justice Act (application by the public prosecutor, decision by the judge of the juvenile court) and the propositions leading to informal juvenile proceedings (Section 76 Juvenile Justice Act) clearly show declining values. Thus, the essential effect of the diversion movement is not to be found in an increase of informal strategies. The main effect is a shift in competence from the judge of the juvenile court to the public prosecutor. Informal proceedings in the competence or under participation of the independent judge have been replaced by decisions by the prosecutor who is subject to political directives.

Referring to the interests of the accused, the conclusion is: An increase in informalization or noninstitutional sanctioning has not come about through the manifold efforts of diversion policy. At the beginning of the diversion campaign as well as today, a formal juvenile court hearing is experienced by 60 out of 100 accused. Now as before, 20 out of 100 juveniles sentenced by a Juvenile Court are sent to a juvenile detention institution and 5 to a youth prison. Besides the increase in the power and status of the prosecutor, the essential practical effect of the diversion movement might be found in the offer of socialization services as conditions of dismissals. Before the diversion campaign, there were no sufficient organizational resources and no sufficient pioneer spirit to let informal proceedings end with educational measures. Today, the public prosecutor has recourse to a considerable range of socialization aids. Presumably, the standard sanction of informal proceedings in the 1970s was the - predominantly written - warning. Today, dismissals are accompanied by community service, victim-offender mediation, supervision order, and so forth.

Accordingly, the diversion campaign of the 1980s has had, at best, no effects; at worse, it has produced a loss of legal safeguards and growing sanction burdens for the accused.

6 Conclusions

The informalization movement has been triggered - at least in the scientific community - through the correct perception that criminal proceedings and criminal punishment have counterproductive, deviance constituting effects. A further containment of these damaging effects does not seem possible through recurrence to opportunity norms of the Code of Criminal Procedure. Rather, more problematic forms of administrative adjudication have emerged. Thus there is a need to look for legislative ways to strengthen the ultima-ratio character of conflict regulation based on the principles of criminal law. I shall sum up the essential consequences of diversion policy:

1. The diversion movement of the 1980s has caused no further decline of prosecutions leading to a formal court hearing that exceeds the increase of dismissals during the 1960s and 1970s. A better position for the accused in the sense of an avoidance of formal proceedings or institutional sanctions has not been achieved.
2. The shift of independent decision variants to the public prosecutor alone has strengthened the institution of prosecution. This has promoted the steering interests

of politics and justice administration. Through the support of the Ministries of Justice and under recourse to opportunity norms and indefinite legal definitions, educational measures have been able to expand and unfold creatively.

3. The criminal justice institutions have by no means reduced their investigatory capacity and their jurisdictional resources in the course of diversion policy. A public loss of importance of criminal law or the criminal justice system is out of the question. The newly created objects of legal protection indicate an unchanged high interest of the state and social norm lobbyists in criminal law.
4. Diversion-oriented trends toward liberalization in the handling of typical youth offenses have no effects on formal criminal proceedings. In cases of juvenile delinquency which reach the level of court proceedings, criminal justice gives no pardon. Under recourse to the preventive purposes of juvenile justice, the court makes use of harder measures than the criminal court does in the case of adults. The assessment of a sanction on the grounds of educational purpose instead of the offense tends to boundlessness: The conviction rate in juvenile cases is still clearly higher than in criminal proceedings facing adults (see Heinz, 1990a: 215). In the juvenile court, institutional sanctions are imposed more frequently than in adult courts (see Heinz, 1990a: 214). Under the responsibility of the educationally oriented juvenile law - also caused by the essentially higher minimum sentence frame - it is clear that longer custodial sentences are imposed than in adult cases (see Heinz, 1990a: 214; Voss, 1983: 112). Current research by Pfeiffer shows that youthful theft offenders get custodial sentences which are more than twice as long compared to adult members of a control group without application of youth criminal law (Pfeiffer, 1991: 363). Through an increasing number of preconvictions, the educational principle intensifies its effect. Sentences for persons convicted unter Juvenile Criminal Law are three to four times higher than for older offenders (Pfeiffer, 1991: 364).

Diversion policy has not been able to meet its own claims. The rate of formal proceedings has not been reduced, the educational principle tending toward a get-tough policy has not been stopped. The essential effect of diversion is to be seen in an intensified political and administrative grip on the criminal justice system accompanied by a cutback of legal safeguards.

References

Albrecht, P.-A. (1990). Exekutivisches Recht. Eine Einführung in empirische Analysen zur staatsanwaltschaftlichen Diversion in Nordrhein-Westfalen. In P.-A. Albrecht (Ed.), *Informalisierung des Rechts* (pp. 1-44). Berlin/New York: de Gruyter.

Beck, U. (1986). *Risikogesellschaft. Auf dem Weg in eine andere Moderne*. Frankfurt/M.: Suhrkamp.

Bettmer, F. (1991). Auswege aus der Pädagogisierungsfalle: Ergeben sich für die Sozialarbeit neue Perspektiven aus der Informalisierung strafrechtlicher Sozialkontrolle? *Neue Praxis, 21*, 33-45.

Dölling, D. (1989). Rechtsprobleme der Jugendstrafrechtsreform durch die Praxis. In Bundesministerium der Justiz (Ed.), *Jugendstrafrechtsreform durch die Praxis* (pp. 243-264). Bonn: Bundesministerium der Justiz.

Feltes, Th., Janssen, H., and Voss, M. (1983). Die Erledigung von Strafverfahren durch Staatsanwaltschaft und Gericht - Brauchen wir die sogenannten Diversionsmodelle in der Bundesrepublik? In H.-J. Kerner, K. Sessar, and H. Kury (Eds.), *Deutsche Forschungen zur Kriminalitätsentstehung und Kriminalitätskontrolle* (pp. 858-895). Köln: Carl Heymanns.

Frehsee, D. (1988). Zur Suche nach "Alternativen Sanktionen" im Jugendstrafrecht. *Monatsschrift für Kriminologie und Strafrechtsreform, 71*, 281-298.

Hassemer, W. (1990a). Grundlinien eines rechtsstaatlichen Strafverfahrens. *Kritische Vierteljahresschrift für Gesetzgebung und Rechtswissenschaft, 5*, 260-278.

Hassemer, W. (1990b). *Kommentar zum Strafgesetzbuch*, Vol. 1, Sections 1, 2. Reihe Alternativkommentare. Neuwied: Luchterhand.

Heinz, Werner, and Korn, S. (1973). *Sozialtherapie als Alibi? Materialien zur Strafvollzugsreform*. Frankfurt/M.: Fischer.

Heinz, W. (1984). Strafrechtliche Sozialkontrolle. Beständigkeit im Wandel? *Bewährungshilfe, 31*, 13-37.

Heinz, W. (1989). Jugendstrafrechtsreform durch die Praxis. Eine Bestandsaufnahme. In Bundesministerium der Justiz (Ed.), *Jugendstrafrechtsreform durch die Praxis* (pp. 13-44). Bonn: Bundesministerium der Justiz.

Heinz, W. (1990a). Die Jugendstrafrechtspflege im Spiegel der Rechtspflegestatistiken. Ausgewählte Zahlen für den Zeitraum 1955 - 1988. *Monatsschrift für Kriminologie und Strafrechtsreform, 73*, 210-226

Heinz, W. (1990b). Diversion im Jugendstrafverfahren. Aktuelle kriminalpolitische Bestrebungen im Spiegel empirischer Untersuchungen. *Zeitschrift für Rechtspolitik, 23*, 7-11.

Heinz, W., and Spiess, G. (1984). *Reaktionsalternativen im Jugendstrafrecht*, 1. Zwischenbericht. Unpublished research report, University of Konstanz, Germany.

Hergenröder, C.S. (1986). *Das staatsanwaltschaftliche Verfahren*. Frankfurt: Peter Lang.

Herzog, F. (1991). *Gesellschaftliche Unsicherheit und strafrechtliche Daseinsvorsorge: Studien zur Vorverlagerung des Strafrechtsschutzes in den Gefährdungsbereich*. Heidelberg: Decker.

Kerner, H.-J. (1981). Diversion - eine wirkliche Alternative? In H. Kury and H. Lerchenmüller (Eds.), *Diversion. Alternativen zu klassischen Sanktionsformen*, Vol. 2 (pp. 688-728). Bochum: Brockmeyer.

Kreissl, R. (1987). Die Krise der Theorie des Wohlfahrtsstaates. Konsequenzen für die Verrechtlichungsdebatte. *Kritische Vierteljahresschrift für Gesetzgebung und Rechtswissenschaft, 2*, 89-111.

Kühl, J. (1987). Zur "Rasterfahndung" und "vorbeugenden Verbrechensbekämpfung". In *10. Strafverteidigertag* (pp. 145-161). Landsberg: Weismann.

Kuhlen, L. (1988). *Diversion im Jugendstrafverfahren. Rechtliche Probleme von Alternativen im Jugendstrafverfahren*. Heidelberg: C.F. Müller.

Kunz, K.-L. (1980). *Die Einstellung wegen Geringfügigkeit durch die Staatsanwaltschaft*. Königstein/Ts.: Athenaeum.

Lüderssen, K. (1989). *Die Krise des öffentlichen Strafanspruchs*. Frankfurt/M.: Metzner.

Ludwig, W. (1989). *Diversion: Strafe im neuen Gewand*. Berlin/New York: de Gruyter.

Ludwig-Mayerhofer, W. (1990). Die staatsanwaltschaftliche Diversionspraxis im Jugendstrafrecht - Eine landesweite Aktenuntersuchung in 19 Staatsanwaltschaften Nordrhein-Westfalens. In P.-A. Albrecht (Ed.), *Informalisierung des Rechts* (pp. 47-225). Berlin/New York: de Gruyter.

Martinson, R. (1974). What works? Questions and answers about prison reform. *The Public Interest, 35*, 22-54.

Matthews, R. (1989). Privatization in perspective. In R. Matthews (Ed.), *Privatizing criminal justice* (pp. 1-23). London: Sage.

Naucke, W. (1986). Versuch über den aktuellen Stil des Rechts. *Kritische Vierteljahresschrift für Gesetzgebung und Rechtswissenschaft, 1*, 189-210.

Naucke, W. (1990). Über die Zerbrechlichkeit des rechtsstaatlichen Strafrechts. *Kritische Vierteljahresschrift für Gesetzgebung und Rechtswissenschaft, 5*, 244-259.

Ostendorf, H. (1991). *Jugendgerichtsgesetz*. Kommentar (2nd ed.). Köln: Carl Heymanns.

Pfeiffer, Chr. (1983). *Kriminalprävention im Jugendgerichtsverfahren*. Köln: Carl Heymanns.

Pfeiffer, Chr. (1989). Diversion - Alternativen zum Freiheitsentzug. Entwicklungstrends und regionale Unterschiede. In Bundesministerium der Justiz (Ed.), *Jugendstrafrechtsreform durch die Praxis* (pp. 74-100). Bonn: Bundesministerium der Justiz.

Pfeiffer, Chr. (1991). Wird nach Jugendstrafrecht härter gestraft? *Strafverteidiger, 11*, 363-370.

Preuss, U.K. (1989). Vorsicht Sicherheit. Am Ende staatlicher Neutralisierung? *Merkur, 43*, 487-498.

Schumann, K.F., and Voss, M. (1981). Versuchte Gefangenenbefreiung. *Zeitschrift für Rechtssoziologie, 2*, 168-224.

Schur, E.M. (1973). *Radical nonintervention. Rethinking the delinquency problem*. Englewood Cliffs, NJ: Prentice-Hall.

Scull, A.T. (1980). *Die Anstalten öffnen? Decarceration der Irren und Häftlinge*. Frankfurt/New York: Campus.

Sessar, K. (1984). Jugendstrafrechtliche Konsequenzen aus jugendkriminologischer Forschung: Zur Trias von Ubiquität, Nichtregistrierung und Spontanbewährung im Bereich der Jugendkriminalität. In M. Walter and G. Koop (Eds.), *Die Einstellung des Strafverfahrens im Jugendrecht* (pp. 26-50). Vechta: Verein für kriminalpädagogische Praxis.

Spiess, G., and Storz, R. (1989). Informelle Reaktionsstrategien im deutschen Jugendstrafrecht: Legalbewährung und Wirkungsanalyse. In Bundesministerium der Justiz (Ed.), *Jugendstrafrechtsreform durch die Praxis* (pp. 127-153). Bonn: Bundesministerium der Justiz.

Staatsanwaltschaften (Arbeitsunterlage), ed. Statistisches Bundesamt Wiesbaden, 1981-1989.

Stangl, W. (1985). *Die neue Gerechtigkeit. Strafrechtsreform in Österreich 1954 - 1975*. Wien: Verlag für Gesellschaftskritik.

Strafverfolgungsstatistik, ed. Statistisches Bundesamt Wiesbaden, 1970-1989.

Teubner, G. (1989). *Recht als autopoietisches System*. Frankfurt/M.: Suhrkamp.

Unger, R.M. (1983). The Critical Legal Studies Movement. *Harvard Law Review, 96*, 563-675.

U.S. Department of Justice (1983). Bureau of Justice Statistics Bulletin, *Prisons in 1982*. Washington, DC: U.S. Government Printing Office.

Voss, M. (1983). Über das keineswegs zufällige Zusammentreffen von Gefängnisausbau und der Einrichtung ambulanter Alternativen. In H.-J. Kerner (Ed.), *Diversion statt Strafe* (pp. 95-116). Heidelberg: Kriminalistik Verlag.

Voss, M. (1986). *Jugend ohne Rechte. Die Entwicklung des Jugendstrafrechts*. Frankfurt/New York: Campus.

Wilkins, L.T. (1964). *Social deviance*. London: Tavistock.

The Incompatibility of Treatment and Punishment

Detlev Frehsee

1 Development of and Discussion on "Erziehung" Within German Juvenile Criminal Law

When talking about diversion, we have to keep in mind that, in Germany, this is linked to the discussion on "Erziehung", because the German juvenile criminal law is ruled by the concept of Erziehung. While general criminal law is based on the principle of guilt and responsibility, juvenile criminal law is based on "Erziehung", and is characterized as an "Erziehungsstrafrecht". The decisive term "Erziehung" in this context is very complex. It has previously been translated as "treatment", as the literally more correct translation "education" is even less apt. However, even treatment only deals with *one* component of the German term Erziehung, to which, nonetheless, the critical problems are certainly linked. The term "welfare" is also available and also deals with an important component. When using one of these English terms, I will be somewhat afraid that neither the English nor the German reader will understand me. Perhaps it is better if I use the German term Erziehung when appropriate.

However, even in Germany, nobody really knows what Erziehung actually is in criminal law. In addition, nobody knows how to describe in any clarity the relationship between Erziehung and punishment. According to Nothacker, the current discussion reveals all possible relationships including Erziehung through, alongside, instead of, despite, as, or in punishment (Heinz, 1989: 15; Nothacker, 1985: 358-360). This is characteristic of the discussion on Erziehung in juvenile criminal law in which great effort has been invested in recent years. Although (on the side of legal experts) this above all concerns attempts to rescue Erziehung (e.g., Beulke, 1990: 677), precisely this is a welcome sign of deep uncertainty. Actually, nobody can deny this any longer since: (a) the understanding of the object of juvenile criminal law, that is, legal behavior and deviance in nonadults, has undergone such fundamental changes; (b) it is not law, but how it is processed, that has clearly changed the emphasis of juvenile criminal law practice; and (c) the organization of reactions has seen a notable growth in autonomy that is, in part, far removed from the judicial system.

The introduction of the Erziehung model into the discussion on juvenile criminal law toward the end of the 19th century was intended originally as a way *out* of criminal law, as an exoneration, as an alternative, and not, in contrast, as a rearmament or new legitimation of criminal law. In his most careful appraisal of the historical process of development, Pieplow (1989) has indicated how the original situation could have developed into the present state that is considered so problematic: "It is conceivable that contemporary changes and their protagonists have *turned* this shield *against* punishment and use it for quite contrary purposes" (p. 6, translated).

In any case, the Juvenile Justice Act of 1923 (*Jugendgerichtsgesetz*; JGG) only recognizes measures of Erziehung or punishment in a clearly separated sense of either/or. The problems arose with the introduction of disciplinary measures (*Zuchtmittel*) as a level of sanction linking Erziehung and punishment in 1943 (Wolff, 1991: 45). This new construction was adopted unchanged into the Juvenile Justice Act of 1953. The so-called "continuity thesis" claims a common conceptual identity of juvenile criminal law in both the Federal Republic of Germany and the Weimar republic and proves to be an autosuggestive attempt of cleaning up. With unconcealed authoritarianism, the criminal anthropologist Richard Lange (1964) buried the alternative and autonomous status of Erziehung and made it the slave of punishment:

"Not Erziehung *instead* of punishment but Erziehung *through* punishment is the idea that asserts itself, inseparable from its correlate of also applying as much atonement as possible in the domain of applied Erziehung." (pp. 372-373, translated)

The ultimate consequence is even to see imprisonment as an instrument of Erziehung. As a matter of fact, the German Federal Supreme Court (*Bundesgerichtshof*; BGH) firmly maintains that the clearest punitive sanction, juvenile prison sentence, does serve "the purpose of Erziehung and the welfare of the juvenile" (BGHSt 16: 261, 263; translated). Unimpaired by the fact that the BGH itself has difficulties in maintaining this conceptually, this contrafactual incantation of a normative ideal develops a truly bitter aftertaste when we consider the actual conditions in juvenile prisons and the unavoidable degradations, psychological wounds, and abuses that occur in them (see, e.g., Albrecht and Schüler-Springorum, 1983; Kersten and von Wolffersdorff-Ehlert, 1980).

Recent years have seen increased attempts to fit modern contours to the concept of Erziehung in juvenile criminal law and make it more compatible with current concepts of criminality through reductionist interpretation and functional operationalization. This primarily concerns an emphasis on constitutional restrictions (*Rechtsstaatlichkeit*) (Albrecht, 1987: 61, 63). This goal should serve, among others, to restrict the personality orientation and regain reference to the offense (Kratzsch, 1989: 161; Walter, 1985: 702). Some authors explicitly argue for the renunciation of the Erziehung principle and recommend to refer to the common aims of sanctioning in juvenile penal law as well (Balbier, 1989: 409; Gerken and Berlitz, 1988: 32; Kuhlen, 1988: 25; Müller, 1991: 347; Ostendorf, 1987: 91, 1989: 104; Voß, 1986a: 215-217; for the separation of Erziehung and punishment *within* juvenile criminal law, see Bohnert, 1983: 522-523).

However, we find a majority of very clear defences of Erziehung as a guiding principle of juvenile criminal law and attempts to differentiate its useful and therefore indispensible functions (Beulke, 1990; Busch, 1990: 133; Dölling, 1989a: 318; Eisenberg, 1987; Heinz, 1989, 1990: 41; Kaiser, 1990: 74-76, 77-78; Rössner, 1990: 18; Schlüchter, 1988; Schüler-Springorum, 1982; Walter, 1989). The decisive role is to support the argument that the goal of Erziehung can provide quantitative and qualitative justifications for reducing or limiting punishment. For instance, Heinz (1989) particularly claims that the significant changes in juvenile criminal policy in recent years such as the shift from formal to informal proceedings, from custodial to non-custodial sanctioning, and the growth of new ambulant measures are a product of the basic principle of Erziehung (see, also, Beulke, 1989: 81-82, 1990: 686; Viehmann, 1989: 118-121).

This is precisely where decisive doubts can be raised as to whether (a) changes in criminal policy would not have been implemented even without the Erziehung principle; (b) whether a decision-making and organizational orientation toward the ideal of Erziehung does not also contain disadvantages; and (c) whether there is still an acceptable relationship between the intended blessings and the negative costs, or whether, in some ways, one evil has not been replaced by another.

The problems can actually be illustrated very well with three dimensions of the modern organization of proceedings and sanctioning that are praised as achievements of the Erziehung orientation: namely, new ambulant measures to which juveniles are referred in informal proceedings. Diversion in Germany is seldom "diversion to nothing" but mostly diversion to something else under the control of prosecutor or court (Voß, 1986a: 80). Here, we can now find a wide range of forms of response and care in the Federal Republic of Germany whose variety is not revealed by the mere reading of the law and has actually developed outside the law. There is group and individual treatment with parent and family counseling, community service orders, job application assistance; and assistance in dealing with authorities, accomodation assistance, supported accomodation, establishment of or advice on residential groups, debt counseling, victim-offender mediation, and behavior modification. There are social competence training courses, courses on education, support courses, courses on experience, and even self-experience, or practical courses, motorbike groups, photography, furniture making, boat building, sport, and games; programs to organize fetes or children's parties, to shoot films, to build playgrounds, educational camping, sailing, and climbing tours, boat trips, trips to islands, and much more (Frehsee, 1988).

It is questionable whether this trend should be praised as an expression of creativity and innovative potential in juvenile criminal justice or more as a market, competition, or even uncontrolled growth. The non-German reader will realize in this a development that is far more advanced elsewhere, particularly in the USA (Ludwig, 1986a). Moreover this development is of a much more innovative kind than elsewhere because German criminal law and procedure law has always been of a very strict legality. For instance, in contradiction to most Western countries, German police have no discretionary power at all. Even the discretionary power of the prosecutor is constructed by the law as an exception, although this is now becoming predominant in practice (Albrecht, 1990: 3-11). So the recent tendencies to deformalization give rise to a new sensitivity for doing "Erziehung" under the rule of penal law (Kuhlen, 1988; Plewig, 1990: 42-44).

2 Criticisms of the "Erziehung" Principle Within Penal Law

I wish to present my criticisms by discussing seven traps and false conclusions or fallacies with which punishment through measures of Erziehung is burdened.

2.1 The False Conclusion on Effects

The false conclusion on effects assumes that measures of Erziehung are appropriate for the prevention of future criminal behavior. Even if success cannot be proved, this assumption is often maintained, because then it is declared to be a matter of simply increasing the intensity of measures or of developing measures that will be truly effective. However, such assumptions are confronted with the general lack of findings in the assessment of efficiency and evaluations of international sanction research. This has shown that, despite repeated hopes invested in the further development of Erziehung programs, there is no support for the idea of any decisive breakthrough in criminal pedagogics. Romig's (1978) comprehensive evaluation of more than 800 studies on custodial and non-custodial social therapy programs for juvenile delinquents in the USA is a good example. Romig analyzed 170 of the programs that contained data on possible behavior modifications and were dealing with: single-case assistance, behavior therapy, intensive instruction, occupational training and work, group therapy, psychotherapy, family therapy, therapeutic camping, diversion programs, probation, residential groups and residential homes, and so forth. The tables of results repeatedly present a sobering "no significant difference". This corresponds to Lipton, Martinson, and Wilks's (1975) famous claim that "nothing works" in the field of adult criminality. Such results have formed the basis for hypothesizing the "exchangeability of sanctions", according to which punitive interventions can be reduced in favor of softer measures without any loss in behavior control (Kaiser, 1988: 895). However, there is hardly any hope that the intensification of Erziehung measures will lead to a decrease in recidivism rates (Albrecht, 1988: 388; Heinz, 1990: 39; Kaiser, 1988: 205; Kraus and Rolinski, 1992: 32).

2.2 The False Criminological Conclusions

The false conclusion on outcome effects corresponds to the false criminological conclusion on the origins of misbehavior. It lies in the assumption that criminality should be understood as an expression of a lack of Erziehung. This, in turn, can be divided into two aspects:

The nature of juvenile delinquency. In a first approach, juvenile delinquency is no longer viewed as a deficit or marginal phenomenon. Rather, it is viewed as ubiquitous and, to a certain extent, as normal (Thiem-Schräder, 1989: 74-77). Even in multiple offenders, intensive delinquent behavior is restricted to episodes or phases (Dölling, 1989b: 9,12; Heinz, 1990: 38; Heinz, Spieß, and Storz, 1988: 649-650; Kerner, 1989: 205). David Matza refers to this in his well-known comment that the deficit theories all explain much too much criminality (Matza, 1964: 21-22). Otherwise, we also find criminality, and even major criminality, among the well-educated, and even more so when this concerns undetected criminality (Sessar, 1984). When, among the clients of the courts, the official offender seems to represent a link between criminality and educational deficits, this is already one of the dire consequences of the Erziehung concept in juvenile criminal law, for the common occurrence of the phenomena only confirms that social control (through all formal stages starting with the reported offense) considers, on the basis of a theory of Erziehung, that it has to provide more intensive care for offenders who *also* exhibit deficits in education (Frehsee, 1988: 290-291).

However, if the concept of Erziehung is narrowed down, and the base rates of developmentally determined "normal" delinquency are viewed as confirming that the mature stage of Erziehung has not yet been achieved, then the concept of Erziehung can be equated with norm compliance, it declines into a mere tautology, and is then, although no longer harmful, completely redundant.

The hypothesized causality between deficits in Erziehung and criminality. This also proves to be inappropriate when the mechanistic demands of measures of Erziehung are considered. Indeed, they cannot (in contrast to incarceration measures) produce immediate behavior modification. They try to achieve this by changing personal dispositions toward legal behavior. This goal assumes that the personality qualities to which the measures are geared relate directly to legal behavior. However, this is not the case. Educational programs try to convey competencies and capacities to juveniles such as technical skills, dexterity, concentration, perseverance, organizational and planning ability, tolerance for frustration, increased self-esteem, community awareness, cooperation, solidarity, ability to face conflict, and so forth. However, all these qualities are completely ambivalent with regard to norm-related behavior. They are just as useful for committing an offense safely, carefully, and reliably as they are for optimizing the performance of a legal activity (Frehsee, 1988: 287).

2.3 The False Sociological Conclusion

The false sociological conclusion hypothesizes that criminality is an individual occurrence. Criminality can be explained in all possible ways. However, from all the conceivable approaches, criminal law selects only the delinquent's voluntary decision to oppose the law as the decisive cause. The discrepancy is attributed to defective motivation in the delinquent. This localizes the error; society, social structure, circumstance, victim, and so forth are freed from all responsibility. This model is functional from the perspectives of general prevention, because criminal law strives to achieve social stability by controlling human behavior.

A conception of criminal law based on the idea of Erziehung only goes one step further insofar as it asks - if not to attribute responsibility but at least to organize the legal consequences - to which (exogenic) causes the defective motivational decision can be traced. Nonetheless, this extension remains individualistic, because the diagnosed deficits (e.g., emotional neglect) are not interpreted as deficits in social living space but as personal deficits in the offender. This resembles a "medical model": The delinquent must be cured but not the social environment that has denied the delinquent opportunities for Erziehung (Ludwig, 1989: 34-35).

This model is criminologically inappropriate in its approach, because criminality is an interactive phenomenon that cannot be conceived outside the context of cultural values, embedments in the life-world, and situational action and social references. Although Erziehung only makes sense *within* the context of social reality, the most well-meaning programs generally do the opposite: They *remove* the client from his or her life space and withdraw into special programs. This particularly applies to very impressive interventions such as client-centered counseling, behavior modification, or adventure pedagogics. Situations are created that should offer a learning field for social interactions, an artificial sociotope, a model of real life in whose protected space appropriate reactions to challenges, conflicts, stress, and borderline situations can be tested. The conceptual error is that such training takes place in play situations and protected zones and does not represent real life where things actually become serious.

The fact that problems with relationships, for example, between the individual and his or her social environment, can be dealt with only when this environment is also included (Erziehung of society) is not mentioned at all.

2.4 The Trap of a State Under the Rule of Law

The Erziehung concept falls into the trap of a state under the rule of law by assuming that treatment is always an appropriate punishment.

First, it has to be considered *conceptually* that Erziehung is not only crime prevention but also a means of influencing the personality. The plan to treat the juvenile naturally follows its own quantitative and qualitative standards. The law opens up the doors and gates to these autonomous standards, as the limiting principle of guilt does not apply here. Moreover a set of special procedural regulations facilitates and intensifies intervention (Pollähne, 1989: 100). Among the rules on measures of Erziehung, Section 5 I JGG most clearly permits the underlying offense to degenerate into a mere "cause" for compulsory measures oriented toward the need for Erziehung. It is stated with regard to Erziehung that, in the individual case, it is possible "to go *beyond* the highest level of punishment assigned to the offense" (Dallinger and Lackner, 1965, Section 18, 6, translated). Thus there is a need to revert to the principle of proportionality for limiting purposes. However, the actual value of this is described as follows in a prominent text book: The relationship can only be "viewed negatively": Offense and measure "may not be beyond any relation to each other. Only the unbearable contradiction between offense and measure is forbidden" (Böhm, 1985: 117, translated). The connection "must not be bound by too strong requirements" (Herz, 1987: 55, translated). However, for the execution of juvenile penal sanctions, "the criterion of future law-abiding cannot reasonably be of a limiting function for the design of the pedagogic program" (Beulke, 1990: 681, translated). Qualitatively speaking, Section 91 JGG reveals the unrestricted totality of Erziehung. This rule regulates the "task of juvenile prison". However, it does not contain a single word on criminality or its prevention. It talks about honest and responsible ways of life, about order, work, instruction, physical training, meaningful leisure-time pursuits, occupational achievements, and pastoral care (cf. Ostendorf, 1991a: 351).

The relationship to criminality steps down; the goal of Erziehung becomes autonomous. As more specific regulations on how to achieve this goal and which methods to apply are not given, juveniles are subject to the specific ideas and preferences of the educators assigned to them.

Gerken and Schumann (1988) have characterized the situation with the very appropriate metaphor of the Trojan Horse: The idea of Erziehung proves to be "a Trojan Horse in the constitutional state". Dinitz' (1978: 225) plea to protect the "right to be left alone" also applies to juveniles (see, also, Hassemer, 1982: 165).

Particularly measures of Erziehung also develop autonomous rules on the intensity of intervention in actual *practise*. In the broadest sense, this problem is discussed under the heading of net-widening (Blomberg, 1980: 572; Janssen, 1983: 39).

Social-pedagogic measures such as training courses and climbing or camping tours have fixed frameworks. A person assigned to such a program has to complete the previously organized course, even when it lasts longer than the time that the offender had "earned" through the offense. Juvenile punishment reveals a trend in which the length of punishment is not determined by the offense but by the amount of time required for the juvenile to complete a training program offered in an institution. New programs of Erziehung, particularly ambulant alternatives, that are additionally set up by private organizations want to have full bookings. They advertise in the courts for client referrals in order to remain economically viable.

This "widening effect" is strengthened by the fact that judges, who would otherwise dismiss a case rather than sentence a juvenile to a sanction that is recognized as meaningless or even damaging (e.g., detention), abandon this reserve if they are convinced that a new measure will do the juvenile some good (for the case of youth prison, see Ludwig, 1986b: 338).

Finally, this problem field also involves the fact that the concerns that guide the activities of social workers differ from those of criminal law. Thus, social workers often have difficulties in letting go of clients who obviously need further assistance, although criminal law offers no further legitimation for intervention (Feltes, 1984: 540-541; Haase-Schur, 1985: 213-214).

As a result, empirical research shows that, under the principle of Erziehung, juveniles are sanctioned more intensively than adults (Heidemann, 1988; Pfeiffer, 1991; Walter, 1990: 57-59). This leads to a disadvantage of nonadult defendants in wide areas (Heinz, 1990: 35-36; for an overview, see Kaiser, 1990: 63-65; see, also, Viehmann, 1989).

There is a particular problem with *young adults*. The group of 18- to 20-year-olds is adult according to German law. Yet the judge has to decide whether they will be processed under the jurisdiction of juvenile or adult criminal law depending on their state of maturity (Section 105, JGG). Thus, although measures of Erziehung from both parents and public youth welfare are no longer permissible, the Federal Constitutional Court confirmed in 1987 that *penal* measures of Erziehung can also be applied to young adults (BVerfG, NStZ 1987: 275). The (juvenile) criminal law thus contains the only possibility of applying Erziehung to a specific group of adults (Balbier, 1989: 405-406; Gerken and Schumann, 1988: 4; Müller, 1991: 347).

By the way, here we see that, within this very same age group, sanctions imposed by juvenile criminal law are evidently harder in comparison to the application of adult criminal law (Pfeiffer, 1991: 118).

It is well-known that the proportion of young adults who have been processed under juvenile criminal law instead of general criminal law has continuously and impressively increased in the last 20 years (Ostendorf, 1991b, introductory remarks on Sections 105-106, marginal number 5; Walter and Eckert, 1985). One possible explanation is that the JGG offers much freer and varied possibilities of exerting hegemonic and colonizing influences by educational measures than naked punishment.

It is possible that this is the decisive factor in the conception of Erziehung in criminal law. Perhaps it has nothing to do with the small number of cases of shoplifting and theft from automobiles. The economic system seems to deal with these quite adequately through its own means of regulation, and they have long become a component of the gross national product as economic factors that increase production and turnover.

The decisive function of Erziehung-oriented criminal law may well be to maintain a means of exerting pressure for generally pleasing conduct and obedience. In view of the density of opportunity achieved by economic developments and the density of rules achieved by normative development as well as with regard to the knowledge about ubiquity, we have possibly already arrived at a situation with regard to the social group of youth in which it has become the hidden function of criminal law to provide immediate and legitimate grounds for applying intervention with Erziehung to anyone whom we want to see disciplined because of secondary motivations (see Treiber, 1973: 44).

On the basis of his comparative empirical research on different styles of sanctioning, Pfeiffer summarizes: "The Erziehung principle has become a dangerous indefinite formula to justify infringements of the rights of juveniles that go far beyond what could be legitimized otherwise by criminal law and criminal procedure law" (1991: 124, translated).

2.5 The Educational Trap

The educational trap opens up through the hierarchical relation between education and criminal law. It has to be recalled that education and criminal law, despite certain agreements, have autonomous and not always identical goal orientations.

Through its involvement in legal protection, criminal law serves to maintain the status quo, to secure the present system of privileges and resources, and to stabilize social structures (Haferkamp, 1980: 78-91). In contrast, education focuses on the human being. Education seeks to help the individual achieve a more self-aware subjective quality in his or her social environment. It seeks to foster human autonomy, emancipation, and responsibility; to grant the individual the power to organize and influence his or her surroundings (Müller, 1991: 346). Education is aimed at giving the individual the ability to claim his or her rights to the benefits of society and participate in society's further development. It is therefore decisively *not* directed toward maintenance but toward change or at least a further development of the status quo.

Wherever education permits itself to become involved in carrying out tasks of criminal law, the goals of *criminal law* become binding (Balbier, 1989: 406; Eckert, 1982: 142; cf. Müller, 1991: 348; Plewig, 1986: 261). The intervention applied is not the one that educational diagnosis shows to be important to the juvenile but the one that the *judge* needs in order to express satisfaction with this alternative of Erziehung (Frehsee, 1990: 55). The judge must consider the measure to be sufficient to meet the goals of criminal law. The educator in criminal law must therefore be prepared to *subordinate* empathy and partisanship toward the delinquent in order to serve the protection of the dominance of criminal law. This is why education sometimes refuses to tolerate such "usurpations": "In that punishment implements that which education is not able to achieve, it becomes clear what is expected of education" (Müller and Otto, 1986: VII-VIII, translated).

2.6 *The Criminal Law Trap*

One falls into the criminal law trap when public opinion views the measures of Erziehung as an undeserved pleasure for the adolescents.

Criminal law seeks to counter specific harmful behaviors. It does this by using the existence of behavioral prohibitions and their exemplary application to create, maintain, and bind normative awareness. The countermotivation to the norm violation is culturally anchored by officially disapproving the norm violation.

This need for disapproval does not require any additional, directed evil. Positive, supportive (above all compensatory) measures are just as sufficient to express the disapproval of behavior, because the delinquent is still confronted with the obligation to modify his or her behavior. It also remains clear that the offender has to face the social costs of the disapproving norm presentation.

This mechanism falls apart if legal proceedings awake the public impression that they are purely a reward (Ludwig, 1986b: 334) as can be the case with popular motorbike courses, canoe tours, climbing tours, or sailing tours. In summer 1989, two 18-year-old recidivist robbers were sentenced in Stockholm to a 6-month sailing cruise in the Caribbean at an estimated cost of half a million

Swedish Kronas. This resulted in such a strong public protest that the sentence had to be withdrawn (Loos, 1989: 57-59). It is easy to understand why. If criminal behavior is viewed as the outcome of sociostructural disadvantage, it is completely possible, from a humanitarian and social perspective, to accept and approve when somebody whose previous life has been characterized by neglect has one occasion when something good is done to them. However, this is certainly not a concern of criminal law, and from its perspective, it is more dysfunctional. It compromises its own symbolic power.

2.7 The Sociopolitical Trap

The Erziehung-oriented criminal law falls into the sociopolitical trap when it provides services that are actually the responsibility of the general system of social welfare and social prevention.

Penal measures of Erziehung in certain forms are mere acts of *welfare*. By this I do not mean that juvenile criminal justice claims all its penal measures to be acts of welfare - the German Federal Supreme Court encourages us to believe that even juvenile prison is welfare (BGHSt 16: 261, 263). No - I now mean real, objective welfare, particularly regarding compensation for structural deficits, such as catching up on lost education or obtaining work or accomodation. However, it has to be considered that, alongside the comparatively small number of *detected* delinquents, there is a much larger group of juveniles in similar situations of psychosocial deficit who do *not* become conspicuous in a comparable way. This raises the question why detected delinquents should benefit from such particular welfare but not equally needy *non*delinquents. Almost 100 years ago, the great German reformer of criminal law, Franz von Liszt (1969) had already asked:

> "There can be no doubt that the qualification for improvement is independent of the commitment of a punishable act. Is it not more than wrong to provide state welfare only to those who have committed an offense?" (p. 38, translated)

From this opposite perspective, when authority only provides support to compensate social deficits to those who have created a public disturbance through their criminal acts, the authority is possibly quite content with this. Because a lot more effort would be required to see that *all in need* receive the same welfare.

This possibly provides the criminal law of Erziehung with a completely different functionality, and, finally, it unfolds as an ultimate *social welfare authority*. For example, whereas general youth welfare is unable to care for young male prostitutes due to lack of resources or inadequate legal access, and has to leave them more or less to themselves, there is sometimes the hope that they will commit an offense and thus provide a possible means of saving them. From this perspective, the liberalization of the new Child and Juvenile Welfare Law (*Kinder- und Jugendhilfegesetz*) in force since the beginning of 1990 must be treated with suspicion: As this law no longer contains such strict access possibilities, will stronger recourse be made to juvenile criminal law? Such reciprocal processes could be observed, for example, when a few years ago in Hamburg closed residential homes were opened whereas remand for juveniles was moved back into the legal system's own closed institutions (Bittscheid-Peters and Koch, 1983: 84).

Finally, from a sociopolitical perspective, the following problem arises regarding the recipient of measures of Erziehung that have a rewarding character: When a juvenile is sentenced to a bicycle tour, a photography course, or a specific sport training as a sanction, it has to be asked whether this is really the most important thing when we consider that the causes of deviant life-styles and harmful behavior are to be sought in the cultural, social, economic, and structural relationships of society. Hence, does not something like a climbing tour or the opportunity to spend time on an island possibly have a little bit of the function (from the perspective of society) of throwing the structurally disadvantaged a sweet, of feeding them with crumbs from the table of the meritocracy in order to leave the unequal (and primarily economically determined) life relationships, the network of "above" and "below", unchanged, and thus contributing in very subtle and seemingly philanthropic ways to the stabilization of the structures that specifically disadvantage these clients?

3 Conclusion

Erziehung is no longer acceptable as a legitimation of criminal law. Even for criminological and sociological reasons, the concept of Erziehung proves to be inappropriate to uphold the goals of criminal law, and, in some ways, it even seems to be damaging or dysfunctional.

Criminal law and also juvenile criminal law is - particularly in view of the empirically demonstrated limitations of the effects of special prevention - only still plausibly explainable and implementable as a *societal* institute of public behavior control that is directed toward the *entire* population of an age cohort and is completely insignificant in the individual case. What remains is a function of social norm stabilization that will become even more acceptable the more other systems that guide norm behavior lose their validity in a pluralistic or even anomic society characterized by uncertainty and individualization.

The more far-reaching question that now arises is whether criminal law is needed to protect this normative orientation function.

References

Albrecht, H.-J. (1988). Zur Reform des Jugendstrafrechts in der Bundesrepublik Deutschland, in Österreich und in der Schweiz. *Recht der Jugend und des Bildungswesens, 36,* 387-398.

Albrecht, P.-A. (1987). *Jugendstrafrecht.* München: C. H. Beck.

Albrecht, P.-A. (1990). Exekutivisches Recht. In P.-A. Albrecht (Ed.), *Informalisierung des Rechts* (pp. 1-44). Berlin/New York: de Gruyter.

Albrecht, P.-A., and Schüler-Springorum, H. (Eds.) (1983). *Jugendstrafe an Vierzehn- und Fünfzehnjährigen.* München: Wilhelm Fink Verlag.

Balbier, R.-W. (1989). Brauchen wir ein neues Jugendstrafrecht? *Deutsche Richterzeitung, 67,* 404-409.

Beulke, W. (1989). Wieviel Erziehung ist im Jugendstrafrecht möglich? In D. Rössner (Ed.), *Toleranz - Erziehung - Strafe* (pp. 65-99). Hofgeismar: Evangelische Akademie Hofgeismar.

Beulke, W. (1990). Brauchen wir eine Wende im Jugendstrafrecht? In K. Geppert and D. Dehnecke (Eds.), *Gedächtnisschrift für Karlheinz Meyer* (pp. 677-697). Berlin/New York: de Gruyter.

Bittscheid-Peters, D., and Koch, U. (1983). Menschen statt Mauern. *Zentralblatt für Jugendrecht und Jugendwohlfahrt, 70,* 81-86.

Blomberg, T.G. (1980). Widening the net: An anomaly in the evaluation of diversion programs. In M.W. Klein and K.S. Teilmann (Eds.), *Handbook of criminal justice evaluation* (pp. 572-592). Beverly Hills, CA: Sage.

Böhm, A. (1985). *Einführung in das Jugendstrafrecht* (2nd ed.). München: C. H. Beck.

Bohnert, J. (1983). Strafe und Erziehung im Jugendstrafrecht. *Juristenzeitung, 38,* 517-523.

Busch, M. (1990). Erziehung als Strafe. *Zeitschrift für Strafvollzug und Straffälligenhilfe, 39,* 133-139.

Dallinger, W., and Lackner, K. (1965). *Jugendgerichtsgesetz* (2nd ed.). München: C. H. Beck.

Dinitz, S. (1978). Nothing fails like a little success. *Criminology, 16,* 225-238.

Dölling, D. (1989a). Kriminologisches Grundlagenwissen zur Jugendkriminalität und zum Umgang mit straffälligen Jugendlichen. In D. Rössner (Ed.), *Toleranz - Erziehung - Strafe* (pp. 7-42). Hofgeismar: Evangelische Akademie Hofgeismar.

Dölling, D. (1989b). Mehrfachauffällige junge Straftäter - kriminologische Befunde und Reaktionsmöglichkeiten der Jugendstrafrechtspflege. *Zentralblatt für Jugendrecht, 76,* 313-319.

Eckert, H.-U. (1982). Zur Technik strafrechtlicher Verhaltenssteuerung. *Zentralblatt für Jugendrecht, 69,* 135-156.

Eisenberg, U. (1987). Zur Verantwortung vor dem Erziehungsgedanken im Jugendstrafrecht. *Juristische Rundschau*, 485-490.

Feltes, Th. (1984). Kriminalisierung und Entkriminalisierung durch Sozialarbeit. *Zentralblatt für Jugendrecht, 71*, 537-543.

Frehsee, D. (1988). Zur Suche nach "Alternativen Sanktionen" im Jugendstrafrecht. *Monatsschrift für Kriminologie und Strafrechtsreform, 71,* 281-298.

Frehsee, D. (1990). Segeln als kriminaltherapeutisches Patentrezept? *Zeitschrift für Erlebnispädagogik, 4,* 41-58.

Gerken, J., and Berlitz, C. (1988). Sanktionseskalation. Zum fatalen Zusammenspiel von Erziehungsideologie und Registerrecht. In J. Gerken and K.F. Schumann (Eds.), *Ein Trojanisches Pferd im Rechtsstaat. Der Erziehungsgedanke in der Jugendgerichtspraxis* (pp. 11-39). Pfaffenweiler: Centaurus.

Gerken, J., and Schumann, K.F. (Eds.) (1988). *Ein Trojanisches Pferd im Rechtsstaat. Der Erziehungsgedanke in der Jugendgerichtspraxis.* Pfaffenweiler: Centaurus.

Haase-Schur, I. (1985). Jugendhilfe und Diversion. *Theorie und Praxis der sozialen Arbeit, 36,* 209-218.

Haferkamp, H. (1980). *Herrschaft und Strafrecht.* Opladen: Westdeutscher Verlag.

Hassemer, W. (1982). Resozialisierung und Rechtsstaat. *Kriminologisches Journal, 14,* 161-166.

Heidemann, A. (1988). Kollisionen zwischen den verfahrensrechtlichen Garantien und dem Erziehungsanspruch des JGG bei der Verteidigung Jugendlicher? Probleme und rechtspolitische Alternativen. In J. Gerken and K.F. Schumann (Eds.), *Ein Trojanisches Pferd im Rechtsstaat. Der Erziehungsgedanke in der Jugendgerichtspraxis* (pp. 85-100). Pfaffenweiler: Centaurus.

Heinz, W. (1989). Jugendstrafrechtsreform durch die Praxis. Eine Bestandsaufnahme. In Bundesministerium der Justiz (Ed.), *Jugendstrafrechtsreform durch die Praxis* (pp. 13-44). Bonn: Bundesministerium der Justiz.

Heinz, W. (1990). Die Bedeutung des Erziehungsgedankens für Normsetzung und Normanwendung im Jugendstrafrecht der Bundesrepublik Deutschland. In J. Wolff and A. Marek (Eds.), *Erziehung und Strafe* (pp. 28-50). Bonn: Forum Verlag.

Heinz, W., Spieß, G., and Storz, R. (1988). Prävalenz und Inzidenz strafrechtlicher Sanktionierung im Jugendalter. In G. Kaiser, H. Kury, and H.-J. Albrecht (Eds.), *Kriminologische Forschung in den 80er Jahren* (pp. 631-660). Freiburg: Eigenverlag Max-Planck-Institut für ausländisches und internationales Strafrecht.

Herz, R. (1987). *Jugendstrafrecht* (2nd ed.). Köln: Heymanns.

Janssen, H. (1983). Entstehungsbedingungen, Hintergründe und Konsequenzen einer veränderten Strategie sozialer Kontrolle. In H.-J. Kerner (Ed.), *Diversion statt Strafe?* (pp. 15-54). Heidelberg: Kriminalistik Verlag.

Kaiser, G. (1988). *Kriminologie. Ein Lehrbuch* (2nd ed.). Heidelberg: C. F. Müller.

Kaiser, G. (1990). Die Behandlung junger Rechtsbrecher zwischen informeller Konfliktregelung und defensivem Formalismus - Erziehungsstrafrecht ohne Chance? In J. Wolff and A. Marek (Eds.), *Erziehung und Strafe* (pp. 62-82). Bonn: Forum Verlag.

Kerner, H.-J. (1989). Jugendkriminalität, Mehrfachtäterschaft und Verlauf. *Bewährungshilfe, 36,* 202-220.

Kersten, J., and Wolffersdorff-Ehlert, Chr. von (1980). *Jugendstrafe - Innenansichten aus dem Knast.* Frankfurt/M.: Fischer.

Kratzsch, D. (1989). Plädoyer für eine Revision des jugendstrafrechtlichen Subsidiaritätsprinzips und der Zuchtmittel. *Heilpädagogische Forschung, 15,* 155-164.

Kraus, L., and Rolinski, K. (1992). Rückfall nach sozialem Training auf der Grundlage offiziell registrierter Delinquenz. *Monatsschrift für Kriminologie und Strafrechtsreform, 75,* 33-46.

Kuhlen, L. (1988). *Diversion im Jugendstrafverfahren.* Heidelberg: C. F. Müller.

Lange, R. (1964). Erziehung und Strafe im heutigen Jugendstrafrecht. In F. Lejman (Ed.), *Festschrift für Karl Olivecrona* (pp. 359-383). Stockholm: Norstedt.

Lipton, D., Martinson, R., and Wilks, J. (1975). *The effectiveness of correctional treatment.* New York: Praeger.

Liszt, F. von (1969). Strafrecht und Jugendkriminalität. In B. Simonsohn (Ed.), *Jugendkriminalität, Strafjustiz und Sozialpädagogik* (2nd ed., pp. 38-42). Frankfurt/M.: Suhrkamp.

Loos, D. (1989). Segeln unter pädagogischem Aspekt. *Zeitschrift für Erlebnispädagogik, 11/12,* 25 et seqq.

Ludwig, W. (1986a). Sozialpädagogik als "weiche Kontrolle"? *Monatsschrift für Kriminologie und Strafrechtsreform, 69,* 193-210.

Ludwig, W. (1986b). Die Funktion des Erziehungsgedankens im Jugendstrafvollzug. *Zentralblatt für Jugendrecht, 73,* 333-339.

Ludwig, W. (1989). *Diversion: Strafe im neuen Gewand.* Berlin/New York: de Gruyter.

Matza, D. (1964). *Delinquency and drift.* New York: Wiley.

Müller, S. (1991). Erziehen - Helfen - Strafen. Zur Klärung des Erziehungsbegriffs im Jugendstrafrecht aus pädagogischer Sicht. *DVJJ-Journal, 2,* 344-351.

Müller, S., and Otto, H.-U. (1986). Sozialarbeit im Souterrain der Justiz. Plädoyer zur Aufkündigung einer verhängnisvollen Allianz. In S. Müller and H.-U. Otto (Eds.), *Damit Erziehung nicht zur Strafe wird* (pp. VII-XXII). Bielefeld: K. T. Böllert.

Nothacker, G. (1985). *"Erziehungsvorrang" und Gesetzesauslegung im Jugendgerichtsgesetz.* Berlin: Duncker & Humblot.

Ostendorf, H. (1987). Zur Ablösung des Erziehungsstrafrechts (statement). In Bundesministerium der Justiz (Ed.), *Verteidigung in Jugendstrafsachen* (pp. 90-91). Bonn: Bundesministerium der Justiz.

Ostendorf, H. (1989). Maßloses Erziehungsstrafrecht oder gebändigtes Präventionsstrafrecht. In M. Walter (Ed.), *Beiträge zur Erziehung im Jugendkriminalrecht* (pp. 91-110). Köln: Heymanns.

Ostendorf, H. (1991a). Erziehung im Jugendstrafrecht - Anspruch und Realität. *DVJJ-Journal, 2,* 351-356.

Ostendorf, H. (1991b). *Jugendgerichtsgesetz. Kommentar* (2nd ed.). Köln: Heymanns.

Pfeiffer, Chr. (1991). Unser Jugendstrafrecht - eine Strafe für die Jugend? Die Schlechterstellung junger Straftäter durch das JGG - Ausmaß, Entstehungsgeschichte und kriminalpolitische Folgerungen. *DVJJ-Journal, 2,* 114-129.

Pieplow, L. (1989). Erziehung als Chiffre. In M. Walter (Ed.), *Beiträge zur Erziehung im Jugendkriminalrecht* (pp. 5-57). Köln: Heymanns.

Plewig, H.-J. (1986). Ist das Jugendstrafrecht durch die Sozialpädagogik zu retten? In S. Müller and H.-U. Otto (Eds.), *Damit Erziehung nicht zur Strafe wird* (pp. 253-269). Bielefeld: K. T. Böllert.

Plewig, H.-J. (1990). *Diversion im Rahmen des Jugendgerichtsgesetzes.* Expertise zum 8. Jugendbericht. Universität Lüneburg. Arbeitsberichte des Fachbereiches Wirtschafts- und Sozialwissenschaften. Unpublished Ms.

Pollähne, H. (1989). Jugendstrafrecht ist Strafrecht - was folgt daraus für seine Anwendung? In D. Rössner (Ed.), *Toleranz - Erziehung - Strafe* (pp. 100-120). Hofgeismar: Evangelische Akademie Hofgeismar.

Rössner, D. (1990). Erziehung und Strafe - die verkannte Zweispurigkeit des Jugendstrafrechts. In J. Wolff and A. Marek (Eds.), *Erziehung und Strafe* (pp. 18-27). Bonn: Forum Verlag.

Romig, D.A. (1978). *Justice for our children.* Lexington, MA: D. C. Heath.

Schlüchter, E. (1988). De nihilo nihil - oder: der Erziehungsgedanke im Jugendstrafrecht. *Goltdammers Archiv für Strafrecht*, 106-128.

Schüler-Springorum, H. (1982). Zur aktuellen Diskussion über Strafe und Erziehung in der deutschen Jugendgerichtsbarkeit. In E.-W. Hanack, P. Rieß, and G. Wendisch (Eds.), *Festschrift für Hanns Dünnebier* (pp. 649-659). Berlin/New York: de Gruyter.

Sessar, K. (1984). Jugendstrafrechtliche Konsequenzen aus jugendkriminologischer Forschung. Zur Trias von Ubiquität, Nichtregistrierung und Spontanbewährung im Bereich der Jugendkriminalität. In M. Walter and G. Koop (Eds.), *Die Einstellung des Strafverfahrens im Jugendrecht* (pp. 26-50). Vechta: Verein für kriminalpädagogische Praxis.

Thiem-Schräder, B. (1989). *Normalität und Delinquenz. Sozialarbeit zwischen Resozialisierung und Nonintervention.* Bielefeld: K. T. Böllert.

Treiber, H. (1973). *Wie man Soldaten macht.* Düsseldorf: Bertelsmann Universitätsverlag.

Viehmann, H. (1989). Anmerkungen zum Erziehungsgedanken im Jugendstrafrecht aus rechtschaffender Sicht. In M. Walter (Ed.), *Beiträge zur Erziehung im Jugendkriminalrecht* (pp. 111-133). Köln: Heymanns.

Voß, M. (1986a). Diversion. Eine neue Form der sozialen Kontrolle. In S. Müller and H.-U. Otto (Eds.), *Damit Erziehung nicht zur Strafe wird* (pp. 79-91). Bielefeld: K. T. Böllert.

Voß, M. (1986b). *Jugend ohne Rechte.* Frankfurt/New York: Campus.

Walter, M. (1985). Ambulante Behandlung im Kriminalrecht. In R. D. Herzberg (Ed.), *Festschrift für Dietrich Oehler* (pp. 693-704). Köln: Heymanns.

Walter, M. (1989). Über die Bedeutung des Erziehungsgedankens für das Jugendkriminalrecht. In M. Walter (Ed.), *Beiträge zur Erziehung im Jugendkriminalrecht* (pp. 59-89). Köln: Heymanns.

Walter, M. (1990). Der Erziehungsgedanke im Jugendrecht - Abschied oder Reformulierung? In J. Wolff and A. Marek (Eds.), *Erziehung und Strafe* (pp. 51-61). Bonn: Forum Verlag.

Walter, M., and Eckert, H.-U. (1985). Zunehmende Anwendung des Jugendrechts gegenüber Heranwachsenden. Änderung der Sanktionsstrukturen oder alte Praxis in neuem Gewande? *Monatsschrift für Kriminologie und Strafrechtsreform, 68,* 69-88.

Wolff, J. (1991). Jugend und Strafrecht im Nationalsozialismus. *Zeitschrift für neuere Rechtsgeschichte, 13,* 41-66.

Cases

BGHSt 16: Entscheidungen des Bundesgerichtshofes in Strafsachen [Rulings of the Federal Supreme Court in Criminal Matters], Vol. 16, 261-264.

BVerfG, NStZ 1987: Ruling of the Federal Constitutional Court, published in Neue Zeitschrift für Strafrechtswissenschaft 1987, 275-276.

Forms of De Facto Decriminalization: Diversion and Defense

*Stephan Barton**

1 Introduction

The previous discussion for and against diversion has paid hardly any attention to the role that the defense takes or should take in diversion procedures (Deichsel, 1987: 163; Hansen-Siedler, 1990: 40). As far as positions are available, these cover the broadest possible spectrum of conceivable opinions: Defense is characterized as the "upholder" of diversion (Zieger, 1986: 132) or as the "agent of diversion par excellence" (Deichsel, 1987: 163; Hansen-Siedler, 1990: 41). Against this background, Juvenile Justice Act commentaries or conference papers also assign defense concrete tasks within the context of diversion programs, namely, that they should take the "initiative themselves in the sense of diversion through dismissal or withdrawal of charges" (Ostendorf, 1991, Section 68, marginal number 5; Eisenberg, 1991a, Section 56, marginal number 12), or that they should work together with the public prosecutor by pulling "pedagogical strings" within diversion proceedings (Breymann, 1987: 113-114). In contrast, it has also been questioned whether defense attorneys, by the nature of their profession, do not belong to the "group who criticize diversion on constitutional grounds" (Hansen-Siedler, 1990: 45). The available definitions of the position of defense in relation to diversion could not be more contradictory.

This article investigates whether there are common points of reference between defense and diversion and where the differences, if any, lie. The perspective requires the inclusion of a superior aspect - that of decriminalization - as a focus of attention.

2 The Common Point of Reference: Decriminalization

Diversion is understood here as refraining from further prosecution after the official determination of a penal norm violation (Kaiser, 1985: 72). Despite strong controversy within science and jurisprudence on the legal position and task of the defense (Beulke, 1980; Eisenberg, 1991b: 1257), it should be unproblematic to summarize defense in criminal proceedings as follows: The defense attorney's task, as the professional support of the accused, is to express everything that is in the interests of the accused and is appropriate to exonerate him or her; or - as Alsberg (1930: 11, translated) succinctly formulated it - "to prevent the high- minded, rash reaching for the truth". In this context, the term defense is not understood in terms of the broader concept of substantive defense. This would mean the "assertion of that which can serve to ascertain the innocence or reduced guilt of the accused, be it through this person him or herself, through the judge, or even through the public prosecutor" (Schott, 1886: 1, translated). In the present context, defense is understood in terms of formal defense, that is, as the "legally regulated (formal) protection of the interests of an accused by a person who is particularly assigned this task" (Schott, 1886: 2, translated). When defense is discussed in the following, I do not mean the broad content of the term in the sense of substantive defense but the legal institution of defense or the practice of substantive defense by the formal defender.

Even this short glance at defense and diversion should suffice to show that both have a common point of reference in their interest in decriminalization. Here, decriminalization is understood as everything that avoids punishment, that fends off the intervention of penal law on the level of the characteristics constituting the criminal act or the sanctions (for a more precise definition, see Naucke, 1984: 199). In this context, both diversion and defense aim toward avoiding punishment de facto or at least minimizing it. In this sense, diversion and defense represent various ways of striving toward de facto decriminalization (Kaiser, 1989: 174) that, despite different historical,[1] disciplinary,[2] and normative origins, can be linked together by the common bond of the idea of decriminalization. The following investigates these two forms of possible decriminalization more closely.

3 A Contrast of Forms of Decriminalization

Although the common reference point - the goal - of diversion and defense is identical, that is, decriminalization, there are major differences in the paths toward it. The means and methods adopted by diversion and defense to achieve decriminalization could not be further apart.

3.1 Deformalization: Formal Guarantees

Diversion means withdrawal from a formal penal social control - with not only its rigorous penal sanctions but also its rigorous legal guarantees of strict criminal procedure for the accused (e.g., assumption of innocence, basic principles of oral proceeding, immediacy of the main proceedings, and giving the accused the benefit of the doubt) - in favor of informal social control. Thus, the path taken toward formalizing conflict is reversed. Although informal social control is associated with softer, under some conditions, less disruptive and more flexible sanctions for the accused, there is also a tendency to lose the legal guarantees given in criminal procedure and the constitution. Proceedings occur increasingly behind closed doors, the guarantees regarding the immediacy and oral proceeding of the trial process, the presumption of innocence and giving the accused the benefit of the doubt lose their rigidity.[3] In this way, diversion means a deformalization of proceedings.

Defense is completely different. The task of the defense is also to monitor the legality of proceedings in the interest of the accused. In this sense, defense watches over the law (Dahs, 1983: marginal number 3), not least, with regard to the formality of proceedings. Without formal procedural guarantees, defense would be inconceivable. It is not just that the legal institution of defense is itself the expression of a formal procedural guarantee - namely, the right to legal counsel (Spaniol, 1990: 198 ff.) - but that the defense can only exert an influence and only have an impact by successfully appealing to formally guaranteed procedural rights, or, at least, being able to appeal to them when necessary. Insofar, it does not matter whether the defense always acts by appealing to formal legal guarantees. The possibility of activating these guarantees if required enables it to be regularly active in the vanguard of current procedural conflicts and to exert influence on them.

Thus, if diversion stands for decriminalization through deformalization, defense means the existence and, if necessary, extension of formal guarantees. Without formalized procedure, defense would be inconceivable. At times, stressing formal guarantees is the only possible way for defense to lead to decriminalization.

3.2 Preconditions, Methods, and Side Effects of Decriminalization Through Diversion or Defense

It is evident that a successful decriminalization as a result of diversion or defense requires different surroundings. The environmental niche in which diversion prospers requires the consensus of those involved; diversion can function only when all participants take a harmonious attitude to each other. If just one of the participants withdraws from this consensus, the chances of decriminalization through diversion are rendered much more difficult if not blocked. This particularly applies to the accused and his or her defense attorney.

Successful defense can, in contrast, happily accept conflict. Defense can and must if necessary raise objections and engage in proceedings contentiously, and sometimes even aggressively: "defense is battle" (Dahs, 1983, marginal number 1, translated). At least it has this potential. Decriminalization through defense does not need a consensus between the legal professionals. At times, it can succeed only when the defense attorney does not shy away from battle and perhaps even seeks conflict - sometimes, even for its own sake - in order to achieve the best possible outcome for the accused.

From the perspective of possible effects that increase or decrease the burdens on proceedings, this means that decriminalization through diversion is, to a large extent, an attempt to relieve the authorities of penal social control from some of their work burden.[4] Diversion serves to lessen the load of the justice system.

Defense is a grain of sand in the gears of justice or can at least be such. The function of defense or the outcome of its activities can certainly be to make the adjudication of legal authorities more difficult. Defense tends to have a justice-inhibiting function;[5] it does not make the work of judges and public prosecutors easier but more difficult. Viehmann (1987) has seen this very clearly, and thus points out that defense and diversion do not fit together:

"Diversion proceedings should be dealt with quickly and simply . . . . The involvement of defense attorneys may have a disproportionate impact on such proceedings, lead to a great deal of complication, to exaggeration, contribute to a solidification of fronts, and may lead to real impairments through ignorance of particular aspects of the Juvenile Justice Act and thereby serve to put the breaks on a desirable exploitation of informal means of adjudication . . . . For these reasons, I would tend to advise against any broadening of the inclusion of defense attorneys in the field of diversion." (p. 110, translated)

Breymann (1987) goes even further in that he wishes to resolve the potential tension between unburdening the justice system through diversion and burdening the justice system through defense. He calls for the defense to speed up proceedings in the interests of diversion and in this sense even abandon central rights and duties of defense[6] in order to promote diversion. The content of such a concept of defense would lead to the abolition of any true defense.

In addition, defense and diversion differ in their normative status, in their legal foundations. The right to defense - the exercise of substantive defense by the formal defense attorney - is, to some extent, a central element of the classical and liberal law of criminal procedure[7] and is codified in central sections of the German Code of Criminal Procedure (StPO). However, the rules for applying diversion (the diversion models) are not fixed in law (apart from the standard tags, that is, Section 153 of the Code of Criminal Procedure and Sections 45, 47 of the Juvenile Justice Act [JGG]) but are regulated in ministerial decrees,[8] directives from attorneys general, or other forms of executive activity. Thus, diversion is based on "soft law", is modern "reflexive law", while decriminalization through defense is based on the "hard", clear, and more durable standards of penal procedure.

Diversion and defense differ not only in the means and methods of planning decriminalization but also in their side effects. In other words, they have different latent functions.[9] Dealing with a norm violation through diversion means that the penal norm itself is not questioned, that the validity and steadfastness of the penal rule or prohibition is confirmed symbolically. Diversion in the face of a delinquent's clear expression of opposition to the norm would appear to contradict the system.

Although defense does not need to attack norms, and generally also does not do so, it has this potential. We only need to consider the defense of "crimes of conviction" or the defense of the abortion process at Memmingen in which the defense created a forum for changes in crime policy.[10] This alone represents a major difference between decriminalization through defense or through diversion.

Naturally, everyday, normal defense is not characterized by an active struggle against the validity of penal norms. Defense attorneys would be overburdened if they were turned into professional crime policy makers. Explicit revolt against the legitimacy of penal norms must remain restricted to exceptional cases. However, even everyday, unspectacular defense is quite capable of evoking sudden insight in those involved in diversion and eventually the general public by discussing the questionability of state punishment and the problem of individual responsibility for social (mis)behavior. Sack (1979) formulates this more critically[11] when he assigns defense the function of "processing crime for productive learning processes in society and its normative structures. In concrete cases of conflict and crime, the defense attorney should show why society has had false expectations regarding his or her client" (p. 148, translated).

In this way, any defense can form a thorn in the side of criminal law; at least any good defense is a protection against exaggerated punitive claims of the state and contains the seeds of a rejection of the state and penal law.

In summary, the two forms of decriminalization, defense and diversion, differ considerably in their means, methods, and side effects. Although both aim at decriminalization in the concrete case, diversion can, nevertheless, in some ways be seen as a "sovereignly" organized decriminalization under the auspices of the shared, "well-understood" interests of the delinquent and justice in an economical application of prevention and resocialization. On the other hand, defense is a decriminalization "from below". Defense primarily acts in the private interest of the accused and may additionally - understood against the background of a clash of interests between the state and private interests - fulfill direct social functions (initiation of learning processes).

4 Defense and Diversion in Practice

If the above-mentioned contrast between "sovereign" decriminalization and decriminalization "from below" is accurate, it could be be anticipated that there are also few common points of reference between defense and diversion - particularly in practice. Above all, it could be assumed that defense attorneys do not really know what to do with diversion in their everyday activities. This assumption can be investigated by looking at a study by Hansen-Siedler (1990).

Part of this work on defense in juvenile court proceedings, which was presented as a master's thesis in criminology at Hamburg, is based on interviews[12] with 10 lawyers who had been appointed as juvenile defense attorneys by the Hamburg justice department (see pp. 70, 73).[13] Although the study was conceived as an exploratory prestudy and makes no claims to be representative, its findings are essentially generalizable.

The study shows that defense attorneys on all levels had "few practical experiences" (p. 102, translated) with the Hamburg diversion model.[14] Although the majority knew that a diversion program has also been implemented at Hamburg, this knowledge did not come from their activity as defense attorneys but from personal contacts with the program initiators or from the crime policy discussion that it had elicited in legal circles (see p. 83). However, in their work, defense attorneys had had almost no contact with the diversion program. They also saw hardly any opportunities of including diversion in their activities, as the majority of cases they dealt with were cases of compulsory representation in which they were court-appointed counsels. The pretrial opportunities for diversion stipulated in Section 45 of the Juvenile Justice Act failed because defense attorneys were appointed only at the opening of the main proceedings (see p. 89). Even during trial, the possibilities of diversion were very slight because of the generally nonpetty nature of the charges (see p. 92). The same applied to the prevention of incarceration measures (one of the alternatives of the Hamburg diversion program). In this field, however, Hansen-Siedler estimated that the defense attorneys "lacked information" (p. 100, translated) on diversion alternatives. He concluded that, because formal defense begins only with the commencement of main proceedings, by which the underlying crime could not be classified as petty, and because the attorneys lacked information on the diversion program, diversion and juvenile defense were mutually exclusive (see p. 93).

5 Conclusions

The theoretical discussion and its confirmation in an inspection of the legal situation seem to provide a clear answer to the question whether defense attorneys are "diversion agents" or "upholders" of diversion: Upholders of diversion are public prosecutors and judges, and maybe further persons and institutions (e.g., police and youth welfare) but not and never defense attorneys. In view of the sovereign nature of decriminalization through diversion, defense attorneys as private individuals cannot be upholders of diversion. Defense attorneys are also anything but "diversion agents par excellence".[15] This is already countered by the fact that practical formal defense only occurs when criminal charges are brought or serves a clientele who do not fit into diversion programs.

The contacts between defense and diversion are thus relatively narrow in practice. The points where defense activities touch diversion programs are restricted to exceptional cases. This does not mean that defense does not have any roles to perform together with diversion, but that these are also exceptions.

The tendency toward incompatibility between diversion and defense reveals that the tasks of defense in the context of diversion can in no way be defined just by stating that defense attorneys should uncritically support a diversion program at every opportunity. There are many indications that diversion, understood as an "all-purpose weapon" for defense to deal with petty crime, does not facilitate the substantive defense of the accused. A defense attorney who simultaneously feels committed to promoting diversion would, in my opinion, be a "double agent".[16] He or she would therefore serve the state's interest in sanctioning. Insofar, the situation is comparable with one in which defense seeks its salvation by striving far too uncritically for a so-called court settlement.[17]

It is more the case that the tasks of the defense could be to test the position of the case and legal situation with a view to entering a clear diversion procedure and providing the client with intensive counseling in this regard. In this context, its task may be to scale down the definition of the charge so that it first becomes possible to enter into diversion. There is also a need to investigate whether the readiness in judges and public prosecutors to scale down a charge can be increased or weakened when refusal might lead to a particularly critical defense. If the client desires to seek decriminalization through diversion, it would seem to be contrary to the system for the defense attorney to strive for this goal only with the means of confrontational defense. His or her activities must consist far more in seeking the consensus and in exchanging the arguments to which the diversion program is geared. This should not mean a complete withdrawal of the defense attorney from the function of a sentinel over the strict observation of procedural law. However, the more the defense stresses formal guarantees, the more difficult it will become for the process of decriminalization through diversion.

Hence, diversion and defense have far less in common than anticipated. They prove to be two such different forms of decriminalization that one can even talk about contrasting decriminalization models. They refer to a different clientele (adolescents - adults), concern different charges (petty crime - intermediate and serious crime), and use completely different means and methods. Defense as the classical 19th century liberal-constitutional concept of decriminalization has little in common with the "sovereignly" initiated and supported diversion programs of the preventive state.

In view of the different catchment areas of decriminalization through diversion or defense, there is also no need to make a choice between the two in an "either/or" sense. Not only can they easily exist and function side by side but also tailoring decriminalization into the alternatives of defense or diversion should not be viewed too narrowly. However, it should not be forgotten that defense and diversion are only two forms of decriminalization among many. Neither mean true decriminalization, that is, the unsubstituted, unconditional withdrawal from crime and punishment (Naucke, 1984: 201). Insofar, it is always worth testing whether the desired solution is not to perform a true decriminalization by removing various sections from the penal code (that primarily concern petty crime), so that diversion could then take a secondary role in the remaining core of penal law. In such a "small area of true, unequivocal penal law", defense would then be indispensable for a constitutional criminal procedure.[18]

Notes

* Translated from German by Jonathan Harrow at University of Bielefeld.

1 Most norms for defense originate in the second half of the 19th century; diversion is a concept formulated in the second half of the 20th century with American origins (see Kaiser, 1985: 72).

2 Defense is a concept from legal and everyday language; diversion a criminological terminus technicus.

3 This has been criticized in various ways on constitutional grounds and does not need to be dealt with in any depth here (see Naucke, 1984; Alternativ-Kommentar StGB 1990, Hassemer, preceding Section 1 marginal number 187 et seq.).

4 "From its very beginnings, diversion seems to have served as an attempt to fight the economic crisis of penal law" (Kaiser, 1985: 73, translated).

5 However, not an inhibition of justice, as could possibly be concluded by extending the previous citation from Kaiser. Justice, to which defense also belongs, is not inhibited by conflicts, complication, or delay in adjudication but may even flower because of it. Only the activities of the authorities of formal social control are possibly inhibited.

6 This includes the right to inspect and read prosecution files, to counsel clients, and even to write a plea for the defense. It is precisely these central duties that Breymann (1987) considers to be in the way: "Not infrequently, cautionary and counseling appointments at the public prosecutor's office or the youth welfare office or the beginning of a measure are postponed because a defense attorney has become involved. First of all, the defense attorney requires at least one week to inspect the files, and then also invites the accused in order to then produce pages of script" (p. 116, translated).

7 Although it is always at risk of being restricted by reforms. See, for example, the proposals for a law to disburden justice (printed in part in Strafverteidiger, 1991: 282 et seq.) or the planned OrgKG [Organized Crime Act] (published in CILIP 39, No. 2, 1991: 49 et seq.).

8 As in the so-called Kiel model (Ostendorf, 1991, Sect. 45, marginal number 16).

9 This discussion on side effects or latent functions addresses whether or not typical side effects occur or are suppressed during decriminalization through defense or diversion that generalize beyond the concrete case and the penal adjudication of the process in question.

10 Another example is the "PKK process" (process against members of the Kurdish Workers' Party, accused of forming a "terrorist association") at Düsseldorf, in which the validity of Sections 129, 129a of the German Penal Code is being attacked.

11 However, in my opinion, assigning defense a quasi-social-sanitary role would overburden it.

12 Semistructured interviews lasting approximately one hour. These were audiotaped and later transcribed.

13 As specialists tend to be consulted for more severe crimes whereas all-round attorneys are consulted more often for petty crimes, this may possibly introduce a degree of bias.

14 A presentation and evaluation of the Hamburg diversion model can be found in Deichsel (1991).

15 As informal legal counselors (juvenile law counseling), lawyers can make a major contribution to assigning juvenile delinquents to diversion programs. However, in their role as informal legal counselors, such lawyers are in no way procedural counsels. Consequently, the paper published by Deichsel (1987: 169) also notes that juvenile law counselors are not active in a forensic sense.

16 Compare Blumberg (1988: 79) who views defense attorneys as being generally at risk of carrying out double-agent activities for the justice system and their clients. Echoes of a double-agent activity can also be seen in Breymann (1987: 114), when he assigns defense attorneys an educational function in the context of diversion programs and urges that they should pull "pedagogic strings" together with the public prosecutor.

17 For a detailed discussion of this issue, see Schünemann (1989: 1895 et seq.).

18 For a procedure "with great constitutional, liberty-protecting assurances in material law, procedural law, and court law," see Naucke (1984: 216).

References

Alsberg, M. (1930). *Die Philosophie der Verteidigung.* Mannheim: Bensheimer.

Alternativ-Kommentar StGB (1990). *Kommentar zum Strafgesetzbuch, Bd. 1.* Neuwied: Luchterhand.

Beulke, W. (1980). *Der Verteidiger im Strafverfahren.* Frankfurt/M.: Metzner.

Blumberg, A. (1988). Anwälte mit Überzeugungen. *Strafverteidiger, 8,* 79-86.

Breymann, K.(1987), Möglichkeiten der Förderung von Diversionsstrategien seitens des Verteidigers. In Bundesministerium der Justiz (Ed.), *Verteidigung in Jugendstrafsachen* (pp. 113-117). Bonn: Bundesministerium der Justiz.

Dahs, H. (1983). *Handbuch des Strafverteidigers.* Köln: O. Schmidt.

Deichsel, W. (1987). Rechtsberatung "vor Ort" im Jugendzentrum, Protokoll über eine vierjährige Tätigkeit. In Bundesministerium der Justiz (Ed.), *Verteidigung in Jugendstrafsachen* (pp. 161-169). Bonn: Bundesministerium der Justiz.

Deichsel, W. (1991). Lenkt Jugendliche ab vom Kriminaljustizsystem, aber lenkt die Aufmerksamkeit nicht ab von den hiermit verbundenen Implikationen, Risiken und Gefahren! Überlegungen anläßlich des Hamburger Diversionsmodells. *Monatsschrift für Kriminologie und Strafrechtsreform, 74,* 224-235.

Eisenberg, U. (1991a). *Jugendgerichtsgesetz mit Erläuterungen* (4th ed.). München: C.H. Beck.

Eisenberg, U. (1991b). Aspekte der Rechtsstellung des Strafverteidigers. *Neue Juristische Wochenschrift, 44,* 1257-1263.

Hansen-Siedler, T. (1990). *Verteidigung im Jugendstrafverfahren,* Diplomarbeit im Aufbaustudium Kriminologie. Hamburg (unpublished).

Kaiser, G. (1985). Stichwort Diversion. In G. Kaiser, H.-J. Kerner, F. Sack, and H. Schellhoss (Eds.), *Kleines Kriminologisches Wörterbuch* (2nd ed) (pp. 72-76). Heidelberg: C. F. Müller.

Kaiser, G. (1989). *Kriminologie* (8th ed). Heidelberg: C. F. Müller.

Naucke, W. (1984). Über deklaratorische, scheinbare und wirkliche Entkriminalisierung. *Goltdammers Archiv, 131,* 199-217.

Ostendorf, H. (1991). *JGG-Kommentar* (2nd ed.). Köln: Heymanns.

Sack, F. (1979). Strafrecht und Kriminalität in einer freiheitlichen Gesellschaft - einige Folgerungen für das Verhältnis zwischen Rechtsanwalt und Mandant. In W. Holtfort (Ed.), *Strafverteidiger als Interessenvertreter* (pp. 132-151). Neuwied: Luchterhand.

Schott, O. (1886). *Die Lehre von der formellen Verteidigung.* Tübingen: Fues Sort.

Schünemann, B. (1989). Die Verständigung im Strafprozeß - Wunderwaffe oder Bankrotterklärung der Verteidigung? *Neue Juristische Wochenschrift, 42,* 1895-1903.

Spaniol, M. (1990). *Das Recht auf Verteidigerbeistand im Grundgesetz und in der Europäischen Menschenrechtskonvention.* Berlin: Duncker & Humblot.

Viehmann, H. (1987). Nutzung und rechtsstaatliche Kontrolle informeller Erledigungsweisen sowie Verhinderung falscher Weichenstellung für die Hauptverhandlung. In Bundesministerium der Justiz (Ed.), *Verteidigung in Jugendstrafsachen* (pp. 101-112). Bonn: Bundesministerium der Justiz.

Zieger, J. (1986). Jugendstrafrecht - Stiefkind der Verteidigung. *Strafverteidiger, 6,* 132.

Juvenile-Specific Forms of Decriminalization

*Dieter Rössner**

1 The Traditional Reasons for a Special Juvenile Criminal Law

Juvenile criminal law only developed into a special area of criminal law in Germany and other countries at the beginning of the 20th century (Voß, 1986; Weber, 1990: 5-6). This development was based on three underlying trends:

1. Since this time, both social life and the scientific discussion have recognized the phase of adolescence as a special form of life between childhood and adulthood in which young persons are confronted with and have to adapt themselves to the normative demands of the adult world (Heidemann, 1988: 97-98; Hurrelmann, Rosewitz, and Wolf, 1989).
2. The emerging "modern" school of criminal law with its new preventive interpretation of punishment emphasizing rehabilitation focuses on a correspondingly intensive treatment of adolescents in particular (Voß, 1986).
3. The decisive impetus for a separate juvenile criminal law results from the close and, for many, convincing combination of the two above-mentioned perspectives in educational concepts (Heinz, 1990). It is assumed that young persons who fail to meet the most obvious norm demands of the adult world - those of criminal law - are in strong need of education. Compliance with these key norms should be attained as long as these young persons are still subject to education. At the same time, the educational purpose is used as a "cipher" to reduce punishment in view of the particular conditions of adolescence (Pieplow, 1989).

The declaration in favor of a preventive and educational perspective in establishing juvenile criminal law has subsequently become so dominant that all considerations regarding special regulations for juvenile criminal law have focused only on the legal consequences of an offense. This is reflected in the state of the law up to the present day. Section 4 of German Juvenile Justice Act categorizes the offenses of juveniles strictly according to the regulations of general criminal law. Only in the following sections does it introduce a sanction and punishment framework that is completely independent from general criminal law. Thus the educational concept is effective only in the legal consequences. Particularly through educational measures, juveniles with criminal tendencies should learn to differentiate more clearly between right and wrong in the future. Even up until recent times, it was still emphasized that success could be facilitated through the earliest possible and most intensive intervention by juvenile criminal law (see Dölling, 1992).

The traditional focus on the means of education disregards the focus of the educational process, namely, the penal norm and its possibly limited claims to validity with regard to juveniles (Engelhard, 1989). Justifications for a special juvenile criminal law on this basis have to deal with the conditions under which juveniles learn norms and the juvenile uncertainties about norms in their environment. The question regarding special regulations for juveniles then becomes more fundamental than in traditional ideas on sanctioning: Should the normative point of reference for the criminalization of juvenile misbehavior not focus on their life-world? This issue points to the intermediate world of adolescence between the freedom from responsibility of childhood and the adult norms as a cultural location where partially contradictory norm demands meet. Such aspects will be discussed in the following.

2 New Reasons for a Juvenile Criminal Law With Special Definitions of Criminality

2.1 The Juvenile Life-World and the Penal Norm System

Because of the assumption of guilt, criminal law assumes that the average adult possesses an at least instinctive knowledge of the norms of criminal law in order to comply with them in general and avoid their violation. Accordingly, the norms are generally applicable to adults, and they are able to adapt their behavior according to the demands of the law (Baumann and Weber, 1985: 175). As these conditions are oriented toward the empirical and pragmatic condition of responsibility, it would seem justifiable to use the specific life-world of young offenders as the basis for a special system of penal norms. It is, after all, only possible to punish a person's autonomous and responsible decision. Therefore, knowledge of norms and the necessary insight to behave accordingly are presumed. Both these elements are essentially influenced by factors of the life-world (Engel and Hurrelmann, 1989: 22; Heitmeyer and Hurrelmann, 1988).

In life-course-oriented biographical models, recent youth research has shown that there are youth-specific age norms that decisively determine behavior in the adolescent phase of life and can clash with general norms (Buchmann, 1983; Engel and Hurrelmann, 1989). Life in the intermediate world of adolescence raises the question of how adaptively the individual is capable of processing social discontinuities (Heitmeyer and Hurrelmann, 1988). In view of the dogmatic principles of criminal law, a specific juvenile criminal law should respond to this question by testing each offense according to its youth-specific criminalization content. Naturally, it is not to be assumed that the decisive elements of the legal principle of responsibility should not have any meaning in juvenile criminal law.

2.2 *Norm Violation and the Learning of Norms as an Element of Socialization*

When it is considered further that the life phase of adolescence is a major phase of socialization and that this process is characterized by the human being developing further across the life course through interaction with life conditions (Heitmeyer and Hurrelmann, 1988), then the adolescent conflict with the adult world is a necessary stage of identity formation (Braun, 1989: 332; Hurrelmann, Rosewitz, and Wolf, 1989; Klima, 1978: 777). The goal of education therefore is the autonomous processing and not the authoritarian repression of conflicts. A prerequisite of the development of an autonomous value and norm system is the formation of a certain structure of cognitive, moral, emotional, verbal, and social competence. The development of such competence requires an openness to the life-world of adolescents, dialogue, and constructive interaction. Autonomous development would be greatly impaired if the definition of social disorder and, in particular, of criminality were to be taken one-sidedly from the adult world (Schumann et al., 1987). The self-discovery of an adolescent is inconceivable without deviance and its discussion. This is confirmed empirically in Schumann's work on the general prevention of penal norms among adolescents. This has revealed that abstention from criminal actions depends decisively on the adolescents' personal values and less on the constraints of penal law (Schumann et al., 1987). Norm education is thus no one-sided process in which the adolescent is so-to-speak the vessel in which social norms only have to be poured (Albrecht, 1987: 57). On balance, it can be concluded that adolescents are required to exhibit a great deal of personal responsibility.

2.3 *Episodic Crime as Part of the Maturation of Personality*

The criminological perspective on juvenile crime also presents a particular picture corresponding to the adolescents' life-world. Juvenile delinquency is no longer viewed as a first step toward a criminal career with the risk of falling into bad ways. In most normal cases, it is less dangerous and mostly characterized by casual petty crimes in the field of property offenses. Insofar, it generally peaks at the age of 16 and is characterized by a temporary, episodic, and fleeting engagement in crime. Crime statistics, research on undetected crime, and studies of age cohorts confirm this (see Dölling, 1989: 9-10; Rössner, 1989). The frequent desistance from criminal behavior is thus in many cases obviously a step toward the adult world and conformity (Heitmeyer and Hurrelmann, 1988: 48, 57).

Conformist behavior and conformist identity grow through a process of adolescent integration into the adult world, particularly through important personal relationships and integration into central institutions of society (Rössner, 1988). The increasingly confirmed theories on control and commitment (see Kirchhoff, 1983) clearly show how the development of criminal careers can be prevented, even in unfavorable conditions. Penal stigmatization and exclusion following a crime are in any case counterproductive factors.

2.4 Overview of Reasons

The present analysis of the reasons for a specific juvenile penal law indicates that the question regarding a material criminalization limit should be an essential element of such a special penal code. The present-day flight into the less binding procedural and broad sanctioning regulations of juvenile criminal law is only partially appropriate to the problem. In particular, the material approach of providing specific legal definitions of juvenile responsibility seems to represent a major constitutional advance. The conceivable approaches toward material decriminalization of juvenile criminal law will be sketched briefly in the following, although a final appraisal is not even approximately possible. They are oriented toward the traditional dogmatic penal prescriptions of the criminal elements. It is promising that the current discussion on crime policy has also adopted the material decriminalization approach very recently. This is particularly thanks to a work group set up by the *Deutsche Vereinigung für Jugendgerichte und Jugendgerichtshilfen* (German Association for Youth Courts and Legal Youth Welfare Services), who have worked out and presented correspondingly differentiated and practice-oriented proposals for the reform of juvenile criminal law.[1]

3 Approaches Toward a Youth-Specific Definition of Criminality

3.1 Total Decriminalization Through the Introduction of a Unified Youth Welfare Law to Also Include Criminal Offenses

The first solution to be considered is the global one of removing the judgment of juvenile misbehavior completely from penal controls. This is supported by the fact that penal prohibitions are directed toward the autonomously deciding person and this level is reached only at the end of a long process of moral development (Kohlberg, 1974; Piaget, 1954). The existing age limit of 14 is also ultimately based on such stages of development. However, the location of the border between juvenile nonresponsibility and the severity of penal law is a continuously open value decision within the entire system of social control. It also cannot be explained uniformly through empirical studies on moral development. Currently, there is much indication that the present 14-year limit should be raised.

Even several years ago, concrete proposals had already been made by, for example, Peters (1965) and the Juvenile Law Commission of the *Arbeiterwohlfahrt* (Workers' Welfare Association; see Hasenclever 1970) on the application of a pure education-oriented youth welfare law or a more communicative and socially oriented youth conflict law to criminal actions by adolescents.

However, these far-reaching demands for reform never had any chances of being implemented at the time, because it was felt that extending childhood into adolescence would lead to an abruptly painful border between adolescence and adulthood. The fluid transition from youth welfare law for the under-14s across educationally oriented juvenile criminal law up to general repressive criminal law is still generally viewed as a meaningful gradual incline. It cannot be rejected that juvenile criminal law can be understood as almost a reflection of the intermediate adolescent world that ranges from tolerance over education to punishment.

3.2 Raising the Age of Criminal Responsibility or the Minimum Age of Imprisonment to 16 or 18 Years

The same direction as the global solution is taken by approaches that call for a general increase in the age of criminal responsibility or the introduction of a relative minimum age for custodial sanctions. As a consequence of such reforms, offenses under the age of responsibility would be processed further under youth welfare law. Since the reform through the Child and Juvenile Welfare Law of 1990 (*Kinder- und Jugendhilfegesetz*; KJHG), this is strongly directed toward confronting juvenile deviance with educational means ranging from social-pedagogic family welfare across day groups to intensive individual pedagogic care. It should be tested how far these means suffice to have a pedagogic impact on 14- to 16-year-old offenders.

It seems to be just as necessary to consider a minimum age of imprisonment for 14- to 18-year-olds. German juvenile prisons are no place for adolescents nowadays, because their climate is characterized by 20- to 24-year-old serious career criminals (Rössner, 1991). They expose adolescents to the world of young (criminal) adults (Gerken and Schumann, 1988: 139). Under such conditions, the education of adolescents and, in particular, their integration into conformist reference systems cannot succeed (Heidemann, 1988: 89; Kersten, 1986). There is an urgent need for crime policy reforms in this sector (Rössner, 1991).

3.3 Restriction to a Catalogue of Serious Offenses

Other considerations address the criterion of the severity of an offense as a means of material decriminalization. Only serious offenses should continue to be subject to penal social controls as juvenile crimes. An example of such a reform proposal is the discussion of a youth welfare law at the Federal Ministry for Youth, Family, and Health in 1973. This discussion proposed that juvenile criminal law should be applied only when the adolescent has committed an offense that normally involves a minimum of 5 years incarceration. Otherwise, youth welfare law should apply.

Such a formal restriction aimed at serious crime, in particular, homicide, is not very convincing in the final analysis. From the penal perspective, it would have to be admitted that, independent from the personality of the adolescent, an unacceptable severity of the offense would basically call for a penal response that would therefore be clear and visible to all. However, a closer inspection shows that it is particularly severe offenses that are frequently based on a disturbed moral development or other major social disorders, and so, from an individual perspective, there are particular impediments to a penal processing of the facts. As severity of offense would also always be accompanied by incarceration, this would additionally result in a contradiction to the possible assumption of a minimum age for imprisonment. Despite its plausibility and its appeal to the principle of proportionality, this approach ultimately remains questionable.

3.4 Decriminalization Through a Youth-Specific Social Adequacy Clause

According to the theory of social adequacy (see, e.g., Jescheck, 1988; Roxin, 1992), actions that remain completely within the framework of the historically produced order of community life and represent either a generally accepted risk or are generally socially tolerated are not criminal. From a criminological perspective, one could then argue that the "normal" episodic juvenile offense represents a general life risk in the world of youth and is therefore penally irrelevant.

Admittedly, this unconventional approach to decriminalization falls down on two points: Currently, it does not seem possible to reliably differentiate "normal" juvenile crime from more intensive forms, and, second, social adequacy is a completely imprecise construct that is more at home in the domain of the sense of justice. Therefore this approach will not be able to fulfill constitutional demands. Additionally, it could be misunderstood by adolescents as a license for socially damaging misbehavior.

3.5 Decriminalization By Removing Criminal Acts That Should Not Be Punishable for Juveniles

It is worth thinking about partially modifying the special part of the Penal Code with respect to juveniles. Each regulation could be examined from the perspective of responsibility in order to ascertain whether differences exist between adolescents in the process of maturation and adults. A first step would be to exclude certain crimes that represent more of a juvenile misdemeanor when committed by adolescents, and therefore do not merit punishment.

Ostendorf (1992) has presented such a concept of material decriminalization for three groups of crimes:

1. *Acts that have not been understood as crimes by juveniles.* These are particularly behaviors that juveniles know to be wrong but that cannot be classified in penal law because of the difficult structure of the evidence, such as forging documents. Adolescents are certainly aware that the self-written letter excusing absence from class is a violation of the behavioral norms of parents and school, but they rarely see it as an act of forgery.
2. *Definitions of crimes that do not fit juveniles.* This particularly concerns the increasing of penalties in situations in which juveniles tend to be exonerated because of their particular social environment. Examples are offenses by juvenile gangs such as theft and robbery.
3. *Definitions of crimes that are unnecessary for juveniles.* These are relatively minor property offenses that are sufficiently protected by civil law as far as juveniles are concerned.

This initial, rough structural classification can only be a beginning. A comprehensive reform must test all crimes precisely regarding their suitability for inclusion in juvenile criminal law.

3.6 Removal of Criminal Liability for Petty Crime

In crime policy and criminology, the heading "petty crime" is viewed as that category of deviant behavior that is located on the borderline between penal tolerance and sanctioned behavior and thus forms the interface between penal control and other forms of social control. Traditionally, crime policy has queried whether no penal sanction is necessary or whether the traditional criminal sanction and the subsequent process is an overreaction by the state when a behavior contains only low criminal content (Rössner, 1993). However, particularly as far as juvenile crime is concerned, it is necessary to ask whether the norm addressees, whose awareness first has to develop, are not overtaxed particularly in this borderline area. Naturally, this is not to say that there should be no reaction to such misdemeanors, but not a penal one. This approach applies equally to both "independent" petty crimes such as infringements of regulations and to "dependent" petty crimes that can only be classified as offenses because of their extremely abstract classification of criminal activity without consideration of the low level of wrong and guilt. At present, dependent petty crime is generally regulated by dropping proceedings according to Sections 45 and 47 of the German Juvenile Justice Act. Here, there exists the possibility of establishing, in terms of material law, a pettiness regulation similar to Section 3 of the former criminal law of the German Democratic Republic. This could also cover, for example, property crimes up to a set amount such as DM 100.

It is also worth considering whether all victimless crimes or crimes with no detectable victim, which are not by themselves visible to juveniles, should be included under a youth-specific petty crime regulation. This could cover, for example, fraudulent exercise of a public office, disturbing the performance of religious rites and the peace of the dead up to exhibitionism, distributing pornography, poaching, and abuse of emergency telephone services.

3.7 Abolition of Juvenile Crime Through Restitution

Restitution can now be considered as a material penal principle with an autonomous character in the restitution of legal peace. Restitution, particularly in the form of victim-offender mediation, is close to other phenomena that lead to a dropping of punishment, for example, in the case of voluntary acts by which the perpetrator of a criminal attempt hinders the consummation of the offense or abandonment of the attempt to commit an offense. Here, there are good juvenile-specific reasons to stretch the borders of nonpunishability by expanding restitution further than is the case with adults. The juvenile offender, who is not so familiar with the norm system as the adult, is given a further chance. It seems appropriate to extend the punishment-free period of restitution awarded after a perpetrator has voluntarily hindered the consummation of an offense to crimes that have actually been committed when the juvenile self-responsibly and voluntarily to a large extent removes, repairs, or otherwise balances out the consequences of the offense. The juvenile who has violated a norm and only then realizes the damaging effects and the validity of the norm should not be punishable. The norm violation and the subsequent learning process are steps on the path toward conformity (see, also, a corresponding proposal in Kerner et al., 1990).

Admittedly, it once more has to be emphasized that restitution only removes the penal aspect of an offense. The juvenile is not disburdened of the civil and above all human responsibility. This leads juveniles toward a constructive confrontation with their offense and with its consequences.

4 Conclusions for Crime Policy

Recent findings on adolescent development and on their life-world call for new considerations on juvenile criminal law. As criminal law above all appeals to the responsibility of persons and cannot be understood as an ideal means of education, it is more fundamental than before to inquire into which norm requirements adolescents have to meet. At various places in the dogma of criminal law, this raises the possibility of material decriminalization. The approaches sketched here should be extended in the further discussion on crime policy. It is to be hoped that particularly the proposals made by the German Association for Youth Courts and Legal Youth Welfare Services (see note 1) will be taken up by the law makers in their future work.

Notes

* Translated from German by Jonathan Harrow at the University of Bielefeld.

1 See the pioneer work on crime policy by the work group on decriminalization in the DVJJ commission on juvenile criminal law. This commendable and productive work was summarized and published by Unterkommission 1 der DVJJ-Kommission zur Reform des Jugendkriminalrechts (1992). See, also, the corresponding findings of the 22. Deutscher Jugendgerichtstag (22nd German Youth Court Conference) at Regensburg (Thesen und Ergebnisse der Arbeitskreise des 22. Deutschen Jugendgerichtstags, 1992). Unfortunately, these important works appeared too late to be considered in this paper.

References

Albrecht, P.-A. (1987). *Jugendstrafrecht.* München: C.H. Beck.

Baumann, J., and Weber, U. (1985). *Strafrecht, Allgemeiner Teil* (9th ed.). Bielefeld: Gieseking Verlag.

Braun, W. (1989). Erziehung - noch gefragt? *Zentralblatt für Jugendrecht, 76,* 331-336.

Buchmann, M. (1983). *Konformität und Abweichung im Jugendalter. Eine empirische Untersuchung zur Biographie- und Identitätsentwicklung und abweichendem Verhalten Jugendlicher.* Diessenhof: Ruegger.

Dölling, D. (1989). Kriminologisches Grundlagenwissen zur Jugendkriminalität und zum Umgang mit jugendlichen Straffälligen. In D. Rössner (Ed.), *Toleranz - Erziehung - Strafe* (pp. 7-42). Hofgeismar: Evangelische Akademie Hofgeismar.

Dölling, D. (1992). Die Bedeutung der Jugendkriminalität im Verhältnis zur Erwachsenenkriminalität. In Bundesministerium der Justiz (Ed.), *Grundfragen des Jugendkriminalrechts und seiner Neuregelung* (pp. 38-59). Bonn: Forum Verlag.

Engel, U., and Hurrelmann, K. (1989). *Psychosoziale Belastung im Jugendalter. Empirische Befunde zum Einfluß von Familie, Schule und Gleichaltrigengruppe.* Berlin/New York: de Gruyter.

Engelhard, H.A. (1989). Jugendstrafrecht - Erziehungsrecht oder Strafrecht. *Zentralblatt für Jugendrecht, 76,* 22-24.

Gerken, J., and Schumann, K.F. (Eds.) (1988). *Ein trojanisches Pferd im Rechtsstaat: Der Erziehungsgedanke in der Jugendgerichtspraxis.* Pfaffenweiler: Centaurus.

Hasenclever, Christa (1970). Vorschläge für ein erweitertes Jugendhilferecht: Denkschrift der Arbeiterwohlfahrt zur Reform und Vereinheitlichung von Jugendwohlfahrtsgesetz und Jugendgerichtsgesetz. *Schriften der Arbeiterwohlfahrt, 22,* Bonn.

Heidemann, A. (1988). Kollision zwischen den verfassungsrechtlichen Garantien und dem Erziehungsanspruch des JGG bei der Verteidigung Jugendlicher? Probleme und rechtspolitische Alternativen. In J. Gerken and K.F. Schumann (Eds.), *Ein trojanisches Pferd im Rechtsstaat: Der Erziehungsgedanke in der Jugendgerichtspraxis* (pp. 85-100). Pfaffenweiler: Centaurus.

Heinz, W. (1990). Die Bedeutung des Erziehungsgedankens für Normsetzung und Normanwendung im Jugendstrafrecht der Bundesrepublik Deutschland. In J. Wolff and A. Marek (Eds.), *Erziehung und Strafe. Jugendstrafrecht in der Bundesrepublik Deutschland und Polen,* Schriftenreihe DVJJ, Vol. 19 (pp. 28-50). Bonn: Forum Verlag.

Heitmeyer, W., and Hurrelmann K. (1988). Sozialisations- und handlungstheoretische Ansätze in der Jugendforschung. In H.-H. Krüger (Ed.), *Handbuch der Jugendforschung* (pp. 47-70). Opladen: Leske und Budrich.

Hurrelmann, K., Rosewitz, B., and Wolf, H.K. (1989). *Lebensphase Jugend: Eine Einführung in die sozialwissenschaftliche Jugendforschung* (2nd ed.). Weinheim: Juventa.

Jescheck, H.-H. (1988). *Lehrbuch des Strafrechts, AT* (4th ed.). Berlin: Duncker & Humblot

Kerner, H.-J., Marks, E., Rössner, D., and Schreckling, J. (1990). Täter-Opfer-Ausgleich im Jugendstrafrecht. *Bewährungshilfe, 37,* 169-176.

Kersten, J. (1986). Zum Vollzug der Freiheitsstrafe an Jugendlichen. In S. Müller and H.-U. Otto (Eds.), *Damit Erziehung nicht zur Strafe wird* (pp. 163-173). Bielefeld: Karin Böllert KT Verlag.

Kirchhoff, G.F. (1983). Kriminalsoziologie. In H.-J. Schneider (Ed.), *Kriminalität und abweichendes Verhalten,* Vol. 1 (pp. 131-154). Weinheim: Beltz.

Klima, R. (1978) Sozialisation. In W. Fuchs (Ed.), *Lexikon der Soziologie* (2nd ed.) (pp. 707-708). Opladen: Westdeutscher Verlag.

Kohlberg, L. (1974). *Zur kognitiven Entwicklung des Kindes.* Frankfurt: Suhrkamp.

Ostendorf, H. (1992). Ansatzpunkte für materiell-rechtliche Entkriminalisierungen von Verhaltensweisen junger Menschen. In Bundesministerium der Justiz (Ed.), *Grundfragen des Jugendkriminalrechts und seiner Neuregelung* (pp. 194-205). Bonn: Forum Verlag.

Peters, K. (1965). Die Grundlagen der Behandlung junger Rechtsbrecher. In *Erstkriminalität und Frühkriminalität. Bericht über die Verhandlungen des 13. Deutschen Jugendgerichtstages in Münster* (pp. 13-29). Hamburg: Selbstverlag der Deutschen Vereinigung für Jugendgerichte und Jugendgerichtshilfen e.V.

Piaget, J. (1954). *Das moralische Urteil beim Kinde.* Zürich: Rascher.

Pieplow, L. (1989). Erziehung als Chiffre. In M. Walter (Ed.), *Beiträge zur Erziehung im Jugendkriminalrecht* (pp. 5-57). Köln: Heymanns.

Rössner, D. (1988). Angewandte Kriminologie und Prävention. In H. Göppinger (Ed.), *Angewandte Kriminologie International* (pp. 138-155). Bonn: Forum Verlag.

Rössner, D. (1989). Gesellschaftliche Toleranz und Jugendkriminalität. In D. Rössner (Ed.), *Toleranz - Erziehung - Strafe* (pp. 43-64). Hofgeismar: Evangelische Akademie Hofgeismar.

Rössner, D. (1991). Reform des Jugendstrafvollzugs bei 14-17jährigen. *DVJJ-Journal, 2,* 219-221.

Rössner, D. (1993). Bagatellkriminalität. In G. Kaiser, H.-J. Kerner, F. Sack, H. Schellhoss (Eds.), *Kleines Kriminologisches Wörterbuch* (3rd ed.) (pp. 48-53). Heidelberg: C.F. Müller.

Roxin, C. (1992). *Strafrecht, AT I.* München: C.H. Beck.

Schumann, K.F., Berlitz, C., Guth, H.-W., and Kaulitzki, R. (1987). *Jugendkriminalität und die Grenzen der Generalprävention.* Neuwied: Luchterhand.

Thesen und Ergebnisse der Arbeitskreise des 22. Deutschen Jugendgerichtstags vom 26.-30.9.1992 Regensburg (1992). *DVJJ-Journal, 3,* 281-292.

Unterkommission 1 der DVJJ-Kommission zur Reform des Jugendkriminalrechts (1992). Entkriminalisierung. *DVJJ-Journal, 3,* 9-16.

Voß, M. (1986). *Jugend ohne Rechte.* Frankfurt/New York: Campus.

Weber, M. (1990). *Die Anwendung der Jugendstrafe.* Frankfurt: Lang.

Self-Incrimination Privilege and Police Interrogation: A Comparative View

Andreas Ransiek

1 The United States and Germany: Same Privilege, Same Problems

Miranda v. Arizona (1966), the U.S. Supreme Court's most important judgment on the self-incrimination privilege and police interrogation, continues to be troublesome. Even more than 25 years after the court handed down the decision under its Chief Justice Earl Warren, there is still a lively discussion on the case's rule and its implications. Although the Miranda warnings[1] and the inadmissibility of confessions if the police have not complied with the Miranda dictates remain the clear law, there is a handful of judgments year after year construing Miranda and the Fifth Amendment self-incrimination privilege. Although most of them narrow the rules or at least the spirit of Miranda (thus giving no need to explicitly overrule it), some nonetheless grant broader protection (e.g., *Edwards v. Arizona*, 1981; *Michigan v. Jackson*, 1986; *Arizona v. Roberson*, 1988; *Minnick v. Mississippi*, 1990; but cf. *McNeil v. Wisconsin*, 1991). Therefore, even if radical changes in the law of police interrogation are unlikely in the United States, the basic problem remains: Did the court go too far in creating the warnings, or did it not go far enough? Are the warnings a dictate of the Fifth Amendment itself, or are they only judge-made, prophylactic rules that can be violated without violating the Fifth Amendment as the Court has argued (*Michigan v. Tucker*, 1974, at 444; *New York v. Quarles*, 1984, at 654; *Duckworth v. Eagan*, 1989, at 209; *O'Connor, Scalia, JJ.*, concurring), giving good reason to doubt whether state court convictions may be reversed if Miranda warnings have not been given (see Grano, 1988; Markman, 1987; Schulhofer, 1987). Thus, the question is whether Miranda should be overruled or replaced by statutes governing police interrogation (Johnson, 1988: 540-550), or whether the case should be taken more seriously and its rules should be broadened.

In Germany, there has also been a lively discussion on police warnings. However, it was led from the opposite starting position. For 25 years, the majority of legal scholars (e.g., Kleinknecht and Meyer, 1991: Section 136, marginal number 20; Roxin, 1991: 154-155) had urged the German Federal Supreme Court (*Bundesgerichtshof*; BGH) - the highest court for questions on the Code of Criminal Procedure[2] - to hold confessions inadmissible at trial if the police had not complied with Sections 163, Subsection 4, 136 of the Code of Criminal Procedure (*Strafprozeßordnung*; StPO), which prescribe police warnings that are quite similar to Miranda. Defendants have to be warned that they are free to talk to the police about the crime they are accused of and that they may consult with defense counsel at any time. In addition, they have to be informed of which crime they are suspected of committing and why they are suspected. Legal scholars do not just refer to Section 136 StPO, but also consider police warnings, at least as far as the right to remain silent is concerned, as a mandate of the German constitution's self-incrimination privilege[3] (Krey, 1988: marginal number 789; Ransiek, 1990: 47-58; Rogall 1988a: before Section 133, marginal number 164). However, until recently, the most important step was still missing in German law: the exclusionary rule. In an earlier decision, the BGH regarded Section 136 StPO as a "second-rank" provision with advisory character only that could not justify the exclusion of a confession (Entscheidungen des BGH in Strafsachen, BGHSt. 22, 170, 173-175). Later, the arguments were replaced, but not the result for police warnings (BGHSt. 31, 395; cf. Pakter, 1985: 29-32). However, the picture finally changed in 1992. Citing Miranda with approval, the BGH acknowledged the inadmissability of a confession if the defendant has not been informed of his or her right to remain silent - at least if the defendant did not know his or her rights (BGHSt. 38, 214).

Thus, German scholars may well have reason to lean back with satisfaction. Defenders of Miranda in the United States may also be pleased, and can refer to the German development as an argument in favor of the warnings, since both Germany and the United States have imported the privilege from England (Eser, 1990: 151-153; *Miranda v. Arizona*, 1966, at 442-443). However, to narrow the view on the warnings would shortcut the discussion and the remaining uncertainty. The Supreme Court's majority was concerned not only with the fact that individuals may not be informed of their rights but mainly with the compulsion inherent to in-custody police interrogations (*Miranda v. Arizona*, 1966, at 445, 457, 461; cf. BGHSt. 38, 214, 222). The Court disapproved of various police interrogation tactics and techniques employed to obtain confessions: tricks like displaying confidence in the suspect's guilt, minimizing the moral seriousness of the crime, casting blame on the victim or society, the friendly-unfriendly act, or faked sympathy for the suspect (*Miranda v. Arizona*, 1966, at 449-455). These are all tricks or pressure on the defendant that could not render a confession involuntary under the traditional voluntariness test of the Fourteenth Amendment.

Since most defendants decide to talk to the police at the outset of interrogation despite the warnings, the broader and more relevant question is which tactics and interrogation methods are prohibited by the privilege. If defendants waive their privilege, are we back to the shortcomings of the voluntariness test? What renders a waiver of the Miranda rights invalid? Miranda continues to be controversial not because the warnings have to be given, but because of the arguments used to justify them. Two conceptions of criminal procedure face each other: one emphasizing the individual rights of defendants that have to be protected in police interrogation and criminal procedure in general; the other stressing that the purpose of criminal procedure is to convict the guilty and free the innocent, but only the innocent, so that defendants' rights should not handcuff the police. Not surprisingly, these positions can also be found in the German discussion on whether or not certain police interrogation techniques are illegal. Once again, the fact that there is a provision in the Code of Criminal Procedure governing defendants' protection in police interrogation is of little help. Section 136a StPO prohibits interrogation methods like cruelty, deception, threatening with illegal actions, or promises of advantages not provided by law, in order to protect defendants' free will, and confessions obtained in this manner are inadmissible. But there are various conflicting opinions on how to construe this provision. The common denominator seems to be that *some* pressure on the defendant to confess and *some* police trickery is allowed, but is unclear where the limit has to be drawn. The resulting situation may be compared roughly with the Supreme Court's voluntariness test, although it is not based on the totality of circumstances and does grant broader protection against deception. The explanation that the defendant's free will and rational choice of confession, or free will against overbearing pressure, is protected hardly gives any clear guidelines on how far the protection of the law does and should extend. In any case, the BGH outlaws only severe impairments of defendant's free will (BGHSt. 31, 395, 399-400). The legal difficulties in the two systems of criminal procedure are congruent - a first hint that the systems are not far apart after all.[4] How can we simultaneously protect individual rights but nonetheless see that justice is done?

2 The Protection of the Self-Incrimination Privilege

2.1 The Rationale of the Privilege: Protection of Individual Rights

The wording of the privilege, which is negative in both German and American, seems to permit various interpretations of its function. Although the state, through its law enforcement officials, may not compel any persons to be witnesses against themselves in criminal cases, no positive right, something a suspect may do, is stated. However, there must be some reason for granting the privilege, some interest that is to be protected in order to explain its existence. This reason seems to be a combination of objective and subjective rationales. There is the systemic interest of the criminal justice system that only guilty persons should be convicted (cf. Dolkino, 1986: 1074-1077) and that power is not abused (cf. Dolkino, 1986: 1077-1087). But the privilege seems to go far beyond the protection of the innocent. The Supreme Court was concerned with threats to civil liberty, emphasizing that the atmosphere of police interrogations can be destructive of human dignity (*Miranda v. Arizona*, 1966, at 457), and that a statement may not be the product of the defendant's free choice (*Miranda v. Arizona*, 1966, at 458) - regardless of whether or not the resulting confession is true. Similarly, the German Federal Constitutional Court (*Bundesverfassungsgericht*; BVerfG) implies that personal freedom is protected by deriving the privilege from Articles 1 and 2 of the German Constitution that guarantee the protection of human dignity and the right to one's own personality (BVerfGE 56, 37, 41-43).

Some scholars argue that the protection granted by the privilege is intended to prevent the defendant from having to make a difficult and unacceptable choice between evils - for example, having to decide between incriminating oneself or enduring various forms of compulsion (BVerfGE, 56, 37, 41-42; Grünwald, 1981: 428; Puppe, 1978: 299; cf. Dripps, 1988: 711-718; Stuntz, 1989: 803). However, the protection of personal liberty emphasized by the Supreme Court and the Federal Constitutional Court goes beyond a conception of choice (Ransiek, 1990: 49-52). It is not crucial that suspects *notice* their confession is not based on their free will (the idea of choice), but whether they actually *are* free to confess. For example, if a defendant confesses after being told that he will be charged with manslaughter if he confesses but with murder if he does not confess, it is not important that he has to choose between alternatives (a choice he may welcome), but that he is unable to reach a self-responsible decision because he is influenced by the promise. The privilege acknowledges that individuals have the freedom to decide whether to incriminate themselves or not; personal autonomy and self-determination are protected (cf. *Miranda v. Arizona*, 1966, at 465). Defendants are allowed to decide on their own and to defend themselves. They are not obliged to assist the state in convicting them.

This is why the Supreme Court regarded police trickery and deception as compulsive within the meaning of the Fifth Amendment, as the examples of critical interrogation methods selected by the Court reveal (*Miranda v. Arizona*, 1966, at 449-455, 461): A defendant tricked into confession does not have to choose between evils. Thus, questioning police trickery under the Fifth Amendment makes sense only if self-determination and autonomy are protected by the privilege. Not only may the defendant not be compelled to give self-incriminating answers; he or she has a right to remain silent. The defendant may decide whether to talk to the police or not. And a confession is admissible only if the defendant intelligently, knowingly, and voluntarily waives his or her rights (*Miranda v. Arizona*, 1966, at 475). It can be argued that not much is left of this standard when one looks at the decisions following Miranda in the Burger and Rehnquist eras (e.g., *Oregon v. Elstad*, 1985; *Moran v. Burbine*, 1986; *Colorado v. Connelly*, 1986; *Spring v. Colorado*, 1987). Although these judgments may be correct in restricting Miranda, the initial standard is, nonetheless, self-determination. Similarly, the BVerfG emphasizes that defendants may self-responsibly take their fate in their own hands in criminal procedure (BVerfGE, 49, 289, 298) and that their free will is protected (BVerfGE, 56, 37, 43). In addition, the Court acknowledges a general right to informational self-determination (BVerfGE, 65, 1, 42): The self-incrimination privilege is pronounced to be part of a broader right.

2.2 *The Scope of the Self-Incrimination Privilege*

The standard: Justice Frankfurter revisited? Starting from the purpose of protecting individual liberty, it is necessary to ask what self-responsibility and self-determination mean within the context of the self-incrimination privilege. On the one hand, they have to mean more than the mere possibility for defendants to choose between self-incrimination and non-self-incrimination. Even the most severely tortured individual still has the choice between continuing to bear torture or confessing (Grano, 1979: 881-882). There is always a choice between alternatives. Unfortunately, impairments of autonomy are only relative and not absolute. On the other hand, self-responsibility also cannot mean that decisions are absolutely uninfluenced by others. In police interrogation, as in any human communication, some influence will always be exerted simply by the fact that somebody is asking questions and interacting with the defendant. Thus, the question of self-responsibility cannot be answered in black and white terms. It is only possible to try to determine to whom the defendant's decision to confess is attributable. If the interrogator's conduct has a material influence on the defendant's will, the defendant's decision cannot be called self-responsible.

This, however, is nothing more than Justice Frankfurter's definition of voluntariness in *Culombe v. Connecticut* (1967, at 602). Justice Frankfurter stated:

> "Is the confession the product of an essentially free will and unconstrained choice of its maker? . . . If it is not, if his will has been overborne and his capacity for self-determination critically impaired, the use of the confession offends due process . . . The line of distinction is that at which governing self-direction is lost and compulsion, of whatever nature or however infused, propels or helps to propel the confession."

However, the Justices concurring with Frankfurter's definition dissented in the result, while the justices who did not share the abstract view reached the same result. Thus, abstract definitions have to be filled with life to be useful. But this is quite easy: Self-responsibility and self-determination only have to be taken seriously. This leads to the next problem: Can we afford and do we want to take self-responsibility seriously?

Privilege and warnings: (1) Warnings and self-determination. First, police warnings enable ignorant defendants to reach self-responsible decisions on whether they want to incriminate themselves or not. They learn that there is a choice, and that they do not have to answer questions. Not knowing one's rights means that one cannot exercise these rights. Thus, under the rationale of self-determination, information is an essential part of the right itself. It seems fair that the state has to provide the relevant information so that not only the well-educated but also the ignorant have an equal chance to exercise their rights. However, this naturally does not explain why those who already know their rights have to be warned of them. This makes it possible to argue that police warnings are not necessary if defendants are already informed of their rights (BGHSt. 38, 214, 225;[5] Kleinknecht and Meyer-Goßner, 1993: Section 136 StPO, marginal number 20).

But warnings have a far more important function than informing the ignorant. I do not share the Supreme Court's view that police warnings can compensate for interrogation techniques such as threats, promises, or trickery (*Miranda v. Arizona*, 1966, at 467), because these tactics are designed specifically to overcome a defendant's resistance to speaking or speaking truthfully: It is of little help to know that there is a right to remain silent when police claim that things are getting worse when this right is exercised (cf. *Miranda v. Arizona*, 1966, at 470). The warnings cannot offset impairments of self-responsibility through interrogation methods like those described in Miranda. But there is something they can do: They can compensate for pressure resulting from the mere fact of police interrogation as such (Rieß, 1980: 300). For defendants who are or feel that they are unable to stand interrogation, for those who are too nervous or cannot express themselves (cf. BGHSt. 38, 214, 222), it is made clear that they do not have to speak or that they may consult a lawyer first. Suspects do not just receive general information on their rights, they gain far more: They do not have to answer any questions *here and now* (Schulhofer, 1987: 447-448). This is important, because a defendant's refusal to talk to the police arouses suspicion in everyday terms. An innocent person should not have any reason to refuse to cooperate with the police and answer questions. Therefore, there is a strong incentive for suspects subjected to interrogation not to reject all communication when they think about how this rejection will be interpreted by the police officer (cf. *Miranda v. Arizona*, 1966, at 454). The warnings are necessary in order to point out that this everyday meaning is not valid in police interrogation. Even if defendants have an abstract knowledge of their rights, they need to know that they are being respected in *this* interrogation and by *this* police officer. Otherwise, the mere fact of being interrogated would create a pressure to speak on the basis of the social rules of question and answer. The warnings that the individual may remain silent and may have the assistance of counsel are essential for a self-determined, responsible decision on whether or not to talk. In addition, defendants should know the seriousness of the crime with which they are being charged if they are to be able to make an intelligent decision on whether they need the assistance of counsel (cf. BGHSt. 37, 48, 53, on illegal deception of defendant suspected of homicide if questioned in a missing-person case; but cf. *Spring v. Colorado*, 1987). Likewise, defendants should be informed that such assistance does not depend on their financial means.

Thus, within the concept of self-determination, at least the warnings that one may remain silent and seek assistance of counsel are not just a safeguard of the self-incrimination privilege (*Michigan v. Tucker*, 1974), "overprotecting the value at stake" (*Duckworth v. Eagan*, 1989, at 209; *O'Connor, Scalia, JJ., concurring*), but are mandated by the Fifth Amendment itself. The warnings ensure that defendants reconsider their situation and then decide what to do. This may not be necessary for *all* defendants, but because it is not possible to perceive whether subjects actually reconsider their rights without warnings, warnings are required without exception; it is ensured that defendants have the chance to do so. Of course, *police* warnings could be substituted "by other fully effective means . . . to notify the person of his right to remain silent" (*Miranda v. Arizona*, 1966, at 479), but not the actual warnings themselves. Criteria for the quality of warnings can be derived from this purpose: The defendant must be able to understand them, and, if necessary, they have to be explained.

Privilege and warnings: (2) Warnings and custody. The above also makes it fairly clear that warnings have to be given before the interrogation starts. If somebody is suspected of having committed a crime and they are going to be interrogated, they have to be warned of their rights regardless of whether or not they are formally charged. However, if the intelligent decisions of defendants are protected, it is irrelevant if they are in custody or not (BGHSt. 38, 214 on roadside questioning, well aware of *Berkemer v. McCarty*, 1984; Herman, 1964: 497). The purpose of the warnings cannot be - as the Supreme Court argued - to overcome interrogation techniques employed by the police. They are designed to inform the ignorant and to overcome the social obligation to answer questions in order to demonstrate one's innocence by cooperating with the police.

Thus, in contrast to U.S. law (*Miranda v. Arizona*, 1966, at 467; *Orozco v. Texas*, 1969; *Beckwith v. U.S.*, 1976; *Dunnaway v. New York*, 1979; *California v. Beheler*, 1983), German law clearly requires that warnings do not just have to be given to persons who are being deprived of their freedom in any significant way. However, Section 136 StPO stipulates that a suspect already is a "Beschuldigter", something between merely being suspected and expressly (but not formally) accused of having committed a crime. According to the BGH, the police are granted some discretion regarding whether they treat somebody as a mere suspect or as a Beschuldigter (BGHSt. 34, 138, 140; 10, 8, 12). When the former is chosen, the law concerning witnesses applies; if the suspect is treated as a Beschuldigter, the warnings come into play. Especially when the police have only some vague suspicion, warnings do not have to be given (BGHSt. 37, 48, 51-52). Although the BGH points out that the police may not misuse this discretion (BGHSt. 38, 214, 228), and warnings have to be given per se if the defendant is arrested (BGHSt. 38, 214, 228), legal scholars have argued for a broader obligation to inform suspects of their rights (Schlüchter, 1983: marginal number 85).

Privilege and warnings: (3) Interrogation. Under the rationale of protecting self-responsibility, the term interrogation should be construed broadly as far as the self-incrimination privilege is concerned. Interrogation does not just mean express questioning, but also includes conduct of police officers that is likely to cause self-incriminating statements by the defendant (*Rhode Island v. Innis*, 1980). Although the Supreme Court gave interrogation this broad meaning here, it surprisingly held that the above definition was not met in the case at the bar: Two officers driving a police car with the defendant in the back talked about the dangers for handicapped children resulting from the fact that the weapon that had been used for the crime was supposed to have been hidden in an area where these children played. Subsequently, the defendant, who had exercised his right to have the assistance of counsel, told the officers where the weapon was. In *Mauro v. Arizona* (1987), the Supreme Court held that it is no interrogation when the defendant is allowed to talk to his wife in the presence of police officers, thereby making incriminating statements. The BGH agreed in a comparable case (BGHSt. 34, 365, 369-370). In all three cases, it seems probable that the police created the situation in order to obtain statements - an argument to hold the confessions inadmissible.

For self-responsible decisions on whether to incriminate oneself, it is also not relevant that suspects realize that they are being interrogated and are dealing with the police. Thus, under this rationale of the self-incrimination privilege, the so-called jail plant should be impermissible (Landgericht Stuttgart NStZ, 1985, 568-569; Wagner, 1989: 34-35; White, 1979: 589-590). Defendants have to know to whom they are confessing: to a real cellmate, an undercover agent, or a police informant. They cannot make a rational decision if they do not know to whom they are really talking. Of course, it is the defendant's risk, if a real cellmate discloses self-incriminating statements, thus violating the defendant's trust. However, if somebody is placed in the same cell in order to elicit statements, this is simply a substitute for direct questioning. Not only is confidence in the cellmate disappointed; defendants cannot realize the significance of their statements. If they confess to a real cellmate, they have to accept the risk that the cellmate may well disclose the secret. If they confess to a police agent, they are only aware of this risk, but the secret will be disclosed with certainty. However, the Supreme Court ruled that the warnings are not required, because defendants do not realize that they are dealing with the police. Thus, the inherent compulsion used by the Warren Court to legitimate the warnings is not given (*Illinois v. Perkins*, 1990). In a comparable case, the BGH disagreed (BGHSt. 34, 362-365). The Court argued that the defendant's pretrial detention is misused to obtain a confession if somebody is placed in the same cell to elicit information. However, a subsequent case narrowed this rule: If fellow inmates obtain incriminating statements on their own behalf, they may continue to do so after they have informed the prosecutor's office and now try to elicit information on the prosecutor's request (BGH NStZ, 1989, 32-33).

Self-incrimination privilege, waiver, and lying defendants. The problems discussed above may be more or less marginal. However, a more basic issue arises if defendants waive their rights and decide to talk to the police without defense counsel present. The waiver of Miranda rights has to be intelligent, knowing, and voluntary, and ". . . any evidence that the accused was threatened, tricked, or cajoled into a waiver will, of course, show that the defendant did not voluntarily waive his privilege" (*Miranda v. Arizona*, 1966, at 475). Even defenders of Miranda argue that after such a waiver, the defendant may be subjected to more subtle forms of compulsion or trickery - those allowed under the Fourteenth Amendment voluntariness test and prohibited only by the Fifth Amendment (Schulhofer, 1987: 444). However, this argument would be convincing only if suspects actually waive their Fifth Amendment privilege against self-incrimination. But, as Justice Marshall has expressed it in a different context, it is hard to imagine that a sane person knowingly relinquishes a right to be free of compulsion (*Schneckloth v. Bustamonte*, 1973, at 281; *Marshall, J.*, dissenting). If defendants agree that compulsion (though only subtle, psychological) can be exerted on them, they indicate that they are not at all capable of a rational decision. Moreover, if defendants waive their privilege, the first Miranda warning itself would be a questionable interrogation method. Defendants have to be warned that they have a right to remain silent. Accordingly, this is the right that they waive. It is not possible to know that they waive the right to be free of compulsion along with the right to remain silent. In Stephen Schulhofer's view, the warning has to be: You have a right to be free of compulsion, and you can waive this right - obviously a rather strange warning. Therefore, I do not think that the Miranda Court was arguing for a waiver of the privilege.

In contrast, the wording in Miranda provides strong support for a general prohibition of police trickery and compulsion even after initial waiver. The right to choose between silence and speech shall "remain unfettered throughout the interrogation process," and the individual should have a continuous opportunity to exercise the right to remain silent (*Miranda v. Arizona*, 1966, at 469). Thus, even after initially having decided to talk to the police, defendants maintain the right to stop talking in the interrogation process. If defendants may choose to remain silent at the outset of interrogation without being tricked, compelled, or cajoled into a waiver, no other rule can apply in the later context (White, 1979: 589-590). Defendants have the right to a rational and intelligent choice throughout the interrogation. From this point of view, all interrogation techniques that impair a rational and intelligent choice are illegal. This interpretation of Miranda is supported by the Court's opinion that the interrogation techniques chosen as examples for inherent compulsion in police interrogation are "destructive of human dignity" (*Miranda v. Arizona*, 1966, at 449-455): Nobody can waive their own dignity.

On the other hand, the Court uses the continuous opportunity to exercise the rights to legitimize why defense counsel should be allowed to be present during interrogation (*Miranda v. Arizona*, 1966, at 469-470). Chief Justice Warren sometimes used the expression waiver with reference to the right to remain silent and sometimes with reference to the privilege. However it makes sense to allow defense counsel to be present during interrogation only when the rationale is to protect the defendant from trickery and compulsion in general. By giving Miranda such a broad meaning, I have to admit that the Fourteenth Amendment voluntariness test no longer has any function in this context. But why should there be two standards for one and the same: the right of defendants to decide on their own whether to confess or not. If Miranda is taken seriously, no space remains for a Fourteenth Amendment test: The Fifth Amendment goes much further. Defendants also do not forfeit these rights if they decide to talk to the police but do not speak truthfully (for an opposite opinion, see Puppe, 1978: 299-306). It is not the defendants' lies that are protected, but their self-determined decision. The police cannot compel defendants to admit to their lies without compelling them to tell the truth at the same time. Uncovering lies cannot be distinguished from uncovering the truth.

Self-incrimination privilege and interrogation tactics. Under the rationale of self-responsibility, the legality of police interrogation tactics cannot depend on the intention of police officers to impair defendants' ability to make rational decisions (White, 1979: 596-601; for an opposite opinion, see BGH StV, 1989, 515). If defendants are to be protected, it is irrelevant whether the police act in good or bad faith, because the function of the privilege is not to condemn officers' conduct. Since actual impairments of defendants' autonomy are not visible, only an objective standard can be applied regarding whether a relevant impairment has occurred. Thus, the question concerns how a certain interrogation technique would have affected a defendant in a comparable and similar situation. If there is a plausible possibility that a defendant's decision has been affected by the police tactic, the tactic is illegal per se in order to guarantee defendants' rights.

Self-incrimination privilege and interrogation tactics: Threats and promises. In line with the purpose of the privilege, it is illegal to arrange the interrogation as a whole in a manner designed to put defendants under pressure, to intimidate them, or to disturb them by creating a menacing atmosphere. The purpose of such an atmosphere can only be to not accept that defendants have the right to remain silent throughout the interrogation. As Chief Justice Warren put it, this is a trade on the weakness of individuals (*Miranda v. Arizona*, 1966, at 455-456). It is also fairly obvious and no surprise that the use of threats and promises to induce a confession is illegal under the privilege. Defendants are pushed to confess either through the fear that threats will be carried out or because of the risk of not receiving possible advantages. Therefore, even a century ago, the Supreme Court ruled the use of threats and promises to obtain confession illegal (*Bram v. U.S.*, 1897). Under the voluntariness test, a confession is regarded as involuntary when caused by "threats of violence, direct or implied promises or exertion of improper influence" (*Hutto v. Ross*, 1976). For example, in one case, a confession was ruled involuntary, because a defendant had been threatened that his sick wife would be interrogated if he did not confess (*Rogers v. Richmond*, 1961); in another, because the suspect had been threatened with losing financial support for her children and that her children would be taken away from her (*Lynumn v. Illinois*, 1963). However, there are other cases maintaining that more violent threats have not affected the defendant's free will (e.g., *Stroble v. California*, 1952), and, nowadays, interrogation techniques seem to have to be offensive or shocking to a civilized system of justice to be outlawed (e.g., *Miller v. Fenton*, 1985).

In Germany, it is disputed whether all promises and threats to obtain a confession are illegal. In accordance with Section 136a StPO, it is argued that only promises of unlawful advantages or threats of illegal actions violate defendants' rights (e.g., Rogall, 1988a: Section 136a, marginal number 67) - an impermissible distinction under the concept of self-responsibility. Otherwise, it should also be illegal to promise defendants a less severe punishment if they confess. The defendant has to pay a price for refusing to confess, and loses the chance to be better off in the case of a confession. However, the illegality of such promises is not acknowledged (BVerfG Wistra, 1987, 134; BGH NStZ, 1987, 217). Thus, a plea-bargaining system is permissible despite the self-incrimination privilege (BVerfG NStZ, 1987: 419; BGHSt. 36, 210; 37, 99; 37, 10; *Brady v. U.S.*, 1970; *North Carolina v. Alford*, 1970; but cf. Schünemann, 1990: B 147-148).[6]

Self-incrimination privilege and interrogation tactics: Police trickery and deception. Apart from the absence of threats and promises, a self-responsible decision by defendants on whether to confess requires that the defendant knows what the interrogation is about. Defendants must have the possibility of realizing that the situation is an interrogation in order to be able to understand the consequences of their statements. Therefore, it is illegal to mislead the subject about the significance of the interrogation (BGHSt. 37, 48, 53). However, it is argued that police trickery or outright deception do not compel defendants to make a statement (Keller, 1989: 136-137; Rogall, 1977: 209). But defendants' self-determination is just as much impaired if they decide on the basis of wrong facts, faked testimony, or a misrepresentation of law. In most cases, defendants still will know that they are confessing. However, it can hardly be argued that deceived defendants knowingly determine their own fate. Nevertheless, in *Frazier v. Cupp* (1969), the Supreme Court held a confession admissible under the voluntariness test although Frazier had been informed incorrectly by the police that his alleged accomplice had confessed and involved Frazier in the crime. Frazier first continued to deny the charge, but he confessed after a police officer suggested that the victim himself might have started a fight after making homosexual advances. In *Oregon v. Mathiason* (1976), the Supreme Court did not consider the defendant's deception, and in *Moran v. Burbine* (1986), the defendant's confession was admissible despite the fact that the police had not informed him that his attorney had tried to contact him prior to interrogation. In addition, the attorney had been falsely informed that the defendant would not be interrogated on that day. On the other hand, deceptions of the defendants rendered the resulting confessions involuntary in *Spano v. New York* (1959) and in *Leyra v. Denno* (1954). In Germany, the BGH considers intentional deceptions of the defendant illegal (BGHSt. 37, 48, 52-53; 35, 328, 329; BGH StV, 1989: 515). Some scholars have tried to distinguish between impermissible deception and permissible trickery (Roxin, 1991: 164; Schlüchter, 1983: marginal number 95). However, it seems to me that the Miranda Court had a different idea: Since the defendant may not be tricked into an initial waiver at the outset of interrogation, police trickery is prohibited throughout the interrogation process. On the other hand, defendants are not protected from making unwise or imprudent decisions. If they are mistaken about the existing evidence, the police do not have to clarify this error. Yet they may not confirm and deepen the defendant's error (BGH StV, 1988, 419, 421).

In view of the protection of self-responsibility, it is also illegal for the police to pretend to be the defendant's friend or counsel in order to obtain a statement (Sasaki, 1988: 1595; White, 1979: 608-617; cf. *Brewer v. Williams*, 1977). It is not relevant that defendants are deceived about the real intent of the police officer or that they are made to believe they have a friend. What is relevant is that an atmosphere is created that is designed to make defendants forget the significance of their statement. Defendants are lulled into believing that everybody will help and understand them (cf. *Miller v. Fenton*, 1986). Therefore, tactics such as an officer pretending that he would advise his own brother to confess, blaming society or the victim for the crime, or minimizing the defendant's moral guilt are impermissible police trickery: They are designed only to cajole the defendant into a confession (cf. *Miranda v. Arizona*, 1966, at 449-455).

2.3 Once Again: Why?

Restrictions of the standard. There seems to be something wrong. If the rationale of the self-incrimination privilege is to protect self-responsibility, and the legitimacy of the warnings follows from this rationale, the consequences of taking self-responsibility seriously seem to show that such a concept is undesirable. It goes too far, and, therefore, neither American or German courts pursue the concept of self-responsibility to its logical end as outlined above. Protecting self-responsibility without restrictions hardly seems to be reconcilable with another function of criminal procedure: to ascertain the truth and punish the guilty. After all, the defendant is suspected of having committed an (outrageous) crime. Thus, the privilege is not and should not be construed in such a one-sided manner in favor of the defendant. Society's interest in an effective enforcement of criminal law has to be taken into account.

The problem is how to restrict the standard. Restrictions are hard to justify without abandoning the concept in total. Attempts can be made to discriminate more or less severe forms of compulsions on defendants to confess. But the results of the voluntariness test have shown that this is not a convincing standard. Although there is clearly a difference between beating defendants into a confession and tricking them, it is impossible to draw a line under the standard of self-responsibility. Although brutality is certainly a more severe violation of defendant's rights, this is arguably only because the defendant is physically hurt as well as being forced to confess. Unfortunately, there is a common denominator: self-determination. Distinguishing between severe or unacceptable and less offensive interrogation techniques is more or less accidental. The warnings could not be explained: Omitting to inform defendants of their rights is not extremely unfair. Some consider deceptions to be unacceptable in a system of law enforcement (Hassemer, 1988: 204; Rogall, 1977: 209), others do not (Grano, 1986: 678-681). If self-responsibility is to be protected, then it has to be protected as a whole. No intermediate step can be ascertained between self-determined and not self-determined. Another possible way out is also barred: Additional requirements alongside the impairment of self-responsibility cannot be added. For example, adding that the interrogation has to be unfair does not help, because interrogation techniques are considered unfair *because* they impair personal autonomy and not for other reasons.

One could try a balancing approach. It has been argued that the privilege should not apply in full force when a defendant is charged with only a minor offense (Günther, 1978: 202-205). But under this view, the privilege could be restricted when justice calls for a least restriction. Defendants would be granted better protection when justice calls for the punishment of the most guilty. The privilege would catch the small fish and let the big fish go free. Therefore, it might be better to try it the other way round: The privilege's standard could be lowered for most serious crimes. Society's interest can be placed above that of the defendant. However, then the privilege would make no sense at all. It would protect defendants most when they are charged with minor crimes, and least when they are accused of major crimes. However, a constitutional right that grants protection when it is least needed is hardly a right of any significance. In any case, the police will not use the arsenal of interrogation techniques to detect minor offenses. There seems to be only one way out: A concept based on defendant's self-determination is wrong.

Why. I think there is another way out. The deadlock above implies that self-responsibility and truth finding are mutually exclusive. Therefore, both sides need to sacrifice some of their logical requirements in order to give both aspects fair meaning in criminal procedure. Whereas it is common opinion that brutality or torture hardly serve to uncover the truth (cf. *Brown v. Mississippi*, 1936), this is not true of more subtle means of obtaining a confession. This is clearly expressed by Fred Inbau (1961: 16): ". . . for I am unalterably opposed to the use of any interrogation technique that is apt to make an innocent person confess . . . I do approve of such psychological tactics and techniques as trickery and deceit . . to secure incriminating information from the guilty."

However, the supposed contrast between defendant's self-responsibility and truth finding does not exist. Protecting the defendant's self-determined decision whether to confess or not throughout the interrogation as outlined above *serves* the purpose of finding the truth and punishing the guilty. Most scholars as well as the courts proceed on the assumption that past events are fixed and unchangeable. They have occurred, and therefore they can be uncovered objectively, even though there are some uncertainties like fading memory. Witnesses can be questioned and the facts can be made visible. Thus, the facts establishing a crime are regarded as something pregiven. However, the events constituting the crime cannot be uncovered as an objective description of the past. The events are not pregiven, but the mutually shared, intersubjective *interpretation* of the events by the persons involved and spectators.

Objects and events become real because they are given a mutual sense within society. They are not real in themselves. This mutual sense is imparted and transmitted through society's language. The words of our language symbolize mutually shared experiences and thus *form* reality. Therefore, we do not see objects and events as something that already exists, but we comprehend and interpret objects and situations. All objects and events are interpretations of being.

Of course, although they are not pregiven, these interpretations are fixed and unchangeable for our society *today*. A chair is a chair and not a table. Thus, the development of language in its historical dimension *creates* reality, but when meaning is accepted, it *is* reality. It is not a fake world with something missing. However, the basic idea is relevant for the context of this article: Events are seen, thought, and recognized in words of our language. They are classified in traditional, prelearned standards of reality. To see and experience situations or events means linguistic comprehension and linguistic order. Therefore, watching or taking part in an event means *interpreting* situations. By choosing words for events, they are defined and created; the situation *becomes* existent. When different persons choose the same interpretations for events, they become reality. Sense is *given*, and not just understood (Grasnick, 1987: 211, 220, 226; for further references, see Ransiek, 1989: 92-99). As reality is interpretation, it depends on the persons who interpret. Different interpretations are possible, depending on social background, learned experiences, and different use of language (Ransiek, 1989: 94-99). So, the same situation may not be the same, because it is not interpreted in the same way. *The* reality is created by agreement only if there is consensus in attributing meaning to events. The truth to be found in criminal procedure is the search for the mutually shared original interpretation by participants and bystanders; the mutually shared definition of events.

This search is, of necessity, a new interpretation. The original one is not available as such, but has to be remembered: a new interpretation of the original comprehension. As a result, questions focus attention on new aspects, and thereby possibly change the original interpretation (Driver, 1968). Reality can be influenced and changed. Truth is not something to be uncovered, but comes into being in a dynamic process and is the result of communication. It can be established only under the condition that the individuals who define the events can give their own interpretations and do not repeat the interpretations expected or suggested by others.

If defendants' statements should contribute to this process of creating and defining truth, it is important that they are *their own* perception of the situation. The process is not served if suspects adopt interpretations offered or forced upon them by the interrogating officer. If the police succeed in rattling defendants or in insisting that defendants' statements are incredible or absurd, defendants may be brought to give up their own view of events. They may even acknowledge that their interpretation is wrong and accept the interrogator's definition of the past - particularly defendants who have little communicative competence to persist with their own perception. Of course, the defendant's version may be nothing more than a fairy-tale. The defendant may lie. But things do not improve if the defendant is made to accept another's definition of events. The result is the same: anything but the truth. However, if a certain version of events is forced upon the defendant, it becomes impossible to decide afterwards which part of the statement is not the defendant's but the interrogator's. However, the dangers are greater if the defendant is made to accept another's view. Nobody will really be surprised if the defendant lies. Nobody will simply believe what the defendant wants to make them believe. However, things are quite different when a defendant confesses: Persons condemning themselves have no rational reason to do so apart from telling the truth. If events are conceded, it does not seem necessary to scrutinize them too closely.

This is not just a theoretical view. It is acknowledged that witnesses of a crime should not be influenced in their testimony by questions offering a certain answer. Changing one word of a question can change answers quite significantly (Loftus

1979: 77-78). Loftus presented a film of an accident to college students. When asked about the accident afterwards, answers differed depending on whether the college students were asked whether they had seen *the* or *any* broken headlight - in fact, there had been no broken headlight. The same was true when they were asked about the color of a station wagon - there was none (Loftus 1979: 83-84; cf. Driver, 1968: 62). If defendants questioned by the police are confused or made confused about the correctness of their view of events, if they are made to believe that their version is unbelievable anyhow, if they are offered an interpretation of events that is attractive to them (through promises, threats, or sympathy), or if they do not realize the difference between their own perception and the one that is offered to them, especially the legal difference, they may not care which version becomes their confession or they may simply give up. To be sure, defendants do not necessarily change their own (true) interpretation. Maybe they are made to speak truthfully. But the problem is: We do not know. What we do know is that there is an inherent danger that defendants will accept definitions of the events that are not their own if they cannot decide self-responsibly what to say. And this danger is sufficient to prohibit incentives to confess. Because we want to punish only those who are really guilty.

It can be argued that it is necessary to discriminate between witnesses and defendants. Defendants seem much more likely to resist if a proposed interpretation condemns them (cf. Grano, 1979: 905-906). But their resistance depends on their communicative abilities and their knowledge of criminal law. Defendants are usually not lawyers who know the legally relevant distinctions and who are used to arguing. The chances of resisting are small for those whose communicative abilities are inferior to the police officer's. This makes it possible to explain why the Supreme Court, under the voluntariness test, was quite favorable to accused who had a poor education, gave a helpless impression, or were juveniles (e.g., *Blackburn v. Alabama*, 1960; *Gallegos v. Colorado*, 1963).

I am not claiming that interrogation tricks and subtle compulsion will make defendants adopt an entirely new interpretation of events. Defendants are not necessarily wholly innocent. But if only parts of the confession can be wrong, it subsequently becomes impossible to separate the interrogator's and the defendant's perceptions. If, for example, police officers affirm a suspect's mistaken assumption that he was videotaped during a bank robbery (BGH StV, 1988, 421; cf. Günther, 1988), all his subsequent statements are not necessarily not his own view of the events. But it is impossible to decide exactly how the police trickery influenced the further course of the interrogation. Interrogation continues, and the suspect may be accepting interpretations offered by the officer because he thinks it would be useless to persist in his own view of other elements of the crime. Of course, the defendant took part in the robbery, but the question is: How exactly?

This also does not mean that police officers intentionally or negligently try to make defendants adopt expected interpretations. But the police have to start their questioning from the suspicion that the defendant is involved in the crime. Thus, they have their own specific interpretation of the events at the outset of the interrogation. In addition, they have to question the suspect on all elements material to a crime. Thus, when questioning, they have to offer a certain interpretation - the one that fits criminal law. This is important, because the interrogator's expectations - the confirmation of his or her suspicion - do not have to be stated explicitly to be recognized by the defendant. Empirical studies have shown that the expectations of researchers influence the test person even when they try to conceal them - which led to the introduction of double-blind studies (cf. Kühne, 1985: 254). Thus, if a certain expectation is signalled by the interrogator, defendants may adjust their statements to this expectation if there are incentives for doing this. Suspects might adhere to the interrogating police officer's authority, given to him or her because he or she decides whether to believe the suspect or not. Once again, this does not imply that innocent persons will confess to all the crimes that they are suspected of committing. But it does imply the possibility that something will be admitted when methods of persuasion are applied, although, in fact, the suspect's perception was different. For example, in *Frazier v. Cupp* (1969), the whole story that Frazier gave to the police may well have been influenced by the faked confession of his alleged accomplice and the suggestion that the victim may also have been culpable. Of course, we do not know this, but there is the unpleasant feeling that this might be so. This is also the reason why the mentally impaired should not be interrogated. The reliability of the confession is extremely doubtful, and conviction should not be based on such a confession (*Colorado v. Connelly*, 1986, at 174-188, *Brennan, Marshall, JJ.*, dissenting).

In summary, the privilege's rationale to protect the defendant's self-responsibility throughout the interrogation process is not an obstacle to seeing that justice is done, but a necessary condition to define past events. Thus, the early Supreme Court decisions excluding confessions because of their unreliability (cf. Caplan, 1985: 1427-1437; Kamisar, 1980: 15-20) are sound. However, reliability does not provide arguments to restrict the exclusion of confessions, but to ban all interrogation tactics that deprive defendants of the chance to determine for themselves whether they are going to confess and what they are going to confess.

2.4 Consequences of Violating the Privilege

As argued above, the self-incrimination privilege requires police warnings to make it effective. Therefore, if the warnings are not administered, confessions are excluded per se (*Miranda v. Arizona*, 1966, at 479). Although it has been argued that a confession has to be excluded to deter further police conduct (Bradley, 1985: 106-108), the main reason is to accept an individual's rights as such: Defendants' statements are only relevant when they present their own view of the crime; their own perceptions are accessible only if the defendants want to tell us them. Therefore, defendants have the right to be informed of their options and they may decide on the basis of this information. The same holds if the police have applied one or more illegal interrogation tactics or created an atmosphere designed either to lull or cajole or to compel a confession from the defendant. First, because defendants' rights have been violated; and, second, because the resulting confession does not serve the truth-finding process.

The inadmissibility of a confession should include the "fruits of the poisonous tree". Any direct or indirect use of a confession obtained in violation of the self-incrimination privilege means that the conviction is based on illegality (Seebode, 1988: 431-432). However, the BGH argues that violations of procedural rights should not have the consequence of blocking the trial (BGHSt. 35, 32, 34; 34, 362, 364; 32, 68, 71) in the sense of simply not convicting the accused. It is also not clear whether indirect evidence will be excluded automatically if illegal interrogation methods have been applied (cf. Wolter, 1984: 276-278). Likewise, in the United States, strong arguments can be made that the "fruit-of-the-poisonous-tree" doctrine is not applicable if police failed to comply with the Miranda requirements. Statements by the defendant are not inadmissible in entirety but may be used to impeach later statements (*Harris v. New York*, 1971; *Oregon v. Haas*, 1974). In *Michigan v. Tucker* (1974), the Court upheld the use of witness testimony, although the witness had become known through the defendant's inadmissible statement. Finally, in *Oregon v. Elstad* (1985), the Court's majority found that Elstad had knowingly and intelligently waived his Miranda rights before confessing a second time, although he had not been told that his first confession was inadmissible. However, the BGH disagrees, at least if the trial judge has not informed the defendant who is not represented by counsel of this inadmissibility before questioning him at trial (BGHSt. 38, 214, 226).

In general, it makes no difference whether the defendant is convicted on the basis of directly or indirectly obtained evidence (BGHSt. 29, 244, 251, on telephone tapping). There is a risk that the combination of illegally obtained indirect evidence and inadmissible confession will create a wrong construction of past events. Although the confession is inadmissible, it is known to exist. Thus, the actual impact on proving the crime and on further investigations can be avoided only when all indirect evidence is also impermissible. Otherwise, the police may feel encouraged to employ illegal tactics until not only a confession but also additional indirect evidence is obtained (Wagner, 1989: 35). Indirectly obtained evidence may be used only when this evidence inevitably would have been uncovered by the law enforcement agencies in any case, or if the evidence can be confirmed by an independent source (*Nix v. Williams*, 1984;[7] Rogall, 1988b:

392). However, the argument that there *always* is the chance that the police would have uncovered the evidence by legal means is inadmissible (but cf. BGHSt. 34, 362, 364; 32, 68, 71).

3 Self-Incrimination Privilege: The Need for Control

Another consequence is necessary: A whole set of legal rules for police interrogation is useless when violations of the law cannot be made visible, particularly when the whole atmosphere of an interrogation is in question. It is not satisfying to seek a solution through the burden of proof. The results do not seem to differ so greatly regardless of whether one has to prove that something happened or did not happen. In Germany, defendants bear the risk that it cannot be proved that their confession was obtained by illegal means (BGHSt. 16, 164, 167) or that warnings were not given (BGHSt. 38, 314, 224, expressly left open if the same is true for the factual basis of other exclusionary rules). When facing police interrogation alone, suspects have a hard time proving a violation of their rights. It seems rather unlikely that police officers will admit to having tricked or pressed defendants into a confession. And it is naturally also unsatisfactory to just believe defendants' stories about what has happened during interrogation. Defendants have good reason to dispose of a confession even if it was obtained legally. Thus, things are not improved very much if the state bears the proof for the voluntariness of a confession under the Fourteenth Amendment (*Lego v. Twomey*, 1977) that warnings have been given and that the defendant has validly waived these rights (*Colorado v. Connelly*, 1986, at 168-169; *Miranda v. Arizona*, 1966, at 475-476). We still do not know what was going on during the interrogation and what the communicative atmosphere was like. For example, in *North Carolina v. Davis* (1966), there is more of a feeling that Davis was mistreated during his 16-day detention than actual knowledge. The result is a swearing contest between defendants and police, which is probably hard for defendants to win if they have signed a written waiver of their Miranda rights (cf. Ogletree, 1988: 1829)

The need for control becomes obvious if defendants' rights and the truth-defining process are to be taken seriously. Police interrogation has to be controlled either by mandatory defense counsel for the defendant or through technical devices such as videotaping the interrogation. Although this proposal sounds rather radical under German law, it is certainly not uncommon in the United States (Caplan, 1985: 1473-1475; Dripps, 1988: 726-734; Herman, 1964: 497-499; Kamisar, 1977: 235-245; Weisberg, 1961: 45; White, 1979: 629). The Supreme Court of Alaska is right to require that in-custody interrogations are to be taped as a mandate of the state constitution's due process clause (*Stephan v. State*, 1985). Otherwise, defendants' rights are not effective. Nonetheless, there are also possible objections to both proposals: If defense counsels are present during interrogations, the danger that defendants will be compelled or tricked into a confession is greatly reduced. However, the number of confessions will naturally tend to be nonexistent, at least during early procedural stages. But the Supreme Court has already expressed this aptly in *Escobedo v. Illinois* (1964):[8]

"No system worth preserving should have to fear that if an accused is permitted to consult with a lawyer, he will become aware of, and exercise these rights. If the exercise of constitutional rights will thwart the effectiveness of a system of law enforcement, then there is something very wrong with that system."

Another objection is that defendants would be forced to be represented by counsel even if they do not wish so (cf. *Faretta v. California*, 1975). But lawyers' roles could be defined narrowly: They would have to control the interview only, and not necessarily represent the defendant. Although videotaping the interrogation is technically possible today, it could reduce the defendants' ability to communicate, because, to some extent, it would transform them into actors on a stage. On the other hand, suspects may become more aware of what they actually admit.

A new definition of police interrogation is necessary. Interrogation is not a fight in which one side tries to uncover the truth while the other tries to hide it, but a process of dialogue in which past events are reconstructed and the truth is defined. This makes it necessary for defendants to have the opportunity to present their own perception of the events if they so wish. The interrogation has to be controlled to ensure the defendants' rights.

Notes

1 Suspects taken into police custody have to be warned prior to interrogation that they have a right to remain silent; that they may consult with a lawyer who may be present during interrogation and will be appointed free of cost if they are indigent; that anything said can be used against them (*Miranda v. Arizona*, 1966, at 479).

2 A short explanation may be helpful here. In Germany, the law of criminal procedure is federal law codified in the Code of Criminal Procedure (StPO). Of course, there is also a constitutional dimension: The highest authority for interpreting the German Constitution is the Bundesverfassungsgericht (BVerfG), the Federal Constitutional Court. Compared to the United States, however, there are only a few BVerfG judgments clearly defining the rights of suspects in criminal cases. There are two main reasons for this: (a) Defendants' rights in criminal procedure are not codified in the Constitution in this article's context. (b) Although basic procedural rights are derived from general principles on human and civil rights in the constitution, the BVerfG is reluctant to give far-reaching constitutional guidelines in order to avoid becoming a superappellate court in this field. All lower courts apply constitutional law as well, and particularly use constitutional principles to construe statutes. Additionally, there is a European dimension: The European Convention of Human Rights is guarded by the European Court for Human Rights.

The Convention is applicable law in Germany; in some ways, it is even superior to ordinary Federal law (BVerfGE, 74, 358, 370).

3 Although the privilege is not codified, it is common opinion that it is nonetheless a constitutional right (BVerfGE 56, 37, 49).

4 The Supreme Court often points out that the American system is an accusatorial and not an inquisitorial one. This does not make it easier to distinguish American and German criminal procedure with regard to defendants' rights. Since 1848, the German system of law enforcement cannot be characterized properly as inquisitorial, although the role of the judge at trial differs particularly from the United States. For the *historical* inquisitorial process, see Roxin (1991: 440-441).

5 This is meant as a rather rare exception. It is not sufficient, for example, that the defendant already has a criminal record. However, no warnings have to be given if the defendant talks to the police with defense counsel present.

6 Germany is *not* a land without plea-bargaining. The legal difficulties, however, had been swept under the carpet until an anonymous article was published by "Detlev Deal" in 1982. The issue is still controversial.

7 The court held that a preponderance standard is sufficient for proving that the indirect evidence would have been obtained (cf. Schlüchter, 1984: 518-520). However, a clear and convincing standard is more appropriate. It has to be ensured that illegal police conduct has not caused a conviction.

8 Another important development in German law should not remain unmentioned. The BGH (BGHSt. 38, 372) followed Escobedo's rule: A suspect wishing assistance of counsel prior to interrogation may not be interrogated. A confession obtained under violation of defendant's right to counsel is inadmissible. The interrogating officer had overcome the defendant's wish by telling him he should know on his own, and would have to decide himself, anyway, whether to make statements or not. In addition, the defendant was told that the questioning was to be continued until things were "clear".

References

Bradley, C.M. (1985). Beweisverbote in der USA und Deutschland. *Goltdammers Archiv für Strafrecht, 132,* 99-113.

Caplan, G.M. (1985). Questioning Miranda. *Vanderbilt Law Review, 38,* 1417-1476.

Deal, D. (1982). Der strafprozessuale Vergleich. *Strafverteidiger, 2,* 545-552.

Dolkino, D. (1986). Is there a rationale for the privilege against self-discrimination? *UCLA Law Review, 33,* 1063-1148.

Dripps, D.A. (1988). Foreword: Against police interrogation - and against the privilege against self-incrimination. *Journal of Criminal Law, Criminology and Police Science, 78,* 699-734.

Driver, E.D. (1968). Confessions and the social psychology of coercion. *Harvard Law Review, 82,* 42-63.

Eser, A. (1990). Die Rechtsstellung des Beschuldigten im Strafprozeß der Bundesrepublik Deutschland. In A. Eser and G. Kaiser (Eds.), *Deutsch-Ungarisches Colloquium über Strafrecht und Kriminologie* (pp.147-167). Baden-Baden: Nomos.

Grano, J.D. (1979). Voluntariness, free will, and the law of confessions. *Virginia Law Review, 65,* 859-945.

Grano, J.D. (1986). Selling the idea to tell the truth: The professional interrogator and modern confessions law. *Michigan Law Review, 84,* 622-690.

Grano, J.D. (1988). Miranda's constitutional difficulties: A reply to Professor Schulhofer. *University of Chicago Law Review, 55,* 174-189.

Grasnick, W. (1987). *Über Schuld, Strafe und Sprache.* Tübingen: Mohr.

Grünwald, G. (1981). Probleme der Gegenüberstellung zum Zwecke der Wiedererkennung. *Juristenzeitung, 36,* 423-429.

Günther, H.-L. (1978). Die Schweigebefugnis des Tatverdächtigen im Straf- und Bußgeldverfahren aus verfassungsrechtlicher Sicht. *Goltdammers Archiv für Strafrecht, 125,* 193-206.

Günther, H.-L. (1988). Anmerkung zu BGH StV 1988, 419. *Strafverteidiger, 8,* 421-424.

Hassemer, W. (1988). Unverfügbares im Strafprozeß. In A. Kaufmann et al. (Eds.), *Festschrift für Werner Maihofer* (pp. 183-204). Frankfurt: Klostermann.

Herman, L. (1964). The Supreme Court and restrictions on police interrogations. *Ohio State Law Journal, 25,* 449-500.

Inbau, F. E. (1961). Police interrogation - a practical necessity. *Journal of Criminal Law, Criminology and Police Science, 52,* 16-20.

Johnson, P. (1988). *Criminal procedure.* St. Paul: West.

Kamisar, Y. (1977). Foreword: Brewer v. Williams - A hard look at a discomforting record. *Georgetown Law Journal, 66,* 209-245.

Kamisar, Y. (1980). *Police interrogations and confessions: Essays in law and policy.* Ann Arbor, MI: Ann Arbor University Press.

Keller, R. (1989). *Rechtliche Grenzen der Provokation von Straftaten.* Berlin: Duncker & Humblot.

Kleinknecht, T., and Meyer, K. (1991). *Kommentar zur StPO* (40th ed.). München: C.H. Beck.

Kleinknecht, T., and Meyer-Goßner, K. (1993). *Kommentar zur StPO* (41st ed.). München: C.H. Beck.

Krey, V. (1988). *Strafverfahrensrecht* (Vol. 1). Stuttgart: Kohlhammer.

Kühne, H.-H. (1985). Der Beweiswert von Zeugenaussagen. *Neue Zeitschrift für Strafrecht, 5,* 252-255.

Loftus E.F. (1979). *Eyewitness testimony.* Cambridge, MA: Harvard University Press.

Markman, S.J. (1987). The Fifth Amendment and custodial questioning: A response to reconsidering Miranda. *University of Chicago Law Review, 54,* 938-949.

Ogletree, C.J. (1988). Are confessions really good for the soul? A proposal to Mirandize Miranda. *Harvard Law Review, 100,* 1826-1845.

Pakter, W. (1985). Exclusionary rules in France, Germany and Italy. *Hastings International Law Review, 9,* 1-57.

Puppe, I. (1978). List im Verhör des Beschuldigten. *Goltdammers Archiv für Strafrecht, 125,* 289-306.

Ransiek, A. (1989). *Gesetz und Lebenswirklichkeit.* Heidelberg: Decker und Schenck.

Ransiek, A. (1990). *Die Rechte des Beschuldigten in der Polizeivernehmung.* Heidelberg: Decker und Schenck.

Rieß, P. (1980). Die Vernehmung des Beschuldigten im Strafprozeß. *Juristische Arbeitsblätter, 12,* 293-301.

Rogall, K. (1977). *Der Beschuldigte als Beweismittel gegen sich selbst.* Berlin: Duncker & Humblot.

Rogall, K. (1988a). Sections 133-136a. In Rudolphi H.J. et al. (1988). *Systematischer Kommentar zur StPO und zum GVG.* Neuwied: Metzner.

Rogall, K. (1988b). Hypothetische Ermittlungsverläufe im Strafprozeß. *Neue Zeitschrift für Strafrecht, 8,* 385-393.

Roxin, C. (1991). *Strafverfahrensrecht* (22nd ed.). München: C.H. Beck.

Sasaki, D. W. (1988). Guarding the guardians: Police trickery and confessions. *Stanford Law Review, 40,* 1593-1616.

Schlüchter, E. (1983). *Das Strafverfahren* (2nd ed.). Köln: Heymanns.

Schlüchter, E. (1984). Anmerkung zu BGHSt. 32, 68. *Juristische Rundschau,* 517-522.

Schulhofer, S.J. (1987). Reconsidering Miranda. *University of Chicago Law Review, 54,* 435-461.

Schünemann, B. (1990). *Absprachen im Strafverfahren? Grundlagen, Gegenstände, Grenzen, Gutachten B zum 58. Deutschen Juristentag.* München: C.H. Beck.

Seebode, M. (1988). Anmerkung zu BGHSt. 34, 362. *Juristische Rundschau,* 427-432.

Stuntz, W.J. (1989). Waiving rights in criminal procedure. *Virginia Law Review, 75,* 761-842.

Wagner, H. (1989). Anmerkung zu BGHSt. 34, 362. *Neue Zeitschrift für Strafrecht, 9,* 34-35.

Weisberg, B. (1961). Police interrogations of arrested persons: A sceptical view. *Journal of Criminal Law, Criminology and Police Science, 52,* 21-46.

White, W.S. (1979). Police trickery in inducing confessions. *University of Pennsylvania Law Review, 127,* 581-629.

Wolter, J. (1984). Anmerkung zu BGHSt. 32, 68. *Neue Zeitschrift für Strafrecht, 4,* 276-278.

Subject Index

Author Index